Economics and Environmental Responsibility in the Global Beverage Industry

Cristina Raluca Gh. Popescu
University of Bucharest, Romania & The Bucharest University of Economic Studies, Romania

Javier Martínez-Falcó
University of Alicante, Spain

Bartolomé Marco-Lajara
University of Alicante, Spain

Eduardo Sánchez-García
University of Alicante, Spain

Luis A. Millán-Tudela
University of Alicante, Spain

IGI Global
PUBLISHER of TIMELY KNOWLEDGE

A volume in the Advances in Business Strategy and Competitive Advantage (ABSCA) Book Series

Published in the United States of America by
IGI Global
Business Science Reference (an imprint of IGI Global)
701 E. Chocolate Avenue
Hershey PA, USA 17033
Tel: 717-533-8845
Fax: 717-533-8661
E-mail: cust@igi-global.com
Web site: http://www.igi-global.com

Library of Congress Cataloging-in-Publication Data

Names: Popescu, Cristina Raluca Gh., 1983- editor. | Martinez Falcó, Javier, 1997- editor. | Marco Lajara, Bartolomé, editor. | Sánchez García, Eduardo (Professor of Management), editor. | Millán-Tudela, Luis A., 1998- editor.
Title: Economics and environmental responsibility in the global beverage industry / edited by Cristina Raluca Gh. Popescu, Javier Martínez-Falcó, Bartolome Marco-Lajara, Eduardo Sánchez-García, Luis Millán-Tudela.
Description: Hershey, PA : Business Science Reference, [2024] | Includes bibliographical references and index. | Summary: "The book serves as a guide for study, reflection and critique in order to understand sustainability in the beverage industry in its triple aspect (economic, social and environmental)"-- Provided by publisher.
Identifiers: LCCN 2024009381 (print) | LCCN 2024009382 (ebook) | ISBN 9798369321492 (hardcover) | ISBN 9798369321508 (ebook)
Subjects: LCSH: Beverage industry--Environmental aspects.
Classification: LCC HD9348.A2 E46 2024 (print) | LCC HD9348.A2 (ebook) | DDC 338.4/7663--dc23/eng/20240423
LC record available at https://lccn.loc.gov/2024009381
LC ebook record available at https://lccn.loc.gov/2024009382

This book is published in the IGI Global book series Advances in Business Strategy and Competitive Advantage (ABSCA) (ISSN: 2327-3429; eISSN: 2327-3437)

British Cataloguing in Publication Data
A Cataloguing in Publication record for this book is available from the British Library.

All work contributed to this book is new, previously-unpublished material. The views expressed in this book are those of the authors, but not necessarily of the publisher.

For electronic access to this publication, please contact: eresources@igi-global.com.

Advances in Business Strategy and Competitive Advantage (ABSCA) Book Series

Patricia Ordóñez de Pablos
Universidad de Oviedo, Spain

ISSN:2327-3429
EISSN:2327-3437

Mission

Business entities are constantly seeking new ways through which to gain advantage over their competitors and strengthen their position within the business environment. With competition at an all-time high due to technological advancements allowing for competition on a global scale, firms continue to seek new ways through which to improve and strengthen their business processes, procedures, and profitability.

The **Advances in Business Strategy and Competitive Advantage (ABSCA) Book Series** is a timely series responding to the high demand for state-of-the-art research on how business strategies are created, implemented and re-designed to meet the demands of globalized competitive markets. With a focus on local and global challenges, business opportunities and the needs of society, the **ABSCA** encourages scientific discourse on doing business and managing information technologies for the creation of sustainable competitive advantage.

Coverage

- Balanced Scorecard
- Economies of Scale
- Foreign Investment Decision Process
- Small and Medium Enterprises
- Ethics and Business Strategy
- Innovation Strategy
- Value Creation
- Core Competencies
- Globalization
- Resource-Based Competition

IGI Global is currently accepting manuscripts for publication within this series. To submit a proposal for a volume in this series, please contact our Acquisition Editors at Acquisitions@igi-global.com or visit: http://www.igi-global.com/publish/.

The Advances in Business Strategy and Competitive Advantage (ABSCA) Book Series (ISSN 2327-3429) is published by IGI Global, 701 E. Chocolate Avenue, Hershey, PA 17033-1240, USA, www.igi-global.com. This series is composed of titles available for purchase individually; each title is edited to be contextually exclusive from any other title within the series. For pricing and ordering information please visit http://www.igi-global.com/book-series/advances-business-strategy-competitive-advantage/73672. Postmaster: Send all address changes to above address.

Titles in this Series

For a list of additional titles in this series, please visit: http://www.igi-global.com/book-series/advances-business-strategy-competitive-advantage/73672

Fostering Innovation in Venture Capital and Startup Ecosystems
Renuka Sharma (Chitkara Business School, Chitkara University, Punjab, India) Kiran Mehta (Chitkara Business School, Chitkara University, Punjab, India) and Poshan Yu (Soochow University, China & Australian Studies Centre, Shanghai University, China)
Business Science Reference • copyright 2024 • 430pp • H/C (ISBN: 9798369313268) • US $270.00 (our price)

Entrepreneurship and Creativity in the Metaverse
Shivani Inder (Chitkara Business School, Chitkara University, India) Byoung-chul Min (Chung-Ang University, South Korea) and Sandhir Sharma (Chitkara Business School, Chitkara University, India)
Business Science Reference • copyright 2024 • 301pp • H/C (ISBN: 9798369317341) • US $275.00 (our price)

Reskilling the Workforce in the Labor Market The Country Cases
Oytun Meçik (Eskişehir Osmangazi University, Turkey)
Business Science Reference • copyright 2024 • 286pp • H/C (ISBN: 9798369336694) • US $295.00 (our price)

Convergence of Digitalization, Innovation, and Sustainable Development in Business
Alper Erturk (Australian University, Kuwait) Stephen Edward Colbran (Central Queensland University, Australia) Erman Coşkun (Izmir Bakircay University, Turkey) Faidon Theofanidis (Australian University, Kuwait) and Oualid Abidi (Australian University, Kuwait)
Business Science Reference • copyright 2024 • 303pp • H/C (ISBN: 9798369307984) • US $275.00 (our price)

Green Economy and Renewable Energy Transitions for Sustainable Development
Rui Alexandre Castanho (WSB University, Poland)
Engineering Science Reference • copyright 2024 • 314pp • H/C (ISBN: 9798369312971) • US $275.00 (our price)

Trends, Challenges, and Practices in Contemporary Strategic Management
Filiz Mızrak (Beykoz University, Turkey)
Business Science Reference • copyright 2024 • 355pp • H/C (ISBN: 9798369311554) • US $275.00 (our price)

Fostering Global Entrepreneurship Through Business Model Innovation
Varun Gupta (Multidisciplinary Research Centre for Innovations in SMEs, Gisma University of Applied Sciences, Potsdam, Germany & Department of Economics and Business Administration, Universidad de Alcalá, Alcalá de Henares (Madrid), Spain)
Business Science Reference • copyright 2024 • 293pp • H/C (ISBN: 9781668469750) • US $275.00 (our price)

IGI Global
PUBLISHER of TIMELY KNOWLEDGE

701 East Chocolate Avenue, Hershey, PA 17033, USA
Tel: 717-533-8845 x100 • Fax: 717-533-8661
E-Mail: cust@igi-global.com • www.igi-global.com

Editorial Advisory Board

Table of Contents

Detailed Table of Contents

The socioeconomic context poses challenges that threaten the economic sustainability of various productive sectors, such as viticulture. In this regard, Valle de Guadalupe in Mexico has experienced exponential growth in the number of its wineries, posing a threat of deterioration of terroir, considering the limited natural resources typical of semi-arid ecosystems. As a result, the competitiveness of the industry is also constrained. In this context, a strategy based on the production of high-end wines, accompanied by marketing strategies that promote the creation of innovative brands, is one possible response to resilience in the sector. This research conducts a diagnosis of innovation by wineries and its impact on their marketing strategies across the four Ps. It is a descriptive study with a sample of 37 wine-producing companies associated with Provino de Ensenada. These analysis results conclude that in the Valle de Guadalupe´s wineries the product and promotion factor shows increase in their innovations, while in the price and place factor, it was found that companies do not innovate.

Sustainability has become a key issue across all economic sectors, but especially in the beverage industry, and the wine industry. Worldwide, an ever-increasing number of manufacturers are committing to reducing their carbon footprint to combat climate change. Bodegas y Viñedos Castiblanque, a winery in the La Mancha area of Spain, stands as an important reference for sustainability. This family-owned company is engaged in a significant project of wine production, manufacturing, and marketing. Simultaneously, it provides visitors with the opportunity to explore the winery, its history, and the latest technological advancements combined with artisan tradition. The case study analyzes this winery's sustainability and innovation management, highlighting key outcomes resulting from its participation in the tourism sustainability plan implemented in the tourism destination of Campo de Criptana (Spain).

environmentally friendly packaging can inspire the next generation of environmentally friendly alternatives. In addition to identifying study gaps and possibilities for customer study, the work's objectives include reviewing existing practices, variables influencing environmental behavior, and customer testing techniques. It also suggests tactics for stakeholders to effectively convey package sustainability to customers.

Enograstronomy has yielded successful results for the wine houses in the Guadalupe Valley by supporting various restaurateurs and establishing typical pairings. The study focuses on four restaurants and four wine houses that attract a high number of wine tourists seeking notable pairings of regional dishes and local wines in Guadalupe Valley. This approach aims to understand the success of such pairings in attracting more tourism to the Valley. Our focus is on understanding the interplay of traditional and modern production elements that contribute to creating a sustainable and productive wine-related environment in the region. Thus, the research scope focuses on identifying the dishes, in combination with wines produced in the Valley, that were highly sought after by visitors between 2015 and 2019, excluding the 2020 and 2021 years due to the impact of COVID-19 on the region and wine tourism. The methodology used for the research is qualitative, based on interviews and bibliographic sources.

The purpose of this study is to investigate how wine tourism influences the adoption of environmentally friendly product and process innovations by Spanish wineries. The research includes control variables like the winery's age, its size, and its association with a Protected Designation of Origin (PDO) to accurately delineate cause-effect relationships. A conceptual model, grounded in existing literature, forms the basis of this study and is empirically examined through Partial Least Squares Structural Equation Modeling (PLS-SEM), drawing on data from 202 Spanish wineries. The results demonstrate that wine tourism substantially and positively impacts the development of green products and process innovations. This research contributes to academic discourse in several ways. It enhances the understanding of the beneficial outcomes linked with wine tourism and adds to the existing knowledge on the nexus between wine tourism and sustainability. This includes the insight that wine tourism can bolster a winery's capacity for green innovation. Additionally, this study is seemingly the first to explore wine tourism as a catalyst for green innovation. The theoretical model introduced in this research is novel, representing a notable advancement in the academic comprehension of the relationship between wine tourism and green innovation in the context of the wine industry.

This research investigates the complex and ever-changing relationship between sustainable practices and the halal food industry. Global economic growth has been driven by the expansion of culinary tourism, but concerns have been raised regarding its long-term effects on ecosystems, cultural heritage, and society. Given the substantial expansion of the halal industry, this study seeks to examine the long-term consequences of sustainability on the community, ecosystem, cultural heritage, and food industry. It is anticipated that the results of this study will make a significant contribution to the travel and hospitality sector by promoting the sustainable viability of ethical and sustainable practices in the halal food industry amid its accelerated growth.

This chapter aims to examine how the patterns of environmental proactivity, fueled by internal, external, or reactive motivations, influence the eco-innovative behaviour and the economic and financial performance of family companies in the wine sector. An empirical study was carried out based on a structural equations model, using a partial least squares technique, for a sample of 79 Spanish family wine companies taken between 2017 and 2018. The study allowed us to highlight the eco-innovative nature of family businesses in the wine sector in Spain. The search for greater effectiveness and efficiency, cost savings, improved profitability, and greater competitiveness, together with regulatory factors (regulatory framework and public incentives) were among the main drivers of environmental proactivity and eco-innovation in the companies analysed. Additionally, the development of environmental innovations results in greater economic and financial performance.

This study focuses on examining the influence of knowledge management (KM) on sustainable performance (SP) within the wine industry. Specifically, it explores how KM affects SP, considering the mediating effect of green innovation (GI) and the moderating effect of collaborative culture (CC). A theoretical model, grounded in prior research, is employed and empirically tested using structural equation modeling (PLS-SEM) with data from 202 Spanish wineries. The findings demonstrate a positive correlation between KM and SP, where GI acts as a mediator and CC serves as a moderator in this relationship. This research is

In many regions of Spain and Portugal, wine is still not very profitable for winegrowers who barely recover the economic and human capital inputs dedicated throughout the year to each harvest. The economic logic of the market is rapidly transforming this landscape and heritage in more and more regions, promoting the mechanization of viticulture for the sake of productivity, giving priority above all to the volume of grapes obtained and the reduction of production costs. In this sense, goblet vines and low vines are giving way to trellising, and the latter to harvesting machinery. However, the value of vine cultivation and winemaking goes far beyond economic profitability as an inseparable part of the cultural landscape and Mediterranean cultures. This chapter delves into cases of good practices for wine tourism and the enormous wealth of the musical heritage and, in general, the intangible cultural heritage (sayings, customs, traditions, agrarian and culinary traditions) surrounding wine.

The COVID-19 pandemic has brought significant changes to people's lifestyles all over the world. Even after the pandemic, many people continue to maintain a healthy lifestyle. As a result, healthy food and drinks have become more popular and are driving consumer preferences in the food and beverage market. It is essential for a healthy lifestyle to consume healthy drinks that are affordable for everyone. In this point, functional foods and beverages have gained significant value. This study investigates the global functional beverage market trends before and after the pandemic. In addition, the study aims to provide a comprehensive analysis of how consumer preferences are changing in response to the trend of functional beverages. It is aimed to give an economic and marketing approach for the rise of functional beverage market.

Preface

In an epoch defined by the inexorable march of environmental degradation and the imperative of sustainable development, the global beverage industry emerges as both protagonist and antagonist. As humanity confronts the repercussions of resource depletion and climate upheaval, the beverage sector finds itself under scrutiny, its practices scrutinized for their complicity in exacerbating ecological crises. In response to this clarion call for accountability and change, *Economics and Environmental Responsibility in the Global Beverage Industry* emerges as a scholarly bastion, offering a profound examination of the intricate interplay between economic imperatives and environmental stewardship within this pivotal sector.

This compendium represents a convergence of scholarly acumen and practical urgency -a testament to the imperative of reconciling economic viability with ecological integrity. Its genesis lies in the recognition of the beverage industry's profound impact on our planet, spanning the gamut from plastic pollution to water scarcity, from carbon emissions to biodiversity loss. Through a kaleidoscope of disciplinary lenses, this volume endeavors to unravel the labyrinthine challenges besetting the industry, offering incisive analyses, innovative frameworks, and pragmatic solutions.

At its core, this book is an intellectual odyssey - a journey through the annals of beverage economics, marketing stratagems, and consumer comportment, illuminated by the guiding beacon of sustainability. Its pages resonate with the reverberations of scholarly discourse, probing the depths of circular economy paradigms, dissecting the nuances of green innovation, and elucidating the intricacies of reverse logistics. Yet, far from being a mere academic exercise, this compendium serves as a clarion call—a rallying cry for collective action and transformative change.

In the labyrinthine landscape of the global beverage industry, each chapter of this compendium represents a distinct facet, a unique vantage point from which to glean insights and chart a course toward sustainability and resilience. Let us embark on a brief journey through the annals of this scholarly tome, exploring the rich tapestry of chapters that await within:

- **Advances in Marketing Innovation to Enhance Resilience in the Wine Industry in Mexico: A Comprehensive Analysis**: This chapter delves into the dynamic realm of marketing innovation within the Mexican wine industry, offering a comprehensive analysis of strategies to enhance resilience in the face of environmental and economic challenges.
- **Among Sustainable Vineyards: The Case of Bodegas Castiblanque**: Through the lens of Bodegas Castiblanque, this chapter offers a nuanced exploration of sustainable practices in viticulture, illuminating the pathways toward ecological integrity and economic viability.

- **Analyzing the Impact of Wine Tourism on the Triple Bottom Line of Spanish Wineries: A Structural Equation Modeling Approach**: Utilizing structural equation modeling, this chapter investigates the multifaceted impacts of wine tourism on the triple bottom line—economic, social, and environmental—of Spanish wineries, providing valuable insights for sustainable development.
- **Encouraging Sustainable Practices and Behaviors in Tourism Consumers and Hotel Management: Côa Valley Region**: Focusing on the Côa Valley Region, this chapter elucidates strategies for fostering sustainable practices and behaviors among tourism consumers and hotel management, contributing to the preservation of cultural and natural heritage.
- **Ethical Exploration of Advertising Impacts: Comparison between Alcohol-Free and Alcoholic Beer Communication of Users' Perceptions and Attitudes**: Through a comparative analysis of alcohol-free and alcoholic beer advertising, this chapter delves into the ethical dimensions of marketing communication, shedding light on consumers' perceptions and attitudes.
- **Evolution of Research on Green Innovation in Wine Industry: A Bibliometric Analysis**: Through a bibliometric analysis, this chapter traces the evolution of research on green innovation in the wine industry, identifying trends, gaps, and future directions for scholarly inquiry.
- **Factors for Consumers to Contemplate Regarding the Adoption of Eco-Friendly Packaging**: This chapter examines the factors influencing consumers' adoption of eco-friendly packaging in the beverage industry, offering valuable insights for sustainable packaging design and marketing strategies.
- **Gastronomy, Wine & Tourism: Development of Regional & Fusion Cuisine in Baja´s Guadalupe Valley**: Focusing on Baja's Guadalupe Valley, this chapter explores the intersection of gastronomy, wine, and tourism, tracing the development of regional and fusion cuisine as a driver of sustainable tourism.
- **Green Innovation in Wine Tourism: Insights from the Spanish Wine Sector**: Drawing on insights from the Spanish wine sector, this chapter delves into green innovation in wine tourism, showcasing best practices and innovative approaches to sustainable tourism development.
- **Halal Food Industry and Sustainability**: Through an exploration of the halal food industry, this chapter examines the intersection of Islamic dietary laws and sustainability principles, offering insights into sustainable practices within the context of halal food production and consumption.
- **How Does Environmental Proactivity Affect Green Innovation? An Assessment of Determinants of Sustainable Practices Adoption in Wine Industry**: This chapter investigates the relationship between environmental proactivity and green innovation in the wine industry, shedding light on the determinants of sustainable practices adoption.
- **Integrating Knowledge Management for Sustainable Growth: Insights from the Spanish Wine Sector**: Focusing on the Spanish wine sector, this chapter explores the role of knowledge management in fostering sustainable growth, highlighting the importance of knowledge sharing and collaboration.
- **Local Fruits for Sustainable Beverage Supply Chains**: Through an examination of sustainable beverage supply chains, this chapter advocates for the integration of local fruits, promoting economic development, and environmental sustainability.

- **Malaysian Oil Palm Industry, a View on the Economy, Social, and Environmental Aspect: Review on Oil Palm Industry in Malaysia**: This chapter offers a comprehensive review of the Malaysian oil palm industry, analyzing its economic, social, and environmental dimensions and exploring strategies for sustainable palm oil production.
- **Navigating the Nexus: Economics and Environmental Responsibility in the Global Beverage Industry**: Serving as the nexus of this compendium, this chapter provides a holistic overview of the economic and environmental challenges facing the global beverage industry, offering insights into pathways for sustainable development.
- **Review and Future Research Direction of Sustainability, Customer Values, Drivers, Attitude and Purchase Intention of Organic Products**: Through a comprehensive review, this chapter examines the nexus between sustainability, customer values, and organic product consumption, charting future research directions in this burgeoning field.
- **The Impact of Firmographics on Philanthropic Engagement in the Global Wine Industry**: Focusing on firmographics, this chapter investigates the factors influencing philanthropic engagement in the global wine industry, shedding light on the intersection of corporate social responsibility and business strategy.
- **The Music of Wine. Resources for Wine Tourism and Wine's Immaterial Cultural Heritage Interpretation**: Exploring the immaterial cultural heritage of wine, this chapter delves into the symbiotic relationship between wine tourism and cultural interpretation, weaving a narrative rich in sensory experiences and historical resonance.
- **The Rise of Functional Beverages Market: Indicators Post COVID-19 Pandemic**: In light of the COVID-19 pandemic, this chapter examines the burgeoning market for functional beverages, analyzing indicators of market growth and consumer trends in a post-pandemic landscape.

The audience for this tome is as diverse as it is expansive—encompassing scholars, students, policymakers, and industry titans alike. For the erudite academic, it offers a rich tapestry of theoretical insights and empirical findings, inviting critical engagement and scholarly dialogue. For the discerning student, it serves as a pedagogical compass, navigating the complex terrain of sustainability in the beverage industry and instilling a profound sense of environmental stewardship. For the visionary policymaker, it provides a roadmap to navigate the nexus of economic growth and ecological resilience, fostering the formulation of evidence-based policies for a sustainable future. And for the impassioned industry professional, it offers a treasure trove of innovative strategies and best practices, catalyzing a paradigm shift toward a more sustainable and equitable beverage landscape.

As we embark on this intellectual odyssey, let us heed the clarion call for collective action. Let us harness the power of knowledge to effectuate meaningful change, a change predicated not on fleeting convenience but on enduring sustainability. For in the crucible of collaboration and innovation lies the promise of a future where the beverage industry thrives in harmony with nature, a future where economic prosperity and environmental responsibility are not mutually exclusive, but inexorably intertwined.

Cristina Raluca Gh. Popescu
University of Bucharest, Romania & The Bucharest University of Economic Studies, Romania

Javier Martínez-Falcó
University of Alicante, Spain

Bartolomé Marco-Lajara
University of Alicante, Spain

Eduardo Sánchez-García
University of Alicante, Spain

Luis A. Millán-Tudela
University of Alicante, Spain

Chapter 1
Advances in Marketing Innovation to Enhance Resilience in the Wine Industry in Mexico:
A Comprehensive Analysis

Creta Cota-Cota
CETYS Universidad, Mexico

Mayer Cabrera-Flores
CETYS Universidad, Mexico

Alicia León-Pozo
CETYS Universidad, Mexico

Marta Peris-Ortiz
Universitat Politècnica de València, Spain

ABSTRACT

The socioeconomic context poses challenges that threaten the economic sustainability of various productive sectors, such as viticulture. In this regard, Valle de Guadalupe in Mexico has experienced exponential growth in the number of its wineries, posing a threat of deterioration of terroir, considering the limited natural resources typical of semi-arid ecosystems. As a result, the competitiveness of the industry is also constrained. In this context, a strategy based on the production of high-end wines, accompanied by marketing strategies that promote the creation of innovative brands, is one possible response to resilience in the sector. This research conducts a diagnosis of innovation by wineries and its impact on their marketing strategies across the four Ps. It is a descriptive study with a sample of 37 wine-producing companies associated with Provino de Ensenada. These analysis results conclude that in the Valle de Guadalupe´s wineries the product and promotion factor shows increase in their innovations, while in the price and place factor, it was found that companies do not innovate.

DOI: 10.4018/979-8-3693-2149-2.ch001

INTRODUCTION

In recent decades, human activity has undergone certain phenomena such as globalization, demographic growth, and the digital revolution. This has resulted in negative effects such as overpopulation, overexploitation of natural resources, more visible social inequality, an acceleration in climate change, and a dehumanization of society, giving rise to what Beck (1998) calls the "Risk Society." A society constantly threatened by extinction faces an ongoing need to deal with dangers and insecurities introduced by modernization. Such are these threats that the UN has set out 17 Sustainable Development Goals to address global challenges such as poverty, hunger, education, climate change, gender equality, and sustainability, aiming to achieve a fairer and more equitable and prosperous world.

Therefore, innovation has become crucial in the current business environment, where competition is intense, and resources are limited. Innovation drives changes in traditional work methods and seeks to improve the products or services offered (Scott & Davis, 2015). To achieve these goals, organizations need distinctive ideas that stimulate creativity and an environment conducive to innovative processes. Managers must also find effective ways to prioritize the distribution and utilization of resources (Gjerding, 2003).Optimal implementation of innovation has become relevant for both managers and organizations, as it can generate competitive advantages and lead to success in the market.

Within this context, the global wine industry faces these same difficulties. However, for wine-producing regions like Baja California, the challenges are even greater. For example, there is a lack of infrastructure for production processes, high costs of inputs such as bottles and corks, weak regulatory frameworks, and no social inclusion approach that would benefit not only wine producers but all stakeholders who help this industry to thrive, including native communities. Additionally, there is a need for greater positioning in the international market, and the sector faces threats to sustainability due to inefficient management of natural resources (water, soil, landscape, etc.) (Consejo Mexicano Vitivinícola, 2018; León-Pozo et al., 2022; Trejo-Pech et al., 2012).

Against this backdrop of resource scarcity in Baja California, a strategy based on the production of high-end wines, accompanied by marketing strategies that promote the development of innovative brands, is one possible response to support the competitiveness and resilience of the sector. This can help to establish a unique, sustainable wine industry in the region, generating a positive impact on internal economic growth and promoting economic development associated with related sectors, such as gastronomy and wine tourism. With this accelerated growth, the industry would transform into a catalyst for regional development and a trigger for the potential of Baja California as a world-class cultural and creative hub (Cabrera-Flores et al., 2024) . As a result, the study of innovation in companies in this wine-producing zone gains particular relevance.

This research aims to diagnose innovation and its impact on marketing strategies in the wine industry in Baja California, Mexico. Thus, the contribution of this research lies in highlighting the role of innovation in marketing as a vehicle to help the wine industry become more resilient. In other words, this study identifies aspects with significant potential for innovation and raises awareness among producers about this potential.

Given the above, the information generated from this work is useful for wineries in the region on their journey towards developing a more innovative wine industry in commercial terms, and more efficient in the use and exploitation of natural resources. In other words, the central expectation is that producers will continue to enhance the quality of their wines, with lower productions that allow for greater environmental preservation and, through marketing innovations, contribute to the development of a high-end wine region.

The article is structured into four sections. The first section describes the conditions in the Baja California wine industry. The second section provides a literature review analyzing the theoretical foundations underlying innovation, seeking to conceptualize innovation and identify its phases, and anticipating its potential relationship with the design, development, and execution of marketing strategies. The third section describes the methodology of the research. The fourth section discusses the results of the fieldwork, presented in relation to the four Ps of marketing: Product, Price, Place, and Promotion. The article closes with a series of arguments emphasizing the contribution, relevance, and pertinence of the study.

THE WINE INDUSTRY IN BAJA CALIFORNIA

Baja California is located in the northwest of Mexico, bordering the U.S. state of California. Its geographical location provides it with a Mediterranean climate that favors the growth of fruits such as vines, mainly in the city of Ensenada and its valleys. Ensenada is considered the capital of Mexican wine, producing 75% of all wine in Mexico and 65% of the grapes for its production (Consejo Mexicano Vitivinícola, 2018).

It is thanks to this microclimate, coupled with the cultural diversity of its inhabitants, that Baja California saw the wine trade become established as a distinctive industry of the local economy. While the origins of the wine industry in this region date back several centuries, it only began to peak in the early 21st century. An industry that had fewer than 10 wineries in the late 1990s now boasts more than 150 wineries established in the region's main valleys (Secretaría de Agricultura, Ganadería, Desarrollo Rural, Pesca y Alimentación [SAGARPA], 2018). Due to this rapid growth, the wine industry has positioned itself as a strategic sector for the development of Baja California (Góngora-Rosado, 2017).

However, this exponential growth has not only brought economic development and cultural transformations, giving rise to new consumption habits and more widespread adoption of wine by the Mexican market; it has also led to unplanned territorial expansion. This has caused environmental deterioration and the overexploitation of natural resources like water. This not only threatens the profitability of the industry but also the quality of wines, and consequently, the sustainability of the sector. Therefore, opting for mass wine production is unfeasible but stimulates the potential emergence of new competitive strategies.

In this context, elevating the quality of wines, following the trend in recent years (Espejel et al., 2014), has emerged as a predominant competitive strategy, surpassing one based on large-scale production. Thus, envisioning Baja California as a region producing high-end wines, with boutique wineries and world-class wine tourism and gastronomy, becomes a value-added strategy. This not only contributes to the international recognition of Mexican wine but also enhances the resilience and sustainability of the sector and the territory it encompasses (Consejo Mexicano Vitivinícola, 2018; Ruiz, 2014; Sánchez & Mungaray, 2010).

In this context, innovation and marketing become relevant as elements that can benefit the economic sustainability of the wine region in Baja California. This approach allows consumers to feel a closer, more special relationship to Baja California brands through more small-scale production. Additionally, reducing mass production helps preserve the terroir (Cabrera-Flores et al., 2024).

LITERATURE REVIEW

This chapter is divided into four sections that address essential topics related to innovation and marketing in the wine industry of Baja California.

Firstly, the study establishes the general context in which the research takes place, examining the importance of sustainability in the wine industry in Baja California and contextualizing it within the current landscape. Subsequently, we address the fundamentals of innovation, and finally, explore marketing in the wine industry and how it can influence the competitiveness of wineries and vineyards.

Sustainability and Resilience in the Wine Industry

The wine industry has a close connection with sustainability, as it makes use of terrain that sustains plant life and is influenced by climate and climatic fluctuations (Ferrer et al., 2022). While the most widely popularized concept of sustainability focuses on the proper use of natural resources, economic issues must not be disregarded. This gives rise to the concept of sustainable entrepreneurship, understood as a business activity that seeks to create economic, social, and environmental value sustainably, without compromising the ability of future generations to meet their own needs. To achieve this, sustainable entrepreneurs innovatively combine resources to meet the needs of people and the planet while reducing or eliminating negative impacts on the environment (Schimmenti et al., 2016).

This approach to the expanded concept of sustainability has received increasing attention from the International Organisation of Vine and Wine and academic institutions in recent decades (Costa et al., 2022). Likewise, it has been observed how wine companies are transitioning to sustainable agricultural and business practices, which may help to differentiate their brand in retail or optimize their economic return on investments with reductions in costs (Gilinsky et al., 2016).

Production challenges vary between regions, products, and grape varieties; hence, it is crucial to adjust production strategies to ensure sustainability. Although assessing the economic impact is complex and requires a thorough analysis with specific scenarios and risk assessments for each region, it is also important to quantify costs and benefits related to climate trends and necessary adaptations for long-term viability (Wagner et al., 2023). Therefore, organizations have begun to recognize the importance of adopting sustainable practices in the supply chain, as one possible outcome is a reduction in costs. Furthermore, the market has shown that consumers not only accept but increasingly demand sustainability in the products they purchase, leading to an increased relevance of sustainability in the business environment (Golicic, 2022). This development in the sector has been accompanied by innovative strategies that enable the industry to find other ways to gain visibility and resilience.

Foundations of Innovation

The term *innovation* comes from the Latin word *innovare*, derived from *novus* allow us to determine innovation as the insertion of something new (Macías, 2005). Schumpeter (1976), meanwhile, defines innovation as a combination of intangible forces that revolutionize the socio-economic structure and dynamics of an organization, community, or region. It destroys old paradigms and generates new elements through a process of creative destruction, which triggers a change in ways of thinking, acting, and organizing. Furthermore, Dosi (1992) points out that innovation processes respond to endogenous capabilities but also to exogenous factors such as the availability of human capital, consumer culture, geographical factors, institutional factors, and the state of science.

Accordingly, innovation is understood to occur when a good or service in the market is created or modified in a manner in which knowledge management plays an important role.

Types of Innovations

The Oslo Manual (OECD, 2005) identifies four types of innovations that cover a wide variety of changes in business activities: product innovations, process innovations, organizational innovations, and marketing innovations. Each of these categories represents a different way in which companies can innovate and improve their market performance.

Product innovation focuses on introducing a new product or service, or an improvement to a product or service, whether technical, material, component-based, software-related, ergonomic, or based on other functional characteristics (OECD, 2005). This innovation is a crucial performance factor in business, as it provides the opportunity to expand into new markets and industries, offering a path for companies to generate profits and improve their economic performance (Rajapathirana & Hui, 2018).

The innovation capability of a product is based on the organization's accumulated knowledge, acquired through a continuous learning process. Therefore, prior knowledge is of great help to enhance a company's ability to learn and assimilate new information, thereby improving its performance through innovation (Haile & Tüzüner, 2022).

Process innovation is defined by the Oslo Manual (OECD, 2005) as the integration of a new form of distribution or production, including improvements in technical aspects, equipment or software. Any method aimed at improving service delivery to customers will have a positive effect on the business. Hence, process innovation will have a significant impact on the growth and performance of a company due to its ability to reduce costs (YuSheng & Ibrahim, 2020).

Organizational innovation involves changes in business practices, workplace organization, and external relationships, according to the definition proposed by Baumane-Vītoliņa et al. (2022). Companies implement organizational innovation to improve operational efficiency, quality control, and learning, and to stimulate other types of innovation or develop new markets.

Finally, *marketing innovation* is described by the OECD (2005) as the introduction of a new form of marketing. It focuses on improving the design or presentation of the product, or its positioning, promotion, or price (the four Ps). Marketing innovation plays a significant role in industry development, as it promotes greater product diversification and expands companies' offerings in the market (Geldes & Felzensztein, 2013).

The Oslo Manual divides innovation not only by objective – product, process, organizational, and marketing – but also by purpose, impact, and the origin of resources (OECD, 2005).

Regarding impact, Aza Payano (2012) describes *radical* or *disruptive innovation*, which can be understood as the impact resulting from the introduction of new products, services, or processes that produce significant changes and create new markets. There is also *incremental innovation*, defined as the improvement and development of established products, services, or processes, with the aim of optimizing customer benefit, reducing costs, repositioning, and adapting to new markets and circumstances, laws, and standards.

A classification by origin of resources defines innovation as open or closed. Aguilar (2014) mentions that open innovation seeks to integrate external partners into the innovation process, including customers, suppliers, and research institutes. In contrast, closed innovation involves only internal resources that generate ideas and then develop and implement them.

Innovation is a fundamental driver for business success, allowing companies to stay competitive and relevant in an ever-changing market. However, innovation alone is not enough; it needs to be combined with effective marketing strategies for innovative products and services to reach consumers.

Therefore, innovation becomes a crucial factor for survival, progress, and growth, consistently ensuring the ability to generate benefits in the context of the wine industry, that is characterized by intense competition and shifts in consumer preferences, it is essential to motivate participants in the wine market towards continuous improvements (Lekics, 2021).

Marketing strategies act as the bridge that connects creativity and innovation with consumers. They identify market needs, communicate the benefits of innovative products and services, and create perceived value that drives adoption and loyalty.

Marketing Strategies

Marketing is "the activity, set of institutions, and processes for creating, communicating, delivering, and exchanging offerings that have value for customers, partners, and society at large" (American Marketing Association, 2017). Drucker (2004) points out that marketing appeals to the satisfaction of human needs.

The literature on marketing proposes a set of elements known as the *marketing mix*, better known as the 4P model, comprising Product, Price, Place, and Promotion. Product refers to investment decisions regarding product attributes and quality. Price refers to the level and structure of prices. The Place variable refers to distribution efforts. Promotion refers to the way a company communicates its products or services to consumers and persuades them to buy them (Pinto et al., 2022).

The use of the marketing mix in any work environment will be of great help in increasing sales and profits, enabling entry into the market. Additionally, the marketing mix helps companies influence current or potential customers to continue doing business, promoting loyalty (Wahab et al., 2016).

Kotler and Armstrong (2017, p. 170) point out that these four steps are fundamental for designing an effective and customer-oriented marketing strategy. Furthermore, once these steps have been established, marketers can implement specific marketing tactics, such as the 4Ps (product, price, promotion, and place, to execute the strategy and achieve the company's objectives (see Table 1).

Marketing and the Wine Industry

In the current context, the wine industry is experiencing sustained growth in its sales, this boom is attributed to a multitude of factors, with the intensification of global competition being a prominent one, in this scenario has prompted companies in the sector to implement more efficient marketing strategies, aimed at customer loyalty and maintaining market participation (Dias et al., 2023).

Marketing is a process that combines the capabilities of a company with the desires of customers with the aim of creating unique value, thereby affording a sustained competitive advantage (Londhe, 2014). Given its potential benefits, marketing has gained great significance, making inroads into different fields beyond business, such as civil society organizations and politics. In the case of business, marketing has become present in all industries.

Consequently, marketing has become a subject of study and the focus of numerous publications on its functioning and impact. Not only have publications on the topic become much more frequent,

Table 1. Marketing strategies

Market segmentation	Selection of target markets
Segmentation of a market into different groups of buyers, with similar characteristics, needs, or behaviors, that require a specific marketing strategy.	Each market group is evaluated in orde select one or more segments.
Differentiation	**Positioning**
Differentiation of market offerings to create value for the customer.	Place where the product or service wil offered. It should be clear, distinctive, desirable in relation to competitors and target market.

Note: Adapted based on Kotler and Armstrong (2017).

but their approaches have diversified. For instance, both Dolan and Goodman (2017) and Galati et al. (2017) have conducted studies from the perspective of social media use in the wine sector. The former analyzed the success of social media associated with the implementation of communication strategies for wine marketing, while the latter validated the efforts of the Sicilian wine industry on social media (Facebook) and examined the relationships between companies' social media efforts and management and company characteristics.

Another approach was taken by Mehta and Bhanja (2017), who worked from a perspective of consumer behavior to identify which attributes determine the selection of wine by young consumers, and found their preferences were influenced first by price and then, in descending order, by type of wine, brand, taste, and origin.

Similarly, from a strategic design perspective, Vergamini et al. (2019) analyzed the marketing strategies of wine producers in Tuscany, concluding that the complex nature of marketing strategies is primarily determined by the national or international market situation.

It has also been noted that the marketing of wine will face various challenges, like customer education will play a crucial role in developing marketing strategies it is imperative to thoroughly understand the market and explore new opportunities (Martinho, 2021).

Finally, in Baja California, García et al. (2018) explore the wine industry and wine tourism from a family business perspective. Meanwhile, Cabrera-Flores et al. (2024) address the issue of marketing in the wine sector from an innovation perspective, with a focus on product image, specifically innovation in wine and craft beer labels.

This literature review has shown a wide diversity of approaches to the study of this industry, emphasizing the importance of analyzing variables such as the competitive environment, consumer behavior, sustainability, the use of social media, and innovation, among other elements that have become essential in designing effective marketing strategies, where technology, innovation, and knowledge management take center stage.

However, the originality of this research lies in the combination of variables to be studied. That is to say, no references have been found that specifically study innovation in marketing strategies, particularly in connection with the wine industry, and even less so, studies conducted with this profile in the Mexican context.

METHOD

The present research is a cross-sectional, non-experimental study with a quantitative and descriptive approach, aimed at analyzing the role of innovation in marketing strategies in the wine industry of Baja California.

The universe was made up of wineries associated with Comité Pro Vino A.C. in Ensenada, the largest organization of wineries in the region. Key informants were selected based on their profile as decision-makers or administrative and marketing personnel working for wine companies. The instrument was administered from May to July 2022.

To calculate the sample, the equation for finite populations was used, considering a population of 73 wineries, a margin of error of 0.5, a confidence level of 95%, and an expected proportion of 0.05, resulting in a total of 37 wineries as the minimum representative sample size.

To measure the innovation variable (Cortés Palacios, 2016; Cuevas-Vargas et al., 2020), four dimensions were considered: product, price, place, and promotion. In turn, these dimensions have their respec-

Table 2. Matrix of operationalization of variables

Definition of the Variable	Dimension	Indicator	Item	Questions
Innovation	**Product**	Experience	10, 11	My company usually makes innovative modifications in the following aspects of the product:
		Presentation		My company makes innovative modifications in the following aspects of packaging:
	Price	Pricing methods	12, 13	In my company, innovative pricing methods have been developed or adopted through:
		Marketing methods		In my company, innovative marketing methods have been developed or adopted through:
	Place	Distribution systems	15,16	In my company, innovative distribution systems are introduced through:
		Product placement		In my company, new marketing methods are introduced in distribution through:
	Promotion	Strategies to boost sales	17, 18	In my company, new strategies are introduced to boost sales through:
		Concepts and means of promotion		In my company, new means of promotion are used to promote products through:
		Development and launch of a new brand image		In my company, the development and launch of a new brand image for a product are carried out through:

tive indicators. For the product dimension, indicators such as product design, packaging modifications, variety in product form, appearance, and taste were used. For the price dimension, indicators included marketing methods and pricing methods. The place dimension included indicators related to product placement, distribution systems, and direct sales. Finally, the promotion dimension used indicators such as concepts and means of promotion, strategies to stimulate sales, and the development and launch of a new brand image (see Table 2).

Based on these variables, dimensions, and indicators, an instrument with closed-ended questions and multiple-choice answers was developed. This instrument was validated by a group of experts, and the survey was administered in person as the data collection technique, with descriptive statistics in SPSS used as the analysis technique for the results.

Among the limitations of the study is the sample size, so a census would add value to the research. Similarly, to delve further into the innovation processes of wineries, a qualitative approach offers the possibility of exploring the level of innovation achieved by the wineries and the opportunities that can be explored in the future.

RESULTS

Our results were obtained through descriptive statistics and are presented in this section separately for each of the four dimensions of marketing (Product, Price, Place, and Promotion), which are in turn associated with their respective indicators, and together comprise the innovation variable.

Product

The Product dimension is composed of experience and presentation. The first indicator was measured on a 6-point hierarchical scale, where one is highest and six is lowest. Product quality and brand are the areas where most changes are introduced, in contrast to after-sales service and type of product (see Figure 1).

Our analysis of the Product dimension found that wineries tended to make modifications to the company's brand and product quality, focusing on the image that the product creates and the quality factor that influences whether customers continue to purchase the product or not. Mehta and Bhanja (2017) revealed five important factors in wine choice among young consumers, namely – in descending order of importance – price, type of wine, brand, taste, and origin, and it is of utmost importance for wineries to take these factors into account when introducing changes. In subsequent studies, variations in marketing strategies employed could be analyzed, considering different types of wine by the same producer, or even comparing different wineries. However, Vergamini et al. (2019) argue that the complex nature of marketing strategies is primarily driven by the national or international market situation, contrary to our findings, which focus on the company's brand and product quality.

Price

For the Price dimension, indicators include pricing methods and marketing methods. These are measured on a scale ranging from one (highest) to six (lowest). Figure 3 shows that wineries establish their pricing based on demand and production costs.

Figure 1. Determinants of the product dimension, associated with the innovation variable

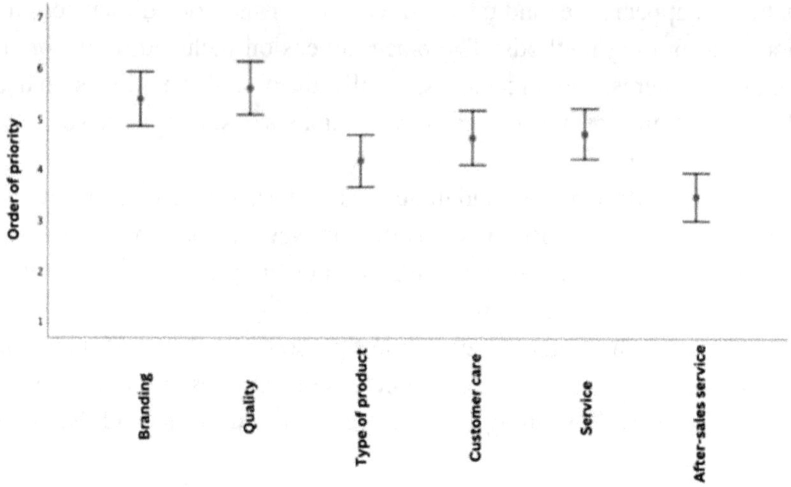

Our analysis of methods of marketing showed that innovation by wineries consisted primarily in advertising on social media (see Figure 4).

For the Price dimension, it was found that companies set their prices based on demand and production costs, as well as the prices in their market. Sadjadi et al. (2012) mention that the demand for a product, its quality, marketing expenses to promote the product, the level of product quality, and the adopted manufacturing process specifications also affect the unit product cost. In this sense, it would be worth analyzing these costs and the investment that wineries make in their marketing strategies, and their effectiveness, because having suitable market strategies provides added value to position a product

Figure 2. Product presentation, associated with the innovation variable

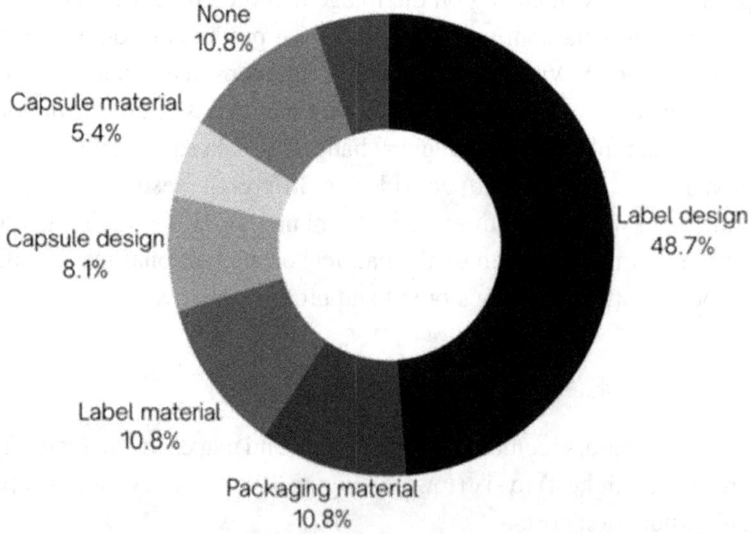

Figure 3. Pricing, associated with the innovation variable

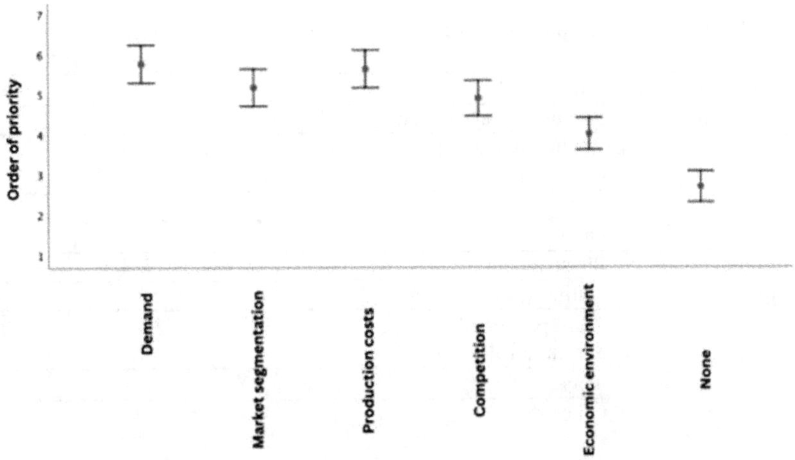

(Kotler et al., 2017). Additionally, it should be considered that online sales are gaining more prominence. The results show that social media are the most important sales channel, with most companies making their sales through accounts on social networks. In this regard, Palmié et al. (2022) point out that as e-commerce has gained more traction in the retail market, companies are innovating their business models and transitioning to digital business models. This highlights a need to evaluate which characteristics of digital media contribute most to promoting Baja California's wine.

Place

The Place dimension is composed of the indicators "distribution systems" and "product placement." For the first indicator, 35.1% of companies have not introduced innovative distribution systems, but 29.7%

Figure 4. Marketing methods, associated with the innovation variable

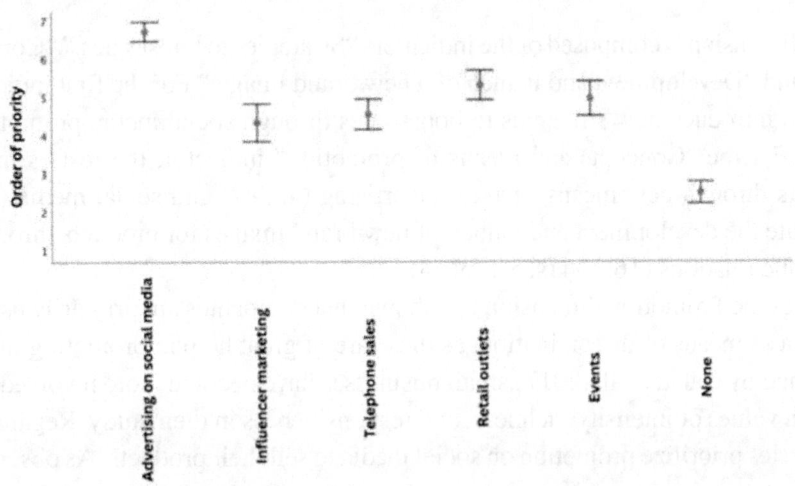

Table 3. Distribution systems and product placement, associated with the innovation variable

Indicator	Response options	Frequency	Valid percentage
Distribution systems	Franchises	3	8.1
	Exclusivity agreements	11	29.7
	Product licensing agreements	9	24.3
	None	13	35.1
	Other	1	2.7
Product placement	Physical stores	14	37.8
	Online stores	10	27.0
	Third parties (Amazon, Mercado Libre)	6	16.2
	None	6	16.2
	Other	1	2.7

distribute through exclusivity agreements and 24.3% through product licensing agreements. For the second indicator of the Place dimension, it was found that wineries usually introduce new marketing methods in distribution through physical stores (37.8%) and online stores (27%) (see Table 3).

In the Place dimension, it was found that companies do not usually introduce new distribution systems, indicating that wineries work independently rather than through third parties. As for product placement, which is closely related to the Price dimension, most wineries sell through physical stores. Additionally, to strengthen their brand, they also use online stores, indicating that they still maintain traditional sales operations but also incorporate digital channels. In this sense, Dolan and Goodman (2017) mention that, within business practice, and especially for brands that rely on direct sales, it is of utmost importance to create strong and favorable brands, a tool that has significant implications for the use of social media as part of marketing strategies. Also, in Baja California, these digital media not only allow for brand positioning but also provide an image that enhances the company's standing.

Promotion

The Promotion dimension is composed of the indicators "Strategies to boost sales," "Concepts and means of promotion," and "Development and launch of a new brand image." For the first indicator, companies were observed to introduce new strategies to boost sales through social media promotion (48.6%) and events (16.2%). For the "Concepts and means of promotion" indicator, the results indicate that they promote products through new means such as advertising (45.9%) and social media (18.9%). Finally, the results indicate the development and launch of new brand images for products through social media (59.5%) and public relations (16.2%) (see Table 4).

Our analysis of the Promotion dimension has shown that companies are primarily using social media and digital media as means of dissemination, as these are of great help in promoting their products. Indeed, as mentioned by Galati et al. (2017),small businesses have become more involved in social media, as shown by high values of intensity, richness, and responsiveness in their study. Regarding strategies to boost sales, wineries prioritize promotion on social media to sell their products. As observed in the previ-

Table 4. Product promotion strategies, associated with the innovation variable

Indicator	Response options	Frequency	Valid percentage
Strategies to boost sales	Loyalty cards	4	10.8
	Discounts	3	8.1
	E-mail marketing	4	10.8
	Social media promotion	18	48.6
	Events	6	16.2
	None	2	5.4
Concepts and means of promotion	Advertising	17	45.9
	Personal selling	5	13.5
	Sales promotion	4	10.8
	Public relations	3	8.1
	Social media	7	18.9
	Advertising leaflets	1	2.7
Development and launch of a new Brand image	Social media	22	59.5
	Personal selling	4	10.8
	Sales promotion	3	8.1
	Public relations	6	16.2
	Other	2	5.4

ous dimensions, wineries have mostly embraced online sales and promotion. Hanaysha (2022) reports significant growth in the use of social media to communicate and promote new or existing products or services in recent years due to their importance in influencing consumer buying behavior. Dolan and Goodman (2017), on the other hand, discuss three communication orientations: experiential messages; brand and product sales and promotion; and the building of a community, relationships, and trust among members. These are not observed in the research results, suggesting that wineries need to start building a community and relationships to foster trust in the brand.

As for the development and launch of a new brand image, again it is clear to see that companies use social media when they have something new to share, indicating that the market is focused on digital media. As mentioned by Covarrubias and Thach (2015), the wine industry in Baja California has made significant advances thanks to innovation and motivation, which producers have sparked through their experiences and the need to create new high-quality products that help attract different markets, whether nationally or internationally.

Based on these results and within each of the marketing strategies (the 4 P's), various commercial trends with the potential to be adopted within the wine industry are observed. For example, as part of product strategies, label innovation emerges as a relevant opportunity niche for attracting new consumers, especially those segments for whom visual appeal is a decisive element in the purchasing decision. In this sense, an effective characterization of the target market becomes indispensable.

On the other hand, concerning place strategies, they also show gradual innovations, and among their areas of opportunity is the utilization of digital transformation in marketing processes. Likewise, this process of digitization is beginning to be experienced in promotion strategies, especially in the use of digital networks, which saw a surge following the pandemic associated with SARS Covid.

This set of business practices is not only applicable to the wine industry, as there are other related industries in the region experiencing a level of maturity similar to the wine industry, such as gastronomy or the craft beer industry. Therefore, the knowledge generated can extend to these sectors as well.

CONCLUSION

While it is true that the wine industry maintains conventional strategies in some processes, such as distribution systems, innovation efforts are more strongly focused on product, price, and promotion strategies, with a notable trend toward digital transformation in methods of marketing and strategies to boost sales. Innovation processes are also observed in brand redesign and product image, including label design.

In this sense, and if a practical application of this research is sought, producers can be sensitized through guidance, courses, or dissemination channels to transfer the knowledge generated about the analyzed variables, emphasizing their focus on the innovation potential found in product and promotion strategies. In this way, producers can direct their efforts towards specific strategies that enable them to be more resilient and transform their brands into vehicles for a high-end market.

These results suggest that the wine industry in Baja California is undergoing a developing digital transformation process. However, the full potential of these technologies has not yet been fully exploited in all marketing strategies. We identified a particular area of opportunity in the Place dimension, which could enhance the sector's presence in the market.

This research has shown that innovation is influencing the wine industry in Baja California, but it is a gradual process. In this sense, it is important to note that the local wine trade only began to truly flourish at the turn of the century. The industry is therefore young and has yet to mature, especially in comparison to Old World regions. However, this can represent an opportunity for wineries looking to reinvent themselves, with innovation being a key factor.

Indeed, innovation can function as a key driver of resilience in the sector and as a trigger for a transition toward an industry centered on high-end products, set apart from other markets that have favored economies of scale, despite the resulting environmental damage and the constant threat they pose to regional sustainability.

In this way, the practical contribution of this research is aimed at wine producers, who will have information that encourages them to generate more innovative marketing strategies, enabling them to position their products in high-end markets.

Furthermore, the information from this research manages to contrast the current growth conditions of the industry in the area and its risks against the opportunities that marketing innovation generates in favor of the sector's resilience. The information generated from this contrast becomes input for the design of public policies seeking to redirect the development of the Baja California wine industry, under a vision of high enological quality, commercial innovation, and environmental preservation.

With this approach, the choice is made for a more comprehensive, better-planned industry development with high value for businesses and the entire economy of a wine tourism zone that is currently perceived as exclusive, with deteriorating environmental conditions, and rapid and disorderly growth.

On the other hand, the proposed approach in this study does not exist in the previous literature of this wine region, so the chapter has the potential to become a theoretical reference for innovation studies in this area. Likewise, the established relationship between innovation, marketing, and the sector's resilience is not a common focus in the international literature of viticulture, hence its contribution to the field of knowledge.

However, the research presents various areas of opportunity for the future. Among them, it is important to conduct qualitative research to understand the creative processes behind marketing innovation and, above all, future work to understand the real impact of these innovations at the market level. For this purpose, a consumer perception study would provide more elements of analysis. Additionally, dedicating a study to the analysis of product and promotion variables – which show the highest degree of innovation – facilitates a better understanding of the phenomenon and allows for more concrete proposals of efficient marketing strategies for producers. These studies can be designed to include more complex statistical analyses, such as structural equations, or, in the case of interviews, applying fuzzy logic techniques. Finally, the possibility of expanding the study sample to achieve a census is an opportunity to reach more accurate conclusions.

REFERENCES

Aguilar, R. (2014). *Innovación Abierta vs Innovación Cerrada I+DEA*. I+DEA. https://www.imasdea.com.mx/innovacion-abierta-vs-innovacion-cerrada/

American Marketing Association. (2017). *What is Marketing? —The Definition of Marketing*. AMA. https://www.ama.org/the-definition-of-marketing-what-is-marketing/

Baumane-Vītoliņa, I., Woschank, M., Apsalone, M., Šumilo, Ē., & Pacher, C. (2022). Organizational Innovation Implications for Manufacturing SMEs: Findings from an Empirical Study. *Procedia Computer Science*, *200*, 738–747. doi:10.1016/j.procs.2022.01.272

Beck, U. (1998). *La sociedad del riesgo: Hacia una nueva modernidad*. Paidós. https://www.gub.uy/sistema-nacional-emergencias/sites/sistema-nacional-emergencias/files/documentos/publicaciones/La%2Bsociedad%2Bdel%2Briesgo%2Bhacia%2Buna%2Bnueva%2Bmodernidad%20-BECK.pdf

Cabrera-Flores, M., Cota-Cota, C., Mellink-Mendez, S., & León-Pozo, A. (2024). Wine and craft beer in Baja California: An approach to innovation through label design. *International Journal of Entrepreneurship and Small Business*, *51*(1), 10060584. doi:10.1504/IJESB.2024.10060584

Consejo Mexicano Vitivinícola. (2018). *Plan Rector 2018*. UVAY Vino. https://uvayvino.org.mx/html/docs/plan_rector_2018.pdf

Cortés Palacios, H. A. (2016). *Influencia del financiamiento y de la innovación en el desempeño de las PyMEs manufacturas en el estado de Aguascalientes*. Universidad Autónoma de Aguascalientes. http://bdigital.dgse.uaa.mx:8080/xmlui/bitstream/handle/11317/1225/416148.pdf?sequence=1&isAllowed=y

Costa, J. M., Catarino, S., Escalona, J. M., & Comuzzo, P. (2022). Achieving a more sustainable wine supply chain—Environmental and socioeconomic issues of the industry. In J. M. Costa, S. Catarino, J. M. Escalona, & P. Comuzzo (Eds.), *Improving Sustainable Viticulture and Winemaking Practices* (pp. 1–24). Academic Press. doi:10.1016/B978-0-323-85150-3.00009-8

Covarrubias, J., & Thach, L. (2015). Wines of Baja Mexico: A qualitative study examining viticulture, enology, and marketing practices. *Wine Economics and Policy*, *4*(2), 110–115. doi:10.1016/j.wep.2015.11.001

Cuevas-Vargas, H., Parga-Montoya, N., & Estrada, S. (2020). Incidencia de la innovación en marketing en el rendimiento empresarial: Una aplicación basada en modelamiento con ecuaciones estructurales. *Estudios Gerenciales*, 66–79. doi:10.18046/j.estger.2020.154.3475

De Aza Payano, E. K. (2012). *Innovación Incremental y Innovación Radical/Disruptiva*. EOI. https://www.eoi.es/blogs/estefanykaryelindeaza/2012/03/07/innovacion-incremental-y-innovacion-radical-disruptiva/

Dias, A., Sousa, B., Santos, V., Ramos, P., & Madeira, A. (2023). Wine Tourism and Sustainability Awareness: A Consumer Behavior Perspective. *Sustainability (Basel)*, *15*(6), 6. doi:10.3390/su15065182

Dolan, R., & Goodman, S. (2017). Succeeding on social media: Exploring communication strategies for wine marketing. *Journal of Hospitality and Tourism Management*, *33*, 23–30. doi:10.1016/j.jhtm.2017.09.001

Dosi, G. (1992). Fuentes, métodos y efectos microeconómicos de la innovación. *Ekonomiaz: Revista vasca de economía, 22*, 269–332.

Drucker, P. F. (2004). *The effective executive: The definitive guide to getting the right things done*. Harper Business.

Espejel, M. I., & Ferrer, Á. Leyva, uana C., & Santos, M. (2014). Turismo en el valle de Guadalupe: ¡Tanto qué hacer! In J. C. Leyva & M. I. Espejel (Eds.), *El Valle de Guadalupe* (pp. 94–101). ENS. http://webfc.ens.uabc.mx/documentos/El%20Valle%20de%20Guadalupe.pdf

Ferrer, J. R., García-Cortijo, M. C., Pinilla, V., & Castillo-Valero, J. S. (2022). The business model and sustainability in the Spanish wine sector. *Journal of Cleaner Production*, *330*, 129810. doi:10.1016/j.jclepro.2021.129810

Galati, A., Crescimanno, M., Tinervia, S., & Fagnani, F. (2017). Social media as a strategic marketing tool in the Sicilian wine industry: Evidence from Facebook. *Wine Economics and Policy*, *6*(1), 40–47. doi:10.1016/j.wep.2017.03.003

García, A., Meraz-Ruiz, L., & Díaz, E. R. (2018). Wine Tourism and Wine Marketing in Family-Owned Micro Wineries in Guadalupe Valley, Mexico. *Rosa dos Ventos, 10*(4), 690–711.

Geldes, C., & Felzensztein, C. (2013). Marketing innovations in the agribusiness sector. *Academia (Caracas)*, *26*(1), 108–138. doi:10.1108/ARLA-05-2013-0042

Gilinsky, A. Jr, Newton, S. K., & Vega, R. F. (2016). Sustainability in the Global Wine Industry: Concepts and Cases. *Agriculture and Agricultural Science Procedia*, *8*, 37–49. doi:10.1016/j.aaspro.2016.02.006

Gjerding, A. N. (2003). The Flexible Firm: New Concepts and Differences Between the Nordic Systems of Innovation. In M. C.; L. Heitor B. Å. (eds), null (Ed.), Innovation, Competence Building, and Social Cohesion in Europe (pp. 122–143). Jessica Kingsley Publishers.

Golicic, S. L. (2022). Changes in sustainability in the global wine industry. *International Journal of Wine Business Research*, *34*(3), 392–409. doi:10.1108/IJWBR-03-2021-0021

Góngora-Rosado, M. A. (2017). *Baja California, México: Puerta norte del vino latinoamericano*. Retos y Oportunidades socioambientales.

Haile, E. A., & Tüzüner, V. L. (2022). Organizational learning capability and its impact on organizational innovation. *Asia Pacific Journal of Innovation and Entrepreneurship*, *16*(1), 69–85. doi:10.1108/APJIE-03-2022-0015

Hanaysha, J. R. (2022). Impact of social media marketing features on consumer's purchase decision in the fast-food industry: Brand trust as a mediator. *International Journal of Information Management Data Insights*, *2*(2), 100102. doi:10.1016/j.jjimei.2022.100102

Kotler, P., Armstrong, G., Araujo, L. A., & Ayala, L. E. P. (2017). *Fundamentos de Marketing*. Pearson Educación de México. https://dialnet.unirioja.es/servlet/libro?codigo=822679

Lekics, V. (2021). Sustainable Innovation in Wine Industry. *Systematic Reviews*, *13*(1), 55–73. PMID:33573701

León-Pozo, A., Robinson Trápaga, D. G., Cabrera-Flores, M. R., & Collins García, R. (2022). *La industria vitivinícola mexicana en el siglo xxi: Retos económicos, sociales y ambientales*. Acento Editores. https://repositorio.cetys.mx/handle/60000/1488

Londhe, B. R. (2014). Marketing Mix for Next Generation Marketing. *Procedia Economics and Finance*, *11*, 335–340. doi:10.1016/S2212-5671(14)00201-9

Macías, A. B. (2005). Una conceptualización comprehensiva de la innovación educativa. *Innovación Educativa (México, D.F.)*, *5*(28), 19–31.

Martinho, V. J. P. D. (2021). Contributions from Literature for Understanding Wine Marketing. *Sustainability (Basel)*, *13*(13), 13. Advance online publication. doi:10.3390/su13137468

Mehta, R., & Bhanja, N. (2017). Consumer preferences for wine attributes in an emerging market. *International Journal of Retail & Distribution Management*, *46*(1), 34–48. doi:10.1108/IJRDM-04-2017-0073

OECD. (2005). Oslo manual: Guidelines for collecting and interpreting innovation data (3rd ed). Organisation for Economic Co-operation and Development : Statistical Office of the European Communities.

Palmié, M., Miehé, L., Oghazi, P., Parida, V., & Wincent, J. (2022). The evolution of the digital service ecosystem and digital business model innovation in retail: The emergence of meta-ecosystems and the value of physical interactions. *Technological Forecasting and Social Change*, *177*, 121496. doi:10.1016/j.techfore.2022.121496

Pinto, L. G., Cavique, L., & Santos, J. M. A. (2022). Marketing Mix and New Product Diffusion Models. *Procedia Computer Science*, *204*, 885–890. doi:10.1016/j.procs.2022.08.107

Rajapathirana, R. P. J., & Hui, Y. (2018). Relationship between innovation capability, innovation type, and firm performance. *Journal of Innovation & Knowledge*, *3*(1), 44–55. doi:10.1016/j.jik.2017.06.002

Ruiz, W. (2014). Elementos para un Diagnóstico Económico de la Vitivinicultura en México | Revista de Economía, Facultad de Economía. *Universidad Autónoma de Yucatán.*, *31*(83), 9. doi:10.33937/reveco.2014.48

Sadjadi, S. J., Yazdian, S. A., & Shahanaghi, K. (2012). Optimal pricing, lot-sizing and marketing planning in a capacitated and imperfect production system. *Computers & Industrial Engineering*, *62*(1), 349–358. doi:10.1016/j.cie.2011.10.006

Sánchez, L., & Mungaray, A. (2010). Vino de calidad: Base de desarrollo endógeno en el Valle de Guadalupe, Baja California. *Frontera Norte*, *22*(44), 109–132.

Schimmenti, E., Migliore, G., Di Franco, C. P., & Borsellino, V. (2016). Is there sustainable entrepreneurship in the wine industry? Exploring Sicilian wineries participating in the SOStain program. *Wine Economics and Policy*, *5*(1), 14–23. doi:10.1016/j.wep.2016.05.001

Schumpeter, J. A. (1976). *Teoría del desenvolvimiento económico: Una investigación sobre ganancias, capital, crédito, interés y ciclo económico (1a* (E. Fondo de Cultura, Ed.).

Scott, W. R., & Davis, G. F. (2015). *Organizations and Organizing: Rational, Natural and Open Systems Perspectives* (1st ed.). Routledge., https://www.perlego.com/book/2192623/organizations-and-organizing-rational-natural-and-open-systems-perspectives-pdf doi:10.4324/9781315663371

Secretaría de Agricultura. Ganadería, Desarrollo Rural, Pesca y Alimentación [SAGARPA]. (2018). *Fomento a la Industria Vitivinícola, impulso y desarrollo del vino mexicano*. gob.mx. https://www.gob.mx/agricultura/es/articulos/fomento-a-la-industria-vitivinicola-impulso-y-desarrollo-del-vino-mexicano

Trejo-Pech, C., Arellano-Sada, R., Coelho, A. M., & Weldon, R. (2012). *Is the Baja California, Mexico, Wine Industry a Cluster? - Trejo-Pech—2012—American Journal of Agricultural Economics—Wiley Online Library*. *94*(1), 569–575.

Vergamini, D., Bartolini, F., Prosperi, P., & Brunori, G. (2019). Explaining regional dynamics of marketing strategies: The experience of the Tuscan wine producers. *Journal of Rural Studies*, *72*, 136–152. doi:10.1016/j.jrurstud.2019.10.006

Wagner, M., Stanbury, P., Dietrich, T., Döring, J., Foerster, C., Freund, M., Friedel, M., Kammann, C., Koch, M., Owtram, T., Schultz, H. R., Voss-Fels, K., & Hanf, J. (2023). Developing a Sustainability Vision for the Global Wine Industry. *Sustainability (Basel)*, *15*(13), 10487. doi:10.3390/su151310487

Wahab, N. A., Hassan, L. F. A., Shahid, S. A. M., & Maon, S. N. (2016). The Relationship Between Marketing Mix And Customer Loyalty In Hijab Industry: The Mediating Effect Of Customer Satisfaction. *Procedia Economics and Finance*, *37*, 366–371. doi:10.1016/S2212-5671(16)30138-1

YuSheng, K., & Ibrahim, M.YuSheng. (2020). Innovation Capabilities, Innovation Types, and Firm Performance: Evidence From the Banking Sector of Ghana. *SAGE Open*, *10*(2), 2158244020920892. doi:10.1177/2158244020920892

KEY TERMS AND DEFINITIONS

Innovation: It is the creative creation or modification of any product or service currently in the market.

Marketing: It involves the cycle of creating, communicating, delivering, and exchanging strategies that add value to consumers.

Place: It is the location or space where the good or service is found in the market.
Price: It is the value assigned to a good or service that is being offered in the market.
Product: It is the good or service that is available in the market.
Promotion: It is the way of making the service or good being offered known.
Resilience: It is the way in which a company can adapt to constant changes.
Sustainability: It is a process that allows maintaining the competitiveness of a company or sector by ensuring a balance with its economic, social, and environmental surroundings.

Chapter 2
Among Sustainable Vineyards:
The Case of Bodegas Castiblanque

Mariangeles García-Haro
Universitat Oberta of Cataunya, Spain

Jorge Linuesa-Langreo
University of Castilla-La Mancha, Spain

Ricardo Martínez-Cañas
https://orcid.org/0000-0003-4629-5513
University of Castilla-La Mancha, Spain

Pablo Ruiz-Palomino
University of Castilla-La Mancha, Spain

ABSTRACT

Sustainability has become a key issue across all economic sectors, but especially in the beverage industry, and the wine industry. Worldwide, an ever-increasing number of manufacturers are committing to reducing their carbon footprint to combat climate change. Bodegas y Viñedos Castiblanque, a winery in the La Mancha area of Spain, stands as an important reference for sustainability. This family-owned company is engaged in a significant project of wine production, manufacturing, and marketing. Simultaneously, it provides visitors with the opportunity to explore the winery, its history, and the latest technological advancements combined with artisan tradition. The case study analyzes this winery's sustainability and innovation management, highlighting key outcomes resulting from its participation in the tourism sustainability plan implemented in the tourism destination of Campo de Criptana (Spain).

INTRODUCTION

The increasing global population means companies and consumers must change the way they produce and consume raw materials, products, and services. It is estimated that, by the year 2030, a 50% increase in global food supplies will be necessary, along with a 50% rise in global energy demand, a 40% growth

DOI: 10.4018/979-8-3693-2149-2.ch002

in global water demand, and a 40% increase in transportation levels in the European Union compared to 2005 (FoodDrinkEurope, 2017). In this context, sustainability has emerged as one of the major challenges that companies must address in the coming years (Moltalvo-Falcón et al., 2023), becoming a leading priority across industries. Sustainability can be defined as meeting the needs of the present without compromising the ability of future generations to meet their own needs (United Nations, 1987).

Environmental instability was particularly notable in 2023, providing an opportunity for companies to reinvent themselves, placing the consumer at the center of their strategy while continuing to give prominence to sustainability, through innovation, agility, and efficiency (Magazine Código 84). According to the CEO Sustainability Guide 2023 report by Bain & Company, consumers are increasingly demanding more sustainable production processes from companies and are willing to pay up to 12% more for sustainable products. For 50% of the respondents, sustainability is one of the top four criteria when making a purchasing decision, although many acknowledge the difficulty in identifying organic production logos or less polluting products.

Sustainability concerns are particularly important for the food and beverage industry, as the raw materials needed for food and beverage production come directly from the natural environment, and their proper conservation entails ensuring sustainable production in the long term (fiab.es). Within the agri-food industry, the wine sector currently faces significant environmental and social challenges that require sustainable solutions (Signori et al., 2017), with balancing sustainability and economic viability being key to the sector's future (Moltalvo-Falcón et al., 2023).

The wine sector is especially important in Spain, being one of the world's leading producers. In terms of sustainability, the wine industry is one of the leaders in adopting sustainable policies as part of its competitive strategy, both in products and in the production and marketing process. Many wineries have succeeded in combining tradition and family ties to the wine culture with the latest technological innovations, instilling a strong commitment to environmental respect and care in their daily activities and policies. Directly associated with sustainability, wine tourism is a growing trend for the industry, acting as a catalyst for enjoyment and passion in the wine industry while contributing to the economic and social development of a region. Vineyard landscapes have significant potential to promote various forms of sustainable tourism, incorporating cultural activities and heritage as visitor attractions, while also allowing for the conservation of natural resources and promoting economic activity (Cañizares-Ruiz and Ruiz-Pulpón, 2020). Spanish wineries are increasingly engaging in this form of sustainable tourism, while simultaneously opting for agricultural practices and the latest technological advances to minimize their carbon footprint and combat climate change in a steadfast commitment to biodiversity and the quality of their wines.

While the wine industry acknowledges the need for more sustainable strategies and the benefits they generate, there are fewer studies on sustainability in the wine sector than in other industries, and so further research is needed (Trigo et al., 2023; Falcó et al., 2023). Although significant changes have occurred in recent decades, there is still a need for greater alignment between the wine industry and sustainability policies (Moltalvo-Falcón et al., 2023). Therefore, with the aim of delving into this line of research, this chapter proposes to analyze the importance of sustainability policy in the wine industry and examine the case of *Bodegas y Viñedos Castiblanque*, a traditional family winery that, by associating artisanal practices with technological innovations, has successfully cultivated, produced, and marketed the highest quality wines in the La Mancha region of Spain.

The chapter is organized as follows. First, we briefly analyze sustainability and its importance in the agri-food industry. Second, sustainability and its application in the wine industry are explored, and the most common sustainability practices in Spanish wineries are examined. Finally, we discuss the case of *Bodegas y Viñedos Castiblanque* and its commitment to sustainability.

LITERATURE REVIEW

Sustainability in the Beverage Industry

In 2015, all the member states of the United Nations approved the 17 Sustainable Development Goals as part of the 2030 Agenda, with the aim of achieving equality for all people worldwide, protecting the planet, and ensuring the prosperity of future generations. Four years later, with the approval of the European Green Deal, the European Union Member States committed to achieving climate neutrality by 2050. To achieve this, a series of proposals were launched to review legislation related to climate, energy, or transportation, reduce greenhouse gas emissions by half by 2030, and achieve zero emissions by 2050.

As stated by the AECOC Manufacturers and Distributors Association, 44% of consumers are now more concerned about caring for the planet, and four out of ten consumers attach importance to brands being transparent about the composition of their products, production processes, and distribution. Thus, as consumers are increasingly involved in such issues, companies that play an active role in sustainability can become leading brands. The circular economy, plastic and emissions reduction, decarbonization, and support for the local economy and society are the major challenges of sustainability that many companies are already addressing, with efforts in this sense to increase in the coming years. Sustainable production includes environmentally sensitive business practices that respond to the interests and needs of society and are economically viable to implement and maintain (Rodríguez-Sánchez and Sellers-Rubio, 2020). To advance in sustainability, in line with the Consumer Sustainability Guide (2020) published by the Spanish Federation of Food and Beverage Industry, the food and beverage industry aims, among other measures, to contribute to sustainable sourcing of raw materials, fight against climate change, reduce food waste, and decrease the environmental footprint of products. In particular, one of the main challenges facing this industry is the reduction of water consumption, an essential element for food production but also for cleaning and disinfection activities. The goal is to reduce its consumption through process optimization and reuse, without affecting the quality and safety of products. Secondly, energy use and combating climate change are one of the foremost priorities for the agri-food industry. In this regard, collaboration with suppliers is promoted in order to optimize the transport and distribution of raw materials and products, use alternative fuels, invest in more efficient and low-carbon technologies, and conduct feasibility studies, among other measures. Thirdly, an important issue is to promote the circular economy and efficiently manage waste. Most of the waste generated by the agri-food industry is packaging (García, 2022), and so the promotion of materials such as paper and cardboard to gradually replace plastics and the use of recycled materials is a central aim (Magazine Código 84).

Currently, more than 70% of food and beverage companies plan to invest in some type of sustainable activity in the short term. These measures include minimizing the use of resources, reusing wasted raw materials, using water utilization systems, and regulating temperature in the production process (García, 2022). In particular, the wine industry is closely linked to sustainability as its processes impact, and are impacted by, the environment, society, and the financial situation of companies (Golicic, 2022).

Importance of Sustainability in the Wine Industry

The Global Wine Industry and Current Situation

The global wine industry has undergone significant changes, particularly in the last ten years, including a rise in the number of producers, market expansion, and changes in wine consumer behavior (Fuentes-Fernández et al., 2022). This requires, on the one hand, assisting farmers in implementing more sustainable practices and, on the other, increasing consumer awareness through marketing techniques to emphasize the importance of purchasing more sustainable wines (Montalvo-Falcón et al., 2023). As San José et al. (2017) report, there is sufficient evidence to link wine culture with sustainable development. Firstly, because it reflects the viticultural exploitation of the environment and shows its social and economic impact on different regions. For example, the rise of wine tourism experiences has boosted the economic and social development of many regions, adding value to many areas.

Sustainability (in its three dimensions: environmental, economic, and social) is part of the main pillars of the strategic plan of the International Organization of Vine and Wine (OIVE) (2020-2024), as can be seen in Axis I "Promoting environmentally friendly viticulture," Axis II "Promoting an economic activity based on the principles of sustainable development, growth, and globalization of markets," and Axis III "Contributing to social development through viticulture." Indeed, the OIV acknowledges its commitment to achieving excellence in sustainability objectives in the environmental, socio-economic, and socio-cultural dimensions to contribute to the Sustainable Development Goals of the 2030 Agenda. Among other measures, this includes assessing the impact of climate change on wine production, protecting and promoting the vineyard landscape, and promoting the circular economy through the reuse of vineyard waste.

The production of grapes and wine is particularly susceptible to applying new technologies and processes that allow for medium and long-term sustainability improvement, while also enhancing the quality of the product obtained (Montalvo et al., 2023). Although it is considered one of the most important crops from a global economic standpoint, due to its strong dependence on terrain and climatic conditions, it is particularly vulnerable to the effects of climate change (Trigo et al., 2023). As Rugani and Lamastra (2023) suggest, the wine sector is one of the most widely studied agri-food sectors from a sustainability perspective, given the volume of its production and commercialization. This has increased in recent years with consumer interest in environmental issues and related health and well-being concerns. As these authors underline, sustainable production and management models in the wine sector have evolved over time due to growing concern for environmental protection and biodiversity, as well as other social aspects.

The Wine Industry in Spain

The Spanish wine industry, according to the Spanish Wine Federation, comprises over 930,000 hectares of vineyards, accounting for 13% of the global total, making Spain the second-largest exporter and the third-largest producer of wine in the world. The wine sector is a significant part of Spain's economy, culture, and society, being a symbol of tradition and history.

Sustainability is also a part of the 2022-2027 strategic plan of the Spanish wine sector (OIVE). The report aims to 'position Spain as a global wine sustainability leader in all its aspects: environmental, social, economic, historical, cultural, and landscape.' The objectives of this axis include the following:

(1) achieving Net Zero by 2035; (2) having 26% of vineyard area for wine grapes under organic cultivation by 2027; (3) ensuring more efficient use of fertilizers, phytosanitary products, and natural resources, such as water or energy; (4) promoting and increasing the area of vineyards that use more efficient and sustainable techniques; (5) adopting a nationally and internationally recognized sustainability seal for the entire sector; and (6) actively communicating the sector's role in sustainability to society and various stakeholders.

Spain is a leader in organic vineyards, with 97 protected designations of origin, making the wine sector a key player in combating depopulation in rural areas. According to the International Organization of Vine and Wine, organic viticulture grew by 13% between 2005 and 2019 (OIVE), and in 2022, 24 Spanish wineries were certified with the 'Wineries for Climate Protection' seal, the first and only specific environmental sustainability certification for the wine sector.

Among the main strategies being implemented by numerous wineries is, firstly, organic farming (Beiro, 2023), which involves eliminating chemical products such as pesticides, fertilizers, and herbicides. An increasing number of Spanish wineries have obtained organic certification, guaranteeing that their wines are sustainably produced. Secondly, biodynamic viticulture is a prominent aspect. To promote the flora and fauna of their environment, wineries perform certain tasks and activities in their vineyards according to the time of year, adapting to climatic conditions. Thirdly, emphasis is placed on recycling and reusing products. Materials previously considered waste, such as grape pomace, are now used as alternative products, being given new applications or reused in the production process. Fourthly, the high-energy consumption in fermentation, conservation, and bottling processes makes the wine industry a significant energy consumer. As a result, Spanish wineries are investing in technologies to reduce this consumption and promote renewable energies such as solar, wind, and geothermal power. Finally, water is one of the most important resources for the wine industry. For this reason, Spanish wineries are investing in more efficient water management processes, such as drip irrigation systems, rainwater collection, or treated wastewater reuse. Some wineries are also using monitoring systems to adjust irrigation based on real-time needs, reducing water consumption and improving grape quality.

Wine and Sustainable Tourism (Enotourism)

One way to promote sustainability in the agri-food industry is through tourism experiences. Currently, experience design has become key for tourist destinations to increase the value perceived by visitors and the sustainability of the destination (Breiby et al., 2020). According to the United Nations World Tourism Organization (UNWTO), for a destination to be sustainable, it must enhance the population of the receiving areas, generate value in the tourist experience, and maintain the quality of the environment through the conservation of natural resources and tangible and intangible heritage, factors that also drive the tourist experience to be authentic (Asociación Española de Ciudades del Vino, 2022). Tourism sustainability is defined by the UNWTOs as "tourism that takes full account of its current and future economic, social, and environmental impacts, addressing the needs of visitors, the industry, the environment, and host communities." As part of the aforementioned Agenda 2030, tourism sustainability is framed within Target 8.9 and 12.b, aiming by 2030 to devise and implement policies to promote sustainable tourism that creates jobs and promotes local culture and products. In recent years, a growing number of individuals have opted to explore destination environments and enjoy experiences related to culture, rural tourism, and ecotourism (Breiby et al., 2020). One of these experience categories is gastronomic tourism, and within it, wine tourism or enotourism.

Enotourism is one of the tourist segments in which sustainability is more feasible due to the involvement of a product such as wine, linked to the natural environment and determined by environmental factors. Additionally, it encompasses other forms of tourism, such as nature tourism, rural tourism, or gastronomic tourism, boosting the development of other types of tourist activities in the related territories (Asociación Española de Ciudades del Vino, 2022). Enotourism integrates gastronomy, culture, architecture, art, leisure, contact with nature, health, and improvement of the quality of life in various wine-growing regions, leading to the consideration of wine-based tourism as a sustainable activity, given its benefits for visitors and landowners (Cañizares-Ruiz and Ruiz-Pulpón, 2020). Enotourism involves a range of recreational activities (such as wine tasting), acquiring knowledge about vineyards and winery operations, interacting with the environment, and on the other hand, vine cultivation has become a mode of development and subsistence, with a multidimensional impact on wine regions (San José et al., 2017).

According to San José (2017), wine tourism is associated with cultural, socio-economic and environmental sustainability. Vineyards are already part of the landscape in many regions, and are a way to observe the contribution of agriculture to the creation of extraordinary landscapes (Rugani and Lamastra, 2023). The wine industry is valued, among other aspects, for the attractive landscapes it creates for tourism and hedonism (International Wine Organization, 2022). The presence of vineyards has shaped the identity of their territories, configuring landscapes, and creating a form of culture and life (Asociación Española de Ciudades del Vino, 2022).

Sustainability is also of particular importance in the so-called Wine Routes, formed by wine-producing regions linked to designations of origin. Enotourism contributes to wealth generation and, at the same time, involves greater knowledge of the efficient and respectful use of the natural environment. Jobs related to vine cultivation are, on occasions, the main driver of the region, being the primary source of income and employment for many families. As stated by Martínez-Falcó et al. (2023), wine tourism is a tourist product that can improve the profitability of wineries while also promoting social and environmental development in the corresponding territories. It also represents a source of differentiation for wineries, as they can sell their products directly to visitors and cross-sell with other products (cheese, oil) (Fuentes-Fernández et al., 2022). At the same time, wine tourism promotes gastronomy and culture by enhancing the consumption of local products, buying from local suppliers, or promoting local traditions and customs, such as crafts or the organization of festivals, generating a cultural exchange between tourists and residents (García-Casajeros et al., 2018).

Additionally, if the winery is part of the Wine Routes, not only the winery, but also the locality to which it belongs, can benefit from increased tourist activity. In this sense, visitors can explore the ecosystem and biodiversity of the landscape where the winery is located, engaging in activities that benefit the territory and helping maintain local identity and culture. Thus, such activity can promote a type of tourism that is more respectful of natural and cultural heritage, less intensive in the number of tourists it receives, and more controlled in the negative impacts derived from tourism activity, fostering the development of future generations (García-Casajeros et al., 2018). Therefore, as Falcó et al. (2023) affirm, to achieve sustainability, the activity of wineries must be based on three pillars: (1) sustainable practices in viticulture, (2) sustainable production in the winery, and (3) the development of sustainable wine tourism.

Wine tourism has become one of the most popular tourist attractions in Spain (Marco-Lájara et al., 2023). Approximately 2.5 million people visit wineries and wine museums along the Wine Routes in Spain each year, representing a 51.59% increase since 2021 (Asociación Española de Ciudades del Vino, 2022). It is not only about wine tasting; rather, it involves a combination of socio-cultural and environmental factors that enhance the tourist's experience. Wine tourism is characterized by its connection to nature, gastronomy, and local products or those from nearby areas (Marco-Lájara et al., 2023). It is a relatively established product in Spain, having been in existence for almost two decades, and has transformed the wine regions where it operates (Asociación Española de Ciudades del Vino, 2022). In fact, Spain is considered one of the best countries to visit for wine lovers, only surpassed by Portugal, Moldova, and Italy, according to a report by the company Bounce. This report highlights Spain as one of the largest wine producers in the world with a wide variety of flavors and types, thanks to its regional character.

In 2022, wine tourism had an economic impact in Spain of over 75 million euros, considering only wineries and museums. The impact would be even greater if other establishments, such as restaurants, accommodations, shops, wine bars, or transportation companies, among many others, were included (Asociación Española de Ciudades del Vino, 2022). Wine tourism in Spain continues to grow (see Figure 1), and although it has not yet returned to pre-COVID-19 levels, the trend is positive. In just two years, visits to wineries and museums along the Wine Routes of Spain has increased by over 80%, making it

Figure 1. Wine lovers index 2023
Source: https://usebounce.com/

Key

Wine consumption (liters per person) · Wine production (liters per person) · Vineyard surface area (as % of country) · Wine tours & tastings (per million people) · Average cost of a bottle of wine ($) · Overall score /10

	Country	Wine consumption	Wine production	Vineyard surface area	Wine tours & tastings	Average cost	Overall score
1	Portugal	58	66	2.09%	263	$4.31	8.83
2	Moldova	-	54	3.60%	55	$4.37	8.16
3	Italy	39	84	2.38%	382	$6.46	7.86
4	Spain	22	75	1.89%	243	$5.39	7.18
5	Georgia	-	57	0.70%	211	$5.91	7.05
6	France	37	67	1.48%	381	$7.54	6.87
7	Hungary	-	30	0.69%	67	$4.29	6.52
8	New Zealand	-	74	0.15%	183	$10.00	5.97
9	Greece	21	20	0.73%	191	$7.54	5.32
10	Chile	12	64	0.26%	220	$5.65	5.31
11	Austria	27	26	0.57%	35	$7.54	4.99
12	Romania	19	20	0.79%	52	$5.42	4.67
13	Argentina	18	25	0.07%	177	$3.00	4.47
14	Germany	23	11	0.29%	35	$5.39	4.33
15	Australia	21	49	0.02%	293	$11.91	4.13
16	South Africa	8	17	0.10%	263	$4.15	4.08
17	Switzerland	30	11	-	29	$14.14	3.19
18	United States	10	7	0.04%	80	$13.00	1.15
19	Brazil	2	1	0.01%	14	$8.05	0.87
20	China	1	0.3	0.08%	1	$12.62	0.65

Table 1. Profile of the wine tourist in Spain 2023

Wineries visited (average)	2.35 wineries	
Travel group	As a couple	42.00%
	In a group	39.80%
Age	18-25 years	12.10%
	26-36 years	23.41%
	36-45 years	23.89%
	46-65 years	36.46%
Sex	Women	46.70%
	Men	53.70%
Relationship with the world of wine	Passionate	32.20%
	Enthusiast	36.80%
	Beginner	15.80%
Bookings	Internet	63.06%
	Telephone	17.83%
	Without reservation	16.72%
Transport	Own or rented vehicle	75.60%
	Bus	19.60%
	Train	11.00%
	Plane	1.60%
Type of accommodation	Rural accommodation	17.19%
	4* Hotel	23.76%
	3* Hotel	15.84%

Source: wineroutesofspain.com

one of the forms of tourism that has most rapidly recovered from the pandemic-driven crisis (Asociación Española de Ciudades del Vino, 2022).

The main sector driving wine tourism in Spain (see Table 1) is that of the wineries affiliated (743) to the Wine Routes of Spain (Asociación Española de Ciudades del Vino, 2022), along with various wine-related leisure companies. In response to increased demand, all categories of accommodations have expanded their offerings, particularly three- and four-star hotels, followed by rural accommodations and campsites. In terms of visitor volume, Castilla-La Mancha is one of the Autonomous Communities with the highest growth rate (118.7%), boasting a total of 31,448 visitors in 2022, mostly of domestic origin.

BODEGAS Y VIÑEDOS CASTIBLANQUE CASE STUDY

Bodegas y Viñedos Castiblanque is a winery located in the town of Campo de Criptana, in the province of Ciudad Real, within the Autonomous Community of Castilla-La Mancha, Spain. It is situated in the "heart of La Mancha," between the municipalities of Alcázar de San Juan and Pedro Muñoz, with direct access to the Vineyards Highway, which connects the provinces of Toledo and Albacete.

Figure 2. Company logo
Source: bodegasyviñedoscastiblanque.com

Bodegas y Viñedos
CASTIBLANQUE

The town of Campo de Criptana, with around 14,000 inhabitants, is known for its famous windmills and the Albaicín neighborhood. According to various studies, its windmills, declared Cultural Heritage Sites, may have inspired Miguel de Cervantes to write Chapter VIII of the first part of Don Quixote: "Just then they came in sight of thirty or forty windmills that rise from that plain…". Indeed, Campo de Criptana is also known as the "Land of Giants", in reference to that episode in the book. Many of its streets are named after characters and adventures from the renowned novel (https://paisdelquijote.es/campo-de-criptana/. History recounts that there were once 34 windmills, but only ten of them are currently preserved (https://www.rutadelvinodelamancha.com/campo-de-criptana/).

In addition to its windmills, the town offers a wide range of cultural and gastronomic experiences and boasts a deeply rooted winemaking tradition.

One of the municipality's main objectives is to become a benchmark for sustainability, and to achieve this, it launched the new Tourism Sustainability Plan in 2023. The strategic pillars of the plan can be summarized into five key areas:

(1) Sustainable mobility: Implementation of a specific parking site for accessing the Sierra de los Molinos, installation of electric vehicle charging points in the car park, and improved accessibility from the parking site to the Sierra de los Molinos.
(2) Recovery and preservation of cultural heritage: Underground wiring, enhancement of archaeological remains, urban beautification, removal of television antennas, and signage.
(3) Sustainable destination management: Implementation of a digitalization plan, adoption of the Integrated System of Spanish Tourist Quality in Destinations (SICTED), and recognition of tourist sustainability within the Natura 2000 Network.
(4) Sustainable destination promotion: Circular economy workshops and sustainable experiences, design and signage of hiking and mountain biking routes, conditioning of the water route, organization of nighttime and theatrical visits, wine school sessions, and Music and Wine Days.
(5) Development of tourist products in collaboration with the Spanish rail company's *Tren de los Molinos* (Windmill Train) for tourists, digital tourist product guides, and promotion campaigns on digital platforms.

As mentioned in Pillar 4 and framed as an action within this Tourism Sustainability Plan, is the "Wine Tasting School," a pioneering project by the Campo de Criptana City Council. It is a communication and training tool aimed at tourists interested in wine culture through workshops and sessions to promote agri-food sector products. The town highlights its passion and tradition for wine through various activities throughout the year. For example, in 2023, one of its famous windmills was redesigned

Figure 3. Winery El Montañés

and converted into a museum to showcase the culture of wine and its wineries, affiliated with the La Mancha Designation of Origin.

Bodegas y Viñedos Castiblanque is located on the slopes of La Mancha, at an altitude of about 800 meters above sea level, with a temperature that fluctuates notably between night and day. It is a family-owned company that began the restoration of a 19th-century winery called "Bodega El Montañés" in 2001 (see Figure 3), founded in 1867. With the intention of preserving its old structure, it retained the stone walls, Arab tile roofing, pine wood interior structure, and initiated the rehabilitation of areas in disuse, while incorporating the latest technological advances in wine production and elaboration (see Figure 4).

The Castiblanque family spans three generations of viticulturists. The beginnings of the winery were the work of Jesús Castiblanque Alberca, better known as "Templao." It was Jesús who manually planted the first Airén vineyards in the 1950s. Over time, with the help of his son Jesús Castiblanque Pintor, they gradually expanded the plantation using traditional methods, planting plots of red grape varieties (Garnacha) and white grape varieties (Airén), eventually reaching a total of 120 hectares. In 1990, the family decided to produce quality bottled wines to ensure the profitability of their agricultural estates, i.e., producing their own grapes on their estates. To do this, they observed market demand at the time and planned a process of changing grape varieties, taking into account the geographical location of the winery, including soil type, regional climate, and the varieties permitted in Castilla-La Mancha.

Five years later, in 1995, the vineyard was restructured, retaining the best quality plots of the Airén grape variety. Additionally, in that year, the planting of the Tempranillo variety began, which the winery had already worked with, and in 2003, the family started to plant Moscatel with the aim of producing a young wine. Additionally, the Chardonnay variety, a typical French wine variety, was planted to obtain a barrel-fermented, high-end white wine. During this period, the planting was completed with other wine varieties, such as Syrah, Petit Verdot, and Cabernet Sauvignon, resulting in a wide range of red wine varieties.

Figure 4. Bodegas y Viñedos Castiblanque
Source: rutadelvinodelamancha.com

Throughout the planting process implemented over the entire period, consideration was given to whether the land could adapt to new technological advances so that all processes could be mechanized. With the vineyard on a trellis system, the company ensures that the fruit is harvested quickly at its optimal moment, especially at night, guaranteeing that the grapes enter the winery fresh. As stated on their website, "before being winemakers, we were viticulturists, and we are clear that the success of a good wine lies in having the best raw material, the highest quality grapes."

Currently, Bodegas y Viñedos Castiblanque *produces, manufactures, and markets some of the best wines in the Castilla-La Mancha region. The company has 120 hectares of its own vineyards and a restored old winery equipped with the most advanced and modern technical resources. Among its facilities, the winery has a technical, commercial, and administrative area, a 180-square-meter tasting room with a specific classroom for training and receiving visitors, and the "*jaraíz*" (winepress), where the grape is processed through destemming and pressing. Additionally, they have what they call the "White Wine Warehouse" and the "Red Wine Warehouse," where they have replaced the old concrete vats with stainless steel tanks for the production of their wines. They also have a cooling system, stabilization and bottling plant, a bottling storage warehouse, a room for 800 barrels and 150,000 bottles, and a fully equipped meeting and conference room.*

One of the aspects the company attaches most importance to is monitoring vine maturation in the field. From winter pruning to spring flowering, they ensure there is no excessive flowering, analyze the actual plant load, and remove surplus clusters in the field to reduce production. Grape harvesting is carried out manually and takes advantage of the cooler hours of the day. The grapes are collected in boxes so that they can be quickly transported and enter the winery at a temperature ranging from 10° to 11°. Consequently, when the grapes are pressed, or the must is fresh, the conditions are more favorable for fermentation.

The rest of the grape harvest is carried out with their own machinery suitable for this purpose, ensuring that the moment of collection is the most appropriate, collecting around 50,000 kg per night. This ensures the must arrives at the right temperature conditions. This entire process allows them to produce high-quality grapes for wines at a reasonable price.

Another fundamental aspect for Bodegas y Viñedos Castiblanque *is their concern for crop maintenance, seeking to reduce the negative impact on crops, with the aim of safeguarding quality and excellence in the vineyards (see Figure 5).*

Figure 5. End of the harvest 2023
Source: Twitter Bodegas y Viñedos Castiblanque

Enotourism Activity

In addition to wine production, manufacturing, and marketing, Bodegas y Viñedos Castiblanque *offers tourists and visitors the opportunity to learn firsthand about the operation of their wineries and the winemaking process through a wide variety of wine tourism activities. Through this project, people visiting their facilities will enjoy a wine tourism experience in which to learn all about wine culture. They will understand the production process and the effort required to obtain and make wine, but they will also be able to participate in the tradition.*

Visitors can choose from six different types of visits. The first involves a tour of the facilities and the 19th-century winery, where the entire grape transformation process is explained. After the activity, visitors can enjoy a snack including local products, such as Manchego cheese, Serrano ham, or olive oil on toast, among others. The second visit consists of a must tasting and a tasting of wines straight from the cask or new harvest (red, white, and rosé wines), giving visitors the exclusive opportunity to taste the wine before its release to the market. This activity takes place in the production warehouses. Thirdly, visitors can enjoy a horizontal tasting of finished wines, similar to the previous one with must and wines exclusively from the new harvest. Another type of visit includes a tour of the winery itself (with tasting and appetizers), with the possibility of visiting the vineyards and savoring a typical Manchego meal while enjoying the spectacular views.

As mentioned, the company seeks to find the right balance between innovation and tradition, based on a family legacy that has emerged as a key strategy for differentiation from other similar wineries. One of the initiatives implemented by Bodegas y Viñedos Castiblanque *is to involve a new type of tourist in the wine industry: children. The tradition of bread with wine and sugar was typically present in children's snacks from previous generations. However, some wineries, like* Bodegas Castiblanque, *aim to partially*

Figure 6. Educational workshops
Source: Twitter Bodegas y Viñedos Castiblanque

recover this tradition by bringing the wine culture closer to children through must, the juice obtained before grape fermentation, characterized by its sweet, alcohol-free taste. In the words of those in charge, "what we learn as children is never forgotten, and the dissemination of wine culture is very necessary for the sector. It's not a matter of prohibiting but of educating properly." Through a workshop, they teach children to taste different grape varieties and the wine transformation process. The children make their own juice by crushing some grapes and then conduct the tasting. Everything taught in the workshop is available in an educational guide drawn up by the winery itself, featuring "Blanquita Castiblanque" *and* "Negrita Castiblanque," *two grape-shaped dolls who find enjoyment in the world of wine.*

If the visitor wishes to add more activities to their experience, they can book the "Family Visit with Bodegas Castiblanque," which includes, in addition to the winery tour to learn about the winemaking process, a children's workshop on must production and tasting, and an educational guide for children related to the world of wine. Parents can enjoy a wine tasting and appetizer at the winery. Additionally, it includes a traditional Manchego cuisine workshop that ends with a tasting meal for adults and a children's menu meal. Lastly, notable is the "Guided Visit to the Sierra de los Molinos", which includes a tour of the Albaicín of Campo de Criptana, where visitors explore the inside of a windmill and the ESART artisan museum. This visit also includes the winery tour and tasting meal.

These experiences can be purchased on their website, as well as on various platforms, such as Groupon and Subasta de Ocio, and the option to buy visit packs through other applications, such as Groupalia, WonderBox, Pangea, among many others.

The route is part of the "La Mancha Wine Route," belonging to the Wine Routes of Spain, with the support of the Spanish administration and the Spanish Association of Wine Cities (Asociación Española de Ciudades del Vino, 2022). It is a wine route that offers a tour of ten municipalities with a great wine tradition in the provinces of Ciudad Real and Toledo, where visitors can have different experiences and personally visit wineries and vineyards controlled by the La Mancha Designation of Origin, explore the surroundings, and participate in tastings not only of wine but also of local products. The association includes more than 50 wineries and cultural attractions, such as medieval castles, windmills, and visits to villages

Figure 7. Wine route of La Mancha
Source: https://rutadelvinodelamancha.com

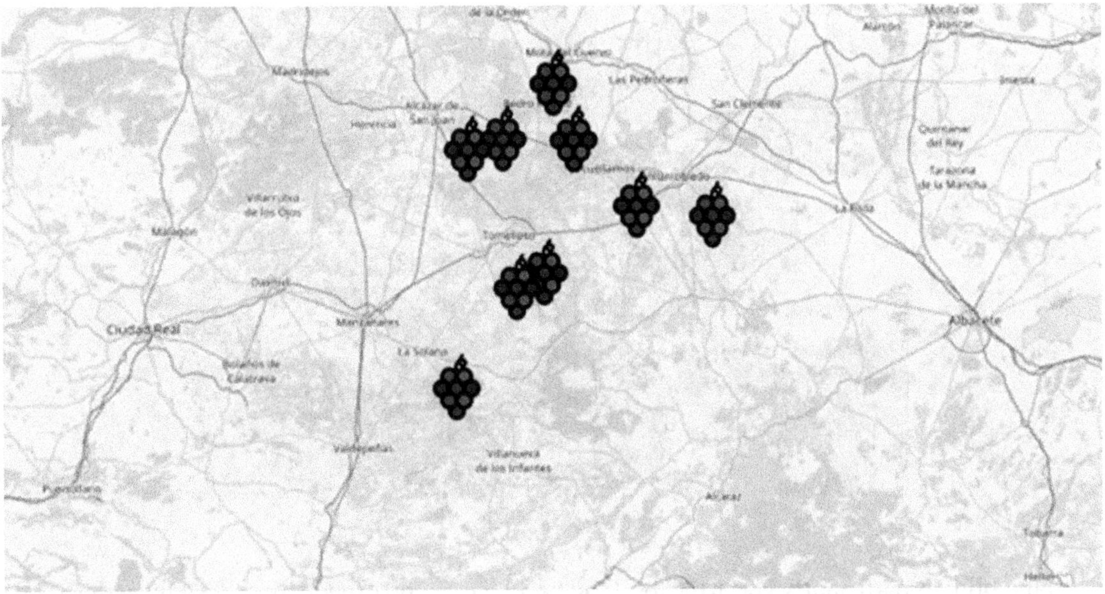

with a tradition of artisanal architecture (https://enoturismospain.com/rutas-vino-espana/ruta-vino-mancha).

Bodegas y Viñedos Castiblanque *participates in a multitude of projects and activities at the regional, national, and even international levels. Among them, its participation at the Airén Festival of Campo de Criptana stands out, as the different concerts take place in the surroundings of the winery, where attendees can enjoy live music while tasting appetizers and a selection of their main wines. In this regard, the winery is the only one in the locality that welcomes travelers from the* Tren de los Molinos *(see Figure 8), a round-trip train journey from Madrid to Campo de Criptana. The journey is enlivened by various historical characters, and, once in the town, tourists embark on different visits, including a tour of the winery with a tasting session included. In 2023, thanks to this initiative, over 150 people visited their facilities, creating a unique experience and a beautiful memory.*

Among other activities, the winery participates in educational workshops (see Figure 9), music and wine events, art exhibitions, presentations at gastronomic fairs, such as the National Wine Fair (FENAVIN), FINE Valladolid, *Feria de los Sabores del Quijote*, and the China Food and Beverage Fair, popular races, and training courses at the University of Castilla-La Mancha.

CONCLUSION

Sustainability has become a significant challenge for businesses. Consumers are increasingly demanding products and services that are transparent and environmentally and socially responsible. Therefore, if companies wish to differentiate themselves and attract consumers, they must not only implement sustainable practices but also communicate them effectively to consumers.

Figure 8. Train of Los Molinos
Source: Twitter Bodegas y Viñedos Castiblanque

Sustainability is particularly key in the food and beverage sector, especially in the wine industry. Wine culture is closely related to territory and its conservation because the activity impacts the environment, and in turn, the environment promotes the climatic conditions that will affect grape cultivation and other viticultural activities. Rationalizing water and energy consumption, recycling and reusing raw materials, reducing waste generation, and minimizing the use of fertilizers and pesticides are all measures wineries have had to adopt to make them efficient and competitive. To achieve these goals, the application of the latest technological innovations is essential alongside traditional artisanship.

Wine tourism, in particular, has become significant for the wine industry and sustainability, emerging as a driver of development for many regions. This activity involves not only boosting the winery itself but also improving the other local economic activities, promoting the consumption of local products and services, fostering local culture, and encouraging the adoption of measures to protect the environment and its biodiversity.

The analysis of *Bodegas y Viñedos Castiblanque* reflects the firm commitment of its managers to sustainability and the diversification of its activities. Over time, the different generations of this family business have adapted to changes in the environment, striking a balance between tradition and innovation,

Figure 9. Wine tasting at the Town Hall of Almodóvar del Campo
Source: Twitter Bodegas y Viñedos Castiblanque

and making a strong commitment to the economic and social development of the Campo de Criptana wine region. To achieve the highest quality wine, innovative agricultural techniques are applied in both the cultivation and harvesting of the product, while the company has also become a reference in wine tourism, providing visitors with the opportunity to learn about the history of their winery, the facilities, and the wine production process.

Indeed, many wineries are already implementing sustainable practices in the production and distribution of wine to reduce their carbon footprint, contribute to the fight against climate change, and preserve the natural and cultural heritage of wine-producing regions. The Spanish wine industry is undergoing a transformation towards a more sustainable model that improves the efficiency and competitiveness of wineries while being perceived as a differential element by consumers.

REFERENCES

Asociación Española de Ciudades del Vino. (2022). *Informe de visitantes a bodegas y museos del vino* [PDF File]. ACEVIN. https://wineroutesofspain.com/wp-content/uploads/2023/06/informe-visitas-a-bodegas-y-museos-rve-2022.pdf

Asociación Española de Ciudades del Vino. (2022). *Guía práctica de turismo sostenible Rutas del Vino de España* [PDF File]. ACEVIN. https://rutadelvinosierradefrancia.files.wordpress.com/2023/02/guia-practica-turismo-sostenible.-rutas-del-vino-de-espana-1.pdf

Bain & Company. (2023, November 24). *El 68% de los millenials en el mundo están preocupados por la sostenibilidad ambiental.* BAIN. https://www.bain.com/es/about/media-center/press-releases/south-america/2023/el-68-de-los-millennials-en-el-mundo-estan-preocupados-por-la-sostenibilidad-ambiental2/

Beiro, R. (2023, April 13). *La apuesta española por la sostenibilidad en la industria del vino.* Vinetur. https://www.vinetur.com/2023041372919/la-apuesta-espanola-por-la-sostenibilidad-en-la-industria-del-vino.html

BOUNCE. (2023). *Wine lovers index 2023.* BOUNCE. https://usebounce.com/blog/wine-lovers-index-2023

Breiby, M. A., Duedahl, E., Øian, H., & Ericsson, B. (2020). Exploring sustainable experiences in tourism. *Scandinavian Journal of Hospitality and Tourism, 20*(4), 335–351. doi:10.1080/15022250.2020.1748706

Cañizares-Ruiz, M. C. C., & Ruiz-Pulpón, Á. R. R. (2020). Paisajes del viñedo, turismo y sostenibilidad: Interrelaciones teóricas y aplicadas. *Investigaciones Geográficas*, (74), 9–28. doi:10.14198/INGEO2020.CRRP

Código 84. (2023 December). *Lo importante para 2024.* AECOC. https://www.aecoc.es/revistas/codigo-84/

Código 84. (2023). *Impacto de la sostenibilidad en la cesta de la compra.* AECOC. https://www.aecoc.es/revistas/codigo-84/

Falcó, J. M., Marco-Lajara, B., García, E. S., & Falcó, J. M. (2023). El enoturismo como catalizador de los objetivos de desarrollo sostenible: Un análisis aplicado a la industria vinícola española. *GeoGraphos: Revista Digital para Estudiantes de Geografía y Ciencias Sociales, 14*(152), 121–140. doi:10.14198/GEOGRA2023.14.156

Federación Española de Industrias de Alimentación y Bebidas. (2020). *Guía al consumidor sobre sostenibilidad* [PDF File]. FIAB. https://fiab.es/wp-content/uploads/2017/11/2017_GUIA-AL-CONSUMIDOR-DE-SOSTENIBILIDAD.pdf

Federación Española del Vino. (2023). *El sector en cifras*. FEV. https://www.fev.es/sector-cifras/

FoodDrink Europe. (2017). *Visión de sostenibilidad ambiental para 2030. Logros, Desafíos y Oportunidades* [PDF File]. FIAB. https://fiab.es/wp-content/uploads/2017/11/2012_VISIO%CC%81N-DE-SOSTENIBILIDAD-MEDIOAMBIENTAL-PARA-2030-FDE.pdf

Fuentes-Fernández, R., Martínez-Falcó, J., Sánchez-García, E., & Marco-Lajara, B. (2022). Does ecological agriculture moderate the relationship between wine tourism and economic performance? A structural equation analysis applied to the ribera del duero wine context. *Agriculture*, *12*(12), 2143. doi:10.3390/agriculture12122143

García, G. (2022, October 26). *Producción sostenible, clave en la industria de alimentos y bebidas*. The Food Tech. https://thefoodtech.com/seguridad-alimentaria/produccion-sostenible-clave-en-la-industria-de-alimentos-y-bebidas/

García-Casarejos, N., Gargallo, P., & Cabanes, B. (2018). Un marco teórico para delimitar el concepto de enoturismo sostenible desde un enfoque multi-nivel. In *E3S Web of Conferences* (Vol. 50, p. 03002). EDP Sciences. doi:10.1051/e3sconf/20185003002

Golicic, S. L. (2022). Changes in sustainability in the global wine industry. *International Journal of Wine Business Research*, *34*(3), 392–409. doi:10.1108/IJWBR-03-2021-0021

González-SanJosé, M. L., Gómez-Miguel, V., & Sotés, V. (2017). La Cultura del Vino, motor del desarrollo sostenible de las regiones vitivinícolas. In *BIO Web of Conferences* (*Vol. 9*, p. 04003). EDP Sciences.

Interprofesional del Vino de España. (2022 July 20). *Estrategia del sector vitivinícola español 2022-2027* [PDF File]. Interprofesional del Vino. https://interprofesionaldelvino.es/wp-content/uploads/2023/11/20072022_Presentacion-Publica_Plan-Estrategico-OIVEE_web-3.pdf

Interprofesional del Vino de España. (2023). *La relevancia económica y social del sector vitivinícola en España* [PDF file]. https://interprofesionaldelvino.es/wp-content/uploads/2023/11/Informe_relevancia_economica_y_social_del_sector_vitivinicola-_en-_Espana_2023_OIVEE_vf.pdf

Malaina, A. (2011). *Niños y vino, se rompe el tabú* [PDF File]. Interprofesional del Vino. https://www.riojatrek.com/wp-content/uploads/2011/02/VV104_22-25_vinos_y_ninos.pdf

Marco-Lajara, B., Úbeda-García, M., Zaragoza-Sáez, P., Poveda-Pareja, E., & Martínez Falcó, J. (2023). Enoturismo y sostenibilidad: Estudio de casos en la Ruta del Vino de Alicante (España). *Pasos (El Sauzal)*, *21*(2), 307–320. doi:10.25145/j.pasos.2023.21.020

Martínez Falcó, J., Marco-Lajara, B., Zaragoza-Sáez, P., & Sánchez-García, E. (2023). Vino, Turismo y COVID-19: El impacto de la COVID-19 en las Rutas del Vino de España. *Pasos (El Sauzal)*, *21*(1), 83–97. doi:10.25145/j.pasos.2023.21.006

Montalvo-Falcón, J. V., Sánchez-García, E., Marco-Lajara, B., & Martínez-Falcó, J. (2023). Sustainability Research in the Wine Industry: A Bibliometric Approach. *Agronomy (Basel)*, *13*(3), 871. doi:10.3390/agronomy13030871

Organización Internacional de la Viña y el Vino. (2020). *Plan Estratégico de la OIVE 2020-2024* [PDF file]. OIVE. https://www.OIVE.int/public/medias/7220/es-OIVE-strategic-plan-2020-2024-web.pdf

Plan de Sostenibilidad Turística de Campo de Criptana. (2023). *About.* Plan de Sostenibilidad Truistica de Camap de Criptata. https://pstdcampodecriptana.es/

Rodriguez-Sanchez, C., & Sellers-Rubio, R. (2020). Sustainability in the beverage industry: A research agenda from the demand side. *Sustainability (Basel)*, *13*(1), 186. doi:10.3390/su13010186

Rugani, B., & Lamastra, L. (2023). A common framework for sustainability indicators in the wine sector: Dream or reality? *Current Opinion in Environmental Science & Health*, *31*, 100408. doi:10.1016/j.coesh.2022.100408

Ruiz, M. C. C., & Pulpón, Á. R. R. (2020). Paisajes del viñedo, turismo y sostenibilidad: Interrelaciones teóricas y aplicadas. *Investigaciones Geográficas*, (74), 9–28. doi:10.14198/INGEO2020.CRRP

San José, M. L. G. (2017). Enoturismo y entornos sostenibles. *Arbor: Ciencia, pensamiento y cultura, 193*(785), 8.

SanJosé, M. L., Gómez-Miguel, V., & Sotés, V. (2017). La Cultura del Vino, motor del desarrollo sostenible de las regiones vitivinícolas. In *BIO Web of Conferences* (Vol. 9, p. 04003). EDP Sciences.

Signori, P., Flint, D. J., & Golicic, S. L. (2017). Constrained innovation on sustainability in the global wine industry. *Journal of Wine Research*, *28*(2), 71–90. doi:10.1080/09571264.2017.1302413

Tecnovino (2022, March). *Sosteniblidad y vino: ¿cómo influye en el consumidor el compromiso medioambiental?* https://www.tecnovino.com/sostenibilidad-y-vino-como-influye-en-el-consumidor-el-compromiso-medioambiental/

Trigo, A., Marta-Costa, A., & Fragoso, R. (2023). Sustainability assessment: Testing and validating a hierarchical framework in the Portuguese wine sector context. In *BIO Web of Conferences* (*Vol. 68*, p. 03008). EDP Sciences. United Nations. https://www.un.org/en/academic-impact/sustainability

Vinos de Castilla-La Mancha Media. (2022, May 20). *La sostenibilidad en el sector del vino: buenas prácticas*. Vinos de Castilla-La Mancha Media. https://vinosdecastillalamancha.es/la-sostenibilidad-en-el-sector-del-vino-buenas-practicas/

Chapter 3
Analyzing the Impact of Wine Tourism on the Triple Bottom Line of Spanish Wineries:
A Structural Equation Modeling Approach

Javier Martínez Falcó
https://orcid.org/0000-0001-9004-5816
University of Alicante, Spain & Stellenbosch University, South Africa

Eduardo Sánchez-García
https://orcid.org/0000-0002-8524-4906
University of Alicante, Spain

Bartolomé Marco-Lajara
https://orcid.org/0000-0001-8811-9118
University of Alicante, Spain

Luis A. Millán-Tudela
https://orcid.org/0000-0003-3669-9960
University of Alicante, Spain

Cristina Raluca Gh. Popescu
https://orcid.org/0000-0002-5876-0550
University of Bucharest, Romania & The Bucharest University of Economic Studies, Romania

ABSTRACT

The research focuses on assessing the impact of wine tourism on the comprehensive sustainability performance, which includes economic, social, and environmental aspects, of Spanish wineries. For a more detailed analysis of the cause-and-effect relationships, factors such as the winery's age, size, and affiliation with a protected designation of origin (PDO) are incorporated as control variables. A conceptual framework is created and subsequently analyzed using partial least squares structural equation modeling (PLS-SEM), based on data from a survey of 202 Spanish wineries. The results indicate a significant and positive relationship between wine tourism activities and the three dimensions of performance in the context of Spanish wineries. This study enhances the existing literature on wine tourism, making a significant contribution as it seems to be the first to explore the impact of wine tourism on the overall sustainable performance of wineries in Spain. Therefore, the research provides important insights for both academic researchers and industry professionals, particularly those considering the initiation or expansion of wine tourism in their business models.

DOI: 10.4018/979-8-3693-2149-2.ch003

INTRODUCTION

The tourism industry has experienced significant transformations recently due to evolving patterns in tourist demand, as Toubes et al. (2021) indicate. Current trends show tourists favoring shorter, more frequent trips, often seeking alternatives to traditional beach destinations. This shift has prompted the creation of new tourist products aligned with emerging demands. Notably, there's an increasing interest in gastronomy, especially wine, which is becoming a central aspect of travel, not just an ancillary activity, as Serra-Cantallops et al. (2021) have observed. Wine tourism, therefore, emerges as a synergy where visitors can explore new experiences while contributing to the development of the regions they visit, a concept discussed by Anderson (2013).

Traditionally, wine tourism is defined as visits to vineyards, wineries, wine festivals, and fairs where tasting wine and experiencing the wine region's characteristics are primary motivators for visitors, as described by Hall and Macionis (1998). The concept, however, has been interpreted from various perspectives. Getz (2000) offers a multifaceted definition, viewing it from the perspectives of wineries, tourist regions, and tourists. For wineries, wine tourism is an opportunity for market differentiation and increasing direct sales. From the perspective of tourist regions, it adds value to the territory and helps preserve viticultural traditions. For tourists, it fulfills the quest for new experiences. In this research, wine tourism is viewed as an activity that enhances the enjoyment of vineyards, wines, and wineries. It's seen as a means to boost the winery's competitiveness, foster territorial development, and introduce innovative products to the market.

The development of wine tourism has seen notable success in regions like Piedmont (Italy), Bordeaux (France), Oporto (Portugal), La Rioja (Spain), Mendoza (Argentina), and Napa Valley (United States). While this activity has long been significant in New World wine countries, its importance is growing in Old World countries as well. This growth is partly due to a decline in domestic wine consumption, an increased focus on exports, and changing tourist demand patterns favoring shorter, more varied trips, as highlighted by Gómez et al. (2019). The focus of this research is on the Spanish context, where wine tourism is emerging as a key contributor to the economic, social, and environmental well-being of the country, according to Zamarreño-Aramendia et al. (2021). Recent data from the Tourist Observatory of the Wine Routes of Spain (OTRVE) indicates that Spain's 35 wine routes attracted over 1.6 million wine tourists in 2021, generating an economic impact exceeding 51 million euros.

Wine tourism is a significant factor in regional development, contributing to economic and social welfare, and preserving the environment where it occurs, as Festa et al. (2020) have pointed out. It embodies the three dimensions of the Triple Bottom Line: economic, social, and environmental sustainability, as discussed by Sun and Drakeman (2022). This study aims to ascertain whether wine tourism positively influences the sustainable performance of Spanish wineries. Despite extensive research on the contribution of wine tourism to territorial development from economic, social, and environmental perspectives, there seems to be a gap in studies focusing on its impact on the sustainable performance of Spanish wineries. This research adopts a micro approach, concentrating on wineries as the main actors in wine tourism.

The structure of the research is as follows: Section 2 examines the relationship between wine tourism and the sustainable performance of wineries. Section 3 details the methodology employed to achieve the research objectives. Section 4 discusses the results of evaluating the global, measurement, and structural model. Lastly, Section 5 concludes with the study's main findings, its limitations, and potential directions for future research.

WINE TOURISM AND SUSTAINABLE PERFORMANCE

The first studies in the field of wine tourism date back to the last decade of the last century, which focused mainly on the link between wine tourism and rural economies, as well as the behavior of wine tourists (Hall, 1996). Among the pioneering works, the books *Wine Tourism Around the World* (Hall *et al.*, 2000) and *Explore Wine Tourism* (Getz, 2000), as well as the research carried out by Charters and Ali-Knigh (2002), Bruwer (2003), Alant and Bruwer (2004), Carlsen (2004), Getz and Brown (2006) and Mitchell and Hall (2006) stand out for their disruptive nature.

Over the last decade, the field of study of wine tourism has expanded to cover a wide range of topics, including the marketing and promotion of wine tourism, its role in regional development, its impact on local communities, its link with sustainability or its social and cultural significance, among others (Kotur, 2023). Among them the link between this type of tourism and sustainability stands out, given that wine tourism can provide a new source of income, promote environmentally responsible practices, increase the demand for sustainable products and practices, as well as improve the environmental awareness of visitors (Lorey *et al.*, 2023).

The increase in temperatures in recent decades has put the survival and viability of wine-growing regions at risk, and the implementation of a sustainable approach by the different members of the wine value chain has gone from being perceived as a mechanism of competitive differentiation to a strategic necessity to guarantee future wine production and, as a consequence, the survival of the sector (Frigon *et al.*, 2020). In this sense, wine tourism activity can contribute to the pillars of sustainability within wineries through the generation of employment, the dissemination of the heritage and history surrounding the activity, as well as the environmental awareness generated among wine tourists (Frost *et al.*, 2020). Wine tourism should not only be understood as a tool to generate higher sales for wineries, but as an activity that can benefit society and the environment in which they operate and that, therefore, favors the success of the wine sector and its survival over time (Andrade-Suárez and Caamaño-Franco, 2020).

In this line of thought, according to González (2017), the authenticity and intrinsic particularities of each wine-growing territory are differential elements that can be capitalized through wine tourism activities, thus favoring not only the economic performance of wineries, but also their social and environmental performance. In this way, all wineries that offer wine tourism activities can increase their level of competitiveness and sustainability at the same time (Nave *et al.*, 2021).

From an economic point of view, wine tourism can be understood as a distribution channel for the direct sale of wine in the winery (Sun and Drakeman, 2022; Montalvo-Falcón *et al.*, 2023). In fact, direct sales in wineries have been the indicator used par excellence by different academics to measure the economic contribution of the activity in wineries (Smyczek *et al.*, 2020), given that they allow: (1) to set a lower price for the wine than in the other channels or a similar price but acquiring the margin kept by intermediaries, (2) to obtain instant liquidity as opposed to other means of distributing wine in which the entry of effect is delayed, (3) benefiting from possible up-selling and/or cross-selling, as well as (4) fostering direct contact with customers, which is fundamental to guarantee future wine sales (generation of sentimental links with the brand and brand ambassadors, increasing knowledge of the wine varieties offered by the winery, etc.) .

Therefore, the wine tourism experience can increase the economic performance of wineries through direct sales in the winery, as well as through the improvement of commercial skills (Canziani *et al.*, 2017). Moreover, from the point of view of economic sustainability, wine tourism can become the main activity of small wineries, given that these are the ones that have the greatest difficulty in accessing large distribution channels, thus representing a profitable and accessible channel through which to market their wines (Karagiannis and Metaxas, 2020; Martínez-Falcó *et al.*, 2023a-j; Martínez-Falcó *et al.*, 2024a-b; Sánchez-García *et al.*, 2023a-b).

From a social point of view, wine tourism is conceived as a means to combat the adverse effects of depopulation, as well as to improve the well-being of society in general and winery workers in particular. Thus, the economic profitability and diversification of activities generated by wine tourism can contribute to the stability of the workers, as well as improve their working conditions (Williams, 2021). Additionally, wine tourism can lead to improved employment opportunities for local residents as well as training and/or retraining opportunities for new jobs linked to the service sector generated by the winery (Kutateladze *et al.*, 2021). However, not only winery workers can see their situation improved through the development of wine tourism, but also the community through the positive externalities generated, such as the beautification of the streets or the expansion of the cultural and leisure offer, among many others (Duarte-Alonso *et al.*, 2021).

Consequently, this activity can play a structuring role in the territory in which the winery is located through the financing of infrastructures (roads, sewage, etc.), the promotion of other sectors related to wine tourism (cultural tourism activities, links with local vendors, etc.) or the extension of services and activities for local residents (recreational facilities, outdoor leisure opportunities, etc.). In the same way, such a tourism typology makes it possible to enhance the wine-growing landscapes, as well as to promote wine culture in the region, thus preserving the tangible and intangible heritage elements inherited from the region's wine-growing tradition (Carvalho *et al.*, 2021).

From an environmental point of view, therefore, wine tourism can be considered as a catalyst for the environmental sustainability of wineries, whether wineries decide to promote their environmental management proactively or reactively, given that, on the one hand, it represents an element of differentiation between them (endogenous factor), and on the other, it improves the environment in which the activity takes place (exogenous factor), through the protection of heritage, the enhancement of gastronomic wealth and the protection of biodiversity (Darnay, 2016). In this way, wine tourism can catalyze environmentally friendly practices in wineries so that they can subsequently act as a pole of attraction for wine tourists with a high level of environmental awareness (Montella, 2017).

The development of wine tourism activities can increase the stock of ecological knowledge, given that, on the one hand, the staff in charge of this activity have to interact with the other employees (oenologist, agronomist, etc.) to be able to transmit the sustainable actions developed by the winery and, on the other hand, they usually receive training courses to learn about the sustainable practices developed by the wineries, which can be translated into a greater capacity to develop ecological innovations and, as a consequence, the improvement of the green performance (Karagiannis and Metaxas, 2020).

Wine tourism, understood as a form of tourism aimed at guaranteeing the use and conservation of this heritage as a cultural resource, must therefore aim to minimize any possible cultural and environmental damage, while at the same time improving the economic and social well-being of the wine region in which the activity takes place. However, despite the growing importance of the activity in favoring economic, social and environmental development, there is still little scientific production that has tried to analyze the effect of this activity on the triple dimension (economic, social and environmental) of winery performance. In order to contribute to this line of research and on the basis of the literature review carried out, the study proposes the following three research hypotheses:

H1. Wine tourism has a positive effect on the economic performance of wineries.

H2. Wine tourism has a positive effect on the social performance of wineries.

Figure 1. Theoretical model to be tested
Source: own elaboration

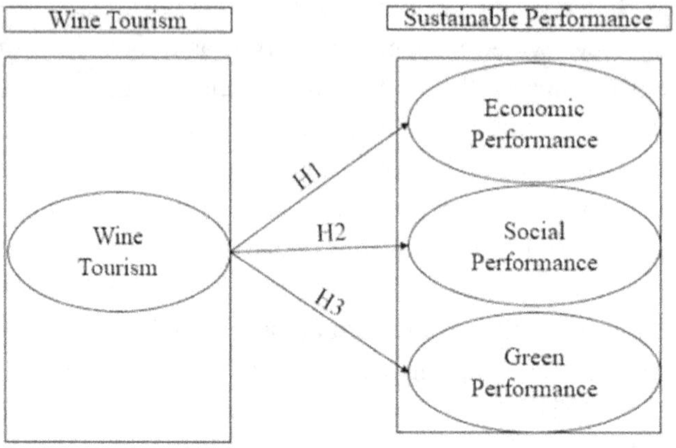

H3. Wine tourism has a positive effect on the green performance of wineries.

A graphical representation of the theoretical model to be tested is shown below in Figure 1.

METHODOLOGY

In order to facilitate the proper understanding of the methodological aspects related to this research, this section is structured in the following four parts: (1) research context, (2) population and sample collection, (3) measurement of variables and (4) analysis technique.

Research Context

There are several reasons for choosing the Spanish wine context for this research. Firstly, according to the latest data provided by the International Organization of Vine and Wine (OIV), Spain is a benchmark in the sector, occupying first place in the world in terms of vineyard surface area and volume of wine exported. However, the importance of the wine industry for Spain is not only determined by economic variables, but also by social and environmental factors, since the sector favors the welfare of citizens, as well as the preservation of the heritage and the environment in which the wineries operate (Marco-Lajara *et al.*, 2022a-d; Marco-Lajara *et al.*, 2023a-d). Secondly, wine tourism is becoming increasingly important for Spanish wineries. Thus, since the creation of the "Wine Routes of Spain" tourism product in 2008, more and more wineries have decided to develop and promote this type of tourism, with 35 wine routes currently existing in the Iberian country (Vázquez-Vicente *et al.*, 2021). Thirdly, wine tourism is an activity with an increasingly strategic component to ensure the survival of Spanish wineries, since it acts as a distribution channel for direct sales in the winery, counteracting the decline in wine consumption in homes, as well as favoring the generation of brand ambassadors (Zamarreño-Aramendia *et al.*, 2021).

Population and Sample

The study population consists of all companies included in the National Classification of Economic Activities (CNAE, by its Spanish abbreviation) code 1102 associated with manufacturing, which according to the data provided by the Iberian Balance Sheet Analysis System (SABI, by its Spanish abbreviation) database is made up of 4,373 companies. For the selection of the sample, based on the literature review conducted and the scales selected, an online questionnaire was developed, managed and administered through the Qualtrics application between September 2021 and January 2022. Initially, 216 responses were obtained in total. Nevertheless, after a filtering and cleaning process, 202 responses were considered valid. It is important to note that the questionnaire was designed to be answered by the top management of the wineries, in particular the CEO of each winery. This is due to the fact that members of senior management have greater skills and knowledge of the overall and strategic functioning of the company and, therefore, a greater mastery of the aspects covered in the questionnaire. Thus, the observations correspond to 202 responses from general managers belonging to 202 different wineries. The CEOs of the wineries had to respond to the questions and items of the constructs explained in the following subsection. Likewise, there is similarity between the population data and the data obtained in the sample, given that the three Autonomous Communities with the highest representation in the population are those with the highest representation in the sample. Similarly, there is a certain proportion between wineries that carry out wine tourism activities (57.43%) and those that do not (42.57%).

Measurement of Variables

Previously validated scales were used to ensure the reliability and validity of the variables. First, to measure wine tourism, a dichotomous variable was used, taking the value 1 when the winery developed wine tourism activities and 0 when it did not carry out such activities. This variable was considered as a dichotomous variable to establish differences between wineries that developed wine tourism activities and those that did not, in order to observe its influence on the development of green innovations. Thus, the objective was to measure whether the activity was performed or not, rather than to measure the degree of intensity of it. To formulate the question associated with the variable, we used the definition of Hall *et al.* (2000), as it is one of the most widely used in the academic literature on wine tourism, as well as because it captures the different characteristics that surround the activity. Second, the sustainable performance variable was considered as a second-order construct consisting of: economic performance (4 items), social performance (5 items) and green performance (5 items). In particular, a sustainable performance scale adapted from Wang and Wang (2012), Paulraj (2012) and Paillé *et al.* (2014) was used (see Table 1). The measurement scale used for this variable was Likert-type with seven response options (1-7), asking respondents to evaluate the average economic, social and green performance of their organization for each item addressed in relation to their competitors, over the last 5 years. Third, age, company size and Protected Designation of Origin (PDO) membership were included as control variables in order to observe the influence that these individual characteristics may have on sustainable performance. On the one hand, PDO was considered as a dichotomous variable, taking the value 1 when the firm was affiliated to at least one PDO and 0 when it was not affiliated to any appellation. On the other hand, the age of the organization was incorporated by measuring the total number of years elapsed from the creation of the company until the time of the study (year 2022). It should be noted that the questions linked to the control variables PDO and age were formulated on the basis of the research

Table 1. Composition of the study variables

Variable	Questions/items	Authors
Control Variables (CV)	CV 1. Is the winery adhered to at least one Protected Designation of Origin?	Marco-Lajara *et al.* (2022b)
	CV 2. When was the winery founded?	Marco-Lajara *et al.* (2022b)
	CV 3. How many employees does the winery have?	OECD (2005)
Wine Tourism (WT)	WT 1. Does the winery conduct tours of its vineyards, facilities, wine festivals or wine tastings so that customers can enjoy and/or experience the attributes of the wine region in which it is located?	Hall *et al.* (2000)
Economic Performance (EP)	EP 1. Our company's average return on investment is above the industry average over the past five years	Wang and Wang (2012)
	EP 2. Our company's average profit is above the industry average over the last five years	
	EP 3. Our company's profit growth is above the industry average over the last five years	
	EP 4. Our company's average sales profitability is above the industry average over the last five years	
Social Performance (SP)	SP 1. Our company has improved the well-being of its stakeholders compared to its competitors over the last five years	Paulraj (2012)
	SP 2. Our company has improved the health and safety of the community in which it operates relative to its competitors over the past five years	
	SP 3. Our company has reduced its environmental impact and risks to the general public relative to its competitors over the past five years	
	SP 4. Our company has improved the occupational health and safety of employees relative to its competitors over the past five years	
	SP 5. Our company has protected the claims and rights of its stakeholders relative to its competitors over the past five years	
Green Performance (GP)	GP 1. Our company has reduced waste and emissions from operations relative to its competitors over the past five years	Paillé *et al.* (2014)
	GP 2. Our company has reduced the environmental impact of its products/services relative to its competitors over the past five years	
	GP 3. Our company has reduced its environmental impact by establishing partnerships with its competitors over the last five years	
	GP 4. Our company has reduced the risk of environmental accidents, spills and emissions compared to its competitors in the last five years	
	GP 5. Our company has reduced purchases of non-renewable materials, chemicals and components relative to its competitors over the past five years	

Source: own elaboration

of Marco-Lajara *et al.* (2022b). With respect to the the size was measured in accordance with the rules of the Organization for Economic Co-operation and Development (OECD, 2005).

Analysis Technique

The technique used to test the proposed theoretical model was structural equation modeling (PLS-SEM) by means of the SmartPLS software version 3.3.9. The technique enables the analysis of a network of relations between variables, which may be unobservable, i.e. latent variables. This makes the technique

Table 2. Global model fit

	Value	HI95	HI99
SRMR	0.048	0.056	0.068
d_ULS	0.742	0.818	0.944
d_G	0.797	0.843	0.951

Source: compiled by authors

particularly useful in the field of management, where this research is framed, given that most of the constructs analyzed are not directly observable (Roldan and Cepeda, 2017). In this sense, the technique is particularly useful for testing the proposed model since sustainable performance is a latent variable. Furthermore, the study sample (n=202) exceeds the minimum sample size of 100 required to apply this technique (Hair *et al.*, 2019). PLS-SEM is also recommended for analyzing direct effects between variables and has been previously used to carry out studies within the field of management in the wine industry, which highlights the suitability of the technique used (Knight *et al.*, 2019).

RESULTS

As recommended by Hair *et al.* (2019), the results have been reported based on three criteria: (1) evaluation of the overall model, (2) evaluation of the measurement model and (3) evaluation of the structural model.

Firstly, with regard to the assessment of the overall model, it should be noted that the model has a Standardized Root Mean Square Residual (SRMSR) of 0.048, which demonstrates that the overall fit of the model is satisfactory as this indicator is less than 0.08 (Hu and Bentler, 1998). In fact, it meets the stricter criterion of Byrne (2008), who states that the SRMSR has to be less than 0.05 for the model to be accepted. Having checked the SRMR criterion, the unweighted least squares discrepancy (d_ULS) and the geodetic discrepancy (d_G9) were verified to be within the confidence range after bootstrapping. All results are lower than HI95 and HI99, as shown in Table 2. Therefore, the findings indicate that this model cannot be discarded (Hair *et al.*, 2019).

Secondly, with regard to the evaluation of the measurement model, it is important to note that the indicators of the studied variables comply with the requirements of individual reliability, since the loadings of these indicators are above 0.707 (Carmines and Zeller, 1979). Likewise, the internal consistency criterion is met for all constructs, with both Conbach's alpha and composite reliability exceeding 0.8 (see Table 3). Similarly, the constructs fulfil the requirement of convergent validity, as the average variance extracted from the variables analyzed exceeds 0.5 (Fornell and Larcker, 1981). This means that every construct explains over half of the indicators' variance. Discriminant validity was analyzed using the Heterotrait-Monotrait (HTMT) criterion. Table 4 demonstrates how the values of the constructs are all lower than 0.80, which shows that the constructs are unique and therefore capture different realities.

Third, before proceeding to the analysis of the structural model, the presence of problems related to collinearity was examined. The reason for this is the necessity to avoid the existence of multi-collinearity between the antecedent variables in each of the endogenous constructs. Following Hair *et al.* (2016), there are signs of collinearity when the Variance Inflation Factor (VIF) is higher than 5. Therefore, values higher than five of the endogenous constructs involve levels of critical collinearity. In this sense, the VIF

Table 3. Evaluation of the measurement model

Construct/Items	Outer Loadings	Rho (Pa)	Cronbach's Alpha	AVE
Wine Tourism (WT)		1.000	1.000	1.000
WT 1	1.000			
Economic Performance (EP)		0.961	0.959	0.892
EP 1	0.915			
EP 2	0.964			
EP 3	0.947			
EP 4	0.951			
Social Performance (SP)		0.920	0.914	0.699
SP 1	0.797			
SP 2	0.774			
SP 3	0.877			
SP 4	0.858			
SP 5	0.869			
Green Performance (GP)		0.923	0.907	0.780
GP 1	0.893			
GP 2	0.851			
GP 3	0.891			
GP 4	0.897			
GP 5	0.806			

Source: compiled by authors

values obtained in this study do not surpass the maximum value in any of the cases. Through Figure 2, the data relatives to R-Squared and β based on a boostrap test with 5000 subsamples can be observed. The direct effects of wine tourism on economic (0.455), social (0.181) and environmental (0.112) performance have been tested, finding both positive and significant effects in all three relationships (see Table 5). The R^2 values for economic, social and green performance are 0.304, 0.262 and 0.149, being

Table 4. Evaluation of discriminant validity

	Age	PDO	EP	WT	GP	Size	SP
Age							
PDO	0.050						
EP	0.023	0.086					
WT	0.123	0.062	0.472				
GP	0.063	0.052	0.471	0.089			
Size	0.113	0.043	0.173	0.134	0.212		
SP	0.097	0.034	0.632	0.193	0.662	0.251	

Source: compiled by authors

Figure 2. Results of the proposed theoretical model
Source: own elaboration

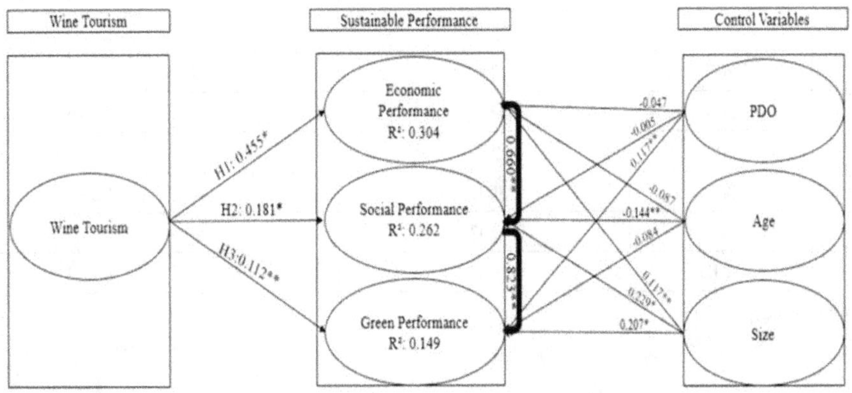

higher than the recommended value of 0.10 by Falk and Miller (1992) for the explained variance of a given endogenous construct to be considered adequate.

The Geisser test (Q^2), which must have estimated values greater than 0 ($Q^2 > 0$), was tested to assess the quality of the model. As can be observed through Table 6, a medium predictive relevance of the model was found as the Q^2 values are above 0.20 (Kline, 2011). Regarding control variables, these findings reveal that PDO membership has a negative relationship with economic and social performance, with only the relationship between PDO membership and green performance being positive and significant. Similarly, age has a negative relationship with economic, social and environmental performance, with only the relationship between age and social performance being negative and significant. Size, on the other hand, has a positive and significant relationship with the three types of performance analyzed.

DISCUSSION AND CONCLUSION

This research is pivotal as it empirically establishes a positive and significant connection between wine tourism and the economic, social, and environmental performance of Spanish wineries. Wine tourism emerges as a novel avenue for diversifying wine companies, enhancing their competitiveness, societal well-being, environmental management, regional development, and the capacity for innovation in an increasingly challenging and dynamic environment.

Table 5. Results of the structural model

Direct Effects	Path Coefficient	t-Value	p-Value	95% BCCI	Hypothesis supported
WT -> EP	0.455	8.967	0.000**	[0.355; 0.553]	H1 supported
WT -> SP	0.181	2.482	0.000**	[0.030; 0.319]	H2 supported
WT -> GP	0.112	2.017	0.044*	[0.022; 0.249]	H3 supported

Source: compiled by authors

Table 6. Construct crossvalidated redundancy

	SSO	SSE	Q^2 (=1-SSE/SSO)
Age	202	202	
PDO	202	202	
EP	808	643.260	0.346
WT	202	202	
GP	808	778.082	0.297
Size	202	202	
SP	1212	1131.203	0.202

Source: compiled by authors

The study reveals the varying impact of wine tourism on the three types of performance, with a more pronounced influence on economic performance, followed by social and environmental aspects. This variation can be attributed to the direct impact of wine tourism on business profitability. Acting as a direct distribution channel, it boosts winery sales, eliminates intermediary profit margins, encourages cross-selling and up-selling of various products, enables direct customer engagement, and fosters the creation of brand ambassadors, thereby establishing emotional connections that drive long-term wine sales. These factors contribute to the economic enhancement of wineries, ensuring their sustainability.

The findings align with those of Lavandoski et al. (2018), who noted a positive correlation between the level of wine tourism development and organizational performance in the Portuguese wine context. However, they differ from Smyczek et al. (2020), who found no direct link between the intensity of wine tourism services and direct sales in Italian wineries. Consequently, the relationship between wine tourism and the economic performance of wineries warrants further exploration to provide clarity in this research domain. The existing scientific literature indicates varied outcomes across different wine-producing countries, highlighting the need for more extensive research in this field.

The study reveals a positive and significant correlation between wine tourism and social performance. This relationship can be attributed to the improved conditions for various stakeholders due to successful wine tourism activities. Wineries engaging in wine tourism can experience increased profitability, leading to enhanced security and stability for employees, thereby improving the winery's competitive position. Additionally, employees may find their roles enriched by the diversification of activities, offering opportunities to specialize in other aspects of the wine sector, particularly wine tourism.

Beyond benefiting employees, wine tourism also positively impacts the society in which the winery operates. It serves as a medium to disseminate the history, heritage, and gastronomic culture associated with the wine-growing region, thus strengthening its wine identity. This alignment with the interests of diverse stakeholders echoes the findings of Poitras and Donald (2006), Andrade-Suárez and Caamaño-Franco (2020), and Frost et al. (2020), who emphasize wine tourism's role in enhancing conditions for winery workers and its contribution to the cultural, historical, and heritage promotion of wine-growing areas.

The relationship between wine tourism and environmental performance, while positive and significant, shows the least intensity. This could be because wine tourism indirectly improves green performance by increasing ecological knowledge among employees. This increase results from interaction among winery members to effectively communicate practices to wine tourists, green training for those conducting wine tourism activities, and environmental inquiries or suggestions from visitors. This enhanced green knowledge positively impacts resource conservation within the winery. Furthermore, wineries may adopt eco-friendly practices to attract environmentally conscious tourists. These findings align with recent research in the field, including studies by Montella (2017), Andrade-Suárez and Caamaño-Franco (2020), and Trigo and Silva (2022), which explore the connections between wine tourism and environmental performance.

This study makes a significant contribution to the field of wine tourism by comprehensively examining the impact of this tourism type on the economic, social, and environmental performance of Spanish wineries. However, the research is not without its limitations. One notable limitation is the cross-sectional nature of the study, which restricts the ability to analyze relationships over an extended period. Additionally, given the importance of the topic, there is a need to expand this analysis to include other wine-producing regions globally.

To address these limitations, future research directions appear to be promising. One such direction involves conducting a longitudinal analysis of the firms that participated in the survey. This approach would allow for a more dynamic understanding of the relationships over time. Another potential area of research is to apply and compare the proposed model in the context of the Californian wine industry. Such a comparative study between Old World and New World wine regions, based on the variables analyzed, could provide deeper insights and broader perspectives on the impact of wine tourism across different wine-producing contexts.

ACKNOWLEDGMENTS

Portions of this work have been previously reported in this research: Martínez-Falcó, J., Marco-Lajara, B., Zaragoza-Sáez, P., & Sánchez-García, E. (2023). The effect of wine tourism on the sustainable performance of Spanish wineries: a structural equation model analysis. *International Journal of Wine Business Research.* Ahead of Print.

REFERENCES

Alant, K., & Bruwer, J. (2004). Wine tourism behaviour in the context of a motivational framework for wine regions and cellar doors. *Journal of Wine Research*, *15*(1), 27–37. doi:10.1080/0957126042000300308

Anderson, K. (2013). Is Georgia the next "new" wine-exporting country? *Journal of Wine Economics*, *8*(1), 1–28. doi:10.1017/jwe.2013.7

Andrade-Suárez, M., & Caamaño-Franco, I. (2020). The Relationship between industrial heritage, wine tourism, and sustainability: A case of local community perspective. *Sustainability (Basel)*, *12*(18), 7453. doi:10.3390/su12187453

Bruwer, J. (2003). South African wine routes: Some perspectives on the wine tourism industry's structural dimensions and wine tourism product. *Tourism Management*, *24*(4), 423–435. doi:10.1016/S0261-5177(02)00105-X

Byrne, B. (2008). *Structural Equation Modeling with EQS: Basic Concepts, Applications, and Programming*. Psychology Press.

Canziani, B., & Byrd, E. (2017). Exploring the influence of regional brand equity in an emerging wine sector. *Journal of Wine Economics, 12*(4), 370–377. doi:10.1017/jwe.2017.30

Carlsen, P. (2004). A review of global wine tourism research. *Journal of Wine Research, 15*(1), 5–13. doi:10.1080/0957126042000300281

Carmines, E., & Zeller, R. (1979). *Reliability and validity assessment* (Vol. 17). Sage Publications. doi:10.4135/9781412985642

Carvalho, M., Kastenholz, E., & Carneiro, M. (2021). Co-creative tourism experiences–a conceptual framework and its application to food & wine tourism. *Tourism Recreation Research*, 1–25.

Charters, S., & Ali-Knight, J. (2002). Who is the wine tourist? *Tourism Management, 23*(3), 311–319. doi:10.1016/S0261-5177(01)00079-6

Darnay, S. (2016). Quality of landscape and sustainability benefit to wine tourism: Contexts and commitments. In *Wine and Tourism* (pp. 15–25). Springer. doi:10.1007/978-3-319-18857-7_2

Duarte Alonso, A., Bressan, A., Kiat Kok, S., & O'Brien, S. (2021). Filling up the sustainability glass: Wineries' initiatives towards sustainable wine tourism. *Tourism Recreation Research*, 1–15. doi:10.1080/02508281.2021.1885801

Falk, R., & Miller, N. (1992). *A primer for soft modeling*. University of Akron Press.

Festa, G., Shams, S., Metallo, G., & Cuomo, M. T. (2020). Opportunities and challenges in the contribution of wine routes to wine tourism in Italy–A stakeholders' perspective of development. *Tourism Management Perspectives, 33*, 100585. doi:10.1016/j.tmp.2019.100585

Fornell, C., & Larcker, D. (1981). Evaluating structural equation models with unobservable variables and measurement error. *JMR, Journal of Marketing Research, 18*(1), 39–50. doi:10.1177/002224378101800104

Frigon, A., Doloreux, D., & Shearmur, R. (2020). Drivers of eco-innovation and conventional innovation in the Canadian wine industry. *Journal of Cleaner Production, 275*, 124115. doi:10.1016/j.jclepro.2020.124115

Frost, W., Frost, J., Strickland, P., & Maguire, J. (2020). Seeking a competitive advantage in wine tourism: Heritage and storytelling at the cellar-door. *International Journal of Hospitality Management, 87*, 102460. doi:10.1016/j.ijhm.2020.102460

Getz, D. (2000). *Explore wine tourism: Management, development and destinations*. Cognizant.

Getz, D., & Brown, G. (2006). Critical success factors for wine tourism regions: A demand analysis. *Tourism Management, 27*(1), 146–158. doi:10.1016/j.tourman.2004.08.002

Gómez, M., Pratt, M., & Molina, A. (2019). Wine tourism research: A systematic review of 20 vintages from 1995 to 2014. *Current Issues in Tourism, 22*(18), 2211–2249. doi:10.1080/13683500.2018.1441267

Hair, J., Hult, G., Ringle, C., & Sarstedt, M. (2016). *A primer on partial least squares structural equation modeling (PLS-SEM)*. SAGE Publications.

Hair, J. F., Sarstedt, M., & Ringle, C. (2019). Rethinking some of the rethinking of partial least squares. *European Journal of Marketing*, *53*(4), 566–584. doi:10.1108/EJM-10-2018-0665

Hall, C. (1996). Wine tourism in New Zealand. Proceedings of tourism down under II: A research conference (pp. 109-119). Donedin: Universidad de Otago.

Hall, C., & Macionis, N. (1998). Wine tourism in Australia and New Zealand. In R. Butler, (Eds.), *Tourism and recreation in rural areas* (pp. 267–298). Wiley.

Hall, C., Sharples, L., Cambourne, B., & Macionis, N. (2000). *Wine tourism around the world: development, management and markets*. Editorial Elsevier.

Hu, L., & Bentler, P. (1998). Fit indices in covariance structure modeling: Sensitivity to underparameterized model misspecification. *Psychological Methods*, *3*(4), 424–453. doi:10.1037/1082-989X.3.4.424

Karagiannis, D., & Metaxas, T. (2020). Sustainable wine tourism development: Case studies from the Greek region of Peloponnese. *Sustainability (Basel)*, *12*(12), 5223. doi:10.3390/su12125223

Kline, R. (2011). *Principles and practice of structural equation modelling*. Guilford Press.

Knight, H., Megicks, P., Agarwal, S., & Leenders, M. (2019). Firm resources and the development of environmental sustainability among small and medium-sized enterprises: Evidence from the Australian wine industry. *Business Strategy and the Environment*, *28*(1), 25–39. doi:10.1002/bse.2178

Kotur, A. (2023). A bibliometric review of research in wine tourism experiences: insights and future research directions. *International Journal of Wine Business Research*.

Kutateladze, R., Koblianidze, T., & Kochlamazashvili, L. (2021). Wine tourism as a mechanism for rural and regional development of Georgia. *Agricultural Economics and Rural Development*, *8*(1), 17–29.

Lavandoski, J., Vargas-Sánchez, A., Pinto, P., & Silva, J. A. (2018). Causes and effects of wine tourism development in organizational context: The case of Alentejo, Portugal. *Tourism and Hospitality Research*, *18*(1), 107–122. doi:10.1177/1467358416634159

Marco-Lajara, B., García, E. S., Larrosa, P. S., & Martínez-Falcó, J. (2022a). Knowledge creation and diffusion inspecialized environments: What are the factors involved? In *Empresa, economía y derecho. Oportunidades ante un entorno global y disruptivo* (pp. 432–459). Dykinson.

Marco-Lajara, B., Martínez-Falcó, J., Millan-Tudela, L. A., & Sánchez-García, E. (2023a). Analysis of the structure of scientific knowledge on wine tourism: A bibliometric analysis. *Heliyon*, *9*(2), e13363. doi:10.1016/j.heliyon.2023.e13363 PMID:36816306

Marco-Lajara, B., Martínez-Falcó, J., Sánchez-García, E., & Millan-Tudela, L. A. (2023b). Analyzing the Role of Renewable Energy in Meeting the Sustainable Development Goals: A Bibliometric Analysis. *Energies*, *16*(7), 3137. doi:10.3390/en16073137

Marco-Lajara, B., Úbeda-García, M., Zaragoza-Sáez, P., Poveda-Pareja, E., & Martínez Falcó, J. (2023c). Enoturismo y sostenibilidad: Estudio de casos en la Ruta del Vino de Alicante (España). *Pasos (El Sauzal), 21*(2), 307–320. doi:10.25145/j.pasos.2023.21.020

Marco-Lajara, B., Zaragoza-Saez, P., & Martínez-Falcó, J. (2022b). Green Innovation: Balancing Economic Efficiency With Environmental Protection. In Frameworks for Sustainable Development Goals to Manage Economic, Social, and Environmental Shocks and Disasters (pp. 239-254). IGI Global.

Marco-Lajara, B., Zaragoza-Sáez, P., Martínez-Falcó, J., & Ruiz-Fernández, L. (2022c). The effect of green intellectual capital on green performance in the Spanish wine industry: A structural equation modeling approach. *Complexity, 2022*, 2022. doi:10.1155/2022/6024077

Marco-Lajara, B., Zaragoza-Sáez, P., Martínez-Falcó, J., & Sánchez-García, E. (2022d). Las rutas del vino de España: el impacto económico derivado de las visitas a bodegas y museos [Spain's wine routes: the economic impact of visits to wineries and museums] In Investigación y transferencia de las ciencias sociales frente a un mundo en crisis [Social science research and transfer in the face of a world in crisis] (pp. 1774–1800).

Marco-Lajara, B., Zaragoza-Sáez, P. C., Martínez-Falcó, J., & Sánchez-García, E. (2023d). Does green intellectual capital affect green innovation performance? Evidence from the Spanish wine industry. *British Food Journal, 125*(4), 1469–1487. doi:10.1108/BFJ-03-2022-0298

Martínez-Falcó, J., Marco-Lajara, B., Sánchez-García, E., & Millan-Tudela, L. A. (2023c). Sustainable Development Goals in the Business Sphere: A Bibliometric Review. *Sustainability (Basel), 15*(6), 5075. doi:10.3390/su15065075

Mártínez-Falcó, J., Marco-Lajara, B., & Zaragoza-Sáez, P. (2023b). Corporate Social Responsibility: A Comprehensive Analysis. In Positive and Constructive Contributions for Sustainable Development Goals (pp. 131-160). IGI Global.

Martínez-Falcó, J., Marco-Lajara, B., Zaragoza-Sáez, P., & Gilinsky, A. (2024b). Wine Tourism in the Valencian Community: A Comparative Analysis. *Investigaciones Turísticas*, (27), 29–52.

Martínez-Falcó, J., Marco-Lajara, B., Zaragoza-Sáez, P., & Millán-Tudela, L. A. (2023f). Analyzing the effect of Corporate Social Responsibility on Green Innovation Performance in the Spanish wine industry: A structural equation modeling analysis. *Agribusiness, 39*(4), 985–1006. doi:10.1002/agr.21820

Martínez Falcó, J., Marco-Lajara, B., Zaragoza-Sáez, P., & Sánchez-García, E. (2023). Vino, Turismo y COVID-19: El impacto de la COVID-19 en las Rutas del Vino de España. *Pasos (El Sauzal), 21*(1), 83–97. doi:10.25145/j.pasos.2023.21.006

Martínez-Falcó, J., Marco-Lajara, B., Zaragoza-Sáez, P., & Sánchez-García, E. (2023g). The effect of knowledge management on sustainable performance: Evidence from the Spanish wine industry. *Knowledge Management Research and Practice*, 1–16. doi:10.1080/14778238.2023.2218045

Martínez-Falcó, J., Marco-Lajara, B., Zaragoza-Sáez, P., & Sánchez-García, E. (2023h). The effect of organizational ambidexterity on sustainable performance: A structural equation analysis applied to the Spanish wine industry. *Agribusiness*. doi:10.1002/agr.21820

Martínez-Falcó, J., Marco-Lajara, B., Zaragoza-Sáez, P. D. C., & Millan-Tudela, L. A. (2023e). Wine tourism as a catalyst for green innovation: Evidence from the Spanish wine industry. *British Food Journal*. doi:10.1108/BFJ-08-2022-0690

Martínez-Falcó, J., Marco-Lajara, B., Zaragoza Sáez, P. D. C., & Sánchez-García, E. (2023d). Wine tourism in Spain: The economic impact derived from visits to wineries and museums on wine routes. *Investigaciones Turísticas*, *25*(25), 168–195. doi:10.14198/INTURI.21219

Martínez-Falcó, J., Martínez-Falcó, J., Marco-Lajara, B., Sánchez-García, E., & Visser, G. (2023i). Aligning the Sustainable Development Goals in the Wine Industry: A Bibliometric Analysis. *Sustainability (Basel)*, *15*(10), 8172. doi:10.3390/su15108172

Martínez-Falcó, J., Sánchez-García, E., Marco-Lajara, B., & Georgantzis, N. (2024a). The interplay between competitive advantage and sustainability in the wine industry: A bibliometric and systematic review. *Discover Sustainability*, *5*(1), 13. doi:10.1007/s43621-024-00196-4

Martínez-Falcó, J., Sánchez-García, E., Marco-Lajara, B., & Millan-Tudela, L. A. (2023j). Do organizational commitment and consumer satisfaction mediate the relationship corporate social responsibility-sustainable performance? Assessing happiness management in Spanish wineries. *Management Decision*. doi:10.1108/MD-02-2023-0217

Martínez-Falcó, J. M., Marco-Lajara, B., & Zaragoza-Saez, P. (2023a). Corporate Social Responsibility vs. Corporate Sustainability: Different Concepts for a Common Goal. In Positive and Constructive Contributions for Sustainable Development Goals (pp. 76-87). IGI Global.

Montalvo-Falcón, J. V., Sánchez-García, E., Marco-Lajara, B., & Martínez-Falcó, J. (2023). Green human resource management and economic, social and environmental performance: Evidence from the Spanish wine industry. *Heliyon*, *9*(10), e20826. doi:10.1016/j.heliyon.2023.e20826 PMID:37860533

Nave, A., do Paço, A., & Duarte, P. (2021). A systematic literature review on sustainability in the wine tourism industry: Insights and perspectives. *International Journal of Wine Business Research*, *33*(4), 457–480.

OECD. (2005). *Eco-innovation in industry: enabling green growth*. OECD.

OTRVE. (2021). *Informe de visitantes a bodegas y museos de las rutas del vino de España. Año 2021 [Report on visitors to wineries and museums on the Wine Routes of Spain. Year 2021]*. OTRVE. https://wineroutesofspain.com/wp-content/uploads/2022/06/informe-visitas-a-bodegas-y-museos-rve-2021.pdf

Paillé, P., Chen, Y., Boiral, O., & Jin, J. (2014). The impact of human resource management on environmental performance: An employee-level study. *Journal of Business Ethics*, *121*(3), 451–466. doi:10.1007/s10551-013-1732-0

Paulraj, A. (2012). Understanding the relationships between internal resources and capabilities, sustainable supply management and organizational sustainability. *The Journal of Supply Chain Management*, *47*(1), 19–37. doi:10.1111/j.1745-493X.2010.03212.x

Piñeiro, M. V., de Salvo, P., & Giommi, F. (2019). Rural tourism and territorial development in Italy. In *Sustainability Assessment at the 21st century*. IntechOpen.

Poitras, L., & Donald, G. (2006). Sustainable wine tourism: The host community perspective. *Journal of Sustainable Tourism*, *14*(5), 425–448. doi:10.2167/jost587.0

Roldan, J., & Cepeda, G. (2017), Modelos de Ecuaciones basados en la Varianza: Partial Least Squares (PLS) para Investigadores en Ciencias Sociales (4a ed.). Universidad de Sevilla.

Sánchez-García, E., Marco-Lajara, B., Martínez-Falcó, J., & Poveda-Pareja, E. (2023a). Cognitive social capital for knowledge absorption in specialized environments: The path to innovation. *Heliyon*, *9*(3), e14223. doi:10.1016/j.heliyon.2023.e14223 PMID:36923853

Sánchez-García, E., Martínez-Falcó, J., Alcon-Vila, A., & Marco-Lajara, B. (2023b). Developing Green Innovations in the Wine Industry: An Applied Analysis. *Foods*, *12*(6), 1157. doi:10.3390/foods12061157 PMID:36981084

Serra-Cantallops, A., Ramón-Cardona, J., & Vachiano, M. (2021). Increasing sustainability through wine tourism in mass tourism destinations. The case of the Balearic Islands. *Sustainability (Basel)*, *13*(5), 2481. doi:10.3390/su13052481

Smyczek, S., Festa, G., Rossi, M., & Monge, F. (2020). Economic sustainability of wine tourism services and direct sales performance–emergent profiles from Italy. *British Food Journal*, *122*(5), 1519–1529. doi:10.1108/BFJ-08-2019-0651

Sun, Y., & Drakeman, D. (2022). The double-edged sword of wine tourism: The economic and environmental impacts of wine tourism in Australia. *Journal of Sustainable Tourism*, *30*(4), 932–949. doi:10.1080/09669582.2021.1903018

Toubes, D. R., Araújo Vila, N., & Fraiz Brea, J. A. (2021). Changes in consumption patterns and tourist promotion after the COVID-19 pandemic. *Journal of Theoretical and Applied Electronic Commerce Research*, *16*(5), 1332–1352. doi:10.3390/jtaer16050075

Trigo, A., & Silva, P. (2022). Sustainable Development Directions for Wine Tourism in Douro Wine Region, Portugal. *Sustainability (Basel)*, *14*(7), 3949. doi:10.3390/su14073949

Vázquez-Vicente, G., Martín-Barroso, V., & Blanco-Jiménez, F. (2021). Sustainable tourism, economic growth and employment—The case of the wine routes of Spain. *Sustainability (Basel)*, *13*(13), 7164. doi:10.3390/su13137164

Wang, Z., & Wang, N. (2012). Knowledge sharing, innovation and firm performance. *Expert Systems with Applications*, *39*(10), 8899–8908. doi:10.1016/j.eswa.2012.02.017

Williams, K. (2021). Wine Tourism: From Winescape to Cellardoorscape. *Tourism Analysis*, *26*(2), 245–248. doi:10.3727/108354221X16079839951529

Zamarreño-Aramendia, G., Cruz-Ruiz, E., & Ruiz-Romero de la Cruz, E. (2021). Sustainable economy and development of the rural territory: Proposal of wine tourism itineraries in La Axarquía of Malaga (Spain). *Economies*, *9*(1), 29. doi:10.3390/economies9010029

Chapter 4
Encouraging Sustainable Practices and Behaviors in Tourism Consumers and Hotel Management: Côa Valley Region

Aquiles Fortes
Polytechnic Institute of Bragança, Portugal

Bruno Miguel Barbosa Sousa
https://orcid.org/0000-0002-8588-2422
Polytechnic Institute of Cávado and Ave, Portugal & CiTUR, Portugal

Aida Carvalho
https://orcid.org/0000-0001-8997-9195
Polytechnic Institute of Bragança, Portugal & CiTUR, Portugal

ABSTRACT

Ecotourism in Portugal is taking hold especially inland, because of an exceptional set of landscapes, protected natural areas, many leisure ac-tivities, and an overwhelming cultural heritage, making this the ideal destination for the responsible traveller. In this sense, the present study, of an exploratory nature, aims to understand the determinants of tourists decision-making process in contexts of ecotourism in the Côa region. A conceptual model was proposed to study the relationship be-tween seven variables, whose results were discussed considering the existing literature. Based on the administration of 136 questionnaires, the data obtained allowed us to conclude that the image of tourist-hotel enterprises has a fundamental role in the experience and satisfac-tion of the tourist, with the need to improve the degree of affectivity in relation to the hotel units. The natural heritage is vital for tourism, for ecotourism, and it is necessary to protect it. The need for greater regu-lation of ecotourism and the promotion of support for the creation of these projects is highlighted.

DOI: 10.4018/979-8-3693-2149-2.ch004

INTRODUCTION

Environmental issues have been the object of reflection due to the ecological footprint they leave in the territories, leading to the emergence of eco-hotels, hotel units that integrate sustainable policies to minimize the impacts generated by their activity, preserving the environment, cultural heritage and economies local (Kirk, 1996; Singh, Cranage & Lee, 2014; Sloan, Legrand & Chen, 2013; Trišić. 2021; Lubowiecki-Vikuk, Sousa, Đerčan & Leal Filho, 2021). At the same time, more and more tourists are aware of this footprint, chal-lenging the entire sector to find ecological solutions for their stays, also emerging green marketing strategies, designed with the aim of captivating guests and integrating the activity competitively (Fortes et al., 2023). For a better understanding of the scope of the theme, it is important to define the concepts of marketing and branding. The con-cept of ecological marketing emerged as a discipline in 1975, in Eu-rope and the United States, from a general awakening of ecological awareness among the population. Polonsky (2011) considers ecological marketing as the activities developed to generate and facilitate any exchanges with the intention of satisfying the desires and needs of con-sumers, provided that the satisfaction of such desires and needs occurs with a minimum of negative impact on the environment. The growing concern with the scarcity of natural resources has not only led to changes in social values, but also to the implementation of teaching good recycling practices in schools. The introduction of the concepts of social and environmental responsibility in children are clear factors of change, which have been making all the difference in society's men-tality and consequently in companies. With this study it is expected not only to better understand the green market and the advantages of adopting sustainability policies by companies, as well as to understand how important it is that marketing efforts are directed towards the con-sumer. green, which has increasingly become a trend (Fortes et al., 2023). Bearing in mind the current dynamics in the global market, and in Portugal, this research aims to identify and contextualize the bene-fits and different green management policies that hotel developments adopt to increase competitive advantages and the determinants of green consumer behavior in tourist contexts -hotel: a study applied to the Côa region in the municipalities of Vila Nova de Foz Côa, Mêda, Figueira de Castelo Rodrigo and Pinhel.

THEORETICAL BACKGROUND

Ecological marketing refers to activities developed to generate and facilitate any exchanges with the intention of satisfying the wants and needs of consumers, provided that the satisfaction of such wants and needs occurs with a minimum of negative impact on the environ-ment (Roseta et al., 2020). Globalization and new market challenges have contributed to the promotion of new trends in commercial scenar-ios. Sustainability and ecology lead companies to adopt green market-ing as true tools at the service of the market to explore business oppor-tunities with the design and conception of green products to supply the needs of the current market (Machado et al., 2022).

Green marketing has been an important academic research topic for at least three decades (Kassarjian, 1971; Kinnear et al., 1974; Cod-dington, 1993; Hopfenbeck, 1993; Peattie, 1995; Polonsky & Mintu - Wimsatt, 1995; Schlegelmilch et al., 1996; Fuller, 1999; Kalafatis et al., 1999; Fernandes et al., 2021; Duarte et al., 2023), but few studies have focused specifically on green branding. In parallel, research on consumer behavior and the marketing applicability to tourism contexts is based on the analysis of tourist motivations and on the ratio of be-havioural intentions (i.e., satisfaction and loyalty), during a period marked by competitivity among tourist destinations (Yoon & Uysal, 2005) (p. 90). In tourism contexts, loyalty is held as the commitment to rebuy or enjoy the product/service again giving consistency to the fu-ture of the same brand, regardless of the influences of the moment or marketing strategies (Oliver, 1999; Prayag & Ryan, 2012). According to Fortes et al. (2023), a visitor's loyalty is related to the in-tention of returning to a tourist destination (revisit) and/or recommending it to relatives, friends and others. The loyalty of the consumer in tourism is no doubt an important factor to assess the success of the development of a tourist destination, being that motivation, image of the tourist des-tination, quality, perceived value and the degree of satisfaction will develop this loyalty according to Fortes et al. (2023).

Among the main business benefits derived from the implementa-tion of ecological marketing, some authors highlight: competitive ad-vantage, added value, green promotion and green distribution. An or-ganization can obtain an advantageous position against the competi-tion if it develops innovative and differentiated ecological products and if its packaging, distribution and other actions generate the least possible impact on the environment (Patel, 2016). Ecological products are perceived by customers as an innovation by organizations to in-crease their levels of satisfaction and allow their introduction into new markets (Kiran, 2012). Green promotion presupposes that the custom-er/consumer is able to differenti-ate an ecological product from a prod-uct without these characteristics. To this end, it is essential that organ-izations know how to use the green label to inform their current and potential customers about the characteristics of their ecological prod-ucts (Dwipamurti, Mawardi & Nuralam, 2018). Regarding green dis-tribution, Hamann (2013) mentions that an inverse distribution system should be created, so that waste can be reincorporated into the produc-tion system as a raw material.

According to the UNWTO database, the number of international tourists reached 1.1 billion people, increasing more than 4% in 2014. In recent years, tourism has proven to be a surprisingly strong and re-silient economic activity, having made a strong contribution to the recovery of the economy, creating millions of jobs and generating bil-lions of euros in exports. This behavior has been observed all over the world, although with greater predominance in Europe, strongly con-tributing to the end of one of the most dramatic economic periods in its history (Fortes et al. 2023).

Therefore, green marketing has been an important academic re-search topic for at least three decades (Mishra & Sharma, 2014; Bhat, 1993; Paço et al., 2009; Oliveira & Sousa, 2020; Meler & Ham, 2012; Saleh et al., 2023), but few studies have focused specifically on green branding and green consumer be-havior in tourism and hotel manage-ment contexts (Fortes et al., 2023). Regarding the growing importance in the development of the connection between the consumer and the brand, it is essential that marketers know and understand which factors affect the brand attachment (Khan, Khalid, Zaman, José & Ferreira, 2021; Japutra, Ekinci & Simkin, 2014). According to Fortes et al. (2023), in their study, the authors realized that the brand attachment can be defined based on three dimensions: emotions, self-connection and importance, which allowed the definition of six determinants of brand attachment: self-congruence, experience, responsiveness, quali-ty, reputation and trust. In this way, the more affection the consumer is to a brand, the more he will be able to transform and control the rela-tionship with the brand (moving from an egocentric to a reciprocal way), in such a way that allows the sharing of resources with brand (Park, Macinnis, Priester, Eisingerich & Iacobucci, 2010).

The attachment varies essentially through strength, that is, stronger attachments are related to stronger feelings as well, namely at the level of connection (emotions of attachment and attachment), af-fection (emotions like love, friendship and passivity) and passion (emotions of enchantment, fascination and attraction). In the meas-urement of attachment, joy, excitement, pride, contentment, relief, nostalgia, or other element that identifies with the individual's memo-ries must also be included. In this way, it can be inferred that the at-tachment, through the evidenced components, manifests an emotional connection in the individual similar to love (Santos, Sousa, Ramos & Valeri, 2022).

METHODOLOGY AND CONTEXT

The present study was inspired by the model presented by Bigné, Sanchez & Sanchez (2001), who sought to investigate the relationship between the image of tourist-hotel units, the purchase determinants and the perception of the green consumer, in which five variables were used: image, quality, satisfaction, recommend and return. In adapting this model to the present investigation, the following variables were defined: image of tourism-hotel undertakings, purchase, experience, affectivity, satisfaction, recommending and returning. Of these seven variables, the following hypotheses were formulated:

Hypothesis 1: There is a relationship between the image of hotels and the purchase of the green product/service offered.

Hypothesis 2: There is a relationship between the image of tour-ist-hotel enterprises/destinations and experience.

Hypothesis 3: There is a relationship between image and affec-tivity on the part of the tourist in relation to the eco-friendly ho-tel/destination.

Hypothesis 4: There is a relationship between experience and the degree of tourist satisfaction.

Hypothesis 5: There is a relationship between affectivity towards eco-friendly hotels/destinations and the degree of satisfaction.

Hypothesis 6: There is a relationship between the degree of satis-faction and the willingness to recommend the eco-friendly ho-tel/destination.

Hypothesis 7: There is a relationship between the degree of satis-faction and the willingness to stay at the eco-friendly hotel/destination.

In this study, and in accordance with the assumptions defended by Santos, Ramos, Sousa, Almeida & Valeri (2022), two sources of data were used. Bibliographical research was first carried out, seeking to be based on the main articles and scientific works published in sci-entific journals related to the theme addressed in this study. The in-depth analysis of these works allowed the construction of the proposed model and its subsequent evaluation, essential for the framework and theoretical foundation of this investigation, as well as for accurately delimiting the area to be investigated and serving as a pillar for the methodological approach. Then, data from the empirical study were obtained, which allowed the investigation of the hypotheses, without any manipulation of the values obtained, and the subsequent extraction of lessons and conclusions. Considering the research of Quivy and Campenhoudt 2005), this study followed the principles of procedures based on the seven steps of scientific procedures: Departure question, exploration, problematic, construction of the analysis model, observa-tion, information analysis and conclusions.

The study was carried out geographically in the northeast of Portu-gal in the Côa region, more specifically in the municipalities: Vila Nova de Foz Côa, Mêda, Figueira de Castelo Rodrigo, Pinhel. With a territory of 4923 Km2, an average population density of 17.3 in-hab/Km2 and a resident population of 84960 inhabitants thanks to its geographical distribution, the Côa region is composed of a heterogeneous mosaic of tradition and history, which can be considered an as-set in terms of tourism and culture. Due to its location in the north and center of the country, with municipalities covering Trás-os-Montes, the Douro and Beira Interior Norte. Consecrated as Cultural Heritage of Humanity, Vale do Côa is a rock art Sanctuary, where it houses the largest Paleolithic rock art complex left by prehistoric men who lived there many millennia ago. The region owns extensive plateaus and mountains of schist and granite, interspersed with large expanses of landscapes of fertile and irrigated valleys, attributes that make the Val-ley not only a National Monument, but also one of the areas with the greatest natural and ecological value of Portugal (Fortes et al., 2023).

According to Fortes et al. (2023), the town is also known for its riv-er, called the Côa River, which rises in Serra das Mesas, next to Serra da Malcata, in the municipality of Sabugal, is one of the few rivers that flows from south to north, crossing a deep valley of landscapes. rocky over 135km. Along its course, the Côa river traces paths that alternate between a schist-Graywakeh complex to the south, granite rocks in the center and again the schist in the area of confluence with the Douro, in the region of Vila Nova de Foz Côa. It is currently considered one of the least polluted rivers in Portugal. Despite its beautiful landscapes and attractiveness, the region is currently considered a poor and low-density region at the national level, with a high rate of aging, popula-tion desertification and a lack of entrepreneurial development initia-tives.

RESULTS AND REFLECTION

The present research had as its general objective the study of the de-terminants in the purchase decision process and the perception of the green consumer in tourist-hotel contexts in the Côa region. The results obtained (132 valid responses, with (eco)touristic consumers in the Northern Portuguese context (from the region of the presented Côa Valley region) in the year 2022) contributed positively to characterize tourists and what determines their choice and perception of eco-hotels. This was verified not only in terms of the characterization of the sam-ple and the Côa Valley region, but also by the opinions expressed re-garding the environment, the market offers of eco-hotels and the re-spective sustainable activities.

In a general perspective, although few tourists have reported having had experiences in eco-hotels to date, there has been a uniform ten-dency towards concern for the environment and for valuing sustainable environmental management policies applied by tourist developments. The items "when you buy a product (e.g. hotel) do you think about how it will affect the environment?", "to what extent is it important for you that hotels use construction materials that are specific to the re-gion where the hotel is located" and that "have installations appropri-ate to the environment (eg: environmentally certified building materi-als, ecological furniture, etc.)", clearly show this. That is, for the pre-sent sample, tourism, in addition to representing leisure and involve-ment in activities that imply getting to know new cultures, is seen as a model adaptable to the natural environment and to sociocultural and economic factors, providing a healthy experience for the individual and/or group with the least possible impact on the local ecosystem. Their concern for the environment was also evident when they stated that "news about environmental problems make them anxious" and that "buying products/services from socially responsible companies can have a positive effect on society". The participants also showed interest in knowing whether the resorts where they are staying have sustainable activities, considering it important that hotels "inform their customers about their good environmental practices".

These results contribute to the understanding that the tourist popula-tion can significantly contribute to the reduction of enterprises with irresponsible tourist exploitations, with a lack of organized systems of selective collection that cause various types of waste, such as bottles and plastic cups, to be discarded without being considered environ-mentally sustainable solutions. Still, the mischaracterization and de-valuation of local communities are problems that cause the degrada-tion of natural resources and compromise the local ecosystem. In fact, the literature has shown that in tourism, unlike other economic activi-ties, there is already a consumer aware of the need to preserve the nat-ural environment and who values the initiatives that are carried out for this purpose. In this way, hotels have a unique opportunity to invest and develop products considered green, with green marketing strate-gies, in order to satisfy the ecological needs of consumers. Tourists are concerned with the environment, as mentioned above, and a solid im-age in this sense, associated with a good marketing strategy, could be a determining factor for tourists in the decision to purchase tourist ser-vices. The more positive the images and perceptions of visitors, the more likely they are to revisit the destination and also to recommend it to others, which leads to a positive financial impact on companies. Marketing strategies associated with image aim to convey the quality of services and this perception of quality has a behavioral impact on customers, associated with the intention to repeat the purchase. The hotel sector is based on providing a set of services and the quality of how they are provided ends up dictating the degree of total customer satisfaction. On the other hand, it is interesting to note that, when the quality variable was not included in the question, most participants stated that "in the near future they intend to stay in an eco-hotel" and that they are "willing to pay a higher price to stay stay in an eco-hotel". This makes us realize that there is indeed a certain level of in-tention to have experiences related to green consumption, as these are people who are willing to choose a product taking into account not only the price, but the fact that it is environmentally sustainable. How-ever, if the quality is very low, compared to conventional hotels, sus-tainable management does not seem to be a sufficiently determining factor in the purchase process. In fact, assessing customers' perception and satisfaction regarding service quality is widely recognized as one of the most effective strategies to increase profitability in the hospitali-ty industry and can be considered as strong determinants for the same.

Participants considered it important for hotels to "train employees to participate in ecological activities with their customers", "adopt ener-gy saving measures, such as the use of occupancy sensors in rooms and bathrooms" and that "they have a swimming pool biological instead of a conventional swimming pool". Since we are talking about people with a very high socio-environmental concern, the results obtained demonstrate that people are open to participating and contributing to good ecological practices and that this contributes to satisfaction in the hotel experience, thus corroborating the fourth hypothesis formulated for this study. That said, it is possible for us to confirm the sixth hy-pothesis formulated for the relationship between tourist satisfaction and the intention to recommend eco-hotels, as a high degree of satis-faction is an important determinant for high loyalty and tendency to recommend tourist destinations. In addition, since there was a tenden-cy for the participants of this study to consider that "there are few eco-hotels available on the market", the eco-hotels in the Côa region are open to improving their attractiveness through differentiation as a driv-ing factor. of competitiveness. Thus, it is proposed that, in line with the procedures in force in the large hotel chains, they invest in perma-nent innovation, creativity, in the continuous training of their employ-ees, in the renovation and updating of their hotel products, in order to adapt and give response to the demands of the new consumer profile.

FINAL CONSIDERATIONS AND NEXT STEPS

According to Oliveira and Sousa (2020), environmental concerns and consumer demand for environmentally friendly products have led to the emergence of a new marketing philosophy called green market-ing.

The great forces behind the green marketing are the demand for green products coupled with concern for the environment. On the other hand, companies seek to balance their sales and profit objectives with social and environmental concerns (McDonagh & Clark, 1995; Paço et al., 2009). With the present chapter, an attempt was made to evaluate the proposed conceptual model, whose objective was to deepen knowledge about the ecotourist profile and identify the determinants in the purchase decision process in the context of ecotourism. It was pos-sible to confirm the formulated hypotheses, by framing the results ob-tained with the existing literature on the subject.

After an in-depth analysis, we can see that people who visit the Côa region have a high level of socio-environmental awareness, help-ing to make tourist-hotel entrepreneurs in the region aware of the need to increase efforts and create management and green marketing strate-gies to captivate consumers in this market segment, considering that consumers do not only take into account the price factor and the quali-ty of the product/service, but also a management that preserves the environment. This requires a permanent effort by tourist-hotel enter-prises to improve, innovate and adapt their environmental practices and policies, in order to respond to the needs and expectations of dif-ferent customers and to respond to the competitive pressures of the tourism activity (Knowles, Diamantis & El-Mourhabi, 2004). In addi-tion to the increase in competition in terms of tourist destinations and the increase in technological innovations, there is a growing demand and awareness on the part of tourists, who are constantly looking for new destinations and new activities to satisfy their need for new, unique and rewarding experiences. In turn, the tourist's positive expe-rience in a given hotel will also be an added value for tourism entre-preneurs (Alves et al., 2022), who need to be up-to-date on future trends in this constantly evolving sector and meet requests and needs of more sophisticated guests (Brunner-Sperdin & Peters, 2009).

This study discusses the growing phenomena of sustainable tour-ism (eco-hotels) and the perspective of relationship marketing. Based on the literature review, we propose a model that connects the dimen-sions of relationship marketing with the consequent satisfaction and the behavioral intention to repeat the experience or reinforce it with a marketing focused on "ecological" motivation. Several studies in mar-keting and tourism contexts have discussed the association of relation-ship marketing with destina-tion and consumer buying behavior, in-cluding the study of satisfaction, loyalty, or quality of service.

The present investigation revealed very pertinent information for the ecotourism area. However, some limitations were identified in the process of carrying out the same, such as the difficulty in collecting data and collaboration on the part of the hotel units, which led to the search for other ways of obtaining the results. If, on the one hand, the use of the digital tool may have influenced the collected data, on the other hand, it appears that the digital medium is currently used mas-sively and the results obtained are congruent with other studies. Still, given the complexity and number of formulated hypotheses, as well as the theoretical nature implicit in their analysis, it was a challenge to give objective answers regarding the relationship between the varia-bles.

In order to circumvent these limitations, it would be very perti-nent, in future studies, to apply instru-ments previously developed to effectively measure the determinants studied in the present investiga-tion, such as the degree of satisfaction with the hotel experience, the degree of affectivity, among others. In this follow-up, it would also be relevant to apply statistical tests that make it possible to ascertain a di-rect and causal relationship between the studied variables. It would also be relevant to extend the study sample to other areas of the na-tional territory and make a comparison of supply and demand and con-sequent factors that may contribute to the choice of ecotourism. Also, take attractive measures for the participation and collaboration of hotel units in filling out questionnaires, helping them to perceive the rele-vance of these studies, in particular because they are the main benefi-ciaries. Finally, it would be extremely important to carry out continu-ous research to measure the impact of the increase in the supply of sus-tainable developments on the demand and degree of customer satisfac-tion and, thus, allow us to understand in what ways offers can be de-veloped that are more adjusted to the demands of consumers.

ACKNOWLEGMENT

This work is financed by national funds through FCT - Foundation for Science and Technology, IP, within the scope of the reference project UIDB/04470/2020.

REFERENCES

Alves, H. M., Sousa, B., Carvalho, A., Santos, V., Lopes Dias, Á., & Valeri, M. (2022). Encouraging brand attachment on consumer behaviour: Pet-friendly tourism segment. [JTHSM]. *Journal of Tourism, Heritage & Services Mar-keting*, *8*(2), 16–24.

Bhat, V. N. (1993). Green marketing begins with green design. *Journal of Business and Industrial Mar-keting*, *8*(4), 26–31. doi:10.1108/08858629310047243

Bigné, J., Sanchez, I., & Sanchez, J. (2001). Tourism Image, Evaluation Vari-ables and After Purchase Be-haviour: Inter-Relationships. *Tourism Management*, *22*(6), 607–616. doi:10.1016/S0261-5177(01)00035-8

Brunner-Sperdin, A., & Peters, M. (2009). What influences guests' emotions? The case of high-quality hotels. *International Journal of Tourism Research*, *11*(2), 171–183. doi:10.1002/jtr.718

Coddington, W. (1993). *Environmental marketing: positive strategies for reaching the green consumer*. McGraw - Hill Companies.

Duarte, M., Dias, Á., Sousa, B., & Pereira, L. (2023). Lifestyle entrepreneur-ship as a vehicle for leisure and sustainable tourism. *International Journal of Environmental Research and Public Health*, *20*(4), 3241. doi:10.3390/ijerph20043241 PMID:36833935

Dwipamurti, I. G. A. N., Mawardi, M. K., & Nuralam, I. P. (2018). The ef-fect of green marketing on brand image and purchase decision (Study on consumer of Starbucks Café Ubud, Gianyar Bali). *Jurnal Administrasi Bisnis*, *61*(3).

Fernandes, S., Ferreira, D., Alves, T., & de Sousa, B. M. B. (2021). Glamp-ing and the development of sustainable tourism: a Portuguese case study. Handbook of Sustainable Development and Leisure Services, 201-222.

Fortes, A., Carvalho, A., & Sousa, B. (2023). Determinants of Green Con-sumer Behavior in Tourism and Hotel Management Contexts: A Study Applied to the Côa Region. In Advances in Tourism, Technology and Sys-tems: Selected Papers from ICOTTS 2022, Volume 2 (pp. 323-332). Sin-gapore: Springer Nature Singapore.

Fuller, D. A. (1999). *Sustainable marketing: Managerial - ecological issues*. Sage Publications. doi:10.4135/9781452220611

Hamann, P. A. (2013). *El marketing verde. Un compromiso de todos. Tiem-po de Opinión. Pág*. Universidad ESAN.

Hopfenbeck, W. (1993). *The green management revolution: Lessons in envi-ronmental excellence*. Prentice Hall.

Japutra, A., Ekinci, Y., & Simkin, L. (2014). Exploring brand attachment, its determinants and outcomes. *Journal of Strategic Marketing*, *22*(7), 616–630. doi:10.1080/0965254X.2014.914062

Kalafatis, S. P., Pollard, M., East, R., & Tsogas, M. H. (1999). Green mar-keting and Ajzen's theory of planned behavior: A cross - market examina-tion. *Journal of Consumer Marketing*, *16*(5), 441–460. doi:10.1108/07363769910289550

Kassarjian, H. H. (1971). Personality and consumer behavior: A review. *JMR, Journal of Marketing Research*, *8*(4), 409–418. doi:10.1177/002224377100800401

Khan, M. I., Khalid, S., Zaman, U., José, A. E., & Ferreira, P. (2021). Green paradox in emerging tourism supply chains: Achieving green consumption behavior through strategic green marketing orientation, brand social re-sponsibility, and green image. *International Journal of Environmental Research and Public Health*, *18*(18), 9626. doi:10.3390/ijerph18189626 PMID:34574552

Kinnear, T. C., Taylor, J. R., & Ahmed, S. A. (1974). Ecologically con-cerned consumers: Who are they. *Journal of Marketing*, 20–24.

Kiran, K. U. (2012). Opportunity and Challenges of Green Marketing with special references to Pune. *International Journal of Management and So-cial Sciences Research*, *1*(1), 18–24.

Kirk, D. (1996). *Environmental management for hotels: A student's hand-book*. Butterworth-Heinemann.

Knowles, T., Diamantis, D., & El-Mourhabi, J. B. (2004). *The Globalization of Tourism and Hospitality. A Strategic Perspective*. Cengage Learning.

Lubowiecki-Vikuk, A., de Sousa, B. M. B., Đerčan, B. M., & Leal Filho, W. (Eds.). (2021). *Handbook of Sustainable Development and Leisure Ser-vices*. Springer. doi:10.1007/978-3-030-59820-4

Machado, A., Vareiro, L., Sousa, B., Figueira, V., & Lavandoski, J. (2022). Green marketing trends in specific contexts of tourism and music festivals: preliminary insights. In *Advances in Tourism, Technology and Systems: Selected Papers from ICOTTS 2021* (Vol. 2, pp. 87–96). Springer Nature Singapore. doi:10.1007/978-981-16-9701-2_8

Meler, M., & Ham, M. (2012). Green marketing for green tourism. In *Facul-ty of tourism and hospitality management in opatija. Biennial In-ternational congress. tourism & hospitality industry* (p. 130). University of Rijeka, Faculty of Tourism & Hospitality Management.

Mishra, P., & Sharma, P. (2014). Green marketing: Challenges and opportu-nities for business. *BVIMR Management Edge, 7*(1).

Oliveira, C. P., & Sousa, B. M. (2020). Green consumer behavior and its implications on brand marketing strategy. In *Green marketing as a posi-tive driver toward business sustainability* (pp. 69–95). IGI Global. doi:10.4018/978-1-5225-9558-8.ch004

Oliver, R. L. (1999). Whence consumer loyalty? *Journal of Marketing*, *63*(4, suppl1), 33–44. doi:10.1177/00222429990634s105

Paço, A., Raposo, M., & Filho, W. L. (2009). "Green" segmentation: An application to the Portuguese consumer market. Journal of Targeting. *Measurement and Analysis for Marketing*, *17*(1), 17–25.

Park, C. W., Macinnis, D. J., Priester, J., Eisingerich, A. B., & Iacobucci, D. (2010). Brand attachment and brand attitude strenght: Conceptual and empirical differentiation of two critical brand equity drivers. *Journal of Marketing*, *74*(6), 1–17. doi:10.1509/jmkg.74.6.1

Patel, R. (2016). Green Marketing: As Tool for Sustainable Development. *Journal of Business and Management*, *18*(8), 139–142. doi:10.9790/487X-180803139142

Peattie, K. (1995). Environmental marketing management: Meeting the green challenge. *Financial Times Management*.

Peattie, K., & Crane, A. (2005). Green marketing: Legend, myth, farce or prophesy. *Qualitative Market Research*, *8*(4), 357–370. doi:10.1108/13522750510619733

Polonsky, M. (2011). Transformative green marketing: Impediments and o:ortunities. *Journal of Business Research*, *64*(12), 1311–1319. doi:10.1016/j.jbusres.2011.01.016

Polonsky, M. J. (1994). An Introduction to Green Marketing. *Electronic Green Journal*, *1*(2). Advance online publication. doi:10.5070/G31210177

Polonsky, M. J. (1995). A stakeholder theory approach to designing envi-ronmental marketing strategy. *Journal of Business and Industrial Marketing*, *10*(3), 29–46. doi:10.1108/08858629510096201

Prayag, G., & Ryan, C. (2012). Antecedents of tourists' loyalty to Mauritius: The role and influence of destination image, place attachment, personal involvement, and satisfaction. *Journal of Travel Research*, *51*(3), 342–356. doi:10.1177/0047287511410321

Quivy. R., & Campenhoudt, L. (2005). Manual de Investigação em Ciências Sociais, Gradiva Publicações Lda., 4.

Roseta, P., Sousa, B. B., & Roseta, L. (2020). Determiners in the consumer's purchase decision process in ecotourism contexts: A Portuguese case study. *Geosciences*, *10*(6), 224. doi:10.3390/geosciences10060224

Saleh, M. M. A., Jawabreh, O., & Abu-Eker, E. F. M. (2023). Factors of applying creative accounting and its impact on the quality of financial statements in Jordanian hotels, sustainable practices. *Journal of Sustainable Finance & Investment*, *13*(1), 499–515. doi:10.1080/20430795.2021.1962662

Santos, V., Ramos, P., Sousa, B., Almeida, N., & Valeri, M. (2022). Factors influencing touristic consumer behaviour. *Journal of Organizational Change Management*, *35*(3), 409–429. doi:10.1108/JOCM-02-2021-0032

Santos, V., Sousa, B., Ramos, P., & Valeri, M. (2022). Emotions and in-volvement in tourism settings. *Current Issues in Tourism*, *25*(10), 1526–1531. doi:10.1080/13683500.2021.1932769

Schlegelmilch, B. B., Bohlen, G. M., & Diamantopoulos, A. (1996). The link between green purchasing decisions and measures of environmental consciousness. *European Journal of Marketing*, *30*(5), 35–55. doi:10.1108/03090569610118740

Singh, N., Cranage, D., & Lee, S. (2014). Green strategies for hotels: Estima-tion of recycling benefits. *International Journal of Hospitality Management*, *43*, 13–22. doi:10.1016/j.ijhm.2014.07.006

Trišić, I. (2021). The Function of Protected Natural Areas of the Vojvodina Province in Sustainable Tourism Development. *TEME: Casopis Za Društvene Nauke*, *45*(1), 315–330. doi:10.22190/TEME200129017T

Yoon, Y., & Uysal, M. (2005). An examination of the effects of motivation and satisfaction on destination loyalty: A structural model. *Tourism Management*, *26*(1), 45–56. doi:10.1016/j.tourman.2003.08.016

KEY TERMS AND DEFINITIONS

Brand: It is an overall experience of a customer that distinguishes an organization or product from its rivals in the perspective of the customer.

Green Consumer: It is a form of consumption that is compatible with the safeguard of the environment for the present and for the next generations.

Green Marketing: It is the process of selling products and/or services based on their environmental benefits. Such a product or service may be environmentally friendly in itself or produced in an environmentally.

Marketing Tools: It is the techniques and materials used by those who are involved in the promotion of goods and services.

Social Marketing: It is the application of the tools and concepts of commercial marketing to social, health and educational problems. Strategy: It describes how the ends (goals) will be achieved by the means (resources).

Chapter 5
Ethical Exploration of Advertising Impacts:
Comparison Between Alcohol-Free and Alcoholic Beer Communication of Users' Perceptions and Attitudes

Jorge Arranz Lago
University of Almería, Spain

Nieves García de Frutos
University of Almería, Spain

ABSTRACT

Governmental regulations and consumer trends towards healthier lifestyle are leading the change to new alcohol-free. However, alcohol consumption is growing, and some critical voices raise concerns about effects of alcohol-free advertisements on their alcoholic counterparts. Yet, little research on alcohol-free advertisement has been developed. This research aims to find out how alcohol-free beer advertisements affect ethical perceptions, brand evaluations and purchasing intention. To do this, an experimental design with two versions of alcoholic and non-alcoholic beer advertisements was performed. In addition, an eye-tracking experiment was developed to reveal which elements attract the attention of the viewer. The results of the analysis performed show that alcohol-free advertisements seem to encourage permissive attitudes towards unethical practices, but not affect brand attitude or beer purchase intention. In turn, eye-tracking analysis revealed that consumers seem to focus on the brand of the advertisement rather than on the specific characteristics of the alcohol-free version.

INTRODUCTION

Over the years, the alcohol industry has played an increasingly important role in our social structure. Beer is undoubtedly the clear example of how a product with such remote origins and addictive char-

DOI: 10.4018/979-8-3693-2149-2.ch005

acteristics has been able to continue to influence our culture today, being the second most consumed processed beverage in Spain, only behind soft drinks (FIAB, 2023). However, new trends point at a change in such consumption patterns. The growing amount of information about the negative effects of alcohol on our organism have led some people to decide to reduce and even eradicate its consumption (Hierro, 2020). In response to the emergence of these concerns, alcoholic beverage brands decided to develop new alcohol-free product lines.

To cite the most popular case, the beer industry was able to anticipate events by producing a line of non-alcoholic beers, making Spain the largest European producer of this product, where almost two out of every ten beers consumed in our territory are non-alcoholic (OCU, 2023). Likewise, the restrictions on sales and promotion that the public sector is gradually imposing on this industry, not allowing them to promote alcoholic drinks, forces them to limit their forms of communication almost exclusively to their non-alcoholic beverages (Sánchez, 2002). As a response, the beer industry has been able to adopt a fragmented type of marketing with the launch of different ranges of beverages, using a segmentation model similar to the one that wine has been developing for decades: adopting more sophisticated production processes and increasing in the perceived quality of its products among the public (Galán et al., 2014). Such strategy meets the demands of an increasing number of consumers who demand higher quality products, providing an escape route for brewers that ensures the survival of an industry that knows how to adapt to new consumer habits. In summary, after the emergence of new trends that at first sight could help a transition away from certain unhealthy drinking habits, it is striking to see how alcohol consumption figures continue to rise, particularly when it comes to beer. The consumption of beer peaked in recent years, while sales figures for the corresponding non-alcoholic versions show a less upward trend over time (Ministry of Agriculture, 2023).

The present work is aimed at clarifying the contrasting evidence between consumption trends and communication strategies of beer companies by answering the following questions: Are there differences in brand perception of advertising stimuli for alcohol-free and alcoholic beers? How do alcohol free beer advertising affect perceptions of brewers' ethical behaviors? To address these questions, a study comparing the effects of viewing an alcohol-free vs. alcoholic beer were compared in order to determine their effects on consumer responses regarding the perceptions of potentially unethical practices performed by brewing companies, brand attitudes and intentions to purchase beer. In addition, in order to achieve a more complete understanding of the potential origin of the (non)differing effects of advertisement for the different products, an eye tracking experiment was developed to examine how individuals visually process alcoholic and non-alcoholic beer advertisements.

The present work is structured as follows: firstly, the theoretical review will be focused on analyzing those factors that intervene in alcohol consumption at different levels (i.e., societal, individual, etc.), placing special interest on communication strategies used by alcohol brands. As for the research methodology, an experimental design will be carried out by means of a survey accompanied by an eye-tracking experiment. The findings of this work show substantial similarities and some differences on the individuals' responses after exposing them to alcoholic beer versus non-alcoholic beer advertisements. In light of the findings, we offer evidence that could be considered for developing future communication campaigns on the one hand and for further developing anti-alcoholic regulations on the other hand.

Figure 1. Socio-ecological model of alcohol consumption
Source: Own elaboration based on information from von Philipsborn et al. (2016).

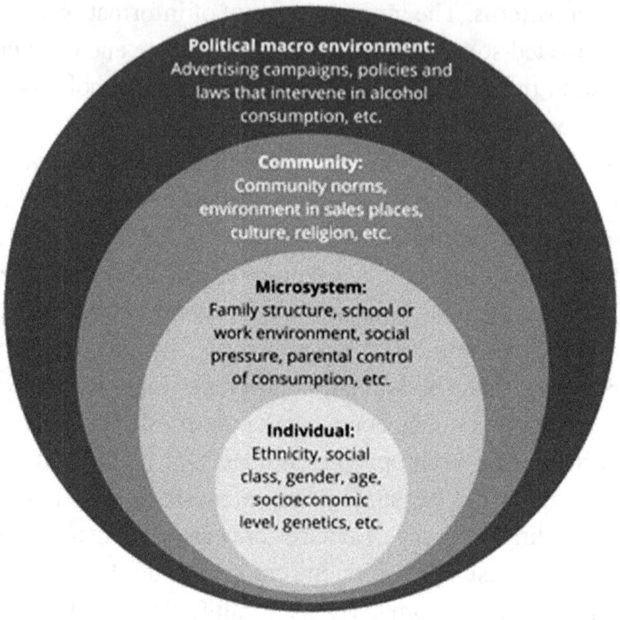

THEORETICAL DEVELOPMENT

The Socio-Ecological Model of Alcohol Consumption

The consumption of alcoholic beverages, as well as its extent and impact, does not affect everyone in the same way: there are factors that condition it depending on the environment and its ability to intervene in the individual's decision. Thus, in line with the socio-ecological model of alcohol consumption (von Philipsborn et al., 2016), we can classify the consumer environment into four levels described in Figure 1. Each circle delimits a level ordered by size according to the number of environments and/or individuals affected. From smallest to largest, we find the individual level, which acknowledges consumers' traits and characteristics; the microsystem level, comprising close friends and familiar environment; the community level, which groups cultural and community; and, finally, the political macro-environment level, representing public sector regulations and laws on the matter.

1) *Individual consumer level*: At the most individual and private level of the person, we can find very diverse factors that affect the consumption of alcoholic beverages, such as socio-economic level, social class, gender, age, ethnicity, or genetics, among other indicators. Additional consumer variables that may explain the preference and consumption of specific alcoholic products are attitudes, intentions, and product-related evaluations (Calvo-Porral et al., 2018)
2) *Consumer microsystem:* The microsystem is defined as the closest environment that affects the individual's decisions. At this level, agents such as the consumer's family, his or her school and work environment, or the social pressure exerted by his or her closest circle stand out.

3) *The consumer's community:* Alcohol has always been rooted in our culture since immemorial times. Alcohol has been the most widely consumed drug in the world and the most widespread drug in terms of geographical areas and ethnic, cultural, and socio-demographic ranges. Its use as a tool for socialization and integration in celebrations and festivities makes its consumption even more widespread, as well as being associated with euphoric, relaxing, and joyful effects, among many others (Sarasa-Renedo et al., 2014).

With regard to our country, alcohol consumption and its derived problems are of great importance, not only because there is an extensive culture regarding the production of alcoholic beverages, but also because of the high level of consumption. Drinking practices are widely accepted as a way of socialization and alcohol is perceived as one more element of our diet (Chamorro-Fernández et al., 2005). In hospitality establishments, the factor that integrates a group is the so-called 'ronda' where all the members ask for a new drink at the same time, so individuals who do not drink like their peers may be excluded from the group (Díez-Hernández, 2003). The same occurs with drinking games and challenges, where the players who participate make use of alcohol as an element of socialization, thus favoring binge drinking at an early age.

In addition, other trends associated with the consumption of alcoholic beverages are present in our culture, such as the so-called 'botellones'. These emerged in the nineties, and they were organized by young people in order to drink, mainly in the street, simply to reach a level of drunkenness that allowed them to achieve a feeling of euphoria and happiness for the rest of the night (Gómez-Fraguela et al., 2008). Recently, due to the rules imposed by the civil authorities regarding drinking in the street, a new trend called 'tardeo' emerged, where the alcoholic consumption takes place in the terraces and under the premises of hospitality establishments. This implies that the consumption of alcoholic beverages also takes place during the afternoon and the evening (Cantó-Gómez & Mantecón, 2020).

Political macro-environment: This last level will be key to this study; it is the largest one, due to its capacity to interfere in the other levels. Thus, it is the one that best explains changes in marketing decisions in recent years in the alcohol industry. The political macro-environment acknowledges current regulations regarding alcohol production, consumption, and especially, advertising.

Currently in Spain, in accordance with Royal Decree 1165/1995 of 7 July 1995, which approves the Regulation of Excise Duties, there is an excise duty on alcohol and alcoholic beverages for the taxation of alcohol and alcoholic beverages. With the exception of the Canary Islands, this tax applies to beer, wine, fermented beverages (cider), intermediate products (sherry or port wine, mistelas, sweet wines, vermouth, etc.), and alcohol and derived or spirituous beverages. The higher the alcohol content of the beverage, the higher the tax rate, with spirits being the most heavily taxed at 958.94 euros per hectoliter of pure alcohol.

With regard to advertising, Law 13/2022, of 7 July, General Audiovisual Communication, also includes an article on unlawful cases in commercial communications of alcoholic beverages. According to this regulation "*audiovisual commercial communication of alcoholic beverages with a level equal to or less than twenty degrees, except when broadcast between 20:30 and 5:00 hours and outside these hours when such audiovisual commercial communications form an indivisible part of the acquisition of rights and the production of the signal to be broadcast*" is prohibited.

In relation to the sale and distribution of alcoholic beverages, it is worth highlighting the case of sporting events. The article 67.3 of Royal Decree 203/2010, of 26 February, which approves the regulation on the prevention of violence, racism, xenophobia, and intolerance in sport, includes the prohibition of selling alcoholic beverages in sports venues, to prevent an escalation of violence among fans. Likewise, the advertising of brands of alcoholic beverages in sports venues is subject to Law 7/2010 of 31 March, General Law on Audiovisual Communication, in those cases where an event is televised.

This work acknowledges how brewing companies have responded to political and community trends by launching and promoting alcohol-free versions of their products, which are likely to reconcile conflicting views on alcohol consumption in current society.

Beverage Industry Communication and Unethical Practices

The consumption habits of the population tend to undergo certain changes over a period of time, mainly due to the progressive knowledge of the products that they habitually consume, as well as the way in which companies use their efforts to address them (Vega-San Sebastián, 1997). Alcoholic beverage brands are no exception: their way of communicating to their audiences has been transformed over time to adapt to new trends, mainly to avoid undermining their profits and positioning (Noel et al., 2020).

Faced with the emerging landscape of behavior in favor of social responsibility and responsible consumption, joint and consensual responses by the different parties were born, such as the creation of ethical conduct manuals on self-regulation in the commercial communication of alcoholic beverages. An example of these manuals of conduct is the Cerveceros de España Advertising Self-Regulation Code (Cerveceros de España, 2003), which establishes the limitation and explicit prohibition of conduct that violates the principle of social responsibility. However, despite such attempts to establish an ethical framework for commercial communication that benefits both parties, it has been found that not all companies comply with what they have signed up to (March et al., 2014).

There is a general agreement that exposure to alcohol advertisements increases the likelihood of non-drinkers starting to drink, particularly among vulnerable consumers, such as children and adolescents (Anderson, Bu2009; Smith, & Foxcroft, 2009). Being exposed to alcohol advertisements tends to enhance positive expectations regarding alcohol consumption, linking it with desirable outcomes (March et al., 2014). A study by March et al. (2014), collected, through an audience analysis of the most important television channels in Spain, a total of 914 advertisements for alcoholic beverages over a period of 11 days, where many of them were broadcasted during advertising spots in children's films, charity galas and football matches. Their analysis revealed how most of these advertisements evoked values such as accomplishment, fun, sexual success, a sense of belonging and group cohesion, among many other social features. Additional evidence shows that young people are exposed to between two and four alcohol advertisements on average during a typical day. It may be likely that those alcohol advertising messages, likely to result in positive responses towards alcohol consumption (Collins et al., 2017; Sargent and Babor, 2020). Vulnerable populations now face an increased risk not only by the prominence of alcohol communication, but they are also more exposed to targeted advertising in social media. Algorithms may detect the greater sensibility of these segments to alcohol communications and thus become the main targets of such campaigns (Goodwin, 2022).Youngsters pay attention to specific advertising elements of alcoholic drinks like characters, music, and humor. This is linked to overall advertising likeability and effectiveness, which in turns affects purchase intention (Chen et al., 2005).

As mentioned above, alcohol consumption has historically been concentrated mainly in social settings, usually associated with the young population. This segment of the population is more likely to make decisions related to experiencing new emotions, even more so when in recent years society has become more permissive and tolerant towards private behavior without the participation of controlling agents (Rodríguez et al., 2004). New ways of communication, such as social media environments, pose new challenges to protect vulnerable consumers (Goodwin, 2022). Not only because they make it easier to create and show ads targeted to those segments that are more likely to show favorable responses to alcohol (Goodwin, 2022), but also because of the prominence of influencers that exhibit alcohol consumption as part of their glamorous lifestyle (Vranken et al., 2023). The role of influencers is especially pervasive for younger audiences that cannot be legally targeted on alcoholic ads, but are very likely to follow influencers that consume alcoholic drinks (Vranken et al., 2023). All the previous circumstances may explain why alcoholic beverage brands have become more involved in the everyday environment of young people (Sargent & Babor, 2020).

Thus, in the face of increasing prohibitionist regulations on the form of advertising and changing trends in the consumption of alcoholic beverages, some brands in the alcohol sector have decided to diversify their product portfolio in favor of reduced (or light) versions and, at the extreme, non-alcoholic variants (Plaza, 2021). In the following section, this new trend employed by a large part of the alcohol industry will be analyzed in more detail.

Emergence of Light and Non-Alcoholic Beverages

According to Sánchez (2023), consumers have become increasingly demanding, not only for qualities such as the taste or quality of the product, but also for the properties that make it beneficial to their health. This is why new movements such as NoLo (no and low alcohol) or mindful drinking are increasingly emerging, some of which advocate minimizing alcohol consumption and demanding beverages that are suitable as substitutes for those that do contain alcohol, mainly among young people and women (Hierro, 2020). In response, just as soft drink brands are launching sugar-free beverages, the alcohol industry has been able to respond to the new social paradigms by choosing to include 'free-from' and reduced-alcohol or light beverages in their product portfolio. There are 0.0 and light drinks in all categories, although we will focus primarily on the beer category.

According to the Organization of Consumers and Users (2023), Spain is the European country with the highest consumption and production of '0.0' beer, with around 15% of total beer consumption. This is undoubtedly due to our pioneering tradition in the brewing of this type of beverage, where it was not until the 1990s that it began to become popular because of new brewing technologies and the increasingly popular campaigns against alcohol (Tobar, 2022).

First non-alcoholic beers were launched under a different brand name to their alcoholic counterparts. The objective of such naming strategy was to differentiate them from the traditional alcoholic brand, given that their taste and properties differed significantly, and it was thought that could negatively affect brand recall. This is the example of the Laiker brand, which belonged to Mahou; or River, brewed by Estrella Galicia. However, after successive restrictions on the advertising of alcoholic beverages were implemented and the formula of non-alcoholic beers was improved, the companies decided to unify them under the same brand. To this end, they simply added the qualifier '0.0' or 'alcohol-free' and reformed their packaging to make them more similar to their alcoholic versions (Broc, 2019). It could be suggested that this change is likely to affect the way the consumers understand and process the advertisements. The more alike two products look (i.e., in terms of branding and packaging), the more likely it is that the individual finds little differences between them, transferring the awareness from the specific alcohol-free product to the general brand (Plaza, 2021).

However, the effects of these advertisements on the recipient are still largely understudied: we do not know yet to what extent an individual processes an advertisement for a non-alcoholic beer in a similar way to its alcoholic counterpart, or how both advertisements affect his or her perception of the brand.

In addition, little is known about the effects of such advertisements beyond the consumption context. Alcohol-free product advertisements have the potential to alter the perception of potentially unethical practices from brewing companies. On the one hand, it is possible that consumers viewing such advertisements become more aware of the possibility of doing things in the right way and thus are more critical when judging such unethical practices. Yet, on the other hand, it is possible that viewing alcohol-free advertisements generates a licensing effect in the consumer (Peloza et al., 2015), making them more permissive with unethical activities.

Following the literature review, this study aims to determine whether there really is a differentiating effect between alcoholic and non-alcoholic beer advertisements in the responses of their recipients. After carrying out a literature review on how the consumer environment and the communication of alcoholic beverage brands work, the following hypotheses are put forward:

H1: Advertisements of alcohol-free and alcoholic beer will exert different effects on consumers' evaluation of brewers' unethical practices.

H2: Advertisements of alcohol-free and alcoholic beer will affect consumers' evaluations of a) the brand object of analysis and b) beer in general.

H3: There will be significant attentional differences depending on whether the advertised product is alcohol-free or not.

OVERVIEW OF STUDIES

In order to respond to the research hypotheses, set out in the previous section, an experimental design would be used as a tool, where one of the following stimuli would be randomly assigned to each respondent: an advertising image of an alcoholic beverage, or, conversely, an advertising image of its non-alcoholic version. Two studies were performed: Study 1, which examined their effects through an online questionnaire, and Study 2, consisting of an eye-tracking experiment.

Beer was chosen as the alcoholic drink to be examined. As previously mentioned, beer is an alcoholic beverage that is deeply rooted in our culture, surpassing any other beverage of this type. Moreover, Spain is the European country with the highest per capita consumption of non-alcoholic beer (OCU, 2019). In addition, as beer is a very popular product in our society, making it easier to obtain realistic answers to the questions related to brand experience and brand choice through the questionnaire.

We selected a well-known Spanish beer brand as the focus of this study. Such brand was selected due to the following reasons: 1) its availability throughout Spain, 2) having a alcohol-free version and 3) frequently advertising both alcohol-free and alcoholic versions of the product. Both the modus operandi of its campaigns and the way in which consumers perceive its brand led us to formulate a study that could provide an answer to our research hypotheses.

Study One

Methodology

Stimulus development

In terms of preparing the survey stimuli, two online advertising posts were chosen: one for their main alcoholic beverage and one for their alcohol-free version. Both images were obtained directly from the beer brand's website. They were selected for their clear similarities between the two images in terms of color, order of elements and slogans used. These images are available in the appendix 2.

Procedure

Data was collected through an auto-administered online questionnaire with two different versions, distinguished only by the stimulus: one would show the alcoholic beer advertisement, and the other its 0.0 version. The dissemination of the questionnaire link mixed convenience with snowball sampling. We randomized the distribution of the different versions with an initial question: '*What digit does your mobile phone number end in?*', where its replica is a closed dichotomous answer with two intervals '0-4'and '5-9'. Depending on the answer, the participant was referred to the questionnaire which contained the alcoholic stimulus if they chose the first interval, or to the alcohol-free advertisement questionnaire if they chose the second interval. This way we would ensure that we would not incur a sampling bias by allocating the stimuli in a non-random way.

The questionnaire had different parts. The first one included questions prior to the appearance of the stimulus. Such questions serve as introduction to the topic and are related to the frequency of beer consumption, preferred alcohol-free and alcoholic beer brands, and features considered when selecting a beer. This way beer brand advertisements selected as stimulus would not interfere with individuals' responses. In the next section, the corresponding stimulus was shown, and the individuals were asked to pay attention to it during a minute. After that, questions regarding potentially unethical practices, brand attitude, and beer purchase attitude were presented. Finally, some demographics were collected, and participants were thanked for their collaboration.

Measurement

Scales were adapted to the specific context of study when necessary. In particular, brand attitude towards the brand from Zarantonello and Schmitt, (2010) and Yoo et al., (2000); purchase intention from Netemeyer et al., (2004); perceived quality from Calvo-Porral, (2018); and evaluation of potential unethical behaviors from brewing companies was adapted from Quiles-Soler, et al., (2005). For the list of items please visit appendix 1 Likert scales were with values ranging from 1 to 5, where chosen, (1 corresponds to 'strongly disagree' and 5 to 'strongly agree'). Individuals were asked to indicate their appreciation of beer features (taste, body, temperature, etc.) on a 5-point scale, where 1 was 'not at all' and 5 was 'very much'. Beer consumption was measured by six items where respondents were asked to indicate how often they drink each type of beer (lager, stout, 0.0, etc.).

Sample description

The final sample consisted of 160 respondents. Table 1 details the demographic data describing the sample. In terms of gender, there is a greater presence of male respondents than female, with 53.5% and 46.5% of the total sample respectively. Likewise, the majority of respondents were between 18 and 24 years of age, with 55.3% of the total, while those over 55 years are the second largest age group (18.2%). Regarding the educational level, we can observe that our sample is highly educated: the vast majority of the individuals who answered the survey are university graduates or students, with 76.1% of

Table 1. Sample description

Variable	Category	Frequence (%)
Gender	Man	53.5%
	Woman	46.5%
	Other	0%
Age	18-24	55.3%
	25-34	5.7%
	35-44	5.7%
	45-54	15.1%
	Over 55	18.2%
Education level	None	0%
	Primary	3.8%
	Secondary	1.3%
	Bachelor	6.3%
	Professional training	11.3%
	University degree	76.1%
Occupation	Still studying	42.1%
	Domestic worker	0.6%
	Unemployed	1.9%
	Self-employed	11.3%
	Employed	34.6%
	Retired	5%
Frequency of drinking	Sporadic or abstemious	31.4%
	Habitual drinker	68.6%

the total, followed by the 11.3% that studied professional training. Considering the occupation, 47.8% of the sample falls into the active population (employed or unemployed), and 47.7% into the inactive population (students, retired people, and domestic workers), so we can say that there are almost identical figures for both types of population. Finally, the majority of the sample identified themselves with habitual drinkers (68.6%)

Results

For the interpretation of the variables studied using the tools described in the previous section, it was decided to carry out different analyses in order to respond to the hypotheses of this research. This study was carried out with the help of the IBM SPSS Statistics v26 statistical software platform.

Differences in perception of brewers' potential unethical practices

Two parametric tests were carried out for independent samples using a one-factor ANOVA analysis to determine potential mean-differences. For both tests, questions related to the potentially unethical practices performed by beer brands and responsible consumption habits were chosen.

Table 2. ANOVA results for type of advertisement

Item	Version	Mean	Sig.
I believe that moderate consumption of beer is not harmful to health	1	3.32	.344
	2	3.50	
I would be willing to collaborate in any campaign against alcohol	1	2.84	.761
	2	2.77	
They should inform about the problems of alcohol on packaging, as they do with tobacco	1	3.52	.252
	2	3.27	
I am happy for celebrities to advertise beers, whether alcoholic or alcohol-free.	1	2.69	.002
	2	3.31	
I welcome the sale of beer at sports venues.	1	2.88	.009
	2	3.45	
I welcome beer brands launching alcohol-free versions.	1	4.06	.710
	2	4.12	
I am happy for minors to drink alcohol-free beer.	1	2.04	.214
	2	2.30	
I am happy for alcohol free beers to sponsor motoring events, such as Formula 1 or MotoGP.	1	2.96	.002
	2	3.61	

Note: 1 represents the alcoholic beer version of the advertisement, 2 represents alcohol-free version of the advertisement.

Firstly, the type of advertisement was chosen as a factor for the analysis. We were able to observe that respondents who were shown the alcohol-free beer advert responded significantly more positively to some of the potentially unethical practices evaluated, like using celebrities for advertising beer, allowing alcohol to be sold in both sporting and motoring events. Furthermore, although the differences are not significant, we can see that the presentation of an advertisement containing a non-alcoholic beer brand to the respondent elicits a general feeling of permissiveness towards potential unethical behavior from brewing companies. By contrast, respondents who watched the alcoholic beer advertisement were more critical with such potential unethical behaviors.

On the other hand, another parametric independent samples test (one-factor ANOVA) was performed, including the same variables as in the previous analysis of means, except that the factor used was a nominal variable created from the beer consumption questions at the beginning of the survey, where respondent 1 corresponds to 'sporadic or abstainer drinker' and respondent 2 to 'regular drinker'. In this way, we were able to find out how the individual felt about unethical and responsible drinking behavior, depending on the drinking pattern that each represented.

To ensure that there is no bias in the sample caused by an unequal distribution of drinker type; descriptive cross-tabulation statistics were performed. Thus, both in the cross-tabulations and in the Pearson's Chi-square test results, we were able to verify that, with a significance value of 0.926, there is no relationship between the two variables, thus assuring us that the type of drinkers was represented almost identically in both questionnaires.

Abstemious and sporadic drinkers were significantly more critical about companies adopting questionable practices in the promotion and sales of beer (i.e., using celebrities or selling beer at sport events),

Table 3. ANOVA results for type of drinker

Item	Participant	Mean	Sig.
I believe that moderate consumption of beer is not harmful to health	1	3.06	.015
	2	3.56	
I would be willing to collaborate in any campaign against alcohol	1	3.12	.044
	2	2.66	
They should inform about the problems of alcohol on packaging, as they do with tobacco	1	3.84	.005
	2	3.20	
I am happy for celebrities to advertise beers, whether alcoholic or alcohol-free beer.	1	2.66	.029
	2	3.13	
I welcome the sale of beer at sports venues.	1	2.80	.030
	2	3.30	
I welcome beer brands launching alcohol-free versions.	1	3.96	.303
	2	4.15	
I am happy for minors to drink alcohol free beer.	1	2.00	.312
	2	2.23	
I am happy for alcohol-free beer to sponsor motoring events, such as Formula 1 or MotoGP.	1	2.98	.065
	2	3.39	

Note: 1 represents sporadic and abstemious, 2 represents habitual drinker.

were more willing to collaborate in campaigns against alcohol and manifested more unfavorable views about the effects of beer consumption than habitual drinkers manifest. Table 3 shows the differences mentioned above.

This analysis allows us to partially accept Hypothesis 1, regarding the valuation towards potentially unethical practices depending on the observed stimulus, since variables of this type have been detected with significant differences in their responses.

Effects of advertisement on brand evaluation and beer purchase intention

In order to test the potential effect of the advertisements presented, linear regression analysis was performed. As for the independent variables, in addition to the type of advertisement it was decided to include other factors: such as attitudes, type of drinker and price. The research involved conducting factor analyses on three questionnaire groups to identify key variables related to beer purchase attitude, brand attitude, and attitude towards unethical practices. These variables were then subjected to reliability analyses, confirming their suitability for subsequent regression analysis. All three factors demonstrated high internal consistency (Cronbach's Alpha > 0.6). The variables comprising each factor were averaged and saved for future regression analysis.

The first regression analysis intended to explain attitude towards the brand. The model was able to explain 21.5% of the variance of the dependent variable. Table 4 shows the coefficients of the different independent variables used in the analysis: attitude towards unethical practices, attitude towards purchasing beer, and type of drinker, exerted a significant effect on the dependent variable, but not type of advertisement. Looking at the column of standardized Beta coefficients, it is possible to see how having more positive attitudes towards unethical practices, having the intention to purchase beer in general and

Table 4. Regression results for the dependent variable: attitude towards the brand

Variables	Standardized coefficients	t	Sig.
(Constant)		3.596	.000
Unethical practices	.261	3.167	.002
Beer consumption intention	.252	3.187	.002
Type of advertisement	.004	0.046	.964
Type of drinker	.159	2.068	.040

being a regular beer drinker lead to greater brand attitude. The type of advertisement (alcohol-free or alcoholic beer) has no influence on brand perception.

A second regression analysis was performed for the dependent variable attitude towards purchasing beer including the independent variables used in the previous analysis except brand attitude in order not to be redundant. The variable price was added to this analysis as an additional control measure. The results of the analysis showed how the independent variables were able to explain 18.4% of the intention to purchase beer. The significance and Beta coefficients shown in Table 5 manifest how that an increase in the convenience of the price of beer, as well as an increase in the attitude towards unethical practices, will in turn lead to a direct increase in beer purchase intentions. We can also see in the same table that neither the type of questionnaire nor the type of drinker were able to influence such general intentions towards purchasing beer.

Both analyses lead us to reject Hypothesis 2a and Hypothesis 2b, concerning the influence of the advertisement shown (alcohol-free vs. alcohol) on brand or product attitudes and intentions. In order to achieve a more complete understanding of the factors that lead these non-significant results of the advertisements showed, a second study, which focuses on the attentional processes of alcohol-free vs alcoholic beer advertisements was performed.

Study 2

Methodology

Stimulus development

For this study, two different stimuli were chosen, this time without providing prior information so as not to condition the visual attention of the respondent. The advertising post of the well-known brand

Table 5. Regression results for the dependent variable: intention to purchase beer.

Variables	Standardized coefficients	t	Sig.
(Constant)		6.312	.000
Price	.312	4.060	.000
Unethical practices	.313	3.936	.000
Type of advertisement	-.041	-0.526	.600
Type of drinkers	.052	0.673	.502

of beer chosen for the study 1 was chosen, specifically its black 0.0 version; due to the fact that it is a novel product for the parent company, and it is likely to receive greater attention from the participants due to its novelty. For this study, the second stimulus was created modifying the alcohol-free version by eliminating the qualifier 0.0', both from the slogan and the packaging. This was achieved by using the software 'RunwayML'. In this way, a fictitious beer advertisement was created to minimize the number of visual differences with respect to the alcohol-free image (see appendix 3).

Data collection

Data was collected with the eye-tracking software Gaze Recorder. For that purpose, a between subject experiment was performed, exposing each respondent to one of the two corresponding posts (i.e., 0.0 dark beer or dark beer). Likewise, to study the hot spots of each version of the advertisement and their potential differences, we determined areas of interest that can collect analytical measures such as the time of visual permanence (i.e., duration of fixations) or the exact second of the first visualization. In this way, it is possible to check to what extent each advertisement is capable of capturing individuals' attention, as well as deciphering the elements that attract the most attention to the image.

This quantitative study focuses on the resident population in Spain, with a convenience sample of 10 respondents. The data collection period occurred in May 2023.The stimuli was randomly assigned to each individual through the same method employed in study 1: telephone numbers ending between 0 and 4 would be presented with black beer image; and telephone numbers ending between 5 and 9 would be presented with 0.0 black beer image.

Areas of interest

The first and second areas of interest comprise the area related to the terms '0.0' in the slogan and packaging of the advertisement respectively. On the other hand, the third and fourth areas of interest correspond to the brand name that appears both in the slogan and on the bottle in both images. Finally, the fifth area of interest covers the space related to the word 'Black' in the advertising slogan.

Results

To perform the mean differences of the eye-tracking experiment, a parametric test for independent samples was carried out by means of a one-factor ANOVA analysis. Such analyses compared the percentages of total fixation duration for the different areas of interest under study.

In this way, we were able to find out how the area of the term '0.0' affects the individual's attention and compare it with other visual elements present in the advertisement. Table 6 shows that there are no differences in the attention devoted to the '0,0' term or the lack of it across advertisements. In fact, there were hardly any differences in the attention received by the different elements of both images. Besides this, the areas with the highest percentage of viewing time (i.e., received higher attention) in both versions of the same advertisement correspond to the brand name in the slogan, followed by the brand name on the beer label.

This analysis leads us to almost reject Hypothesis 3 completely. This hypothesis was related to the existence of significant attentional differences between alcohol-free and alcoholic beer advertisements. However, the results show that the different elements of the advertisement received similar levels of attention regardless of the version.

Table 6. ANOVA results for eye-tracking experiment

Variable	Advertisement	Average (%)	Sig.
Brand name in the advertising slogan	1	25.6%	.099
	2	30.4%	
Qualifier '0.0' in the advertising slogan	1	2.4%	.326
	2	8.2%	
Qualifier 'Black' in the advertising slogan	1	12.2%	.037
	2	4.8%	
Text field below the advertising slogan	1	10.8%	.210
	2	8.4%	
Brand name on the product labeling	1	22.4%	.598
	2	20.8%	
'0.0' qualifier on the product labeling	1	6.2%	.385
	2	3.6%	
Top label on bottle	1	5.4%	.676
	2	4.4%	

Note: 1 represents alcoholic beer version of the advertisement, 2 represents alcohol-free version of the advertisement

DISCUSSION

Beer consumption and consumers' perception of alcohol continues to be an issue of special attention in current society. Our culture has been developing in recent decades a role of acceptance towards alcohol consumption, which, according to Sarasa-Renedo et al. (2014), would be responsible for normalizing a drug with all the dangers and harm that it conveys. On the other hand, the new trends of responsible consumption are having an increasing impact on the commercial actions of the alcohol industry, leading to the emergence of responses in line with these ethical demands, such as the launch of alcohol-free beer (Noel et al., 2020). Thus, social responsibility codes have been put forward, such as the current self-regulation code for beer companies (Cerveceros de España, 2003), where they commit themselves to develop a series of ethical aspects mainly related to the commercial communication of their products. However, in practice these ethical codes are not sufficient to give rise to positive ethical behavior, as some companies do not follow their own communication and sales principles (March, 2014) or find new and more subtle ways to overcome traditional communication restrictions (Vranken et al., 2023). Such ways of acting especially affect vulnerable consumers, which may be in addition inadvertently targeted by automated communications (Goodwill, 2022).

This research, therefore, stems from the question of whether the new consumer trends really favor the development of a change in business strategy aimed at eradicating alcohol consumption, or, on the contrary, serve as an incentive to continue selling its main product under the promotion of a less harmful alternative. Key to this is whether there is a differentiated consumer response to commercial encouragement of alcoholic beverages with and without alcohol. To our knowledge, there is scant attention to the effects that alcohol-free advertising exerts on its viewers, and even less in comparison with their alcoholic counterparts.

To address such research questions, two studies were performed. The first one consisted of a survey with 160 respondents whereas the second one focused on an eye-tracking experiment with data from 10 respondents. Overall, our primary results point that viewing an alcohol-free beer advertisement does not necessarily lead to negative evaluations of unethical practices of brewing companies (Ugalde, 2014), but rather the opposite: it seems to produce a generalized feeling of rejection towards the prohibitionist movements of these practices. This may destabilize the idea of Noel et al. (2020) that the promotion of non-alcoholic alternatives could be a beneficial response to pro-healthy trends, as it seems that it only generates a greater sense of permissiveness towards alcohol promotion and consumption. However, and in agreement with Quiles-Soler (2005), unethical business practices were less accepted by the population that did not consume beer or consumed it sporadically than those who consumed it regularly. This confirms Hierro's (2020) hypothesis about the new NoLo or mindful drinking movements where he points out that this type of consumers advocate a change of trends by the alcohol industry in order to eradicate the widespread perception of alcohol acceptance.

On the other hand, it was observed that the intention to purchase beer (Netemeyer et al., 2004) does not seem to be conditioned by the type of advertisement or by the type of drinker who observed it. According to Calvo-Porral et al. (2018) and Quiles-Soler (2005), the findings show the possibility that beer purchase intention could be best explained by variables such as price evaluations or the consumer's attitude towards unethical brewers' practices. The same occurs with the attitude towards the brand, where the fact that the individual holds a favorable opinion towards unethical business practices and a favorable opinion towards alcohol consumption and sales does not affect a better brand perception.

Finally, the eye-tracking results show the possibility that there are no significant differences in the attention time of the receiver when faced with two advertisements of similar appearance and different types of products. In this case, with an advertisement for beer with and without alcohol. On the other hand, we were able to observe that the name of the beer brand may be a factor that stands out fundamentally due to its high percentage of time visualized in both ads. Thus, it would be coherent to affirm that the brand is a characteristic that predominates over others when it comes to capturing viewers' attention. This lends support to the change of the naming strategy developed by beer companies in the latest years (Broc, 2019; Plaza, 2021).

PUBLIC POLICY IMPLICATIONS

Several recommendations for action can be drawn for the benefit of sustainable consumption and the improvement of society's quality of life. Beyond the challenges that new forms of communication of alcoholic brands in social media pose (Goodwin, 2022; Vranken et al., 2023), our results warn about the switch to non-alcoholic versions of the same products. We have been able to observe that advertisements for alcohol-free beers do not generate a desire to buy, but they rather improve their perception of the unethical practices employed by some beer companies when developing their communication activities. Thus, the measures imposed by the authorities concerning broadcasting hours and places may have little effect in curbing beer consumption to the extent that '0.0 beer' advertisements help to generate a greater brand presence because of their ease of promotion (Plaza, 2021). Lately, we are witnessing some advancements in this light, since the latest version of self-regulation code for alcoholic beverages addresses emitting hours and targets of alcohol-free alternatives (EFE:Agro, 2024).

Considering beer consumption as a seemingly immovable element of our culture, it would be unrealistic to implement legislation that would further regulate beer advertising, even if we know that an advertising for a non-alcoholic substitute provokes very similar brand evaluations to those generated by the alcoholic version. For their part, sustainable drinking trends have put pressure on an industry that for decades offered only a single variety of beer to diversify its product portfolio in favor of new, healthier substitutes. Thus, a proper way to promote healthy habits stems from accepting that beer consumption is an indispensable part of our society and recognizing that its non-alcoholic equivalents can serve to focus attention on a large proportion of consumers who have not had the opportunity to try them, either because of price or logistical reluctance.

On the other hand, according to the literature review, there are doubts as to whether the type of institutional campaigns against alcohol consumption can actually generate attitudes of rejection of these drinks by those who consume them. In fact, inconsistencies are found in some public campaigns, such as in the case of beer fairs like the 'Oktoberfest' organized by public administrations, where they promote through a festive event the incitement to alcohol consumption, even offering free admission to the event. As a result, a single, clear message regarding the problems of alcohol consumption is not disseminated, but rather contradictory communications are used in a way that can lead to confusion among citizens.

Public policy makers need to extend their surveillance to new communication environments and formats, present mainly in social media (Goodwill, 2022; Vranken, et al., 2023). Some steps in this regard can be found in the new regulation of spirit beverages, which restricts the promotion of alcoholic beverages among those influencers who have a follower base that is composed of adults (+25 years) and do not transmit narratives that foster irresponsible consumption of alcoholic drinks (EFE:Agro, 2024).

After observing in this research that a large part of the population has never tried an alcohol-free beer, and knowing that beer consumption continues to reach its absolute maximums, it is suggested that the authorities classify this issue as a matter of state in order to redirect their communication efforts towards the promotion of healthy substitutes. Given the strength of brand and branding strategies pushed by brewing companies, it is logical to expect that new products (i.e., alcohol-free beer) try to capitalize on them. However, if a real reduction of alcohol consumption is sought, both public institutions and companies need to consider using different brand names for the different (i.e., alcohol-free vs. alcoholic) versions of the products. All this, would ultimately facilitate the development of dealcoholizing processes for beverages. Once again, the normalization of these alternatives could put an end to a large part of alcohol consumption in our country and would put an end to malicious practices that currently benefit their alcoholic counterparts.

FUTURE DIRECTIONS AND LIMITATIONS

As we have been able to observe, this research has managed to gather very interesting data on alcohol consumption in our society, as well as contributing to a study on the effects of the communication of alcohol-free products on consumers' brand value and their perception of the unethical practices performed by the industry. Similarly, these analyses have been complemented by an experiment that was able to determine the attentional similarities between advertisements for two beers from the same brand, although different in terms of their alcohol content. However, it is worth highlighting several issues that limit the reach and generalizability of the findings obtained.

Firstly, the current work is limited by its focus on a single brand and type of advertisement (i.e., static image). In the future, it may be of interest to replicate this study in different settings. For example, due to the recent significant increase in low-alcohol spirits it would be interesting to evaluate the impact of such advertisements on the consumption of their main alcoholic version., it would also be worth extending the study to different beer brands and advertising formats and styles. In this way, it could be possible to eliminate the potential brand bias caused by the choice of a well-known brand in the current study.

On the other hand, this research focused on whether there is a causal relationship between the observation of an advertisement for non-alcoholic beer and an increase in the consumption of regular beer. This ended up being a limitation when it came to studying such consumer behavior, given the difficulty of clearly measuring this type of data. Sometimes, the fact of estimating information that may be very obvious a priori causes reluctance in the respondent's response, as it results in involuntary and unplanned attitudes that are difficult to measure. For this reason, the survey omitted questions related to direct purchase behavior in favor of questions on purchase intention and brand evaluation.

Finally, although the eye-tracking experiment was able to provide a heat map where the attentional time devoted to the brand was predominant, it was not possible to measure how such fixation affects the individual's subsequent purchase decision. Moreover, individual factors, such as the level of beer consumption or the familiarity with the beer were not acknowledged Therefore, as a future line of research, an experimental study could be developed where individual characteristics are controlled. In addition, or separately in another study, advertisements for a non-alcoholic beer of one brand can be shown to one group of individuals and another advertisement of a different brand to another group, in order to observe their purchase behavior afterwards. In this way, we could consider three possible scenarios: whether the 'brand' factor affects the individual's purchase, whether it is the 'non-alcoholic' element that influences their consumption decision, or whether both variables have an impact on their ultimate choice of product.

CONCLUSION

The current work offers novel evidence on the effects of alcohol-free beer advertising, which have received little attention. More specifically, we compared the effects of alcohol-free vs. alcoholic beer advertisements on consumer responses such as attitudes towards unethical behaviors, brand attitude and beer purchase intention. Moreover, we compared the attentional effects of the advertisements of these two types of products.

As we have been able to analyze, recent policy regulations and consumer trends are clear and decisive in the approach to new product diversification strategies for a large part of the beer industry in our country. The non-alcoholic versions of beer, therefore, reflect this change in business vision, turning out to be alternatives that are less harmful to health, with an increasingly sophisticated preparation and similar to their alcohol-based equivalents.

However, after analyzing the data obtained in the survey, it seems that non-alcoholic beer advertisements do not provoke a positive purchase desire towards the product they advertise, regardless of whether they are regular or sporadic drinkers or teetotalers. In this way, what at first glance may seem like a beneficial strategy to reduce unhealthy behaviors could end up being innocuous and ineffective in its ability to generate purchasing desires of non-alcoholic products. Furthermore, these results seem to communicate that these advertisements encourage greater permissiveness when assessing unethical practices performed by certain beer brands in their commercial communication strategy.

On the other hand, the complementary experiment by eye-tracking showed us the possibility that the element of a beer advertisement with or without alcohol that most attracts the attention of the individual who observes it is the brand of the beer itself, prevailing over the elements remaining visuals that may appear on an advertising billboard. This discovery makes us reflect on the usefulness of promoting an advertisement with different alcohol content to influence the consumption of the person receiving the stimulus. According to our results, these activities seem to favor the development of a brand positioning more than generating awareness of the product itself. In this way, we believe that advertising alcohol-free beer versus alcoholic beer, exerts little effect on a company's branding objectives, since increasing their brand awareness is indifferently satisfied in both ways. Although some measures to limit alcohol-free advertising have been recently adopted, it is still early to consider their effect. In the meantime, all our findings make us question whether the rise of new varieties of non-alcoholic beers, that are visually similar and use the same name as their alcoholic counterparts, is objectively worth it as an engine of progress towards a healthier society.

REFERENCES

Agro, E. F. E. (2024). *Las bebidas espirituosas amplían su autorregulación con normas para 'influencers' y las 0,0.* EFE:Agro https://efeagro.com/bebidas-espirituosas-amplian-autorregulacion/

Anderson, P. (2009). Is it time to ban alcohol advertising? *Clinical Medicine, 9*(2), 121–124. doi:10.7861/clinmedicine.9-2-121 PMID:19435114

Broc, Ò. (2019). Cerveza sin alcohol para vender más alcohol. *El Comidista.* https://elcomidista.elpais.com/elcomidista/2019/10/10/articulo/1570720904_131455.html

Calvo-Porral, Orosa-González, J., & Blazquez-Lozano, F. (2018). A clustered-based segmentation of beer consumers: From "beer lovers" to "beer to fuddle". *British Food Journal, 120*(6), 1280–1294. doi:10.1108/BFJ-11-2017-0628

Cantó-Gómez, A., & Mantecón, A. (2020). El "tardeo" en Alicante: la mercantilización del espacio en una ciudad turística. *Ciudad y terriorio. Estudios territoriales, 52*(2006), 2659-3254. doi:10.37230/CyTET.2020.206.06

Cerveceros de España. (2003). Código de Autorregulación Publicitaria de Cerveceros de España. *Cerveceros de España.* https://cerveceros.org/uploads/60ad057cdcd31__CAP _CE_envigor.pdf

Chamorro-Fernández, A., Alonso Sardón, M., & Mirón Canelo, J. (2005). Valoración de la producción científica y epidemiológica sobre alcoholismo en España (1996-2002). *A tu. Salud (Barranquilla), 49,* 16–19.

Chen, M. J., Grube, J. W., Bersamin, M., Waiters, E., & Keefe, D. B. (2005). Alcohol advertising: What makes it attractive to youth? *Journal of Health Communication, 10*(6), 553–565. doi:10.1080/10810730500228904 PMID:16203633

Collins, R. L., Martino, S. C., Kovalchik, S. A., D'Amico, E. J., Shadel, W. G., Becker, K. M., & Tolpadi, A. (2017). Exposure to alcohol advertising and adolescents' drinking beliefs: Role of message interpretation. [h]. *Health Psychology, 36*(9), 890–897. doi:10.1037/hea0000521 PMID:28639822

Federación Española de Industrias de Alimentación y Bebidas (FIAB). (2023). Volumen de bebida consumido por persona en el hogar en 2021, desglosado por grupos de productos (en litros). *Statista*. https://es.statista.com/estadisticas/475374/consumo-per-capita-de-bebida-en-el-hogar-en-espana-por-producto/

Galán, I., González, M., & Valencia-Martín, J. (2014). Patrones de consumo de alcohol en España: Un país en transición. *Revista Española de Salud Pública*, *88*(4), 529–540. doi:10.4321/S1135-57272014000400007 PMID:25090408

Gómez-Fraguela, J. A., Fernández Pérez, N., Romero Tríñanes, E., & Luengo Martín, A. (2008). El botellón y el consumo de alcohol y otras drogas en la juventud. *Psicothema*, *20*(2), 211–217. PMID:18413080

Goodwin, I. (2022). Programmatic alcohol advertising, social media and public health: Algorithms, automated challenges to regulation, and the failure of public oversight. *The International Journal on Drug Policy*, *109*, 103826. doi:10.1016/j.drugpo.2022.103826 PMID:35994939

March Cerdá, J. C., Martín Barato, A., López Doblas, M., Luque Martín, N., Prieto Rodríguez, M. A., & Danet Danet, A. (2014). La publicidad de bebidas alcohólicas en España y su repercusión en la población adolescente. *Revista Española de Drogodependencias*, *39*(4), 59–76.

Ministerio de Agricultura, P. y A. (MAPA). (2023). Volumen de cerveza consumida con y sin alcohol en los hogares españoles entre 2011 y 2021 (en miles de kilos). *Statista*. https://es.statista.com/estadisticas/487254/consumo-de-cerveza-de-los-hogares-por-tipo-en-espana/

Ministerio de Sanidad. (2022). *Informe del Plan Nacional sobre Drogas*. PNSD. https://pnsd.sanidad.gob.es/home.htm

Netemeyer, R. G., Krishnan, B., Pullig, C., Wang, G., Yagci, M., Dean, D., Ricks, J., & Wirth, F. (2004). Developing and validating measures of facets of customer-based brand equity. *Journal of Business Research*, *57*(2), 209–224. doi:10.1016/S0148-2963(01)00303-4

Noel, J. K., Sammartino, C. J., & Rosenthal, S. R. (2020). Exposure to Digital Alcohol Marketing and Alcohol Use: A Systematic Review. *Journal of Studies on Alcohol and Drugs*, *19*(s19), 57–67. doi:10.15288/jsads.2020.s19.57 PMID:32079562

Observatorio Español de las Drogas y las Adicciones. (2021). INFORME 2021: Alcohol, tabaco y drogas ilegales en España. *Ministerio de Sanidad. Delegación del Gobierno para el Plan Nacional sobre Drogas*, 52-65.

Organización de Consumidores y Usuarios. (2023). Cervezas sin y 0,0%, ¿la alternativa? *OCU.org*. https://www.ocu.org/alimentacion/alimentos/noticias/cervezas-sin-y-00

Paniagua-Repetto, H. (2007). Vacaciones y ausencia de publicidad de alcohol alrededor de los centros educativos: ¿una casualidad? *Anales de Pediatría (Barcelona, Spain)*, *66*(2), 224. doi:10.1016/S1695-4033(07)70383-1

Peloza, J., Ye, C., & Montford, W. J. (2015). When companies do good, are their products good for you? How corporate social responsibility creates a health halo. *Journal of Public Policy & Marketing*, *34*(1), 19–31. doi:10.1509/jppm.13.037

Plaza, A. (2021). ¿Anuncios de whisky y ginebra en TV? Llevan décadas prohibidos pero cuelan con versiones «light». *eldiario.es*. https://www.eldiario.es/ economia/anuncios-whisky-ginebra-tv-llevan-decadas-prohibidos-cuelan-versiones-light_1_7946458.html

Quiles-Soler, M. (2005). *Análisis de la publicidad de bebidas al- cohólicas: valores percibidos y consumo en población universitaria*. Universitat d'Alacant.

Rodríguez, E., Sánchez, L., & Megías, I. (2004). Jóvenes y publicidad. Valores en la comunicación publicitaria para jóvenes. *Injuve FAD*. http://www.injuve.es/ sites/default/files/completojovenesypublicidad.pdf

Sánchez, M. (2023). Bebidas alcohólicas: cuatro tendencias que marcan el rumbo. AEOC. https://www.aecoc.es/articulos/c84-bebidas-alcoholicas-4-tendencias-que-marcan-el-rumbo

Sánchez, R. (2002). Publicidad de bebidas alcohólicas. Algunas razones para establecer unos límites. *Adicciones*, *13*(1), 133–140.

Sarasa-Renedo, A., Sordo, L., Molist, G., Hoyos, J., Guitart, A. M., & Barrio, G. (2014). Principales daños sanitarios y sociales relacionados con el consumo de alcohol. *Revista Española de Salud Pública*, *88*(4), 469–491. doi:10.4321/S1135-57272014000400004 PMID:25090405

Sargent, J. D., & Babor, T. F. (2020). The Relationship Between Exposure to Alcohol Marketing and Underage Drinking Is Causal. *Journal of Studies on Alcohol and Drugs*, *19*(s19), 113–124. doi:10.15288/jsads.2020.s19.113 PMID:32079567

Smith, L. A., & Foxcroft, D. R. (2009). The effect of alcohol advertising, marketing and portrayal on drinking behaviour in young people: Systematic review of prospective cohort studies. *BMC Public Health*, *9*, 1–11. doi:10.1186/1471-2458-9-S1-S1 PMID:19200352

Tobar, S. (2022). España, paraíso de la cerveza sin alcohol: ¿qué y quién está detrás del éxito de las 0,0? *El Español*. https://www.elespanol.com/invertia/empresas/distribucion/ 20220702/espana-paraiso-cerveza-sin-alcohol-detras-exito/684431923_0.html

Ugalde, C. (2014). Influencia de la actitud hacia la marca y su calidad percibida hacia sus anuncios: ¿afectan la intención de compra? *REDMARKA UIMA - Universidad de A Coruña – CIECID*, *13*, 43-62.

Vega San Sebastián, A. (1997). El alcohol en los medios de comunicación: La presión para su consumo-abuso. *Revista Científica Iberoamericana de Comunicación y Educación*, *9*, 105–110.

von Philipsborn, P., Stratil, J., Burns, J., Busert, L., Pfadenhauer, L., Polus, S., Holzapfel, C., Hauner, H., & Rehfuess, E. (2016). Environmental interventions to reduce the consumption of sugar-sweetened beverages and their effects on health (Protocol). *Cochrane database of systematic reviews (Online)*.

Vranken, S., Beullens, K., Geyskens, D., & Matthes, J. (2023). Under the influence of (alcohol) influencers? A qualitative study examining Belgian adolescents' evaluations of alcohol-related Instagram images from influencers. *Journal of Children and Media*, *17*(1), 134–153. doi:10.1080/17482798.2022.2157457

Yoo, B., Donthu, N., & Lee, S. (2000). An Examination of Selected Marketing Mix Elements and Brand Equity. *Journal of the Academy of Marketing Science*, *28*(2), 195–211. doi:10.1177/0092070300282002

Zarantonello, L., & Schmitt, B. (2010). Using the Brand Experience Scale to Profile Consumers and Predict Consumer Behavior. *Journal of Brand Management*, *17*(7), 532–540. doi:10.1057/bm.2010.4

KEY TERMS AND DEFINITIONS

Advertising Impact: effects that advertising efforts exert on consumer perceptions, purchasing decisions, and societal norms. In the case of breweries, these effects include shaping brand image, creating positive associations, and foster demand for their products.

Alcohol-Free Advertising: Advertisement efforts devoted to versions of alcoholic products that contain substantially less alcohol or no alcohol at all. Given the regulations that ban most promotions of alcoholic drinks, this format of advertising has received greater attention in the latest years.

Brand Attitude: Evaluations (combinations of affect and belief) that consumers hold towards a given brand. In the case of alcohol-free vs. alcoholic advertisement no differences for brand attitude were found.

Evaluations of Unethical Behavior in Brewing Industry: Consumer evaluations of the appropriateness of controversial practices, such as, targeting vulnerable populations, placing products in sportive venues or using alcoholic-free products to create awareness of alcoholic brands.

Eye-Tracking: Technology used to monitor and measure eye movement. It involves tracking gaze patterns when the person is viewing a given object. In this chapter, eye-tracking was employed to understand attentional differences between alcohol-free and alcoholic advertisements.

NoLo: Societal movement that is worried abput the negative effects of alcohol consumption and seeks to enjoy a lifestyle which comprises No or Low levels of alcohol. Alcohol-free or low alcoholic beverages are targeted at followers of this movement.

Vulnerable Population: Population that is more sensible to the effects of alcohol advertisements because they have more problems to discern marketing exaggerations and protect themselves from different types of advertising.

APPENDIX

Appendix 1: Constructs and Items for Regression Analysis

CONSTRUCTS	ITEMS
Beer purchase intention	This advertising makes me want to consume that beer
Brand attitude	If I had to choose between (brand) and a foreign beer, I would select the former, even if its not as good as the second one.
	Even if there is a great variety of beers, I would still choose (brand)
	I would choose (brand) over other brands because I think it is the best one.
Price	When I select a beer, I pay attention to its price
Perceived unethical practices	They should inform about the problems of alcohol on packaging, as they do with tobacco
	I am happy for celebrities to advertise beers, whether alcoholic or alcohol-free.
	I welcome the sale of beer at sports venues.
	I welcome beer brands launching alcohol-free versions.
	I am happy for minors to drink alcohol-free beer.

Appendix 2: Stimuli Presented in Study One

Figure 2.

Appendix 3. Stimuli Presented in Study Two

Figure 3.

Chapter 6
Evolution of Research on Green Innovation in the Wine Industry:
A Bibliometric Analysis

Marcos Carchano
University of Castilla-La Mancha, Spain

Inmaculada Carrasco
https://orcid.org/0000-0002-3844-4569
University of Castilla-La Mancha, Spain

Ángela González
University of Castilla-La Mancha, Spain

ABSTRACT

Green innovation has been recognized as a crucial element in achieving sustainable development, capturing the interest of researchers and professionals. This has led to a significant number of publications analyzing how green innovation can reduce the environmental impact of business activities. Simultaneously, the negative impact of climate change on wine production has pushed wineries to shift their practices towards more sustainable production models. The main aim of this study is to analyze the scientific state, trends, and gaps in the field of green innovation in the wine industry. To achieve this goal, a bibliometric analysis was carried out using VOSviewer software. The results indicate that sustainability has attracted considerable attention in the wine industry in the last three years. Specifically, green innovation has been studied as a vehicle to improve the environmental performance of this sector. Moreover, the results provide a comprehensive overview of the current situation in the field, serving as a valuable starting point for future research.

DOI: 10.4018/979-8-3693-2149-2.ch006

INTRODUCTION

Nowadays, wineries are pressured to develop more ecological practices to reduce negative impacts, fight climate change effects, meet environmental preferences of consumers and institutional organizations. The increasing global wine demand required to identify new strategies and practices to embrace sustainability. Wine production, distribution and consumption implies negative environmental effects like deforestation, natural resources consumption, increase of GHG emissions, pesticides use, generation of waste, among others (Christ and Burrit, 2013). Additionally, climate change exerts a significant negative effect on wine production (Petriashvili et al., 2023; Galbreath et al., 2020). Phenomena such as heatwaves, torrential rains, frost, rising temperature can affect to agricultural operations (Marx et al., 2017), so climate is a key driver of wine production and productivity (Neethling et al., 2019). A significant consequence of warming and reduced precipitation is an earlier harvest that affects grape composition and quality, resulting in higher sugar levels and lower phenolic, acidity, and aromatic levels (Marín et al., 2021; Mozell and Thach, 2014). Consequently, climate change is currently a significant concern for winemakers (Chieco et al., 2023).

Moreover, ecological transition is one of the main priorities for stakeholders in the wine industry (Beber et al., 2023). The current demand for ecological and sustainable products has grown considerably in this industry (Galati et al., 2019; Fiore et al., 2017), forcing companies to adopt alternative approaches to adapt to new market conditions (Frigon et al., 2020; Carchano et al., 2023). In fact, one of the main motivations for transitioning towards sustainability in the wine world lies in the changing consumer behavior, now oriented towards ecological products (Sellers-Rubio and Nicolau-Gonzalbez, 2016). Thus, increased consumer concern about environmental issues has boosted the demand for organic wines (Barber et al., 2009). For instance, Pomarici et al. (2018) find that younger consumers show more interest in wines with a lower environmental impact in terms of water consumption. Similarly, Moscovi et al. (2022) analyze the differences in consumer perception of ecological wine and their purchasing intentions. The results show that sustainable production and ecological certification are gaining prominence among consumers in this industry, to the extent that they are willing to pay a higher price for ecological wines. The trend towards acquiring sustainably produced wines is on the rise, with an increasing number of consumers opting for this choice (Rabadán and Bernabéu, 2021). In fact, consumers are willing to pay a premium for organic wines. Mos existing studies declare the willingness to pay more for sustainable products (Moscovici et al., 2022; Schäufele and Hamm, 2017). The shift towards consumption patterns based on sustainable products opens up new opportunities for wine companies.

Institutional pressure (legal rules, guidelines, and standards) can also stimulate green initiatives in wine industry (Flores et al., 2018; Galbreath et al., 2016). Recently, the European Commission has emphasized the necessity to implement environmental practices to favor sustainable development. In this regard, European wine producers face a wide variety of regulations (Meloni et al., 2019). For example, currently the production and labeling of organic products regarding control systems, commercial regimes, and production standards are regulated by Regulation (EU) 2018/848. The regulation sets out the different principles and requirements that organic farming must meet, as well as standards relating to the labeling of various organic foods. The recently implemented regulation replaces the previous Regulation (EC) 834/2007. At the same time, the Common Agricultural Policy 2023-2027 (in effect since January 1, 2023) includes a variety of stricter environmental measures and standards to promote organic farming and responsible input management. Additionally, it also integrates a wide range of voluntary environmental measures. In this sense, the CAP is established as a key instrument for combating climate change in agriculture. Thanks to the measures incorporated into the various agricultural policies, agricultural emissions have decreased by 24% between 1990 and 2017 (European Commission, 2019). Along with compliance with different European directives, wineries face a wide variety of sustainability guidelines and indicators used to assess sustainability performance in different countries. In this respect, Flores (2018) conducts a cross-analysis in six different countries to identify the main existing frameworks for sustainability assessment. Some specific examples include South Africa (Sustainable Wine South Africa, SWSA), New Zealand (Sustainable Winegrowing New Zealand, SWNZ), Australia (McLaren Vale Sustainable Winegrowing Australia, MVSWGA), Chile (National Code of Sustainability for Chilean Wine Industry), US/California (California Sustainable Winegrowing Alliance, CSWA), and France (Terra Vitis). Most national frameworks are based on certifications or environmental labels. In conclusion, wine producers face different EU and national directives to improve sustainability. This idea is in line with the results of previous studies exploring the main drivers in the adoption of sustainability practices in the wine industry (for example, De Steur et al., 2020)

Therefore, be green is becoming a critical element in company survival. Consequently, nowadays wineries have incorporated sustainability in their operations (Pomarici and Vecchio, 2019; Ferri et al., 2024), adopting sustainable-oriented innovations to achieve environmental benefits (e.g. protection of biodiversity or landscape) (De Steur et al., 2020). Galbreath et al., (2020) find that climate change effects (changes in temperature and rainfall) lead to develop sustainable adaptative practices.

The wine industry is one of the most important economic activities for several countries worldwide. According to data from International Organisation of Vine and Wine (OIV) (2023), there are 7,3 million hectares of vineyard surface in the world in 2022. Spain is the largest vineyard in the world (955.000 hectares), followed by France (812.0000 hectares) an Italy (718 hectares), together represent over 75% of the worldwide vineyard surface. The European Mediterranean countries have been traditionally the main world area in wine cultivation and production. However, in the last decades, new wine countries like United States, Argentine, South Africa or New Zealand have experimented an expansion in vineyard surfaces, resulting in a more complex and competitive market (Hussain et al., 2007). Following the same OIV report, the global wine production and consumption is estimated at 258 million hectoliters and 232 million hectoliters respectively in 2022. To better understand its importance in the world economy, we can focus on its operations volume. The acceleration of wine industry globalization has result in an expansion of wine trade. Specifically, as detailed in OIV (2023) global wine exports reached 107 million hectoliters in 2022 with a monetary record-breaking value of 37,6 billion euros.

Considering this context, wineries must design strategies to increase competitiveness and sustainability. In this sense, Golicic et al., (2017) highlight three main strategies for wine companies to incorporate sustainability into their businesses and survive in a highly competitive environment: (1) innovation and experimentation are positioned as one of the main elements for the development of resilience, the introduction of product innovations (new labeling, packaging, etc.). Process innovations (customer relationship management system, marketing processes) or organizational innovations can increase the efficiency and effectiveness of production systems, cost savings, use of resources, etc. (2) Another strategy that works to build resilience and mainstream sustainability is resource sourcing and capacity building. Companies require the resources, skills, competencies, or experience that are indispensable means to produce and innovate. (3) Finally, supply chain connections are the third strategy, which according to the authors helps companies build resilience. Cooperation and connection with other companies in the sector provide resources, ideas and even innovations. These are very valuable means, especially for smaller companies, which are the predominant ones in the wine sector.

Companies face various pressures and challenges to find alternative methods that allow them to improve their environmental performance, increase their profits, and remain competitive. The role of green innovation in addressing issues related to sustainable development has been widely recognized in the literature (e.g. Bag et al., 2022 or Ahmad and Wu, 2021), to the extent that nowadays these practices are positioned as a key mechanism to ensure the survival of the company (Eryigit and Özcüre, 2015). Specifically, in recent decades there has been a growing interest among researchers, professionals, and public agents towards environmental conservation, which has simultaneously led to an increasing focus on environmentally innovative practices (Polzin et al., 2016). Green innovation, known also as green innovation or environmental innovation (Tariq et al., 2017; Díaz-García et al., 2015) is defined as "production, assimilation or exploitation of a product, production process, service or management or business method that is novel to the organization (developing or adopting it) and which results, throughout its life cycle, in a reduction of environmental risk, pollution and other negative impacts of resources use (including energy use) compared to relevant alternatives" (Kemp y Pearson, 2007). Specifically, development of green innovations can result in a win-win situation for consumers, institutions, and companies. First, it allows companies to simultaneously achieve environmental and competitive benefits (Moyano-Fuentes et al., 2019). The introduction of these types of practices can help to reduce negative impact of business activities on environment, making its more circular and respectful (Valero Gil et a., 2023; Zheng and Latridis 2022). Indeed, green innovation is a key element for transition to a circular economy (De Jesús et al., 2018). Recent studies have shown that conventional agricultural practices generate a greater environmental impact than other forms of sustainable production, such as biodynamic farming (Villanueva-Rey et al., 2014). On the other hand, environmental practices allow companies to satisfy pressure from stakeholder pressures (Demirel and Kesidou, 2019). In addition, green innovation has become and effective vehicle to improve competitiveness, increase efficiency, reduce cost, strengthening company´s differentiation strategies and increase market share (Berrone et al., 2017; Afshari et al., 2020; Hizarci-Payne et al., 2021).

Despite, be sustainable can give competitive advantages and growth opportunities to wineries (Ferrer et al., 2023; Forbes et al., 2009; Atkin et al., (2012), the effort to implement sustainable practices remains limited in some wineries (Broccardo and Zicare, 2020). The explanation behind this fact may lie in the risk and high costs associated with this type of innovations. Most wineries are characterized by their small size and limited resources, which can become a barrier to the advancement of sustainability in this sector. Recently Carchano et al., (2023) carried out empirical study which highlight the financial rewards associated to environmental proactivity in wine industry, however, there arises the need to conduct studies that demonstrate the economic benefits derived from green investments.

The renewed interest in green innovation has led to a significant growth in the existing literature in this field. Recently, several studies have utilized bibliometric methodology to analyze the state of knowledge in the field of eco-innovation. For instance, authors such as Frrukh et al. (2021), Albort-Morant et al. (2017), and Takalo et al. (2021) have conducted bibliometric reviews to examine the state of the art and the development of research in green innovation. Similarly, Qing et al. (2022) contribute to understanding the relationship between green technology innovation and financial performance through a review of existing literature. Other studies focus on providing a comprehensive insight into the various motivations that drive companies to engage in eco-innovation (Passaro et al., 2023; López-Pérez et al., 2024), how green innovation facilitates expansion in international markets (Šūmakaris et al., 2020), and how these practices contribute to sustainable development (Zheng and Latreidis, 2022). Despite these valuable contributions, there is currently a lack of bibliometric analysis on the concept of eco-innovation in the wine industry. Specifically, there is a shortage of studies in environmental management literature on the wine sector, and much less in the specific field on green innovation. Recognizing that the sector can significantly influence the nature and impact of environmental practices' drivers and outcomes (Passaro et al., 2023), there is a need to better understand the current state, structure, and future directions of academic literature on green innovation in wine.

The main aim of this study is to analyze the scientific state, trends, and gaps on green innovation in the field of wine sector in order to provide a general overview and guide researchers in the identification of potential lines of research. Therefore, we want to identify the main works, authors, journals, institutions, and countries. To achieve this end, this study carries out a bibliometric analysis using VOSviewer software. Following this aim a three key research questions have been established:

RQ1: What are the current trends about green innovation in wine industry?

RQ2: Which are the most important and relevant studies, authors, journals, and countries on green innovation in wine industry?

RQ3: Which are the relevant research topics addressed in this field?

To our knowledge, despite growing interest in sustainable development has accelerated the increase of the research on green innovation, there are still scant systematic literature reviews studies focused on wine industry. This research contributes providing a comprehensive framework to advance in the knowledge of how green innovation can help wineries to improve their environmental impacts, and obtain a complete helicopter view of the state of the art. In addition, the study can serve as a guide to help researchers to identify the current gaps and provide a reference to identify directions for future research.

The article is structures as follows. After this introduction, in section 2 data and research methodology used in this study are presented. In section 3, the main findings and result are provided. Finally, in section 4 implications of the results are discussed and conclusions, limitations and future research directions are given.

METHODOLOGY

To address our research questions, this study focuses on the bibliometric analysis of scientific publications on wine industry and green innovation. Bibliometric analysis is a quantitative research method based on a mathematical and statistical element that allow to map scientific information, study the different trends of the publications, identify popular contributions and authors and recent gaps, collaboration patterns, among others (Donthu et al., 2021; Krause et al., 2020). Moreover, bibliometric analysis provides a helicopter view of scientific production in a specific field, its represents and innovative approach in contrast to the traditional theoretical framework building (Bjork et al., 2014; Merigó et al., 2015). With the use of this research method the reliability and replicability of the results is guaranteed over time due to the transparent and reproducible review process (Stechemesser and Guenther, 2012). For these reasons, the use of this technique has gained popularity in various research areas, including wine industry (Marco-Lajara et al., 2023).

Specifically, to carry out the bibliometric analysis and represent the current state of the literature on green innovation and wine industry, Web of Science database was selected. This decision is justified because Wos is the leading database of publications in many fields (Ye et al., 2020), it is composed of three indices: the Science Citation Index Expanded (SCI-E), Social Sciences Citation Index (SSCI), and Emerging Sources Citation Index (ESCI), included over 21.100 journals indexed and published in

Figure 1. PRISMA diagram

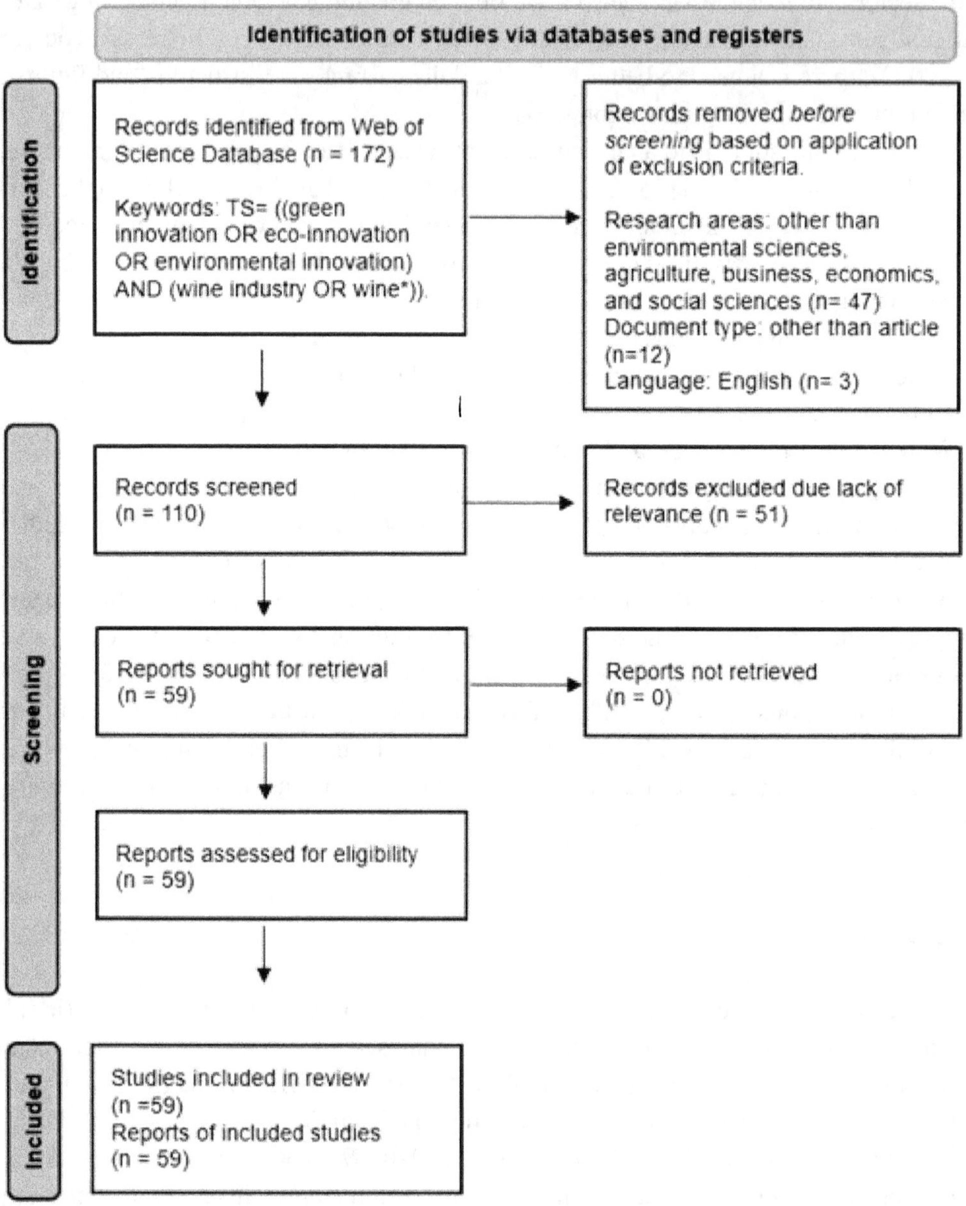

over 250 scientific disciplines, that guaranteed the high quality of the indexed articles (Rey-Marti et al., 2016). Furthermore, WoS database has been used as the main data source for recent existing bibliometric analysis (e.g. Albort-Morant et al., 2017 or López-Pérez et al., 2023)

We followed the PRISMA guidelines (Preferred Reporting Items for Systematic Reviews and Meta-Analyses) for conducting the bibliometric study due to its better accuracy (Moher et al., 2010). It consists of 3 steps (see figure 1): the first step was identification of relevant literature, for this purpose, and based on the preliminary assessment of the literature, we have chosen the following research equation "TS= ((green innovation OR eco-innovation OR environmental innovation) AND (wine industry OR wine*))". In the environmental literature, the concepts of green, eco and environmental have been used like synonymous to identify innovations aimed to reduced environmental impact (Tariq et al., 2017; Díaz-García et al., 2015). Based on the search query a total of 172 records were provided by WoS database in the initial phase. We have excluded the articles not belonging to the areas of environmental sciences, agriculture, business, economics, and social sciences. Moreover, we have excluded document types other than peer-reviewed articles or review articles and languages other than English. We removed 11 conference papers and 1 book chapter and 2 Spanish and Portuguese's, articles. The next step was screening, after carefully reading of titles and abstracts, we excluded 51 publications due to lack of relevance. After completing the selection process, a total of 59 articles were returned for analysis.

Additionally, the software VOSviewer (Van Eck and Waltman, 2010) was used to carry out the bibliometric analysis and visually present the main results. VOSviewer have a user-friendly interface that allow build comprehensive graphic maps, and run out different analyses, like citations, co-citations, co-authorship, or co-occurrences networks. The analysis and interpretation of the results are presented in the next section.

RESULTS

Publications Trends Analysis

As already mentioned in the introduction section, green innovation has been recognized as a key factor to minimize negative environmental impact from business activity. At the same time, various studies have emerged pointing out the significant negative impact of climate change on the production of the wine sector. Moreover, these studies highlight the importance of taking measures to promote sustainable development to ensure the survival and adaptation of the wine sector. Consequently, it has attracted a significant attention from researchers, policy makers and managers, resulting in a growing number of articles published in the last years. Figure 1 shows the number and trend of publications on green innovation in wine industry. First work in the field was published in 2009 by Saint-Ges and Bélis-Bergouignan behind the name: Ways of reducing pesticides use in Bordeaux vineyards. The work focuses on studying the behavior of French winegrowers towards the adoption of sustainable practices through environmental innovations. Other of the initial studies emphasizing the importance of green innovations in the wine industry is conducted by Atkin et al. (2012) and Leenders and Chandra (2013). The first investigates diverse environmental practices that wineries should adopt for gaining competitive advantages. The second delves into the examination of various catalysts for green innovation and their impact on business performance. Despite no publications being recorded in the years 2010, 2011, and 2014, the number of works has slowly increased from the year 2009 to 2019, reaching a total of 28 publications. Over the past four years, there has been a significant increase in the number of publications. Specifically, 31 articles were published during this period.

Among the publications developed in recent years, notable examples include the study conducted by Frigon et al. (2020), aimed at identifying the main drivers of eco-innovation in the Canadian wine industry. Rabadán and Bernabéu (2021) examine eco-innovation from the consumer perspective to identify predisposition towards purchasing new products produced sustainably. Oricain et al. (2022) attempt to determine the main factors driving the adoption of practices. More recently, authors such as

Figure 2. Number of articles published by year
Source: Own elaboration with data from WOS

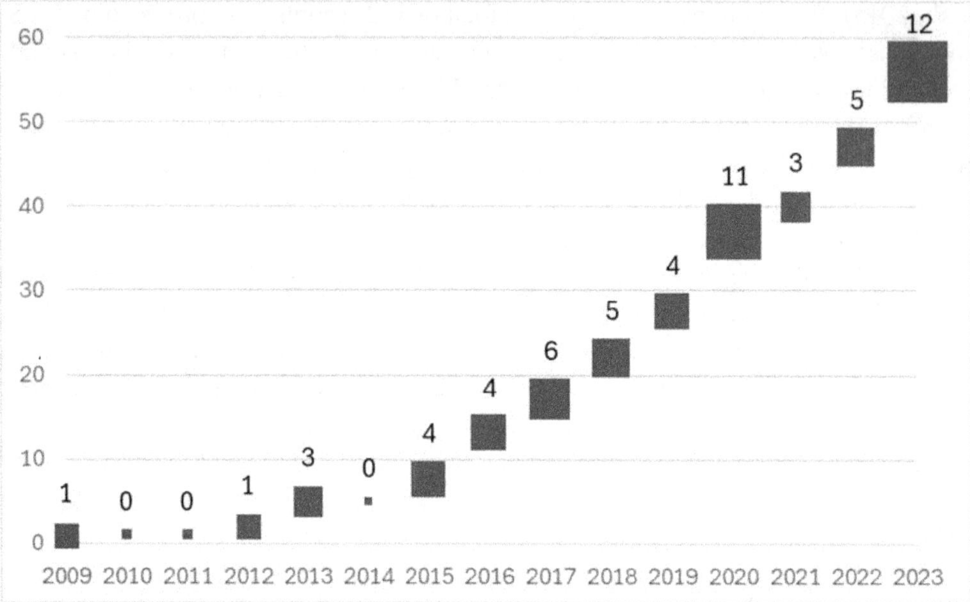

Martínez-Falcó et al. (2023b), Lichy et al. (2023), Carchano et al. (2023), or Wang et al. (2023) have analyzed the production of organic wine from various perspectives.

Journals Analysis

In relation to the journals with most articled published in the field of green innovation in wine economics, figure 3 summarizes main journals in terms of number of publications. The seven most influential journals are: (1) Journal of Cleaner Production; (2) Sustainability; (3) British Food Journal; (4) International Journal of Wine Business Research; (5) Agribusiness; (6) Science of the Total Environment; (7) Journal of Business Ethics. Specifically, over 60% of the articles published on this topic were concentrated in 7 journals. It suggests that these journals are the most significant and influential in this field. Additionally, 22 journals only have 1 published article. The two most popular journals are the Journal of Cleaner Production and Sustainability, both have a Journal Impact Factor (JIF) index (considered a representative index to measure journals´ quality) on Environmental Sciences´ Category, belonging to the 1st and 2nd quartile respectively. Furthermore, journals such as British Food Journal, Agribusiness, Science of the Total Environment or Journal of Business Ethics are also listed in the JIF index, indicating that main literature on green innovation in wine industry has been published on high quality and research impact journals. It is important to highlight that main journal are dedicated to environmental sciences, business, and economics.

Figure 3. Journal publications
Source: Own elaboration with data from WOS

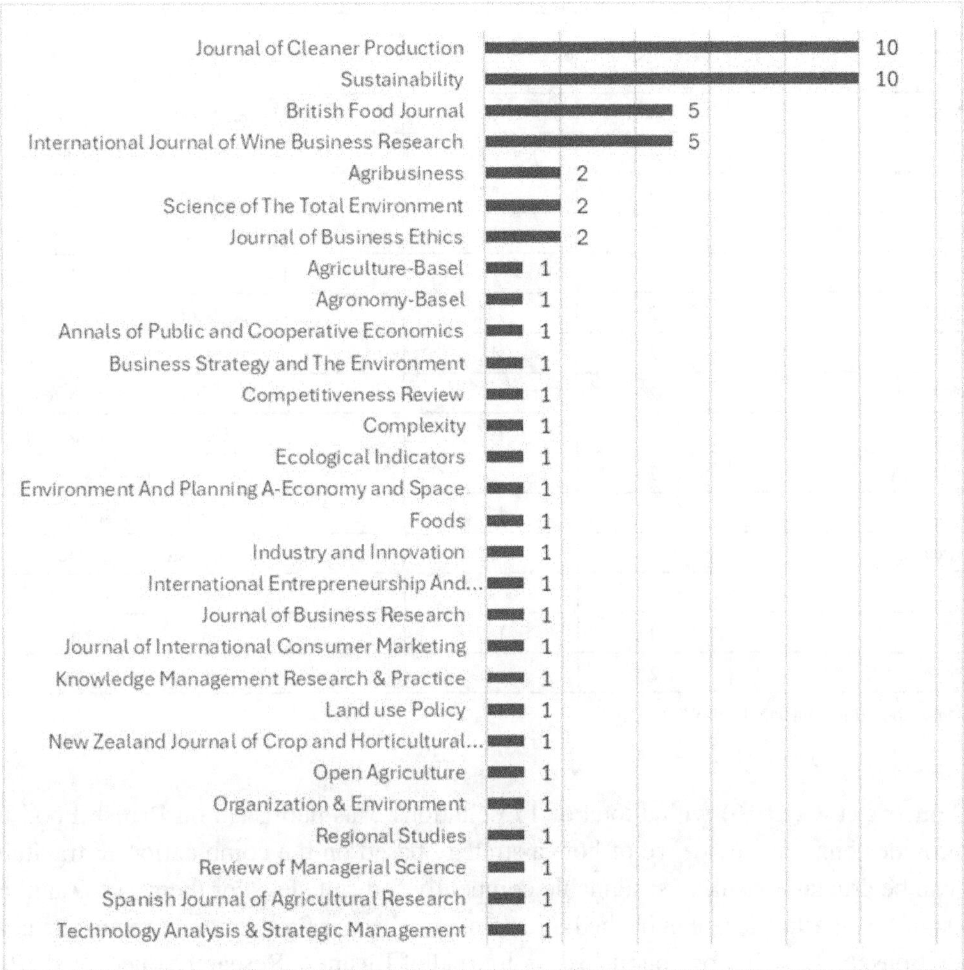

Authors Analysis

Once the journals trends have been analyzed, the study continue with the analysis of author contribution, focus on number of articles, co-authorship author and co-citation network. As already mentioned in methodological section, VOS viewer software has been used to obtained bibliometric maps. Table 1 presents the main authors with at least two papers published. As shown, the five most prominent authors with 4 articles published in the field of green innovation and the wine industry are Carrasco (University of Castilla-La Mancha), Galbreath (Curtin University), González-Moreno (University of Castilla-La Mancha), Marco-Lajara (University of Alicante), and Martínez-Falco (University of Alicante). The remaining authors (12) have only published two studies. Shifting focus to citations, the most cited author is Giacosa from the University of Turin, followed by Pucci (University of Siena), Zanni (University of Siena), and Galbreath (Curtin University), representing over 70% of the total citations for the main author contributions. Giacosa has the highest number of citations (192) with two articles. The prominent

Table 1. Ranking of main authors

Author	Articles	Citations	Institution
Carrasco, I	4	14	University of Castilla-La Mancha
Galbreath, J	4	139	Curtin University
Gonzalez-Moreno, A	4	14	University of Castilla-La Mancha
Marco-Lajara, B	4	27	University of Alicante
Martinez-Falco, J	4	27	University of Alicante
Barba-Sanchez, V	2	64	University of Castilla-La Mancha
Calle, F	2	13	University of Castilla-La Mancha
Carchano, M	2	1	University of Castilla-La Mancha
Doloreux, D	2	47	HEC Montreal
Dressler, M	2	4	University of Ludwigshafen
Giacosa, E	2	192	University of Turin
Millan-Tudela, L.A.	2	5	University of Alicante
Pucci, T	2	157	University of Siena
Sanchez-Garcia, E	2	22	University of Alicante
Spielmann, N	2	36	NEOMA Business School
Zanni, L	2	157	University of Siena
Zaragoza-Saez, P	2	4	University of Alicante

Source: Own elaboration with data from WOS

article (Demetris et al., 2016) with a total of 173 citations, was published on British Food Journal in 2016. It provides empirical evidence of how a strategy based on the combination of tradition and innovation can be crucial in achieve sustainable competitive advantages. For their part, Zanni and Pucci have two significant articles, one published on Journal of Cleaner Production (Annunziata et al., 2018) with 98 citations, and another one published on Journal of Business Research (Pucci et al., 2020) with 59 citations. Finally, Galbreath held and important position thanks to a recent study that investigates the potential influence of exports intensity on the implementation of green innovations (Galbreath, 2019). All prominent citing articles have been published in first quartiles of Journal Impact Factor; therefore, it is expected that the number of citations for these articles will increase significantly in the coming years.

Co-authorship analysis was carried out to identify collaborative patterns among authors. The results are presented in Figure 4, where only 17 out of 166 total authors met the minimum criteria for the number of documents (n=2). In the red cluster, the most productive authors are Martínez-Falco and Marco-Lajara from the University of Alicante. They collaborated in most of their works with Millán-Tudela, Sánchez-García, and Zaragoza-Sáez, also from the University of Alicante. Another significant collaboration network is shown in the green cluster. The leading authors, with 4 articles, are Carrasco and González-Moreno from the University of Castilla-La Mancha. Their main collaborators are Carchano and Calle, who have co-authored two out of the four articles. Additionally, there is a link between Pucci and Zanni (see blue cluster), who have published all their documents together.

Finally, Figure 5 illustrates the different relationships between cited authors. Co-citation analysis examines the frequency with which two authors are cited together in other publications. To perform the

Figure 4. Density visualization cluster of main authors
Source: Own elaboration with data from WoS and using VOSviewer

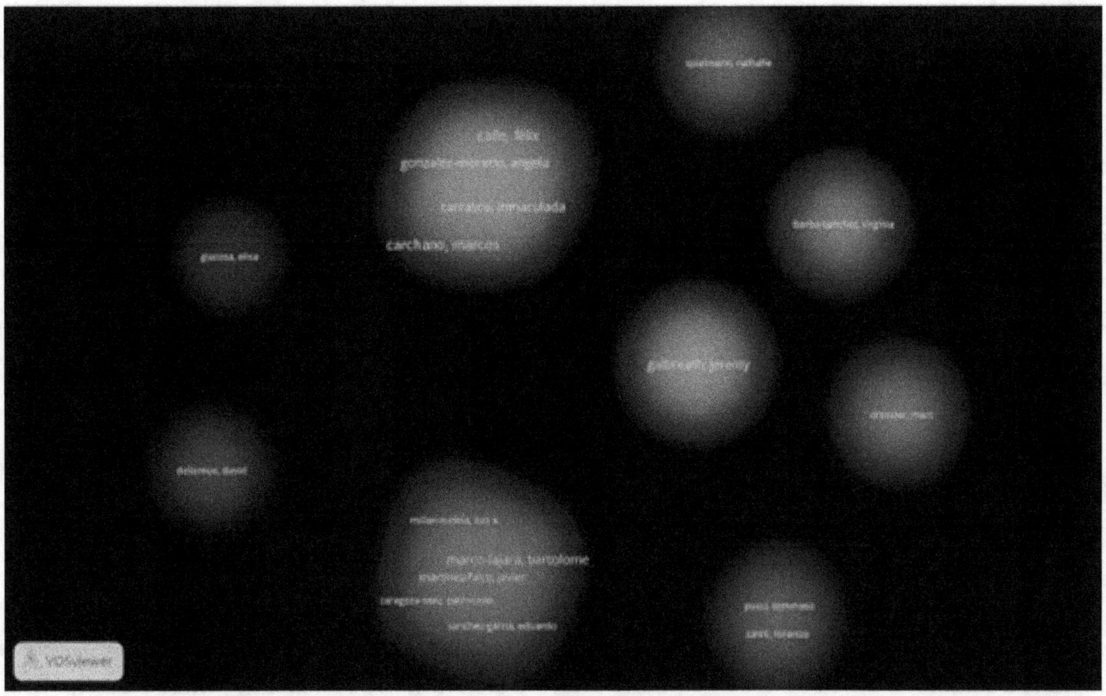

Figure 5. Co-citation analysis map
Source: Own elaboration with data from WoS and using VOSviewer

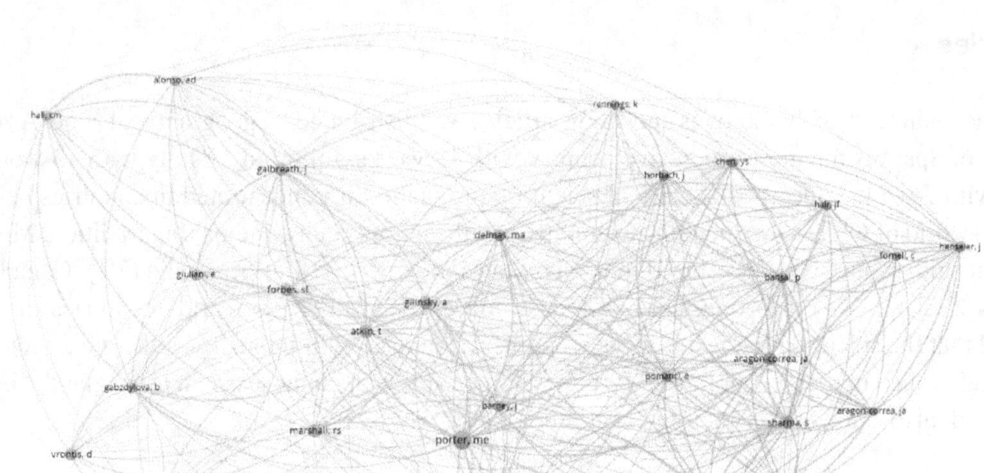

Figure 6. Geographical distribution of articles
Source: Own elaboration with data from WoS

present analysis, a minimum threshold of 10 citations per author has been established, resulting in a sample of 30 authors (based on the 59 initially selected articles). We can identify three clusters: Cluster 1 (red) with 13 items, Cluster 2 (green) with 11 items, and Cluster 3 (blue) with 6 items. According to the results, the most frequently cited author in other works is Porter, with a total of 42 citations. In the green cluster, Marshall has the highest number of citations (23), while in the red cluster, Aragón-Corea is the leading author with 30 citations.

Countries

One of the main aims of this study is know how articles was distributed by geographical zone. As evident in figure 6, Spain is the most productive country with 18 works, followed by Italy with 15 works, and France with 7 works. Specifically, 48% of scientific production is concentrated in countries belonging to the old world of wine, corresponding to countries with an important winemaking tradition. Moreover, important studies have been developed in United States of America (8%), Australia (7%), Canada (4%), and New Zeeland (4%). Existing research is less concentrated in "New world" countries. It is to be expected that the scientific interest in wine from these countries will intensify as the wine sector gains more significance in their economies. Moreover, some European countries such as England, Germany, or Denmark also stand out for their interest in this field.

Research Trends

To explore research trends, we conducted a co-occurrence analysis of keywords in the selected articles using VOSviewer. This method is widely employed to characterize research content, understand current patterns within a specific field and identify the frequency of a word is used. Co-occurrence assumes that keywords accurately reflect the primary content of the articles. The highest word that appears in the

Figure 7. Main keywords appeared in the studied field
Source: Own elaboration with data from WoS and using VOSviewer

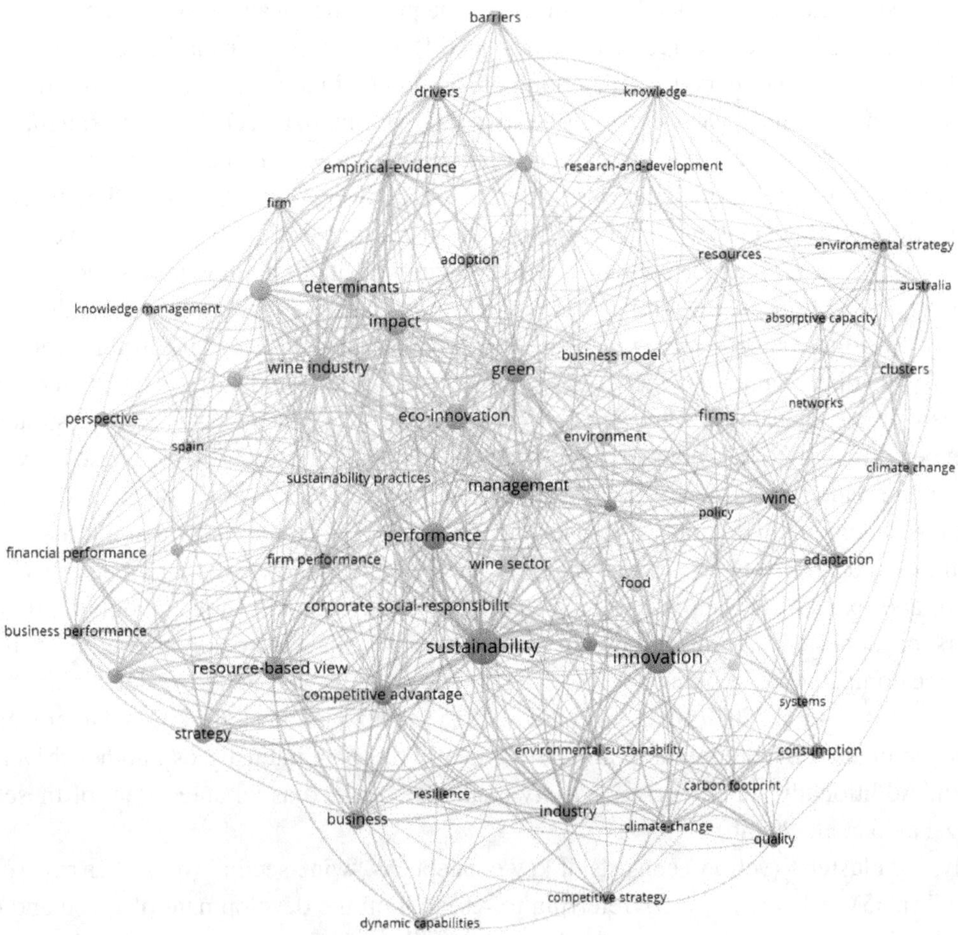

studies of green innovation in wine industry are "sustainability", "innovation", "management", "wine industry", "green", "eco-innovation", and "performance" (see figure 7). These keywords account for a number of co-occurrences greater than 10, indicating that researchers are currently involve into the study of these topics. The identified trend may be attributed to several reasons. The fight against climate change has become one of the essential issues for organizations, communities, and public entities in the wine industry. For this reason, there exists a growing literature examining how wineries can reduce their negative environmental impact. In this regard, green innovation is positioned as a viable option to achieve this goal. However, managers still consider green investments as risky and costly. This is why research has increased its effort to provide empirical evidence of how green innovation can improve economic performance and contribute to developing competitive advantages. Recent works, such as those conducted by Carchano et al., (2023), Martínez-Falcó et al., (2023) or Dressler (2023), highlight increasing interest in achieving sustainability in the wine sector.

In addition, clustering analysis show the relationship between keywords. The cluster 1 (red) is focuses on key concepts as "sustainability", which achieve the highest co-occurrences (n=22), "innovation" (n=19), "performance" (n=12) and "competitive advantage" (n=8). Cluster 1 refers to works focusing on investigate how innovation can serve as a vehicle to achieve sustainable development and better performance. The adoption of sustainable practices in wine production leads to significant benefits such as improved resource efficiency, cost reduction, product differentiation in the market, enhanced reputation, increased sales levels, and market share, among others. Green innovations can help improve wineries' financial performance and achieve competitive advantages (Annunziata et al., 2018; Ratten, 2018). Furthermore, they enable the development of clean production processes characterized by the use of fewer resources and less energy, producing fewer emissions and a lower volume of waste, thereby contributing to reducing the environmental impact of the wine industry (Wang et al., 2023; Carchano et al., 2023). In this sense, investment in green technologies leads to a win-win situation for wineries and society at large.

Moreover, as can be seen, most relevant keyword in the cluster 2 (green) is "wine industry" (n=12), followed by "eco-innovation" (n=11), "green" (n=11) and "impact" (n=11). Cluster 2 refers to works focusing on providing empirical evidence about the different drivers and barriers that influence wineries to implement green innovation. "Management" (n=12), "resource-based view" (n=10), "strategy" (n=7) and "firm performance" (n=5) are main keywords associated to cluster 3 (blue). These keywords focus on the strategic management of green innovation, and it impact on firm performance. Studies focused on analyzing sustainability drivers are the most predominant. The results show that internal factors such as capabilities and financial and human resources, technological knowledge, or green transformational leadership, and external factors such as competitive pressure, demand for ecological products from consumers, or increased environmental concern among policymakers are among the main motivations leading wine companies to implement ecological practices (Calle et al., 2022; Tyler et al., 2020; Frigon et al., 2020; Muscio et al., 2017; Oricain et al., 2022; Sánchez-García et al., 2023). Other studies, such as the one conducted by Galbreath et al. (2019), identify export intensity as another driver of green innovation. Additionally, wine tourism activity is also recognized as an antecedent of these practices (Martínez-Falcó et al., 2023b).

Finally, the cluster 4 (yellow) consists of key concepts as "wine sector" (n=7), "firms" (n=6), "environment" (n=5) and "food" (n=5), referring to research on the development of green and corporate social responsibilities strategies in agri-food sector. Finally, the highest keywords involved on cluster 5 (purple) are "wine" (n=9), "cluster" (n=5) "absorptive capacity" (n=3), and "australia" (n=3).

CONCLUSION

Currently, the wine industry faces various threats related, firstly, to the impact of its activity on sustainable development and, secondly, to the negative effects of climate change on wine production. Moreover, the increasing environmental awareness of consumers, organizations, and policymakers has driven wineries to design and implement environmental management systems with the aim of enhancing their sustainable practices, meeting the growing demand for eco-friendly products, and adapting to environmental policies. Regarding this context, green innovation has been proposed in literature as a tool for achieving competitive advantages (reduction costs, better productivity and efficient in resources used), and both environmental and economic performance. Despite the growing interest in contributing to sustainable development goals in the wine industry, existing literature on environmental management has focused on sectors with high pollution rates, overlooking traditional and less polluting sectors such as the wine industry. Consequently, it is necessary to conduct studies that expand the knowledge on the potential effects of green innovation in the wine industry to achieve sustainable development.

The aim of this article was to analyze the scientific state, trends, and gaps in the field of green innovation in wine industry. To achieve this goal, a bibliometric analysis using VOSviewer was performed based on a total of 59 articles from Webs of Science database published in 2009-2023. As a general conclusion, the study revealed that the literature on green innovation and wine industry has grown in the past years, focusing on how it can help at wineries to achieve sustainable development, improve firm performance, and achieve competitive advantages.

Our results confirm that the research progress in this field has become more relevant in last four years, passing from 28 articles published between 2009-2019, to 59 articles in 2023. These results highlight that the research on environmental practices in wine industry is still in an early stage, which also evidence the potential importance of this scientific area can eventually attain. Regarding to geographical distribution, countries belonging to Old World Wine (Spain, Italy and France) are the most popular with the 48% of the scientific production, while United States of America, Australia, Canada and New Zeeland has contributed to the field with less intensity. In addition, Journal of Cleaner Production, Sustainability, British Food Journal, and International Journal of Wine Business Research are the most productive journals.

Related to the influential authors, Carrasco (University of Castilla-La Mancha), Galbreath (Curtin University), González-Moreno (University of Castilla-La Mancha), Marco-Lajara (University of Alicante), and Martínez-Falco (University of Alicante) are the most influential authors in terms of published articles, and Giaco (University of Turin), Pucci (University of Siena), Zanni (University of Siena), and Galbreath (Curtin University), representing most popular authors in terms of citations with over 70% of the total citations for the main author contributions.

Moreover, bibliometric analysis has allowed us to identify research trends. Current research is mainly focusing on providing empirical evidence of the different factors that encourage wineries to implement green innovation and how it can contribute to improving environmental performance in the agri-food sector. Additionally, there is another significant part of the literature focusing on investigating the economic benefits of green investment to increase managers' commitment to opportunities derived from the implementation of green innovations.

This study makes three significant contributions to the existing literature. First, we conducted a bibliometric analysis to identify influential works and research trends, providing a helicopter view of research in green innovation in the wine industry. This can be used as a starting point for future articles. Secondly, our study provides insights to researchers and practitioners to understand the current situation in this field. Finally, the results contribute to the theory of environmental management, advancing in the knowledge of how wineries can face environmental and social challenges through green innovations.

In addition to theoretical implications, this study also has significant ramifications for managers and policymakers. This analysis provides a comprehensive view of the growing interest in the topic, especially in recent years. Managers should focus their strategies on the development of environmental innovations that can address the increasing concerns of various stakeholders regarding sustainable development. This shift in organizational culture can have positive repercussions both on society and the company itself. The production and marketing of eco-friendly products can minimize the negative impact of business activities on the environment while enhancing consumer satisfaction, potentially renewing their purchasing intentions and boosting the company's reputation, thereby gaining a competitive advantage. Management must recognize the value that eco-innovation can bring to the company. In this regard, managers should establish collaboration networks with consumers, as the information provided by them can help improve companies' understanding of market needs. Thus, eco-innovation emerges as a crucial element for the sustainable growth of the industry and business survival.

On the other hand, policy measures should focus on designing a regulatory framework of incentives and rewards that lead to the adoption of environmental practices. Measures should be articulated to enhance managers' understanding of the impact of climate change on the future development of the wine industry. Policy effectiveness could be enhanced by considering the unique business structure of the wine sector. Policymakers should consider the resources and capabilities of different companies (SMEs, cooperatives, large enterprises, multinationals) when designing regulatory frameworks. For example, while larger companies may opt for eco-innovations to avoid potential penalties under strict regulatory frameworks, smaller companies may lack the necessary human and financial resources to undertake green initiatives and may not be affected by regulations. For such companies, an incentive-focused regulatory framework would be more effective. Additionally, recognizing the significant role that green investments play in terms of competitiveness and business growth, public authorities should focus on designing efficient policies that promote green technology innovation activities. Likewise, they should increase efforts to raise environmental awareness, both among management and consumers, who can play an important role in transitioning towards a sustainable wine model.

Considering current trends identified, further research is needed to assess sustainable practices in the wine industry. The business structure of this sector is very complex, involving a significant number of small or medium-sized wineries (mainly family-owned or cooperatives) coexisting with a few large companies. In this regard, future research should examine internal and external drivers and barriers fostering green innovation adoption, considering the different types of companies. Characteristics such as size, age, or resource and capability availability can influence environmental behavior and perceived risk. For example, large wineries, with more resources (financial and human) and capabilities, can be more proactive in addressing environmental issues than smaller-sized companies with limited resource availability. To date, there is scant literature examining motivations that can drive green innovation considering the specific characteristics of family firms or cooperatives in the wine industry. These research studies can achieve an important impact on wine literature by providing empirical evidence to policymakers about the differential behavior of wine companies. In this regard, policymakers could enhance efficiency in designing environmental policy.

Furthermore, is important to provided more empirical evidence on the relationships between green innovation and economic performance in order to change traditional managers vision about risky and costly of sustainable investments. Managers should perceive these practices as an opportunity to improve competitiveness, opens up new business opportunities, increase market sales, profits and reputation. In addition, adopting green innovation can also contribute to develop differentiation strategy, improving customer loyalty and satisfaction. On the other hand, regarding the key role management values or perceptions on strategic decisions, it is necessary to advance in the examination of how top management green commitment can influence the implementation of green innovations. There are no studies that examine management characteristics effects on environmental strategies in wine industry.

However, the findings are limited due to database and software used. For conduct the bibliometric analysis, we have only considered Web of Science database. Although it is a widely used in this type of analysis, maybe there are relevant studies in wine industry published on other databases (for example Scopus or Google Scholar), so we can´t guarantee that our study covers all relevant published articles. In this regard, future researchers can consider use other databases and include other types of publications (book chapters and conference proceedings) to increase number of articles included. Additionally, the use of a single software (VOSviewer) can be considered a limitation. Bibliometric analysis can be improved by using other tools and methods.

REFERENCES

Afshari, H., Searcy, C., & Jaber, M. Y. (2020). The role of eco-innovation drivers in promoting additive manufacturing in supply chains. *International Journal of Production Economics, 223*, 107538. doi:10.1016/j.ijpe.2019.107538

Albort-Morant, G., Henseler, J., Leal-Millán, A., & Cepeda-Carrión, G. (2017). Mapping the field: A bibliometric analysis of green innovation. *Sustainability (Basel), 9*(6), 1011. doi:10.3390/su9061011

Annunziata, E., Pucci, T., Frey, M., & Zanni, L. (2018). The role of organizational capabilities in attaining corporate sustainability practices and economic performance: Evidence from Italian wine industry. *Journal of Cleaner Production, 171*, 1300–1311. doi:10.1016/j.jclepro.2017.10.035

Atkin, T., Gilinsky, A. Jr, & Newton, S. K. (2012). Environmental strategy: Does it lead to competitive advantage in the US wine industry? *International Journal of Wine Business Research, 24*(2), 115–133. doi:10.1108/17511061211238911

Bag, S., Dhamija, P., Bryde, D. J., & Singh, R. K. (2022). Effect of eco-innovation on green supply chain management, circular economy capability, and performance of small and medium enterprises. *Journal of Business Research, 141*, 60–72. doi:10.1016/j.jbusres.2021.12.011

Barber, N., Taylor, C., & Strick, S. (2009). Wine consumers' environmental knowledge and attitudes: Influence on willingness to purchase. *International Journal of Wine Research, 1*(null), 59-72. doi:10.2147/IJWR.S4649

Beber, C. L., Lecomte, L., Rodrigo, I., Canali, M., Pinto, A. S., Pomarici, E., ... Malorgio, G. (2023). The Agroecological Challenges in the Wine Sector: Perceptions from European Stakeholders. *Wine Economics and Policy, 12*(2), 1–32. doi:10.36253/wep-15244

Berrone, P., Fosfuri, A., Gelabert, L., & Gomez-Mejia, L. R. (2013). Necessity as the mother of 'green' inventions: Institutional pressures and environmental innovations. *Strategic Management Journal, 34*(8), 891–909. doi:10.1002/smj.2041

Bjork, S., Offer, A., & Söderberg, G. (2014). Time series citation data: The Nobel Prize in economics. *Scientometrics, 98*(1), 185–196. doi:10.1007/s11192-013-0989-5

Broccardo, L., & Zicari, A. (2020). Sustainability as a driver for value creation: A business model analysis of small and medium entreprises in the Italian wine sector. *Journal of Cleaner Production, 259*, 120852. doi:10.1016/j.jclepro.2020.120852

Carchano, M., Carrasco, I., & González, A. (2023). Examining environmental proactivity in the Spanish wine industry: The moderating role of size. *Agribusiness, n/a*(n/a). doi:https://doi.org/ doi:10.1002/agr.21882

Carchano, M., Carrasco, I., & González, Á. (2023). Eco-innovation and environmental performance: Insights from Spanish wine companies. *Annals of Public and Cooperative Economics, n/a*(n/a). doi:https://doi.org/ doi:10.1111/apce.12421

Chieco, C., Morrone, L., Magli, M., Gelmetti, A., Pedo, S., Roman Villegas, T., & Eccel, E. (2023). Italian winegrowers' and wine makers' attitudes toward climate hazards and their strategy of adaptation to the change. *Italian Journal of Agrometeorology*, (1), 47–65. doi:10.36253/ijam-1874

Christ, K. L., & Burritt, R. L. (2013). Critical environmental concerns in wine production: An integrative review. *Journal of Cleaner Production, 53*, 232–242. doi:10.1016/j.jclepro.2013.04.007

de Jesus, A., Antunes, P., Santos, R., & Mendonça, S. (2019). Eco-innovation pathways to a circular economy: Envisioning priorities through a Delphi approach. *Journal of Cleaner Production, 228*, 1494–1513. doi:10.1016/j.jclepro.2019.04.049

De Steur, H., Temmerman, H., Gellynck, X., & Canavari, M. (2020). Drivers, adoption, and evaluation of sustainability practices in Italian wine SMEs. *Business Strategy and the Environment, 29*(2), 744–762. doi:10.1002/bse.2436

Díaz-García, C., González-Moreno, Á., & Sáez-Martínez, F. J. (2015). Eco-innovation: Insights from a literature review. *Innovation (North Sydney, N.S.W.), 17*(1), 6–23. doi:10.1080/14479338.2015.1011060

Doloreux, D., & Kraft, L. (2019). A Taxonomy of Eco-Innovation Types in SMEs: Exploring Different Firm Profiles in the Canadian Wine Industry. *Sustainability (Basel), 11*(20), 5776. doi:10.3390/su11205776

Donthu, N., Kumar, S., Mukherjee, D., Pandey, N., & Lim, W. M. (2021). How to conduct a bibliometric analysis: An overview and guidelines. *Journal of Business Research, 133*, 285–296. doi:10.1016/j.jbusres.2021.04.070

Dressler, M. (2023). Sustainable Business Model Design: A Multi-Case Approach Exploring Generic Strategies and Dynamic Capabilities on the Example of German Wine Estates. *Sustainability (Basel), 15*(5), 3880. doi:10.3390/su15053880

Eryigit, N., & Özcüre, G. (2015). Eco-Innovation as Modern Era Strategy of Companies in Developing Countries: Comparison Between Turkey and European Union. *Procedia: Social and Behavioral Sciences, 195*, 1216–1225. doi:10.1016/j.sbspro.2015.06.246

European Commision. (2019). *Agricultural Policy: COP21 United for climate*. EC. https://agriculture.ec.europa.eu/document/download/7c24c51f-55d1-4015-90d9-0fd8e974b525_en?filename=cop21-what-eu-agricultural-policy-does-for-climate_en.pdf&prefLang=es

Farrukh, M., Javed, S., Raza, A., & Lee, J. W. C. (2021). Twenty years of green innovation research: Trends and way forward. *World Journal of Entrepreneurship, Management and Sustainable Development, 17*(3), 488–501. doi:10.1108/WJEMSD-06-2020-0068

Ferrer, J. R., García-Cortijo, M.-C., Pinilla, V., Castillo-Valero, J.-S., & Serrano, R. (2023). Sustainability and growth: Evidence from Spanish wine industry. *Spanish Journal of Agricultural Research, 21*(2), e0104. doi:10.5424/sjar/2023212-20241

Fiore, M., Silvestri, R., Contò, F., & Pellegrini, G. (2017). Understanding the relationship between green approach and marketing innovations tools in the wine sector. *Journal of Cleaner Production, 142*, 4085–4091. doi:10.1016/j.jclepro.2016.10.026

Flores, S. S. (2018). What is sustainability in the wine world? A cross-country analysis of wine sustainability frameworks. *Journal of Cleaner Production, 172*, 2301–2312. doi:10.1016/j.jclepro.2017.11.181

Forbes, S. L., Cohen, D. A., Cullen, R., Wratten, S. D., & Fountain, J. (2009). Consumer attitudes regarding environmentally sustainable wine: An exploratory study of the New Zealand marketplace. *Journal of Cleaner Production, 17*(13), 1195–1199. doi:10.1016/j.jclepro.2009.04.008

Fraga, H., García de Cortázar Atauri, I., & Santos, J. A. (2018). Viticultural irrigation demands under climate change scenarios in Portugal. *Agricultural Water Management, 196*, 66–74. doi:10.1016/j.agwat.2017.10.023

Frigon, A., Doloreux, D., & Shearmur, R. (2020). Drivers of eco-innovation and conventional innovation in the Canadian wine industry. *Journal of Cleaner Production, 275*, 124115. doi:10.1016/j.jclepro.2020.124115

Galati, A., Schifani, G., Crescimanno, M., & Migliore, G. (2019). "Natural wine" consumers and interest in label information: An analysis of willingness to pay in a new Italian wine market segment. *Journal of Cleaner Production, 227*, 405–413. doi:10.1016/j.jclepro.2019.04.219

Galbreath, J. (2019). Drivers of Green Innovations: The Impact of Export Intensity, Women Leaders, and Absorptive Capacity. *Journal of Business Ethics, 158*(1), 47–61. doi:10.1007/s10551-017-3715-z

Galbreath, J., Charles, D., & Oczkowski, E. (2016). The Drivers of Climate Change Innovations: Evidence from the Australian Wine Industry. *Journal of Business Ethics, 135*(2), 217–231. doi:10.1007/s10551-014-2461-8

Golicic, S. L., Flint, D. J., & Signori, P. (2017). Building business sustainability through resilience in the wine industry. *International Journal of Wine Business Research, 29*(1), 74–97. doi:10.1108/IJWBR-02-2016-0005

Hizarci-Payne, A. K., İpek, İ., & Kurt Gümüş, G. (2021). How environmental innovation influences firm performance: A meta-analytic review. *Business Strategy and the Environment, 30*(2), 1174–1190. doi:10.1002/bse.2678

Kemp, R., & Pearson, P. (2007). Final report MEI project about measuring eco-innovation. *UM Merit, Maastricht, 10*(2), 1–120.

Leenders, M. A. A. M., & Chandra, Y. (2013). Antecedents and consequences of green innovation in the wine industry: The role of channel structure. *Technology Analysis and Strategic Management, 25*(2), 203–218. doi:10.1080/09537325.2012.759203

Lichy, J., Kachour, M., & Stokes, P. (2023). Questioning the business model of sustainable wine production: The case of French "Vallée du Rhône" wine growers. *Journal of Cleaner Production, 417*, 137891. doi:10.1016/j.jclepro.2023.137891

López Pérez, G., García Sánchez, I. M., & Zafra Gómez, J. L. (2023). A systematic literature review and bibliometric analysis of eco-innovation on financial performance: Identifying barriers and drivers. *Business Strategy and the Environment, n/a*(n/a). doi:10.1002/bse.3550

Marco-Lajara, B., Martínez-Falcó, J., Millan-Tudela, L. A., & Sánchez-García, E. (2023). Analysis of the structure of scientific knowledge on wine tourism: A bibliometric analysis. *Heliyon*, *9*(2), e13363. doi:10.1016/j.heliyon.2023.e13363 PMID:36816306

Marín, D., Armengol, J., Carbonell-Bejerano, P., Escalona, J. M., Gramaje, D., Hernández-Montes, E., Intrigliolo, D. S., Martínez-Zapater, J. M., Medrano, H., Mirás-Avalos, J. M., Palomares-Rius, J. E., Romero-Azorín, P., Savé, R., Santesteban, L. G., & de Herralde, F. (2021). Challenges of viticulture adaptation to global change: Tackling the issue from the roots. *Australian Journal of Grape and Wine Research*, *27*(1), 8–25. doi:10.1111/ajgw.12463

Martínez-Falcó, J., Marco-Lajara, B., Zaragoza-Sáez, P., & Sánchez-García, E. The effect of knowledge management on sustainable performance: evidence from the Spanish wine industry. *Knowledge Management Research & Practice*, 1-16. doi:10.1080/14778238.2023.2218045

Martínez-Falcó, J., Marco-Lajara, B., Zaragoza-Sáez, P. d. C., & Millan-Tudela, L. A. (2023b). Wine tourism as a catalyst for green innovation: evidence from the Spanish wine industry. *British Food Journal*. doi:10.1108/BFJ-08-2022-0690

Marx, W., Haunschild, R., & Bornmann, L. (2017). Climate change and viticulture-a quantitative analysis of a highly dynamic research field. *Vitis*, *56*(1).

Meloni, G., Anderson, K., Deconinck, K., & Swinnen, J. (2019). Wine Regulations. *Applied Economic Perspectives and Policy*, *41*(4), 620–649. doi:10.1093/aepp/ppz025

Merigó, J. M., Mas-Tur, A., Roig-Tierno, N., & Ribeiro-Soriano, D. (2015). A bibliometric overview of the Journal of Business Research between 1973 and 2014. *Journal of Business Research*, *68*(12), 2645–2653. doi:10.1016/j.jbusres.2015.04.006

Moscovici, D., Gow, J., Alonso Ugaglia, A., Rezwanul, R., Valenzuela, L., & Mihailescu, R. (2022). Consumer preferences for organic wine - Global analysis of people and place. *Journal of Cleaner Production*, *368*, 133215. doi:10.1016/j.jclepro.2022.133215

Moyano-Fuentes, J., Maqueira-Marín, J. M., & Bruque-Cámara, S. (2018). Process innovation and environmental sustainability engagement: An application on technological firms. *Journal of Cleaner Production*, *171*, 844–856. doi:10.1016/j.jclepro.2017.10.067

Mozell, M. R., & Thach, L. (2014). The impact of climate change on the global wine industry: Challenges & solutions. *Wine Economics and Policy*, *3*(2), 81–89. doi:10.1016/j.wep.2014.08.001

Muscio, A., Nardone, G., & Stasi, A. (2017). How does the search for knowledge drive firms' eco-innovation? Evidence from the wine industry. *Industry and Innovation*, *24*(3), 298–320. doi:10.1080/13662716.2016.1224707

Neethling, E., Barbeau, G., Coulon-Leroy, C., & Quénol, H. (2019). Spatial complexity and temporal dynamics in viticulture: A review of climate-driven scales. *Agricultural and Forest Meteorology, 276-277*, 107618. doi:10.1016/j.agrformet.2019.107618

Oricain, N. D., Olmos, M. F., & Castel, A. G. (2022). Determinants of organic wine production: An application in the DOC Rioja wine industry. *Spanish Journal of Agricultural Research, 20*(3), 18.

Passaro, R., Quinto, I., Scandurra, G., & Thomas, A. (2023). The drivers of eco-innovations in small and medium-sized enterprises: A systematic literature review and research directions. *Business Strategy and the Environment, 32*(4), 1432–1450. doi:10.1002/bse.3197

Petriashvili, A., Mach, J., Štěbeták, M., Prášilová, M., Svoboda, R., Navrátilová, M., Beranová, M., Veselá, K., Hofman, V., & Němec, O. (2023). The impact of climate change on the sustainability of wine production and the structure of its consumption in Czechia. *Heliyon, 9*(7), e17882. doi:10.1016/j.heliyon.2023.e17882 PMID:37539305

Pomarici, E., Asioli, D., Vecchio, R., & Næs, T. (2018). Young consumers' preferences for water-saving wines: An experimental study. *Wine Economics and Policy, 7*(1), 65–76. doi:10.1016/j.wep.2018.02.002

Pomarici, E., & Vecchio, R. (2019). Will sustainability shape the future wine market? *Wine Economics and Policy, 8*(1), 1–4. doi:10.1016/j.wep.2019.05.001

Pucci, T., Casprini, E., Galati, A., & Zanni, L. (2020). The virtuous cycle of stakeholder engagement in developing a sustainability culture: Salcheto winery. *Journal of Business Research, 119*, 364–376. doi:10.1016/j.jbusres.2018.11.009

Qing, L., Chun, D., Ock, Y.-S., Dagestani, A. A., & Ma, X. (2022). What Myths about Green Technology Innovation and Financial Performance’s Relationship? A Bibliometric Analysis Review. *Economies, 10*(4), 92. doi:10.3390/economies10040092

Rabadán, A., & Bernabéu, R. (2021). An approach to eco-innovation in wine production from a consumer's perspective. *Journal of Cleaner Production, 310*, 127479. doi:10.1016/j.jclepro.2021.127479

Ratten, V. (2018). Eco-innovation and competitiveness in the Barossa Valley wine region. *Competitiveness Review, 28*(3), 318–331. doi:10.1108/CR-01-2017-0002

Saint-Ges, V., & Bélis-Bergouignan, M.-C. (2009). Ways of reducing pesticides use in Bordeaux vineyards. *Journal of Cleaner Production, 17*(18), 1644–1653. doi:10.1016/j.jclepro.2009.05.006

Sánchez-García, E., Martínez-Falcó, J., Alcon-Vila, A., & Marco-Lajara, B. (2023). Developing Green Innovations in the Wine Industry: An Applied Analysis. *Foods, 12*(6), 1157. doi:10.3390/foods12061157 PMID:36981084

Schäufele, I., & Hamm, U. (2017). Consumers' perceptions, preferences and willingness-to-pay for wine with sustainability characteristics: A review. *Journal of Cleaner Production, 147*, 379–394. doi:10.1016/j.jclepro.2017.01.118

Stechemesser, K., & Guenther, E. (2012). Carbon accounting: A systematic literature review. *Journal of Cleaner Production, 36*, 17–38. doi:10.1016/j.jclepro.2012.02.021

Šūmakaris, P., Ščeulovs, D., & Korsakienė, R. (2020). Current Research Trends on Interrelationships of Eco-Innovation and Internationalisation: A Bibliometric Analysis. *Journal of Risk and Financial Management, 13*(5), 85. doi:10.3390/jrfm13050085

Takalo, S. K., & Tooranloo, H. S. (2021). Green innovation: A systematic literature review. *Journal of Cleaner Production, 279*, 122474. doi:10.1016/j.jclepro.2020.122474

Tariq, A., Badir, Y. F., Tariq, W., & Bhutta, U. S. (2017). Drivers and consequences of green product and process innovation: A systematic review, conceptual framework, and future outlook. *Technology in Society*, *51*, 8–23. doi:10.1016/j.techsoc.2017.06.002

Tyler, B., Lahneman, B., Beukel, K., Cerrato, D., Minciullo, M., Spielmann, N., & Discua Cruz, A. (2018). SME Managers' Perceptions of Competitive Pressure and the Adoption of Environmental Practices in Fragmented Industries: A Multi-Country Study in the Wine Industry. *Organization & Environment, 33*(3), 437–463. doi:10.1177/1086026618803720

Valero-Gil, J., Surroca, J. A., Tribo, J. A., Gutierrez, L., & Montiel, I. (2023). Innovation vs. standardization: The conjoint effects of eco-innovation and environmental management systems on environmental performance. *Research Policy*, *52*(4), 104737. doi:10.1016/j.respol.2023.104737

Van Eck, N., & Waltman, L. (2010). Software survey: VOSviewer, a computer program for bibliometric mapping. *Scientometrics*, *84*(2), 523–538. doi:10.1007/s11192-009-0146-3 PMID:20585380

Vega-Bayo, A., Mariel, P., Meyerhoff, J., Corsi, A. M., & Chovan, M. (2023). Climate change adaptation preferences of winemakers from the Rioja wine appellation. *Journal of Choice Modelling*, *48*, 100434. doi:10.1016/j.jocm.2023.100434

Villanueva-Rey, P., Vázquez-Rowe, I., Moreira, M. T., & Feijoo, G. (2014). Comparative life cycle assessment in the wine sector: Biodynamic vs. conventional viticulture activities in NW Spain. *Journal of Cleaner Production*, *65*, 330–341. doi:10.1016/j.jclepro.2013.08.026

Vrontis, D., Bresciani, S., & Giacosa, E. (2016). Tradition and innovation in Italian wine family businesses. *British Food Journal*, *118*(8), 1883–1897. doi:10.1108/BFJ-05-2016-0192

Wang, Y., Li, Y., Sun, T., Milne, E., Yang, Y., Liu, K., Li, J., Yan, P., Zhao, C., Li, S., Duan, B., Li, J., & Wan, X. (2023). Environmental impact of organic and conventional wine grape production, a case study from Wuwei wine region, Gansu Province, China. *Ecological Indicators*, *154*, 110730. doi:10.1016/j.ecolind.2023.110730

Ye, N., Kueh, T. B., Hou, L., Liu, Y., & Yu, H. (2020). A bibliometric analysis of corporate social responsibility in sustainable development. *Journal of Cleaner Production*, *272*, 122679. doi:10.1016/j.jclepro.2020.122679

Zheng, L., & Iatridis, K. (2022). Friends or foes? A systematic literature review and meta-analysis of the relationship between eco-innovation and firm performance. *Business Strategy and the Environment*, *31*(4), 1838–1855. doi:10.1002/bse.2986

Chapter 7
Factors for Consumers to Contemplate Regarding the Adoption of Eco-Friendly Packaging

Uttam Kaur
Chandigarh University, India

Prashant Kumar Siddhey
https://orcid.org/0000-0002-4236-0966
Chandigarh University, India

ABSTRACT

The rising adoption of environmentally friendly development principles at different levels in industrial and organizational platforms has coincided with the evolution of packaging sustainability ideas. Several obstacles, including intricate value chains and unfavorable customer perceptions stemming from the financial, societal, and ecological implications of sustainable practices, may dissuade businesses from adopting more environmentally friendly packaging. Packages with increased sustainability could thus never reach the market. However, initiatives that encourage a favorable customer perception towards environmentally friendly packaging can inspire the next generation of environmentally friendly alternatives. In addition to identifying study gaps and possibilities for customer study, the work's objectives include reviewing existing practices, variables influencing environmental behavior, and customer testing techniques. It also suggests tactics for stakeholders to effectively convey package sustainability to customers.

INTRODUCTION

Packaging now plays a crucial role in sustainability alongside its traditional functions of preserving product security, aiding shipping, and enabling communication. Despite recent strides in sustainable packaging, there remain chances for enhancement. Much like other businesses, the packaging sector

DOI: 10.4018/979-8-3693-2149-2.ch007

finds itself at the intersection of environmental preservation, societal fairness, and economic developing, defining the contemporary commercial and societal landscape of the early 21st century. To bolster sustainability in the packaging value chain, efforts can be directed towards improving the collection and sorting processes for recycling, composting, reuse, and waste-to-energy processing (Nguyen et al., 2020). Additionally, there is a need for responsible removal and handling of organized packaging, along with a focus on sustainable material sourcing. The goal is to reduce substantial and supply usage while maintaining the crucial purposes of packaging. As constraints on water, land, energy, and food intensify, and issues like declining air quality and overpopulation become more pronounced, the packaging industry faces a critical juncture (Orzan et al., 2018). The choice lies between adopting more sustainable packaging practices or redirecting efforts towards fostering consumer appreciation for packaging. This aware decision can have extensive consequences, with the final selection potentially resulting in improved rules, and enforced constraints on the value chain and resources (Martinho et al., 2015). While consumer familiarity with sustainable packaging is growing, there is a lack of awareness regarding the role of food packaging in reducing food waste (Popovic et al., 2019). Scenes of ocean plastics and environmental pollution contribute to this lack of appreciation. It is important to acknowledge that the term "eco-friendly packaging" is consistently used in this discourse, even though packaging will inevitably have some environmental impact.

In response to a growing demand from consumers for sustainable initiatives driven by a recognized shared value, companies and policymakers have taken action. The challenges faced by advertising and packaging progress players, material suppliers, and consultants in balancing sustainability considerations were evident. Decision-makers grappled with issues such as cost, technical hurdles, and team coordination (Nguyen et al., 2021). Consequently, numerous ecological packaging solutions, lacking favorable economic and temporal parameters, remained unimplemented. Without clear evidence that sustainable packaging positively impacts sales or reduces costs, companies struggled to justify pursuing such initiatives despite promoting their commitment to sustainability. This disconnection between rhetoric and action, as well as between intentions and viability, hindered progress. A more effective approach emerged when defining options for food protection before assessing ecological packaging. This contrasted sharply with the common practice of selecting a packaging material and then adding essentials for product safety, which often resulted in higher costs and/or compromised product safety, leading to increased food waste (Zeng & Durif, 2019). Failure to effectively convey the essential functions and role of packaging in the food value chain led to consumers developing incomplete understandings of both packaging and sustainable packaging. This gap in understanding influenced consumer preferences, with many believing their choices were sustainable when, in reality, they were not. Various factors contributed to the limited achievement of ecological packaging solutions in the market. These included consumer resistance to unfamiliar technologies, cost concerns, regulatory challenges, insufficient item safety, manufacturing obstacles (due to sourcing or material properties), and competitive disadvantages. To address these challenges, stakeholders should gain a better knowledge of existing customer drivers guiding ecologically conscious buying choices. This understanding can inform strategies to promote sustainable consumer behaviors and build a compelling business case for the adoption of more sustainable packaging (Lan et al., 2023).

Given the intricacies posed by factors such as alternative food packaging, escalating packaging regulations, and the recognition that a compelling business case is essential for shared value with customers, there is a pressing need for in-depth assessments and research into the dynamics shaping consumer attitudes towards sustainable packaging. The motivation behind this review and exploration stems from the necessity to provide comprehensive insights and solutions for stakeholders in the food and packaging industry, particularly those engaged in customer study and ecological packaging choices (Petljak et al., 2019). The main objective of this investigation is to compile the body of customer studies on packaging that is more environmentally friendly, highlighting potential, pointing out gaps in the literature, and laying out the need for more study. Many customer test results are not made available because developing packaging and goods are private. A comprehensive search was carried out using terms including "ecological packaging," "customer + study, behavior, attitudes," and "environmentally friendly packaging," among others, throughout the Scopus and Web of Science databases. The investigation needs that have been explicitly identified in books, reviewed by expert publications, reviews, governmental reports, and comments from industry and multi-stakeholder organizations have been the basis for the investigation suggestions made in this study (Ahmad et al., 2020). The writers also make use of their wealth of knowledge from customer testing and study, as well as from the packaging sectors. Examining customer opinions of environmentally friendly packaging against life cycle assessments (LCAs) of sustainable purchase and post-buy behaviors, the review explores this relationship. Customer reactions and attitudes impacted by changing norms, demography, packaging design components, signals, and regional and cultural variations are among the many topics that are investigated. Strategies aimed at enhancing customer getting of ecological packaging, particularly in situations involving known trade-offs, are also shared (Nguzen et al., 2021). This latest customer study on eco-friendly packaging amalgamates recent findings to provide a comprehensive overview of contemporary issues in consumer considerations.

Furthermore, this document includes a table that consolidates latest customer study findings on eco-friendly packaging. In essence, it offers a comprehensive overview of contemporary issues, references, and potential future endeavors relevant to stakeholders such as investigators, businesses, legislators, customers, and others within the production.

ENVIRONMENTALLY FRIENDLY PACKAGING

This part examines the concept of sustainability in packing from the standpoints of formal definitions, the packaging process, ecology, and the food value chain. When it comes to consumer communication, it can be deceptive to assume that environmentally friendly packaging is the same as compostable or reusable materials or materials with allowed restoration (Dharmadhikari, 2012). Other criteria, like economic viability and social impacts, are frequently overlooked. To successfully explain environmentally friendly packaging to customers, it is necessary to first examine the formal definitions and historical background. The fundamental idea of sustainability has been understood for generations (Singh et al., 2011). Sustainability was employed in food packing in ancient civilizations and is still used in contemporary societies to store food till the following harvest season. Protecting the environment while advancing social and economic advancements are central to the idea of a more sustainable future, which has grown to be one of the most significant tenets for ongoing global development programs (Kumar et al., 2014).

CONSUMER PERCEPTIONS OF ENVIRONMENTALLY FRIENDLY PACKAGING

Communication approaches are preferably achieved in the design process with input from preliminary descriptive consumer research, after the establishment of a shared understanding of environmentally friendly packaging and its relationship to the product along the whole value chain. However, customer misconceptions and prejudices regarding the package aspects may hinder a product's commercial success. Many on-label promises fall short of conveying the businesses' sustainability message because of customer misinterpretations (Scott & Vigar-Ellis, 2014). However, research on real-life life costs and consumer assessments of sustainability revealed disparities because of pre-existing beliefs about environmentally friendly packaging. Such disparities can be attributed, in part, to earlier green washing-inspired efforts. This section contains literature material on these topics (Esvandiari, 2023).

Misinterpretations by Consumers

While many customers support initiatives to use environmentally friendly packaging, most have misunderstandings about sustainability in general. "Packaging design that evokes explicitly or implicitly the eco-friendliness of the packaging" is how consumers describe environmentally friendly packaging (Seo & Scammon, 2017). The phrase "eco-friendliness" is wide and does not encompass the social and economic components of environmentally friendly packaging. Environmentally friendly packaging definitions are always changing in tandem with the ideals of environmentally friendly growth. However, studies have shown that customers are not well informed on environmentally friendly packaging (Norton et al., 2022). The concepts of social justice and customer demands for packaging's performance, affordability, and ease of use may all influence how sustainable growth in packaging affects society. As was previously said, the fact that there are misunderstandings over what constitutes sustainability is crucial to customer study on environmentally friendly packaging. As a result, attitudes both during and after purchases may be impacted (Grebmer & Diefenbach, 2022).

Measured Sustainability

When faced with little knowledge of sustainability, consumers typically rely on cue-inferring processes to help them make decisions. For the packaging business to grow sustainably, customers must be aware of the findings of life cycle analyses conducted on packaging materials and procedures. The study replicated the decisions that customers make when they buy. The true ecology of a package may not always coincide with consumer perceptions of what constitutes a sustainable package (Campbell et al., 2015). When evaluating the environmentally friendly qualities of packaging, the production aspect is disregarded in favor of concentrating solely on the post-consumption utilization mode. Reusable glass, plastic, and paperboard were found to be the most sustainable materials, while non-returnable plastic, plastic, and paperboard components were thought to be the least sustainable (Seo et al., 2016).

Green Washing

"Green washing" is the term used to describe deceptive statements made about a package's environmental sustainability compared to other types of packaging, for as using the terms "eco-friendly," "green "or" green leaf." This is common. The visible environment is directly impacted by the packing material; it's noteworthy to observe that this visibility may influence customers' opinions of sustainability (Butt et al., 2021). This information can help designers of cutting-edge packaging solutions encourage customers to make more environmentally friendly decisions, which will enhance the purchasing process (Fouziya & Gracious, 2018). The 1990s saw advances in consumer research that paved the way for the use of behavioral studies to integrate sustainability into marketing campaigns. Although many package designs for more environmentally friendly packaging attempted to convey this sustainability to customers, these attempts sometimes led to vague or false "green" claims on product packaging. The packaged food industry's attempts to promote sustainability have been misguided because of the potential to link packaging sustainability to sales (Felix et al., 2022). Green washing claims have been dropped as a result of customer outrage and inquiries about false and misleading claims. Since the promotion of environmentally friendly packaging is associated with previously made fraudulent promises, there is an actual or perceived high risk involved (Martinez et al., 2020). Many businesses don't tell customers about their attempts to use more environmentally friendly packaging to avoid being accused of "green washing" and maybe receiving unfavorable reviews. Customers' mistrust and beliefs about green washing have made genuine brands less competitive, which has demoralized them. Customers are demanding that environmentally friendly objectives and their relationship to the business be indicated in the claims and labeling on the packaging (Kahraman & Kazancoglu, 2019). According to research, sustainable advertising mistakes include selling standard items as premium, depending only on promotions rather than product development, directing marketing efforts towards compliance, and engaging in environmentally conscious business. There is a dearth of crucial information that customers need to make decisions as a result of this incapacity to communicate with them properly (Qayyum et al., 2023).

CONSUMER BEHAVIOUR THEORIES ON SUSTAINABILITY

Over the past few decades, the utilization of marketing and consumer research has played a pivotal role in shaping trades and buying behaviors. The foundation of active advertising and advertising movements has been laid upon consumer theories, forming a complex field that delves into people's behaviors and favouritisms both throughout the buying process and post-consumption (Han, 2021). As depicted in Figure 2, the increasing number of research studies indicates a eco-friendly packaging and consumers behaviour over the past decade. The significance of consumer behaviors in driving purchase intentions has led to a surge in research on sustainable packaging. Addressing consumer confusion regarding sustainable packaging requires a consideration of the part packaging plays in the overall value chain. While it is true that consumers recognize the importance of sustainable practices in theory, there exists a disconnection between their opinions and their actual environmentally friendly actions (Milfont & Markowitz, 2016). This disparity is evident in the value-action gap observed in recycling behavior, where compartmentalized sectors and compensated behaviors contribute to conflicting decisions. Figure 1. Shows the research carried out in the top ten countries using the keywords related to eco-friendly packaging. In the realm of consumer attitudes, it is noted that positive sentiments in one sector, such as energy conservation, do not necessarily translate to similar behaviors in another sector, such as recycling. This understanding underscores the complexity of connecting consumers to more sustainable packaging choices (David Lee et al., 2016). Consumers often exhibit a disconnection between their observed and real engagement with ecological packaging. When assessing rewarded behavior, it becomes apparent that an excess of eco-friendly actions in one area, like opting for ecological shippings, may be offset by unsustainable behaviors in another area, such as neglecting to recycle a recyclable package. This intricate interplay highlights the challenges in promoting consistent environmentally conscious choices among consumers (White et al., 2019). The exploration of the packaging value-action gap involves delving into well-established behavioral concepts in consumer studies. Meta motivation, theories of reasoned action

Figure 1. Studies conducted in top ten countries on the keywords of eco-friendly packaging

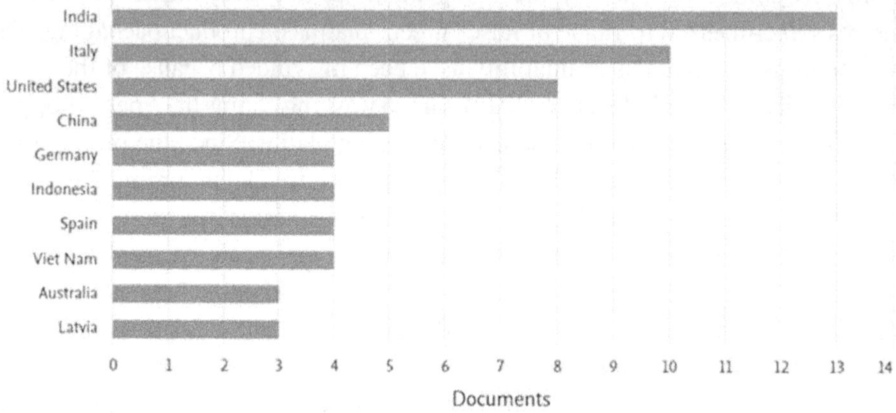

and planned behavior, and social desirability bias are among the frequently studied and cited concepts in understanding and addressing the complexities surrounding consumer behaviors in the context of sustainable packaging (Castaneda et al., 2015).

Value-Action Gap

Consumers may be required to compromise on quality, performance, and cost in exchange for some sustainable packaging, which leads to a discrepancy in "attitude-behavior" known as the value-action gap. Customers may choose not to buy the goods from the business for economic, social, and demographic reasons, even if they express a preference in surveys. Therefore, willingness to pay (WTP) may not necessarily correlate with packaging's sustainability qualities (Chauhan, 2020). On the other hand, buyers tended to choose ecologically friendly items more when trade-offs were eliminated. This might help explain why category-wide changes to packaging that is more environmentally friendly are more successful. Customers were forced to choose between the more environmentally friendly packaging and the product features. Customer misunderstanding arises from the absence of any category-wide effort in addition to the more environmentally friendly packing (ElHaffar et al., 2020).

Motivation in the Met Averse

It is difficult to persuade customers to adopt a certain, sustainable behaviour because of how several elements combine and create false perceptions. Due to these misconceptions, decisions are made based more on their own opinions about sustainable items than on sound sustainability principles. Attitudes and behaviours can spread between domains. The link between ecology and customer behaviour, including purchasing and post-buy attitudes, is the subject of several ideas and studies (Boz et al., 2020). Maslow invented the phrase "meta motivation," which states that if fundamental requirements (clothes, food, and shelter) are met, people tend to care more about topics unrelated to their immediate well-being. Consequently, societal and ecological reasons—like ecological packaging—become increasingly important after consumers' fundamental needs are met. Environmental concerns associated with packaging sustainability do become a worry, according to consumer studies on the environment conducted with

Figure 2. Quantify the studies conducted over different years in the Scopus database that incorporate the keywords "eco-friendly packaging" and "consumers"

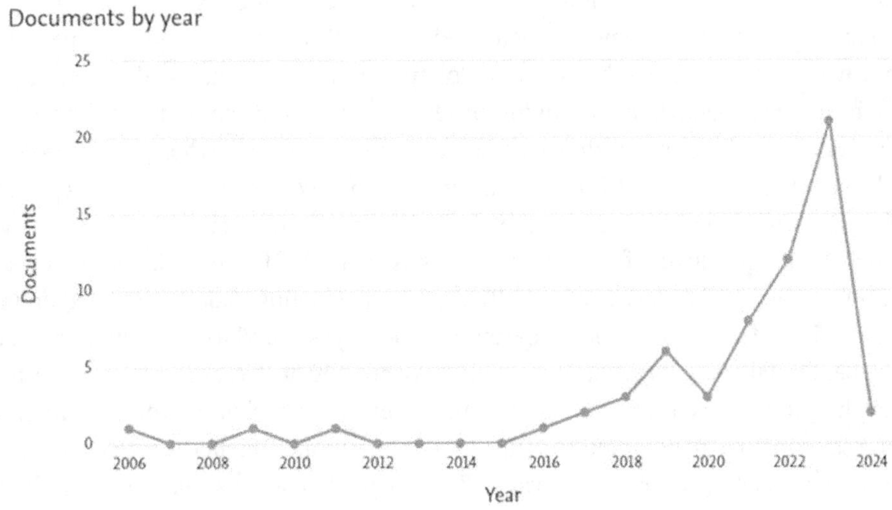

consumer groups where basic demands (such as price and taste) are satisfied. To link environmentally friendly packaging with customers with low incomes is extremely crucial (Scholer & Miele, 2016).

Barriers to Sustainable Behaviors

Inspirational intellectual and behavioural obstacles can all be indicators of environmentally conscious behaviour. Psychological and social identification, which manifests in an individual's interests in rights for people or responsibility for the environment, can present impediments to motivation. Customers are more likely to choose an ecologically friendly product if they think their purchase will have a beneficial effect on the particular issue (Orzan et al., 2018). While behavioural obstacles can be attributed to factors like time, money, travel distance, and other trade-offs, intellectual barriers are determined by the knowledge accessible about the product or the firm providing environmentally friendly solutions. It has been demonstrated that a variety of factors, such as accessible knowledge and individual motivation, influence customers' decisions to make environmentally conscious purchases. Customers are shifting to more "ecological" packaging (Zeng & Durif, 2019). According to this survey, customers would swap brands, healthier options, and the convenience of carrying, availability, and design for packaging that is more environmentally friendly, even though they were unwilling to compromise on flavour or cost (Petljak et al., 2019). This study demonstrated that "ecological" packaging might lead to brand switching in terms of addressed needs; nevertheless, taste and price criteria still need to be met. The same study evaluated the association between environmentally concerned customers' buying behaviors and their post-consumer package disposal practices. The findings imply that post-consumer disposal is important for customers who feel that eco-friendly packaging is necessary (Monteiro et al., 2019).

Spillover Effect

A further idea that is frequently brought up is the spillover effect, which is the result of engaging in one behaviour and having an impact on a non-targeted behaviour. Both positive and negative effects are possible from spillovers on non-targeted behaviours. Positive spillover effects, on the other hand, can result in one pro-environmental behaviour improving or leading to another unintentional pro-environmental behaviour (Choi & Lee, 2020). On the other hand, adverse spillover occurs when pro-environmental action in one area eliminates the essential for pro-environmental behaviour in alternative zone. For instance, when someone who would like to live sustainably at home decides to not be environmentally concerned, there may be detrimental spillover effects (Micheaux & Aggeri, 2021). Once the product was consumed, customers who were inclined to buy ecologically friendly packaging usually recycled and returned the packets. The overview of ecological consumption behaviors was found to be limited due to the frequent reports of both beneficial and adverse spillover effects occurring at the same time. Engaging in separate waste and recycling initiatives has been demonstrated to enhance packaging minimization. Conversely, committing to recycling has been found to reduce the inclination to feel compelled to make ecological behavioral variations, such as minimizing waste. These findings suggest that there are both beneficial and adverse contagion effects (Wang et al., 2022).

The Bias of Socially Desirableness

The bias of socially desirableness calls on customers to express their opinions rather than just how they behave after making a certain choice. Sustainability and related problems are sensitive by nature, and customers are unlikely to come across as unsustainable (Zeng & Durif, 2019). Various tactics have been devised to identify, diminish, or eradicate social desirability bias. Such tactics' efficacy is called into doubt because of their poor capacity to discern bias in particular domains, the implicit problems they raise, the expense and unethical nature of their use (Dinh et al., 2022).

FACTORS RELATED TO SUSTAINABILITY PERCEPTIONS

Investigations evaluating the impact of environmentally friendly packaging on buyer choices are rather rare, even though the fact that there are many consumer reactions toward packaging design components. The fact that environmentally friendly packaging frequently falls short of market expectations while being heavily advertised might be attributed to this lack of information with a clear direction (Zeng & Durif, 2019). Furthermore, customers might not want to transition from their known items to ecological novel packaging, or ecological packaging could not cover the item that they seek. This section included several elements that have been found to have an impact on customer views.

Demographics

The following demographic factors may influence sustainable buying behaviours favourably or unfavourably: age, gender, income, and education. Factors related to age, political party affiliation, and time constraints on recycling all had an impact on customer WTP for the recyclable materials of packaging made of various materials, such as aluminium, glass, plastic, and paper. The existence of eco-labels and environmental mindset, as well as education level, all influenced the desire to make green purchases. Because of the focus on human nature and eco-labels, buying intention was influenced by gender (Martinho et al., 2015). Higher educated respondents' purchasing intentions were shown to be enhanced by environmental attitudes and eco-labels on items; female respondents were also more likely to purchase green products when these factors were combined. According to customer recycling research, women recycle more frequently than males. According to the analyzed research, women are more likely than males to purchase and dispose of things sustainably and are also more in charge of choosing what goes in the home. The demographics don't seem to have much to do with recycling behaviors, other than gender (Orzan et al., 2018).

Country of Origin

Variations in customer behaviors towards sustainability may also be attributed to origin nation and location. Numerous research with customers from various nations and areas have been carried out. The definition of "sustainability" differed throughout nations and areas. There are divergent opinions on the post-consumer disposal of packaging depending on the country of origin. Depending on the place of origin, consumer opinions regarding ecologically friendly packaging differ in how important recyclability, reusability, and biodegradability (Popovic et al., 2019). Regardless matter where they are from, customers have little to no knowledge about how packaging's manufacturing, transportation, and sale phases affect sustainability. Additionally, container end-of-life was a bigger concern for customers than the source. According to empirical findings, high-income nations often care more about ecological issues than low-income nations do (Petljak et al., 2019). Few studies have been conducted on the relationship between customer opinions and poor, lower-middle, and middle or upper economic position. However as customer behavior is influenced by different economic groupings, it is important to comprehend their viewpoints to design environmentally friendly packaging that would appeal to them the most. The product's price, usefulness, and packaging ease were the key determinants of impression among younger Indian buyers (Wandosell et al., 2021). It's interesting to note that consumers who were not vegetarians cared more about the environment than those who were. There is a dearth of environmental legislation and business support for environmentally friendly packaging and the use of green concepts. Improved sustainable post-consumption behaviors like recycling are made much more difficult when these efforts are coupled with inadequate infrastructure. Geographical parallels and variances in reaction patterns within and within nations were also discovered in a similar study (Alam, 2023).

Norms and Values

It has been studied how role identity, whether social or personal, influences and explains sustainable behaviors. However, when the individual thought of recycling as a crucial part of their self-identity, self-identity was a solid forecaster of reutilizing intent and enhanced desire to recycle. Moral standards dictate that consumers should use ecologically friendly packaging when making purchases (Orzan et al., 2018). An individual's environmental concerns serve as their moral justification. Reduced-waste packaging was preferred due to moral considerations and perceived conformity with expectations. Moreover, it was discovered that perceived societal norms influenced personal norms. Social pressure to purchase and dispose of packaging sustainably had little effect on consumers, and it was discovered that they had a low sense of control over the issues surrounding package waste (Popovic et al., 2019).

Package Design

The procedure of using cues involves making decisions about one characteristic based on another. For instance, a customer's taste decisions during testing and when buying might be influenced by the color of the package. To identify cues utilizing short customer attention spans, the number of cues paired with regulated time can be used in specific contexts. This can result in misidentified stimuli and a reliance primarily on prominent ones. Because consumer-identified signals are the basis for the approaches and because consumers differ in their time lags before registering cues, this emphasis may yield very variable findings. Consumer signals on packaging may be created via the use of graphical, structural, and linguistic elements (Zeng & Durif, 2019). Among the most popular indications in packaging design to indicate sustainability are visuals and colours. Sustainability is also communicated verbally through claims and statements on packaging. For consumer goods, consumer perceptions of product efficiency decreased when an ecological label or the colour was utilized on the labelling as opposed to using a dissimilar colour without a labelling. Green is also negatively associated with buying when it is used alone. This adverse effect was lessened when environmentally friendly packaging with the eco-label was applied. Customers who rely only on their own informal opinions regarding such matters may not be familiar with the concept of sustainability. The pricing, ecological characteristics, and quality of the item took precedence over packaging design (Dinh et al., 2022).

On-Label Claims

The claims made both orally and visually about the environmental friendliness of the packaging, as well as how they affect customers' attitudes and intent to buy. Individuals with a high level of knowledge about the environment were responsive to verbal statements and package design, but those with a low level of ecological knowledge were not (Petljak et al., 2019; Zeng & Durif, 2019).

Price

Prior consumer studies on sustainable goods and eco-friendly packaging frequently identified price as a deterrent and a determining factor in purchase intentions. In comparison to purchasing ecological product packaging and recycling, the impact of pricing, product quality, package functioning, and packaging design was evaluated among customers who originally self-identified as environmentally conscious and indifferent to such matters. The two main elements that determined whether or not to buy were taste and pricing (Petljak et al., 2019). The cost for environmentally friendly packaging must be equivalent to that of less environmentally friendly packaging, or it should be able to indicate increased disposal costs. However, switching to environmentally friendly packaging may cost enterprises more money owing to variations in materials, manufacturing, processing, and supply. Both the proportion of consumers willing to pay more for environmentally friendly items and the number of persons reporting energy-saving behaviors at home are declining. Purchase intentions for sustainable products are based on customer environmental views, the availability of eco-labels, and willingness to pay for eco-friendly goods (Zeng & Durif, 2019).

Product Factors

Sustainably designed packaging improved consumers' perceptions of the quality of products. It's interesting to note that when product quality was cued, environmentally friendly packaging had no further impact on sustainability metrics or perceived product quality. This indicates that organic products' perceived quality is improved by environmentally friendly packaging, but their actual quality is unaffected. This correlation between chocolate quality and organic content may result from buyers' willingness to forego environmentally friendly packaging (Zeng & Durif, 2019). Product protection is not as important to consumers as material selection when it comes to environmentally friendly packaging. Customers choose packing materials, nonetheless, when determining what an ecologically friendly package's most crucial component should be. The material-based perspective is consistent with other studies showing that customers misunderstood what environmentally friendly packaging meant (Popovic et al., 2019).

Over Packaging

The impact of excessive packaging on customer opinions and the perception of ecologically friendly brands. According to the findings, excessive packaging did not directly affect consumers' connection to green brands. The customer's perception of green companies, however, determines their connection to and unfavorable attitude towards excessive packaging. For items sold under private labels, excessive packaging may be a delicate topic since, while businesses might choose to reduce or do away with it and project an environmentally friendly image, doing so puts their reputation and customer acceptance in jeopardy (Zeng & Durif, 2019). We tracked how excessive packaging affected consumers' opinions of private-label items' affordability, ease of use, durability, and sustainability. As excessive packaging was eliminated, perceptions of cost and environmental friendliness rose but convenience declined. Additionally, they noted that only private-label items were assessed to be of lower quality (Orzan et al., 2018).

PACKAGING THAT ENCOURAGES BETTER POST-CONSUMPTION ENVIRONMENTAL PRACTICES

Packaging may also help customers engage with environmentally friendly behaviours, such as post-consumption actions, and raise the perceived value of packaging by facilitating these actions, which in turn can influence customer and packaging-related aspects. The majority of the material currently in publication focuses on general attitude assessments and post-consumption behaviours about shifts in customer WTP and enhanced recyclability (Widayat et al., 2021). The study on the relationship between environmentally friendly packaging and customer opinions after consumption is highlighted in this section. The rising acceptance of sustainability ideals hasn't always been directly linked to environmentally friendly actions like recycling routines (Boz et al., 2020). The shopping and post-consumption disposal behaviours associated with environmentally conscious decisions are linked to customers' environmental consciousness and environmentally conscious mindset. Except for pricing, buyers were also prepared to give up nearly all product features in favor of packaging that is more ecologically friendly. Customers who preferred eco-friendly packaging were inclined to recycle the packaging or give it back to the retailer. Regretfully, customers are being misled by information on sustainability (Chen et al., 2023). The study revealed that WTP answers were significantly influenced by recycling objectives, such as enhancing water quality, and that there was no significant correlation between demographics and recycling behavior. It's interesting to see that states with return incentives did not have greater WTP. This suggests that customers are growing accustomed to paying high costs or receiving small deposits in exchange for returning goods. Time-sensitive customers tended to pay less for packaging made of recyclable materials (Chirilli et al., 2022).

CUSTOMER STUDY AND ASSESSMENT TECHNIQUES FOR ENVIRONMENTALLY FRIENDLY PACKAGING

In the realm of behavioral studies, our comprehension of the choices made by individuals or groups regarding environmental alternatives remains constrained. Prior to formulating and executing sustainable packaging strategies, it is imperative to conduct thorough consumer testing that simulates target behaviors. Various methodologies have been devised to evaluate consumer preferences, such as conjoint and discrete choice analysis, which involve identifying both continuous and discrete properties. However, certain limitations persist in consumer studies on the sustainability features of products, including the absence of concurrent measurement of visual and descriptive stimuli and the exclusion of an environmental impact variable as an independent variable in discrete analysis (Nguyen et al., 2021). The study approach used to evaluate how environmentally friendly packaging affects customer tastes includes analytical techniques to measure the influence of particular design signs, multifaceted opinions (consisting of customer opinions), and overall attitude-related theories. Overall attitude-related theories, guided by the theory of planned behavior (TPB), posit that customer attitudes toward ecological goods are shaped by perceived behavior. For instance, an individual's environmental consciousness and knowledge serve as motivating factors to contribute to resolving environmental issues such as packaging waste. Holistic approaches assess packaging characteristics as a unified entity, disregarding individual elements (Scott & Vigar-Ellis, 2014). This approach is rooted in the notion that packaging, composed of multiple elements, collectively influences attitudes or behaviors. Findings from such methods indicate that material cues play a significant role in evaluating the sustainability of packaging, with packaging material types surprisingly absent in responses. Previous analyses have examined cues like color, labels, and transparency. While studies investigating the influence of individual ecological characteristics on packaging are inadequate, they prove effective in discerning behaviors, purchase attitudes, and the correlation among ecological components and useful and expense features. Analytical methods reveal that sustainable features involve both graphical and essential elements, such as material form. In addition to diverse approaches for consumer testing on sustainability, the test setting can significantly influence outcomes (Popovic et al., 2019). It is crucial to exercise caution when extrapolating results from studies relying on questionnaires rather than observable purchasing activities. For a more accurate assessment of pro-environmental consumer behavior, an ideal setting would replicate actual purchasing scenarios, and the test group should represent a subset of the target demographic. Notably, consumers with higher education levels tend to exhibit a positive response to environmental aspects of packaging, underscoring the importance of screening respondents based on their educational backgrounds (Ketelsen et al., 2020).

ANALYSIS AND PROSPECTS FOR THE FUTURE

Marketing of more environmentally friendly packaging to customers is a challenge, as was said. Furthermore, if packaging suppliers and businesses just rely on customers' ideas of sustainability, then the most ecologically friendly packaging options won't be adopted since customers don't always select the most responsible package. Alternatively, if food packaging firms use more dependable environmentally friendly containers and make sure that consumers are made aware of this packaging in a meaningful way, they will accept it. Examining factors influencing the adoption of eco-friendly packaging, the research becomes a pivotal resource for various stakeholders, including researchers, businesses, legislators, and customers. By synthesizing current insights, the study not only informs businesses seeking alignment with sustainable practices but also aids legislators in crafting effective policies. The findings resonate with researchers exploring the evolving landscape of consumer behavior in the context of eco-conscious choices. As the production landscape shifts towards sustainability, this consolidated study serves as a roadmap, guiding stakeholders towards informed decisions and innovative solutions, fostering a harmonious relationship between consumer preferences and environmentally responsible packaging practices. Taking advantage of possibilities requires leadership, involve customers in a discussion about environmental packaging, and do customer studies to find out how customers may be won over to more environmentally friendly packaging. A thorough customer study with the intended audience is required before designing and implementing environmentally friendly packaging methods. The influence of environmentally friendly packaging on customer preferences for environmentally friendly packaging is studied using analytic methods to evaluate the effects of particular design cues, comprehensive opinions (customer opinions and sign-based interaction), and overall attitude-related theories. A summary of the potential, research requirements, and initiatives is provided in the next section. Most importantly, building customer relationships around more environmentally friendly packaging can help create the business situation required to put more environmentally friendly packaging into practice. The study on factors influencing consumers' considerations of eco-friendly packaging presents valuable contributions to both academia and industry. The research provides a comprehensive understanding of the multifaceted elements influencing consumers' decisions in adopting environmentally sustainable packaging. Real-world implications include insights for businesses to develop more effective marketing strategies, tailored to the identified factors. Theoretical contributions lie in the advancement of consumer behavior theories within the context of eco-friendly choices. However, limitations may arise from the dynamic nature of consumer preferences and the potential influence of cultural and regional variations. Future research should delve deeper into the long-term impact of eco-friendly packaging adoption, exploring potential shifts in consumer behavior over time, as well as investigating emerging technologies and innovative solutions that could further enhance the practical feasibility and acceptance of sustainable packaging options.

Possibilities

1. Create a situation for more environmentally friendly packaging. According to meta-motivation research, people behave more responsibly when they are given concrete knowledge about sustainability. The secret to encouraging customers to move to a more environmentally friendly package is to provide them with continuous, concrete information.
2. Learn from nations with strong recycling rates that have high group environmental norms.

3. Ensure that companies and localities comply with rules by managing suppliers, inventing novel approaches to business and ecological goods and services, and setting up forums for best practices.
4. There's a chance to introduce low-income groups to environmentally friendly packaging.
5. Make sustainable collecting and sorting profitable, create employment and revenue, and add creativity to initiatives to support the ecological economy in lower and middle income zones.
6. Packaging is not seen as a big deal for small and medium-sized businesses, and packaging methods are not reviewed and modified in light of new developments in materials science. One tends to take packaging optimization for granted because it immediately impacts the company's budget in addition to influencing the environment, but this isn't always the case.
7. Modify the value chain for packaging to facilitate a healthier food system that reduces food waste and promotes environmentally friendly packaging.
8. Low-income communities make decisions about what packaged food to buy based on certain price-determining criteria, therefore it's critical to create packaging that is both economical and sustainable.
9. The industry has to adopt a common concept of sustainability.

Approaches for Explaining Sustainable Development to Customers

1. Use package design as a vehicle for innovation in informing customers about sustainability. This is due to the fact that cue utilisation has shown that different consumer messages about sustainability are not well communicated by colours, materials, vocal language, or visuals.
2. Establish sustainable standards that may be utilised to convey features of sustainability that appeal to customers, much as clean label standards. Checklists that emphasise features like recyclable materials, decreased package volume, and recycled content, for instance, could be appealing to customers.
3. Understand that businesses promoting socially conscious business practices will only be more credible in the eyes of customers if their environmental claims are substantiated and have a significant impact on them.
4. Employ thorough life cycle assessments (LCAs) that include an evaluation of the packaging's capacity to reduce food waste, which is crucial for a food system that is more environmentally friendly.
5. Go after category-wide campaigns to convert to more eco-friendly designs and materials, as well as smaller volume containers, that are effective and provide customers the sustainability leadership they require.
6. Integrate environmental data with mobile device technology to provide customers with information on how to properly dispose of packaging in the area where the item is utilized and to track their ecological exertions. This will give customers the guidance and relationships they sorely need.
7. Explain the societal and commercial effects of packaging life cycle assessments by incorporating customer food waste and recycling practices.
8. Find out which product categories' best package design cues are for promoting environmentally friendly practices (packaging value is quite category-specific).
9. Encourage actions that have a good knock-on impact and steer clear of those that have a negative one.
10. Encourage behaviors that enhance customers' sense of self and enhance their social desirability.

11. Create labels or indications for disposable and reusable containers that are universal rather than culturally particular.
12. Use a set of standard criteria to evaluate contenders' sustainability when deciding which innovative packaging concepts and models to honor.
13. Pay attention to recognizing models that have the potential to affect larger-scale shifts, including packaging that is ready for recycling, which makes it simple to remove labels at recyclers, and the use of workable compatibilizers.

Research Needs

1. Recognize that when customers learn that environmentally friendly packaging reduces food waste and costs associated with bad food, their readiness to pay (RTP) for ecological characteristics is not diminished. To establish a more ecological supply, research on ways to counteract customer inclination to lose money by discarding food is crucial.
2. Get a deeper comprehension of customer behavior, including recycling and eco-friendly shopping choices.
3. Acquire knowledge of the most prevalent packaging myths to inform your clients and achieve shared value objectives.
4. Raise the awareness of environmentally conscious and indifferent customers about sustainable packaging practices. Since men are less likely than women to buy environmentally friendly packaging, there needs to be research on how to get men to buy more of it.
5. Identify the views of lower, middle, and upper class groups to define environmentally friendly packaging that appeals to all customers.
6. Help customers internalize packaging and usage. It is best to evaluate environmentally friendly packaging and supply together for a more sustainable end product. The price of packaged goods does not account for the environmental costs of packaging use.

REFERENCES

Ahmad, N., Ghazali, N., Abdullah, M. F., Nordin, R., Nasir, I. N. M., & Farid, N. A. M. (2020). Green marketing and its effect on consumers' purchase behaviour: An empirical analysis. *Journal of International Business. Economics and Entrepreneurship*, *5*(2), 46–55.

Alam, M. Z. (2023). A Study on The Selection Motives and Challenges Faced by Consumers Concerning Green Packaged Products. *TEM Journal*, *12*(4), 2273. doi:10.18421/TEM124-38

Boz, Z., Korhonen, V., & Koelsch Sand, C. (2020). Consumer considerations for the implementation of sustainable packaging: A review. *Sustainability (Basel)*, *12*(6), 2192. doi:10.3390/su12062192

Butt, A., Khan, S. N., Zakir, M. M., Rana, W., & Laila, A. (2021). Firms greenwashing practices and consumers' perception: Role of marketing and non-marketing external stake holders in firms greenwashing practices. *Indian Journal of Economics and Business*, *20*(3), 689–706.

Campbell, B., Khachatryan, H., Behe, B., Dennis, J., & Hall, C. (2015). Consumer perceptions of eco-friendly and sustainable terms. *Agricultural and Resource Economics Review*, *44*(1), 21–34. doi:10.1017/S1068280500004603

Castaneda, M. G., Martinez, C. P., Marte, R., & Roxas, B. (2015). Explaining the environmentally-sustainable consumer behavior: A social capital perspective. *Social Responsibility Journal*, *11*(4), 658–676. doi:10.1108/SRJ-02-2014-0019

Chauhan, V. Z. (2020). Value-Action Gap Towards Green Consumer Behavior: A Theoretical Review and Analysis. [IJCRT]. *International Journal of Creative Research Thoughts*, *8*(4), 497–505.

Chen, C. C., Sujanto, R. Y., Bui, T. D., & Tseng, M. L. (2023). Sustainable recyclate packaging in Indonesian food and beverage industry: A hybrid decision-making analysis in consumption stages. *Quality & Quantity*, *57*(3), 2053–2089. doi:10.1007/s11135-022-01458-x

Chirilli, C., Molino, M., & Torri, L. (2022). Consumers' awareness, behavior and expectations for food packaging environmental sustainability: Influence of socio-demographic characteristics. *Foods*, *11*(16), 2388. doi:10.3390/foods11162388 PMID:36010389

Choi, S., & Lee, S. (2020). Eco-Packaging and its Market Performance: UPC-level Sales, Brand Spillover Effects, and Curvilinearity. *Sustainability (Basel)*, *12*(21), 9061. doi:10.3390/su12219061

David Lee, J., Bahl, A., Black, G. S., Duber-Smith, D. C., & Vowles, N. S. (2016). Sustainable and non-sustainable consumer behavior in young adults. *Young Consumers*, *17*(1), 78–93. doi:10.1108/YC-08-2015-00548

Dharmadhikari, S. (2012). Eco-friendly packaging in supply chain. *IUP Journal of Supply Chain Management*, *9*(2), 7.

Dinh, M. T. T., Su, D. N., Tran, K. T., Luu, T. T., Duong, T. H., & Johnson, L. W. (2022). Eco-designed retail packaging: The empirical conceptualization and measurement. *Journal of Cleaner Production*, *379*, 134717. doi:10.1016/j.jclepro.2022.134717

ElHaffar, G., Durif, F., & Dubé, L. (2020). Towards closing the attitude-intention-behavior gap in green consumption: A narrative review of the literature and an overview of future research directions. *Journal of Cleaner Production*, *275*, 122556. doi:10.1016/j.jclepro.2020.122556

Esvandiari, M. (2023). The Effect of Eco-Friendly Packaging on Purchase Intention with Consumer Perception as an Intervening Variable. *International Journal of Entrepreneurship and Sustainability Studies*, *3*(2), 62–80. doi:10.31098/ijeass.v3i2.1818

Felix, R., Gonzalez, E. M., Castano, R., Carrete, L., & Gretz, R. T. (2022). When the green in green packaging backfires: Gender effects and perceived masculinity of environmentally friendly products. *International Journal of Consumer Studies*, *46*(3), 925–943. doi:10.1111/ijcs.12738

Fouziya, R., & Gracious, J. (2018). Awareness of green marketing and its influence on consumer perception: An exploratory study. *Sumedha Journal of Management*, *7*(2), 62–68.

Grebmer, C., & Diefenbach, S. (2022). Perceiving and believing? The subjective persuasiveness of graphic design elements and eco-friendly packaging materials on consumers' environmental consciousness. *International Journal of Sustainable Development, 4*(3-4), 234–252.

Han, H. (2021). Consumer behavior and environmental sustainability in tourism and hospitality: A review of theories, concepts, and latest research. *Journal of Sustainable Tourism, 29*(7), 1021–1042. doi:10.1080/09669582.2021.1903019

Kahraman, A., & Kazançoğlu, İ. (2019). Understanding consumers' purchase intentions toward natural-claimed products: A qualitative research in personal care products. *Business Strategy and the Environment, 28*(6), 1218–1233. doi:10.1002/bse.2312

Ketelsen, M., Janssen, M., & Hamm, U. (2020). Consumers' response to environmentally-friendly food packaging-A systematic review. *Journal of Cleaner Production, 254*, 120123. doi:10.1016/j.jclepro.2020.120123

Kumar, Y., Shukla, P., Singh, P., Prabhakaran, P. P., Tanwar, V. K., & Kumar, Y. (2014). Bio-plastics. A perfect tool for eco-friendly food packaging: A Review. *Journal of Food Product Development and Packaging, 1*(1), 01-06.

Lan, B. T. H., Phuong, T. T. L., Dat, T. T., & Truong, D. D. (2023). Factors affecting the purchase intention of products with environmentally friendly packaging of urban residents in Ho Chi Minh City, Vietnam. *Sustainability (Basel), 15*(9), 7726. doi:10.3390/su15097726

Martínez, M. P., Cremasco, C. P., Gabriel Filho, L. R. A., Junior, S. S. B., Bednaski, A. V., Quevedo-Silva, F., & Padgett, R. C. M. L. (2020). Fuzzy inference system to study the behavior of the green consumer facing the perception of greenwashing. *Journal of Cleaner Production, 242*, 116064. doi:10.1016/j.jclepro.2019.03.060

Martinho, G., Pires, A., Portela, G., & Fonseca, M. (2015). Factors affecting consumers' choices concerning sustainable packaging during product purchase and recycling. *Resources, Conservation and Recycling, 103*, 58–68. doi:10.1016/j.resconrec.2015.07.012

Micheaux, H., & Aggeri, F. (2021). Eco-modulation as a driver for eco-design: A dynamic view of the French collective EPR scheme. *Journal of Cleaner Production, 289*, 125714. doi:10.1016/j.jclepro.2020.125714

Milfont, T. L., & Markowitz, E. (2016). Sustainable consumer behavior: A multilevel perspective. *Current Opinion in Psychology, 10*, 112–117. doi:10.1016/j.copsyc.2015.12.016

Monteiro, J., Silva, F. J. G., Ramos, S. F., Campilho, R. D. S. G., & Fonseca, A. M. (2019). Eco-design and sustainability in packaging: A survey. *Procedia Manufacturing, 38*, 1741–1749. doi:10.1016/j.promfg.2020.01.097

Nguyen, A. T., Parker, L., Brennan, L., & Lockrey, S. (2020). A consumer definition of eco-friendly packaging. *Journal of Cleaner Production, 252*, 119792. doi:10.1016/j.jclepro.2019.119792

Nguyen, A. T., Yến-Khanh, N., & Thuan, N. H. (2021). Consumers' purchase intention and willingness to pay for eco-friendly packaging in Vietnam. *Sustainable Packaging*, 289-323.

Nguyen, N. T., Nguyen, L. H. A., & Tran, T. T. (2021). Purchase behavior of young consumers toward green packaged products in Vietnam. *The Journal of Asian Finance. Economics and Business*, *8*(1), 985–996.

Norton, V., Waters, C., Oloyede, O. O., & Lignou, S. (2022). Exploring consumers' understanding and perception of sustainable food packaging in the UK. *Foods*, *11*(21), 3424. doi:10.3390/foods11213424 PMID:36360036

Orzan, G., Cruceru, A. F., Bălăceanu, C. T., & Chivu, R. G. (2018). Consumers' behavior concerning sustainable packaging: An exploratory study on Romanian consumers. *Sustainability (Basel)*, *10*(6), 1787. doi:10.3390/su10061787

Paidari, S., Ahari, H., Pasqualone, A., Anvar, A., Allah Yari Beyk, S., & Moradi, S. (2023). Bio-nanocomposites and their potential applications in physiochemical properties of cheese: An updated review. *Journal of Food Measurement and Characterization*, *17*(3), 1–12. doi:10.1007/s11694-022-01800-9

Petljak, K., Naletina, D., & Bilogrević, K. (2019). Considering ecologically sustainable packaging during decision-making while buying food products. *Ekonomika Poljoprivrede*, *66*(1), 107–126. doi:10.5937/ekoPolj1901107P

Popovic, I., Bossink, B. A., & van der Sijde, P. C. (2019). Factors influencing consumers' decision to purchase food in environmentally friendly packaging: What do we know and where do we go from here? *Sustainability (Basel)*, *11*(24), 7197. doi:10.3390/su11247197

Qayyum, A., Jamil, R. A., & Sehar, A. (2023). Impact of green marketing, greenwashing and green confusion on green brand equity. *Spanish Journal of Marketing-ESIC*, *27*(3), 286–305. doi:10.1108/SJME-03-2022-0032

Ramesh, M. (2020). Impact Of Packaging On The Purchase Decision Of Consumers: A Special Reference To The Online Purchase Of Green Products. *Journal of Engineering Sciences, 11*(1).

Sandeepani, D. M. M., & Samaraweera, G. C. (2021). How green marketing tools shape consumer purchase behavior. *Tropical Agricultural Research and Extention*, *24*(3), 206. doi:10.4038/tare.v24i3.5523

Scholer, A. A., & Miele, D. B. (2016). The role of metamotivation in creating task-motivation fit. *Motivation Science*, *2*(3), 171–197. doi:10.1037/mot0000043

Scott, L., & Vigar-Ellis, D. (2014). Consumer understanding, perceptions and behaviours with regard to environmentally friendly packaging in a developing nation. *International Journal of Consumer Studies*, *38*(6), 642–649. doi:10.1111/ijcs.12136

Sekar, K. C., Thapliyal, N., Pandey, A., Joshi, B., Mukherjee, S., Bhojak, P., & Bahukhandi, A. (2023). *Plant species diversity and density patterns along altitude gradient covering high-altitude alpine regions of west Himalaya*. Geology, Ecology, and Landscapes. doi:10.1080/24749508.2022.2163606

Seo, J. Y., & Scammon, D. L. (2017). Do green packages lead to misperceptions? The influence of package colors on consumers' perceptions of brands with environmental claims. *Marketing Letters*, *28*(3), 357–369. doi:10.1007/s11002-017-9420-y

Seo, S., Ahn, H. K., Jeong, J., & Moon, J. (2016). Consumers' attitude toward sustainable food products: Ingredients vs. Packaging. *Sustainability (Basel), 8*(10), 1073. doi:10.3390/su8101073

Silva, G., Ramos, S. F., Campilho, R. D. S. G., & Fonseca, A. M. (2020). ScienceDirect ScienceDirect Eco-Design Eco-Design and and Sustainability Sustainability in in Packaging: Packaging: A A Survey. *Procedia Manufacturing, 38*(2019), 1741–1749. doi:10.1016/j.promfg.2020.01.097

Singh, A., Sharma, P. K., & Malviya, R. (2011). Eco friendly pharmaceutical packaging material. *World Applied Sciences Journal, 14*(11), 1703–1716.

Su, D. N., Duong, T. H., Thanh, M., Dinh, T., Nguyen-phuoc, D. Q., & Johnson, L. W. (2020). Jo ur l P re of. *Journal of Cleaner Production, 123683*. Advance online publication. doi:10.1016/j.jclepro.2020.123683

Veflen, N., Velasco, C., & Kraggerud, H. (2023). Signalling taste through packaging: The effects of shape and colour on consumers' perceptions of cheeses. *Food Quality and Preference, 104*, 104742. doi:10.1016/j.foodqual.2022.104742

Wandosell, G., Parra-Meroño, M. C., Alcayde, A., & Baños, R. (2021). Green packaging from consumer and business perspectives. *Sustainability (Basel), 13*(3), 1356. doi:10.3390/su13031356

Wang, L., Elahi, E., Zhou, Y., Wang, L., & Zhang, S. (2022). A Review of Packaging Materials' Consumption Regulation and Pollution Control. *Sustainability (Basel), 14*(23), 15866. doi:10.3390/su142315866

White, K., Habib, R., & Hardisty, D. J. (2019). How to SHIFT consumer behaviors to be more sustainable: A literature review and guiding framework. *Journal of Marketing, 83*(3), 22–49. doi:10.1177/0022242919825649

Widayat, W., Praharjo, A., Putri, V. P., Andharini, S. N., & Masudin, I. (2021). Responsible consumer behavior: Driving factors of pro-environmental behavior toward post-consumption plastic packaging. *Sustainability (Basel), 14*(1), 425. doi:10.3390/su14010425

Yeo, S. F., Khoo, Y. H., Tan, C. L., & Lim, K. B. (2020). Product packaging: Impact on customers' purchase intention. *International Journal of Business and Society, 21*(2), 857–864. doi:10.33736/ijbs.3298.2020

Zeng, T., & Durif, F. (2019). The influence of consumers' perceived risks towards eco-design packaging upon the purchasing decision process: An exploratory study. *Sustainability (Basel), 11*(21), 6131. doi:10.3390/su11216131

Zhang, W., & Luo, B. (2021). Do environmental concern and perceived risk contribute to consumers ' intention toward buying remanufactured products? An empirical study from China. *Clean Technologies and Environmental Policy, 23*(2), 463–474. doi:10.1007/s10098-021-02061-8

Chapter 8
Gastronomy, Wine, and Tourism:
Development of Regional and Fusion Cuisine in Baja´s Guadalupe Valley

Francisco Alberto Núñez-Tapia
https://orcid.org/0000-0003-4771-6869
CETYS Universidad, Mexico

Ricardo Collins-García
CETYS Universidad, Mexico

Mayer Cabrera-Flores
CETYS Universidad, Mexico

ABSTRACT

Enograstronomy has yielded successful results for the wine houses in the Guadalupe Valley by supporting various restaurateurs and establishing typical pairings. The study focuses on four restaurants and four wine houses that attract a high number of wine tourists seeking notable pairings of regional dishes and local wines in Guadalupe Valley. This approach aims to understand the success of such pairings in attracting more tourism to the Valley. Our focus is on understanding the interplay of traditional and modern production elements that contribute to creating a sustainable and productive wine-related environment in the region. Thus, the research scope focuses on identifying the dishes, in combination with wines produced in the Valley, that were highly sought after by visitors between 2015 and 2019, excluding the 2020 and 2021 years due to the impact of COVID-19 on the region and wine tourism. The methodology used for the research is qualitative, based on interviews and bibliographic sources.

DOI: 10.4018/979-8-3693-2149-2.ch008

INTRODUCTION

By the beginning of the twenty-first century, the emergence of a modern oenological culture in the Guadalupe Valley has been catalyzed by the proliferation of diverse wines available worldwide, leading to a surge in opportunities for wine tourism.

Concurrently, the cultural significance surrounding wine has reshaped consumer preferences, heightening awareness of distinctive elements such as varietals, vintages, and terroirs, among other attributes. This cultural shift has fueled an increased interest in visiting wine regions, driven by a desire for engaging sensory and cultural experiences that underscore the physical and symbolic elements inherent in vineyards.

The exploration of viticultural development in the Guadalupe Valley, situated in Ensenada, Baja California, Mexico, represents a burgeoning research area. Its focal point is the understanding and acknowledgment of the ancestral link between vine cultivation and wine consumption in the northwestern region of Mexico. This comprehension is underpinned by significant advancements in both regional and industrial wine production within the locality.

This connection of elements is further enhanced by the emergence of a regional cuisine that, despite being in a gestational process, has already become a driving force for success in the sale and consumption of wine in this territory, and one of its most emblematic elements of regional identity.

Despite its recent rise and relevance, Baja California cuisine continues to search for its own identity, anchored in the use of local ingredients, traditional techniques, and unique combinations resulting in flavors and dishes recognized by residents and visitors as part of a cultural identity under construction.

In this scenario, the proximity between wine and food has become the main attraction of tourism in the Valle de Guadalupe, and one of the most important in the entire region. The perceived quality of this pairing has brought benefits to the so-called Wine Route, both for restaurants and wineries, strengthening the enogastronomic fabric of the region.

However, despite the success of the Wine-Food pairing in the Guadalupe Valley, its evolutionary process as a symbol of cultural identity of Baja California is unknown, making the analysis of the nature, behavior, and perception of the enogastronomic proposal and culture the central objective of this research. It is important to highlight that studies on the viticultural region of Guadalupe Valley are limited, especially those regarding the evolution process of enogastronomic culture. Therefore, this research adds to the scarce background in this field of knowledge, thus constituting a relevant theoretical contribution.

The relevance and pertinence of analyzing the factors that make up the enogastronomic scene of the Guadalupe Valley lies in being able to explain its processes of cultural insertion, in search of generating a framework of productive, respectful, inclusive, and sustainable development.

Primarily, the scope of this research aims to enrich the discourse on wine tourism in the Guadalupe Valley, recognized as a hub for over 60% of Mexico's national wine production and renowned as one of the most prolific regions in the country for winemaking. Through its Wine Route, visitors are afforded the opportunity to delve into the rich tapestry of traditions, customs, culture, and history inherent in this viticultural terrain, partaking in enogastronomic tours and exploring various wine estates and restaurants scattered across the area. The gastronomic landscape of the Guadalupe Valley serves as a cornerstone in attracting a burgeoning number of tourists, with the proliferation of diverse dining establishments—ranging from traditional to haute cuisine—since 2010 catering to the diverse palate preferences of visitors. This culinary diversity enables tourists to savor the regional fare and indulge in a myriad of unique dishes that epitomize the essence of the valley's gastronomy.

To achieve this, a qualitative methodology with an exploratory scope was adopted, and semi-structured interviews were conducted as the data collection technique, in addition to bibliographic, hemerographic, and private collection sources.

Thus, this chapter consists of five sections; The first section presents a historical analysis of the viticultural region under study. The second section provides a literature review focused on the analysis of the relationship between gastronomy, wine, and tourism. The third section briefly describes the method adopted for the research development. Meanwhile, the fourth section presents the main findings, concluding with a series of conclusions in the fifth section

HISTORICAL CONTEXT

Guadalupe Valley presently stands as a major hub for extensive wine production. However, its historical significance in the northern sector of the municipality of Ensenada extends to the early 19th century. The establishment of the Our Lady of Guadalupe of the North mission in 1834 marked the inception of viticulture in what is now known as Guadalupe Valley. This mission, the last to be constructed in Mexican territory, operated for six years under the administration of Félix Caballero from the Dominican Order. It featured storage facilities, workshops, soldier quarters, and a flourishing agricultural landscape with 5,000 heads of cattle, sheep, goats, and abundant crops of wheat and beans. The mission also boasted an orchard of fruit trees and a vineyard, contributing significantly to the region's agricultural and viticultural heritage (Magoni, 2009).

Although in the previous data it is mentioned that the mission came to have a vineyard, it should be remembered that the vines and subsequently the small wine production made at this time, were to be used in sacramental and religious acts derived from the activities of the mission. Also, a fact that draws attention is the large number of cattle with which the mission came to have at one point, a figure that glimpsed the economic activity that would be predominant in this place in the rest of the nineteenth century, where in this area when the mission was destroyed in 1840, it became the main commercial activity until the entry of the twentieth century.

The narrative concerning livestock serves as a window into the predominant commercial endeavors in the Guadalupe region during the 19th century. During this period, the area wasn't primarily conceived for large-scale grape production and harvest for subsequent winemaking. However, the existence of a vineyard within the mission's premises, coupled with the favorable climatic conditions of the Valley and, notably, the abundant water resources at that time, prompted certain individuals to contemplate the prospective development of winemaking. This foresight was particularly significant, considering that artisanal wine production had been underway in the southern territory of Ensenada since the mid-eighteenth century. The confluence of these factors laid the foundation for envisioning a future where winemaking could flourish, setting the stage for the eventual transformation of the region into a notable winemaking hub.

For this, it is necessary to mention that the mission of Our Lady of Guadalupe of the North was built by Kumiai hands, indigenous people settled in the area with whom Father Caballero supported himself to erect it, as well as that, from the same hand of these, it was destroyed six years after its foundation. The Kumiai, a Yumano group native to the region of northwestern Mexico and southwestern United States, near the Pacific, were described as the largest native population group in the area between the seventeenth, eighteenth and nineteenth centuries which were known to be the most radical, proud and courageous group, always willing to defend and fight for their freedom, independence and ancestral values (Bendímez, 1987).

Likewise, this particular Yumano group was characterized by constantly migrating in the area following the aguajes, where they collected various edible fruits such as wild corn, acorns, prickly pears, mesquite among others; in relation to the local fauna, they were dedicated to hunting rabbits, squirrels, deer and sheep to mention a few, which formed for many decades' part of their food diet (Garduño, 2015).

For Father Caballero, they were key for him and his men to survive in the region, since the Kumiai helped them build the mission of Our Lady of Guadalupe of the North, as well as that they worked in it the six years in which it was in operation, and protected from attacks by other settled Yumano groups, and in constant movement, in the vicinity of the mission. In turn, for the Kumiai it was important to build the mission in the area, which in a certain way linked them to settle in it and its surroundings, and momentarily leave their nomadic life to which they were accustomed; also, with the establishment of soldiers and missionaries in the region, came cattle ranching to which some of the Kumiai began to quickly annex to work on the new ranches that were formed in their old lands.

This is how this Yumano group, hand in hand with the activities promoted by the mission, began to become sedentary and acquired knowledge about new cultural elements, alien to their traditions, such as the cultivation of the vine, a new religion and language, as well as forms of agricultural and livestock processes, unknown to them before the arrival of the Spaniards, although without leaving the practice of fishing, hunting and harvesting of wild fruits that had been developing in the centuries prior to the nineteenth century (Santiago, 2007).

When the mission was destroyed in 1840, the practice of harvesting and making wine continued to occur in the Guadalupe Valley by the Kumiai. The purpose of teaching vine cultivation was to obtain wine to carry out the religious practices, also the remnant was sold or given to the natives with whom they began to trade and exchange belongings.

Thus, from the 1830s, in the area that is known today as the Guadalupe Valley, wine began to be part of the food culture of the inhabitants settled in the area that, after the destruction of the mission and departure of the religious orders from Baja California, in the ranches that remained, the planting of the vine on a larger scale was continued and in the family gardens of the Yumano groups, to a lesser extent where in addition to the elaboration of artisanal wine, the Kumiai began to consume table grapes and raisins, as well as unfermented grape juice (Santiago, 2001).

Guadalupe Valley, a place where climatic and hydrological conditions favor wine development, a lot of stories of indigenous Yumano settlements from past eras converge along with the missionary development carried out by religious orders; but in the turn of the twentieth century and with the arrival of Russian Molokan migrants who, together with investors and merchants dedicated to the wine industry, a legacy and oenological heritage that constitute part of the Baja California identity associated to wine making, started to form, take shape, and define itself as the main commercial activity in the Valley.

By the 1920s, the promotion of Baja California, particularly Ensenada and Tijuana, as tourist destinations for businessmen and citizens residing in the United States of America, a country that had prohibited all consumption and production of alcoholic beverages through the enactment of the 18th amendment to the Constitution of the United States, through the so-called Volstead Act, began effective from October 8, 1919, until December 5, 1933, date on which it was abrogated. In this way, U.S. businessmen from the gaming industry moved to the mexican border, who erected tourist complexes such as Agua Caliente in Tijuana and Playa Ensenada in Ensenada (Núñez, 2017); in these years there was an exponential growth among foreigners, who became the main consumers and disseminators of consumption of the wine produced in Baja California.

Although the Baja California peninsula is considered a pioneer area in the production and consumption of wine, whose missionary past brought the first branches were there has been a favorable land for its cultivation, being between regions with a Mediterranean climate and extreme climate, surrounded by the Sea of Cortez and the Pacific Ocean, the north part of the peninsula, where ideal land and the climatic conditions were an important factor for its adoption, the production of wine in Guadalupe Valley, as well as its past roots in the region, represents today a distinctive feature of the regional identity of the residents of Baja California.

Gastronomy, Wine, and Tourism

By the turn of the twentieth first century, the modern oenological culture aroused in Guadalupe Valley, propelled by the increase of different wines that are offered worldwide, has multiplied the opportunities for its appreciation and delight through wine tourism. Similarly, the cultural phenomenon around wine has modified the profile of the consumer, increasing their awareness about distinctive elements such as varietals, vintages and terroirs, among other characteristics of wine. In addition to this movement, interest grew in visiting the wine regions in search of playful, sensory and cultural experiences, which among other contents values elements present, physically and symbolically, in the vineyards.

The cultural landscape of the vineyards is manifested in the work of fields and wineries, work impregnated with history and identity of the terroir, as well as farmers and vintners, the practices surrounding them, the artifacts and knowledge linked to the culture of wine in wineries and production centers. The oenological culture has its origin in the cultivation of the vine and the aging of wine, as well as the trades that emerge from it. The work of cultivating vineyards transforms the natural landscape, assigning areas for tillage, maceration and aging, while initiating productive cycles of planting, care and harvesting, but also fermentation, aging and packaging; with this it establishes a calendar, whose phases integrate cycles of production, distribution and consumption. Of equal importance is to preserve aspects of an immaterial nature, in the landscape of the vineyard, as well as the narratives of tillage activities, fermentation of the grape and socialization activities that lie in the history of wine producers. It goes without saying that both elements are intimately linked and form part of wine tourism, which includes a form of thematic tourism, related to rural and cultural tourism (Elías, 2008) and similarly, in the tourism strategies linked to wineries, the production and promotion of wine converge in the same place, which implies a significant effort to manage the space for its commercial use (Vaquero, 2013).

Thanks to the association of wine with the popular festival of the harvest, known as Fiestas de la Vendimia, more than a sign of social distinction, it is possible to conceptualize the consumption of wine as one of a social and cultural nature, particularly in the localities where it is produced; municipalities, rural areas, semi-urban areas and cities belonging to wine-growing areas. The recreation of the harvest festivals, especially in Guadalupe Valley, were born on the necessity to create new festivals that are a manifestation of the culture of the moment (Torrego, 2002).

The elements linked to the territory give competitive advantages to the wine routes whose characteristics rest on their geography and history, their social and cultural values, as well as ecological, which claim conservation; at the same time, the continuous improvement of the services present comparative advantages. Visits to vineyards, wineries, museums and sites of interest that accompany the wine tasting, can go along with experiences for different audiences, be they family, professionals, vacationers, hikers, cyclists, among others. Likewise, the gastronomic offer, festivals and cultural traditions, renew the opportunity to visit the wine-growing regions.

The global interest in wine consumption, accompanied by the increase in wine production around the world, represents opportunities and challenges for Guadalupe Valley as well as for wine-growing areas in Baja California. Among various resources that this production demands, the role of industrial heritage can be highlighted as a resource that can promote social and cultural values (Gámez & Núñez, 2020), in addition to producing economic gains. The cultural landscape of wine-growing areas is a resource to preserve and protect, and the imperative of tourism profitability jeopardizes agricultural viability, as well as the environmental resources necessary for sustainability. In order to balance the relationship between wine tourism and cultural heritage, it is recommended to act, conserving, recovering or creating new elements, and generating landscape wealth to benefit from its development (Ramírez & García, 2013).

The Wine Route, located in the Guadalupe Valley, in Ensenada, Baja California, is one of the most important and popular tourist attractions in northwestern Mexico. Year after year, tourists from the surrounding cities of Tijuana, Tecate, Rosarito and Mexicali, as well as from the counties of the neighboring state of California, United States, come to travel the traditional route, followed by national visitors predominantly from the states of Sonora, Sinaloa and Mexico City, to taste, learn and rejoice with everything related to the wine industry.

The bulk of the tourism that traditionally arrives in Ensenada, is that attracted to the natural and majestic scenarios that the municipality has, where its large stretches of beach stand out, which have been the main tourist destination since the late nineteenth century, and exploited to a greater extent in the twentieth century when they came to erect tourist complexes stationed in the town. The beach is the great tourist attraction of the municipality that, for more than 100 years approximately (1890-1990), was the main factor of attraction for those visitors who came to explore the state (Núñez Tapia, 2017). However, this changed in the beginning of twentieth first century, when Ensenada began to promote, in a complementary way to beach tourism, wine tourism, strengthening the promotion of the wine regions, such as Guadalupe Valley.

It is then that, with the turn of the new century, the wine route in Baja California began to be managed. For this, it must be understood that a wine route, as a thematic concept, is one where tourist services are offered in an area or region in which the wine industry predominates; it is established and built in order to create an identity of the destination where it is developed having as its central axis the oenological value of the local product, to which are added different components such as the gastronomic, accommodation and historical, which exalt it. Then, the fact of having luxury spaces, implied a sumptuous consumption associated with wine, as is noted in the haute cuisine of the restaurants that began operating in the Valley.

With the establishment of a wine route, what followed was a fast development of wine tourism, which involves recreational activities associated with the knowledge, recreation and cultural enjoyment of a wine territory. In addition to what is meant by a wine and wine tourism route, we must take into consideration that the primary objectives of visitors are to know the traditions, customs, culture and history that the wine territory entails. That is why tourists not only seek to visit the wineries and production factories, but to also know and walk through the vineyards, buy typical products of the territory, taste the local cuisine, and of course, consume the local wine. That is why, technically, a wine route is a tourist product that is developed thanks to a vast business network of mutual cooperation, where the public and private sectors converge in order to offer different tourist services associated with enhancing regional viticulture (Vaquero, 2013).

In the picturesque Guadalupe Valley, which contributes to over 60% of the national wine production, emerging as a pivotal center for Mexican winemaking, the momentum of wine tourism gained significant traction at the turn of the twentieth century. In the early 2000s, a strategic push for promoting the wine route as a key tourist attraction in Baja California took shape. The aim was to entice visitors, drawn by the allure of Baja California wines, to explore the largest wine-producing region in Mexico. Spearheaded by the State's Secretary of Tourism, a comprehensive national campaign was launched. This initiative not only highlighted the opportunity for wine enthusiasts to traverse the wine route and visit regional wineries but also emphasized the chance to discover the beauty of the Guadalupe Valley. Additionally, the campaign sought to showcase the vibrant local hospitality industry by promoting hotels in the town, inviting tourists to savor the delectable offerings of traditional cuisine that define the unique identity of the region.

Likewise, with the promotion carried out by the State's Secretary of Tourism, this same governmental structure financially supported different wineries located on the wine route, to improve and modernize their facilities with the aim of attracting and entertaining potential tourists who came to know the region. The role of this Secretary has been key given that it has become the main regional, national and international promoter regarding the wine production that arises in the state, as well as the regional gastronomy that accompanies it. It was for this reason that, in one of its promotions of tourist offer, the Secretary of Tourism announced that, visitors to the wine route could make an enogastronomic tour when visiting different wine houses and restaurants in the area.

To this tourist promotion, tours were included to the surroundings of the Valley to publicize the sites and landscapes that make it up, in addition to telling them the history and culture of the region in the different sites they visited; in this way tourists could know the natural landscape, history and folklore of the largest and most famous wine route in Mexico from the hand and voice of local agents, since the Secretary of Tourism promoted the training of personnel working in wineries, as in their surroundings, to transmit and raise awareness among visitors of the history and importance of wine production that takes place in the region (Núñez et al. 2022).

This is how the offer of different attractions and services to tourists close to the wine route in Baja California begins, where in addition to visiting the facilities of large national wine houses, such as Bodegas de Santo Tomás, Casa Pedro Domecq and L.A. Cetto, they can meet smaller wineries which have increased in number due to having ventured local entrepreneurs in the elaboration and production of wine; it was noted that, in the first decade of the twenty-first century, wine companies went from 10 to 70; currently, there are more than 150 dedicated to this turn.

In turn, thanks to the tourism promotion of the region, where the manufacture and sale of products made from the vine predominated almost exclusively, the development of industries previously non-existent in Guadalupe Valley was promoted, such as different places of accommodation and restaurants, together with the promotion of tourist tours, that arrive to Ensenada by sea (Mac Kay Tepper, 2013).

In addition, since 2010, the region experienced a boom in the emergence of different restaurants, from traditional to haute cuisine, which are accompanied by various art galleries, museums, camping sites, spas and boutique hotels, where visitors can learn about local history, taste regional food and stay the night. Also, from the month of May and until mid-September approximately, visitors can go to different celebrations and festivals that take place on the wine route and get to know part of the oenological culture as well as acquiring local souvenirs.

On the other hand, this route also offers other products such as traditional artisanal breads, olive oil, jams, a variety of cheeses, among others. In terms of lodging, few spaces are offered that have a high quality in service and comfort for the visitor, focused on sustainability and care of the native nature of the place, which are mostly surrounded by the traditional roots of the vine and wine (Meraz Ruiz 2013).

It is important to note that much of the success of the wine route has been given by the edible products sold in the region, such as those mentioned above, to the regional dishes that tourists can taste. The cuisine of Baja California is known for combining foods from the land and sea located in the state, with various elements of Mediterranean and Asian cuisine, to create typical combinations of the region that, over the years, these dishes have been mixed with the consumption of different Baja California wines which is a key factor to understand the enogastronomic tourism that seeks it and the complementary success for the Wine Route (Morgan et al., 2016).

Regional cuisine enhances the intangible cultural heritage of the region, when combined with the production, consumption and sale of wine, which contributes to consolidate different intangible and tangible elements of Baja California, which lead to generate its own identity alluding to viticulture. This is how, together with gastronomy in conjunction with the consumption of wine, some wine houses have revalued traditional elements and production tools that they have put as ornaments to decorate their wineries and transmit their different historical legacies.

This is a common characteristic that occurs in different parts of the world where different oenological routes have been established, as it occurs in Spain or Chile because, by valuing the tangible heritage, such as wineries, farming utensils or jars, it is when you can find value and identity of a specific region by publicizing how wine production has evolved in a certain area and thus be able to appreciate the affinity of viticulture and sensitize people about the customs, traditions and innovations of their production. That is why, through the wine tourism raised in the Wine Route of Baja California, modern sociocultural and socioeconomic tourist demands can be interrelated, as well as knowing what the wine houses of the region can promote as components of the Baja California identity.

An integral and noteworthy facet defining the identity of the wine route in Baja California finds expression in the vibrant harvest festivals. These celebratory events play a pivotal role in shaping the symbolic landscape where the urban and rural realms seamlessly intersect. The festivities, in essence, contribute significantly to the formation of the sociocultural fabric of Baja California. As these celebrations unfold, they not only serve as a local identity marker but also establish a connection that extends beyond the region's borders. This interconnected identity is intricately woven into the evolving culinary landscape of the Valley, representing a fundamental aspect of the state's wine cultural heritage and the burgeoning culinary identity that defines the essence of Baja California.

METHODOLOGY

Collaborative Methodology: Qualitative Research and Personal Interviews

The methodology used in this research is qualitative, where the four interviews that were carried out to chefs relate to four restaurants that operate in Guadalupe Valley and provided substantial data to try to understand, at a first glimpse, the cuisine and enogastronomic scene developing in the Valley. For purpose of confidentiality, the 4 chefs are classified as C1, C2, C3, C4, and in no particular order are linked to the following restaurants: Malva, Hacienda Guadalupe, Yumano, & Pinar. The personal interviews were divided into 3 segments, or operating blocs: 1) *Characterization of the restaurant*; 2) *Nature and behavior of the enogastronomic proposal*; & 3) *Perception of enogastronomic culture and its evolution*

Table 1. Chefs classification of their kitchens

Participants	Traditional, Regional or Fusion
C1	Regional. The kitchen "*is a regional cuisine, influenced by the traditional cuisine that is in Mexico. We work with the ingredients that you have in the region, with the seasonal ingredient & also work with recipes of aforetime, of the traditional Mexican cuisine with its own variations depending on the seasonal foods (vegetables), the restaurant menu changes but mostly with fresh (natural) products.*"
C2	Fusion. "*Our cuisine is governed by three things, one is that it is a local ingredient, the second is that the ingredient has something to do with Mexico and the third is that it has to do with some personal experience, that is, that we have worked and lived with that ingredient or that technique because, we do not do Baja California cuisine, although they are ingredients from Baja California, it is not traditional cuisine or cuisine from here.*"
C3	Regional. "*Of the physical type, it is a field kitchen that could be similar to a typical family kitchen that someone puts together on their ranch when the family visits.*"
C4	Regional. "*We decided to be in contact with the region to offer a gastronomic proposal, and also a cultural one that encompassed everything, wine, food, drinks. A large percentage of our products are from the region, we use local cuisine, you will not find other proteins that are not from the region.*"

in the region; where each individual described the personal points of view related to the wine tourism and the cuisine they have saw developed in the Valley between 2015 & 2019.

Related to the first bloc, *Characterization of the restaurant*, chefs C1, C2 & C4 agree that the profile of the tourists that they received between 2015 to 2019 consisted of roughly 70-80% of Mexican tourists, for Tijuana, Mexicali predominantly, as well as other states of the Mexican Republic, and 20-30% of American tourists, mainly from California in low winter seasons but is more well balanced on high summer seasons (50-60% Mexican to 40-50% American). C3 stated that roughly 90% of the restaurant clientele was Mexican.

The chefs were asked to try to classify their kitchens from traditional, regional, or fusion cuisines declaring the following as seen in Table 1:

DISCUSSION AND FINDINGS

The majority of the chefs interviewed leaned towards the regional cuisine, as their kitchens intertwine with the traditional Mexican cuisine but mixed with regional or native ingredients. In this last point, C4 emphasizes that they were more prone to trying to get back to the roots of the Valley, when the Kumiai and other tribes proliferated as stated in the following:

"The herbs are collected from the hills as holy herb, rosemary, sage; we have our own garden but we go out to collect in the nearby hills here, we go out with our baskets in search of these wild herbs that they used and still use some of these ethnic groups, especially the Kumiai; then their techniques are also applied to the kitchen, such as cooking with smoke, slow on the coals, the way to salt or marinate the protein, all that is on the menu."

Related to the second bloc, *Nature and behavior of the enogastronomic proposal*, the chefs were asked about their own gastronomic proposals related to the wines of the region, as well as if there are dishes that they served accompanied by wines from the region. In this particular bloc, the chefs were also asked how was their cuisine inserted in the regional gastronomy in developing in Guadalupe Valley, as well as if they had created emblematic dishes in regards to the high in-demand consumption of them, or being a benchmark of the restaurants they work in. The following, are some of the statements we were able to obtain from them in this regard.

C2 argued the following:

"I did not want to be employed by anyone, I wanted to put my kitchen but I had no money to put the restaurant of my dreams and so I partnered with a winemaker, she opened the doors of the winery and suggested me to do something together in summer nothing more, like a grill, which before there were many in the Valley in the summer but, after the end of my first the summer I did not want to close and she did not want to close either because in the end she was selling her wines so we decided to remain open [...] I was motivated to open a commensal, with a good sociocultural level, because the tourist who comes to the Valley comes chosen, in which the tourist does not eat many things, then we opened with a garden menu, there in the ranch we had our little orchard, then we started with that, we approached producers from the Valley, from small ranches, and neighbors who farmed, quail producers too, so the first menu was born and obviously, a lot of seafood from the black market or, shops that bought from local farms [...] Over time a lot of producers approached us, for example that of ducks, rabbits, vegetables, you are getting to know and also more market, more portfolio of suppliers and because that has always been the engine of our restaurant, local, regional or Baja California product. There came a time when 100% of the product was from Ensenada, but the cost goes up a lot when you buy local, organic, then we reached a point that the cost of the menu was very high and then the ensenadense is no longer your target customer because, from studies they have done, the per capita income of the ensenadense is very low. [...] Then we had to start seeing other products that we did have or were so much organic, the local but no longer so local, so artisanal, so we began to evolve to reach that average because we also had an orchard, we raised our sheep, goats, ducks but when the alfalfa began to rise, because all the straw that comes to us is American and suddenly it was pricey and maintaining it the hatchery came out very expensive, it was a very expensive hobby, but you turned to see the animals the nearby meat industries, for example sheep from those place, and no, it was horrible, so was the quality. So, what do you do? You either cultivate it, you raise it or you buy it of poor quality or better not have it, and this is how we evolved from our initial gastronomic proposal."

This experience was a little different for C1:

"We started when we heard from tourists that went to have breakfasts in the few place available in the Valley a couple of years ago, that they had a bad experience with the food. We started with a kitchen, and with a garden, because before there was nothing here, there were people, there was a market but they lacked much produce, then I started the kitchen, I was the founder of the kitchen and I started to cook with what I had on hand because if I ran out of something I couldn't run to Ensenada to get it, so we planted a garden and started with the species, we had rosemary, thyme, chives, various herbs there and I left very early, about 6 in the morning, to Ensenada to bring fresh vegetables because also at that time nobody came here to bring or distribute those products and what I harvested here it was not enough, so I went there and bought everything, brought it back and we started working. This is how the kitchen arose, working with what we had at the time in the season and fresh, so it was something that I have never wanted to change because it represents us as a good kitchen, we do not use processed products or preservatives or monosodium glutamates, that is how our kitchen was born."

C4 did not have a clear comment on this but C3 shed some light on how the started:

"The chefs with whom I started working, owned Italian, Spanish and Peruvian restaurants, so I approached the latter with the pure nostalgia of working with fish and seafood in Mexico City and one of the things I learned in my childhood raised in Ensenada was that the most delicious fish comes from cold waters and the waters of Peru are similarly cold to those of Ensenada. So I can say that in my training there was related to Mediterranean cuisine because of the Italians and Spaniards with whom I worked, a very good training in fish and shellfish in Ensenada, with the chefs from here and because I assisted them in the events they participated in, they worked traditional Mexican stew, dried peppers, moles, traditional Mexican sauces, with European cuts and European cooking styles but with the flavor of Mexican peppers. I think I have a very Mediterranean approach to local ingredients with a glimpse of the kitchens that resonate with them, and if I try to label what I do in the restaurant is to pass on my experience through a filter and say I like this and I do this, for example, I used black beans a lot because I grew up eating black beans as a garnish for steaks or beef because it is the bean that I like, and also with avocado leaves because it tastes very good, and a lot of olive oil and a lot of cheese from the region."

Having been questioned about their first approached in working in Guadalupe Valley, the chefs were asked if they had created pairings of dishes served with wines of Baja California, and they expressed the following as shown in table 2:

Table 2. Have you developed own gastronomic dishes served with wines of the region?

Participants	Creation of dishes paired with local wine
C1	*"Yes. And well, we have created some house wine and done successful tastings already, we have already done the pairing so that when the tourists come we already know what wine goes with the dishes being served and yes, the pairing is a very important part of everything and complement the cuisine here in the Valley. When we design a protein recipe for lunch or dinner, we are very careful to bring the ingredient of the recipe, but that the ingredient is not too abrasive to collide with the wine, so that they are agreeable to any of the wines that we have, that way, for example, at a table of 8 people, one can order fish, the other a ceviche, the other a rib eye, another ordered a steak and the rest can order octopus. So, what wine is everything paired with? We designed 3 wines that are very versatile so that in some way they are pleasant for those types of dishes that I just mentioned. The wines that we sell the most our restaurant and in the winery are the white wine, the rosé, and a mixture of reds, which we design to be versatile; this last one is a wine that has little time in barrel, they are 9 months in barrel, it is a mixture of three grapes, Nebbiolo, Tempranillo and Merlot, and we design it in such a way that it is pleasant for the dishes we have. Those 3 wines are the best sellers paired up with our dishes."*
C2	*"No. For me, pairing is equal to a marriage and you must sell a pairing and as my wine list is not very extensive I do not want to deceive people by selling more and many years ago we removed the pairing and sell them as harmony that is when a wine harmonizes your dish but it is not a perfect pairing. Because there is also a lot of risk in pairing, as in marriage, that is, if it sticks or it could also burst, then we handle it as a harmony and we don't have it on the menu and if someone asks about a pairing then we recommend a harmony. Sometimes it is not even wine per course, but it can be a red or a white for two courses."*
C3	*"Yes. The restaurant always has house wines paired up with our dishes, and although there is a variety of reds, there is only one white, we did not have rosé and so the menu had to be made taking into account the wines available to work with a 6-course menu because by having it fixed, the menu, I knew that the first two courses would go with the glass of white wine or with the light red wine and from there forward."*
C4	*"No. But we always did the pairing with the wine in mind. And whenever we put together a menu we sit down with the glass, adjust the flavor, make the dish and taste it, but we make a small harmony related to the dish and wine, not defined as a regular pairing."*

Related to the third bloc, one topic stood out for the chefs, the *Perception of the enogastronomic culture and its evolution in the region*, specifically in Guadalupe Valley. In this regard, we present the different points of view that these chefs stated, in the following order: C4, C1, C2, & C3:

C4 stated the following:

"All restaurants have something from the cuisine that is classified as Baja Mediterranean but we are not aware of it but we fall into this concept, but not contemporary cuisine. Our cuisine is highlighted by roasted meats, and typical Mexican food. But, talking today about a typical cuisine from Guadalupe Valley is a bit complicated and I even think it will not be easy to achieve it because unlike other places that already have something rooted and traditional, the Valley, and as an advantage over these other places we have adopted many people from outside, many investors, and although there are many people from Ensenada, the vast majority are from outside. There is no clear trend in local gastronomy, and it has been difficult to unify, but the advantage is that there is diversity. A dish could be grilled octopus, tomahawk, tuna, ceviche as the main regional ones, and meat dishes are mostly accompanied by beans with some vegetables, very showy and we complement it with some other things."

C1 stated the following:

"Yes, there is a closely related evolution and the combination of these factors that have turned the Valley into a very important destination in terms of tourism in Mexico at a national level. Obviously, the offer we have of wines in the Valley is of high quality, the truth here is I always say that in the Valley wine began to be made the other way around than in other wine regions in the world. Here the wineries that arrived at the end of the 90's, began making quality wine and the other wineries that arrived after them were focused on making quality Mexican wine and that began to give a lot of prestige to our wines, to the Valley, little by little they became known. [Later] it attracted the scene of talented chefs from all over Mexico, who came to settle here because good wine always goes hand in hand with good food, with good gastronomy, and together, oenology and gastronomy, is a good line that is drawn straight, they go hand in hand but always, some of the businessmen and families that were here always want to privilege the agricultural vocation of the Valley and wine, because wine is what has made this region, not the great restaurant, not a great chef, but the wine, the production of wine because we are in a privileged area, because of the climate, the land, etc., and the natural thing is that the quality wine scene has brought quality restaurants to the Valley. [These factors] attract good tourism, it brings good visitors and that visitor needs to, apart from drinking wine and dining, a place to sleep, and it comes naturally to have those places to stay. In those years [2000-2010] there were small hotels, with 6 rooms, 12 at most, B&B´s with 6 rooms that were already here, well-designed places and so far we are doing well, oenology, gastronomy and hospitality has grown."

C2 stated the following:

"Well, right now we are at a little a small venue, I think we are at the most critical moment in the Valley, or in Baja California in theory, because it is not only this Valley, but also the other Valleys that make wine in this region. We were doing very well, we were going slowly and I told people to come and open restaurants in the Valley but I told them not to get rich, not to make millions of pesos, but to live in peace, live at ease and stay the course. But then these big developers arrived to open these massive restaurants

with very commercial cuisine, to offer another market. I remember perfectly the day [one of those big ones] opened, because two vans arrived with intoxicated people, already drunk, wanting to eat in our restaurant, with their cans of Coors or Bud Light, throwing them into the planters and wanting to go on a rampage in our restaurant. And they saw the menu and literally said: What is this? no hamburgers, no pizzas? Well no. And the best thing that could have happened to us is that they stood up and left. That had never happened to me. Before we had a natural filter because there weren't those places for those people, so those people, that market, didn't come to the Valley. Since those places began to open because those predators arrived, & started doing raves for example, and because they saw the amount of money that was being thrown into the bags, others followed. We were doing very well, we had a very good quality tourist. […] Then everything that we had taken care of began to crumble with the arrival of all these people because the regulations were not heeded because they exist but don´t do matter. So, right now we are half the people who want to take care of the Valley and the other half who want to exploit the Valley. What we don't want is to make a Tulum here [Yucatán], we don't want to make a Rosarito Spring Break because in the end wine is culture and wine is not a high-grade alcoholic beverage, so in order to get intoxicated as those people want, it's that other drinks have entered the Valley and that today people that arrive at the wineries are asking for things that are not wine, then that is what we do not want, [because you are saying that] your wine is not good enough to drink it in a glass that you have to add Sprite to make a sangria. So what is happening right now? We are waiting to see what route the local authorities are going to take. If the next one [mayor of Ensenada] enters and is in favor of the Valley, it could go very well for us and if not, it could end up going very badly for us."

Finally, C3 stated the following:

"Well, I think that from that equation [enogastronomic culture and its evolution in the region] the first was wine, wine brought food and that pair brought tourism. I think that first the wine ran on its own and teamed up with the food and those 2 ran on their own for a while, designing, for example, the wine and the bottle, as well as a school of thought about the gastronomy that was going to be served here. I think that food and wine did click much faster than with tourism because the latter still hasn't quite fit in with the duo and I think that the lack of harmony between the 3 is because as Mexicans, we have a very poor idea of what heritage is, of what gives us identity and how to take care of it. When I started learning about native plants, I realized that people don't know how important they are in an arid zone like this, to have water in the subsoil and on the hill close to our restaurant, it is possible to see the Valley in all its extension and each time it looked more deserted, granite color instead of green and although there is a season of the year in which the hill looks brown, there is less and less green and one already knows the water problems that exist, and already having information of its importance and using it gave me the need to tell more people of how much you want your business to grow so that the landscape you want your clients to see is maintained, the landscape through which your clients come to sit here, and these ideas occurred to me when I discovered other new destinations in the Valley and saw places covered in granite, or grass, or had a fountain where the water was just splashing and evaporating in the sun and I was wondering, are we putting too much water on this grass and that is why I can't develop my own orchard? Because in the end that water is also mine, we are both grabbing it from the same subsoil and I was stressed by the need to want to do something else and I felt like part of the problem and not of the solutions and I am not going to lie to you, this grown exponentially and is growing more and more with projects of this type that are not aware of what is happening in the community where they come to

do business, they do not see this community as their home, as the home they are going to inherit their children and that is the patrimony of a family and that if this continues to grow in the stupid way that tourism projects grow in Mexico eventually the water and the landscape will run its course badly. The people who come to see this landscape are going to stop coming and the people who do not come to see this type of landscape are the ones who are going to continue coming and, who do you want to serve? What kind of house do you want to leave your family? […] There are many people interested in the well-being of the Valley and there are efforts to try to make things more environmentally friendly but not all the world sees it as necessary, as the economic interest is above this vision of the future, but only for people who want things to happen in the friendliest way. What threats do I see? What I see is that people are well divided and are not looking for the points in common that they have, there is a mutual pointing out of those who are very ecologists and those who are not and are very commercial, like to hold massive events and very late and if they do not accept each other with their differences and fight for things that are common, this is going to go downhill. I think there is a very stupid mindset on the part of the municipality that is hitting the industry very hard and the truth is that everyone is right, it's the worst. Also, water is a major problem. Look, we all thought that water was going to be what was going to limit growth, but right now, even though we lack water, growth continues. In the last 15 years everyone has made their wells deeper. They have been wanting to pipe Tijuana's gray water and bring it here for a few years now. If we were in Switzerland this would not be a bad idea, but we are not in Switzerland. Who is really going to guarantee that this water arrives clean? If it doesn't arrive clean and you put it in, you're going to ruin the Valley but there are still people who support doing that because they want to have a larger production of wine when they could dedicate themselves to making a more limited production of wine, of much higher quality and sell it to a selective clientele and not to hordes of people. I do not know. I think that in reality there is no remedy, that what remains for us is to take care of the parts that can still be taken care of, the little nature that remains and try to raise awareness, but it is very slow."

CONCLUSIONS AND FUTURE RESEARCH

As stated in the methodology section of this paper, there is a different mindset regarding what we understand as the cuisine that is developing in Guadalupe Valley, and for the most part, grew in consideration with the arrival of more restaurants, wineries and tourists that seek them. The personal interviews shed some similarities and big contrasts as well. For instance, in the first operation bloc related to *Characterization of the restaurant*, 3 out of the 4 chefs interviewed for this research stated that they follow a regional cuisine, based mostly on traditional recipes, and only one chef, C2, that they preferred a fusion cuisine, that even though they use almost all of the ingredients from the region, for them, it is not something created wholeheartedly form the regional sense, but a mixture of different factors, as C2 stated in his answer shown in Table 1.

In regards to the second bloc, where the chefs were asked about the *Nature and behavior of the eno-gastronomic proposal*, a part of shining some light on how they started working in the Valley, they were divided in how they paired up their dishes with the local wine of their region, as C1 & C4 rely on these methods to create and serve their dishes, as in contrast to C2 & C4 who prefer not to pair them, but create a harmony between what they serve to eat and drink. This information became relevant finding as one of the mainstays of quality cuisine associated with wine, always tries to pair, in the most perfect way, how both (food & wine) intertwine with one and other, where most chefs that work with different kinds of wine strive to pair up their dishes in sync with the wines that accompanied them. But shown in this research, some chefs are opting to not create the perfect pairing, between wine & food, but a harmony, as they called it, were the flavors don't match sometimes accordingly, but are good enough for the tourists that are not that much familiarized on how food should be accompany by with wines.

As for the last bloc, *Perception of enogastronomic culture and its evolution in the region*, this question poised different answers as C1 & C4 were mostly in favor of a growth in developing services that accompany pairing of dishes with wine, like places where tourists can stay in the Valley as to C2 & C3 were more critical of the outburst growth Guadalupe Valley has experienced since 2015, were, in their mindset, the lack of organization, lack of regulations, and unfriendly development for not taking care of the landscape associated with geographical features of the Valley, mostly related to the agricultural development of wine-making, is changing the scenery in bad a way.

The intermediate outcome of the results we have obtained from the interviews of the 4 chefs that work in successful restaurants in Guadalupe Valley gave us a glimpse of the enogastronomic scene that is developing since 2015 in this region, and although COVID-19 create a halt on the tourism flow and development in recent years, since the start of 2022 various activities have resumed with a steadier and frequent movement of tourists to the Valley. Future research is needed to get a general sense of the activities related to the cuisine and pairings with regional wines that are happening in the Valley, as well as to try to understand the controversy regarding the rapid development, its pros & cons as well as if the issue of the lack of water will interfere and cause and imminent and irreversible damage to the sustainability of Guadalupe Valley. Further research should also be aim to analyze the relationship between the gastronomic offer that has been developing in Wine Route established in Guadalupe Valley, mainstreamed specially by the tourism sector, and its relationship and influence on the gastronomy consumed by residents of the Valley as well as the rest of the municipality of Ensenada to know if the local residents value and adapt some of them to their diet as part of their cultural identity and heritage. Increasing the number of case studies, and segmenting them based on their nature, focus and dimension, should be considered in order to analyze the diversity of perspectives on the evolution of Guadalupe Valley´s wine and gastronomy route, as to incorporating more case studies that take into account both small traditional restaurants as well as those with gourmet or innovative cuisines from a broader perspective.

REFERENCES

Bendímez Patterson, J. (1987, September – December). Antecedentes históricos de los indígenas de Baja California. *Estudios Fronterizos (México)*, *5*(14), 11–46. doi:10.21670/ref.1987.14.a01

Elías, L. (2008). Paisaje del viñedo: Patrimonio y recurso. *Pasos (El Sauzal)*, *6*(2), 137–158. doi:10.25145/j.pasos.2008.06.012

Gámez, M., & Núñez Tapia, F. A. (2020). Investigaciones, enfoques interdisciplinarios y perspectivas sobre el patrimonio industrial. In *M. Gámez y F.A. Núñez (Coords.), Y se detuvieron las máquinas. Lenguajes, reconversión y espacios simbólicos sobre el Patrimonio Industrial*. El Colegio de San Luis.

Garduño, E., (2015). *Pueblos Indígenas de México en el Siglo XXI; Yumanos, cucapá, kiliwa, pa ipai, kumiai*, México, Comisión Nacional para el Desarrollo de los Pueblos Indígenas.

Mac Kay Tepper, C. (2013). Hilando fino con el agua y el vino. In J. Leyva & M. Espejel (Eds.), *El Valle de Guadalupe. Conjugando tiempos* (pp. 37–47). Universidad Autónoma de Baja California., http://webfc.ens.uabc.mx/documentos/El Valle de Guadalupe.pdf

Magoni, C. (2009). *Historia de la Vid y el Vino en Baja California*. Universidad Iberoamericana.

Meraz Ruiz, L. (2013). La trascendencia histórica de la zona vitivinícola de Baja California. *Multidisciplinaria, 16*, 66–87. http://www.revistas.unam.mx/index.php/multidisciplina/article/view/50080

Morgan, J., Cuamea, O., & Minaverry, C. (2016). El enoturismo en México: comportamiento de viaje y patrones de consumo en la ruta del vino, Baja California. *RED Sociales, 3*(6), 73–98. http://www.redsocialesunlu.net/wp-content/uploads/2016/10/RSOC017-004-Morgan-Medina-J.-

Núñez Tapia, F. A. (2017). Jack Dempsey's Hotel in Baja California: The Playa Ensenada. *The Journal of San Diego History*, *63*, 147–170. https://sandiegohistory.org/journal/2018/march/summer-2017-2/

Núñez Tapia, F. A., Cabrera-Flores, M., Sánchez López, J., & Collins García, R. (2022). Ruta del vino y fiestas de la vendimia: expresiones de la vocación enoturística, el patrimonio cultural y la identidad bajacaliforniana. In A. Vázquez, N. Borrego, A. Herrera, & E. Sánchez (Eds.), *La industria vitivinícola mexicana en el siglo XXI: retos económicos, sociales y ambientales* (pp. 509–536). Centro de Investigación y Asistencia en Tecnología y Diseño del Estado de Jalisco A.C.

Ramírez, L., & García, I. (2013). Los paisajes de la vid en Ribera del Guadiana como recurso turístico. In S. Pérez & J. Blánquez (Eds.), *Patrimonio cultural de la vid y el vino* (pp. 307–3017). Universidad Autónoma de Madrid.

Santiago Guerrero, B. (2001). La industria vitivinícola en el Valle de Guadalupe, de 1956 a nuestros días. In P. R. David & A. S. O. José (Eds.), *Memoria del primer simposio Baja California en el siglo XX. Una reflexión histórica*. Universidad Autónoma de Baja California/Sociedad Histórica de Tijuana/Seminario de Historia de Baja California.

Santiago Guerrero, B. (2007). *Genealogía e la migración y la comunidad kumiai de San José de la Zorra. El Valle de Guadalupe, Ensenada, Baja California. Miguel Olmos (coord.) Antropología de las fronteras. Alteridad, historia e identidad más allá de la línea*. El Colegio de la Frontera Norte/Miguel Ángel Porrúa.

Torrego, F. (2002). Las fiestas populares en la oferta turística cultural. In *Boletín de la Real Sociedad Geográfica* (pp. 325–339). Real Sociedad Geográfica., https://realsociedadgeografica.com/wp-content/uploads/2018/02/BOLETIN-RSG-2001-2002-CXXXVII-CXXXVIII.pdf

Vaquero, D. (2013). Rutas del Vino de España, o el arte de conocer y experimentar el patrimonio de la vid y el vino. In S. Pérez & J. Blánquez (Eds.), *Patrimonio cultural de la vid y el vino* (pp. 293–305). Universidad Autónoma de Madrid.

KEY TERMS AND DEFINITIONS

Enogastronomic: experience that blends culinary and oenological aspects.

Enotourism: it is a form of tourism that focuses on exploring wine regions, as well as visiting wineries and vineyards.

Ensenadense: This refers to a person, aspect, or characteristic related to the city of Ensenada.

Harvest Festivals: Celebrations that take place at the end of the wine harvest, intended to celebrate a successful conclusion.

Oenological Culture: Abset of knowledge, practices, traditions, and values related to the production and appreciation of wine.

Wine CULTURAL HERITAGE: This focuses on the cultural, historical, and traditional elements associated with a specific region dedicated to wine production.

Wine Route: The action of touring regions dedicated to wine production in a tourist manner.

Chapter 9
Green Innovation in Wine Tourism:
Insights From the Spanish Wine Sector

Javier Martínez Falcó
https://orcid.org/0000-0001-9004-5816
University of Alicante, Spain & Stellenbosch University, South Afric

Eduardo Sánchez-García
https://orcid.org/0000-0002-8524-4906
University of Alicante, Spain

Bartolomé Marco-Lajara
https://orcid.org/0000-0001-8811-9118
University of Alicante, Spain

Luis A. Millán-Tudela
https://orcid.org/0000-0003-3669-9960
University of Alicante, Spain

Cristina Raluca Gh. Popescu
https://orcid.org/0000-0002-5876-0550
University of Bucharest, Romania & The Bucharest University of Economic Studies, Romania

ABSTRACT

The purpose of this study is to investigate how wine tourism influences the adoption of environmentally friendly product and process innovations by Spanish wineries. The research includes control variables like the winery's age, its size, and its association with a Protected Designation of Origin (PDO) to accurately delineate cause-effect relationships. A conceptual model, grounded in existing literature, forms the basis of this study and is empirically examined through Partial Least Squares Structural Equation Modeling (PLS-SEM), drawing on data from 202 Spanish wineries. The results demonstrate that wine tourism substantially and positively impacts the development of green products and process innovations. This research contributes to academic discourse in several ways. It enhances the understanding of the beneficial outcomes linked with wine tourism and adds to the existing knowledge on the nexus between wine tourism and sustainability. This includes the insight that wine tourism can bolster a winery's capacity for green innovation. Additionally, this study is seemingly the first to explore wine tourism as a catalyst for green innovation. The theoretical model introduced in this research is novel, representing a notable advancement in the academic comprehension of the relationship between wine tourism and green innovation in the context of the wine industry.

DOI: 10.4018/979-8-3693-2149-2.ch009

INTRODUCTION

Since the early 1990s, wine tourism has garnered significant interest from researchers, initially driven by winemaking countries in the New World, as noted by Bonn et al. (2018). These countries spearheaded the generation of scientific knowledge in this research area. However, Old World wine-producing countries are increasingly recognizing the role of wine tourism in mitigating domestic wine consumption decline and reliance on wine exports, as Gómez et al. (2019) have pointed out. Additionally, this activity is acknowledged as an opportunity for diversification in the wine business and meeting new market demands in an environment that is competitive, technological, and international.

Australia, ranking as the fifth largest wine-producing region globally, attracts over eight million tourists to its wineries annually, including more than one million international wine tourists, a figure that has seen a threefold increase over two decades (Wine Australia, 2020). In the United States, California's Napa Valley alone contributed $54.8 billion to the state economy and supported 875,000 direct and indirect jobs in 2021 (Wine Institute, 2021). In Spain, the focus of this research, wine tourism is strategically important for winery management, attracting over one and a half million wine tourists in 2021 through its 34 wine routes (Wine Routes Tourism Observatory, 2021).

Wine tourism is conceptualized diversely. Some academics, like Bruwer and Alant (2009), view it as a journey aimed at exploring wineries, wine regions, and local traditions. Others, such as Getz and Brown (2006), regard it as a cultural experience where wine and heritage intertwine, a strategy for regional development, and a channel for wine distribution. In this study, wine tourism is perceived as an activity linked to the enjoyment of vineyards, wine, and wineries, aiming to enhance the competitiveness of wineries (acting as a direct wine sales channel), support territorial development (benefiting the area where the activity occurs), and foster innovation (by offering new products to the market).

According to Gómez et al. (2019), current research on wine tourism encompasses several key areas: territorial development, wine routes, the behavior of wine tourists, the wine tasting and winery experience, the development of theoretical models, wine-related events and festivals, and strategies for wine marketing and promotion. Wine tourism can also boost a winery's innovation capacity, necessitating the modernization of equipment, adaptation to new trends, enhancement of wine quality, commercial skills improvement, and creation of tourism products, as Booyens (2020) suggests. Despite its significance, the link between wine tourism and organizational innovation remains underexplored in literature, even though this relationship is crucial for the future viability of wineries and their respective regions. This research seeks to bridge this gap, exploring the connection between wine tourism and sustainability, specifically examining if wine tourism influences the development of green product and process innovations in wineries.

In the competitive global market, wineries face the challenge of innovating to sustain a competitive edge over time, a point emphasized by Fernández-Olmos et al. (2021). Innovation in the wine sector is increasingly aligning with environmental management principles. Innovations related to environmental protection can enhance the economic, social, and environmental profitability of wineries and combat challenges like water scarcity, energy shortages, and global warming, thus ensuring the sector's survival, as indicated by Signori et al. (2017). Wineries are recognized as developing green innovations when they show sustainable behavior through radical or incremental improvements in their products and/or processes, thereby enhancing competitiveness while benefiting the environment and society (Booyens, 2020).

Green product innovations in wine tourism encompass goods and services significantly improved to benefit the environment and activities that engage wine tourists in the wine region, raising their environmental awareness, as Baird et al. (2022) have noted. Green process innovations, on the other hand, involve the development of new or improved production methods to enhance productivity and resource efficiency, often linked with the adoption of new technologies that optimize organizational processes, as discussed by Baird et al. (2018).

The evolving demands of wine tourists necessitate continuous innovation for wineries' survival, as noted by Sigala (2023). The increasing sophistication of wine tourists' expectations has spurred wineries to innovate, modernize, and adapt their practices to contemporary challenges, a trend identified by Alonso et al. (2022). Wine tourists are becoming more environmentally conscious, showing a preference for sustainable practices in wineries and the purchase of organic, natural, and biodynamic wines, as indicated by Szolnoki and Tafel (2022). Consequently, wineries are increasingly focusing on ecological innovations that not only adapt to environmental needs but also cater to the preferences of wine tourists, as Angelova and Pastarmadzhieva (2020) have observed. Despite the growing importance of this area, there appears to be a lack of empirical studies examining the influence of wine tourism on fostering green innovations. This study aims to fill this gap by proposing and testing a theoretical model using structural equation modeling.

This research enriches academic literature in several aspects. Firstly, it enhances the understanding of the benefits associated with wine tourism. Secondly, it contributes to the discourse on the link between wine tourism and sustainability, positing that this form of tourism can augment the capacity for ecological innovation. Thirdly, it appears to be the first to analyze wine tourism as a driving force for green innovation. Finally, the theoretical model introduced in this study is novel, representing a significant contribution to scientific knowledge.

To address the research question, the paper is structured as follows: after the introduction, section 2 examines the relationship between wine tourism and green innovation. Section 3 describes the methodology employed to meet the study's objectives. Section 4 details the main findings, and section 5 concludes with the key takeaways, limitations, and directions for future research.

TOURISM AND WINE PRODUCTION: A PERFECT SYMBIOSIS

This section is divided into two subsections. First, it reflects on the potential benefits that wineries can achieve by offering wine tourism activities and, subsequently, it analyses the effect of this activity on the wineries' green innovation capacity.

Wine Tourism and its Benefits

The development of wine tourism activities represents an innovative process since a new wine-themed tourism product must be articulated (Giacomarra *et al.*, 2020). Wine tourism, therefore, implies the tertiarization of wineries, which now offer a set of service activities complementary to the main activity: wine production (Carlsen, 2004; Smyczek *et al.*, 2020; Brochado *et al.*, 2021).

Current tourism activity shows a clear evolution towards more frequent and shorter trips, so that travelers, in addition to the demand for mature sun and beach destinations, are increasingly looking for new experiences (Martínez-Falcó *et al.*, 2023a-j; Martínez-Falcó *et al.*, 2024a-b). To meet these new patterns in tourism demand, public and private agents have begun to create new tourism products linked to heritage conservation and gastronomic enjoyment (Serra-Cantallops *et al.*, 2021). In this sense, it should be noted that tourists are increasingly interested in the gastronomic offer of the territories they visit and, within this, in everything related to the world of wine (Gu *et al.*, 2020).

The symbiosis between wine and tourism therefore represents a different experience for tourists, also allowing to promote the economic, social and environmental development of the wine regions where the activity is carried out (Oltean and Gabor, 2022). In fact, any tourist, regardless of their knowledge in oenology, can appreciate the facilities of the winery, taste its wines, listen to the sound when opening a bottle or toast with the right glasses, thus allowing everyone to enjoy a complete sensory experience (Brochado *et al.*, 2021). This means that wine, in general, and wine tourism, in particular, have become one of the main motivations for travel rather than a complementary activity to it (Bruwer and Rueger-Muck, 2019).

Likewise, wine tourism is a new opportunity to diversify wine businesses, improve business viability and wineries' sustainability (Bruwer, 2003; Acuti *et al.*, 2019; Santos et al., 2021). In fact, there are a number of benefits derived from the activity. The literature review identified three main advantages of developing this activity: (1) increased competitiveness, (2) territorial development and (3) promotion of innovation.

Firstly, the wine tourism strategy allows the wineries to promote their main products (wines), diversify their core business and improve their long-term survival (Teixeira and Ferreira, 2018; Bruwer and Rueger-Muck, 2019). Competitiveness through wine tourism activity can be achieved, therefore, through direct sales in the wineries made by wine tourists, obtaining higher margins and adding value to the main product (Hall *et al.*, 2009; Scorrano *et al.*, 2019). Likewise, there is empirical evidence that when wine tourism is aligned with the pillars of sustainability, wineries' competitiveness increases. In this sense, González (2017) points out that the competitiveness of wine companies is closely linked to wine tourism and sustainable practices. In addition, according to this author, the attributes of the wine-growing territories, such as authenticity, can also be clear dynamic elements to promote the competitiveness of wineries. Pulpón and Ruiz (2019), for their part, point out that wine tourism involves the interconnection between nature, technical knowledge and winemaking activity, with the aim of increasing the competitiveness and sustainability of wineries. In this sense, Filopoulos and Frittella (2019) highlight the role played by wine tourism activity to increase the competitiveness of the organization through cooperation, diversity of activities and experiences, as well as through the co-creation of new tourism products.

Secondly, one of the inherent objectives of wine tourism activity is to contribute to community development, especially when it is carried out in depopulated wine regions (González-SanJose *et al.*, 2017). Under the vision Martin *et al.* (2020), wine tourism not only contributes to the preservation of the environment, but also to the economic and social welfare of the territories in which the activity is carried out. In this line of thought, Bujok *et al.* (2016) argue that wine tourism is one of the tourism typologies that most contributes to territorial development, given that it helps to promote wine-growing territories and, at the same time, enhances knowledge of the local gastronomy and the unique landscape of each region. Likewise, hiring workers from the territories where wineries are located for the development of wine tourism activities is an essential measure to mitigate the adverse effects of population, especially considering that, on many occasions, wineries are located in rural areas (Alonso and O'Neill, 2010). In addition to hiring workers, wineries that offer wine tourism activities invest in socially responsible programs and constantly collaborate in projects that favour the surrounding communities culturally, socially and economically (Martin *et al.*, 2020). Wine tourism is also capable of raising tourists' awareness of the importance of local culture, the preservation of cultural heritage and the wine-growing landscape, as well as the identity value treasured by territories with a wine-growing tradition.

Thirdly, the wine tourism activity can act as a catalyst for organizational innovation since it can lead to improved efficiency, modernization of equipment, adaptation to new trends and improved wine quality (Alonso and Bressan, 2016; Vukovic *et al.*, 2020; Carvalho et al., 2021). In this order of ideas, Baird *et al.* (2018) indicate that innovations developed by wineries can derive as a consequence of the sustainable and wine tourism practices developed by them. Therefore, winery innovation is determined by the proactive assumption by wineries of practices linked to sustainability and wine tourism (Grimstad, 2011; Cantino *et al.*, 2019; Rachao *et al.*, 2020; Sánchez-García *et al.*, 2023a-b). Academic literature indicates that the sustainable development of wineries requires the implementation of innovations that are able to balance their economic benefit with social and environmental welfare in the environment in which they operate (Amarando *et al.*, 2019). In this context, wine tourism is a product innovation capable of generating wealth for wineries, society and the environment (Flores and Medeiros, 2016; Crespi-Vallbona and Mascarilla-Miró, 2020). In the following section, the link between wine tourism and green innovations is explored in more detail, given that this typology of green innovations can be explained through the increase in the stock of ecological knowledge derived from the development of wine tourism activities.

Wine Tourism and Green Innovation

Green innovation represents the combination of two activities necessary for proper business management: innovation and environmental management (Borsatto and Bazani, 2021). In this research we define this type of innovation as a radical or incremental improvement of product and/or process focused on saving energy, preserving the environment, as well as promoting waste recycling and eco-efficient design. Therefore, green innovation originates when the organization focuses on preserving the environment as a differential competitive element and, to this end, develops innovative solutions.

There are two schools of thought when it comes to conceiving green innovation. On the one hand, there is a current of academics who consider that this type of innovation represents a superfluous expense which, in addition, limits the free competition of organizations (e.g. Gallarotti, 1995; Wong *et al.*, 1996). On the other hand, from another point of view, eco-innovation has been conceived as an essential element to proactively meet new changes in environmental regulations, as well as the growing environmental awareness of stakeholders linked to the organization (e.g. Chen, 2008; Schiederig *et al.*, 2012; Zhou *et al.*, 2021). The latter current of thought dominates current business and academic thinking, given that the implementation of this type of innovation can increase the productivity of the company while improving its differentiation.

Within this framework, the global wine industry has had to satisfy the environmental pressures of different stakeholders by developing new innovative products and processes to respond to this strategic need (Andrade-Suárez and Caamaño-Franco, 2020; Bandinelli *et al.*, 2020). Green innovation in the wine industry can manifest itself in different ways, including: organic farming, the use of innovative organic compounds for pest control, the development of computer programs for water and energy management in the winery, the implementation of robots to carry out the harvest, or the implementation of temperature control equipment to preserve the barrels (Leenders and Chandra, 2013).

Leenders and Chandra (2013) identify the existence of two groups of antecedent variables that catalyze green innovation in wineries. On the one hand, the authors identify external variables, being those under which wineries cannot influence but can be influenced when developing green innovations. Such factors may include government regulation, environmental associations, market competition, or dwindling natural resources (Takalo and Tooranloo, 2021). On the other hand, Leenders and Chandra (2013) also point to the existence of internal variables as catalysts of green innovations in wineries, these being the triggers under which wineries can act. Some examples of this typology of variables would be ethical motivations, environmental sensitivity or concern for society and employees (Arici and Uysal, 2022). However, it should be noted that internal drivers sometimes arise in reaction to external drivers, so the grouping of factors is not always clear (Marco-Lajara *et al.*, 2022a-d; Marco-Lajara *et al.*, 2023a-d).

In the academic literature, numerous studies highlight the role of the environmental management developed by wineries as an internal factor to drive green innovations, being also important both to improve environmental awareness and to increase wineries' business performance (Bandinelli *et al.*, 2020; Ouvrard *et al.*, 2020; Marco-Lajara *et al.*, 2022b). Pomarici *et al.* (2021) consider, for their part, that leadership is a fundamental building block to improve environmental practices in the wine value chain, as well as to increase green innovations in wineries. Frigon *et al.* (2020), on the other hand, argue that one of the fundamental internal factors driving the development of green innovations is the need for wineries to reduce costs, given that this type of innovation can result in the reduction of energy consumption or the reuse of waste. In fact, green innovation not only allows the reuse of the resources employed by wineries, but also reduces the need to purchase new materials from abroad (Rabadán *et al.*, 2019).

There are different motivations for wineries to develop green innovations. First, this type of innovation allows wineries to reduce their costs while improving their differentiation (Galbreath, 2019). Second, green innovations enable wineries to comply with environmental regulations and reduce dependence on chemicals (Li *et al.*, 2020). Third, the development of innovations linked to environmental protection can improve the corporate image and reputation of wineries (Zhao *et al.*, 2021). Fourth, wineries can develop green innovations to adhere to environmental regulations in order to enjoy tax incentives (Pucci *et al.*, 2020). Fifth, wineries can meet the environmental needs of their different stakeholders through such innovations (Alonso *et al.*, 2019).

These benefits derived from the development of green innovations can be increased in wineries that develop wine tourism activities, since this type of tourism can also include ecological innovations of products and processes focused on the activity itself (Correia *et al.*, 2022). In this sense, green product innovations linked to the wine tourism activity involve enhancing the wine tourists' experience in the winery while promoting the territory and the environment in which it is developed (Karagiannis and Metaxas, 2020). The diversification of the tourist offers by the winery through food and beverage options, accommodations integrated into the facilities or the organization of events are clear examples of this type of innovation (Alonso and Kok, 2020). In addition, this type of innovation also includes the pairing of wine with other food products, such as cheese, chocolate or cold meats, as well as activities in nature that are included with the wine tourism activity, such as mountain bike routes or horseback riding.

Gastronomy, in general, and wine, in particular, have become an essential part of tourism, contributing to the dissemination of the gastronomic, heritage and economic wealth of wine regions. In this sense, Sigala (2019) states that wine tourism can be employed to engage consumers emotionally with the values that wine symbolizes. Therefore, given the growing international competition in the global wine industry, constant innovation in the wine tourism product is a decisive factor for the long-term survival of wineries, given that, on the one hand, innovation in the wine tourism offer will make it possible to attract both old and new wine tourists and, on the other hand, it will increase the economic diversification of wineries (Portela and Domínguez, 2020; Montalvo-Falcón *et al.*, 2023).

Therefore, wine tourism can play a decisive role in the development of green product innovations, since this type of tourism allows the acquisition of external organic knowledge through suggestions for improvement from wine tourists who come to the facilities, while improving the transfer of organic knowledge between the different members working in the winery. This increase in the pool of green knowledge in wineries can lead to the development of organic, natural and biodynamic wines, as well as the creation of wine tourism products in which environmental protection is a priority. However, despite the ability of wine tourism to catalyse the development of green product innovations, to the best of our knowledge there are no previous studies that have analysed this linkage. In order to overcome this gap in the academic literature and based on the literature review carried out, the following hypothesis is proposed:

H1: Wine tourism activity has a positive effect on green product innovation of wineries

The green process innovations associated with this activity, on the other hand, are made up of the information and communication technologies used for the commercialization and marketing of wine, as well as the subsequent savings in resources that this entails (Booyens, 2020). Some specific examples of this type of innovation could be: electronic portals to advertise wine tourism offerings, online reservation systems, the development of electronic wine tourism management systems or the issuing of personalized tickets for the activity (dedications, gift tickets, etc.).

Wineries that develop wine tourism activities transmit the history, gastronomy and local culture to tourists who come to their facilities, since they are not isolated from the social, historical and cultural reality that surrounds them (Santos *et al.*, 2019; Wu and Liang, 2020). For the proper transmission of winemaking practices, employees are trained under the pillars of sustainability so that they can subsequently transmit the organization's sustainable approach to tourists. In addition, the employees in charge of the wine tourism activity must interact with other employees (winemakers, agronomists, environmental managers, etc.) in order to know and be able to adequately transmit the sustainable practices developed

Figure 1. Proposed theoretical model
Source: own elaboration

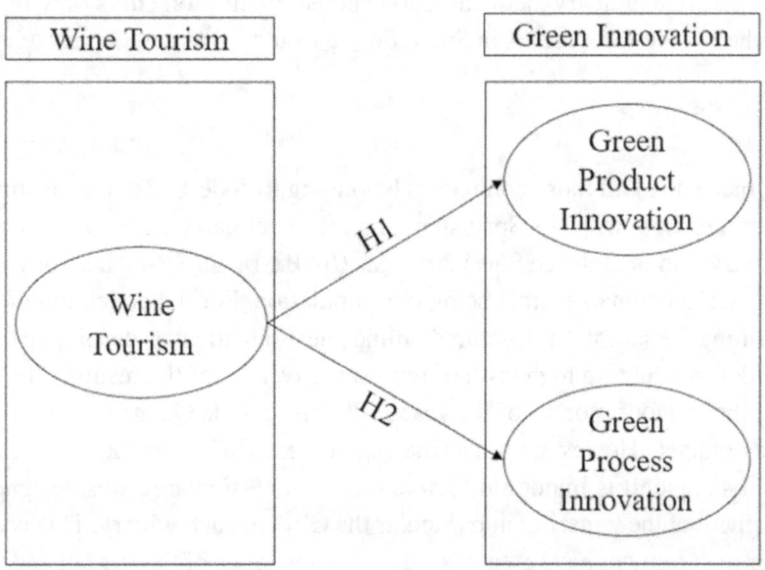

by the organization (Nave *et al.*, 2021). This allows increasing the stock of ecological knowledge of the wineries, thus affecting the green innovation processes developed by them.

Wine tourism can therefore catalyse the development of green process innovations both through the suggestions of wine tourists and through the improvement of workers' ecological knowledge. In this way, this type of tourism can favour the reduction or elimination of polluting materials, the use of alternative energies in the wine production process, as well as the development of new technologies to offer the wine tourism activity. As in the case of the wine tourism-green product innovation link, to the best of our knowledge, there is no previous research that has analysed wine tourism as an antecedent variable of green process innovation. In order to address this research gap and making use of the literature review developed, the following hypothesis is proposed:

H2: Wine tourism activity has a positive effect on green process innovation of wineries

Figure 1 shows a graphic representation of the theoretical model to be tested.

METHODOLOGY

This section is divided into four blocks to facilitate its correct understanding: (1) research context, (2) population and sample, (3) questionnaire and (4) analysis technique. Each of these sections is presented in detail below.

Research Context

The research is contextualized in the Spanish wine industry for three main reasons. Firstly, Spain has a privileged position in this industry, being the third largest wine producer in the world, the largest vineyard surface area in the world, as well as the largest exporter in volume according to the latest data provided by the International Organization of Vine and Wine (OIV). In second place, the wine subsector is the most important after the meat subsector within the Food and Beverages sector in Spain, according to data provided by the Central Director of Companies. Thirdly, wine tourism has an increasingly important weight in the Spanish wine industry, being able to generate 91 million euros only in visits to museums and wineries attached to the wine routes in Spain (Wine Routes Tourism Observatory, 2021).

Population and Sample

The population is made up of all those companies belonging to code 1102 of the National Classification of Economic Activities (CNAE, by its Spanish acronym). After carrying out a search through the database of the Iberian System of Balance Sheet Analysis (SABI, by its Spanish acronym), it is possible to state that there are 4.373 companies, this being our population. For the collection of primary data and, therefore, for obtaining the sample, a structured online questionnaire was developed through a review of the literature in order to achieve a high level of representativeness of the results. The questionnaire was distributed during the last four months of the year 2021 through the Qualtrics application. Initially, 216 observations were obtained. However, after a filtering process, 202 observations were considered valid, this being our final sample. It is important to note that the questionnaire was designed to be answered by the top management of the wineries, in particular the CEO of each winery. This is due to the fact that members of senior management have greater skills and knowledge of the overall and strategic functioning of the company and, therefore, a greater mastery of the aspects covered in the questionnaire. Thus, the observations correspond to 202 responses from general managers belonging to 202 different wineries. The CEOs of the wineries had to respond to the questions and items of the constructs explained in the following subsection. Likewise, it should be noted that there is consonance between the population and the sample obtained, given that, according to the data provided by the SABI database, the three Autonomous Communities with the greatest representation in the population are also those with the greatest representation in the sample, these being: Castilla and Leon, Catalonia and Castilla La-Mancha. In addition, there is a certain balance between the wineries in the sample that carry out wine tourism activities and those that do not, since 57.43% of the wineries carry out wine tourism activities and the remaining 42.57% focus solely on winemaking. It should also be noted that the Spanish autonomous communities with the greatest representation in the sample are Castilla and Leon (14.36%), Catalonia (13.37%), Castilla La-Mancha (10.89%) and La Rioja (9.90%), with all the autonomous communities that make up Spain being present in the study. The geographical distribution is in line with the population under study, since, according to the data provided by the SABI database, the Spanish communities with the most wineries are Castilla an Leon (17.35%), Catalonia (15.64%) and Castilla La-Mancha (11.31%).

Research Questionnaire

To carry out the study, previously validated scales were used to guarantee the consistency, reliability and validity of the variables used. First, a dichotomous variable was used to measure the wine tourism variable, taking the value 1 when wine tourism activities were carried out and 0 when no such activities were carried out. This variable was considered as a dichotomous variable to establish differences between wineries that developed wine tourism activities and those that did not, in order to observe its influence on the development of green innovations. Thus, the objective was to measure whether the activity was performed or not, rather than to measure the degree of intensity of it. To formulate the question associated with the variable, we used the definition of Hall *et al.* (2000), as it is one of the most widely used in the academic literature on wine tourism, as well as because it captures the different characteristics that surround the activity. Secondly, to measure green innovation, the Likert scale developed by Chen (2008) was used, consisting of: green product innovation (4 items) and green process innovation (4 items). Third, Protected Designation of Origin (PDO), size and age were introduced as control variables. On the one hand, PDO was considered as a dichotomous variable, taking the value 1 when the company was adhered to at least one PDO and the value 0 when it was not adhered to any appellation. On the other hand, the age of the organization was measured through the total number of years elapsed from the creation of the company until the time of the study (year 2022). It should be noted that the questions linked to the control variables PDO and age were formulated on the basis of the research of Marco-Lajara et al. (2022a). As regards the size of the organization, this variable was measured according to the standards followed by the Organization for Economic Co-operation and Development (OECD, 2005). Table 1 provides information on the validated scales selected for the study.

Analysis Technique

To test the proposed theoretical model, partial least squares structural equation modelling (PLS-SEM) was used, using the SmartPLS v 3.3.9 software. This technique allows the analysis of a network of relationships between variables, some of which may not be observable, i.e. latent variables. This makes

Table 1. Composition of the study variables

Variable	Questions/items	Authors
Control Variables (CV)	CV 1. Is the winery adhered to at least one Protected Designation of Origin?	Marco-Lajara *et al.* (2022a)
	CV 2. When was the winery founded?	Marco-Lajara *et al.* (2022a)
	CV 3. How many employees does the winery have?	OECD (2005)
Wine Tourism (WT)	WT 1. Does the winery conduct tours of its vineyards, facilities, wine festivals or wine tastings so that customers can enjoy and/or experience the attributes of the wine region in which it is located?	Hall *et al.* (2000)
Green product innovation (GPTI)	GPTI 1. The company chooses the product materials that produce the least amount of contamination to carry out product development or design	Chen (2008)
	GPTI 2. The company chooses the product materials that consume the least energy and resources to carry out product development or design	
	GPTI 3. The company uses the least amount of materials to compose the product to carry out the development or design of the product	
	GPTI 4. The company chooses materials that are easy to recycle, reuse and decompose to carry out the development or design of the product	
Green process innovation (GPSI)	GPSI 1. The emission of hazardous substances or wastes is effectively reduced in the manufacturing process	Chen (2008)
	GPSI 2. In the manufacturing process, waste and emissions are recycled to enable their treatment and reuse	
	GPSI 3. Water, electricity, coal, or oil consumption is reduced in the manufacturing process	
	GPSI 4. In the manufacturing process, the use of raw materials is reduced	

Source: own elaboration

the technique a particularly useful tool for research in the field of social sciences, given that most of the variables used in the field are not directly observable (Roldan and Cepeda, 2017). There are three main reasons why PLS-SEM is employed for the conduct of the present study. First, the minimum sample size to be able to employ PLS-SEM is 100 observations (Reinartz *et al.*, 2009), which represents an opportunity for our research, since the sample obtained (n=202) exceeds the minimum size established. Second, our study establishes direct relationships between constructs, being recommended the use of PLS-SEM in this case. Third, the PLS-SEM technique has been used previously to analyse the wine industry and wine tourism activity, so it is a valid method for our research.

RESULTS

Based on the recommendations of Hair *et al.* (2019), the proposed model results are reported in three blocks: (1) global model evaluation, (2) measurement model evaluation, and (3) structural model evaluation.

First, regarding the global model evaluation, it is worth noting that the proposed model has a Standardized Root Mean Square Residual (SRMSR) of $0.036 < 0.08$, which highlights the adequate global fit of the model. Moreover, the model meets the more stringent requirement proposed by Byrne (1979), who considers that in order to have an adequate global fit of the model, the SRMSR must be less than

Table 2. Overall model fit

	Value	HI95	HI99
SRMR	0.036	0.041	0.058
d_ULS	0.103	0.268	0.329
d_G	0.164	0.293	0.357

Source: compiled by authors

0.05. Once the SRMR criterion was checked, we proceeded to verify if the results of the unweighted least squares discrepancy (d_ULS) and the geodesic discrepancy (d_G) were within the confidence range after bootstrapping. Table 2 shows that these indicators are below HI95 and HI99, which implies that the model cannot be rejected.

Secondly, regarding the evaluation of the measurement model, the following criteria were followed to proceed with this analysis: (1) the individual reliability of the indicators was analysed through their external loadings (λ), (2) internal consistency was evaluated through Cronbach's Alpha and composite reliability (ρc), (3) convergent validity was tested through the Average Variance Extracted (AVE) and (4) discriminant validity was analysed through the Heterotrait-Monotrait criterion (HTMT).

Table 3 shows that all the loadings of the indicators are greater than 0.707, so they meet the requirement of individual item reliability. Likewise, the constructs meet the criterion of internal consistency, given that the Cronbach's Alpha and composite reliability indicators exceed 0.8. The constructs, in turn, meet the requirement of convergent validity, since the AVE values exceed the 0.5 level. This means that each construct is able to explain more than half of the variance of its indicators. Finally, Table 4 shows the results of the discriminant validity following the HTMT criterion. As can be seen, the values of the six variables are lower than 0.85, which means that each construct is unique and, therefore, each of them captures different realizations (Hair *et al.*, 2016).

Thirdly, once it was confirmed that the construct measures were reliable and valid, the structural model was evaluated. To perform this task, we proceeded to evaluate: (1) multicollinearity problems, (2) the path coefficients, (3) the R-squared level and (4) the predictive relevance of Q^2.

According to Hair et al. *(2019), there are indications of collinearity when the Variance Inflation Factor (VIF) is greater than 5 (VIF >5). Therefore, values greater than five for endogenous constructs imply critical levels of collinearity. In this sense, the VIF values obtained in the present investigation do not exceed the maximum value in any of the cases. Moreover, there is no unobserved heterogeneity in the sample data. Figure 2, on the other hand, shows the results regarding the path coefficients, their significance and the R-Squared based on a bootstrap test with 5.000 subsamples. The direct effects of the wine tourism variable on green product innovation (β=0.493; 0.000) and process innovation (β=0.491; 0.000) are positive and significant (see Table 5). Therefore, both hypotheses are accepted. Finally, in order to analyse the quality of the proposed model, the Geisser test (Q^2) was performed, which should report values greater than 0 (Q^2> 0). As can be seen in Table 6, there is an average predictive relevance of the model, since the Q^2 values are greater than 0.25 (Turner, 2010). Regarding the variables, the results show that only membership in at least one PDO has a positive and significant influence on both types of green innovation analysed, since while age shows a negative but non-significant influence, size shows a positive but non-significant relationship. Therefore, it could be interesting to analyse the exist-*

Table 3. Measurement model: external loadings, construct reliability and convergent validity

Construct/Items	Outer Loadings	Rho (Pa)	Cronbach's Alpha	AVE
Wine Tourism (WT)		1.000	1.000	1.000
WT1	1.000			
Green Product Innovation (GPTI)		0.963	0.961	0.895
GPTI 1	0.956			
GPTI 2	0.955			
GPTI 3	0.930			
GPTI 4	0.941			
Green Process Innovation (GPSI)		0.927	0.918	0.803
GPSI 1	0.931			
GPSI 2	0.898			
GPSI 3	0.931			
GPSI 4	0.821			

Source: compiled by authors

Table 4. Measurement model: discriminant validity

	PDO	Age	Wine Tourism	Green Product Innovation	Green Process Innovation	Size
PDO						
Age	0.080					
Wine Tourism	0.260	0.123				
Green Product Innovation	0.263	0.061	0.553			
Green Process Innovation	0.290	0.019	0.545	0.752		
Size	0.065	0.127	0.162	0.150	0.111	

Source: compiled by authors

ing differences in the development of green innovations by wineries according to their size, age and membership in a given PDO.

The results of the present research suggest that the development of wine tourism activities by wineries can lead towards an increased ability to implement green product and process innovations. The results are in line with Grimstad (2011) and Baird *et al.* (2018) who indicate that innovations developed by wineries can derive as a consequence of the sustainable and wine tourism practices developed by these, given that, based on the results of the study, it can be affirmed that wine tourism activity acts as a catalyst for innovations that aim to protect the environment. However, the study aims to overcome an existing gap in the literature, given that, although wine tourism has been analysed as an antecedent variable of organizational innovation, to the best of our knowledge, there are no previous studies that have analysed the effect of wine tourism on green innovation. Based on the results obtained in this research, the catalytic role of wine tourism on green innovation in wineries is demonstrated.

Figure 2. Theoretical model with R-squared, path coefficients (β) and significance
*Notes: * p < 0.05 ** p < 0.001*
Source: own elaboration

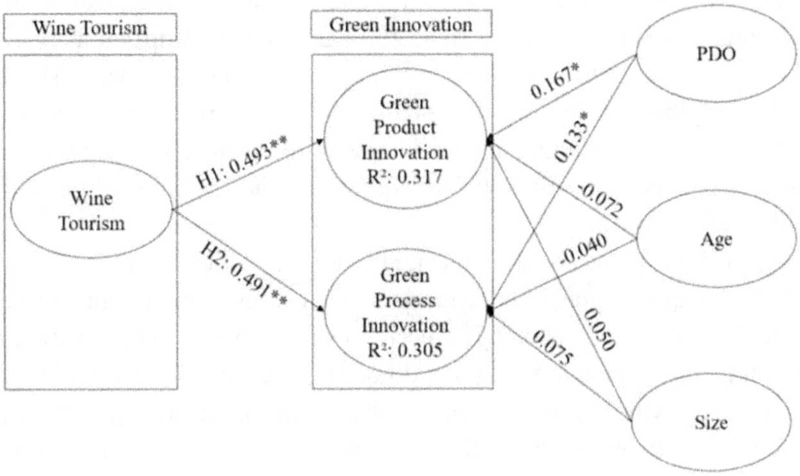

Table 5. Results of the structural model for the mediation model

Direct Effects	Path Coefficient	t-Value	p-Value	95% BCCI	Hypothesis supported
Wine Tourism -> Green Product Innovation	0.493	8.341	0.000**	[0.387; 0.577]	Hypothesis 1 supported
Wine Tourism -> Green Process Innovation	0.491	8.412	0.000**	[0.379; 0.573]	Hypothesis 2 supported

BCCI: bias corrected confidence intervals
Source: compiled by authors

Table 6. Construct crossvalidated redundancy

	SSO	SSE	Q^2 (=1-SSE/SSO)
PDO	202	202	
Age	202	202	
Wine Tourism	202	202	
Green Process Innovation	808	618.336	0.255
Green Product Innovation	808	584.174	0.277
Size	202	202	

Source: compiled by authors

CONCLUSION

This research empirically establishes a significant and positive link between wine tourism and green innovation, making it a valuable resource for both academics and professionals in the wine sector interested in the potential benefits of wine tourism. Wine tourism is identified as a product innovation, requiring wineries to create a tourism product centered on the wine experience. This activity opens up new avenues for diversifying wine businesses, enhancing their competitiveness, regional development, and innovation capacity in a challenging and evolving environment. The study underscores the role of wine tourism in spurring green innovations, thereby boosting wineries' competitiveness while safeguarding their surrounding environment.

Several factors contribute to the positive and significant correlation between wine tourism and green innovation. Firstly, wineries engaging in wine tourism may possess more financial resources, leading to better environmental management. Secondly, wineries involved in wine tourism are likely to adopt eco-friendly practices and convey these to visitors, promoting wider implementation of green innovations. Thirdly, wineries offering wine tourism products often demonstrate strategic vision, recognizing the potential of this activity to enhance organizational competitiveness. This perspective may increase their inclination to pursue green innovations, improving their competitive stance. Fourthly, the development of wine tourism activities can augment ecological knowledge, as employees involved in these activities interact with others and often receive training in sustainable practices, potentially leading to enhanced ecological innovation capabilities. Lastly, wine tourists, especially those deeply interested in wine, can be a crucial influence on the organization to adopt environmentally friendly practices and, consequently, foster the development of green innovations.

This research makes significant contributions to both academic literature and the wine sector through various channels. Theoretically, it enhances understanding of the benefits that wine tourism activity brings to wineries. It addresses a gap in academic literature by exploring the relationship between wine tourism and green innovation, a linkage that, to our knowledge, has not been previously studied. The theoretical model proposed in this study is novel and its analysis marks a considerable advancement in scientific knowledge. The research contributes to the academic discourse on factors that drive green innovation in the wine industry, identifying wine tourism as a previously unexplored antecedent variable.

Practically, this study offers insights for wine managers considering the introduction of a tourism product in their wineries. The empirical evidence suggests that engaging in wine tourism enhances an organization's capacity for green innovation. Managers can also gain an PDO. The research demonstrates that association with a PDO can positively and significantly influence green innovation. This may be attributed to the fact that PDO-affiliated wineries are required to adhere to quality certification standards, which involves developing quality winemaking practices and seeking innovation to enhance wines.

Regarding winery size, there is a positive, albeit not significant, relationship with green innovation. This relation might be explained by the growth in green knowledge as the number of employees increases. Conversely, age has a negative but not significant relationship with green innovation. This negative association could be due to contemporary trends in winemaking and aging processes, and perspectives on wine tourism. While younger wineries might be more inclined to produce organic, natural, and biodynamic wines and view wine tourism as vital for increasing sales, some older wineries may be hesitant to innovate in terms of wine type and have not yet developed their commercial capabilities, making wine tourism a challenge for them.

This research is valuable for policymakers in wine-growing regions, as it provides insights into developing policies that encourage or enhance wine tourism activities in wineries. Policymakers can promote the formation of wine routes in their areas to foster collaboration among public and private entities in the wine sector, thereby creating an environment conducive to wine tourism. This initiative can boost the intensity of wine tourism in wineries, leading to innovations that contribute to environmental improvement. Additionally, policymakers can support the creation of wine festivals in wine-producing municipalities, enabling wineries to utilize their wine tourism facilities effectively. This strategy can encourage wineries to consider or enhance wine tourism, which may lead to the development of green innovations.

Furthermore, local politicians can develop programs to boost gastronomic tourism, increasing the influx of wine tourists and making it more appealing for wineries to develop or promote this type of tourism. As demonstrated in this study, such initiatives can motivate wineries to implement eco-friendly innovations to protect their operating environment.

Despite the study's significant contributions, it has limitations. One inherent limitation is the cross-sectional nature of the study, which does not allow for examining relationships over an extended period. Future research could involve a longitudinal analysis of the surveyed companies, requiring their ongoing participation to track their evolution in a competitive, technological, and international business environment. Additionally, given the relevance of the subject, extending the analysis to other wine-producing countries would be beneficial. Analyzing the effect of wine tourism on green innovation in wineries internationally could yield interesting comparisons between New and Old World wine-producing countries.

Another future research direction is to explore the impact of wine tourism on the green intangible assets of organizations. While this study argues that wine tourism increases ecological knowledge, introducing a mediating variable like green intellectual capital could further illuminate the relationship. Lastly, this research focuses on wine tourism as a single antecedent variable for green innovation. Future studies could investigate the catalytic roles of environmental proactivity, environmental management, and adherence to ecological certifications in developing green innovations in Spanish wineries.

ACKNOWLEDGMENTS

Portions of this work have been previously reported in this research: Martínez-Falcó, J., Marco-Lajara, B., Zaragoza-Sáez, P. D. C., & Millan-Tudela, L. A. (2023). Wine tourism as a catalyst for green innovation: evidence from the Spanish wine industry. *British Food Journal.*

REFERENCES

Acuti, D., Mazzoli, V., Grazzini, L., & Rinaldi, R. (2019). New patterns in wine consumption: The wine by the glass trend. *British Food Journal, 122*(8), 2655–2669. doi:10.1108/BFJ-04-2019-0299

Alonso, A., & Bressan, A. (2016). Micro and small business innovation in a traditional industry. *International Journal of Innovation Science, 8*(4), 311–330. doi:10.1108/IJIS-06-2016-0013

Alonso, A., Bressan, A., Kim, O., Kok, S., & Atay, E. (2022). Integrating tradition and innovation within a wine tourism and hospitality experience. *International Journal of Tourism Research*, *25*(1), 169–182. doi:10.1002/jtr.2561

Alonso, A., & Kok, S. (2020). Identifying key wine product and wine tourism attributes in an ultra-peripheral wine region: Implications for wine consumers and wine tourism. *Tourism Recreation Research*, *45*(4), 469–484. doi:10.1080/02508281.2020.1746999

Alonso, A., Kok, S., & O'brien, S. (2019). Understanding approaches to innovation through the dynamic capabilities lens: A multi-country study of the wine industry. *International Journal of Innovation Management*, *23*(6), 1950054. doi:10.1142/S1363919619500543

Alonso, A., & O'Neill, M. (2010). Wine tourismin Spain: The case of three wine regions. *Tourism: An International Interdisciplinary Journal*, *57*(4), 405–420.

Amarando, M., Assenov, I., & Visuthismajarn, P. (2019). A systematic review of sustainable wine tourism research in asia 2000-2018. *African Journal of Hospitality, Tourism and Leisure*, *8*(4), 2223–814X.

Andrade-Suárez, M., & Caamaño-Franco, I. (2020). The Relationship between industrial heritage, wine tourism, and sustainability: A case of local community perspective. *Sustainability (Basel)*, *12*(18), 7453. doi:10.3390/su12187453

Angelova, M., & Pastarmadzhieva, D. (2020). Development of bio-based economy: Entrepreneurial endeavors and innovation across Bulgarian wine industry. *Journal of International Students*, *13*(2), 149–162. doi:10.14254/2071-8330.2020/13-2/11

Arici, H., & Uysal, M. (2022). Leadership, green innovation, and green creativity: A systematic review. *Service Industries Journal*, *42*(6), 280–320. doi:10.1080/02642069.2021.1964482

Baird, T., Hall, C., & Castka, P. (2018). New Zealand winegrowers attitudes and behaviours towards wine tourism and sustainable winegrowing. *Sustainability (Basel)*, *10*(3), 797. doi:10.3390/su10030797

Baird, T., Hall, C., Castka, P., & Ramkissoon, H. (2022). Innovation, wine tourism, and sustainable winegrowing in cool climate regions: A longitudinal international comparative analysis. In *Handbook of innovation for sustainable tourism* (pp. 167–191). Edward Elgar Publishing.

Bandinelli, R., Acuti, D., Fani, V., Bindi, B., & Aiello, G. (2020). Environmental practices in the wine industry: An overview of the Italian market. *British Food Journal*, *122*(5), 1625–1646. doi:10.1108/BFJ-08-2019-0653

Bonn, M., Cho, M., & Um, H. (2018). The evolution of wine research: A 26-year historical examination of topics, trends and future direction. *International Journal of Contemporary Hospitality Management*, *30*(1), 286–312. doi:10.1108/IJCHM-09-2016-0521

Booyens, I. (2020). Tourism innovation in the Western Cape, South Africa: Evidence from wine tourism. In *New directions in South African tourism geographies* (pp. 183–202). Springer. doi:10.1007/978-3-030-29377-2_11

Borsatto, J., & Bazani, C. (2021). Green innovation and environmental regulations: A systematic review of international academic works. *Environmental Science and Pollution Research International*, *28*(45), 63751–63768. doi:10.1007/s11356-020-11379-7 PMID:33141379

Brochado, A., Stoleriu, O., & Lupu, C. (2021). Wine tourism: A multisensory experience. *Current Issues in Tourism*, *24*(5), 597–615. doi:10.1080/13683500.2019.1649373

Bruwer, J. (2003). South African wine routes: Some perspectives on the wine tourism industry's structural dimensions and wine tourism product. *Tourism Management*, *24*(4), 423–435. doi:10.1016/S0261-5177(02)00105-X

Bruwer, J., & Alant, K. (2009). The hedonic nature of wine tourism consumption: An experiential view. *International Journal of Wine Business Research*, *21*(3), 235–257. doi:10.1108/17511060910985962

Bruwer, J., & Rueger-Muck, E. (2019). Wine tourism and hedonic experience: A motivation-based experiential view. *Tourism and Hospitality Research*, *19*(4), 488–502. doi:10.1177/1467358418781444

Bujok, P., Kempla, M., Porzer, M., Jelinek, J., & Janeckova, N. (2016). Example of the development and changes in tourism presented on historical growth of the city of hodonn. *Ecology, Economics, Education and Legislation*, *1*, 345–352.

Byrne, B. (2008). *Structural Equation Modeling with EQS: Basic Concepts, Applications, and Programming*. Psychology Press.

Cantino, V., Giacosa, E., & Cortese, D. (2019). A sustainable perspective in wine production for common-good management: The case of Fontanafredda biological "reserve. *British Food Journal*, *121*(2), 259–274. doi:10.1108/BFJ-06-2018-0351

Carlsen, P. (2004). A review of global wine tourism research. *Journal of Wine Research*, *15*(1), 5–13. doi:10.1080/0957126042000300281

Carvalho, M., Kastenholz, E., & Carneiro, M. (2021). Co-creative tourism experiences–a conceptual framework and its application to food & wine tourism. *Tourism Recreation Research*, 1–25. doi:10.1080/02508281.2021.1948719

Chen, Y. (2008). The driver of green innovation and green image – green core competence. *Journal of Business Ethics*, *81*(3), 531–543. doi:10.1007/s10551-007-9522-1

Correia, A., Melo, C., & Carvalho, C. (2022). Wine Tourism Experiences: An Exploratory Approach to Innovation Potential in the Douro Valley, Portugal. In *Advances in Tourism, Technology and Systems* (pp. 243–253). Springer. doi:10.1007/978-981-16-9701-2_20

Crespi-Vallbona, M., & Mascarilla-Miró, O. (2020). Wine lovers: Their interests in tourist experiences. *International Journal of Culture, Tourism and Hospitality Research*, *14*(2), 239–258. doi:10.1108/IJCTHR-05-2019-0095

Fernández-Olmos, M., Gargallo-Castel, A., & Malorgio, G. (2021). Do institutional networks affect winery survival? *British Food Journal*, *123*(7), 2478–2491. doi:10.1108/BFJ-09-2020-0836

Filopoulos, S., & Frittella, N. (2019). Designing sustainable and responsible wine tourism experiences *BIO Web of Conferences*. IEEE. 10.1051/bioconf/20191203006

Flores, S., & Medeiros, R. (2016). Wine tourism moving towards sustainable viticulture? Challenges, opportunities and tools to internalize sustainable principles in the wine sector. In: Peris-Ortiz, M., Del Río Rama, M., Rueda-Armengot, C. (eds) Wine and Tourism. Springer, Cham. doi:10.1007/978-3-319-18857-7_16

Frigon, A., Doloreux, D., & Shearmur, R. (2020). Drivers of eco-innovation and conventional innovation in the Canadian wine industry. *Journal of Cleaner Production, 275*, 124115. doi:10.1016/j.jclepro.2020.124115

Galbreath, J. (2019). Drivers of green innovations: The impact of export intensity, women leaders, and absorptive capacity. *Journal of Business Ethics, 158*(1), 47–61. doi:10.1007/s10551-017-3715-z

Gallarotti, G. (1995). It pays to be green: The managerial incentive structure and environmentally sound strategies. *The Columbia Journal of World Business, 30*(4), 38–57. doi:10.1016/0022-5428(95)90004-7

Getz, D., & Brown, G. (2006). Critical success factors for wine tourism regions: A demand analysis. *Tourism Management, 27*(1), 146–158. doi:10.1016/j.tourman.2004.08.002

Giacomarra, M., Galati, A., Crescimanno, M., & Vrontis, D. (2020). Geographical cues: Evidences from New and Old World countries' wine consumers. *British Food Journal, 122*(4), 1252–1267. doi:10.1108/BFJ-08-2019-0580

Gómez, M., Pratt, M., & Molina, A. (2019). Wine tourism research: A systematic review of 20 vintages from 1995 to 2014. *Current Issues in Tourism, 22*(18), 2211–2249. doi:10.1080/13683500.2018.1441267

Gonzalez-SanJose, M. Gómez-Miguel, V. & Sotés, V. (2017). The wine culture, a driver of the sustainable development of wine regions. *BIO web of conferences, 40th World Congress of Vine and Wine*. IEEE.

Grimstad, S. (2011). Developing a framework for examining business-driven sustainability initiatives with relevance to wine tourism clusters. *International Journal of Wine Business Research, 23*(1), 62–82. doi:10.1108/17511061111121416

Gu, Q., Qiu, H., King, B., & Huang, S. (2020). Understanding the wine tourism experience: The roles of facilitators, constraints, and involvement. *Journal of Vacation Marketing, 26*(2), 211–229. doi:10.1177/1356766719880253

Hair, J., Hult, G., Ringle, C., & Sarstedt, M. (2016). *A primer on partial least squares structural equation modeling (PLS-SEM)*. Sage publications.

Hair, J., Sarstedt, M., & Ringle, C. (2019). Rethinking some of the rethinking of partial least squares. *European Journal of Marketing, 53*(4), 566–584. doi:10.1108/EJM-10-2018-0665

Hall, C., Johnson, G., Cambourne, B., Macionis, N., Mitchell, R., & Sharples, L. (2009). Wine tourism: an introduction. In *Wine tourism around the world* (pp. 1–23). Routledge. doi:10.4324/9780080521145-1

Hall, C., Sharples, L., Cambourne, B., & Macionis, N. (2000). *Wine tourism around the world: development, management and markets*. Editorial Elsevier.

Karagiannis, D., & Metaxas, T. (2020). Sustainable wine tourism development: Case studies from the Greek region of Peloponnese. *Sustainability (Basel)*, *12*(12), 5223. doi:10.3390/su12125223

Leenders, M., & Chandra, Y. (2013). Antecedents and consequences of green innovation in the wine industry: The role of channel structure. *Technology Analysis and Strategic Management*, *25*(2), 203–218. doi:10.1080/09537325.2012.759203

Li, M., Tian, Z., Liu, Q., & Lu, Y. (2022). Literature review and research prospect on the drivers and effects of green innovation. *Sustainability (Basel)*, *14*(16), 9858. doi:10.3390/su14169858

Marco-Lajara, B., García, E. S., Larrosa, P. S., & Martínez-Falcó, J. (2022a). Knowledge creation and diffusion inspecialized environments: What are the factors involved? In *Empresa, economía y derecho. Oportunidades ante un entorno global y disruptivo* (pp. 432–459). Dykinson.

Marco-Lajara, B., Martínez-Falcó, J., Millan-Tudela, L. A., & Sánchez-García, E. (2023a). Analysis of the structure of scientific knowledge on wine tourism: A bibliometric analysis. *Heliyon*, *9*(2), e13363. doi:10.1016/j.heliyon.2023.e13363 PMID:36816306

Marco-Lajara, B., Martínez-Falcó, J., Sánchez-García, E., & Millan-Tudela, L. A. (2023b). Analyzing the Role of Renewable Energy in Meeting the Sustainable Development Goals: A Bibliometric Analysis. *Energies*, *16*(7), 3137. doi:10.3390/en16073137

Marco-Lajara, B., Úbeda-García, M., Zaragoza-Sáez, P., Poveda-Pareja, E., & Martínez Falcó, J. (2023c). Enoturismo y sostenibilidad: Estudio de casos en la Ruta del Vino de Alicante (España). *Pasos (El Sauzal)*, *21*(2), 307–320. doi:10.25145/j.pasos.2023.21.020

Marco-Lajara, B., Zaragoza-Saez, P., & Martínez-Falcó, J. (2022b). Green Innovation: Balancing Economic Efficiency With Environmental Protection. In Frameworks for Sustainable Development Goals to Manage Economic, Social, and Environmental Shocks and Disasters (pp. 239-254). IGI Global.

Marco-Lajara, B., Zaragoza-Sáez, P., Martínez-Falcó, J., & Ruiz-Fernández, L. (2022c). The effect of green intellectual capital on green performance in the Spanish wine industry: A structural equation modeling approach. *Complexity*, *2022*, 2022. doi:10.1155/2022/6024077

Marco-Lajara, B., Zaragoza-Sáez, P., Martínez-Falcó, J., & Sánchez-García, E. (2022d). Las rutas del vino de España: el impacto económico derivado de las visitas a bodegas y museos [Spain's wine routes: the economic impact of visits to wineries and museums] In Investigación y transferencia de las ciencias sociales frente a un mundo en crisis [Social science research and transfer in the face of a world in crisis] (pp. 1774–1800).

Marco-Lajara, B., Zaragoza-Sáez, P. C., Martínez-Falcó, J., & Sánchez-García, E. (2023d). Does green intellectual capital affect green innovation performance? Evidence from the Spanish wine industry. *British Food Journal*, *125*(4), 1469–1487. doi:10.1108/BFJ-03-2022-0298

Martin, H., Hernández, B., & Herrero, A. (2020). Social consciousness and perceived risk as drivers of crowdfunding as a socially responsible investment in tourism. *Journal of Travel Research*, *60*(1), 16–30. doi:10.1177/0047287519896017

Martínez-Falcó, J., Marco-Lajara, B., Sánchez-García, E., & Millan-Tudela, L. A. (2023c). Sustainable Development Goals in the Business Sphere: A Bibliometric Review. *Sustainability (Basel), 15*(6), 5075. doi:10.3390/su15065075

Mártínez-Falcó, J., Marco-Lajara, B., & Zaragoza-Sáez, P. (2023b). Corporate Social Responsibility: A Comprehensive Analysis. In Positive and Constructive Contributions for Sustainable Development Goals (pp. 131-160). IGI Global.

Martínez-Falcó, J., Marco-Lajara, B., Zaragoza-Sáez, P., & Gilinsky, A. (2024b). Wine Tourism in the Valencian Community: A Comparative Analysis. *Investigaciones Turísticas*, (27), 29–52.

Martínez-Falcó, J., Marco-Lajara, B., Zaragoza-Sáez, P., & Millán-Tudela, L. A. (2023f). Analyzing the effect of Corporate Social Responsibility on Green Innovation Performance in the Spanish wine industry: A structural equation modeling analysis. *Agribusiness, 39*(4), 985–1006. Advance online publication. doi:10.1002/agr.21820

Martínez Falcó, J., Marco-Lajara, B., Zaragoza-Sáez, P., & Sánchez-García, E. (2023). Vino, Turismo y COVID-19: El impacto de la COVID-19 en las Rutas del Vino de España. *Pasos (El Sauzal), 21*(1), 83–97. doi:10.25145/j.pasos.2023.21.006

Martínez-Falcó, J., Marco-Lajara, B., Zaragoza-Sáez, P., & Sánchez-García, E. (2023g). The effect of knowledge management on sustainable performance: Evidence from the Spanish wine industry. *Knowledge Management Research and Practice*, 1–16. doi:10.1080/14778238.2023.2218045

Martínez-Falcó, J., Marco-Lajara, B., Zaragoza-Sáez, P., & Sánchez-García, E. (2023h). The effect of organizational ambidexterity on sustainable performance: A structural equation analysis applied to the Spanish wine industry. *Agribusiness*. doi:10.1002/agr.21820

Martínez-Falcó, J., Marco-Lajara, B., Zaragoza-Sáez, P. D. C., & Millan-Tudela, L. A. (2023e). Wine tourism as a catalyst for green innovation: Evidence from the Spanish wine industry. *British Food Journal*. doi:10.1108/BFJ-08-2022-0690

Martínez-Falcó, J., Marco-Lajara, B., Zaragoza Sáez, P. D. C., & Sánchez-García, E. (2023d). Wine tourism in Spain: The economic impact derived from visits to wineries and museums on wine routes. *Investigaciones Turísticas, 25*(25), 168–195. doi:10.14198/INTURI.21219

Martínez-Falcó, J., Martínez-Falcó, J., Marco-Lajara, B., Sánchez-García, E., & Visser, G. (2023i). Aligning the Sustainable Development Goals in the Wine Industry: A Bibliometric Analysis. *Sustainability (Basel), 15*(10), 8172. doi:10.3390/su15108172

Martínez-Falcó, J., Sánchez-García, E., Marco-Lajara, B., & Georgantzis, N. (2024a). The interplay between competitive advantage and sustainability in the wine industry: A bibliometric and systematic review. *Discover Sustainability, 5*(1), 13. doi:10.1007/s43621-024-00196-4

Martínez-Falcó, J., Sánchez-García, E., Marco-Lajara, B., & Millan-Tudela, L. A. (2023j). Do organizational commitment and consumer satisfaction mediate the relationship corporate social responsibility-sustainable performance? Assessing happiness management in Spanish wineries. *Management Decision*. doi:10.1108/MD-02-2023-0217

Martínez-Falcó, J. M., Marco-Lajara, B., & Zaragoza-Saez, P. (2023a). Corporate Social Responsibility vs. Corporate Sustainability: Different Concepts for a Common Goal. In Positive and Constructive Contributions for Sustainable Development Goals (pp. 76-87). IGI Global.

Montalvo-Falcón, J. V., Sánchez-García, E., Marco-Lajara, B., & Martínez-Falcó, J. (2023). Green human resource management and economic, social and environmental performance: Evidence from the Spanish wine industry. *Heliyon*, *9*(10), e20826. doi:10.1016/j.heliyon.2023.e20826 PMID:37860533

Nave, A., Do Paço, A., & Duarte, P. (2021). A systematic literature review on sustainability in the wine tourism industry: Insights and perspectives. *International Journal of Wine Business Research*, *33*(4), 457–480.

OECD. (2005). *Oslo Manual: A Guide to Collecting and Interpreting Innovation Data*. OECD. http://www.itq.edu.mx/convocatorias/manualdeoslo.pdf

Oltean, F., & Gabor, M. R. (2022). Wine Tourism—A Sustainable Management Tool for Rural Development and Vineyards: Cross-Cultural Analysis of the Consumer Profile from Romania and Moldova. *Agriculture*, *12*(10), 1614. doi:10.3390/agriculture12101614

Ouvrard, S., Jasimuddin, S. M., & Spiga, A. (2020). Does sustainability push to reshape business models? Evidence from the European wine industry. *Sustainability (Basel)*, *12*(6), 2561. doi:10.3390/su12062561

Pomarici, E., Corsi, A., Mazzarino, S., & Sardone, R. (2021). The Italian wine sector: Evolution, structure, competitiveness and future challenges of an enduring leader. *Italian Economic Journal*, *7*(2), 259–295. doi:10.1007/s40797-021-00144-5

Portela, J., & Domínguez, M. (2020). Las rutas del vino como motores de dinamización socio-territorial: El caso de Castilla y León. *Boletín de la Asociación de Geógrafos Españoles*, *84*(2789), 1–36.

Pucci, T., Casprini, E., Galati, A., & Zanni, L. (2020). The virtuous cycle of stakeholder engagement in developing a sustainability culture: Salcheto winery. *Journal of Business Research*, *119*, 364–376. doi:10.1016/j.jbusres.2018.11.009

Pulpón, A. & Ruiz, M. (2019). *Potential of vineyard landscapes for sustainable tourism.*

Rabadán, A., González-Moreno, Á., & Sáez-Martínez, F. (2019). Improving firms' performance and sustainability: The case of eco-innovation in the agri-food industry. *Sustainability (Basel)*, *11*(20), 5590. doi:10.3390/su11205590

Rachao, S., Breda, Z., Fernandes, C., & Joukes, V. (2020). Cocreation of tourism experiences: Are food-related activities being explored? *British Food Journal*, *122*(3), 910–928. doi:10.1108/BFJ-10-2019-0769

Reinartz, W., Haenlein, M., & Henseler, J. (2009). An empirical comparison of the efficacy of covariance-based and variance-based SEM. *International Journal of Research in Marketing*, *26*(4), 332–344. doi:10.1016/j.ijresmar.2009.08.001

Roldan, J., & Cepeda, G. (2017), Modelos de Ecuaciones basados en la Varianza: Partial Least Squares (PLS) para Investigadores en Ciencias Sociales (4a ed.), Universidad de Sevilla.

Sánchez-García, E., Marco-Lajara, B., Martínez-Falcó, J., & Poveda-Pareja, E. (2023a). Cognitive social capital for knowledge absorption in specialized environments: The path to innovation. *Heliyon*, *9*(3), e14223. doi:10.1016/j.heliyon.2023.e14223 PMID:36923853

Sánchez-García, E., Martínez-Falcó, J., Alcon-Vila, A., & Marco-Lajara, B. (2023b). Developing Green Innovations in the Wine Industry: An Applied Analysis. *Foods*, *12*(6), 1157. doi:10.3390/foods12061157 PMID:36981084

Santos, V., Ramos, P., Almeida, N., & Santos-Pavón, E. (2019). Wine and wine tourism experience: A theoretical and conceptual review. *Worldwide Hospitality and Tourism Themes*, *11*(6), 718–730. doi:10.1108/WHATT-09-2019-0053

Santos, V., Ramos, P., Sousa, B., & Valeri, M. (2021). Towards a framework for the global wine tourism system. *Journal of Organizational Change Management*, *35*(2), 348–360. doi:10.1108/JOCM-11-2020-0362

Schiederig, T., Tietze, F., & Herstatt, C. (2012). Green innovation in technology and innovation management–an exploratory literature review. *R & D Management*, *42*(2), 180–192. doi:10.1111/j.1467-9310.2011.00672.x

Scorrano, P., Fait, M., Maizza, A., & Vrontis, D. (2019). Online branding strategy for wine tourism competitiveness. *International Journal of Wine Business Research*, *31*(2), 130–150. doi:10.1108/IJWBR-06-2017-0043

Serra-Cantallops, A., Ramón-Cardona, J., & Vachiano, M. (2021). Increasing sustainability through wine tourism in mass tourism destinations. The case of the Balearic Islands. *Sustainability (Basel)*, *13*(5), 2481. doi:10.3390/su13052481

Sigala, M. (2019). The synergy of wine and culture: The case of Ariousios wine, Greece. In *Management and marketing of wine tourism business* (pp. 295–312). Palgrave Macmillan. doi:10.1007/978-3-319-75462-8_15

Sigala, M. (2023). Thriving in Wine Tourism Through Technology and Innovation: A Survival or a Competitiveness Need? In *Technology Advances and Innovation in Wine Tourism* (pp. 3–11). Springer. doi:10.1007/978-981-19-8277-4_1

Signori, P., Flint, D., & Golicic, S. (2017). Constrained innovation on sustainability in the global wine industry. *Journal of Wine Research*, *28*(2), 71–90. doi:10.1080/09571264.2017.1302413

Smyczek, S., Festa, G., Rossi, M., & Monge, F. (2020). Economic sustainability of wine tourism services and direct sales performance–emergent profiles from Italy. *British Food Journal*, *122*(5), 1519–1529. doi:10.1108/BFJ-08-2019-0651

Szolnoki, G., & Tafel, M. (2022). Environmental Sustainability and Tourism—The Importance of Organic Wine Production for Wine Tourism in Germany. *Sustainability (Basel)*, *14*(19), 11831. doi:10.3390/su141911831

Takalo, S., & Tooranloo, H. (2021). Green innovation: A systematic literature review. *Journal of Cleaner Production*, *279*, 122474. doi:10.1016/j.jclepro.2020.122474

Teixeira, S., & Ferreira, J. (2018). Entrepreneurial artisan products as regional tourism competitiveness. *International Journal of Entrepreneurial Behaviour & Research*, *25*(4), 652–673. doi:10.1108/IJEBR-01-2018-0023

Turner, S. (2010). Networks of learning within the English wine industry. *Journal of Economic Geography*, *10*(5), 685–715. doi:10.1093/jeg/lbp053

Vukovic, D., Maiti, M., Vujko, A., & Shams, R. (2020). Residents' perceptions of wine tourism on the rural destinations development. *British Food Journal*, *122*(8), 2739–2753. doi:10.1108/BFJ-04-2019-0291

Wine Australia. (2020). *Wine Tourism Snapshot 2018-2019*. Wine Australia. https://www.wineaustralia.com/market-insights/australian-wine-tourism-snapshot

Wine Institute. (2021), *Economic Impact of California Wine*. Wine Institute. http://www.wine-economy.com/

Wine Routes Tourism Observatory. (2021). *Informe de visitantes a bodegas y museos de las rutas del vino de españa. Año 2021*. WRTO. https://wineroutesofspain.com/observatorio-turistico-rve/

Wong, V., Turner, W., & Stoneman, P. (1996). Marketing strategies and market prospects for environmentally-friendly consumer products. *British Journal of Management*, *7*(3), 263–281. doi:10.1111/j.1467-8551.1996.tb00119.x

Wu, G., & Liang, L. (2020). Examining the effect of potential tourists' wine product involvement on wine tourism destination image and travel intention. *Current Issues in Tourism*, 1–16. doi:10.1080/13683500.2020.1828310

Zhao, N., Liu, X., Pan, C., & Wang, C. (2021). The performance of green innovation: From an efficiency perspective. *Socio-Economic Planning Sciences*, *78*, 101062. doi:10.1016/j.seps.2021.101062

Zhou, M., Govindan, K., Xie, X., & Yan, L. (2021). How to drive green innovation in China's mining enterprises? Under the perspective of environmental legitimacy and green absorptive capacity. *Resources Policy*, *72*, 102038. doi:10.1016/j.resourpol.2021.102038

Chapter 10
Halal Food Industry and Sustainability

Early Ridho Kismawadi
https://orcid.org/0000-0002-9420-5212
IAIN Langsa, Indonesia

ABSTRACT

This research investigates the complex and ever-changing relationship between sustainable practices and the halal food industry. Global economic growth has been driven by the expansion of culinary tourism, but concerns have been raised regarding its long-term effects on ecosystems, cultural heritage, and society. Given the substantial expansion of the halal industry, this study seeks to examine the long-term consequences of sustainability on the community, ecosystem, cultural heritage, and food industry. It is anticipated that the results of this study will make a significant contribution to the travel and hospitality sector by promoting the sustainable viability of ethical and sustainable practices in the halal food industry amid its accelerated growth.

INTRODUCTION

Many of the challenges facing the food industry have the capacity to compromise sustainability(Bai et al., 2020; Kouhizadeh et al., 2021; Naylor et al., 2021). Excessive consumption of vital resources, including energy, water, and land, is a significant problem because of its potential to cause damage to the environment. The management of waste and contamination resulting from the application of agricultural chemicals and pesticides is a significant additional challenge. Ecological degradation and biodiversity loss can be triggered by intensive agricultural practices, whereas economic inequality between farmers and small producers can occur due to uneven supply chain architecture. Dangers to food safety, food wastage and concerns about animal welfare further complicate the food industry's already complex problems. The industry's unsustainability is further exacerbated by rising greenhouse gas emissions and the consequences of climate change associated with traditional food production. To address these challenges and advance the food industry's sustainability efforts, it is critical to put consumer awareness, responsible regulation, and innovation at the forefront of the sustainable food selection process.

DOI: 10.4018/979-8-3693-2149-2.ch010

By participating in various initiatives addressing social, economic, and environmental issues, the halal food sector makes a major contribution to promoting sustainability (Rejeb, Keogh, et al., 2021). Limited production techniques exemplify an organization's commitment to sustainability; These techniques emphasize the use of environmentally friendly materials, prudent resource allocation, and low-impact manufacturing processes. Focus is placed on sustainable agricultural practices, including crop rotation and organic cultivation(Meena et al., 2020; Sharma et al., 2020; Wu et al., 2020). Combining a rigorous work ethic and selecting business partners committed to fair social and economic practices are fundamental elements of responsible supply chain management. Further emphasizing eco-friendly options is the promotion of inventive sustainable products, including organic and locally sourced foods. Promoting domestic manufacturing and ensuring that business practices have a direct positive impact on the economic and social well-being of local communities are important methods of empowering these communities. Consumer education on sustainability is becoming an increasingly important component of marketing initiatives that emphasize sustainable product attributes in an effort to raise customer awareness and encourage behaviour modification. Sustainability certification is considered an important measure to reflect the halal food industry's commitment to sustainable principles, including but not limited to social justice, environmental management, and animal welfare. The Responsible Halal Food Industry is actively contributing to the advancement of a more sustainable food industry in the future through the implementation of this comprehensive strategy(Ali et al., 2021; Rejeb, Rejeb, et al., 2021; Tseng et al., 2022).

Due to the significant impact that gastronomic heritage and culinary experiences can have on the local economy and the environment as a whole, the intersection of food tourism and sustainability has gained prominence as a field of study in recent times. This article aims to examine the dynamic relationship between sustainable practices and culinary tourism so as to illuminate potential opportunities for collaboration as well as challenges in this complex environment.

Food tourism that includes culinary excursions and other gastronomic cultural explorations has been instrumental in stimulating economic development in various regions around the world. To attracting a growing number of international tourists seeking authentic dining experiences, the unique appeal of local gastronomy and culinary customs has also given rise to an intricate network of food-focused businesses, ranging from high-end restaurants to street vendors.

However, as a consequence of its meteoric rise, the sustainability and long-term effects of culinary tourism on people, ecosystems, and cultural heritage are of serious concern. The study seeks to deconstruct the intricacies by exploring the correlation between food tourism and sustainable practices, as well as by addressing related subjects such as cultural preservation, resource management, and the socioeconomic consequences of culinary tourism.

To incorporate sustainable practices into the culinary tourism industry, it is imperative to conduct a comprehensive analysis of the entire value chain, which includes production, distribution, consumption and waste management. The aim of this study is to investigate innovative approaches and ideal methodologies that can be adopted by destination managers, policy makers, and food entrepreneurs to ensure that food tourism is sustainable and has a positive impact on surrounding ecosystems and communities.

Through case study analysis, survey administration, and application of qualitative and quantitative research methods, the study aims to contribute substantial insights to the body of knowledge. The results of this study are expected to serve as a foundation for the development of sustainable and ethical culinary tourism practices, thus assisting stakeholders in the hospitality and tourism sector in their strategic decision making.

The study underscores the critical intersection between culinary tourism and sustainability, a growing academic discipline, with a particular focus on halal cuisine. Halal refers to food and drinks that adhere to the teachings of Islamic Sharia. Food labelled halal must be produced with approved ingredients, in an ethical and hygienic manner, and without haram substances. Evaluation of the halal status of a product requires careful examination of factors including sanitation, fairness, and adherence to Islamic teachings.

The food tourism sector has undergone substantial expansion in recent years as more and more individuals become aware of the environmental and economic benefits that culinary traditions and experiences can provide. The halal industry is experiencing significant growth, attracting everything from street vendors to high-end eateries, due to the unique appeal of regional cuisine and culinary traditions(M. A. Abdullah & Azam, 2020; Adham et al., 2020; Azmi et al., 2020).

The research presented here is particularly important in the realm of halal product-based culinary tourism, as it tackles critical questions related to sustainability and its enduring impact on cultural heritage, ecosystems, and society. This study uses a holistic methodology to examine significant issues such as cultural heritage preservation, resource management, and socio-economic consequences of the rapidly growing halal culinary tourism sector. The aim is to clarify the complex correlation that exists between culinary tourism and sustainable practices. Especially with regard to halal products, the incorporation of sustainable practices into food tourism is a major concern. The investigation is expected to contribute to a body of knowledge regarding the integration of sustainability principles into halal food tourism through a comprehensive examination of the entire value chain, including consumption, waste management, production, and distribution. The study's findings are anticipated to provide valuable insights to the travel and hospitality industry and lay the foundation for the development of sustainable and ethical halal culinary tourism practices. The research has significant relevance in addressing the complex challenges arising from the rapid expansion of the industry and advocating for the long-term viability of the halal culinary tourism sector.

The study is expected to make a substantial contribution to the body of knowledge regarding the relationship between sustainable practices and culinary tourism, particularly in terms of halal products. This research effort will contribute to the existing literature by explaining the different challenges and prospects in the domain of sustainable food tourism. With a focus on resource management, cultural preservation, and the socioeconomic consequences of the burgeoning halal culinary tourism industry, it is hoped that this research will result in a deeper understanding. As a result, it is expected that innovative approaches and exemplary methods will be identified in the industry. It can be adopted by legislators, destination managers, and stakeholders in the food sector to ensure the long-term viability of food tourism, particularly in terms of halal products. The findings of this study are expected to provide participants in the travel and hospitality industry with strategic guidance, enabling them to make more informed and sustainable decisions. In conclusion, it is hoped that this study will establish a basis for the development of ethical food tourism practices, thus emphasizing its positive influence on the expansion of the food tourism industry as a whole.

ENVIRONMENTAL IMPACT OF FOOD INDUSTRY

The food industry, being a prominent economic sector on a global scale, engenders substantial environmental repercussions that demand diligent consideration in the pursuit of sustainability(Coppola et al., 2021; Kakani et al., 2020; Rana et al., 2021; C. Tan & McClements, 2021). The industry poses several

Figure 1. Muslim consumer expenditure on food and beverages worldwide in 2019, by leading country (in billion U.S. dollars)
Source: Thomson Reuters (Graph by Statista)

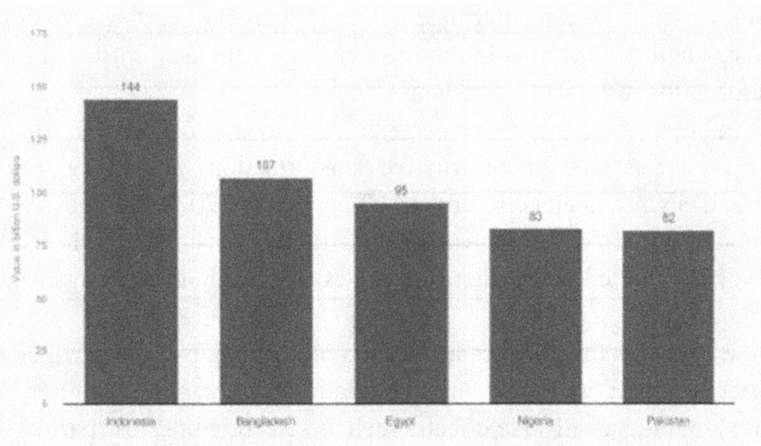

challenges pertaining to waste management, greenhouse gas emissions, production, and consumption, as well as environmental resource utilisation. One of the most significant factors to consider is the utilisation of natural resources. Agriculture and food processing both necessitate substantial quantities of energy, water, and soil. Particularly in agriculture, inefficient water usage can degrade water quality and damage aquatic ecosystems. Additionally, transportation, storage, and food processing energy consumption significantly contribute to the carbon footprint of the industry.

The emission of greenhouse gases, particularly from the livestock industry, represents a significant obstacle. Methane and nitrogen oxides are significant contributors to global warming as byproducts of animal digestion on farms(Fawzy et al., 2020; Mat Aron et al., 2020; Mohsin et al., 2021). To mitigate these effects, a transition to more environmentally benign and sustainable livestock practises is essential in this context. Food waste constitutes an additional concern that demands substantial consideration. Overproduction, over purchasing, and consumer discharges are all components of the food supply chain that contribute to worldwide food waste. Food waste not only contributes to environmental issues but also disregards the resources that were utilised during production.

With 2019 spending reaching around 144 billion US dollars, Indonesia has an important role in the global halal food market which is valued at more than 1.17 trillion US dollars. Aspects of environmental impacts generated by the food industry, including greenhouse gas emissions, water use, and land use, as well as the implications of halal food consumption on the environment also need to be anticipated.

Plastic contamination is a significant concern regarding the use of plastic in food packaging, as it negatively impacts the environment. Plastics that are mismanaged have the potential to affect marine life, pollute oceans, and cause a worldwide waste crisis(Al-Tayyar et al., 2020; Bhargava et al., 2020; Kumar et al., 2020). Important measures to tackle this issue include initiatives to reduce the usage of single-use plastics and advancements in sustainable packaging. The application of chemical fertilisers and pesticides in intensive agriculture can result in soil degradation and the extinction of species. It is necessary to implement sustainable agricultural practises, including crop rotation and organic cultivation, in order to mitigate these adverse effects. Furthermore, irregular supply chain architecture frequently gives rise to economic inequality among small producers and farmers, thereby exacerbating the challenges faced in achieving social and economic sustainability. Animal welfare, food safety, and food waste are increasingly significant concerns that add to the already complex landscape of the food industry. Strategies including the implementation of organic food production methods, effective waste management practises, and judicious resource selection can contribute to the mitigation of certain challenges. In addition, the significance of sustainability education for consumers is growing as it influences consumer behaviour and stimulates demand for sustainable products.

The halal food industry can significantly contribute to the promotion of sustainability in this regard. The industry can serve as a catalyst for constructive transformation by engaging in endeavours that tackle social, economic, and environmental concerns (Al-Tayyar et al., 2020; Bhargava et al., 2020; Kumar et al., 2020). The implementation of low-impact manufacturing processes and the use of environmentally favourable materials are limited production techniques that exemplify an organization's dedication to sustainability.

Increasingly, the transition towards a more sustainable food industry is placing significant emphasis on sustainable agricultural practises, including crop rotation and organic cultivation. Significant measures can be implemented to mitigate adverse effects, such as selecting business partners who advocate sustainable products, organic and local foods, and are dedicated to equitable social and economic practises.

HALAL LIFESTYLE AND SUSTAINABILITY

The adoption of a halal lifestyle facilitates constructive transformations towards sustainability across multiple facets of everyday existence, encompassing consumables, apparel, cosmetics, and dining patterns (Huriah et al., 2022; Nugroho et al., 2022; Susanti, 2021). The halal lifestyle places significant emphasis on sustainability through the implementation of minimalism, the abolition of excessive consumption, and the promotion of durable products(Ngah et al., 2021; Rejeb, Keogh, et al., 2021; Rejeb, Rejeb, et al., 2021; Secinaro & Calandra, 2021). Regarding food consumption, a halal lifestyle can foster sustainability through the recognition of food as a fundamental necessity as opposed to an indulgent inclination. This can be manifested through the adoption of a more regional and seasonal food intake, thereby diminishing reliance on imported goods that necessitate extended transportation and supplementary energy. Furthermore, by promoting sustainable agriculture and mitigating environmental harm, the halal lifestyle instils a sense of esteem for the entire food supply chain.

Regarding apparel, the halal lifestyle can serve as a catalyst for a paradigm shift regarding clothing consumption(Ariffin & Hamid, 2021; Masudin et al., 2021; Rejeb, Keogh, et al., 2021; Tayob, 2021). In order to adhere to the principle of minimalism, one should select garments crafted from eco-friendly materials and refrain from engaging in excessive purchasing, which contributes to the accumulation of textile waste. Consumers adopting a positive stance by prioritising quality over quantity are inclined to select apparel items that exhibit durability and versatility across multiple occasions. As an effort to promote sustainability in the fashion industry, the selection of eco-friendly apparel materials, such as recycled or organic, is rapidly gaining popularity. Regarding personal care and cosmetics, halal lifestyle places an emphasis on the selection of sustainable and risk-free products. This consists of utilising constituents that are non-toxic, environmentally sustainable, and have undergone no animal testing. The adoption of a halal lifestyle encourages the use of environmentally responsible cosmetics, thereby increasing demand for goods produced with ethical consideration for their health and environmental impact.

Figure 2. Value of the modest apparel market in selected countries in 2021 (in billion U.S. dollars)
Source: DinarStandard; SalaamGateway.com (Graph by Statista)

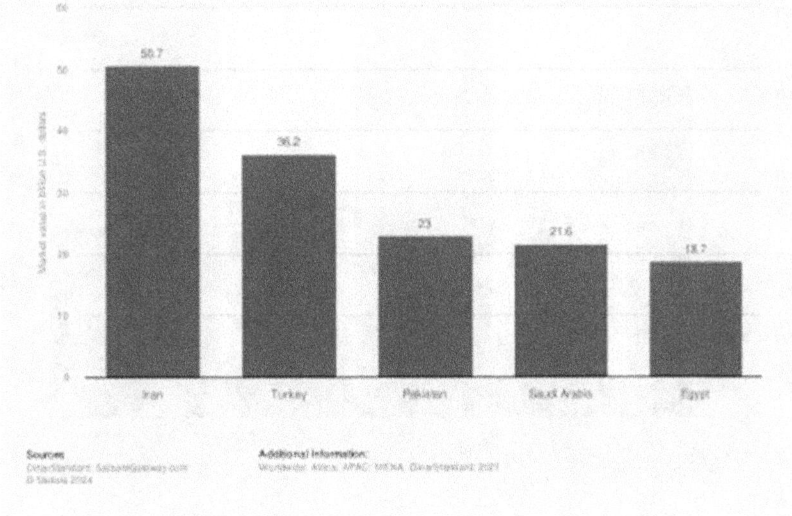

The halal lifestyle can stimulate the regional economy through its patronage of regional goods and services. This encompasses endorsing regional producers who embrace sustainable methodologies, acquiring locally produced products that demonstrate ethical labour practises, and fostering community empowerment through engaged involvement in the local economy. Creating economic sustainability at the local level and minimising the environmental impact of long-distance transportation are both advanced by the decision to support local markets and products(Nor Zaidi et al., 2022; Yaka, 2022).

The value of the Muslim clothing market in 2021, focusing on the comparison between Iran and Turkey as the two largest markets in the industry in 2022. In 2021, the market value of Muslim clothing in various countries is an important concern in the context of the global economy. The data cited shows that in 2022, Iran became the largest market for Islamic clothing, with a market value of slightly more than 50 billion US dollars. This shows the economic significance of Iran in the Muslim clothing industry. Furthermore, a comparison was made with Turkey, which took second place in terms of the market value of Muslim clothing in the same year. Although Iran dominates as the largest market, the market value of Muslim clothing in Turkey is also quite significant, although lower compared to Iran. In 2022, the market value of Muslim clothing in Turkey reached a little more than 36 billion US dollars. A comparison between Iran and Turkey shows a significant difference in the market value of Muslim clothing between the two countries. Nonetheless, both remain major players in the Muslim clothing industry in 2021, demonstrating the importance of Iran and Turkey in the global market for products that meet the needs and preferences of Muslim consumers around the world.

Social awareness and education are crucial components in promoting sustainability via a halal lifestyle. Halal lifestyles can influence a more conscientious and accountable society by disseminating knowledge regarding the environmental and social consequences that can arise from choices regarding consumption. Social awareness campaigns may incorporate discourse pertaining to the environmental ramifications of plastic waste disposal, sustainable agricultural practises, or the adverse effects of hazardous substances present in beauty products. Individuals' perspectives regarding the correlation between their consumption patterns and their ecological footprint may be altered by this education.

*Figure 3. Muslim consumer expenditure on cosmetics worldwide in 2021, by leading country (in billion U.S. dollars) **
Source: Thomson Reuters (Graph by Statista)

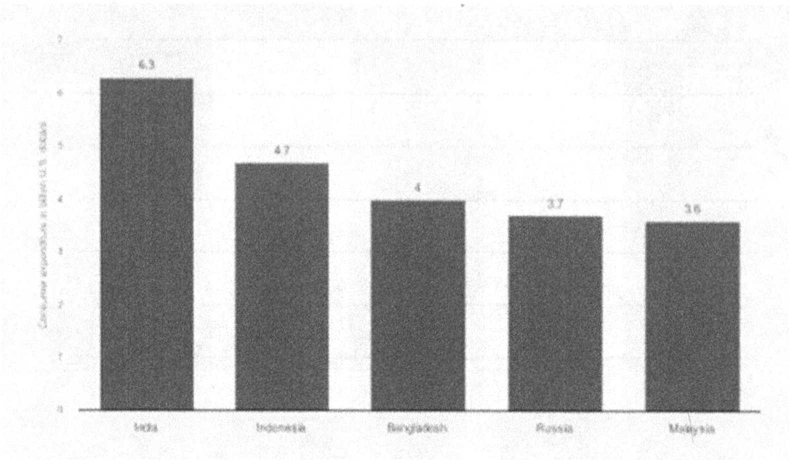

Top five Muslim consumer cosmetics markets globally in 2021, with emphasis on India and Indonesia as the two largest markets. According to the above data, in 2021, India took the top spot as the largest Muslim consumer cosmetics market globally. Consumer spending on cosmetics in India reached about $6.3 billion that year. This shows the significance of the Indian economy in the cosmetics industry specializing in meeting the needs of Muslim consumers. Followed by India, Indonesia occupies the second position in terms of consumer spending on cosmetics by Muslims. Although lower than India, Indonesia remains an important cosmetics market, with consumer spending of around four billion US dollars in the same year.

Technology can be utilised to encourage sustainable halal lifestyles(Ariffin & Hamid, 2021; Masudin et al., 2021; Rejeb, Keogh, et al., 2021; Tayob, 2021). Innovative technologies, such as intelligent applications that enable users to monitor the carbon footprint of a product or select items that adhere to sustainability principles, can assist consumers in making sustainable choices. By implementing blockchain technology, supply chains can be made more transparent, ensuring that halal products are manufactured and distributed in an ethical and sustainable manner(Ali et al., 2021; Bux et al., 2022; Surjandari et al., 2021; A. Tan et al., 2022).

The value of the halal pharmaceutical market is based on expenditure by country in 2021, with emphasis on Turkey's role as a leader in such spending. According to the data above, in 2021, Turkey occupied the top position in spending on halal pharmaceutical products, with total spending reaching around 9.7 billion US dollars in the year. This shows Turkey's significance in the halal pharmaceutical industry, as well as the strong need and demand for pharmaceutical products that meet halal standards. During the same time period, total spending on halal pharmaceutical products globally is estimated at around 100 billion US dollars. This shows that the halal pharmaceutical market constitutes a fairly significant part of the overall pharmaceutical market, with growth continuing to increase along with the increasing awareness and demand for pharmaceutical products that comply with halal principles. Spending on halal pharmaceutical products is a reflection of a variety of factors, including the level of need and accessibility of health products in a country, public health policies, and people's religious preferences and beliefs towards products considered halal.

Figure 4. Value of halal pharmaceutical markets by spending worldwide in 2021 (in billion U.S. dollars)
Source: DinarStandard (Graph by Statista)

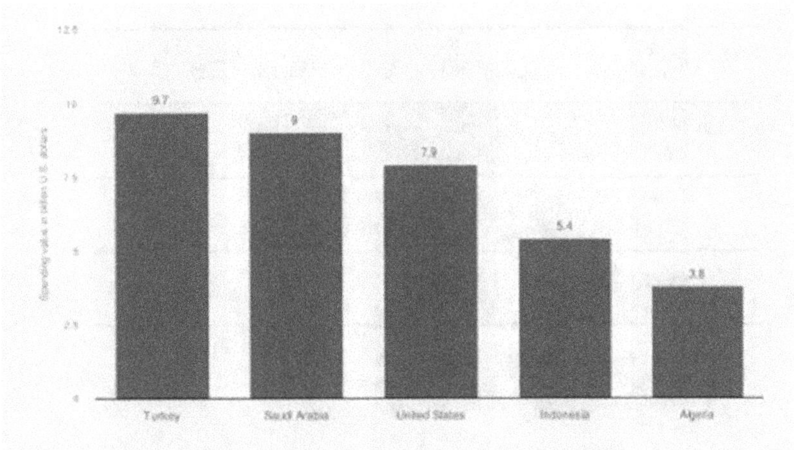

HALAL FOOD INDUSTRY AND RESOURCE EFFICIENCY

There is a strong correlation between resource efficiency and the halal industry, as both pertain to endeavours to enhance sustainable business practises encompassing social, environmental, and economic dimensions(Ab Talib & Zulfakar, 2023; Haleem et al., 2021; Islam et al., 2023). Within this framework, the halal sector possesses substantial capacity to enhance resource efficiency by means of environmentally responsible energy, water, and raw material management. In the halal industry, effective resource management not only generates sustainable economic advantages but also acknowledges the social and environmental accountability of the organisation.

The world's largest halal food market by member countries of the Organization of Islamic Cooperation (OIC) in 2021, with emphasis on Indonesia and Bangladesh as the top two markets. According to the data above, in 2021, Indonesia occupies the top position as the largest halal food market in the world among OIC member countries. The market value of halal food in Indonesia reached around 146.7 billion US dollars that year. This shows Indonesia's important role in the halal food industry globally, given its large Muslim population and strong domestic market demand. Followed by Indonesia, Bangladesh occupies the second position in terms of halal food market value. Bangladesh had a market value of about $125.1 billion in the same year. Despite being lower than Indonesia, Bangladesh remains a major player in the halal food industry, demonstrating significant market potential in the country. The data shows that overall, the total value of halal food imports to OIC member countries is estimated at around 200 billion US dollars.

In the halal industry, energy management is one of the primary areas that can be enhanced. As the world's energy demand rises, production processes that integrate sustainable energy technologies with judicious energy management strategies have the potential to mitigate energy usage and minimise environmental repercussions(Andoni et al., 2019; M. I. Khan et al., 2018; Manthiram, 2020). Implementing renewable energy sources, such as biomass or solar power, could constitute a substantial stride in the halal industry's effort to reduce its carbon imprint. By placing emphasis on energy efficiency, halal companies have the potential to not only reduce their environmental footprint but also enhance their competitiveness in a worldwide market that is progressively priming sustainable business practises.

*Figure 5. Leading markets of halal food in 2021, by OIC country (in billion U.S. dollars) **
Source: International Trade Centre; DinarStandard; SalaamGateway.com (Graph by Statista)

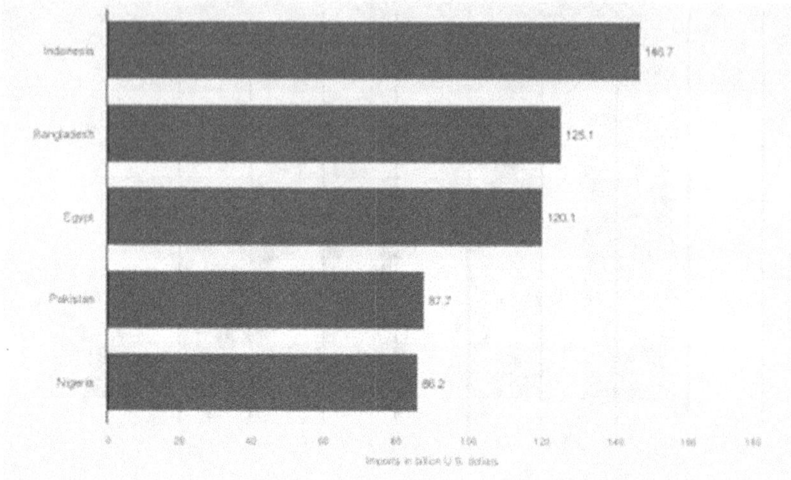

*Figure 6. Forecasted halal food revenue worldwide from 2014 to 2024, by category (in billion U.S. dollars) **
Source: Statista estimates, Hexa Research

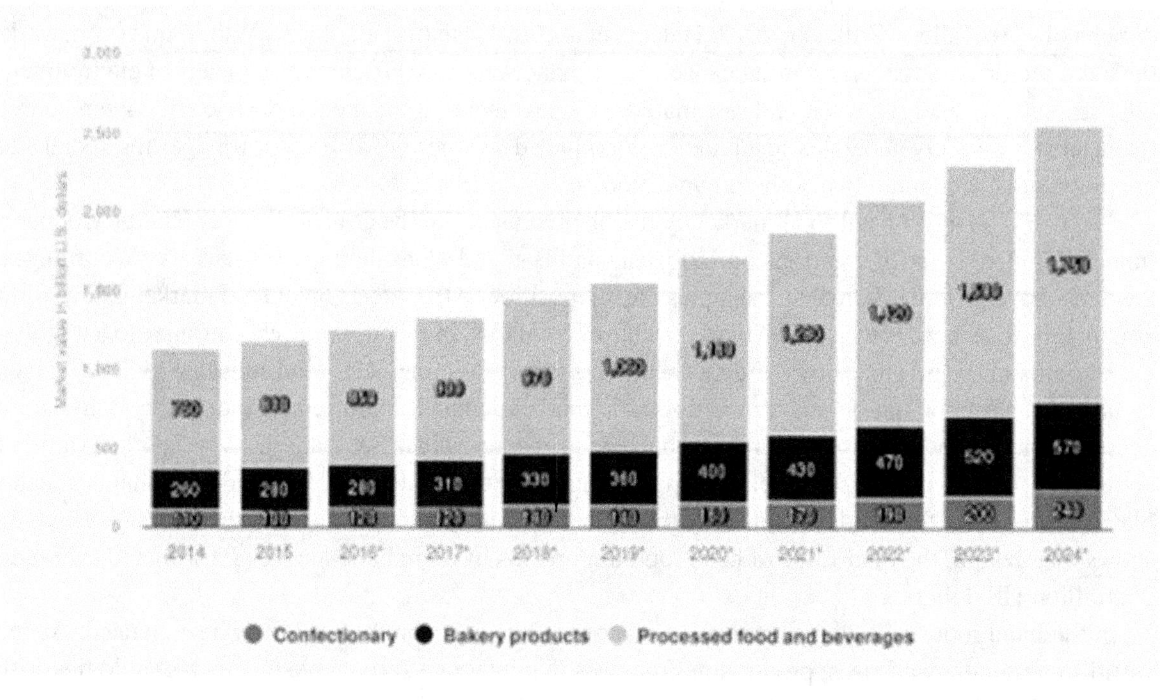

Estimated revenue of the halal food market globally from 2014 to 2024, with emphasis on specific food categories. According to the data above, from 2014 to 2024, the revenue of the halal food market globally is expected to experience significant growth. In 2016, the global halal processed food and beverage market revenue was estimated at around 850 billion US dollars. Projections show that the halal processed food and beverage market revenue will continue to increase substantially until 2024. It is projected that by that year; the revenue of the global halal food market will reach around 1.75 trillion US dollars. Revenue from halal processed food and beverages is one of the important aspects in the overall halal food market. It covers a wide range of processed food products and beverages manufactured in accordance with established halal standards, which include ingredients, production processes, and processing in accordance with the teachings of the Islamic religion. This growth in the revenue of the halal processed food and beverage market reflects the increasing consumer awareness of halal products, both among Muslim and non-Muslim populations. It can also be influenced by factors such as global Muslim population growth, urbanization, lifestyle changes, and changing consumption trends.

Furthermore, judicious water management constitutes an additional critical element in endeavours to establish the sustainability of the halal sector. Halal industry production processes, including animal processing and slaughter, frequently necessitate substantial water consumption(Ab Rashid & Bojei, 2020; Azmi et al., 2018; Elseidi, 2018; Surjandari et al., 2021). Consequently, sustainable and effective water management is critical. Water conservation practises and water recycling technologies can be implemented by the halal industry to mitigate the effects of natural water resource extraction. Halal enterprises can provide environmental support and ensure the sustainability of water resources by allocating resources towards wastewater recovery and investments in water-sensitive technologies.

In the halal industry, sustainable selection and utilisation of raw materials is an additional crucial element that can be implemented to promote sustainability. Supporting local producers while utilising recyclable raw materials, halal production processes can reduce the environmental impact of transportation and promote the sustainability of the local economy. By utilising environmentally favourable raw materials, a more sustainable supply chain can be established in addition to a reduction in environmental damage. The halal industry has the potential to contribute positively to the reduction of natural resource exploitation and the promotion of environmentally sustainable business practises.

The sustainability of the halal industry is significant not only at the local level but also on an international scale(Abdul Rahim et al., 2022; Ismail et al., 2023; Laila et al., 2023). The exponential expansion of halal markets globally underscores the criticality for the halal sector to conform its operational procedures to sustainability principles. The halal industry may implement technology-driven energy management as a strategic measure to reduce energy usage and enhance production processes. By identifying areas where efficiency can be increased, the implementation of intelligent sensors and automation can contribute to the development of a more sustainable and effective operational environment.

The development of sustainable products is fundamental to the halal industry's contribution to global sustainability. Manufacturing advancements in basic materials, packaging, and production processes can yield halal products that not only adhere to halal standards but also uphold the tenets of sustainability. Halal products manufactured with a commitment to sustainability may appeal to consumers who are becoming more conscious of the ecological consequences associated with the goods they purchase(Endri et al., 2020; Katuk, 2019; M. I. Khan et al., 2022).

Moreover, sustainable partnerships are essential to the halal industry's achievement of its sustainability objectives. Collaboration with sustainability agencies and non-governmental organisations can facilitate the exchange of information, the development of sustainable technologies, and collaborative research. These types of collaborations have the potential to fortify sustainability endeavours, facilitate the establishment of optimal methodologies, and offer novel approaches to intricate sustainability dilemmas.

Amid a heightened international consciousness regarding sustainability concerns, the halal industry possesses the potential to act as a catalyst for constructive transformation by prioritising environmental and social well-being alongside economic considerations. By practising holistic resource efficiency, intelligent energy management, prudent water management, and sustainable raw material selection, the halal industry has the capacity to contribute to a more sustainable business future, thereby safeguarding the planet's survival and promoting collective prosperity.

RECYCLING AND WASTE MANAGEMENT

The halal industry contributes significantly to the pursuit of sustainability via a multitude of initiatives, with recycling and waste management constituting a critical area of emphasis(Abdul Rahim et al., 2022; Mat et al., 2020). Given the circumstances, the halal industry considers sustainability not only a social obligation but also an imperative that requires the participation of the entire production chain in an effort to safeguard the environment and promote a sustainable economic system. The halal industry contributes significantly to recycling through its promotion of recycled products and implementation of efficient recycling systems(Huang et al., 2018; Vollmer et al., 2020). A comprehensive comprehension of the life cycle of halal products enables organisations to strategically plan and produce commodities with recycling in mind. Sustainability consciousness is integrated into each phase of production, ranging from packaging to the final product. The use of recyclable eco-friendly packaging, for instance, can help reduce environmental pollution and carbon emissions caused by plastic refuse.

Consumers are also involved in the implementation of an effective recycling system, in addition to producers. Education programmes and incentives that promote the return of used products for recycling can be implemented by the halal industry to engage consumers in recycling activities. The presence of recycling labels on halal products can provide consumers with information regarding the company's dedication to sustainability, thereby fostering a sense of shared accountability and consciousness(Haleem et al., 2021; Rizkitysha & Hananto, 2022). Waste management is emerging as a significant obstacle, particularly in sectors that engage in animal processing. In order to minimise waste, the halal industry can implement novel strategies that optimise the utilisation of every animal byproduct. As an illustration, by repurposing scraps that were formerly regarded as waste into ancillary products like organic fertiliser or animal fodder, for instance, cutting process byproducts can acquire additional value.

The halal industry prioritises the implementation of sustainable and secure waste treatment techniques(Anssari et al., 2020; Mor & Ravindra, 2023). Implementing appropriate waste management practises, such as effluent recycling or composting, can effectively mitigate the adverse environmental effects. Actively participating in community waste management programmes and developing waste management systems that adhere to safety and sustainability standards are both capabilities of the halal industry. Waste management and recycling practises that are effective can provide economic benefits in addition to environmental ones. Businesses can optimise available resources and reduce production expenses by repurposing existing materials. At this level of the economy, sustainability fosters a more sustainable and stable business environment. Consumer trust and brand image are additional indicators of the significance of waste management and recycling in the halal industry. There is a growing trend among environmentally conscious societies to favour products sourced from companies that actively engage in recycling initiatives and responsible refuse management. Consequently, such sustainability initiatives can provide a competitive advantage, fortify consumer relationships, and establish a positive reputation that endures over time.

Modern technology can facilitate the optimisation of waste management and recycling processes(Fernando, 2019; Munasinghe et al., 2019). By integrating advanced information and monitoring systems, halal organisations can enhance their waste tracking and management capabilities. Additionally, waste processing technology is in a constant state of development, enabling the halal industry to benefit from environmentally favourable and cost-effective innovations. Achieving sustainability via waste management and recycling requires the cooperation of the halal industry, the government, and society at large. Incentives and regulations that promote sustainable recycling and waste management practises may be implemented by governments. In the context of sustainability initiatives, community engagement in local recycling programmes and support for such endeavours can serve as catalysts for constructive transformation.

HALAL FOOD INDUSTRY AND ENVIRONMENTAL SUSTAINABILITY

The halal food industry significantly contributes to environmental sustainability by engaging in numerous initiatives, such as the preservation of habitats and biodiversity, mitigation of greenhouse gas emissions, and prevention of other forms of pollution(Crippa et al., 2021; Hannan et al., 2018; Sarkodie & Strezov, 2019). As environmental challenges become more tangible, the halal food industry must lead the way in environmentally responsible business practises that preserve the earth's ecosystem while ensuring adherence to halal principles.

Habitat and biodiversity conservation is a primary methodology employed by the halal food industry to promote environmental sustainability. Raw materials utilised in the production of halal foods are frequently derived from natural sources, such as animal and agricultural products. In this instance, the halal food industry's selection of sustainable natural resources may have an impact on the ecological equilibrium (Azhar & Tu, 2021; E R Kismawadi, Irfan, M., Al Muddatstsir, U. D., & Abdulkarim, 2023). Sustainable agriculture, encompassing ecological preservation and biodiversity-promoting agricultural methods, has the potential to serve as the bedrock for halal food raw material production. Not only does ensuring sustainability in this supply chain benefit producers and consumers in the short term, but it also preserves an ecological equilibrium that is conducive to long-term viability.

Utilising regionally sourced ingredients can serve as an additional approach to sustainability within the halal food sector. The reduction of reliance on long-distance imports of basic materials can effectively mitigate the environmental consequences associated with transportation. Furthermore, by endorsing local producers who embrace sustainable agricultural methods, communities can be economically motivated to preserve biodiversity and preserve the equilibrium of local ecosystems. For instance, halal food manufacturers may form partnerships with nearby farmers to guarantee that their agricultural practises do not negatively impact the environment, but rather preserve the ecological equilibrium.

Waste management is a crucial component of the halal food industry's commitment to sustainability. As an additional resource, waste from the halal food production procedure can be processed and repurposed. This practise not only mitigates the environmental consequences of waste but also generates value from resources that were previously regarded as refuse. For instance, food scraps can be utilised as organic fertiliser, and the recycling procedure can convert organic waste into energy. The implementation of this methodology is propelling the halal food sector towards enhanced sustainability of natural resources.

At a higher level, the halal food industry places significant emphasis on the reduction of greenhouse gas emissions and other forms of pollution as a means to promote environmental sustainability.

Specifically, energy efficiency is emerging as a critical factor in the effort to decrease emissions. By implementing practises that reduce overall energy consumption, utilising more efficient technologies, and incorporating renewable energy sources, the halal food industry can increase energy efficiency at every stage of production. By adopting renewable energy sources, such as wind and solar power, the sector can mitigate its reliance on finite fossil fuels and make a positive contribution towards the global effort to reduce carbon emissions.

The implementation of sustainable transport and logistics practises is an additional critical aspect in the effort to mitigate greenhouse gas emissions. Logistics providers that prioritise vehicle fleets powered by renewable energy, optimise delivery routes to reduce emissions, and employ information technology to enhance delivery efficacy are options available to the halal food industry. By doing so, the consumption of fossil fuels can be curtailed, thereby mitigating the effects of climate change.

The choice of packaging materials is a critical component in endeavours to mitigate emissions and pollution. Biodegradable or recyclable packaging materials are available to the halal food industry. Furthermore, reducing the use of single-use plastics and implementing innovations in eco-friendly packaging design are constructive measures towards mitigating the environmental impact of plastic waste.

Sustainability in the halal food industry encompasses the entire value chain and extends beyond operational procedures(Ali et al., 2021; Rejeb, Rejeb, et al., 2021; Secinaro & Calandra, 2021). It requires a systemic approach. It is essential to involve stakeholders, such as governments, consumers, farmers, and producers, in the development of an ecosystem that promotes sustainable business practises. Such as the use of sensor technology to monitor carbon footprints or blockchain technology to ensure supply chain transparency, technological innovation can also be a useful instrument in accelerating the transition to sustainability.

INNOVATIVE TECHNOLOGY IN HALAL FOOD PRODUCTION

Addressing the challenges associated with sustainable and halal products has led to a significant emphasis on the implementation of cutting-edge technology in halal food production. Investigating the potential implementations of cutting-edge technologies like blockchain, Internet of Things (IoT), and artificial intelligence (AI) not only enhances operational efficacy but also safeguards the integrity of halal food products and the sustainability of supply chains. This emphasis signifies the dedication of the halal food sector to not only adhere to halal criteria, but also satisfy consumer expectations regarding openness, security, and ecological responsibility.

Use of Artificial Intelligence (AI) in Halal Food Production

The implementation of artificial intelligence yields substantial beneficial outcomes within the halal food sector (Kismawadi, 2023; Ridho Kismawadi et al., 2023; Sumarliah & Al-hakeem, 2023) Real-time monitoring and optimisation of production processes is a capability of AI systems. Using historical data as an example, halal food companies can utilise AI to forecast market demand, manage inventory, and optimise production. In addition to enhancing quality control, AI can detect potential contamination or noncompliance with halal standards automatically. This not only enhances the efficacy of production but also more effectively guarantees the halal of the products. The visual inspection of product quality through the use of image processing technology is a concrete instance of AI in action. By utilising cameras and AI image recognition technology, a halal food factory can verify that every product item adheres to predetermined quality criteria. By rapidly detecting anomalies or flaws in products, the system guarantees that consumers exclusively receive halal products of the highest quality.

Internet of Things and Halal Food Supply Chain Sustainability

Throughout the halal food supply chain, improved integration and connectivity are made possible by the Internet of Things (IoT)(Ahmad Tarmizi et al., 2020; Ali et al., 2021; Ali & Suleiman, 2018; E R Kismawadi, Irfan, M., Al Muddatstsir, U. D., & Abdulkarim, 2023; S. Khan et al., 2022; Kismawadi, 2024) From agriculture to distribution, Internet of Things (IoT) sensors can be deployed at various nodes in the supply chain to monitor temperature, humidity, and environmental conditions, among other factors critical to preserving product safety and quality. At the agricultural stage, for instance, sensors can provide producers with real-time data on crop and soil conditions, enabling them to optimise resource utilisation and reduce waste. One tangible illustration of the Internet of Things' implementation pertains to the transportation and storage of goods. Temperature sensors may be installed in storage facilities or delivery vehicles by halal food manufacturers in order to ensure that temperatures adhere to food safety regulations. Automated alerts can be generated by the system in the event that the temperature deviates from the intended range, enabling prompt intervention to avert product damage.

Security and Transparency With Blockchain in the Halal Food Industry

In the halal food industry, blockchain technology introduces the concepts of decentralisation and data security. With regard to sustainability, the food supply chain can be made completely transparent via blockchain technology(Ali et al., 2021; Bux et al., 2022; Hew et al., 2020; A. Tan et al., 2022). The blockchain can record each stage from production to consumption, thereby increasing transparency regarding the distribution, production processes, and source materials. This ensures that halal food products adhere to the desired sustainability standards of consumers. Blockchain implementation is demonstrated in the traceability of halal meat. The entire meat production process, including animal husbandry, slaughtering, and distribution, is meticulously documented in the blockchain. The sustainability and halal certification of the meat that consumers purchase can be readily verified by scanning QR codes located on product packaging. This fosters a significant degree of openness and confidence among consumers.

Technology Integration for Full Sustainability

In practise, these three technologies can be integrated by halal food manufacturers to attain complete sustainability(Allam & Dhunny, 2019; Bonilla et al., 2018; Kamble et al., 2018; Kusiak, 2018). A halal food facility, for instance, could optimise production utilising AI and data collected by IoT sensors. A midway, blockchain technology can be employed to guarantee an immutable and transparent ledger of each transaction occurring within the supply chain. This integration establishes a technological ecosystem characterised by mutual support, enhanced efficiency, and comprehensive sustainability. An instance of this technology being effectively integrated is in the manufacturing process of halal milk. Farms may employ IoT sensors to monitor the production and health of cattle. AI systems are capable of utilising the gathered data to forecast the ideal quantity of milk production. The blockchain records each stage of production and distribution in order to guarantee data security and transparency. By doing so, businesses can guarantee that the halal milk they manufacture is not only sustainable but also of superior quality.

Implementing cutting-edge technologies in halal food production, including blockchain, Internet of Things, and artificial intelligence, is a strategic move to ensure the products' halal and sustainability. The aforementioned instances serve to demonstrate the practical implementation of these technologies in order to enhance transparency, quality control, and efficiency throughout the halal food supply chain. Not only does the incorporation of cutting-edge technology into the halal food sector ensure compliance with technological developments, but it also establishes a robust framework for a sustainable and reputable future.

INDUSTRY COLLABORATIONS AND PARTNERSHIPS

The correlation between sustainability and the halal food industry is mediated through elements of industry collaboration and robust partnerships. This approach is crucial in guaranteeing that the manufacturing of halal food not only complies with halal requirements but also makes a positive impact on sustainability in the realms of the environment, society, and economy.

Business Partnership Model

Business alliances are essential for the sustainable operation of the halal food industry(Donner et al., 2020; Sullivan et al., 2018; Veleva & Bodkin, 2018; Wamba-Taguimdje et al., 2020). The establishment of alliances among corporations, governmental bodies, and non-governmental organisations (NGOs) facilitates the realisation of sustainable objectives through synergies. A partnership between a halal food manufacturer and a local government, for instance, could be established to support local farmer development programmes. Under this partnership programme, the company can support economic development in local communities and ensure a sustainable supply of raw materials by providing farmers with training and resources.

Partnerships between businesses and non-governmental organisations (NGOs) with a concentration on sustainability are also possible. Together with environmental non-governmental organisations, halal food companies can identify and mitigate the environmental impacts of their operations. For instance, the organisation may collaborate with non-governmental organisations (NGOs) to redesign waste management initiatives or implement ecologically sustainable agricultural methods. To provide a tangible example, halal food company A engages in a partnership with an environmental NGO and the local government to aid in the advancement of organic farming among local producers. By means of this collaboration, the organisation imparts knowledge and expertise on organic farming methodologies, furnishes organic fertilisers, and ensures the procurement of agricultural commodities at equitable prices. Local governments facilitate the acquisition of suitable land for organic cultivation and incentivize farmers to participate by offering tax breaks. Monitoring the positive environmental effects of sustainable agricultural practises is a function of environmental non-governmental organisations (NGOs). These organisations provide an in-depth understanding of such practises.

Industry Collaboration Model

Industry collaboration, apart from commercial partnerships, plays a pivotal role in advancing sustainability within the halal food sector(R. Abdullah et al., 2018). By means of this partnership, businesses are able to exchange expertise, resources, and knowledge in order to develop collective solutions that advance sustainability objectives. Within the halal food industry, retailers, distributors, and producers can work together to establish a more sustainable supply chain through collaboration. The halal food industry forum serves as a tangible illustration of industry collaboration, as it convenes participants from various phases of the supply chain(Ab Rashid & Bojei, 2020; Ali et al., 2021; Ali & Suleiman, 2018; Mohamed et al., 2020; Secinaro & Calandra, 2021). By sharing best practises to reduce carbon footprint, optimise resource utilisation, and increase production efficiency, businesses can participate in this forum. This form of collaboration facilitates the interchange of valuable information and presents prospects for organisations to acquire knowledge from one another.

To illustrate, a collaborative effort was initiated by halal food manufacturer B, distributor C, and retailer D with the aim of diminishing the utilisation of single-use plastics in product packaging. They acknowledge that plastic contributes significantly to environmental degradation. Retailers are providing incentives for consumers to utilise reusable shopping bags, while manufacturers are committed to developing environmentally friendly packaging and distributors are attempting to optimise distribution by reducing the use of secondary packaging. By collaborating, they are developing comprehensive strategies to mitigate the ecological consequences associated with the packaging of halal food products.

Integration of Partnerships and Collaboration in Sustainability

It is critical to emphasise that industry collaborations and business partnerships are not inseparable; instead, they work in tandem to accomplish sustainability objectives. By means of business alliances with governmental bodies and non-governmental organisations (NGOs), a halal food company can augment its sustainability initiatives, whereas industry collaboration facilitates the interchange of insights and advancements that generate industry-wide best practises. To illustrate integration, halal food company E collaborated on agroforestry initiatives with the local government and an industry forum. With the assistance of the local government, the corporation provides unused land to local farmers for the planting of nut trees as part of this partnership. Industry forums facilitate the exchange of sustainable agriculture and forest management best practises. By means of these collaborations and partnerships, the organisation not only fosters local economic expansion but also contributes to the conservation of the environment.

The correlation between the halal food sector and sustainability yields advantages that span across multiple domains(Ali et al., 2021; Rejeb, Keogh, et al., 2021; Secinaro & Calandra, 2021). To begin with, business partnerships facilitate the distribution of resources and obligations among various stakeholders, thereby augmenting the overall positive influence. Furthermore, industry collaboration enables the expedited integration of optimal methodologies by means of knowledge and expertise sharing. Collectively, they constitute an ecosystem that fosters the halal food industry's sustainable expansion.

Halal food companies can foster local economic development, promote sustainable agriculture, and guarantee the sustainability of their supply chains by means of collaborative alliances. Concurrently, collaboration within industries facilitates the interchange of concepts and advancements, thereby enhancing industry-wide best practises. By integrating collaboration and partnership, organisations in the halal food sector can develop comprehensive and efficient sustainability solutions. Consequently, establishing this connection signifies not only catering to consumer needs but also ensuring the long-term viability of the halal food sector and the environment.

SUSTAINABILITY CERTIFICATION AS A HALAL FOOD INDUSTRY STANDARD

Sustainability certification has emerged as an essential pillar within the halal food sector, serving as a pivotal factor in the establishment of universally acknowledged industry standards (Arieftiara et al., 2022; Bux et al., 2022; Mat et al., 2020; Secinaro & Calandra, 2021). The fundamental objective of this certification is to harmonise sustainability and halal elements, guaranteeing that the manufacturing of halal food not only adheres to religious standards but also promotes ecological sustainability, energy efficiency, responsible waste management, and corporate social responsibility.

Waste management is an area that is given significant emphasis by sustainability certification within the halal food industry. Halal food companies are obligated to implement measures that promote waste reduction, recycling, and management in adherence to sustainability principles, as part of this certification process. For instance, a certified halal food manufacturer may implement a programme for the recycling of plastic waste generated during production. By means of cooperative efforts with external entities, this plastic refuse can be effectively administered, thereby diminishing its ecological impact and fostering a more sustainable setting. Energy efficiency is an additional critical element that sustainability certification facilitates within the halal food industry. Organisations that receive certification are required to supplement their energy requirements with renewable energy sources, such as wind or solar power. Additionally, energy efficiency technology implementation during production is a crucial measure in minimising environmental impact. Certified halal food companies, for instance, are able to utilise more energy-efficient production equipment, thereby reducing carbon emissions and energy consumption (Iranmanesh et al., 2020; Parvin Hosseini et al., 2020; Usman et al., 2022).

In the halal food industry, corporate social responsibility (CSR) is an essential component of sustainability certification as well. Partnerships between businesses are essential to attaining robust social responsibility. Establishing partnerships among the company, governmental bodies, and non-governmental organisations (NGOs) is a prerequisite for certification. A halal food company, for instance, may establish alliances with environmental non-governmental organisations in order to identify and mitigate the environmental effects of its operations. This may encompass participation in tree-planting initiatives, endorsement of environmental education programmes, or engagement in other community-based endeavours that yield beneficial outcomes. Furthermore, sustainability certification should mandate that halal food companies actively engage in community-based social responsibility initiatives. Certified businesses can guarantee that all workers in their supply chain are treated fairly and safely in this situation. This encompasses the provision of appropriate working conditions, fair compensation, and sufficient amenities. Businesses can support local community programmes or initiate initiatives that enhance the quality of life in the vicinity of their facilities by donating a portion of their profits.

Consistent with the incorporation of halal elements, halal components must be an integral part of sustainability certification in the halal food industry. This includes ensuring strict adherence to halal standards in both the production process and the basic materials utilised. It is anticipated that halal food companies with this certification will act as positive social change agents and incorporate sustainability into every aspect of their operations. Ongoing reporting and monitoring are essential components of sustainability certification within the halal food sector. Companies obtaining this certification are obligated to engage in ongoing surveillance of their operations with regard to sustainability and halal considerations.

Collecting information regarding carbon footprint, water consumption, social impacts, and energy efficacy is required. Subsequently, these reports ought to be incorporated into yearly sustainability reports that are made available to investors, consumers, and other stakeholders. The establishment of accountability through this transparency guarantees that the organisation rigorously adheres to the sustainability criteria established by the certification.

Therefore, sustainability certification within the halal food sector serves as a strategic measure to attain sustainability objectives, in addition to satisfying the needs of a market that is becoming more environmentally aware. It establishes a comprehensive perspective on ethical business conduct by harmonising halal certification with sustainability. By obtaining this certification, the halal food industry can enhance its ability to address the concerns of contemporary consumers, contribute positively to society and the environment, and contribute to the development of a more sustainable industrial future.

PUBLIC POLICY

It is crucial that the government develop public policies that promote the halal food industry's sustainability in order to guarantee that the sector not only adheres to halal standards but also contributes positively to the environment, society, and economy. By implementing appropriate frameworks, regulations, and incentives, governments have the ability to stimulate the adoption of sustainable practises by businesses.

Government Incentives

Government-sponsored sustainable practises can be reciprocated by halal food companies through economic incentives. Tax incentives or tax breaks may be provided to businesses, for instance, in exchange for investments in environmentally beneficial technologies or improved waste management. Such an incentive would motivate businesses to consider sustainability as an astute investment strategy in addition to a social responsibility. A nation has implemented a fiscal incentive initiative whereby halal food companies that meet or surpass specific sustainability criteria are granted substantial tax reductions. As a reaction, the organisation allocated supplementary financial resources towards enhancing the energy efficacy of their manufacturing facilities and executing more efficient waste management initiatives.

Strict Environmental Regulations

Proactive government intervention in the establishment of stringent environmental regulations pertaining to the halal food sector is feasible. Potential regulations may encompass emission limits, standards for chemical use, and refuse management obligations. The establishment of stringent sustainability criteria by the government serves as a clear indication to businesses that engagement in sustainable operations is mandatory.

A nation has the ability to enact policies mandating that halal food manufacturers comply with stringent emission standards and utilise eco-friendly ingredients throughout the manufacturing process. Nonconforming businesses risk incurring penalties or even being prohibited from operations, whereas compliant businesses earn the support of the government and the confidence of consumers.

Framework for Sustainability Reporting

By establishing transparent structures for sustainability reporting, governments have the ability to promote the implementation of sustainable ideas (Arieftiara et al., 2022). Government-issued reporting standards and guidelines can aid businesses in measuring and disclosing the social and environmental impacts of their operations in a transparent manner. Moreover, it facilitates the comparison of ongoing business performance across organisations.

A sustainability reporting framework that mandates halal food companies to regularly disclose their carbon emissions, water consumption, and social responsibility initiatives could be established by the government (Arieftiara et al., 2022). Businesses that are proactive and forthright in this reporting can enhance their reputation and receive additional government support.

Investment in Research and Innovation

Funding sustainable research and innovation can assist the government in promoting the halal food industry's sustainability(Deku et al., 2023; Secinaro & Calandra, 2021; Sumarliah & Al-hakeem, 2023). The implementation of this research support programme has the potential to foster the advancement of novel technologies, enhanced production processes, and inventive resolutions to sustainability obstacles within the halal food industry.

Government funding may be allocated to research initiatives that seek to enhance the energy efficacy of halal food manufacturing. These funds are subsequently invested in the installation of renewable energy systems at the production facilities of a halal food company, thereby reducing energy costs and carbon emissions.

Engaging in Joint Partnership

To accomplish shared sustainability objectives, governments can facilitate partnerships between the private sector, governments, and NGOs. Establishing this type of partnership can facilitate the exchange of information, resources, and novel approaches, thereby fortifying collaborative endeavours aimed at attaining sustainability within the halal food sector. The government can convene forums on sustainability that include environmental non-governmental organisations, halal food corporations, and local governments. Governments can furnish current information on regulations, businesses can exchange best practises, and non-governmental organisations (NGOs) can offer unbiased perspectives on the environmental repercussions of industrial operations via this forum.

Increased Consumer Awareness

The government has the capacity to influence consumer consciousness with respect to the environmental impact of the halal food sector(Arifin et al., 2021; Rachmawati & Suroso, 2022; Zuraini et al., 2019). The government may organise counselling and education campaigns to enlighten the public about the significance of selecting sustainable halal food products. An initiative by the government to instruct consumers on how to interpret sustainability labels present on halal food product packaging could be implemented via social media (Krisharyanto et al., 2019; Osman et al., 2020; Prayuti, 2020). It facilitates the decision-making process of consumers regarding the products they purchase, thereby motivating companies to enhance their sustainability practises in order to maintain market competitiveness.

By employing a blend of regulatory measures, incentive schemes, and supportive structures, governmental bodies can furnish businesses with the essential drive to embrace sustainable practises. Within this particular framework, tangible illustrations demonstrate that governmental intervention can foster an atmosphere conducive to constructive transformation, promote inventive thinking, and furnish optimal resolutions to sustainability obstacles within the halal food sector. Therefore, in addition to its regulatory role, the government assumes the role of a strategic partner in directing the sector towards greater sustainability.

CONCLUSION

This article describes, in the context of sustainability challenges facing the food industry, specifically in the field of halal food, the sector's crucial role in fostering environmentally, socially, and economically responsible business practises. Critical issues that require attention include excessive resource consumption, refuse management, and the environmental repercussions of intensive agricultural practises. The halal food industry can be a catalyst for sustainability by virtue of its dedication to limited production methods, sustainable agricultural approaches, accountable supply chain administration, and advocacy for sustainable products. Sustainability certification is regarded as a significant indicator of the halal food industry's dedication to sustainable principles in this context.

This study investigates the intricate correlation that exists between culinary tourism and sustainability, with a specific focus on halal products. The establishment of ethical and sustainable culinary tourism practises is widely regarded as a critical measure in the protection of ecosystems, communities, and cultural heritage. By employing an integrative methodology and conducting case study analyses, this research endeavours to provide significant contributions to the field of travel and hospitality. Furthermore, significant areas of interest include the environmental ramifications of the food industry, the extent to which a halal lifestyle contributes to sustainability, the advantages of resource efficiency within the halal sector, and the function of technological innovation in halal food manufacturing. Sustainability certification, industry collaboration, and strong partnerships have been recognised as crucial approaches to guarantee that halal food manufacturing not only complies with halal standards but also makes a positive contribution to sustainability as a whole.

This study makes a substantial scholarly contribution, particularly to the domains of sustainability and the halal food sector. Through an investigation into the correlation between halal products, culinary tourism, and sustainable practises, this study contributes to the body of knowledge and paves the way for additional inquiries in this domain. Destination managers, halal food producers, and industry stakeholders will be able to make more informed decisions regarding the enhancement of the sustainability of their operations with the assistance of the findings of this study, which can serve as a strategic manual for halal food industry participants seeking to boost sustainable business practises. The study's results have significant implications for the advancement of sustainable and ethical culinary tourism. They establish a fundamental basis for stakeholders in the hospitality and tourism industry to create initiatives that promote the conservation of cultural heritage, effective management of resources, and consideration of the socio-economic impacts of culinary tourism.

This research's significance extends beyond the industry level and influences public policies concerning sustainability, particularly as it pertains to the halal food sector. The implications of these results may significantly influence the formulation of policies by policymakers that encourage sustainable business practises, such as the implementation of sustainability certification as a prevailing standard in the industry. Furthermore, this research may serve as a model for other scholars who are intrigued by investigating the correlation between the halal food sector, sustainability, and culinary tourism. It may also encourage additional investigations into specific facets that have yet to be thoroughly examined.

To offering scholarly perspectives, the ramifications of this research also manifest in a tangible way for consumers. Consumers can be educated on the significance of selecting halal food products that also support sustainable practises in light of these findings. Consequently, this study possesses the capacity to induce a shift in consumer conduct and stimulate the market for goods that adhere to halal and sustainability criteria.

Furthermore, the ramifications of this study foster greater collaboration among pertinent stakeholders in the halal food sector, thereby stimulating the expansion of cooperation in that sector. Enhanced collaboration can bolster collective endeavours to enhance the sector's sustainability, thereby fostering an atmosphere conducive to innovation and sustainable expansion. Furthermore, the research emphasises the significance of cutting-edge technologies in the halal food manufacturing process, thereby stimulating the implementation of such technologies throughout the sector. The halal food industry may be able to leverage technological advantages to increase resource efficiency and overall sustainability as a result of these ramifications.

CONFLICT OF INTEREST

The author states that there is no conflict of interest.

REFERENCES

Ab Rashid, N., & Bojei, J. (2020). The relationship between halal traceability system adoption and environmental factors on halal food supply chain integrity in Malaysia. *Journal of Islamic Marketing*, *11*(1), 117–142. doi:10.1108/JIMA-01-2018-0016

Ab Talib, M. S., & Zulfakar, M. H. (2023). Sustainable halal food supply chain management in a small rentier halal market. *Arab Gulf Journal of Scientific Research*. doi:10.1108/AGJSR-11-2022-0251

Abdul Rahim, N. R., Abdullah, I., Yahya, N. A., Awang, M. N., Muhammad, S. Z., Ahmad Sabri, S., & Ahmad, N. N. (2022). Negotiation of needs towards halal talents sustainability. *Journal of Islamic Marketing*, *13*(1), 20–44. doi:10.1108/JIMA-11-2019-0245

Abdullah, M. A., & Azam, M. S. E. (2020). Halal entrepreneurship from maqasid-al-sharia'h perspective: Inseparable concept for halalpreneurs. *Food Research*, *4*(S1), 34–42. doi:10.26656/fr.2017.4(S1).S07

Abdullah, R., Sabar, R., & Mustafar, M. (2018). Green Halal supply chain in Malaysian halal food companies: A conceptual framework. *International Journal of Supply Chain Management*, *7*(5), 502–510. https://www.scopus.com/inward/record.uri?eid=2-s2.0-85060870564&partnerID=40&md5=04ca49f07d21949606b68e3ce6c0a3c1

Adham, K. A., Muhamad, N. S., & Said, M. F. (2020). Diagnosing the Halal Industry of Taiwan: A viable system model approach. *Jurnal Pengurusan*, *58*, 169–179. doi:10.17576/pengurusan-2020-58-14

Ahmad Tarmizi, H., Kamarulzaman, N. H., Abd Rahman, A., & Atan, R. (2020). Adoption of internet of things among Malaysian halal agro-food smes and its challenges. *Food Research*, *4*(S1), 256–265. doi:10.26656/fr.2017.4(S1).S26

Al-Tayyar, N. A., Youssef, A. M., & Al-hindi, R. (2020). Antimicrobial food packaging based on sustainable Bio-based materials for reducing foodborne Pathogens: A review. *Food Chemistry*, *310*, 125915. doi:10.1016/j.foodchem.2019.125915 PMID:31841936

Ali, M. H., Chung, L., Kumar, A., Zailani, S., & Tan, K. H. (2021). A sustainable Blockchain framework for the halal food supply chain: Lessons from Malaysia. *Technological Forecasting and Social Change*, *170*, 120870. Advance online publication. doi:10.1016/j.techfore.2021.120870

Ali, M. H., & Suleiman, N. (2018). Eleven shades of food integrity: A halal supply chain perspective. *Trends in Food Science & Technology*, *71*, 216–224. doi:10.1016/j.tifs.2017.11.016

Allam, Z., & Dhunny, Z. A. (2019). On big data, artificial intelligence and smart cities. *Cities (London, England)*, *89*, 80–91. doi:10.1016/j.cities.2019.01.032

Andoni, M., Robu, V., Flynn, D., Abram, S., Geach, D., Jenkins, D., McCallum, P., & Peacock, A. (2019). Blockchain technology in the energy sector: A systematic review of challenges and opportunities. *Renewable & Sustainable Energy Reviews*, *100*, 143–174. doi:10.1016/j.rser.2018.10.014

Anssari, O. M., Alkaldy, E. A., Almudhaffar, N., AlTaee, A. N., & Ali, N. S. (2020). A feasibility study of electrical energy generation from municipal solid waste in Iraq: Najaf case study. *Iranian Journal of Electrical and Computer Engineering*, *10*(4), 3403–3411. doi:10.11591/ijece.v10i4.pp3403-3411

Arieftiara, D., Nawir, J., & Julianisa, I. A. (2022). Halal Food Certification, Financial Performance, and Sustainability Reporting: Comparative Study of Food and Beverage Firms in Malaysia and Indonesia. *AgBioForum*, *24*(2), 12–22. https://www.scopus.com/inward/record.uri?eid=2-s2.0-85144748584&partnerID=40&md5=a70dde874837ebf5eaf159d6bbcf378c

Ariffin, M. F. M., & Hamid, M. F. A. (2021). Negotiating Halal Crimes: The Use Of Block-Chain Technology. *Global Journal Al-Thaqafah*, *11*(1), 41–48. https://www.scopus.com/inward/record.uri?eid=2-s2.0-85114418195&partnerID=40&md5=2a7ff7dcf4aa9c4c66ec2d6dfb550f8e

Arifin, A., Wyman, F., & Hendijani, R. B. (2021). An investigation of the aspects affecting non-Muslim customers' purchase intention of halal food products in Jakarta, indonesia. *Future of Food: Journal on Food, Agriculture and Society*, *9*(2), 1–13. doi:10.17170/kobra-202102163257

Azhar, A., & Tu, Y. T. (2021). The investigation of key factors for successful implementation of sustainable halal food supply chain management. *Food Research*, *5*(6), 221–228. doi:10.26656/fr.2017.5(6).235

Azmi, F. R., Abdullah, A., Bakri, M. H., Musa, H., & Jayakrishnan, M. (2018). The adoption of halal food supply chain towards the performance of food manufacturing in Malaysia. *Management Science Letters*, *8*(7), 755–766. doi:10.5267/j.msl.2018.5.0010

Azmi, F. R., Abdullah, A., Musa, H., & Wan Mahmood, W. H. (2020). Perception of food manufacturers towards adoption of halal food supply chain in Malaysia: Exploratory factor analysis. *Journal of Islamic Marketing*, *11*(3), 571–589. doi:10.1108/JIMA-12-2018-0236

Bai, C., Dallasega, P., Orzes, G., & Sarkis, J. (2020). Industry 4.0 technologies assessment: A sustainability perspective. *International Journal of Production Economics*, *229*, 107776. doi:10.1016/j.ijpe.2020.107776

Bhargava, N., Sharanagat, V. S., Mor, R. S., & Kumar, K. (2020). Active and intelligent biodegradable packaging films using food and food waste-derived bioactive compounds: A review. *Trends in Food Science & Technology*, *105*, 385–401. doi:10.1016/j.tifs.2020.09.015

Bonilla, S. H., Silva, H. R. O., da Silva, M. T., Gonçalves, R. F., & Sacomano, J. B. (2018). Industry 4.0 and sustainability implications: A scenario-based analysis of the impacts and challenges. *Sustainability (Basel)*, *10*(10), 3740. doi:10.3390/su10103740

Bux, C., Varese, E., Amicarelli, V., & Lombardi, M. (2022). Halal Food Sustainability between Certification and Blockchain: A Review. *Sustainability (Basel)*, *14*(4), 2152. doi:10.3390/su14042152

Coppola, G., Gaudio, M. T., Lopresto, C. G., Calabro, V., Curcio, S., & Chakraborty, S. (2021). Bioplastic from Renewable Biomass: A Facile Solution for a Greener Environment. *Earth Systems and Environment*, *5*(2), 231–251. doi:10.1007/s41748-021-00208-7

Crippa, M., Solazzo, E., Guizzardi, D., Monforti-Ferrario, F., Tubiello, F. N., & Leip, A. (2021). Food systems are responsible for a third of global anthropogenic GHG emissions. *Nature Food*, *2*(3), 198–209. doi:10.1038/s43016-021-00225-9 PMID:37117443

Deku, W. A., Wang, J., & Das, N. (2023). Innovations in entrepreneurial marketing dimensions: Evidence of Halal food SMES in Ghana. *Journal of Islamic Marketing*, *14*(3), 680–713. doi:10.1108/JIMA-03-2021-0098

Donner, M., Gohier, R., & de Vries, H. (2020). A new circular business model typology for creating value from agro-waste. *The Science of the Total Environment*, *716*, 137065. Advance online publication. doi:10.1016/j.scitotenv.2020.137065 PMID:32044489

Elseidi, R. I. (2018). Determinants of halal purchasing intentions: Evidences from UK. *Journal of Islamic Marketing*, *9*(1), 167–190. doi:10.1108/JIMA-02-2016-0013

Endri, E., Syafarudin, A., Santoso, S., Imaningsih, E. S., Suharti, T., & Rinda, R. T. (2020). Consumption behavior patterns of generations Y Halal products in Indonesia. *Academy of Entrepreneurship Journal*, *26*(2), 1–10. https://www.scopus.com/inward/record.uri?eid=2-s2.0-85087295237&partnerID=40&md5=c9cf2090de2186839b0aef47463b286a

Fawzy, S., Osman, A. I., Doran, J., & Rooney, D. W. (2020). Strategies for mitigation of climate change: A review. *Environmental Chemistry Letters*, *18*(6), 2069–2094. doi:10.1007/s10311-020-01059-w

Fernando, R. L. S. (2019). Solid waste management of local governments in the Western Province of Sri Lanka: An implementation analysis. *Waste Management (New York, N.Y.)*, *84*, 194–203. doi:10.1016/j.wasman.2018.11.030 PMID:30691892

Haleem, A., Khan, M. I., & Khan, S. (2021). Conceptualising a framework linking halal supply chain management with sustainability: An India centric study. *Journal of Islamic Marketing*, *12*(8), 1535–1552. doi:10.1108/JIMA-07-2019-0149

Hannan, M. A., Hoque, M. M., Hussain, A., Yusof, Y., & Ker, P. J. (2018). State-of-the-Art and Energy Management System of Lithium-Ion Batteries in Electric Vehicle Applications: Issues and Recommendations. *IEEE Access : Practical Innovations, Open Solutions*, *6*, 19362–19378. doi:10.1109/ACCESS.2018.2817655

Hew, J.-J., Wong, L.-W., Tan, G. W.-H., Ooi, K.-B., & Lin, B. (2020). The blockchain-based Halal traceability systems: A hype or reality? *Supply Chain Management*, *25*(6), 863–879. doi:10.1108/SCM-01-2020-0044

Huang, B., Pan, Z., Su, X., & An, L. (2018). Recycling of lithium-ion batteries: Recent advances and perspectives. *Journal of Power Sources*, *399*, 274–286. doi:10.1016/j.jpowsour.2018.07.116

Huriah, T., Permana, I., Octavia, M., & Abdul Hamid, S. H. B. (2022). Understanding the purchasing behaviors of halal cosmetics of teenagers in Indonesia using the theory of planned behavior and theory of consumption value. *Bali Medical Journal*, *11*(3), 1608–1613. doi:10.15562/bmj.v11i3.3704

Iranmanesh, M., Mirzaei, M., Parvin Hosseini, S. M., & Zailani, S. (2020). Muslims' willingness to pay for certified halal food: An extension of the theory of planned behaviour. *Journal of Islamic Marketing*, *11*(1), 14–30. doi:10.1108/JIMA-03-2018-0049

Islam, M. M., Ab Talib, M. S., & Muhamad, N. (2023). Developing theoretical lenses for upstream halal businesses. *Journal of Islamic Marketing*. doi:10.1108/JIMA-05-2022-0156

Ismail, M. B., Mohamad, N. B., & Ahamat, A. (2023). Learning Orientation as Mediator between International Entrepreneurial Orientation and International Firm Performance in Global Halal Industry. *Global Journal Al-Thaqafah*, *SI*(Special Issue), 53–64. doi:10.7187/GJATSI072023-5

Kakani, V., Nguyen, V. H., Kumar, B. P., Kim, H., & Pasupuleti, V. R. (2020). A critical review on computer vision and artificial intelligence in food industry. *Journal of Agriculture and Food Research*, *2*, 100033. Advance online publication. doi:10.1016/j.jafr.2020.100033

Kamble, S. S., Gunasekaran, A., & Gawankar, S. A. (2018). Sustainable Industry 4.0 framework: A systematic literature review identifying the current trends and future perspectives. *Process Safety and Environmental Protection*, *117*, 408–425. doi:10.1016/j.psep.2018.05.009

Katuk, N. (2019). The application of blockchain for halal product assurance: A systematic review of the current developments and future directions. *International Journal of Advanced Trends in Computer Science and Engineering*, *8*(5), 1893–1902. doi:10.30534/ijatcse/2019/13852019

Khan, M. I., Khan, S., & Haleem, A. (2022). Analysing barriers towards management of Halal supply chain: A BWM approach. *Journal of Islamic Marketing*, *13*(1), 66–80. doi:10.1108/JIMA-09-2018-0178

Khan, M. I., Shin, J. H., & Kim, J. D. (2018). The promising future of microalgae: Current status, challenges, and optimization of a sustainable and renewable industry for biofuels, feed, and other products. *Microbial Cell Factories*, *17*(1), 36. doi:10.1186/s12934-018-0879-x PMID:29506528

Khan, S., Khan, M. I., Haleem, A., & Jami, A. R. (2022). Prioritising the risks in Halal food supply chain: An MCDM approach. *Journal of Islamic Marketing*, *13*(1), 45–65. doi:10.1108/JIMA-10-2018-0206

Kismawadi, E. R. (2023). Improving Islamic bank performance through agency cost and dual board governance. *Journal of Islamic Accounting and Business Research*. doi:10.1108/JIABR-01-2023-0035

Kismawadi, E. R. (2024). Contribution of Islamic banks and macroeconomic variables to economic growth in developing countries: Vector error correction model approach (VECM). *Journal of Islamic Accounting and Business Research*, *15*(2), 306–326. doi:10.1108/JIABR-03-2022-0090

Kismawadi, E. R., Irfan, M., Al Muddatstsir, U. D., & Abdulkarim, F. M. (2023). Fintech innovations: Risk mitigation strategies in Islamic finance. In *Fintech Applications in Islamic Finance* (pp. 35–58). AI, Machine Learning, and Blockchain Techniques. doi:10.4018/979-8-3693-1038-0.ch003

Kouhizadeh, M., Saberi, S., & Sarkis, J. (2021). Blockchain technology and the sustainable supply chain: Theoretically exploring adoption barriers. *International Journal of Production Economics*, *231*, 107831. doi:10.1016/j.ijpe.2020.107831

Krisharyanto, E., Retnowati, E., & Hastuti, N. T. (2019). Regulation and provisions for supervision of halal products in Indonesia. *Journal of Legal, Ethical and Regulatory Issues, 22*(1). https://www.scopus.com/inward/record.uri?eid=2-s2.0-85063267345&partnerID=40&md5=65f177af5906f2dab2f098ca6562db8a

Kumar, S., Mukherjee, A., & Dutta, J. (2020). Chitosan based nanocomposite films and coatings: Emerging antimicrobial food packaging alternatives. *Trends in Food Science & Technology*, *97*, 196–209. doi:10.1016/j.tifs.2020.01.002

Kusiak, A. (2018). Smart manufacturing. *International Journal of Production Research*, *56*(1–2), 508–517. doi:10.1080/00207543.2017.1351644

Laila, N., Ratnasari, R. T., Ismail, S., Mohd Hidzir, P. A., & Mahphoth, M. H. (2023). The intention of small and medium enterprises' owners to participate in waqf: The case of Malaysia and Indonesia. *International Journal of Islamic and Middle Eastern Finance and Management*, *16*(3), 429–447. doi:10.1108/IMEFM-01-2022-0014

Manthiram, A. (2020). A reflection on lithium-ion battery cathode chemistry. *Nature Communications*, *11*(1), 1550. doi:10.1038/s41467-020-15355-0 PMID:32214093

Masudin, I., Jie, F., Djajadikerta, H., & Widayat, W. (2021). The effect of halal retail and manufacturing technology readiness on halal meat logistics performance. *International Journal of Logistics Systems and Management*, *40*(1), 1–27. doi:10.1504/IJLSM.2021.117688

Mat, N. K. N., Sulaiman, Y., Abdghani, N. H., & Mohamad, M. (2020). Halal consumption determinants: The mediating role of risk perception and muslim lifestyle. *Malaysian Journal of Consumer and Family Economics*, *24*, 63–78. https://www.scopus.com/inward/record.uri?eid=2-s2.0-85094201810&partnerID=40&md5=57285140ec6a05c8f5b9da0479241126

Mat Aron, N. S., Khoo, K. S., Chew, K. W., Show, P. L., Chen, W.-H., & Nguyen, T. H. P. (2020). Sustainability of the four generations of biofuels – A review. *International Journal of Energy Research*, *44*(12), 9266–9282. doi:10.1002/er.5557

Meena, R. S., Kumar, S., Datta, R., Lal, R., Vijayakumar, V., Brtnicky, M., Sharma, M. P., Yadav, G. S., Jhariya, M. K., Jangir, C. K., Pathan, S. I., Dokulilova, T., Pecina, V., & Marfo, T. D. (2020). Impact of agrochemicals on soil microbiota and management: A review. *Land (Basel)*, *9*(2), 34. doi:10.3390/land9020034

Mohamed, Y. H., Abdul Rahim, A. R., & Ma'aram, A. (2020). The effect of halal supply chain management on halal integrity assurance for the food industry in Malaysia. *Journal of Islamic Marketing*, *12*(9), 1734–1750. doi:10.1108/JIMA-12-2018-0240

Mohsin, M., Kamran, H. W., Atif Nawaz, M., Sajjad Hussain, M., & Dahri, A. S. (2021). Assessing the impact of transition from nonrenewable to renewable energy consumption on economic growth-environmental nexus from developing Asian economies. *Journal of Environmental Management*, *284*, 111999. doi:10.1016/j.jenvman.2021.111999 PMID:33556829

Mor, S., & Ravindra, K. (2023). Municipal solid waste landfills in lower- and middle-income countries: Environmental impacts, challenges and sustainable management practices. *Process Safety and Environmental Protection*, *174*, 510–530. doi:10.1016/j.psep.2023.04.014

Munasinghe, M., Jayasinghe, P., Deraniyagala, Y., Matlaba, V. J., Santos, J. F. D., Maneschy, M. C., & Mota, J. A. (2019). Value–Supply Chain Analysis (VSCA) of crude palm oil production in Brazil, focusing on economic, environmental and social sustainability. *Sustainable Production and Consumption*, *17*, 161–175. doi:10.1016/j.spc.2018.10.001

Naylor, R. L., Hardy, R. W., Buschmann, A. H., Bush, S. R., Cao, L., Klinger, D. H., Little, D. C., Lubchenco, J., Shumway, S. E., & Troell, M. (2021). A 20-year retrospective review of global aquaculture. *Nature*, *591*(7851), 551–563. doi:10.1038/s41586-021-03308-6 PMID:33762770

Ngah, A. H., Gabarre, S., Han, H., Rahi, S., Al-Gasawneh, J. A., & Park, S.-H. (2021). Intention to purchase halal cosmetics: Do males and females differ? a multigroup analysis. *Cosmetics*, *8*(1), 1–14. doi:10.3390/cosmetics8010019

Nor Zaidi, F. L. A., Jamaludin, M. A., & Tukiran, N. A. (2022). MUSLIM CONSUMERS' PERCEPTIONS ON COUNTERFEIT COSMETICS. *Malaysian Journal of Syariah and Law*, *10*(1), 76–82. doi:10.33102/mjsl.vol10no1.385

Nugroho, A. J. S., Ihalauw, J. J. O. I., & Kristian, N. A. N. A. (2022). The Moderating Effect of Trust and Product Involvement on Antecedents of Halal Brands to Purchase Intention towards the Competitiveness of the Sharia Economic System in Indonesia. *Journal of System and Management Sciences*, *12*(5), 374–396. doi:10.33168/JSMS.2022.0522

Osman, S., Ab. Rahman, S., & Jalil, A. (2020). Issues in halal food product labelling: A conceptual paper. *Food Research*, *4*, 214–219. doi:10.26656/fr.2017.4(S1).S15

Parvin Hosseini, S. M., Mirzaei, M., & Iranmanesh, M. (2020). Determinants of Muslims' willingness to pay for halal certified food: Does religious commitment act as a moderator in the relationships? *Journal of Islamic Marketing*, *11*(6), 1225–1243. doi:10.1108/JIMA-02-2018-0043

Prayuti, Y. (2020). MUSLIM FOOD CONSUMER PROTECTION THROUGH THE REGULATION OF HALAL LABELS IN INDONESIA. *Jurnal IUS Kajian Hukum Dan Keadilan*, *8*(1), 17–25. doi:10.29303/ius.v8i1.716

Rachmawati, E., & Suroso, A. (2022). A moderating role of halal brand awareness to purchase decision making. *Journal of Islamic Marketing*, *13*(2), 542–563. doi:10.1108/JIMA-05-2020-0145

Rana, R. L., Tricase, C., & De Cesare, L. (2021). Blockchain technology for a sustainable agri-food supply chain. *British Food Journal*, *123*(11), 3471–3485. doi:10.1108/BFJ-09-2020-0832

Rejeb, A., Keogh, J. G., Rejeb, K., & Dean, K. (2021). Halal food supply chains: A literature review of sustainable measures and future research directions. *Foods and Raw Materials*, *9*(1), 106–116. doi:10.21603/2308-4057-2021-1-106-116

Rejeb, A., Rejeb, K., & Zailani, S. (2021). Are Halal Food Supply Chains Sustainable: A Review And Bibliometric Analysis. *Journal of Foodservice Business Research*, *24*(5), 554–595. doi:10.1080/15378020.2021.1883214

Ridho Kismawadi, E., Irfan, M., & Shah, S. M. A. R. (2023). Revolutionizing islamic finance: Artificial intelligence's role in the future of industry. In The Impact of AI Innovation on Financial Sectors in the Era of Industry 5.0 (pp. 184–207). doi:10.4018/979-8-3693-0082-4.ch011

Rizkitysha, T. L., & Hananto, A. (2022). Do knowledge, perceived usefulness of halal label and religiosity affect attitude and intention to buy halal-labeled detergent? *Journal of Islamic Marketing*, *13*(3), 649–670. doi:10.1108/JIMA-03-2020-0070

Sarkodie, S. A., & Strezov, V. (2019). Effect of foreign direct investments, economic development and energy consumption on greenhouse gas emissions in developing countries. *The Science of the Total Environment*, *646*, 862–871. doi:10.1016/j.scitotenv.2018.07.365 PMID:30064112

Secinaro, S., & Calandra, D. (2021). Halal food: Structured literature review and research agenda. *British Food Journal*, *123*(1), 225–243. doi:10.1108/BFJ-03-2020-0234

Sharma, R., Kamble, S. S., Gunasekaran, A., Kumar, V., & Kumar, A. (2020). A systematic literature review on machine learning applications for sustainable agriculture supply chain performance. *Computers & Operations Research*, *119*, 104926. doi:10.1016/j.cor.2020.104926

Sullivan, K., Thomas, S., & Rosano, M. (2018). Using industrial ecology and strategic management concepts to pursue the Sustainable Development Goals. *Journal of Cleaner Production*, *174*, 237–246. doi:10.1016/j.jclepro.2017.10.201

Sumarliah, E., & Al-hakeem, B. (2023). The effects of digital innovations and sustainable supply chain management on business competitive performance post-COVID-19. *Kybernetes*, *52*(7), 2568–2596. doi:10.1108/K-09-2022-1326

Surjandari, I., Yusuf, H., Laoh, E., & Maulida, R. (2021). Designing a Permissioned Blockchain Network for the Halal Industry using Hyperledger Fabric with multiple channels and the raft consensus mechanism. *Journal of Big Data*, *8*(1), 10. doi:10.1186/s40537-020-00405-7

Susanti, C. E. (2021). The effect of push motivational factors and pull motivational factors on tourist loyalty through satisfaction on halal tourists in east java. *WSEAS Transactions on Environment and Development*, *17*, 510–519. doi:10.37394/232015.2021.17.49

Tan, A., Gligor, D., & Ngah, A. (2022). Applying Blockchain for Halal food traceability. *International Journal of Logistics*, *25*(6), 947–964. doi:10.1080/13675567.2020.1825653

Tan, C., & McClements, D. J. (2021). Application of advanced emulsion technology in the food industry: A review and critical evaluation. *Foods*, *10*(4), 812. doi:10.3390/foods10040812 PMID:33918596

Tayob, S. (2021). Halal consumption as ethical practice: Negotiating halal certification in South Africa. *Islamic Africa*, *11*(1), 71–93. doi:10.1163/21540993-01101006

Tseng, M.-L., Ha, H. M., Tran, T. P. T., Bui, T.-D., Lim, M. K., Lin, C.-W., & Helmi Ali, M. (2022). Data-driven on sustainable food supply chain: A comparison on Halal and non-Halal food system. *Journal of Industrial and Production Engineering*, *39*(6), 430–457. doi:10.1080/21681015.2022.2040622

Usman, H., Chairy, C., & Projo, N. W. K. (2022). Impact of Muslim decision-making style and religiosity on intention to purchasing certified halal food. *Journal of Islamic Marketing*, *13*(11), 2268–2289. doi:10.1108/JIMA-01-2021-0027

Veleva, V., & Bodkin, G. (2018). Corporate-entrepreneur collaborations to advance a circular economy. *Journal of Cleaner Production*, *188*, 20–37. doi:10.1016/j.jclepro.2018.03.196

Vollmer, I., Jenks, M. J. F., Roelands, M. C. P., White, R. J., van Harmelen, T., de Wild, P., van der Laan, G. P., Meirer, F., Keurentjes, J. T. F., & Weckhuysen, B. M. (2020). Beyond Mechanical Recycling: Giving New Life to Plastic Waste. *Angewandte Chemie International Edition*, *59*(36), 15402–15423. doi:10.1002/anie.201915651 PMID:32160372

Wamba-Taguimdje, S.-L., Fosso Wamba, S., Kala Kamdjoug, J. R., & Tchatchouang Wanko, C. E. (2020). Influence of artificial intelligence (AI) on firm performance: The business value of AI-based transformation projects. *Business Process Management Journal*, *26*(7), 1893–1924. doi:10.1108/BPMJ-10-2019-0411

Wu, K., Wang, S., Song, W., Zhang, J., Wang, Y., Liu, Q., Yu, J., Ye, Y., Li, S., Chen, J., Zhao, Y., Wang, J., Wu, X., Wang, M., Zhang, Y., Liu, B., Wu, Y., Harberd, N. P., & Fu, X. (2020). Enhanced sustainable green revolution yield via nitrogen-responsive chromatin modulation in rice. *Science*, *367*(6478), eaaz2046. Advance online publication. doi:10.1126/science.aaz2046 PMID:32029600

Yaka, Z. (2022). The Effects Of Measures Taken In The Scope Of The Islamic Price Policy On Investment, Production, Employment, And Stability. *Ilahiyat Studies*, *13*(1), 83–117. doi:10.12730/13091719.2022.131.234

Zuraini, M. I., Muhammad Afiq, M., & Nurzulain, Z. (2019). The influence of cross-generation attitude on halal food products. *Malaysian Applied Biology*, *48*(2), 41–46. https://www.scopus.com/inward/record.uri?eid=2-s2.0-85070731515&partnerID=40&md5=1c34445544f5c856f727f11789899a91

Chapter 11
How Does Environmental Proactivity Affect Green Innovation?
An Assessment of Determinants of Sustainable Practices Adoption in the Wine Industry

Marcos Carchano Alcaraz
University of Castilla-La Mancha, Spain

Inmaculada Carrasco
https://orcid.org/0000-0002-3844-4569
University of Castilla-La Mancha, Spain

Ángela González
University of Castilla-La Mancha, Spain

ABSTRACT

This chapter aims to examine how the patterns of environmental proactivity, fueled by internal, external, or reactive motivations, influence the eco-innovative behaviour and the economic and financial performance of family companies in the wine sector. An empirical study was carried out based on a structural equations model, using a partial least squares technique, for a sample of 79 Spanish family wine companies taken between 2017 and 2018. The study allowed us to highlight the eco-innovative nature of family businesses in the wine sector in Spain. The search for greater effectiveness and efficiency, cost savings, improved profitability, and greater competitiveness, together with regulatory factors (regulatory framework and public incentives) were among the main drivers of environmental proactivity and eco-innovation in the companies analysed. Additionally, the development of environmental innovations results in greater economic and financial performance.

DOI: 10.4018/979-8-3693-2149-2.ch011

INTRODUCTION

Family companies are the main form of business worldwide; two thirds of businesses are family firms, creating between 50% and 80% of jobs and contributing to a large part of global GDP (between 70% and 90%) (De Massis et al., 2018). In Spain, family businesses account for 88.8% of the total business fabric, generating 67% of employment and 57% of GDP. By sectors, family firms are the main type of company in construction (88%), other services (88%), agriculture, livestock and forestry (86%) and retail (86%), and in the wine sector, more than 80% of companies are family businesses, according to recent data published by the Family Business Institute.

These companies are characterised by sharing values, principles and a culture in which prudence, austerity, a long-term vision, or a commitment to the environment are factors that condition their structure and behaviour. Familiness determines decision-making (De Massis et al., 2013; Carnes e Irlanda, 2013), which, in turn, influences aspects such as expansion, internationalization, investment or innovation. Thus, without abandoning economic objectives, family businesses behave responsibly towards both the environment and their employees (Chrisman et al., 2005); due to features such as their long-term focus (Miller and Le Breton-Miller, 2005), they tend to be socially responsible and more environmentally proactive, all with a view to benefiting future generations (Cennamo et al., 2012; Berrone et al., 2012). Along the same lines, Craig and Dibrell (2006) highlight the commitment of family businesses to compliance with environmental policies, which subsequently enhances their environmental performance (Block and Wagner, 2014).

Thus, in a context of growing competitiveness, climate emergency and socio-economic uncertainty because of the COVID-19 crisis, family businesses are aware that their prosperity and viability depend on their ability to adapt to changes in the environment, where innovation plays a key role (Calabrò et al., 2019; Porter, 1980, Kraus et al., 2020). More specifically, environmental innovation is a tool that firms can use to combat the negative environmental effects of economic activity (Del Río et al., 2011), thus contributing to the achievement of the Sustainable Development Goals (Tamayo-Orbegozoetal, 2016) by combining economic prosperity with environmental benefits (OECD, 2012; Barbieri et al., 2016). In fact, the concept of eco-innovation refers to sustainability-focused innovation that enables improved environmental performance (Carrillo-Hermosilla et al., 2010; Horbach et al., 2012; Díaz-García et al., 2015; Bossle et al., 2016; He et al., 2018). From an eco-innovation perspective, family businesses are among the most innovative organizations worldwide (Urbinati et al., 2017; De Massis et al., 2018), since their inimitable resources in terms of family participation (Krappe et al., 2011) and their inherent characteristics drive innovation as a source of growth and wealth (Zhara et al., 2004), while at the same time driving their success (Duran et al., 2016).

The wine sector accounts for an important part of world economic activity (Bigliardi and Galati, 2013; Dascalau et al., 2019). In Spain, this sector has acquired certain economic, social, cultural and environmental relevance. According to data published by the International Wine Observatory (OIV, 2023), in 2022 the size of the world vineyard was estimated at 7.3 million ha, of which 13.1% belong to Spain, making it the country with the largest vineyard area in the world. World wine production in 2022 was estimated at 258 million hl, the largest producers being Italy (54.8 million hl), France (49.2 million hl) and Spain (44.9 million hl). For its part, the world wine trade generated 37.6 million euros. Exports were dominated by Spain, Italy and France, which together represented more than 50% of world market value and volume. Spain was the second largest exporter in volume with 21.2 million hl, behind Italy, and the third in value with 3.000 million euros behind France (12.300 million euros) and Italy (7.800 million euros).

One of the defining characteristics of the wine sector in Spain is the wide variety of wine producing companies (limited companies, cooperatives; individual and family companies; small and medium-sized companies; business groups, etc.). As a result, the eco-innovative behaviour of the sector is not homogeneous. For this reason, existing cross-sectional research (Barba-Sánchez and Atineza-Sahuquillo, 2016; del Brío-González and Barba-Sánchez, 2020) needs to be complemented with other studies that illustrate the particularities of each type of company.

As in other sectors, the wine sector faces pressures related to the impact of its activity on the environment and climate change. Consumers are major agents of change, demanding stronger social and environmental commitment from companies and governments, and prioritising value for money and personal safety in their purchases. However, environmental regulations (Román-Sánchez and Belmonte-Ureña, 2013) and the internal capacities of wineries (Angelova and Pastarmadzhieva, 2020) may also be key factors in explaining environmental proactivity and eco-innovation in Spanish family wineries.

Given the precedents in literature, this article aims to examine how proactive environmental practices, fuelled by internal, external, or reactive motivations, influence the eco-innovative behaviour and the economic and financial performance of family companies in the wine sector. To this end, an empirical study was carried out based on a structural equation model using a partial least squares technique is presented for a sample of 79 family wine companies, sampled in 2017, based on the Aragón-Correa questionnaire (1998). With this objective in mind, the study is divided into five parts. This introduction is followed by a presentation of the theoretical framework which establishes the relationships between family businesses, environmental proactivity, eco-innovation, and economic and financial performance. The third section develops the empirical analysis and section four presents evidence on the eco-innovative behaviour of family businesses. The fifth and final section presents the conclusions.

CONCEPTUAL FRAMEWORK

Family Businesses

Research on family businesses has grown significantly in recent years (Debicki et al., 2009; Swab et al., 2020). Family businesses are the main type of business entity (Gedajlovic et al., 2012; Poza, 2013; Morck and Yeung, 2004), representing approximately 90% of all companies worldwide (Aldrich and Cliff, 2003). Thus, they play an important role in the economy (La Porta et al., 1999; Faccio and Lang, 2002) through the generation of employment, well-being, and wealth (Fan et al., 2011; Astrachan and Shanker, 2003).

A wide variety of definitions of "family business" have been provided (Chrisman et al., 2005; Westhead and Cowling, 1998; Chua et al., 2012). Traditionally, the most common approach has focused on family participation in ownership, management, or control (Chua et al., 1999; Chrisman et al., 2012; Zahra, 2010). This approach establishes that family participation in the ownership of the company and presence in the governing board are sufficient conditions to classify a company as a family business (Pearson et al., 2008; Mazzi, 2011), in such a way that the family intervenes in the company's objectives, strategies and behaviours (Miller et al., 2013; Steier, 2003; Zahra et al., 2007). In contrast, the "essence approach" is based on the way in which the family contributes to the business, i.e., it is a resource-based approach

(Habbershon and Williams, 1999) in which the behaviour, resources, and capacities contributed by the family are valued. Thus, the essence approach focuses on the family's relevance in management, ownership and control (Dyer, 2006; Zellweger et al., 2011; Chrisman et al., 2005). The essential approach can be used to explain the different behaviours existing among the same group of family businesses, thus considering the existing heterogeneity (Chrisman et al., 2012; Westhead and Howoth, 2007; Nordqvist et al., 2014; Chua et al. al., 2012). In our case study, family businesses were defined as companies in which the family owned more than 50% of share capital.

Regardless of the specific definition of a family business, family involvement provides a valuable resource compared to other non-family businesses (Sharma, 2008; Zellweger et al., 2010; Berrone et al., 2012). This set of resources deriving from the interaction between the family and the business is known as "familiness" (Habbershon et al., 2003). They are considered to be inimitable resources (Krappe et al., 2011) that favour business growth and survival (Frank et al., 2010) and serve as a source of competitive advantage for innovation (Zahra et al., 2004, Röd, 2016).

Additionally, it should be noted that family businesses have their own characteristics, which differentiate them from other non-family firms, such as transgenerational succession, reciprocal altruism, family social capital, overlapping of business activities and family matters, family control in decision-making without external interference, long-term orientation, among other features (Gómez-Mejía et al., 2007; Le Breton-Miller and Miller 2006; Corbetta and Salvato 2004; Arregle et al. 2007; Dudaroğlu, et al., 2018; Chua et al., 1999).

Eco-Innovation

Innovation, in the business framework, is recognized as one of the main elements necessary to guarantee the survival of companies (Shumpeter, 1934). Furthermore, taking into account the current environmental framework, innovation plays a key role in combating the harmful effects of economic activity on the environment. As regards the concept of environmental innovation, also known as eco-innovation or "green" innovation (Karakaya et al., 2014; Tariq et al., 2017), the European Commission (2007) defines this as "any innovation that makes progress towards the goal of sustainable development by reducing impacts on the environment, increasing resilience to environmental pressures or using natural resources more efficiently and responsibly". In general, all current definitions of eco-innovation emphasize its role in enhancing environmental and social performance (Carrillo-Hermosilla et al., 2010; Chang and Chen, 2013; Horbach et al., 2012; Díaz-García et al., 2015; Boons et al., 2013; Ben Arfi et al., 2018). Therefore, eco-innovation constitutes a critical element for ensuring sustainable and smart growth (Dangelico and Pujari, 2010; Horbach, 2008; Jabbour et al., 2015; Tamayo-Orbegozo et al., 2016), by simultaneously supporting the achievement of economic and environmental benefits (Schiedering et al., 2012; Berrone et al., 2013; Kemp, 2010). Thus, the development and application of eco-innovations will allow companies to contribute to the achievement of the sustainable development goals (Wong et al., 2013; Bhutta et al., 2021; Ding et al., 2021) and, at the same time, help them to develop competitive advantages (Weng et al., 2015; Chiou et al., 2011; Dangelico, 2016; Block, 2012, Chu et al., 2019), improve competitiveness (Sarkar, 2013; Stari and Kanashiro, 2013; Sellitto et al., 2020; Fernando et al., 2021), increase cost efficiency and make more efficient use of resources (Albort-Morant et al., 2018; Porter and Der Linde, 1995; Wang et al., 2017; Díaz-García et al., 2015), reduce pollution rates (Stanocvic et al., 2015; Amore and Bennedsen, 2016), among others. Moreover, the incorporation of these types of innovations has been positively related with the economic, environmental, and financial performance of companies (Porter and Van del Linde, 1995; Danso and Adomako, 2019; Zhang et al., 2019; Ar, 2012; Horváthová, 2012; Hojnik et al., 2018; Roy and Khastagir, 2016; Moyano-Fuentes et al., 2019). In this sense, eco-innovative companies are defined as firms immersed in sustainable development through green innovations (Marcus and Fremeth, 2009).

In the literature on eco-innovation, three large groups of determining factors of eco-innovation have been identified: normative, internal, and external (Pereira and Vence, 2012; Horbach et al., 2012; Barbieri et al., 2016; Lin et al., 2013). Regulatory factors refer to business behaviour driven by legislative pressure in relation to environmental aspects. Many authors have claimed that regulations are an important determinant of eco-innovation (Huang et al., 2009; De Marchi, 2012). For example, the study carried out by Horbach, Rammer, and Rennings (2012) identified that companies subject to environmental regulations are more likely to innovate than those that are not. Kammerer (2009) showed how companies implement environmental innovations when faced with a strict regulatory framework. Failure to comply with the regulatory framework can lead to increased costs for companies, prompting them to be more reactive to eco-innovation (Berrone et al., 2013; Carrillo-Hermosilla et al., 2010; Chen et al., 2012; Kammerer, 2009), to the extent that sometimes the mere announcement of strict environmental regulations are conducive to business innovation (Khanna et al., 2009). Similarly, public incentives also play a major role in the application of environmental innovations (Horbach et al., 2013). The internal characteristics of companies also influence innovation processes (Fagerberg et al., 2005). Internal factors refer to the possession of capacities for the implementation of innovative strategies. These capabilities derive from the know-how held and developed by these companies. Internal drivers include the search for greater effectiveness and efficiency, environmental concerns, cost savings, search for greater performance (financial and economic), environmental culture, technological and organisational capabilities, degree of corporate social responsibility, employee training, degree of investment in R&D (Del Río et al., 2013; Kesidou and Demirel, 2012; Sarkis et al., 2010; Cainelli et al., 2012; De Marchi, 2012; Chang and Chen, 2013).

Finally, the literature identifies another group of factors that influence the eco-innovation process, namely, external factors, defined as pressures exerted by stakeholders in generic or specific environments (e.g. consumers, pressure groups, public administrations, etc.). The main external factors are technology development, market demand, and cooperation. Market demand appears to be related to the demands of consumers, suppliers, public institutions, and competitors (Huang et al., 2009; Gauthier and Wooldridge, 2012; Del Rio González, 2009). In this sense, cooperation between business and market forces is essential to promote eco-innovation. De Marchi (2012) carried out a study on manufacturing companies in Spain and concluded that formal cooperation with external partners is positively correlated with the development of environmental innovations. Similar conclusions were obtained by Triguero, Moreno-Mondéjar, and Davia (2013), who showed how collaboration networks with research institutes, agencies, and universities are essential for promoting eco-innovation. Cooperation between companies and suppliers is equally crucial, especially when it comes to guaranteeing the supply of ecological inputs (Albino et al., 2009). Therefore, external demands, which pressure companies to improve their environmental performance, help such firms to develop skills related to eco-innovation (Hicks and Dietmar, 2007; Wu et al., 2021; Triguero et al., 2017; Tu et al., 2021).

Family Businesses and Eco-Innovation

The family nature of a business has implications for the performance of family-owned firms (Jaskiewicz and Dyer, 2017). In particular, due to their family culture and a long-term orientation, family businesses are more likely to develop environmental strategies to benefit future generations (Delmas and Gergaud, 2014; Block and Wagner, 2014; Lumpkin et al., 2010, Cassia et al., 2011; Kammerlander and Ganter, 2015). In other words, these characteristics drive these companies to adopt more sustainable environmental behaviour (Doluca et al., 2018; Zahra et al., 2004), which, in turn, strengthens their innovation capacity (Perri and Peruffo, 2017; Llach and Nordquist, 2010; Laguir et al., 2016). Similarly, family social capital has been positively related with the development of innovations (Andrade et al., 2011). Academics have highlighted the negative implications of their greater conservatism and aversion to risk, maintenance of control and ownership, and propensity to preserve family resources (Cassia et al., 2011; Gómez -Mejía et al., 2014; Block et al., 2013; Souder et al., 2017; Chrisman and Patel, 2012; Sciascia et al., 2015). These latter characteristics pose an obstacle to innovation (Roessl et al., 2010). In this sense, it has been observed that family participation in ownership, management, and governance has a positive and negative influence on the innovation strategies adopted by family businesses (Chrisman et al., 2015).

Deriving from the strategic importance of eco-innovation, we will focus on the innovative nature of family businesses. As mentioned previously, family businesses have traditionally been seen as conservative from an innovation standpoint (Gómez-Mejía et al., 2007). This is far from the case, as some studies have highlighted the proactive approach adopted by such firms when investing in environmental strategies (Sharma and Sharma, 2011; Classen et al., 2014), resulting in a positive relationship between family ownership and innovation (Craig and Moores, 2006; Zahra, 2005; Classen et al., 2014; Matzler et al., 2015). In this sense, family businesses are innovative (Nieto et al., 2013). Specifically, Calabró, Vecchiari, Gast, Campopiano, De Massis, and Kraus (2019) carried out a systematic review of 78 articles in the literature and found that 67% of the articles comparing family and non-family businesses reported that the former ones were more innovative than the latter. On this point, authors such as Duran et al., (2016) have highlighted that although family businesses achieve greater innovation results than non-family firms, the former present lower levels of investment than the latter, i.e. comparatively speaking family businesses invest less in innovation, but do so more efficiently, resulting in the achievement of incremental innovations (Nieto et al., 2013; Röd, 2016). Thus, it has been shown that family businesses have a greater capacity to invest in innovation but do so less intensively due to their specific characteristics (Chrisman et al., 2015; Classen et al., 2014).

METHODOLOGY AND DATABASE

In accordance with the previous theoretical aspects, this empirical analysis attempted to verify the following hypotheses:

Hypothesis 1 (H_1): The internal factors of family businesses in the Spanish wine sector are positively associated with environmental proactivity.

Hypothesis 2 (H_2): Regulatory factors are positively associated with the environmental proactivity of family businesses in the Spanish wine sector.

Hypothesis 3 (H_3): External factors are positively associated with the environmental proactivity of family businesses in the Spanish wine sector.

Hypothesis 4 (H_4): The environmental proactivity of family businesses in the Spanish wine sector is positively associated with process eco-innovation.

Hypothesis 5 (H_5): The environmental proactivity of family businesses in the Spanish wine sector is positively associated with product eco-innovation.

Table 1. Details of the sample and data collection

Population Size	4093 Wineries Located in Spain (3520 family firms)
Sampling method	Questionnaire for the complete population
Final sample size	251 companies (79 family firms)
Subsample analyzed	79 family firms
Response rate	33% (4,6%)
Sampling error	6% (10,90%)
Data collection	Electronic questionnaire
Collection period	2017–2018

Hypothesis 6 (H_6): Process eco-innovations in family businesses in the Spanish wine sector will have a positive impact on company performance.

Hypothesis 7 (H_7): Product eco-innovations in family businesses in the Spanish wine sector will have a positive impact on company performance.

To contrast the hypotheses, a partial least squares (PLS) model was used with data from 79 family businesses. The analysed information was gathered using an electronic questionnaire, validated by Aragón-Correa (1998), and implemented at 251 wineries in the wine sector during 2017. Of the sample, 88 corresponded to family businesses. However, only 79 presented valid answers. This represents a 4,6% response rate and a sampling error of 10,9% for a confidence interval of 95%.

This technique allowed us to establish dependency relationships between variables that were not directly measurable (latent variables) (Hair et al., 2017; Ringle et al., 2018) by combining principal component analysis and multiple regressions. This methodology offers a series of practical advantages over its alternatives, hence its growing popularity in a wide variety of scientific fields (Ringle et al., 2012; Hair et al., 2012; Henseller et al., 2009), including research on family businesses (e.g. Sarstedt et al., 2014; Chua et al., 1999; Segaro et al., 2014). This method is suitable for small samples, in highly complex situations, with abnormally distributed variables, in non-experimental research with data obtained from surveys, and for testing a proposed theoretical framework (Sarstedt et al., 2018; Hair et al., 2013; Reinatz et al., 2009; Hair et al., 2019; Roldán and Sánchez-Franco, 2012; Rigdon et al., 2017). Therefore, PLS is one of the main methodologies for causal-predictive analysis (Fritzsche & Oz, 2007).

The structural equation model has two elements or sub-models (Henseler et al., 2015): the structural or internal model representing the dependency relationships between exogenous and endogenous variables, according to the theoretical model, enabling the calculation of structural coefficients and the evaluation of the weights and magnitudes of these relationships; and the measurement or external model, which shows the relationships between the construct (circles) and the factors (rectangles), analyses factorial loads and verifies that they are all correctly incorporated in each construct. The SEM model was estimated using the PLS technique with SmartPLS 3 software (Ringle et al., 2015).

Following the proposed theoretical framework, seven constructs were defined, fed by 29 indicators, referring to the sample of 79 family businesses. Within the model, the endogenous construct (financial performance) was directly explained by two exogenous constructs (product and process eco-innovation), which, in turn, acted as endogenous constructs, explained by environmental proactivity, which acted as an exogenous construct and endogenous. The latter was fed by three exogenous constructs: internal,

Table 2. Constructs and indicators

CONSTRUCT	INDICATORS
Financial performance (ξ_1)	Reference to satisfaction with the level of sales (RF1)
	Reference to satisfaction with sales growth (RF2)
	Reference to satisfaction with market share (RF3)
	Reference to satisfaction with profitability (RF4)
	Reference to satisfaction with a gross profit margin (RF5)
	Reference to satisfaction with operating profit (RF6)
	Reference to satisfaction with the achievement of objectives (RF7)
Product eco-innovation (ξ_2)	Reference to leadership in product eco-innovations (ET1)
	Reference to number of product eco-innovations (ET1)
	Reference to the intensity of product eco-innovation (ET3)
Process eco-innovation (ξ_3)	Reference to leadership in process eco-innovation (ET4)
	Reference to the number of process eco-innovations (ET5)
	Reference to the intensity of process eco-innovation (ET6)
Environmental proactivity (ξ_4)	Reference to the existence of environmental objetives and plans (PM1)
	Reference to explicit definition of company environmental policy (PM2)
	Reference to environmental criteria considered in selection of suppliers (PM3)
	Reference to environmental standards considered in selection of suppliers (PM4)
	Reference to environmental criteria considered in distribution (PM5)
	Reference to emphasis on commitment to the environment in marketing campaigns (PM6)
	Reference to collaboration with environmental organizations (PM7)
	Reference to sponsorship of environmental events (PM8)
Internal motivation (ξ_5)	Reference to the extension of the range of products (M1)
	Reference to the expansion of markets (M2)
	Reference to the improvement of profitability (M3)
	Reference to competitiveness (M4)
Reactive motivation (ξ_6)	Reference to the adaptation of the legal framework (M5)
	Reference to public incentives (M6)
External motivation (ξ_7)	Reference to adaptation to demand (M7)
	Reference to the actions of organizations and pressure groups (M8)
	External link: local industry associations (M9)

reactive, and external motivation. The definitions of the indicators of the latent variables were as follows (see Table 2).

4. Results and discussion

Figure 1 shows the results of the model obtained through SmartPLS 3. The proposed model is reflective. The arrows indicate the regression relationships between the indicators with the constructs (measurement model) and between the constructs (structural model). The space between the arrows

Figure 1. Structural equations model estimated through PLS

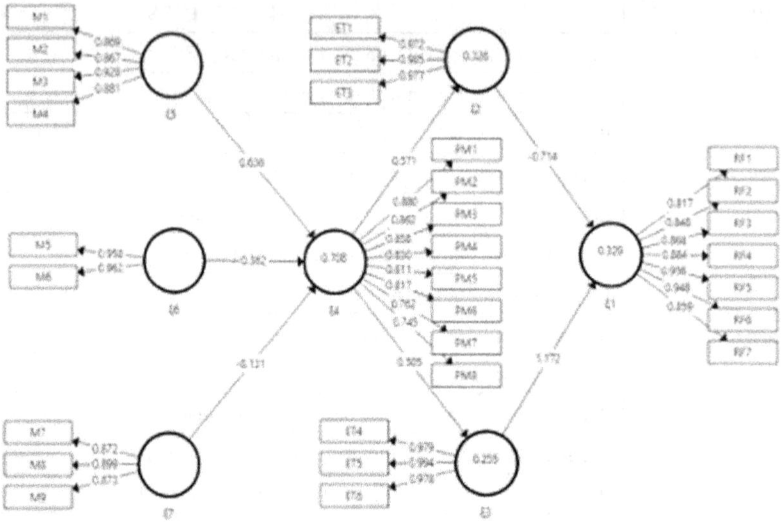

indicates the partial regression coefficients. In addition, the coefficient R^2 associated with each construct appears within each circle.

The PLS results were evaluated in two stages. First, the measurement model was examined through individual reliability, internal consistency, and validity. The factor loads were greater than 0.70, which indicated that the construct explained more than 50% of the variance of the indicator (see Figure 1). The next step consisted in evaluating the internal consistency of the constructs; this is normally evaluated through Jöreskog's rho to assess composite reliability (1971). Fornell and Larcker (1981) recommend values greater than 0.7 for this criterion; higher values correspond to a higher level of reliability. Another measure of internal consistency of each item and its respective construct is Cronbach's alpha value (Diamantopoulos et al., 2008), which indicates the internal coherence of the indicators; this must be greater than 0.7. As shown in Table 3, high internal consistency was observed for all the latent variables.

Convergent validity was evaluated using average variance extracted (AVE) (see Table 3) with a minimum acceptable value of 0.5 (Chin, 1998; Fornell and Larcker, 1981). A value of 0.5 or higher indicates that the construct explains more than 50% of the variance of its indicators. In our case, all the constructs

Table 3. Reliability and validity of the measurement model

	Cronbach's Alpha	Composite reliability	AVE
ξ_1	0.953	0.962	0.782
ξ_2	0.977	0.985	0.957
ξ_3	0.933	0.939	0.967
ξ_4	0.931	0.943	0.676
ξ_5	0.910	0.936	0.736
ξ_6	0.915	0.959	0.921
ξ_7	0.862	0.913	0.777

Table 4. Discriminant validity based on Fornell-Larcker.

	ξ1	ξ2	ξ3	ξ4	ξ5	ξ6	ξ7
ξ1	0.884						
ξ2	0.374	0.978					
ξ3	0.509	0.928	0.984				
ξ4	0.338	0.571	0.505	0.822			
ξ5	0.379	0.700	0.646	0.796	0.887		
ξ6	0.351	0.346	0.304	0.762	0.733	0.960	
ξ7	0.514	0.821	0.854	0.562	0.805	0.502	0.882

presented an AVE greater than 0.78. Discriminant validity was evaluated using Fornell-Larcker criterion (Fornell and Larcker, 1981) (see Table 4). This criterion establishes that the square AVE root of each construct must be greater than its correlation with the rest of the constructs. All correlations are smaller than the square root of AVE.

As regards the structural model, the ability of the model to predict endogenous constructs was studied. The coefficient R^2 associated with the regressions of the latent variables of the endogenous constructs was used. The value of R^2, which is reflected within the circles of the endogenous constructs (see Figure 1), indicated the variance of the construct explained by the model. The higher the value of R^2, the greater the predictive capacity of the model. In this sense, Falk and Miller (1992) indicate that endogenous latent variable values greater than 0.1 are acceptable for the goodness of fit of the model. The model showed that all latent variables (environmental proactivity, process eco-innovation, product eco-innovation, and company performance) presented an acceptable goodness of fit. However, although the R^2 coefficients were higher than 0.1, they were not high, a fact justified by the context of the study.

The technique used to evaluate the statistical significance of the latent regression coefficients was *bootstrapping*, which analyses the importance of the relationship between the variables. In terms of relevance, coefficients close to +1 indicate strong positive relationships, while coefficients close to -1 indicate strong negative relationships. The results revealed that five of the seven structural relationships were significant ($p \leq 0.05$) (see Table 5).

The latent internal motivation variable showed a significant positive correlation with the latent environmental proactivity variable (β_{eleven}= 0.636), which confirmed that the internal motivational factors of family businesses were positively associated with environmental proactivity (H1). Our results also confirmed the second hypothesis. Regulatory factors drive the environmental proactivity of family businesses (β_{12}= 0.362). Moreover, considering the specific indirect effects between the latent variables: 1. Internal motivation → environmental proactivity → eco-innovation (process and product) β_6 = 0.321 and β_4 0.363, and, 2. Reactive motivation → environmental proactivity → eco-innovation (process and product) β_7 = 0.183 and β_5 = 0.206, it was observed that family experience and reactive motivations have a significant indirect effect on environmental innovation. The results of the indirect and direct effects analysis confirmed the theoretical approach. Internal factors, which refer to the internal characteristics of companies, influence the innovation process (Fagerberg et al., 2005). Specifically, the greater product variety, market expansion, and improvement of profitability and competitiveness have been identified as internal factors. For their part, regulatory factors have also been confirmed as drivers of eco-innovation (Huang et al., 2009; De Marchi, 2012). The results obtained in this study coincide with the conclusions

Table 5. Structural model path coefficient values

	Original Sample	T statistics	Coefficient	Hypothesis accepted
$\xi_{5\rightarrow}\ \xi_4$	β_{11}= 0.636	3.862	0.000	H_1
$\xi_{6\rightarrow}\ \xi_4$	β_{12}= 0.362	3.959	0.000	H_2
$\xi_{7\rightarrow}\ \xi_4$	β_{13}= -0.131	0.743	0.458	
$\xi_{4\rightarrow}\ \xi_3$	β_{21}= 0.505	4.516	0.000	H_4
$\xi_{4\rightarrow}\ \xi_2$	β_{22}= 0.571	6.946	0.000	H_5
$\xi_{3\rightarrow}\ \xi_1$	B_{31}= 1,172	2.186	0.029	H_6
$\xi_{2\rightarrow}\ \xi_1$	β_{32}= -0.714	1.241	0.215	
Specific indirect effects		**Original Sample**	**T statistics**	**Coefficient**
$\xi_{5\rightarrow}\ \xi_{4\rightarrow}\ \xi_2$		B_4= 0.363	3.362	0.001
$\xi_{6\rightarrow}\ \xi_{4\rightarrow}\ \xi_2$		β_5= 0.206	4.131	0.000
$\xi_{5\rightarrow}\ \xi_{4\rightarrow}\ \xi_3$		β_6= 0.321	3.797	0.000
$\xi_{6\rightarrow}\ \xi_{4\rightarrow}\ \xi_3$		β_7= 0.183	3.052	0.002

reported by authors such as Horbach et al., (2012), Kammerer (2009), Carrillo-Hermosilla, et al., (2010), or Horbach et al., 2013, who showed how public incentives and the existence of a strict regulatory framework play a major role in the implementation of environmental innovations. However, the weight of these types of motivations is much lower than that of internal motivations.

Additionally, with respect to hypotheses 4 and 5, the results showed that the environmental proactivity of family businesses has positive and significant effects on both process (β_{21}= 0.505) and product (β_{22}= 0.571) innovation. This study supports the thesis that family businesses, due to their specific characteristics (Gómez-Megía et al., 2007; Corbetta and Salvato, 2004; Dudaroglu et al., 2018), behave proactively towards the development of environmental strategies (Cassia et al., 2011; Delmas and Gergaud, 2014; Doluca et al., 2018; Classen et al., 2014), thus enhancing their innovative capacity (Laguir et al., 2016; Perri and Perufflo, 2017). A positive relationship exists between family ownership and innovation (Matzler et al., 2015), thus confirming the findings reported by Nieto et al., (2013), who defended the innovative nature of family businesses. The sample did not offer significant results on moderation that could stem from factors such as age, degree of openness, belonging to a denomination of origin, etc.

Finally, a positive and significant correlation was observed between environmental process innovation and the economic and financial performance of companies (Porter and Van del Linde, 1995; Zhan et al., 2019; Hojnik et al., 2018; Roy and Khastagir, 2016; Moyano-Fuentes et al., 2019). In this sense, hypothesis 6 was confirmed.

CONCLUSION

In recent years, issues related to climate change and sustainable development have had a tremendous impact on society, driving companies to adopt environmental innovations as a means to achieve environmental objectives, respond to the growing demand for green products and services from *stakeholders* and meet regulatory requirements. Eco-innovation allows companies to develop sustainable activities, from both an economic and environmental standpoint.

This study examines the eco-innovative behaviour of family businesses in the wine sector. The choice of the sample was justified by several factors. On the one hand, family businesses account for a large proportion of the global and national business fabric (67% and 88.8%, respectively). This reveals their important role as generators of employment, wealth, and well-being. The wine sector is no exception and represents, in aggregate terms, approximately 1.5% of the national Gross Value Added (GVA).

The proposed empirical analysis contributes to the debate on eco-innovation within family businesses. Specifically, the innovative nature of such companies may be highlighted. The search for greater effectiveness and efficiency, cost savings, improved profitability, and greater competitiveness, coupled with regulatory factors (regulatory framework and public incentives), were among the main drivers of environmental proactivity and eco-innovation in family businesses in the wine sector. Additionally, the development of environmental innovations enhances their economic and financial performance.

These results are relevant for managers of family businesses in the sector, as they may benefit from evidence of how eco-innovation can help them to respond to stakeholder pressure and at the same time obtain better competitive advantages and enhance financial performance. They are also interesting for political decision-makers because they show that, although the current regulatory framework exerts a positive influence by fuelling environmental proactivity and eco-innovation in the companies analysed, its influence is much less relevant than internal factors. Therefore, there is room for improvement in the design and implementation of necessary measures. Future research should focus on more concrete aspects in this specific field.

The study had certain limitations, such as the fact that it was based on a cross-sectional sample. More in-depth research should be carried out in this field in the future through longitudinal studies. The size of the sample may also have posed limitations, since, although the employed methodology was adapted to the size of the sample and allowed interesting conclusions to be drawn, size may not be sufficient to obtain significant results regarding the potential moderating effects of factors such as age, the degree of openness, belonging to a designation of origin, etc. On the other hand, the study conducted focuses on the Spanish wine sector, which limits the generalization of results to other sectors and/or countries. Future research should develop similar studies applied to different sectors and/or countries.

REFERENCES

Albino, V., Balice, A., & Dangelico, R. M. (2009). Environmental strategies and green product development: An overview on sustainability-driven companies. *Business Strategy and the Environment*, *18*(2), 83–96. doi:10.1002/bse.638

Albort-Morant, G., Leal-Rodríguez, A. L., & De Marchi, V. (2018). Absorptive capacity and relationship learning mechanisms as complementary drivers of green innovation performance. *Journal of Knowledge Management*, *22*(2), 432–452. doi:10.1108/JKM-07-2017-0310

Aldrich, H. E., & Cliff, J. E. (2003). The pervasive effects of family on entrepreneurship: Toward a family embeddedness perspective. *Journal of Business Venturing*, *18*(5), 573–596. doi:10.1016/S0883-9026(03)00011-9

Amankwah-Amoah, J., Danso, A., & Adomako, S. (2019). Entrepreneurial orientation, environmental sustainability and new venture performance: Does stakeholder integration matter? *Business Strategy and the Environment*, *28*(1), 79–87. doi:10.1002/bse.2191

Amore, M. D., & Bennedsen, M. (2016). Corporate governance and green innovation. *Journal of Environmental Economics and Management*, *75*, 54–72. doi:10.1016/j.jeem.2015.11.003

Andrade, D. M., De Lima, J. B., Antonialli, L. M., & De Muylder, C. F. (2011). The family social capital impact in practices of learning, change and innovation in entrepreneurial family businesses. *African Journal of Business Management*, *5*, 12819–12828.

Angelova, M., & Pastarmadzhieva, D. (2020). Development of bio-based economy: Entrepreneurial endeavors and innovation across Bulgarian wine industry. *Journal of International Students*, *13*(2), 149–162. doi:10.14254/2071-8330.2020/13-2/11

Ar, I. M. (2012). The impact of green product innovation on firm performance and competitive capability: The moderating role of managerial environmental concern. *Procedia: Social and Behavioral Sciences*, *62*, 854–864. doi:10.1016/j.sbspro.2012.09.144

Aragón-Correa, J. A. (1998). Strategic proactivity and firm aroach to the natural environment. *Academy of Management Journal*, *41*(5), 556–567. doi:10.2307/256942

Arfi, W. B., Hikkerova, L., & Sahut, J. M. (2018). External knowledge sources, green innovation and performance. *Technological Forecasting and Social Change*, *129*, 210–220. doi:10.1016/j.techfore.2017.09.017

Arregle, J.-L., Hitt, M. A., Sirmon, D. G., & Very, P. (2007). The development of organizational social capital: Attributes of family firms. *Journal of Management Studies*, *44*(1), 72–95. doi:10.1111/j.1467-6486.2007.00665.x

Astrachan, J. H., & Shanker, M. C. (2003). Family businesses' contribution to the US economy: A closer look. *Family Business Review*, *16*(3), 211–219. doi:10.1177/08944865030160030601

Barba-Sánchez, V., & Atienza-Sahuquillo, C. (2016). Environmental proactivity and environmental and economic performance: Evidence from the winery sector *Sustainability*, *8*.

Barbieri, N., Ghisetti, C., Gilli, M., Marin, G., & Nicolli, F. (2016). A survey of the literature on environmental innovation based on main path analysis. *Journal of Economic Surveys*, *30*(3), 596–623. doi:10.1111/joes.12149

Berrone, P., Cruz, C., & Gomez-Mejia, L. (2012). Socioemotional wealth in family firms: Theoretical dimensions, assessment aroaches, and agenda for future research. *Family Business Review*, *25*(3), 258–279. doi:10.1177/0894486511435355

Berrone, P., Fosfuri, A., Gelabert, L., & Gomez-Mejia, L. R. (2013). Necessity as the mother of green inventions: Institutional pressures and environmental innovations. *Strategic Management Journal*, *34*(8), 891–909. doi:10.1002/smj.2041

Bhutta, M. K. S., Muzaffar, A., Egilmez, G., Huq, F., Malik, M. N., & Warraich, M. A. (2021). Environmental sustainability, innovation capacity, and supply chain management practices nexus: A mixed methods research approach. *Sustainable Production and Consumption*, *28*, 1508–1521. doi:10.1016/j.spc.2021.08.015

Bigliardi, B., & Galati, F. (2017). Family firms and collaborative innovation: Present debates and future research. *European Journal of Innovation Management*. doi:10.1108/EJIM-05-2017-0054

Block, J., Miller, D., Jaskiewicz, P., & Spiegel, F. (2013). Economic and technological importance of innovations in large family and founder firms: An analysis of patent data. *Family Business Review*, *26*(2), 180–199. doi:10.1177/0894486513477454

Block, J. H. (2012). R&D investments in family and founder firms: An agency perspective. *Journal of Business Venturing*, *27*(2), 248–265. doi:10.1016/j.jbusvent.2010.09.003

Block, J. H., & Wagner, M. (2014). The effect of family ownership on different dimensions of corporate social responsibility: Evidence from large U.S. firms. *Business Strategy and the Environment*, *23*(7), 475–492. doi:10.1002/bse.1798

Boons, F., Montalvo, C., Quist, J., & Wagner, M. (2013). Sustainable innovation, business models and economic performance: An overview. *Journal of Cleaner Production*, *45*, 1–8. doi:10.1016/j.jclepro.2012.08.013

Bossle, M. B., de Barcellos, M. D., Vieira, L. M., & Sauvée, L. (2016). The drivers for adoption of eco-innovation. *Journal of Cleaner Production*, *113*, 861–872. doi:10.1016/j.jclepro.2015.11.033

Cainelli, G., Mazzanti, M., & Montresor, S. (2012). Environmental innovations, local networks and internationalization. *Industry and Innovation*, *19*(8), 697–734. doi:10.1080/13662716.2012.739782

Calabrò, A., Vecchiarini, M., Gast, J., Campopiano, G., De Massis, A., & Kraus, S. (2019). Innovation in family firms: A systematic literature review and guidance for future research. *International Journal of Management Reviews*, *21*(3), 317–355. doi:10.1111/ijmr.12192

Carnes, C. M., & Ireland, R. D. (2013). Familiness and innovation: Resource bundling as the missing link. *Entrepreneurship Theory and Practice*, *37*(6), 1399–1419. doi:10.1111/etap.12073

Carrillo-Hermosilla, J., Del Río, P., & Könnölä, T. (2010). Diversity of eco-innovations: Reflections from selected case studies. *Journal of Cleaner Production*, *18*(10), 1073–1083. doi:10.1016/j.jclepro.2010.02.014

Cassia, L., De Massis, A., & Pizzurno, E. (2011). An exploratory investigation on NPD in small family businesses from Northern Italy, *International Journal of Business, Management, and social sciences*, *2*, 1-14.

Cennamo, C., Berrone, P., Cruz, C., & Gomez-Mejia, L. R. (2012). Socio-emotional wealth and proactive stakeholder engagement: Why family-controlled firms care more about their stakeholders. *Entrepreneurship Theory and Practice*, *36*(6), 1153–1173. doi:10.1111/j.1540-6520.2012.00543.x

Chain, M. M., Vermeulen, W. J., Meeus, M. T., & Hekkert, M. P. (2009). Enhancing our understanding of the role of environmental policy in environmental innovation: Adoption explained by the accumulation of policy instruments and agent-based factors. *Environmental Science & Policy*, *12*(7), 934–947. doi:10.1016/j.envsci.2009.06.001

Chang, C., & Chen, Y. (2013). Green organizational identity and green innovation. *Management Decision*, *51*(5), 1056–1070. doi:10.1108/MD-09-2011-0314

Chen, Y., Chang, C., & Wu, F. (2012). Origins of green innovations: The differences between proactive and reactive green innovations. *Management Decision*, *50*(3), 368–398. doi:10.1108/00251741211216197

Chin, W. W. (1998). Issues and Opinion on Structural Equation Modeling. *Management Information Systems Quarterly*, *22*, 1, 7–15.

Chiou, T. Y., Chan, H. K., Lettice, F., & Chung, S. H. (2011). The influence of greening the suliers and green innovation on environmental performance and competitive advantage in Taiwan. *Transportation Research Part E, Logistics and Transportation Review*, *47*(6), 822–836. doi:10.1016/j.tre.2011.05.016

Chrisman, J., Chua, J., De Massis, A., Frattini, F., & Wright, M. (2015). The ability and willingness paradox in family firm innovation. *Journal of Product Innovation Management*, *32*(3), 310–318. doi:10.1111/jpim.12207

Chrisman, J., & Patel, P. (2012). Variations in R&D investments of family and nonfamily firms: Behavioral agency and myopic loss aversion perspectives. *Academy of Management Journal*, *55*(4), 976–997. doi:10.5465/amj.2011.0211

Chu, Z., Wang, L., & Lai, F. (2018). Customer pressure and green innovations at third party logistics providers in China: The moderation effect of organizational culture. *International Journal of Logistics Management*, *30*(1), 57–75. doi:10.1108/IJLM-11-2017-0294

Chua, J. H., Chrisman, J. J., & Sharma, P. (1999). Defining the family business by behavior. *Entrepreneurship Theory and Practice*, *23*(4), 19–39. doi:10.1177/104225879902300402

Chua, J. H., Chrisman, J. J., Steier, L. P., & Rau, S. B. (2012). Sources of heterogeneity in family firms: An introduction. *Entrepreneurship Theory and Practice*, *44*(6), 1, 3–19. doi:10.1111/j.1540-6520.2012.00540.x

Classen, N., Carree, M., Van Gils, A., & Peters, B. (2014). Innovation in family and non-family SMEs: An exploratory analysis. *Small Business Economics*, *42*(3), 595–609. doi:10.1007/s11187-013-9490-z

Corbetta, G., & Salvato, C. (2004). Self-serving or self-actualizing? Models of man and agency costs in different types of family firms: A commentary on Comparing the agency costs of family and non-family firms: Conceptual Issues and Exploratory Evidence. *Entrepreneurship Theory and Practice*, *28*(4), 355–362. doi:10.1111/j.1540-6520.2004.00050.x

Craig, J. B., & Dibrell, C. (2006). The natural environment, innovation, and firm performance: A comparative study. *Family Business Review*, *19*(4), 275–288. doi:10.1111/j.1741-6248.2006.00075.x

Craig, J. B. L., & Moores, K. (2006). A 10 year longitudinal investigation of strategy, systems, and environment on innovation in family firms. *Family Business Review*, *19*(1), 1–10. doi:10.1111/j.1741-6248.2006.00056.x

Dangelico, R. M. (2016). Green product innovation: Where we are and where we are going. *Business Strategy and the Environment*, *25*(8), 560–576. doi:10.1002/bse.1886

Dascalu, I., Manescu, C., & Sirb, N. M. (2019). The impact of the wine sector on economy. *Journal of Biotechnology*, *305*, S86. doi:10.1016/j.jbiotec.2019.05.296

De Marchi, V. (2012). Environmental innovation and R&D cooperation: Empirical evidence from Spanish manufacturing firms. *Research Policy*, *41*(3), 614–623. doi:10.1016/j.respol.2011.10.002

De Massis, A., Frattini, F., & Lichtenthaler, U. (2013). Research on technological innovation in family firms: Present debates and future directions. *Family Business Review*, *26*(1), 10–31. doi:10.1177/0894486512466258

De Massis, A., Kotlar, J., Wright, M., & Kellermanns, F. W. (2018). Sector-based entrepreneurial capabilities and the promise of sector studies in entrepreneurship. *Entrepreneurship Theory and Practice*, *42*(1), 1, 3–23. doi:10.1177/1042258717740548

Debicki, B. J., Matherne, C. F. III, Kellermanns, F. W., & Chrisman, J. J. (2009). Family business research in the new millennium: An overview of the who, the where, the what, and the why. *Family Business Review*, *22*(2), 151–166. doi:10.1177/0894486509333598

Del Brío González, J., & Barba-Sanchez, V. (2020). The Mediating Effect of Environmental Proactivity on the Influence of Stakeholder Pressure and Environmental Strategy of Wineries in Spain. *International Journal of Environmental Research*, *14*(6), 771–783. doi:10.1007/s41742-020-00281-2

Del Río, P., Carrillo-Hermosilla, J., Könnölä, T., & Bleda, M. (2011). *Business strategies and capacities for eco-innovation*. Instituto de Empresa Business School Working Paper, EC8-124-I.

Del Río, P., Peñasco, C., & Romero-Jordán, D. (2015). Distinctive features of environmental innovators: An econometric analysis. *Business Strategy and the Environment*, *24*(6), 361–385. doi:10.1002/bse.1822

Del Río González, P. (2009). The empirical analysis of the determinants for environmental technological change: A research agenda. *Ecological Economics*, *68*(3), 861–878. doi:10.1016/j.ecolecon.2008.07.004

Delmas, M. A., & Gergaud, O. (2014). Sustainable certification for future generation: The case of family business. *Family Business Review*, *27*, 228–243. doi:10.1177/0894486514538651

Diamantopoulos, A., Riefler, P., & Roth, K. P. (2008). Advancing formative measurement models. *Journal of Business Research*, *61*(12), 1203–1218. doi:10.1016/j.jbusres.2008.01.009

Díaz-García, C., González-Moreno, Á., & Sáez-Martínez, F. J. (2015). Eco-innovation: Insights from a literature review. *Innovation (North Sydney, N.S.W.)*, *17*(1), 1, 6–23. doi:10.1080/14479338.2015.1011060

Ding, Q., Khattak, S. I., & Ahmad, M. (2021). Towards sustainable production and consumption: Assessing the impact of energy productivity and eco-innovation on consumption-based carbon dioxide emissions (CCO2) in G-7 nations. *Sustainable Production and Consumption*, *27*, 254–268. doi:10.1016/j.spc.2020.11.004

Doluca, H., Wagner, M., & Block, J. (2018). Sustainability and environmental behavior in family firms: A longitudinal analysis of environment-related activities, innovation and performance. *Business Strategy and the Environment*, *27*(1), 152–172. doi:10.1002/bse.1998

Dudaroğlu, M., Öner, M. A., & Önday, Ö. (2018). Impact of family influence on top management team in family businesses: A path-analytic study on automotive parts industry in Turkey. *International Journal of Contemporary Alied Researches*, *5*(3), 123–161.

Duran, P., Kammerlander, N., Van Essen, M., & Zellweger, T. (2016). Doing more with less: Innovation input and output in family firms. *Academy of Management Journal*, *59*(4), 1224–1264. doi:10.5465/amj.2014.0424

Dyer, W. G. (2018). Are family firms really better? Reexamining examining the 'family effect'on firm performance. *Family Business Review*, *31*(2), 240–248. doi:10.1177/0894486518776516

European Commission. (2017). *Special Eurobarometer 459: Climate change*. EC. https://ec.europa.eu/clima/sites/clima/files/suort/docs/report_2017_en.pdf

Faccio, M., & Lang, L. H. P. (2002). The ultimate ownership of Western European corporations. *Journal of Financial Economics*, *65*(3), 365–395. doi:10.1016/S0304-405X(02)00146-0

Fagerberg, J., Mowery, D. C., & Nelson, R. R. (Eds.). (2005). *The Oxford handbook of innovation*. Oxford university press.

Falk, R. F., & Miller, N. B. (1992). *A primer for soft modeling*. University of Akron Press. University of Akron Press.

Fernando, Y., Tseng, M. L., Sroufe, R., Abideen, A. Z., Shaharudin, M. S., & Jose, R. (2021). Eco-innovation impacts on recycled product performance and competitiveness: Malaysian automotive industry. *Sustainable Production and Consumption*, *28*, 1677–1686. doi:10.1016/j.spc.2021.09.010

Flores, S. S. (2018). What is sustainability in the wine world? A cross-country analysis of wine sustainability frameworks. *Journal of Cleaner Production*, *172*, 2301–2312. doi:10.1016/j.jclepro.2017.11.181

Fornell, C., & Larcker, D. F. (1981). Evaluating structural equation models with unobservable variables and measurement error. *JMR, Journal of Marketing Research*, *18*(1), 39–50. doi:10.1177/002224378101800104

Frank, H., Lueger, M., Nosé, L., & Suchy, D. (2010). The concept of Familiness: Literature review and systems theory-based reflections. *Journal of Family Business Strategy*, *1*(3), 119–130. doi:10.1016/j.jfbs.2010.08.001

Fritzsche, D., & Oz, E. (2007). Personal values' influence on the ethical dimension of decision making. *Journal of Business Ethics*, *75*(4), 335–343. doi:10.1007/s10551-006-9256-5

Gauthier, J., & Wooldridge, B. (2012). Influences on sustainable innovation adoption: Evidence from leadership in energy and environmental design. *Business Strategy and the Environment*, *21*(2), 98–110. doi:10.1002/bse.716

Gedajlovic, E., Carney, M., Chrisman, J. J., & Kellermanns, F. W. (2012). The adolescence of family firm research: Taking stock and planning for the future. *Journal of Management*, *38*(4), 1010–1037. doi:10.1177/0149206311429990

Gomez-Mejia, L., Campbell, J., Martin, G., Hoskisson, R., Makri, M., & Sirmon, D. (2014). Socioemotional wealth as a mixed gamble: Revisiting family firm RandD investments with the behavioral agency model. *Entrepreneurship Theory and Practice*, *38*(6), 1351–1374. doi:10.1111/etap.12083

Gómez-Mejia, L. R., Hynes, K. T., Nunez-Nickel, M., & Moyano-Fuentes, H. (2007). Socioemotional wealth and business risk in family-controlled firms: Evidence from Spanish olive oil mills. *Administrative Science Quarterly*, *52*(1), 106–137. doi:10.2189/asqu.52.1.106

Habbershon, T. G., Williams, M., & MacMillan, I. C. (2003). A unified systems perspective of family firm performance. *Journal of Business Venturing*, *18*(4), 451–465. doi:10.1016/S0883-9026(03)00053-3

Habbershon, T. G., & Williams, M. L. (1999). A resource-based framework for assessing the strategic advantages of family firms. *Family Business Review*, *12*(1), 1–25. doi:10.1111/j.1741-6248.1999.00001.x

Hair, J. F. Jr, Hult, G. T. M., Ringle, C. M., & Sarstedt, M. (2021). *A primer on partial least squares structural equation modeling (PLS-SEM)*. Sage publications. doi:10.1007/978-3-030-80519-7

Hair, J. F. Jr, Ringle, C. M., & Sarstedt, M. (2013). Partial least squares structural equation modeling: Rigorous alications, better results, and higher acceptance. *Long Range Planning*, *46*(1-2), 1–12. doi:10.1016/j.lrp.2013.01.001

Hair, J. F., Risher, J. J., Sarstedt, M., & Ringle, C. M. (2019). When to use and how to report the results of PLS-SEM. *European Business Review*, *31*(1), 1, 2–24. doi:10.1108/EBR-11-2018-0203

Hair, J. F., Sarstedt, M., Pieper, T. M., & Ringle, C. M. (2012). The use of partial least squares structural equation modeling in strategic management research: A review of past practices and recommendations for future alications. *Long Range Planning*, *45*(5-6), 5–6, 320–340. doi:10.1016/j.lrp.2012.09.008

Hair, J. F., Sarstedt, M., & Ringle, C. M. (2019). Rethinking some of the rethinking of partial least squares. *European Journal of Marketing*, *5*(4), 566–584. doi:10.1108/EJM-10-2018-0665

He, F., Miao, X., Wong, C. W., & Lee, S. (2018). Contemporary corporate eco-innovation research: A systematic review. *Journal of Cleaner Production*, *174*, 502–526. doi:10.1016/j.jclepro.2017.10.314

Henseler, J., Ringle, C. M., & Sarstedt, M. (2015). A new criterion for assessing discriminant validity in variance-based structural equation modeling. *Journal of the Academy of Marketing Science*, *43*(1), 115–135. doi:10.1007/s11747-014-0403-8

Henseler, J., Ringle, C. M., & Sinkovics, R. R. (2009). The use de partial least squares path modeling in international marketing. *Advances in International Marketing*, *20*, 277–320. doi:10.1108/S1474-7979(2009)0000020014

Hicks, C., & Dietmar, R. (2007). Improving cleaner production through the alication of environmental management tools in China. *Journal of Cleaner Production*, *15*(5), 395–408. doi:10.1016/j.jclepro.2005.11.008

Hojnik, J., Ruzzier, M., & Manolova, T. S. (2018). Internationalization and economic performance: The mediating role of eco-innovation. *Journal of Cleaner Production*, *171*, 1312–1323. doi:10.1016/j.jclepro.2017.10.111

Horbach, J. (2008). Determinants of environmental innovation—New evidence from German panel data sources. *Research Policy*, *37*(1), 163–173. doi:10.1016/j.respol.2007.08.006

Horbach, J., Oltra, V., & Belin, J. (2013). Determinants and specificities of eco-innovations compared to other innovations—An econometric analysis for the French and German industry based on the community innovation survey. *Industry and Innovation*, *20*(6), 523–543. doi:10.1080/13662716.2013.833375

Horbach, J., Rammer, C., & Rennings, K. (2012). Determinants of eco-innovations by type of environmental impact—The role of regulatory push/pull, technology push, and market pull. *Ecological Economics*, *78*, 112–122. doi:10.1016/j.ecolecon.2012.04.005

Horváthová, E. (2012). The impact of environmental performance on firm performance: Short-term costs and long-term benefits? *Ecological Economics*, *84*, 91–97. doi:10.1016/j.ecolecon.2012.10.001

Huang, Y. C., Ding, H. B., & Kao, M. R. (2009). Salient stakeholder voices: Family business and green innovation adoption. *Journal of Management & Organization*, *15*(3), 309–326. doi:10.5172/jmo.2009.15.3.309

Jabbour, C. J. C., Jugend, D., de Sousa Jabbour, A. B., Gunasekaran, A., & Latan, H. (2015). Green product development and performance of Brazilian firms: Measuring the role of human and technical aspects. *Journal of Cleaner Production*, *87*, 442–451. doi:10.1016/j.jclepro.2014.09.036

Jaskiewicz, P., & Dyer, W. G. (2017). Addressing the elephant in the room: Disentangling family heterogeneity to advance family business research. *Family Business Review*, *30*(2), 111–118. doi:10.1177/0894486517700469

Kammerer, D. (2009). The effects of customer benefit and regulation on environmental product innovation., Empirical evidence from aliance manufacturers in Germany. *Ecological Economics*, *68*(8-9), 2285–2295. doi:10.1016/j.ecolecon.2009.02.016

Kammerlander, N., & Ganter, M. (2015). An attention-based view of family firm adaptation to discontinuous technological change: Exploring the role of family CEOs' noneconomic goals. *Journal of Product Innovation Management*, *32*(3), 361–383. doi:10.1111/jpim.12205

Karakaya, E., Hidalgo, A., & Nuur, C. (2014). Diffusion of eco-innovations: A review. *Renewable & Sustainable Energy Reviews*, *33*, 392–399. doi:10.1016/j.rser.2014.01.083

Kemp, R. (2010). Eco-Innovation: Definition, measurement, and open research issues. *Economics and Politics*, *27*(3), 397–420.

Kesidou, E., & Demirel, P. (2012). On the drivers of eco-innovations: Empirical evidence from the UK. *Research Policy*, *41*(5), 862–870. doi:10.1016/j.respol.2012.01.005

Khanna, M., Deltas, G., & Harrington, D. R. (2009). Adoption of pollution prevention techniques: The role of management systems and regulatory pressures. *Environmental and Resource Economics*, *44*(1), 85–106. doi:10.1007/s10640-009-9263-y

Krae, A., Goutas, L., & von Schlie, A. (2011). The family business brand: An inquiry into the construction of the image of family businesses. *Journal of Family Business Management*, *1*(1), 37–46.

Kraus, S., Rehman, S. U., & García, F. J. S. (2020). Corporate social responsibility and environmental performance: The mediating role of environmental strategy and green innovation. *Technological Forecasting and Social Change*, *160*, 120262. doi:10.1016/j.techfore.2020.120262

La Porta, R., Lopez-de-Silanes, F., & Shleifer, A. (1999). Corporate ownership around the world. *The Journal of Finance*, *54*(2), 471–517. doi:10.1111/0022-1082.00115

Laguir, I., Laguir, L., & Elbaz, J. (2016). Are family small and medium sized enterprises more socially responsible than nonfamily small and medium sized enterprises? *Corporate Social Responsibility and Environmental Management*, *23*(6), 386–398. doi:10.1002/csr.1384

Le Breton-Miller, I., & Miller, D. (2006). Why do some family businesses out-compete? Governance, long-term orientation, and sustainable capability. *Entrepreneurship Theory and Practice*, *30*(6), 731–746. doi:10.1111/j.1540-6520.2006.00147.x

Lin, R. J., Tan, K. H., & Geng, Y. (2013). Market demand, green product innovation, and firm performance: Evidence from Vietnam motorcycle industry. *Journal of Cleaner Production*, *40*, 101–107. doi:10.1016/j.jclepro.2012.01.001

Llach, J., & Nordquist, M. (2010). Innovation in family and non-family businesses: A resource perspective. *International Journal of Entrepreneurial Venturing*, *2*(3/4), 381–399. doi:10.1504/IJEV.2010.037119

Lumpkin, G. T., Brigham, K. H., & Moss, T. W. (2010). Long-term orientation: Implications for the entrepreneurial orientation and performance of family businesses. *Entrepreneurship and Regional Development*, *22*(3-4), 3–4, 241–264. doi:10.1080/08985621003726218

Marcus, A., & Fremeth, A. (2009). Green management matters regardless. *The Academy of Management Perspectives*, *23*(3), 17–26. doi:10.5465/amp.2009.43479261

Matzler, K., Veider, V., Hautz, J., & Stadler, C. (2015). The impact of family ownership, management, and governance on innovation. *Journal of Product Innovation Management*, *32*(3), 319–333. doi:10.1111/jpim.12202

Mazzi, C. (2011). Family business and financial performance: Current state of knowledge and future research challenges. *Journal of Family Business Strategy*, *2*(3), 166–181. doi:10.1016/j.jfbs.2011.07.001

Miller, D., & Le Breton-Miller, I. (2005). *Managing for the Long Run: Lessons in Competitive Advantage from Great Family Businesses*. Harvard Business School Press.

Miller, D., Le Breton-Miller, I., & Lester, R. H. (2013). Family firm governance, strategic conformity and performance: Institutional versus strategic perspectives. *Organization Science*, *24*(1), 189–209. doi:10.1287/orsc.1110.0728

Morck, R., & Bernard, Y. (2004). Family control and the rent–seeking society. *Entrepreneurship Theory and Practice*, *28*(4), 391–409. doi:10.1111/j.1540-6520.2004.00053.x

Moyano-Fuentes, J., Maqueira-Marín, J. M., & Bruque-Camara, S. (2018). Process innovation and environmental sustainability engagement: An alication on technological firms. *Journal of Cleaner Production*, *171*, 844–856. doi:10.1016/j.jclepro.2017.10.067

Nieto, M. J., Santamaria, L., & Fernandez, Z. (2015). Understanding the innovation behavior of family firms. *Journal of Small Business Management*, *53*(2), 382–399. doi:10.1111/jsbm.12075

Nordqvist, M., Sharma, P., & Chirico, F. (2014). Family firm heterogeneity and governance: A configuration aroach. *Journal of Small Business Management*, *52*(2), 192–209. doi:10.1111/jsbm.12096

OECD. (2012). *The future of eco-innovation: The role of business models in green transformation.* OECD. https://www.oecd.org/innovation/inno/49537036.pdf

Organización Internacional de la Viña y el Vino. (2023). *Aspectos de la coyuntura mundial: Situación del sector en 2022.* OIV. https://www.oiv.int/public/medias/7903/actualidad-oiv-de-la-coyuntura-del-sector-vitivin-cola-mundi.pdf

Pearson, A. W., Carr, J. C., & Shaw, J. C. (2008). Toward a theory of familiness: A social capital perspective. *Entrepreneurship Theory and Practice*, *32*(6), 949–969. doi:10.1111/j.1540-6520.2008.00265.x

Pereira, A., & Vence, X. (2012). Key business factors for Eco-innovation: An overview of recent firm-level empirical studies. *Cuadernos de Gestión*, *12*(Especial - Innovación), 73–103. doi:10.5295/cdg.110308ap

Perri, A., & Peruffo, E. (2017). *Family business and technological innovation. Empirical insights from the Italian pharmaceutical industry.* Palgrave Macmillan., doi:10.1007/978-3-319-61596-7

Porter, M., & Van der Linde, C. (1995). Green and competitive: Ending the stalemate. *Harvard Business Review*, *73*, 120–134.

Poza, E. J. (2013). *Family business.* Cengage Learning.

Reinartz, W., Haenlein, M., & Henseler, J. (2009). An empirical comparison of the efficacy of covariance-based and variance-based SEM. *International Journal of Research in Marketing*, *26*(4), 332–344. doi:10.1016/j.ijresmar.2009.08.001

Rigdon, E. E., Sarstedt, M., & Ringle, C. M. (2017). On comparing results from CB-SEM and PLS-SEM: Five perspectives and five recommendations, *Marketing: ZFP–Journal of Research and Management, 39*, 4-16.

Ringle, C. M., Sarstedt, M., Mitchell, R., & Gudergan, S. P. (2018). Partial least squares structural equation modeling in HRM research. *International Journal of Human Resource Management*, *31*(12), 1617–1643. doi:10.1080/09585192.2017.1416655

Ringle, C. M., Sarstedt, M., & Straub, D. W. (2012). A critical look at the use of PLS-SEM in MIS quarterly. *Management Information Systems Quarterly*, *36*(1), 1, 3–14. doi:10.2307/41410402

Ringle, C. M., Wende, S., & Becker, J. M. (2015). *SmartPLS 3.* SmartPLS 3. http://www.smartpls.com (2015)

Röd, I. (2016). Disentangling the family firm's innovation process: A systematic review. *Journal of Family Business Strategy*, *7*(3), 85–201. doi:10.1016/j.jfbs.2016.08.004

Roessl, D., Fink, M., & Kraus, S. (2010). Are family firms fit for innovation? Towards an agenda for empirical research. *International Journal of Entrepreneurial Venturing*, *2*(3/4), 366–380. doi:10.1504/IJEV.2010.037118

Roldán, J. L., & Sánchez-Franco, M. J. (2012). Variance-based structural equation modeling: guidelines for using partial least squares in information systems research. In M. Mora, O. Gelman, & A. L. Steenkamp (Eds.), *Research Methodologies, Innovations and Philosophies in Software Systems Engineering and Information Systems*. IGI Global. doi:10.4018/978-1-4666-0179-6.ch010

Román-Sánchez, I. M., & Belmonte-Ureña, L. J. (2013). Araisal of environmental regulations on sustainable consumption of water in the wine-producing Spanish industry [EEMJ]. *Environmental Engineering and Management Journal*, *12*(10), 1979–1987. doi:10.30638/eemj.2013.247

Roy, M., & Khastagir, D. (2016). Exploring role of green management in enhancing organizational efficiency in petro-chemical industry in India. *Journal of Cleaner Production*, *121*, 109–115. doi:10.1016/j.jclepro.2016.02.039

Sarkar, A. N. (2013). Promoting eco-innovations to leverage sustainable development of eco-industry and green growth. *European Journal of Sustainable Development*, *2*(1), 171–171.

Sarkis, J., Gonzalez-Torre, P., & Adenso-Diaz, B. (2010). Stakeholder pressure and the adoption of environmental practices: The mediating effect of training. *Journal of Operations Management*, *28*(2), 163–176. doi:10.1016/j.jom.2009.10.001

Sarstedt, M., Bengart, P., Shaltoni, A. M., & Lehmann, S. (2018). The use of sampling methods in advertising research: A gap between theory and practice. *International Journal of Advertising*, *37*(4), 650–663. doi:10.1080/02650487.2017.1348329

Sarstedt, M., Ringle, C. M., Henseler, J., & Hair, J. F. (2014). On the emancipation of PLS-SEM: A commentary on Rigdon (2012). *Long Range Planning*, *47*(3), 154–160. doi:10.1016/j.lrp.2014.02.007

Schiedering, T., Tietze, F., & Herstatt, C. (2012). Green innovation in technology and innovation management—An exploratory literature review. *R & D Management*, *42*(2), 180–192. doi:10.1111/j.1467-9310.2011.00672.x

Schumpeter, J. A. (1934). *The theory of economic development*. Harvard University Press.

Sciascia, S., Nordqvist, M., Mazzola, P., & De Massis, A. (2015). Family ownership and RandD intensity in small and medium-sized firms. *Journal of Product Innovation Management*, *32*(3), 349–360. doi:10.1111/jpim.12204

Segaro, E. L., Larimo, J., & Jones, M. V. (2014). Internationalization of family small and medium sized enterprises: The role of stewardship orientation, family commitment culture and top management team. *International Business Review*, *23*(2), 381–395. doi:10.1016/j.ibusrev.2013.06.004

Sellitto, M. A., Camfield, C. G., & Buzuku, S. (2020). Green innovation and competitive advantages in a furniture industrial cluster: A survey and structural model. *Sustainable Production and Consumption*, *23*, 94–104. doi:10.1016/j.spc.2020.04.007

Sharma, P. (2008). Commentary: Familiness: Capital stocks and flows between family and business. *Entrepreneurship Theory and Practice*, *32*(6), 971–977. doi:10.1111/j.1540-6520.2008.00266.x

Sharma, P., & Sharma, S. (2011). Drivers of proactive environmental strategy in family firms. *Business Ethics Quarterly*, *21*(2), 309–334. doi:10.5840/beq201121218

Souder, D., Zaheer, A., Sapienza, H., & Ranucci, R. (2017). How family influence, socioemotional wealth, and competitive conditions shape new technology adoption. *Strategic Management Journal*, *38*(9), 1774–1790. doi:10.1002/smj.2614

Stanovcic, T., Pekovic, S., & Bouziri, A. (2015). The effect of knowledge management on environmental innovation: The empirical evidence from France. *Baltic Journal of Management, 10*, 413.

Starik, M., & Kanashiro, P. (2013). Toward a theory of sustainability management: Uncovering and integrating the nearly obvious. *Organization & Environment*, *26*(1), 7–30. doi:10.1177/1086026612474958

Steier, L. (2003). Variants of agency contracts in family-financed ventures as a continuum of familial altruistic and market rationalities. *Journal of Business Venturing*, *18*(5), 597–618. doi:10.1016/S0883-9026(03)00012-0

Swab, R. G., Sherlock, C., Markin, E., & Dibrell, C. (2020). SEW what do we know and where do we go? A review of socioemotional wealth and a way forward. *Family Business Review*, *33*(4), 424–445. doi:10.1177/0894486520961938

Tamayo-Orbegozo, U., Vicente-Molina, M. A., & Villarreal-Larrinaga, O. (2017). Eco-innovation strategic model. A multiple-case study from a highly eco-innovative European region. *Journal of Cleaner Production*, *142*, 1347–1367. doi:10.1016/j.jclepro.2016.11.174

Tariq, A., Badir, Y. F., Tariq, W., & Bhutta, U. S. (2017). Drivers and consequences of green product and process innovation: A systematic review, conceptual framework, and future outlook. *Technology in Society*, *51*, 8–23. doi:10.1016/j.techsoc.2017.06.002

Triguero, A., Fernández, S., & Sáez-Martinez, F. J. (2018). Inbound open innovative strategies and eco-innovation in the Spanish food and beverage industry. *Sustainable Production and Consumption*, *15*, 49–64. doi:10.1016/j.spc.2018.04.002

Triguero, A., Moreno-Mondéjar, L., & Davia, M. A. (2013). Drivers of different types of eco-innovation in European SMEs. *Ecological Economics*, *92*, 25–33. doi:10.1016/j.ecolecon.2013.04.009

Tu, Y., & Wu, W. (2021). How does green innovation improve enterprises' competitive advantage? The role of organizational learning. *Sustainable Production and Consumption*, *26*, 504–516. doi:10.1016/j.spc.2020.12.031

Urbinati, A., Franzò, S., De Massis, A., & Frattini, F. (2017). Innovation in Family Firms: A Review of Prior Studies and a Framework for Future Research. In A. Brem & E. Viardot (Eds.), *Revolution of Innovation Management* (pp. 213–246). Palgrave Macmillan. doi:10.1057/978-1-349-95123-9_8

Wang, W., Yu, B., Yan, X., Yao, X., & Liu, Y. (2017). Estimation of innovation's green performance: A range-adjusted measure aroach to assess the unified efficiency of China's manufacturing industry. *Journal of Cleaner Production*, *149*, 919–924. doi:10.1016/j.jclepro.2017.02.174

Weng, H. H., Chen, J. S., & Chen, P. C. (2015). Effects of Green Innovation on Environmental and Corporate Performance: A Stakeholder Perspective. *Sustainability (Basel)*, *7*(5), 4997–5026. doi:10.3390/su7054997

Westhead, P., & Cowling, M. (1998). Family firm research: The need for a methodological rethink. *Entrepreneurship Theory and Practice*, *23*(1), 31–56. doi:10.1177/104225879802300102

Westhead, P., & Howorth, C. (2007). Types of private family firms: An exploratory conceptual and empirical analysis. *Entrepreneurship and Regional Development*, *19*(5), 405–431. doi:10.1080/08985620701552405

Wong, W. P., Tseng, M., & Tan, K. H. (2013). A business process management capabilities perspective on organization performance. *Total Quality Management & Business Excellence*, *25*, 5–6, 602–617.

Wu, W., Sheng, L., Tang, F., Zhang, A., & Liu, J. (2021). A system dynamics model of green innovation and policy simulation with an application in Chinese manufacturing industry. *Sustainable Production and Consumption*, *28*, 987–1005. doi:10.1016/j.spc.2021.07.007

Zahra, S. A. (2005). Entrepreneurial Risk Taking in Family Firms. *Family Business Review*, *18*(1), 23–40. doi:10.1111/j.1741-6248.2005.00028.x

Zahra, S. A. (2010). Harvesting family firms organizational social capital: A relational perspective. *Journal of Management Studies*, *47*(2), 345–366. doi:10.1111/j.1467-6486.2009.00894.x

Zahra, S. A., Hayton, J. C., & Salvato, C. (2004). Entrepreneurship in family vs. non-family firms: A resource-based analysis of the effect of organizational culture. *Entrepreneurship Theory and Practice*, *28*(4), 363–381. doi:10.1111/j.1540-6520.2004.00051.x

Zahra, S. A., Neubaum, D. O., & Larrañeta, B. (2007). Knowledge sharing and technological capabilities: The moderating role of family involvement. *Journal of Business Research*, *60*(10), 1070–1079. doi:10.1016/j.jbusres.2006.12.014

Zellweger, T. M., Eddleston, K. A., & Kellermanns, F. W. (2010). Exploring the concept of familiness: Introducing family firm identity *Journal of family business strategy, 1*, 54-63.

Zellweger, T. M., Nason, R. S., Nordqvist, M., & Brush, C. G. (2011). Why do family firms strive for nonfinancial goals? An organizational identity perspective. *Entrepreneurship Theory and Practice*, *37*(2), 229–248. doi:10.1111/j.1540-6520.2011.00466.x

Zhang, D., Rong, Z., & Ji, Q. (2019). Green innovation and firm performance: Evidence from listed companies in China. *Resources, Conservation and Recycling*, *144*, 48–55. doi:10.1016/j.resconrec.2019.01.023

Chapter 12
Integrating Knowledge Management for Sustainable Growth:
Insights From the Spanish Wine Sector

Javier Martínez Falcó
https://orcid.org/0000-0001-9004-5816
University of Alicante, Spain & Stellenbosch University, South Africa

Eduardo Sánchez-García
https://orcid.org/0000-0002-8524-4906
University of Alicante, Spain

Bartolomé Marco-Lajara
https://orcid.org/0000-0001-8811-9118
University of Alicante, Spain

Luis A. Millán-Tudela
https://orcid.org/0000-0003-3669-9960
University of Alicante, Spain

Cristina Raluca Gh. Popescu
https://orcid.org/0000-0002-5876-0550
University of Bucharest, Romania & The Bucharest University of Economic Studies, Romania

ABSTRACT

This study focuses on examining the influence of knowledge management (KM) on sustainable performance (SP) within the wine industry. Specifically, it explores how KM affects SP, considering the mediating effect of green innovation (GI) and the moderating effect of collaborative culture (CC). A theoretical model, grounded in prior research, is employed and empirically tested using structural equation modeling (PLS-SEM) with data from 202 Spanish wineries. The findings demonstrate a positive correlation between KM and SP, where GI acts as a mediator and CC serves as a moderator in this relationship. This research is distinctive in its approach: it is among the first to investigate the KM-SP relationship in the context of the wine industry and the first to incorporate the CC variable as a moderator in examining this relationship.

DOI: 10.4018/979-8-3693-2149-2.ch012

INTRODUCTION

The challenge of maintaining a competitive advantage has become more complex due to the increasing social and environmental pressures faced by organizations, as noted by Khouroh et al. (2020). In response, dynamic organizations are adopting strategies like Knowledge Management (KM), Green Innovation (GI), and Collaborative Culture (CC) to enhance their economic, social, and environmental performance, a trend identified by Shehzad et al. (2022).

Companies increasingly recognize knowledge as a strategic asset crucial for achieving Sustainable Performance (SP). The processes of acquiring, transferring, and applying knowledge, i.e., KM, enable organizations to adapt to environmental dynamism, endorse sustainable practices, gain advantages, and build trust among customers and shareholders. These benefits are reflected in improved performance across economic, social, and environmental dimensions, as Demir et al. (2021) have articulated. KM is instrumental in facilitating organizational change where social and environmental sustainability are as important as economic viability.

KM is also a catalyst for the development of eco-friendly products and processes, integral to GI. Knowledge-based resources are key to sustainable innovation, as companies improve their knowledge acquisition, transfer, and application, their capacity for implementing green product and process innovations increases due to a larger stock of green knowledge and its wider dissemination among employees, as Abbas and Sağsan (2019) have observed. Thus, KM is a vital component in developing organizational capabilities that encompass economic, social, and environmental aspects, a concept explored by Wang et al. (2022).

Within the context of capabilities and intangible assets, CC is crucial for promoting knowledge sharing within a company, which can lead to improved SP. An organization's values should emphasize collaboration, knowledge sharing, acceptance of failure, and fostering social interaction among its members, as Yang et al. (2018) suggest. This cultural framework facilitates the effective sharing and application of knowledge, ultimately enhancing an organization's sustainable performance.

In the wine industry, effective management of winery knowledge is a critical strategic factor for market competition, primarily for two reasons. First, effective Knowledge Management (KM) enhances the flow and application of green knowledge within wineries, aiding them in addressing climatic challenges like climate change, energy, and water scarcity, which are crucial for the sector's survival, as noted by Obermayer et al. (2022). Second, KM facilitates the competitiveness and distinctiveness of wineries from their competitors by encouraging the creation of environmentally friendly products and processes, such as organic, natural, and biodynamic wines, as discussed by Marco-Lajara et al. (2022a). This approach can improve winery performance, especially since customers often prefer organic wines, despite a general lack of understanding about what this entails, as Fuentes-Fernández et al. (2022) have shown.

Recent studies have explored the impact of KM on Sustainable Performance (SP) through Green Innovation (GI) (Abbas and Sagsan, 2019; Shahzad et al., 2020; Shahzad et al., 2021). However, there appears to be a gap in research that simultaneously examines the relationships among KM, SP, GI, and Collaborative Culture (CC). To address this, the study aims to analyze the positive influence of KM on SP, along with the mediating role of GI and the moderating role of CC. Understanding these relationships is crucial, as it identifies antecedent, mediating, and moderating variables of SP, offering pathways to enhance not just the competitiveness of business organizations but also societal and environmental well-being. This is particularly relevant in the wine industry, where winery survival is contingent on achieving economic profitability while respecting the environment and the vine-growing conditions

(Bandinelli et al., 2020). Moreover, the role of KM in winemaking and ageing processes, and therefore in the future of wineries, warrants special attention (Thrassou et al., 2020).

The study seeks to address three Research Questions (RQs): (RQ1) Does KM positively affect the SP of wineries? (RQ2) Does GI mediate the KM-SP link in wineries? (RQ3) Does CC moderate the KM-SP relationship in wineries? A theoretical model based on a literature review is formulated and tested using structural equation modeling. Primary data is collected through a questionnaire conducted from September 2022 to January 2023.

The Spanish wine industry serves as the focal point of this research, presenting a unique opportunity for analysis, especially given the absence of previous studies examining these relationships in this sector. Knowledge has become a pivotal element in the competitive landscape of the wine industry, with the enhancement of winemaking and ageing processes playing a crucial role in sustaining a winery's competitive edge. This underscores the importance of studying KM and its impact on other organizational variables, as highlighted by Marco-Lajara et al. (2022b). The novelty of this study lies in both the joint examination of the constructs and the contextualization of the research within the Spanish wine industry.

This research enriches academic literature in multiple ways. Firstly, it addresses the unexplored relationship between KM and SP within the wine industry, thereby providing new scientific insights into the dynamics of these variables. Secondly, it pioneers the use of the CC variable as a moderator in this relationship, offering a novel perspective on the theoretical foundations of this interaction. Thirdly, the theoretical model proposed in this study is a significant advancement in understanding the benefits of KM for organizations, having not been previously tested. Fourthly, the research sheds light on the role of intangible assets, particularly knowledge, in enhancing economic, social, and environmental performance. Fifthly, it integrates the Resource-Based View (RBV), the Knowledge-Based View (KBV), and the theory of SD as theoretical foundations to substantiate the analyzed relationships, drawing on diverse approaches to elucidate these complex interactions.

To achieve the research objectives, the study is organized as follows: after this introduction, Section 2 establishes the theoretical basis for the research hypotheses. Section 3 details the methodology employed in the study. Section 4 presents the findings, Section 5 discusses these results, and Section 6 concludes the study with key takeaways. Finally, Section 7 outlines the research's limitations and suggests directions for future research.

THEORETICAL UNDERPINNING: RESOURCE-BASED VIEW, KNOWLEDGE-BASED VIEW AND THEORY OF SUSTAINABLE DEVELOPMENT

RBV was developed in the 1990s with the aim of understanding the factors of business success after a previous period dominated by the thought that the industry effect was the fundamental determinant of competitive advantage (Barney et al., 2011). Under this approach, the organization is conceived as a set of resources and capabilities that, when combined and used effectively, can ensure the sustained performance of the firm. The RBV, therefore, has been widely used to understand the relationship between resources and organizational performance.

However, when studies focus their analysis on knowledge, they tend to be framed under the premises of the KBV, since, under this perspective, knowledge is conceived as the main driver of organizational performance (Grant, 1997). This approach, considered as a split of the KBV, was developed and stimulated at the end of the nineties of the last century, to postulate the priority role of knowledge over other assets, since, under the premises of the theory, KM is the fundamental requirement to achieve sustained performance over time (Blome et al., 2014).

Three dimensions of KM are used in this study: the creation, transfer and application of knowledge. Knowledge acquisition relates to the process of collecting, organizing and analyzing information and data to create new knowledge. It involves gathering information from a variety of sources, such as internal documents, external sources and customer feedback, as well as organizing and analyzing the information to create new knowledge (Caputo et al., 2019). In terms of knowledge transfer, this refers to the process of sharing knowledge between members of the organization and between different departments, as well as with external stakeholders such as customers, suppliers and partners (Ouakouak et al., 2019). As regards knowledge application, this relates to the process of using knowledge and information to create value. This includes the use of knowledge to develop new products and services, to improve existing ones, or to identify and develop new growth opportunities and organizational strategies (Singh et al., 2021). Through the present research we intend to know how KM affects the economic performance of organizations, so that, in the relationship we propose, underlies the idea that the resources and capabilities of the organization are essential elements to achieve a sustained competitive advantage over time -RBV-, being knowledge the primary factor for this purpose -KBV-.

Furthermore, the study is also linked to the theory of SD, since through the dependent variable analyzed, the aim is to determine not only the economic performance generated by KM, but also the social and environmental performance. The origins of this approach date back to the report of the Brutland Commission entitled "Our Common Future" (UN, 1987). This report highlighted the need to strike a balance between economic development and social and environmental well-being, defining SD as "development that meets the needs of the present generation without compromising the ability of future generations to meet their needs". It should be noted that this theory is closely related to environmental management, since it focuses on the adoption by companies of green strategies that enable the organization to obtain economic performance while improving society and the environment in which they operate, including the development of environmentally friendly products and processes.

Subsequently, in 1994, John Elkington coined the term Triple Bottom Line (TBL) to identify the dimensions that organizations had to pursue in order to pursue a SP and thus contribute to SD: economic, social and environmental (Elkington, 1994). The economic dimension of performance focuses on maximizing profits by increasing sales and decreasing costs, the social dimension is based on enriching the relationship between the organization and the surrounding society, and the environmental dimension focuses on preserving the environment, reducing natural resources and decreasing emissions of gases and hazardous substances (Silvestre and Ţirca, 2019).

Under the joint understanding of the three dimensions, i.e., RBV, KBV and SD theory, the present research aims to explain the link between KM and SP, as well as the mediating effect of GI and the moderating effect of CC on this relationship. In the following sections, the study of these relationships is explored in greater depth.

Knowledge Management and Sustainable Performance

Appropriate KM enables organizations to ensure that their employees have access to the right information at the right time, thereby enhancing their competitiveness and creativity (Sahibzada et al., 2020). It allows for the proper management and control of the flow of tacit knowledge, linked to the development of organizational capabilities and routines, and explicit knowledge, associated with codified knowledge, which can be translated into improved economic performance of companies (Asiaei and Bontis, 2019).

However, KM is not only linked to a company's economic variables, but also to social and environmental ones. In this regard, Breznik (2018) argues that knowledge-based organizations are not only more likely to develop innovations, but also explore new ways to develop their operations in a sustainable way. Thus, KM can be used to create and manage knowledge resources while considering the economic, social and environmental concerns of stakeholders that influence the operation of the firm.

KM is an increasingly important capability in the global wine industry, given that it has had to face numerous transformations through the acquisition, transfer and application of new knowledge, among which stand out the increase of professionalization in wine production, the growing importance of environmental management as a strategic element to improve the competitiveness of wineries or the search for positive externalities for wine-growing territories (Ouvrard et al., 2020). Therefore, the processes of creation, transfer and application of knowledge in this sector have become fundamental to improve the competitiveness of wineries, as well as to favor social and environmental welfare in the area in which they operate (Iannone, 2015; Montalvo-Falcón *et al.*, 2023; Sánchez-García *et al.*, 2023a-b).

Global knowledge sharing is one of the fundamental requirements for achieving SD, and organizational KM can play a key role in achieving this goal, given its ability to incentivize the acquisition, transfer and application of knowledge among its members (Martins et al., 2019; Martínez-Falcó *et al.*, 2023a-j; Martínez-Falcó *et al.*, 2024a-b). In addition, the increasing demand from stakeholders for environmental aspects means that KM processes need to be improved to identify the economic, social and environmental impacts generated by organizations (Vrabcová et al., 2022; Marco-Lajara *et al.*, 2022a-d).

In fact, nowadays, KM is playing an increasingly important role in achieving the principles of sustainability in companies, since the United Nations Global Compact (UNGC) urges organizations, with special emphasis on manufacturing, to implement the most advanced technologies to efficiently use the resources employed, with KM, in this context, being an essential element to this end (UNGC, 2018). Such technologies are used by dynamic firms to develop products and processes that enable the organization not only to improve its economic, but also its social and environmental performance (Stanovcic et al., 2015; Marco-Lajara *et al.*, 2023a-d).

KM can therefore trigger a change in the way organizations compete, assuming the social and environmental responsibility they have towards their environment along with the need to be economically viable (Martins et al., 2019). For this reason, in the context of sustainability, KM can be conceived as a new business paradigm to achieve economic, social and environmental sustainability of companies (Abbas, 2020). In this sense, the development and improvement of KM enables companies to operationalize and implement the principles of sustainability (Caniglia et al., 2021).

Several researchers have tried to empirically demonstrate the relationship between KM and SP. On the one hand, López-Torres et al. (2019) revealed that knowledge acquisition had a positive effect on organizational sustainability. On the other hand, Muñoz-Pascual et al. (2019) demonstrated how organizational knowledge sharing enabled the achievement of economic, social and environmental goals in Portuguese SMEs. Similarly, Abbas and Sagsan (2019) empirically demonstrated the positive KM-SP relationship in manufacturing firms in Pakistan. Subsequently, Abbas (2020) analyzed the influence of knowledge acquisition on the total quality management-corporate sustainability relationship in Pakistani manufacturing and service firms, corroborating the positive influence of knowledge acquisition on the improvement of economic, social and environmental variables of the organization. As can be seen, the results of these studies focus mainly on the manufacturing sector, given its recognized capacity to generate economic wealth and improve the society and environment in which the companies are located.

In the wine context, Gil and Carrillo (2016) analysed knowledge transfer processes within Riojan wineries, showing an increase in human capital in these firms in recent years. Woodfield and Husted (2017), on the other hand, argue that knowledge sharing in New Zealand family wineries is bidirectional and, moreover, improves the innovative performance of these wineries. Similarly, Marco-Lajara et al. (2022a) demonstrated a positive and significant relationship between KM and the innovative performance of Spanish wineries. However, the academic literature that has analysed KM, or one of its dimensions, in the wine context has not addressed its link with SP. In order to overcome this research gap and, based on the existing academic literature, the following hypothesis is put forward:

H1. KM has a positive effect on SP of wineries

Knowledge Management, Green Innovation, and Sustainable Performance

KM is one of the fundamental antecedent variables to explain the success of GIs, since the improvement of firms' innovative processes is associated with the way in which they use their previously learned knowledge (Kianto et al., 2017). In fact, the connection between both variables occurs when top management decides to invest in the development of GIs and, for this purpose, they use employees' knowledge and competencies (Pérez-Luño et al., 2019).

GI represents a mechanism to eliminate or minimize the negative externalities that organizations generate with their operations on the environment through the reduction in the consumption of resources, waste and the proper management of pollution (Fernando et al., 2019). The academic literature identifies two main types of GIs: green product innovation and green process innovation. Thus, while green product innovation focuses on the modification of the design of products offered to the market or the development of new products made from renewable or non-toxic materials, green process innovation focuses on improving production processes that allow moving from raw materials to final products (Albort-Morant et al., 2016). In this way, green product innovation enables the achievement of energy efficiency while reducing the company's detrimental impact on the environment, and green process innovation, on the other hand, enables the minimization of natural resources and waste (Zhang et al., 2019). Therefore, GIs not only provide a competitive advantage for the organization, but also promotes environmental protection as well as social welfare (Cillo et al., 2019).

Recent research has highlighted the role of knowledge acquisition, transfer and application in achieving both types of GI. Abbas and Sagsan (2019) demonstrated that knowledge acquisition, transfer and application led to improved GI and, as a consequence, corporate sustainability. In the same line of thought, Shahzad et al. (2019) defend the role of KM in improving GI, given that, as they argue, as knowledge flow is higher, knowledge sharing between hierarchical levels and subsidiaries will also be higher, thus increasing the innovative capacity of the organization. Similarly, Awan et al. (2021) argue that social interaction and cooperation within a company can improve GI processes. Moreover, GI enables performance to be improved in its triple dimension, i.e. economic, social and environmental performance (Asadi et al., 2020).

Firstly, with regard to the economic dimension, GI can positively affect the reduction of organizational costs through the reduction of energy, the reduction of costs associated with waste treatment and disposal, the elimination of environmental penalties or the improvement of the green image of the organization (Zhang and Ma, 2021). Secondly, as far as the social dimension is concerned, the development of GIs by companies can act as a mechanism to recruit and retain the best employees, while increasing their awareness of environmental issues (Mehta and Chugan, 2015). In fact, as suggested by Boons et al. (2013), companies that develop GIs contribute to a greater extent to the satisfaction of their customers and their staff, which influences the improvement of their social performance. Thirdly, as regards the environmental dimension, environmentally friendly innovations can drive the decrease of emissions, waste, hazardous and poisonous substances, as well as reduce environmental incidents, thus improving the green performance of the organization (Rehman et al., 2021). Scientific production indicates, therefore, that KM can positively impact the development and implementation of GIs in organizations, which, in turn, can be translated into higher SP.

KM is one of the main strategies to improve the development of GIs in organizations (Polas et al., 2021). This is because the capacity to innovate is knowledge-intensive, so the better the KM, the greater the capacity of organizations to develop and implement innovations within companies (Migdadi, 2021). Thus, when KM contributes to the adoption and utilization of green resources through the knowledge and skills of workers, firms will be more likely and more successful in developing GIs (Cui et al., 2021).

In turn, GIs help to prevent pollution, promote recycling, minimize the negative impact of production and manufacturing operations, meet the environmental demands of stakeholders, and improve business competitiveness, leading to improved SP (Asadi et al., 2020). This type of innovation also leads to a more satisfied workforce and improved labor retention, as well as positively affecting the reduction of organizational costs (Aftab et al., 2022). In this way, GIs can reduce the costs of energy consumption and waste treatment and disposal, while improving the image and competitive advantage of companies, resulting in a higher SP (Kiranantawat and Ahmad, 2022).

GI can therefore act as a mediating variable in the KM-SP relationship as it can be determined by the way in which the firm acquires, transfers and applies its knowledge, in turn impacting on the economic, social and environmental performance of firms (Shahzad et al., 2020). In order to make further progress in the study of the above relationships, as well as to provide new knowledge through their analysis in an industry in which they had not been previously contextualized, such as the wine industry, the following hypotheses is proposed:

H2. GI mediates the relationship between KM and SP of wineries

The Moderating Effect of Collaborative Culture in the Knowledge Management-Sustainable Performance Relationship

CC refers to the set of values, beliefs and behaviors shared by the members of the organization that determine the collaborative way in which the organization behaves, thus playing an essential role in achieving business objectives in the long term (Wen et al., 2021). Culture, therefore, shapes the processes that determine how members create and disseminate knowledge flows in the organization (Le et al., 2020). Thus, if culture is built on the premises of collaboration, organizations can generate greater trust and commitment among their members, enabling them to improve their KM. The central aspect of CC, therefore, is the predisposition to share knowledge among the members of the company, which translates into greater competitiveness of the organization (Kumar et al., 2021).

Organizational culture thus allows strengthening the creation, transfer and application of knowledge. In fact, the link between these two variables has been analyzed in an extensive number of academic publications. Chang and Lin (2015), through their research applied to 315 public and private companies in Taiwan, demonstrated that under a results-based organizational culture, creativity among collaborators, knowledge sharing and the application of knowledge in innovative proposals in order to achieve organizational goals were fostered. Additionally, recent findings indicate that employees were reluctant to exchange knowledge when there was a culture oriented to the possession of knowledge, since the fear of losing the power implied by its possession led to selfish behavior of employees, thus using knowledge for their individual and not organizational benefit (Rahman et al., 2018).

The main source of organizational knowledge resides in people, whose values and beliefs can determine the ease or difficulty with which knowledge is transferred and, therefore, can influence business success. Thus, for knowledge to be created, transferred and used successfully, organizational culture must be based on knowledge sharing (Atapattu and Jayakody, 2014). In this regard, Serenko et al. (2016), based on their study of 691 employees in the financial sector, indicate that organizational culture can positively influence knowledge sharing, contributing to improved business performance. According to the results of their research, companies can increase their efficiency through an organizational culture that advocates knowledge sharing among its members. Along the same lines, Prabhakar et al. (2018), corroborate that an organizational culture based on openness to new experiences, learning and knowledge sharing positively affects KM processes, which has an impact on business performance. In addition, organizations with a CC are aware of their surroundings, of the socioeconomic and environmental problems that surround them, show a clear sensitivity to environmental preservation and seek to improve the well-being of the community in which they operate, which allows them to improve not only their economic performance, but also their social and environmental performance (Di Vaio and Varriale, 2020).

An organisational culture in which members cooperate with each other, support one another and understand mistakes as a mechanism for progress can facilitate knowledge acquisition by encouraging interaction between employees and exposure to mistakes, promote knowledge transfer by conceiving that knowledge increases in value when it is shared and disseminated, and create the right organisational environment so that the company can translate acquired knowledge into organisational capabilities and routines that improve its economic, social and environmental performance (Lam et al., 2021).

In fact, CC can enhance job satisfaction by allowing employees to share their ideas and foster a good working environment, increase economic profitability by increasing employee productivity and efficiency, and improve environmental performance, as employees can have greater trust and support from the organisation to develop programmes to reduce the negative externalities generated by the company's activity on the environment (Sudusinghe and Seuring, 2021).

CC can thus strengthen the relationship between KM and SP, as it can generate an organizational environment conducive to improving the acquisition and flow of knowledge among workers and, at the same time, favoring the economic, social and environmental performance of companies. However, despite the acknowledged capacity of CC to boost the KM-SP relationship, to the best of our knowledge, there are no previous studies that have analyzed this relationship in the sector under study . In order to overcome this research gap and based on the literature review, the following hypothesis is put forward:

H3. CC moderates the KM-SP relationship of wineries

Figure 1 shows a graphical representation of the relationships outlined above.

Figure 1. Proposed theoretical model
Source: own elaboration

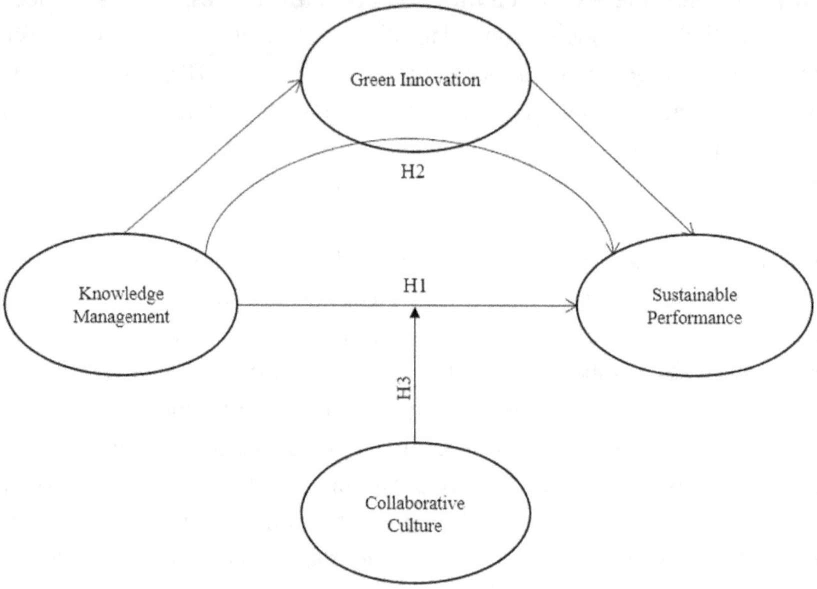

METHODOLOGY

The methodological section has been divided into four blocks to facilitate its correct understanding: (1) context of the research, (2) population and sample, (3) questionnaire and (4) analysis technique. Each of the following sections is detailed below.

Research Context

The present study is contextualized in the wine industry given its economic, social and environmental weight in the Spanish economy, as well as its suitability for the subject matter under study. Firstly, it is important to highlight the fact that Spain is a benchmark in this industry, given that, according to the latest data provided by the International Organization of Vine and Wine (OIV), the Iberian country is the one with the largest vineyard surface area, as well as the largest exporter of wine in volume, which shows the economic weight of the sector in this country. Secondly, the modern wine industry is based on knowledge and its correct management in order to obtain sustainable competitive advantages over time, given that these intangibles play a fundamental role in obtaining quality wines in which care is taken over the winemaking and ageing process, as well as the grape varieties used, among other aspects (Pradana et al., 2019). For this reason, we consider it important to analyze the effect of KM on the improvement of SP, given the growing importance of knowledge in the business success of wineries. Thirdly, to our knowledge, no previous research has addressed the relationships raised in the Spanish wine industry, which represents a research opportunity to contribute new knowledge to the study of capabilities and intangible assets in organizations.

Population and Sample

The study population is made up of the 4,373 companies belonging to code 1102 of the National Classification of Economic Activities (CNAE, by its acronym in Spanish) according to the data provided by the database of the Iberian System of Balance Sheet Analysis (SABI, by its acronym in Spanish), as these are all the companies dedicated to wine production in Spain. For the selection of the sample, an online questionnaire was elaborated and distributed through the Qualtrics application between September 2021 and January 2022 (five months). Initially, 216 responses were obtained, but after a filtering and filtering process, 202 were considered valid, which is the total number of companies that represent our sample. At this point, the analysis of non-response bias was checked, as 216 samples were collected at the initial stage and 202 were finally considered after the filtering process. To this end, the T-test was used to verify both questionnaires, obtaining in all cases p-values greater than 0.05 at a significant level of 0.05, indicating that there are no significant differences in the questionnaires analyzed. In addition, the response rate amounts to 4.62%, which is lower than the average online questionnaire response rate in the field of organizational research, being around 40% (Kreamer et al., 2021). However, as noted by Stedman et al. (2019), response rates for online questionnaires in social sciences have declined sharply since 1970, ranging from 77% in the 1970s to 43% in the 2010s, further suggesting that the average response rate in the 2030s will be around 21%. Also, recent research in wine business shows response rates below 5%, such as the studies by Marco-Lajara et al. (2020a) and Marco-Lajara et al. (2022b).

It is important to note that the sample obtained is consistent with those of the population, given that, from the point of view of geographical origin, the three autonomous communities with the greatest representation in the population are also those with the greatest weight in the sample and the size of the companies in the sample follows the same pattern as the size of the companies in the population. Table 1 shows in detail the exact percentages relating to the geographical distribution of the wineries in the sample and the population analyzed, as well as their size. Thus, it can be seen that Castilla and Leon, Catalonia and Castilla La Mancha are the regions with the highest representation in the sample and in the population. Similarly, the size of the wineries in the sample bears a certain similarity to the size of the wineries in the population, given that more than 60% in both cases are made up of micro-companies, i.e. they have fewer than 10 workers. Likewise, as far as the sample is concerned, 30.20% are small enterprises (between 10 and 49 workers), 4.95% are medium-sized (between 50 and 199 workers) and 1.98% are large (more than 200 workers), these percentages being slightly higher for the wineries in the population.

Research Questionnaire

Validated scales were used to construct the questionnaire in order to ensure the reliability and validity of the constructs used. Firstly, we used the 13-item scale proposed by Pérez-López and Alegre (2012) to measure KM, in which the variable is broken down into three second-order constructs: knowledge acquisition (5 items), knowledge transfer (4 items) and knowledge use (4 items). Secondly, to measure GI we used the scale developed by Chen (2008), which conceives the variable as a second-order construct formed by: green product innovation (4 items) and green process innovation (4 items) as first-order constructs. Thirdly, to measure SP, multidimensional constructs were required, thus integrating the economic, social and environmental dimension. In particular, a SP scale adapted from Wang and Wang (2012), Paulraj (2012) and Paillé et al. (2014) was used. This scale consists of 15 items, considering SP as a second-order variable made up of: economic performance (4 items), social performance (5 items) and environmental

Table 1. Percentage of wineries in the sample and in the study population based on geographic distribution and size

	Population	Sample
Autonomous Community		
Andalucia	4.36%	6.93%
Aragon	3.40%	3.47%
Asturias	4.20%	0.99%
Balearic Islands	1.02%	1.98%
Canary Islands	0.10%	2.48%
Cantabria	0.08%	0.50%
Castilla La-Mancha	12.36%	10.89%
Castilla and Leon	17.49%	14.36%
Catalonia	16.87%	13.37%
Community of Madrid	3.31%	4.46%
Valencian Community	4.53%	6.44%
Extremadura	3.29%	3.96%
Galicia	9.31%	7.92%
La Rioja	8.12%	9.90%
Murcia	1.28%	3.47%
Navarra	1.96%	1.49%
Basque Country	8.31%	7.43%
Winery size		
Micro	71.26%	62.38%
Small	24.96%	30.20%
Medium	2.67%	4.95%
Large	1.11%	1.98%

Source: Prepared by the authors based on sample information and the SABI database

performance (5 items). The measurement scale used for this variable was Likert-type, asking respondents to evaluate the average economic, social and environmental performance of their winery for each item in relation to their competitors over the last 5 years. Fourth, the 5-item Likert-type scale used to measure CC was employed by Lee et al. (2012). It is important to note that all scales were measured using 7-point Likert-type scales and that the four variables analysed were understood as reflective constructs, with the first-order construct being reflective (CC) and the second-order constructs being reflective-reflective (KM, GI and SP). Finally, Protected Designation of Origin (PDO), winery size and age were introduced as control variables. On the one hand, PDO was considered as a dichotomous variable, taking the value 1 when the firm was affiliated to at least one PDO and 0 when it was not affiliated to any appellation. On the other hand, the size of each organization was measured according to the standards followed by the Organization for Economic Co-operation and Development (OECD, 2005). With respect to the age of the organization, this variable was incorporated by measuring the total number of years elapsed from the creation of the company until the time of the study (year 2022).

Analysis Technique

Partial least squares structural equation modelling (PLS-SEM) was the analysis technique employed for the development of this research, using the SmartPLS v. 3.3.9 software. This technique is useful for analyzing various theoretical relationships between constructs, which may be latent. This makes the technique particularly useful in the discipline of Management, in which the present study can be framed, given that most of the variables analyzed are not directly observable (Cepeda-Carrión et al., 2019). The decision to use PLS-SEM as the analysis technique is based on three reasons. First, most of the variables (KM, GI, SP) are second-order constructs, being this technique a particularly effective tool in this type of multidimensional variables (Henseler et al., 2016). Secondly, in the present research there are measured and purple effects, being advisable to use PLS-SEM in these cases (Cepeda-Carrión et al., 2019). Thirdly, the minimum sample size for the application to have statistical power is 100, so the minimum sample requirement of the technique used (n=202) is met.

RESULTS

For the calculation of the results of the proposed model, the two-stage model based on the scores of the latent variables was used, given that most of the constructs used employ multidimensional constructs. Thus, first, the aggregate scores of the latent variables were calculated and then these scores were converted into indicators of the second-order variables. As recommended by Hair et al. (2019), the results are reported following three blocks: (1) the global model evaluation, (2) the structural model evaluation and (3) the structural model evaluation.

The model to be tested has a standardized root mean square residual of 0.051, which shows that the model has an adequate overall fit since this value is lower than the maximum value recommended in the literature of 0.08 (Byrne, 2008). This shows that the model cannot be rejected, so the analysis of the structural model evaluation and the evaluation of the measurement model can continue (see Table 2).

Regarding the evaluation of the measurement model, it is important to highlight that the steps recommended by Hair et al. (2019) were followed, based on: (1) analyzing the reliability of the indicators through their loadings (λ), (2) examining the composite reliability through Cronbach's alpha and composite reliability, (3) reviewing the convergent validity through the Average Variance Extracted (AVE) and, finally, assessing the discriminant validity through the Heterotrait-Monotrait criterion (HTMT).

First, as regards the evaluation of the measurement model, Table 3 shows that all the indicators meet the individual reliability criteria, since the values of the indicators are greater than 0.707 (Fornell and Larcker, 1981). This confirms that the indicators present adequate levels of individual reliability, thus

Table 2. Overall model fit

	Value
SRMR	0.051
d_ULS	0.200
d_G	0.165

Source: own elaboration

Table 3. Measurement model indicators: external loadings, construct reliability and convergent validity

Construct/Items	Outer Loadings	Rho (Pa)	Cronbach's Alpha	AVE
Knowledge Management (KM)		0.901	0.895	0.691
KM 1	0.926			
KM 2	0.867			
KM 3	0.934			
Green Innovation (GI)		0.832	0.827	0.590
GI 1	0.916			
GI 2	0.931			
Sustainable Performance (SP)		0.871	0.843	0.837
SP 1	0.778			
SP 2	0.902			
SP 3	0.933			
Collaborative Culture (SP)		0.924	0.918	0.929
CC 1	0.963			
CC 2	0.965			
CC 3	0.856			
CC 4	0.838			
CC 5	0.925			

Note: The indicators for the second-order variables are: KM 1= Knowledge Acquisition; KM 2= Knowledge Transfer; KM 3= Knowledge Utilization; GI 1= Green Product Innovation; GI 2= Green Process Innovation; SP 1= Economic Performance; SP 2= Social Performance; SP 3= Environmental Performance.

Source: compiled by authors

being able to measure the constructs in question. Secondly, the results obtained serve to corroborate that the variables analyzed meet the criterion of internal consistency reliability, given that both Cronbach's alpha indicator and the composite reliability (pc) exceed the minimum established value of 0.8. Third, the constructs have an AVE greater than 0.5, which shows that they meet the convergent validity requirement (Kline, 2011). This means that each construct is able to explain more than half of the variance of its indicators. Fourth, through Table 4, it can be affirmed that all the analyzed constructs follow the criteria of discriminant validity, given that the HTMT is lower than 0.85 (Hair et al., 2016). Therefore, each construct is different and, as a consequence, captures different realities.

Once the reliability and validity of the constructs had been verified, the next step was to evaluate the structural model. However, before proceeding to such an assessment, the presence of collinearity-related problems in the structural model was examined. This is due to the need to avoid the presence of multicollinearity between the antecedent variables of each of the endogenous constructs. In this sense, according to Hair et al. (2019), there is evidence of collinearity when the variance inflation factor is greater than 5 (VIF >5). Therefore, values higher than five of the endogenous constructs imply critical levels of collinearity. In this sense, the VIF values obtained in this work do not exceed the maximum value in any of the cases (see Table 5), so there are no collinearity problems. The evaluation of the measurement model for its part consisted of analyzing the predictive capacity, as well as the relationships between the constructs studied. To perform this task, we followed the indications proposed by Hair et al. (2016)

Table 4. Evaluation of discriminant validity through the HTMT criterion

	CC	GI	KM	SP	PDO	SIZE	AGE
Collaborative Culture (CC)							
Green Innovation (GI)	0.521						
Knowledge Management (KM)	0.746	0.766					
Sustainable Performance (SP)	0.602	0.613	0.724				
Protected Designation of Origin (PDO)	0.070	0.073	0.123	0.059			
SIZE	0.026	0.045	0.061	0.061	0.316		
AGE	0.053	0.027	0.037	0.077	0.080	0.106	

Source: compiled by authors

based on the evaluation of the path coefficients and the R-squared level. Figure 2 shows the results for these indicators based on a bootstrap test of 5,000 subsamples. As can be seen, the direct, indirect and moderate effects of KM on the SP of the wineries are positive and statistically significant (see Table 6). This implies that GI partially mediates the relationship between KM and SP, since both direct (0.368) and indirect (0.098) effects are positive and significant, with a strong total effect of KM on SP of 0.466 ($p \leq= 0.001$). Furthermore, the impact of KM on SP varies significantly as a function of the degree of CC, given that the CC interaction term is significant at the 95% confidence level. Therefore, all five hypotheses formulated are accepted. As for the control variables, while PDO membership and size have a negative but non-significant relationship, age has a positive and significant relationship.

Likewise, going deeper into the effect of wine tourism on the main relationship, Figure 3 shows the interaction effect by means of a simple slope analysis. The three lines that appear represent the relationships between KM (X axis) and SP (Y axis). On the one hand, the central line represents this relationship for a situation where the CC would take a midpoint (i.e., a medium level of CC). The other two lines represent the same relationship when the moderating variable takes high and low levels, respectively. In this case we can observe that as the CC intensifies the relationship between KM and SP grows significantly, while at lower levels of CC the aforementioned relationship loses strength.

Table 5. Analysis of collinearity in the model through VIF values

	KM	SP	GI	CC
Knowledge Management (KM)		1.778	1.000	
Sustainable Performance (SP)				
Green Innovation (GI)		1.779		
Collaborative Culture (CC)				
SIZE		1.013		
Protected Designation of Origin (PDO)		1.486		
AGE		1.629		

Source: compiled by authors

Figure 2. Theoretical model with R-squared, path coefficients (β), and significance
*Notes: **p<0.05 *p<0.001*
Source: own elaboration

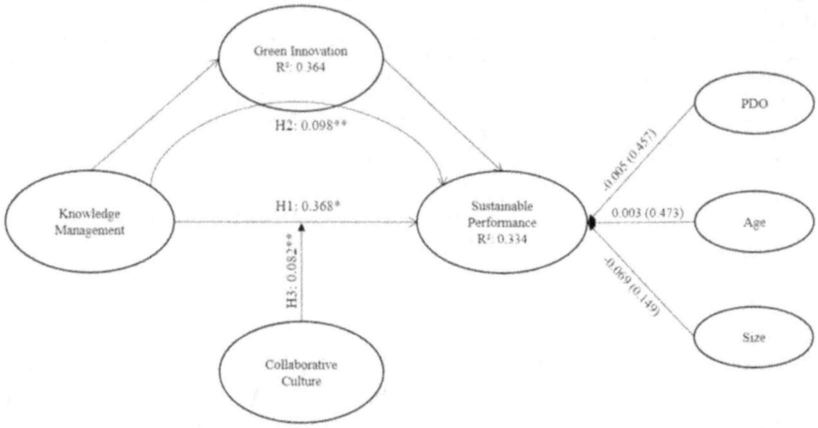

Table 6. Results of the structural model

Direct Effects	Path Coefficient	t-Value	P Value	95% BCCI	Hypothesis supported
Knowledge Management (KM) -> Sustainable Performance (SP)	0.368	4.507	0.000*	[0.202; 0.543]	H1 supported
Indirect Effect	**Path Coefficient**	**t-Value**	**P Value**	**95% BCCI**	**Hypothesis supported**
Knowledge Management (KM)-> Green Innovation (GI)-> Sustainable Performance (SP)	0.098	2.012	0.045**	[0.050; 0.159]	H2 supported
Moderating Effect	**Path Coefficient**	**t-Value**	**P Value**	**95% BCCI**	**Hypothesis supported**
Knowledge Management (KM)-> Collaborative Culture (CC)-> Sustainable Performance (SP)	0.082	2.043	0.042**	[0.006; 0.150]	H3 supported

Notes: **p<0.05 *p<0.001
Source: compiled by authors

Finally, the quality of the model is analyzed by means of the Gesisser test (Q^2), in which the estimated values must be greater than 0 ($Q^2 > 0$). As can be seen in Table 7, there are average levels of productive relevance in the model, given that the values of Q^2 are higher than 0.25 (Turner, 2010).

DISCUSSION

The results of the present research therefore suggest that proper KM in wineries can lead to higher SP. Moreover, the acquisition, transfer and application not only generate higher economic, social and environmental performance, but also favors the development of GIs, thus reinforcing the KM-SP relationship. The positive and significant relationship between KM and SP is in line with the latest published

Figure 3. Slope analysis for the moderation effect of CC
Source: prepared by the authors through SmartPLS

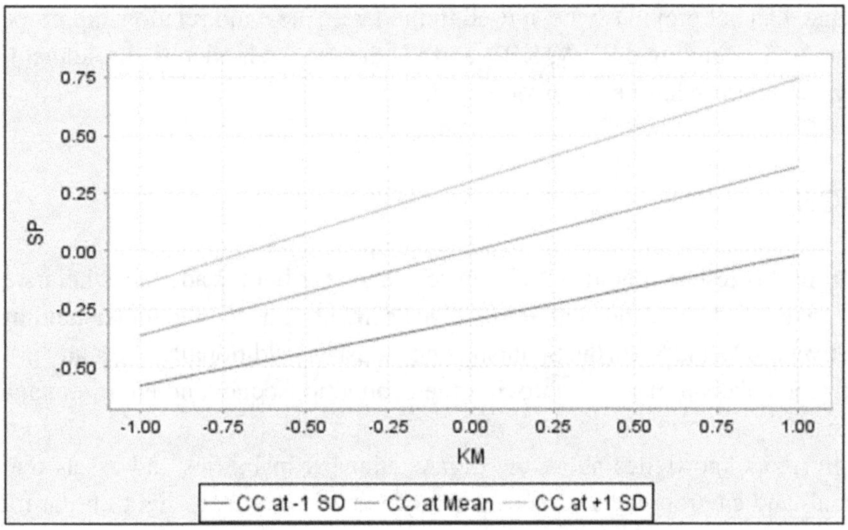

Table 7. Construct cross validated redundancy

	SSO	SSE	Q^2 (=1-SSE/SSO)
Collaborative Culture (CC)	202.000	202.000	
Green Innovation (GI)	404.000	256.815	0.364
Knowledge Management (KM)	606.000	606.000	
Sustainable Performance (SP)	606.000	403.420	0.334
Protected Designation of Origin (PDO)	202.000	202.000	
SIZE	202.000	202.000	
AGE	202.000	202.000	

Source: compiled by authors

research on the subject, such as Shahzad et al. (2021), Shahzad et al. (2020) and Abbas and Sagsan (2019), all contextualized in the manufacturing industry of Pakistan. In particular, Abbas and Sagsan (2019) investigated how KM processes influenced technological innovation, ecological management and economic, social and environmental sustainability. Shahzad et al. (2020), on the other hand, examined the role of KM process in improving SP by integrating GIs and organizational agility. Similar to the results reported in the present research, this study also shows how GI partially mediates the KM-SP relationship. Shahzad et al. (2021), for their part, demonstrate how KM processes significantly improve economic, social and environmental performance, as well as the mediating role of the development of sustainable practices in this linkage.

Furthermore, the present study is also in line with various investigations showing the positive effect of GI on SP. In this sense, Sezen and Cankaya (2013) examined the GI-SP relationship in firms in the automotive, chemical and electronics sector in Turkey. In the same vein, Asadi et al. (2020) demonstrated a positive and significant relationship in the Malaysian hotel sector. Aftab et al. (2022) and Kiranantawat and Ahmad (2022), moreover, empirically proved the relationship between GI and SP in Pakistan's manufacturing industry and Thailand's service sector respectively. CC, on the other hand, to the best of our knowledge, had not previously been used to moderate the main relationship proposed. However, through the joint understanding of RBV, KBV and SD theory, the moderating role that the CC variable can play in this relationship has been corroborated.

CONCLUSION

The findings from this research hold significant relevance for both academic scholars and professionals in the wine industry. They contribute to the enhancement of academic understanding regarding the relationship between KM and SP in the Spanish wine industry. Additionally, the study provides practical guidelines for winemakers aimed at improving the economic, social, and environmental performance of their wineries.

This study furthers knowledge about the organizational capabilities and assets that influence the economic, social, and environmental performance of wineries. It sheds light on the mechanisms that enable wineries not only to sustain their market presence but also to enhance their competitiveness while respecting the environment and the society they operate within.

Wineries are confronted with various pressures to maintain their competitive edge, simultaneously improving societal well-being and environmental stewardship. They can serve as pillars of their regions, demonstrating sustainable practices. The wine sector faces both exogenous and endogenous challenges that impact and drive economic, social, and environmental performance. Exogenous factors include rising energy prices, water scarcity, increasing environmental awareness, and climate change. Endogenous factors involve proactive measures by winery managers to foster development.

This research is particularly significant as it empirically demonstrates the positive and significant impact of KM on SP in wineries. The study also reveals that this effect is partially mediated by GI and moderated by CC. Wineries that focus on acquiring, transferring, and applying knowledge can enhance their SP and develop environmentally friendly innovations. Moreover, the KM-SP relationship is strengthened when supported by a collaborative culture.

IMPLICATIONS

The study provides both practical and theoretical insights. Theoretically, it enriches the academic discourse on environmental management by offering empirical evidence of the KM and SP relationship in the Spanish wine industry. This is a significant advancement, as no previous study has tested the proposed model in this sector, enhancing the understanding of the constructs and environmental management in wineries. The research's conclusions, with their internal and external validity, could be applicable to the wine sector in other countries, although future research is encouraged to test the model in various Old and New World wine contexts to identify similarities and differences. Uniquely, the study incorporates CC as a moderator in the KM-SP relationship, advancing knowledge about CC and its relationship with other constructs. The study also integrates the RBV, KBV, and SD theories to substantiate the relationships, providing nuanced insights into these dynamics. The theoretical implications answer the three

RQ): (RQ1) KM and SP have a positive and significant relationship; (RQ2) GI partially mediates this relationship; and (RQ3) CC moderates the KM-SP relationship.

Practically, the findings are crucial for winemakers' economic, social, and environmental management decisions. For knowledge acquisition, wineries could encourage employee participation in sustainability seminars and establish benchmarking partnerships with companies specializing in SP improvement practices. In knowledge transfer, wineries should create environments for sharing sustainable knowledge and implement IT systems for disseminating explicit knowledge like good practice manuals. In implementing knowledge, wineries can develop eco-friendly products and processes, including organic, natural, and biodynamic wines, using grape stems for compost, constructing eco-efficient buildings, and developing energy self-management and carbon footprint measurement systems. These KM practices can enhance SP and GI. The study also underscores the importance of CC in strengthening the KM-SP relationship, suggesting wine managers build a collaborative organizational culture, fostering cooperation, tolerance for failure, and idea exchange. CEOs should cultivate a culture where cooperation and mutual support are paramount, and mistakes are seen as opportunities for growth.

LIMITATIONS AND FUTURE RESEARCH LINES

Despite the valuable contributions made by this research, it is essential to acknowledge its limitations. Firstly, given the significance of this study, there is a need to expand its geographical scope to facilitate comparisons between New World and Old World wine-producing countries. Therefore, as a potential avenue for future research, we aim to extend our analysis to include the California wine region, enabling a comprehensive comparison between these two prominent wine regions. Secondly, a limitation inherent to cross-sectional studies is their inability to capture longitudinal relationships over an extended period. To address this limitation, a potential future research direction involves conducting a longitudinal analysis involving the same companies that participated in this study. This approach will provide insights into how these relationships evolve over time. Additionally, we intend to delve deeper into the impact of control variables, such as age, size, and PDO membership, on the Sustainable Performance (SP) of wineries through the application of multigroup analysis. Lastly, it is important to acknowledge that the response rate to the survey utilized in this research fell below the average response rate typically observed in the field of social sciences. As a part of future research efforts, we aim to enhance response rates in subsequent investigations. This will be crucial in improving the external validity of future studies, ensuring that results are representative of a broader population.

ACKNOWLEDGMENTS

Portions of this work have been previously reported in this research: Martínez-Falcó, J., Marco-Lajara, B., Zaragoza-Sáez, P., & Sánchez-García, E. (2023). The effect of knowledge management on sustainable performance: evidence from the Spanish wine industry. *Knowledge Management Research & Practice*, 1-16.

REFERENCES

Abbas, J. (2020). Impact of total quality management on corporate sustainability through the mediating effect of knowledge management. *Journal of Cleaner Production*, *244*, 118806. doi:10.1016/j.jclepro.2019.118806

Abbas, J., & Sagsan, M. (2019). Impact of knowledge management practices on green innovation and corporate sustainable development: A structural analysis. *Journal of Cleaner Production*, *229*, 611–620. doi:10.1016/j.jclepro.2019.05.024

Aftab, J., Abid, N., Sarwar, H., & Veneziani, M. (2022). Environmental ethics, green innovation, and sustainable performance: Exploring the role of environmental leadership and environmental strategy. *Journal of Cleaner Production*, *378*, 134639. doi:10.1016/j.jclepro.2022.134639

Albort-Morant, G., Leal-Millán, A., & Cepeda-Carrión, G. (2016). The antecedents of green innovation performance: A model of learning and capabilities. *Journal of Business Research*, *69*(11), 4912–4917. doi:10.1016/j.jbusres.2016.04.052

Asadi, S., Pourhashemi, S., Nilashi, M., Abdullah, R., Samad, S., Yadegaridehkordi, E., & Razali, N. (2020). Investigating influence of green innovation on sustainability performance: A case on Malaysian hotel industry. *Journal of Cleaner Production*, *258*, 120860. doi:10.1016/j.jclepro.2020.120860

Asiaei, K., & Bontis, N. (2019). Translating knowledge management into performance: The role of performance measurement systems. *Management Research Review*, *43*(1), 113–132. doi:10.1108/MRR-10-2018-0395

Atapattu, A., & Jayakody, J. (2014). The interaction effect of organizational practices and employee values on knowledge management (KM) success. *Journal of Knowledge Management*, *18*(2), 307–328. doi:10.1108/JKM-07-2013-0276

Awan, U., Nauman, S., & Sroufe, R. (2021). Exploring the effect of buyer engagement on green product innovation: Empirical evidence from manufacturers. *Business Strategy and the Environment*, *30*(1), 463–477. doi:10.1002/bse.2631

Bandinelli, R., Acuti, D., Fani, V., Bindi, B., & Aiello, G. (2020). Environmental practices in the wine industry: An overview of the Italian market. *British Food Journal*, *122*(5), 1625–1646. doi:10.1108/BFJ-08-2019-0653

Barney, J., Ketchen, D. Jr, & Wright, M. (2011). The future of resource-based theory: Revitalization or decline? *Journal of Management*, *37*(5), 1299–1315. doi:10.1177/0149206310391805

Blome, C., Schoenherr, T., & Eckstein, D. (2014). The impact of knowledge transfer and complexity on supply chain flexibility: A knowledge-based view. *International Journal of Production Economics*, *147*, 307–316. doi:10.1016/j.ijpe.2013.02.028

Boons, F., Montalvo, C., Quist, J., & Wagner, M. (2013). Sustainable innovation, business models and economic performance: An overview. *Journal of Cleaner Production*, *45*, 1–8. doi:10.1016/j.jclepro.2012.08.013

Breznik, K. (2018). Knowledge management–from its inception to the innovation linkage. *Procedia: Social and Behavioral Sciences, 238*, 141–148. doi:10.1016/j.sbspro.2018.03.017

Bucci, M., & El-Diraby, T. (2018). The functions of knowledge management processes in urban impact assessment: The case of Ontario. *Impact Assessment and Project Appraisal, 36*(3), 265–280. doi:10.1080/14615517.2018.1445179

Byrne, B. (2008). *Structural Equation Modeling with EQS: Basic Concepts, Applications, and Programming*. Psychology Press.

Caniglia, G., Luederitz, C., von Wirth, T., Fazey, I., Martin-López, B., Hondrila, K., & Lang, D. J. (2021). A pluralistic and integrated approach to action-oriented knowledge for sustainability. *Nature Sustainability, 4*(2), 93–100. doi:10.1038/s41893-020-00616-z

Caputo, F., Garcia-Perez, A., Cillo, V., & Giacosa, E. (2019). A knowledge-based view of people and technology: Directions for a value co-creation-based learning organization. *Journal of Knowledge Management, 23*(7), 1314–1334. doi:10.1108/JKM-10-2018-0645

Cepeda-Carrion, G., Cegarra-Navarro, J., & Cillo, V. (2019). Tips to use partial least squares structural equation modelling (PLS-SEM) in knowledge management. *Journal of Knowledge Management, 23*(1), 67–89. doi:10.1108/JKM-05-2018-0322

Chang, C., & Lin, T. (2015). The role of organizational culture in the knowledge management process. *Journal of Knowledge Management, 19*(3), 433–455. doi:10.1108/JKM-08-2014-0353

Chen, Y. (2008). The driver of green innovation and green image–green core competence. *Journal of Business Ethics, 81*(3), 531–543. doi:10.1007/s10551-007-9522-1

Cheng, H., Chen, C., Wu, S., Mirza, Z. A., & Liu, Z. (2017). Emergy evaluation of cropping, poultry rearing, and fish raising systems in the drawdown zone of Three Gorges Reservoir of China. *Journal of Cleaner Production, 144*, 559–571. doi:10.1016/j.jclepro.2016.12.053

Cillo, V., Garcia-Perez, A., Del Giudice, M., & Vicentini, F. (2019). Blue-collar workers, career success and innovation in manufacturing. *Career Development International, 24*(6), 529–544. doi:10.1108/CDI-11-2018-0276

Cillo, V., Rialti, R., Bertoldi, B., & Ciampi, F. (2019). Knowledge management and open innovation in agri-food crowdfunding. *British Food Journal, 121*(2), 242–258. doi:10.1108/BFJ-07-2018-0472

Cui, R., Wang, J., Xue, Y., & Liang, H. (2021). Interorganizational learning, green knowledge integration capability and green innovation. *European Journal of Innovation Management, 24*(4), 1292–1314. doi:10.1108/EJIM-11-2019-0325

Demir, A., Budur, T., Omer, H., & Heshmati, A. (2021). Links between knowledge management and organisational sustainability: Does the ISO 9001 certification have an effect? *Knowledge Management Research and Practice*, 1–14. doi:10.1080/14778238.2020.1860663

Di Vaio, A., & Varriale, L. (2020). Blockchain technology in supply chain management for sustainable performance: Evidence from the airport industry. *International Journal of Information Management, 52*, 102014. doi:10.1016/j.ijinfomgt.2019.09.010

Elkington, J. (1997). *The triple bottom line sustainability's accountants.*

Fernando, Y., Jabbour, C., & Wah, W. (2019). Pursuing green growth in technology firms through the connections between environmental innovation and sustainable business performance: Does service capability matter? *Resources, Conservation and Recycling*, *141*, 8–20. doi:10.1016/j.resconrec.2018.09.031

Fornell, C., & Larcker, D. (1981). Evaluating structural equation models with unobservable variables and measurement error. *JMR, Journal of Marketing Research*, *18*(1), 39–50. doi:10.1177/002224378101800104

Gil, A., & Carrillo, F. (2016). Knowledge transfer and the learning process in Spanish wineries. *Knowledge Management Research and Practice*, *14*(1), 60–68. doi:10.1057/kmrp.2014.12

Grant, R. (1997). The knowledge-based view of the firm: Implications for management practice. *Long Range Planning*, *30*(3), 450–454. doi:10.1016/S0024-6301(97)00025-3

Hair, J., Hult, G., Ringle, C., & Sarstedt, M. (2016). *A primer on partial least squares structural equation modeling (PLS-SEM).* SAGE Publications.

Hair, J., Hult, G., Ringle, C., Sarstedt, M., Castillo-Apraiz, J., Cepeda Carrion, G., & Roldán, J. (2019). *Manual de Partial Least Squares Structural Equation Modeling (PLS-SEM) (2ª Edición).* OmniaScience Scholar. doi:10.3926/oss.37

Henseler, J., Hubona, G., & Ray, P. (2016). Using PLS path modeling in new technology research: Updated guidelines. *Industrial Management & Data Systems*, *116*(1), 2–20. doi:10.1108/IMDS-09-2015-0382

Iannone, B. (2015). Sustainability to Improve Knowledge Values and Intangible Capital: A Case Study in Wine Sector. In *European Conference on Knowledge Management* (p. 367). Academic Conferences International Limited.

Kianto, A., Sáenz, J., & Aramburu, N. (2017). Knowledge-based human resource management practices, intellectual capital and innovation. *Journal of Business Research*, *81*, 11–20. doi:10.1016/j.jbusres.2017.07.018

Kiranantawat, B. & Ahmad, S. (2022). Conceptualising the relationship between green dynamic capability and SME sustainability performance: the role of green innovation, organisational creativity and agility. *International Journal of Organizational Analysis*. doi:10.1108/IJOA-04-2022-3246

Kline, R. (2011). *Principles and practice of structural equation modeling.*

Kreamer, L., Albritton, B., Tonidandel, S., & Rogelberg, S. G. (2021). The use and misuse of organizational research methods 'best practice'articles. *Organizational Research Methods*, *1*(1), 1–19. 10944281211060706

Kumar, G., Meena, P., & Difrancesco, R. (2021). How do collaborative culture and capability improve sustainability? *Journal of Cleaner Production*, *291*, 125824. doi:10.1016/j.jclepro.2021.125824

Lam, L., Nguyen, P., Le, N., & Tran, K. (2021). The relation among organizational culture, knowledge management, and innovation capability: Its implication for open innovation. *Journal of Open Innovation*, *7*(1), 66. doi:10.3390/joitmc7010066

Le, P., Lei, H., Le, T., Gong, J., & Ha, A. (2020). Developing a collaborative culture for radical and incremental innovation: The mediating roles of tacit and explicit knowledge sharing. *Chinese Management Studies, 14*(4), 957–975. doi:10.1108/CMS-04-2019-0151

Lee, S., Kim, B., & Kim, H. (2012). An integrated view of knowledge management for performance. *Journal of Knowledge Management, 16*(2), 183–203. doi:10.1108/13673271211218807

López-Torres, G., Garza-Reyes, J., Maldonado-Guzmán, G., Kumar, V., Rocha-Lona, L., & Cherrafi, A. (2019). Knowledge management for sustainability in operations. *Production Planning and Control, 30*(10), 813–826. doi:10.1080/09537287.2019.1582091

Marco-Lajara, B., García, E. S., Larrosa, P. S., & Martínez-Falcó, J. (2022a). Knowledge creation and diffusion inspecialized environments: What are the factors involved? In *Empresa, economía y derecho. Oportunidades ante un entorno global y disruptivo* (pp. 432–459). Dykinson.

Marco-Lajara, B., Martínez-Falcó, J., Millan-Tudela, L. A., & Sánchez-García, E. (2023a). Analysis of the structure of scientific knowledge on wine tourism: A bibliometric analysis. *Heliyon, 9*(2), e13363. doi:10.1016/j.heliyon.2023.e13363 PMID:36816306

Marco-Lajara, B., Martínez-Falcó, J., Sánchez-García, E., & Millan-Tudela, L. A. (2023b). Analyzing the Role of Renewable Energy in Meeting the Sustainable Development Goals: A Bibliometric Analysis. *Energies, 16*(7), 3137. doi:10.3390/en16073137

Marco-Lajara, B., Úbeda-García, M., Zaragoza-Sáez, P., Poveda-Pareja, E., & Martínez Falcó, J. (2023c). Enoturismo y sostenibilidad: Estudio de casos en la Ruta del Vino de Alicante (España). *Pasos (El Sauzal), 21*(2), 307–320. doi:10.25145/j.pasos.2023.21.020

Marco-Lajara, B., Zaragoza-Saez, P., & Martínez-Falcó, J. (2022b). Green Innovation: Balancing Economic Efficiency With Environmental Protection. In Frameworks for Sustainable Development Goals to Manage Economic, Social, and Environmental Shocks and Disasters (pp. 239-254). IGI Global.

Marco-Lajara, B., Zaragoza-Sáez, P., Martínez-Falcó, J., & Ruiz-Fernández, L. (2022c). The effect of green intellectual capital on green performance in the Spanish wine industry: A structural equation modeling approach. *Complexity, 2022*, 2022. doi:10.1155/2022/6024077

Marco-Lajara, B., Zaragoza-Sáez, P., Martínez-Falcó, J., & Sánchez-García, E. (2022d). Las rutas del vino de España: el impacto económico derivado de las visitas a bodegas y museos [Spain's wine routes: the economic impact of visits to wineries and museums] In Investigación y transferencia de las ciencias sociales frente a un mundo en crisis [Social science research and transfer in the face of a world in crisis] (pp. 1774–1800).

Marco-Lajara, B., Zaragoza-Sáez, P. C., Martínez-Falcó, J., & Sánchez-García, E. (2023d). Does green intellectual capital affect green innovation performance? Evidence from the Spanish wine industry. *British Food Journal, 125*(4), 1469–1487. doi:10.1108/BFJ-03-2022-0298

Martínez-Falcó, J., Marco-Lajara, B., Sánchez-García, E., & Millan-Tudela, L. A. (2023c). Sustainable Development Goals in the Business Sphere: A Bibliometric Review. *Sustainability (Basel), 15*(6), 5075. doi:10.3390/su15065075

Mártínez-Falcó, J., Marco-Lajara, B., & Zaragoza-Sáez, P. (2023b). Corporate Social Responsibility: A Comprehensive Analysis. In Positive and Constructive Contributions for Sustainable Development Goals (pp. 131-160). IGI Global.

Martínez-Falcó, J., Marco-Lajara, B., Zaragoza-Sáez, P., & Gilinsky, A. (2024b). Wine Tourism in the Valencian Community: A Comparative Analysis. *Investigaciones Turísticas*, (27), 29–52.

Martínez-Falcó, J., Marco-Lajara, B., Zaragoza-Sáez, P., & Millán-Tudela, L. A. (2023f). Analyzing the effect of Corporate Social Responsibility on Green Innovation Performance in the Spanish wine industry: A structural equation modeling analysis. *Agribusiness*, *39*(4), 985–1006. doi:10.1002/agr.21820

Martínez Falcó, J., Marco-Lajara, B., Zaragoza-Sáez, P., & Sánchez-García, E. (2023). Vino, Turismo y COVID-19: El impacto de la COVID-19 en las Rutas del Vino de España. *Pasos (El Sauzal)*, *21*(1), 83–97. doi:10.25145/j.pasos.2023.21.006

Martínez-Falcó, J., Marco-Lajara, B., Zaragoza-Sáez, P., & Sánchez-García, E. (2023g). The effect of knowledge management on sustainable performance: Evidence from the Spanish wine industry. *Knowledge Management Research and Practice*, 1–16. doi:10.1080/14778238.2023.2218045

Martínez-Falcó, J., Marco-Lajara, B., Zaragoza-Sáez, P., & Sánchez-García, E. (2023h). The effect of organizational ambidexterity on sustainable performance: A structural equation analysis applied to the Spanish wine industry. *Agribusiness*. doi:10.1002/agr.21820

Martínez-Falcó, J., Marco-Lajara, B., Zaragoza-Sáez, P. D. C., & Millan-Tudela, L. A. (2023e). Wine tourism as a catalyst for green innovation: Evidence from the Spanish wine industry. *British Food Journal*. doi:10.1108/BFJ-08-2022-0690

Martínez-Falcó, J., Marco-Lajara, B., Zaragoza Sáez, P. D. C., & Sánchez-García, E. (2023d). Wine tourism in Spain: The economic impact derived from visits to wineries and museums on wine routes. *Investigaciones Turísticas*, *25*(25), 168–195. doi:10.14198/INTURI.21219

Martínez-Falcó, J., Martínez-Falcó, J., Marco-Lajara, B., Sánchez-García, E., & Visser, G. (2023i). Aligning the Sustainable Development Goals in the Wine Industry: A Bibliometric Analysis. *Sustainability (Basel)*, *15*(10), 8172. doi:10.3390/su15108172

Martínez-Falcó, J., Sánchez-García, E., Marco-Lajara, B., & Georgantzis, N. (2024a). The interplay between competitive advantage and sustainability in the wine industry: A bibliometric and systematic review. *Discover Sustainability*, *5*(1), 13. doi:10.1007/s43621-024-00196-4

Martínez-Falcó, J., Sánchez-García, E., Marco-Lajara, B., & Millan-Tudela, L. A. (2023j). Do organizational commitment and consumer satisfaction mediate the relationship corporate social responsibility-sustainable performance? Assessing happiness management in Spanish wineries. *Management Decision*. doi:10.1108/MD-02-2023-0217

Martínez-Falcó, J. M., Marco-Lajara, B., & Zaragoza-Saez, P. (2023a). Corporate Social Responsibility vs. Corporate Sustainability: Different Concepts for a Common Goal. In Positive and Constructive Contributions for Sustainable Development Goals (pp. 76-87). IGI Global.

Martins, V., Rampasso, I., Anholon, R., Quelhas, O., & Leal Filho, W. (2019). Knowledge management in the context of sustainability: Literature review and opportunities for future research. *Journal of Cleaner Production*, *229*, 489–500. doi:10.1016/j.jclepro.2019.04.354

Mehta, K., & Chugan, P. (2015). Green HRM in pursuit of environmentally sustainable business. Pursuit of Environmentally Sustainable Business. *Universal Journal of Industrial and Business Management*, *3*(3), 74–81. doi:10.13189/ujibm.2015.030302

Migdadi, M. (2021). Knowledge management, customer relationship management and innovation capabilities. *Journal of Business and Industrial Marketing*, *36*(1), 111–124. doi:10.1108/JBIM-12-2019-0504

Montalvo-Falcón, J. V., Sánchez-García, E., Marco-Lajara, B., & Martínez-Falcó, J. (2023). Green human resource management and economic, social and environmental performance: Evidence from the Spanish wine industry. *Heliyon*, *9*(10), e20826. doi:10.1016/j.heliyon.2023.e20826 PMID:37860533

Muñoz-Pascual, L., Galende, J., & Curado, C. (2019). Human resource management contributions to knowledge sharing for a sustainability-oriented performance: A mixed methods approach. *Sustainability (Basel)*, *12*(1), 161. doi:10.3390/su12010161

OECD. (2009). *Eco-innovation in industry: enabling green growth*. OECD.

Ouakouak, M., & Ouedraogo, N. (2019). Fostering knowledge sharing and knowledge utilization: The impact of organizational commitment and trust. *Business Process Management Journal*, *25*(4), 757–779. doi:10.1108/BPMJ-05-2017-0107

Ouvrard, S., Jasimuddin, S., & Spiga, A. (2020). Does sustainability push to reshape business models? Evidence from the European wine industry. *Sustainability (Basel)*, *12*(6), 2561. doi:10.3390/su12062561

Paillé, P., Chen, Y., Boiral, O., & Jin, J. (2014). The impact of human resource management on environmental performance: An employee-level study. *Journal of Business Ethics*, *121*(3), 451–466. doi:10.1007/s10551-013-1732-0

Paulraj, A. (2011). Understanding the relationships between internal resources and capabilities, sustainable supply management and organizational sustainability. *The Journal of Supply Chain Management*, *47*(1), 19–37. doi:10.1111/j.1745-493X.2010.03212.x

Pérez-López, S., & Alegre, J. (2012). Information technology competency, knowledge processes and firm performance. *Industrial Management & Data Systems*, *112*(4), 644–662. doi:10.1108/02635571211225521

Pérez-Luño, A., Alegre, J., & Valle-Cabrera, R. (2019). The role of tacit knowledge in connecting knowledge exchange and combination with innovation. *Technology Analysis and Strategic Management*, *31*(2), 186–198. doi:10.1080/09537325.2018.1492712

Polas, M., Tabash, M., Bhattacharjee, A. & Dávila, G. A. (2021). Knowledge management practices and green innovation in SMES: The role of environmental awareness towards environmental sustainability. *International Journal of Organizational Analysis*. doi:10.1108/IJOA-03-2021-2671

Prabhakar, G., Reddy, P., Savinkina, L., Gantasala, S., & Ankireddy, S. (2018). Influence of organisational culture dimensions on knowledge management processes in higher educational institutions. *International Journal of Knowledge Management Studies*, *9*(1), 51–71. doi:10.1504/IJKMS.2018.089693

Pradana, M., Pérez-Luño, A., & Fuentes-Blasco, M. (2019). Revisiting measure of absorptive capacity: Applying the scales in Spanish wine industry. *Journal of Management Information and Decision Sciences, 22*(4), 515–526.

Rahman, M., Moonesar, I., Hossain, M., & Islam, M. (2018). Influence of organizational culture on knowledge transfer: Evidence from the Government of Dubai. *Journal of Public Affairs, 18*(1), 1696. doi:10.1002/pa.1696

Rehman, S. U., Kraus, S., Shah, S. A., Khanin, D., & Mahto, R. (2021). Analyzing the relationship between green innovation and environmental performance in large manufacturing firms. *Technological Forecasting and Social Change, 163*, 120481. doi:10.1016/j.techfore.2020.120481

Sahibzada, U. F., Jianfeng, C., Latif, K. F., Shah, S. A., & Sahibzada, H. F. (2020). Refuelling knowledge management processes towards organisational performance: Mediating role of creative organisational learning. *Knowledge Management Research and Practice*, 1–13.

Sánchez-García, E., Marco-Lajara, B., Martínez-Falcó, J., & Poveda-Pareja, E. (2023a). Cognitive social capital for knowledge absorption in specialized environments: The path to innovation. *Heliyon, 9*(3), e14223. doi:10.1016/j.heliyon.2023.e14223 PMID:36923853

Sánchez-García, E., Martínez-Falcó, J., Alcon-Vila, A., & Marco-Lajara, B. (2023b). Developing Green Innovations in the Wine Industry: An Applied Analysis. *Foods, 12*(6), 1157. doi:10.3390/foods12061157 PMID:36981084

Serenko, A., Bontis, N., & Hull, E. (2016). An application of the knowledge management maturity model: The case of credit unions. *Knowledge Management Research and Practice, 14*(3), 338–352. doi:10.1057/kmrp.2014.37

Sezen, B., & Cankaya, S. (2013). Effects of green manufacturing and eco-innovation on sustainability performance. *Procedia: Social and Behavioral Sciences, 99*, 154–163. doi:10.1016/j.sbspro.2013.10.481

Shahzad, K., Arenius, P., Muller, A., Rasheed, M., & Bajwa, S. (2019). Unpacking the relationship between high-performance work systems and innovation performance in SMEs. *Personnel Review, 48*(4), 977–1000. doi:10.1108/PR-10-2016-0271

Shahzad, M., Qu, Y., Zafar, A., & Appolloni, A. (2021). Does the interaction between the knowledge management process and sustainable development practices boost corporate green innovation? *Business Strategy and the Environment, 30*(8), 4206–4222. doi:10.1002/bse.2865

Shahzad, M., Qu, Y., Zafar, A. U., Rehman, S., & Islam, T. (2020). Exploring the influence of knowledge management process on corporate sustainable performance through green innovation. *Journal of Knowledge Management, 24*(9), 2079–2106. doi:10.1108/JKM-11-2019-0624

Shehzad, M., Zhang, J., Dost, M., Ahmad, M., and Alam, S. (2022). Knowledge management enablers and knowledge management processes: a direct and configurational approach to stimulate green innovation. *European Journal of Innovation Management*. . doi:10.1108/EJIM-02-2022-0076

Silvestre, B., & Ţirca, D. (2019). Innovations for sustainable development: Moving toward a sustainable future. *Journal of Cleaner Production, 208*, 325–332. doi:10.1016/j.jclepro.2018.09.244

Singh, S. K., Gupta, S., Busso, D., & Kamboj, S. (2021). Top management knowledge value, knowledge sharing practices, open innovation and organizational performance. *Journal of Business Research*, *128*, 788–798. doi:10.1016/j.jbusres.2019.04.040

Stanovcic, T., Pekovic, S., & Bouziri, A. (2015). The effect of knowledge management on environmental innovation: The empirical evidence from France. *Baltic Journal of Management*, *10*(4), 413–431. doi:10.1108/BJM-01-2015-0012

Stedman, R., Connelly, N., Heberlein, T., Decker, D., & Allred, S. (2019). The end of the (research) world as we know it? Understanding and coping with declining response rates to mail surveys. *Society & Natural Resources*, *32*(10), 1139–1154. doi:10.1080/08941920.2019.1587127

Sudusinghe, J., & Seuring, S. (2021). Supply chain collaboration and sustainability performance in circular economy: A systematic literature review. *International Journal of Production Economics*, *245*, 1–19.

Thrassou, A., Vrontis, D., Crescimanno, M., Giacomarra, M., & Galati, A. (2020). The requisite match between internal resources and network ties to cope with knowledge scarcity. *Journal of Knowledge Management*, *24*(4), 861–880. doi:10.1108/JKM-06-2019-0291

Turner, S. (2010). Networks of learning within the English wine industry. *Journal of Economic Geography*, *10*(5), 685–715. doi:10.1093/jeg/lbp053

UNGC. (2018). *United Nations Global Compact*. United Nations.

Vrabcová, P., Urbancová, H., & Petříček, M. (2022). Knowledge and its transfer–key prerequisite for long-term competitive advantage and sustainable business. *Knowledge Management Research and Practice*, *20*(4), 630–640. doi:10.1080/14778238.2021.2015262

Wang, Z., & Wang, N. (2012). Knowledge sharing, innovation and firm performance. *Expert Systems with Applications*, *39*(10), 8899–8908. doi:10.1016/j.eswa.2012.02.017

Wen, Q., Wu, Y., & Long, J. (2021). Influence of ethical leadership on employees' innovative behavior: The role of organization-based self-esteem and flexible human resource management. *Sustainability (Basel)*, *13*(3), 1359. doi:10.3390/su13031359

Wong, S. (2013). Environmental requirements, knowledge sharing and green innovation: Empirical evidence from the electronics industry in China. *Business Strategy and the Environment*, *22*(5), 321–338. doi:10.1002/bse.1746

Woodfield, P., & Husted, K. (2017). Intergenerational knowledge sharing in family firms: Case-based evidence from the New Zealand wine industry. *Journal of Family Business Strategy*, *8*(1), 57–69. doi:10.1016/j.jfbs.2017.01.001

Yang, Z., Nguyen, V., & Le, P. (2018). Knowledge sharing serves as a mediator between collaborative culture and innovation capability: An empirical research. *Journal of Business and Industrial Marketing*, *33*(7), 958–969. doi:10.1108/JBIM-10-2017-0245

Zhang, D., Rong, Z., & Ji, Q. (2019). Green innovation and firm performance: Evidence from listed companies in China. *Resources, Conservation and Recycling*, *144*, 48–55. doi:10.1016/j.resconrec.2019.01.023

Zhang, Q., & Ma, Y. (2021). The impact of environmental management on firm economic performance: The mediating effect of green innovation and the moderating effect of environmental leadership. *Journal of Cleaner Production*, *292*, 126057. doi:10.1016/j.jclepro.2021.126057

APPENDIX

Table 8. Measures of variables used in the research

Variable		Questions/items	Authors
Control Variables (CV)		CV 1. Is the winery adhered to at least one Protected Designation of Origin?	Marco-Lajara et al. (2022a)
		CV 2. When was the winery founded?	Marco-Lajara et al. (2022a)
		CV 3. How many employees does the winery have?	OECD (2005)
Knowledge Management (KM)	Knowledge Acquisition (KA)	KA 1. We meet regularly with our customers to find out what their needs will be in the future.	Pérez-López and Alegre (2012)
		KA 2. We have processes in place to gain knowledge about our suppliers.	
		KA 3. We have a system in place that allows us to learn successful practices from other organizations	
		KA 4. We have processes in place to generate new knowledge from existing knowledge	
		KA 5. New ideas and approaches to work performance are continually being piloted	
	Knowledge Transfer (KT)	KT 1. Regular meetings are held to inform all employees of the latest developments in the company.	
		KT 2. The company has formal mechanisms in place to ensure the sharing of best practice across different areas of the business.	
		KT 3. The company has employees who are involved in several teams or divisions and who also act as liaisons between them.	
		KT 4. Employees are responsible for collecting, collating and distributing employee feedback internally.	
	Knowledge Application (KA)	KA 1. The company has processes in place to apply the knowledge learned from experiences.	
		KA 2. The company makes knowledge available to those who need it.	
		KA 3. Our company has processes in place to use knowledge to develop new products/services	
		KA 4. Our company is able to localize and apply knowledge to changing competitive conditions.	
Green Innovation	Green Product Innovation (GPDI)	GPDI 1. The company chooses materials that produce the least amount of pollution to carry out product development or design.	Chen (2008)
		GPDI 2. The company chooses the materials that consume the least energy and resources to carry out the product development or design.	
		GPDI 3. The company uses the least amount of materials to compose the product to carry out the product development or design.	
		GPDI 4. The company takes into account that the product is easy to recycle, reuse and decompose in order to carry out the development or design of the product.	
	Green Process Innovation (GPSI)	GPSI 1. The manufacturing process effectively reduces the emission of hazardous substances or wastes.	
		GPSI 2. The manufacturing process recycles waste and emissions allowing for treatment and reuse.	
		GPSI 3. The manufacturing process reduces the consumption of water, electricity, coal or oil	
		GPSI 4. The manufacturing process reduces the use of raw materials.	

<table>
<tr><th colspan="2">Variable</th><th>Questions/items</th><th>Authors</th></tr>
<tr><td rowspan="14">Sustainable Performance (SP)</td><td rowspan="4">Economic Performance (EP)</td><td>EP 1. Our company's average return on investment is above the industry average over the last five years.</td><td rowspan="4">Wang and Wang (2012)</td></tr>
<tr><td>EP 2. Our company's average profit is above the industry average over the last five years.</td></tr>
<tr><td>EP 3. Our company's profit growth is above the industry average over the last five years.</td></tr>
<tr><td>EP 4. Our company's average return on sales is above the industry average over the last five years.</td></tr>
<tr><td rowspan="5">Social Performance (SOP)</td><td>SOP 1. Our company has improved the well-being of its stakeholders relative to its competitors over the past five years.</td><td rowspan="5">Paulraj (2012)</td></tr>
<tr><td>SOP 2. Our company has improved the health and safety of the community in which it operates relative to its competitors over the past five years.</td></tr>
<tr><td>SOP 3. Our company has reduced environmental impact and risks to the general public relative to its competitors over the past five years.</td></tr>
<tr><td>SOP 4. Our company has improved the occupational health and safety of employees relative to its competitors over the past five years.</td></tr>
<tr><td>SOP 5. Our company has protected the claims and rights of its stakeholders relative to its competitors over the past five years.</td></tr>
<tr><td rowspan="5">Green Performance (GP)</td><td>GP 1. Our company has reduced waste and emissions from operations relative to its competitors over the past five years.</td><td rowspan="5">Paillé et al. (2014)</td></tr>
<tr><td>GP 2. Our company has reduced the environmental impact of its products/services relative to its competitors over the past five years.</td></tr>
<tr><td>GP 3. Our company has reduced environmental impact by establishing partnerships compared to its competitors in the last five years.</td></tr>
<tr><td>GP 4. Our company has reduced the risk of environmental accidents, spills and emissions compared to its competitors over the last five years.</td></tr>
<tr><td>GP 5. Our company has reduced purchases of non-renewable materials, chemicals and components relative to our competitors over the last five years.</td></tr>
<tr><td colspan="2" rowspan="5">Collaborative Culture (CC)</td><td>CC 1. Members of our company are willing to take responsibility for mistakes they make.</td><td rowspan="5">Lee et al. (2012)</td></tr>
<tr><td>CC 2. The members of our company cooperate with each other</td></tr>
<tr><td>CC 3. The members of our company are willing to support each other.</td></tr>
<tr><td>CC 4. The members of our company share an atmosphere of interdepartmental cooperation in the performance of tasks</td></tr>
<tr><td>CC 5. The members of our company are satisfied with their level of co-operation</td></tr>
</table>

Source: compiled by authors

Chapter 13
Local Fruits for Sustainable Beverage Supply Chains

Umesh Somashekharayya Kollimath
https://orcid.org/0000-0002-5173-3461
SBSPM's APIMR, Pune, India

ABSTRACT

The process of connecting local fruit growers with consumers, fostering sustainability, bolstering local economies, and facilitating access to fresh, wholesome food are all made possible by the short food supply chain (SFSC). The demand-supply imbalance in India sometimes results in an underdeveloped local fruit market. This chapter identifies mismatch between cultivators and consumers, suggesting action plan to improve alternative supply chains at a local level. These may foster local fruits supply chains connecting farmers to retailers. Considering local and indigenous fruits located in Maharashtra; 1000 households and ten food supply chain stakeholders were studied. Actors in the traditional fruit supply chain proposed strategies to cater to consumer preferences. Ten specialists in the food supply chain endorsed the findings and the fifteen measures that need to be changed between 2023 and 2030. By increasing the availability of local fruits on the market, this would assist growers and processors in making business plans for the future and in disclosing shifts in consumer preferences or market dynamics.

INTRODUCTION

According to the EU's rural development policy, a short food supply chain (SFSC) is a chain of supply that involves a small number of economic actors and is dedicated to local economic development, cooperation, and the preservation of close social and geographic ties between food producers, processors, and consumers. The program offers co-financing from the European Agricultural Fund for Rural Development, which incentivizes European farmers to participate in SFSC projects. Because of this, farmers in both urban and rural areas who sell their produce to customers directly and with few middlemen have recently expanded both in number and reach.

SFSCs are available in many formats. Direct sales from the farmer to the final customer (farm-gate, farmers' markets, and online delivery) are among the easiest. Other formats include 'choose your own',

DOI: 10.4018/979-8-3693-2149-2.ch013

box delivery services, and community-supported agriculture (CSA), in which customers subsidize local farmers by purchasing a'subscription' to their fresh fruit for a specific growing season. Fresh seasonal fruit and vegetables are usually the primary goods exchanged in an SFSC, followed by dairy items, beverages, and animal products (mostly fresh and prepared meat).

A change in consumer behavior that has demonstrated a greater respect for local food and associated characteristics like the location of origin, traditional production methods, and processing processes is largely responsible for the emergence of SFSCs. Furthermore, according to a 2016 EU-wide survey, four out of five Europeans believe that increasing the importance of farmers in the food chain is either very or extremely significant. Consistent with this pattern, the European Commission funds multi-actor projects that involve active collaboration between researchers and agri-food practitioners (farmers' associations, trade associations, advisors, and small businesses) over the course of the projects. The European Commission sees SFSCs as a significant issue due to their ability to promote sustainable urban and rural development. Likewise, in India, the need for wholesome, high-quality food has also grown among consumers. Customers are becoming increasingly willing to spend more for organic and sustainably produced food, indicating an increase in conscious consumerism. As a result, the producers now have access to new markets.

Government initiatives have also contributed to the alteration of India's food supply network. Among the projects are those that promote Farmer Producer organizations, build cold storage facilities, and use sustainable agricultural methods.

Literature Review: The researcher has carried out literature review of 10 research articles chosen on the basis of their relevance the present article. While choosing the literatures, care has been taken to ensure that the articles cover issues spanning global to local concerns.

"Sustainable Food Systems in Fruits and Vegetables Food Supply Chains" by Lucía Cassani Andrea and Gomez-Zavaglia; Frontier in nutrition, Volume 9 – 2022

This review examines the current state of fruit and vegetable wastes (characterization, availability) as sources of useful constituents (fiber, polyphenols, pigments) that can be added to food, medicine, and cosmetic products. Furthermore, a comprehensive and methodical strategy is discussed, which encompasses sustainable methods often employed in lab and commercial settings for the effective extraction of bioactive components from fruit and vegetable wastes. All things considered, this review offers a general updated overview of the state of the fruit and vegetable chain supplies in the post-pandemic era, providing an integrative perspective that focuses on whole processes and their social and economic impacts rather than just recovering fiber and phytochemicals from the wastes previously mentioned.

"A Systematic Review of Sustainable Fresh Fruit and Vegetable Supply Chains" by Ömer Özgür Tort,Özalp Vayvay, and Emine Çobanoğlu

The purpose of this study is to review the current state of knowledge and practices around fresh fruit and vegetable supply chains (FFVSC). The examined articles have been divided into groups according to their conclusions, study objectives, and messaging. Our intention is to guide future academics and practitioners by emphasizing significant research directions associated with these categories. For a better understanding, the instruments and procedures employed by these subgroups are detailed, which are mostly based on their shared study goals. Therefore, this study offers insight into FFVSC research for those who are inexperienced with the topic or want to go deeper into the directions that earlier research in the field has highlighted.

"Short Food Supply Chains (SFSC) as Local and Sustainable Systems" by Sebastian Jarzębowski, Michael Bourlakis, and Agnieszka Bezat-Jarzębowska; Sustainability 2020, 12(11), 4715

The paper is divided into three pieces. Section 2 provides an explanation of the Materials and Methods. In Section 3, common topics for short food supply chain analysis are introduced together with the typology of short food supply chains. We then look at the advantages of SFSCs in three areas of sustainable development. Furthermore, a classification, compilation, and analysis of the optimal approaches for short food supply chains with an emphasis on sustainability are conducted. A summary of potential roadblocks and prospects for the establishment of SFSCs is included in Section 4's conclusion. The concluding remarks are included in the last section.

"Business strategy pathways for short food supply chains: Sharing value between consumers and producers" by F. Cirone, M. Masotti, P. Prosperi, S. Bosi, G. Dinelli, M. Vittuari; Sustainable Production & Consumption; Volume 40, September 2023

The paper is divided into three pieces. Section 2 provides an explanation of the Materials and Methods. In Section 3, common topics for short food supply chain analysis are introduced together with the typology of short food supply chains. We then look at the advantages of SFSCs in three areas of sustainable development. Furthermore, a classification, compilation, and analysis of the optimal approaches for short food supply chains with an emphasis on sustainability are conducted. A summary of potential roadblocks and prospects for the establishment of SFSCs is included in Section 4's conclusion. The concluding remarks are included in the last section. A home survey comprising a representative sample of 1122 Italian households yielded four customer profiles. After that, from two focus groups with ten participants representing different stakeholders in the food supply chain, six topic areas of action were chosen. By employing the backcasting method, outdated granules.

"Need for a balance between short food supply chains and integrated food processing sectors: COVID 19 takeaways from India" by Venkatesh Thulasiraman, M.S.Giri Nandgopal & Anjineyulu Kothakota; Journal of Food Science & Technology

The integrated food processing businesses of today face several challenges, such as excessive energy consumption, greenhouse gas emissions, and food insecurity during pandemics and disasters. These issues are discussed in this article. Furthermore, we emphasize a more sustainable approach that better comprehends and reconciles SFSC and integrated food processing. In this case, resurrecting SFSC and traditional food processing techniques along with integrated food processing units would be a workable solution. This strategy opens up new possibilities for the process-supply system of the future.

"Scoping study on fruits and vegetables" by Xuezhen Guo, Thomas Tichar, Balraj Sikka, Agarwal Bhoormal, Kumar Gesh, Narula Sapna,4 Kumar Anand and Singh Kshyama; Wageningen Economic Research Report 2021-104 | Project code 2282500391

The research examines significant problems with the fruit and vegetable industry. The Bill & Melinda Gates Foundation (BMGF) recommended that four states—Andhra Pradesh, Bihar, Odisha, and Uttar Pradesh—be included in this study due to the size of the country. Seven fruit and vegetable products were chosen for in-depth analysis in this study: aubergine, litchi, mango, onion, orange, pea, and tomato.. The crops chosen were chosen based on four factors: 1) consumption by low- and middle-class urban and rural customers; 2) economic significance and income production for farmers; 3) nutritional value; and 4) chances for women to advance economically. To give a response, the study used a combination of 12 key informant interviews (KIIs), 20 focus group discussions (FGDs), and a literature review.

The study shows that the (fruit and vegetable) sector has a major impact on people's livelihoods, particularly in rural India. With 12.6% of all horticultural crops produced in India, the state of Uttar Pradesh produces the most, followed by West Bengal and Madhya Pradesh with 10.4% and 8.5%, respectively. The World Health Organization's recommended daily intake of fruits and vegetables is far more than the per-capita daily consumption of 262 g per person. Despite advancements, the Indian fruit and vegetable industry remains underdeveloped compared to its potential. Rather than productivity improvement, land expansion has been the primary driver of the increase in fruit and vegetable output during the past ten years.

"Underutilized Fruits and Vegetables in Hot Arid Regions of India: Status and Prospects: A Review" by P. R. Meghwal, Akath Singh, Dalpat Singh; Agricultural Reviews · January 2021, DOI: 10.18805/ag.R-2087

This article examines the prospects for fruits cultivated in hot and arid climate. As the article reveals; majority of the India's 31.7 million hectares of hot, dry regions are located in Rajasthan (61%). With scanty rainfall, extreme weather conditions and poor soil type,. The annual crops frequently fail. Notwithstanding these drawbacks, the area has a high population of people and livestock due to its good floral and faunal diversity. To supplement agricultural income, a variety of drought-resistant perennial fruits and vegetables are cultivated alongside annual crops. Commercial fruit crops planted in irrigated areas. Alongside annual crops, a range of drought-resistant perennial fruits and vegetables are grown to enhance agricultural income. Many of the less-used fruit crops are also farmed or grown organically.

"Underutilized wild fruits of North Maharashtra" by Kshirsagar Prachi P, Prabha Y. Bhogaonkar, and Vishal R. Marathe; Journal of Research in Plant Sciences, 071-076 | JRPS | 2012 | Vol 1 | No 1.

The article examines how local communities' and tribes' food needs, among other everyday necessities, are met by forest products. The current study set out to catalogue the wild fruits that the rural and tribal populations of North Maharashtra used as food. 46 species of fruits, representing 25 families, 23 of which are dicotyledonous and 02 of which are monocotyledonous, are known to be edible. Of these, twenty-four are trees, nine are shrubs, seven are climbers, and six are herbs. Fruits from several tree species are used most often. Of the 28 types of fruits, 24 are cooked, and 2 are consumed uncooked (i.e., unripe). Four species of fruits are pickled, while one species' fruits are utilised to make oil. A market study on commercially valuable fruits was also conducted. This is an effort to bring neglected wild fruits in the forefront. The current study makes it clear that more research is urgently needed to identify more underutilised fruits, which will undoubtedly improve the fruit basket. Since common cultivar fruits are too expensive and inaccessible for many marginalised rural populations and forest dwellers, underutilised wild fruits provide as a source of sustenance. Promoting wild edibles can undoubtedly help rural residents financially.

"Issues and Challenges in the Supply Chain of Fruits & Vegetables Sector In India: A Review" by Saurav Negi and Neeraj Anand; International Journal of Managing Value and Supply Chains (IJMVSC) Vol. 6, No. 2, June 2015.

The authors point out that the Indian F&V industry is the most lucrative of all farming operations in terms of job prospects and farm earnings. They also highlight the industry's enormous potential to promote the expansion of agriculture. India offers a vast range of meteorological and physio-geographical circumstances, making it the perfect location to develop a variety of F&V. The current analysis highlights the variables influencing India's fruit and vegetable supply chain. The primary conclusions of the study are to the following areas: finance, infrastructure, information, processing & value addition, and processing. Among the major problems that have been identified are a lack of infrastructure, low processing and value addition, low farmer income, inefficiencies in the supply chain, a large number of intermediaries and a fragmented supply chain, and insufficient quality and safety regulations. Resolving these issues will assist farmers, the state government, transporters, and food processing facilities by lowering losses and waste, raising the farmer's price share, generating employment opportunities for the community, and providing other advantages.

"Creating sustainable fresh produce supply chains by managing uncertainties" by Samir Gokran and Thyagaraj Kuthambalayan; Journal of Cleaner Production Volume 207, 10 January 2019, Pages 908-919.

This empirical study aims to investigate the effects of supply, demand, and price uncertainty in fresh produce supply chains (FSC) in an effort to improve sustainability. Fresh produce is made from plants and has a short shelf life. The intrinsic qualities of the product—such as seasonality, quality volatility, and perishability—are what cause the uncertainty in FSC.

According to the resource-based view (RBV), an organization's performance is determined by its resources and capabilities. The RBV theory states that both internal and external integration—achieved through relational, operational, and information technology capabilities—are viewed as resources that assist businesses in improving their FSC performance and their sustainability metrics, as well as their suppliers' delivery performance. It is proposed that there exists a positive correlation between the firm's performance and its FSC performance, and that FSC uncertainty acts as an adverse mediating factor in the positive correlations between firms' capabilities and FSC success. Survey data is used to independently calibrate and validate a structural equation model. The results are consistent with the theoretical underpinnings of the concept. In conclusion, businesses need to manage uncertainty by striking a balance between resource investments and benefits. Large organizations that participate in integrative operations usually have to make large resource commitments, and performance improvement may take some time. Sustainability measures demonstrate that without requiring significant resource investments, the small enterprises in this study have enhanced their performance through internal and external integration.

LOCAL FRUITS SCENARIO ANALYSIS

India has a diverse natural environment that makes it possible to develop any kind of horticultural crop. It ranks second in the world for producing fruits and vegetables, after China. 2021–2022 will see the production of 107.24 million metric tonnes of fruits, according to the National Horticulture Board. Fruit crops were grown on 7.05 million hectares of arable land.

India, an Emerging Fruits Basket of the World

The Food and Agriculture Organization (FAO) reports that India is currently the world's top producer of papayas (39.30%), mangoes (including mangosteens and guavas) (43.80%), and bananas (26.45%). India's broad production base allows it to capitalize on significant export possibilities. In 2022–2023, India exported fresh fruits and juices worth USD 737.81 million, or Rs. 5,944.49 crores.

Fruits including grapes, pomegranates, mangoes, bananas, and oranges make up the majority of the country's exports; however, there are no incentives for growing or marketing other regional fruits like papaya, custard apple, guava, etc.

Indian fresh produce is mostly exported to the United Arab Emirates, Bangladesh, Nepal, Malaysia, the Netherlands, Sri Lanka, the United Kingdom, Qatar, Oman, and Iraq. Indian processed fruits and vegetables are mostly exported to the United States, United Arab Emirates, Bangladesh, China, Saudi Arabia, and the Netherlands.

India's horticulture products are growing in popularity while holding a meager 1% global market share. This is due to concurrent developments in the sectors, such as state-of-the-art quality control and cold chain infrastructure. The government has started APEDA to build several Centers for Perishable Cargoes and integrated post-harvest processing facilities across the country, in addition to major contributions from the private sector. This attempt has also benefited from initiatives targeted at building the ability of farmers, processors, and exporters.

Fruit Zones of Maharashtra

This article centers on the very nutritious, less commercialized fruits that the local people have historically produced and consumed. Both the growers and the customers have shown indifference toward these crops. They are therefore either suffering from a lack of promotion or from low commercial worth. Long-term, this can cause them to become extinct, endangering a lot of nutrient-dense desi fruits at the expense of more well-known and unusual fruit species.

The seven fruits that are featured in this article are mostly grown with less focus on commerce but are nonetheless popular in the region's cuisine. The consumption pattern and nutritional information for these fruits are displayed in the following table:

Table 1. The important fruit zones of Maharashtra

Sr.No.	Region	Districts	Crops grown
1.	Warm Coastal Region Rainfall 80" to 200" with humid climate	Ratnagiri, Kolaba, Thana, Sindhudurg.	Mango, Cashewnut Coconut, Chiku, Banana, Pine Apple Jack fruit, Aracanut
2.	Western Deccan region partly dry and humid with 30 to 50" rainfall.	Parts of Kolhapur, Nasik, Satara, Sangli and Poona.	Mango, Banana, Chiku, Limes, Guava, Jack fruits.
3.	Eastern Deccan fairly dry and hot with 15 to 25" rainfall	Jalgaon, Dhule Ahmednagar, Solapur, Aurangabad, Beed, Osmanabad, Eastern parts of Pune	Mosambi, Limes, Grapes, Papaya Banana, Guava, Pomogranate, Fig, Phalsa
4.	Western Vidarbha and Eastern Marathwada. Fairly hot with 20" – 30" rainfall during monsoon.	Buldhana, Akola, parts of Yeotmal, Parbhani, Nanded, Hingoli, Washim, parts of East Khandesh and Aurangabad	Mango Banana, Grape, Mosambi, Santra, Fig, Custard apple, Guava and Phalsa.
5.	North East Region of Vidarbha. Hot and dry with partly humid region, with 30" – 40" rainfall	Amravati, Wardha, Nagpur, Chanda, Bhandara, parts of Akola	Orange (Santra), Mosambi, Mango, Papaya, Guava and Limes.

Principal Problems With the Fruit and Vegetable Supply Chain

Demand for functional foods, penetration of private labels and organized retail, and rising expenditure on health foods are the main factors propelling this industry's expansion. Typical Supply Chain for fresh fruits in India has multiple market intermediaries, leading to significant break ups in average rupees per consumer that ultimately reaches the farmers, the largest risk takers in any form of farming.

Apart from dwindling profits, farmers also are the net sufferers on account of wastage of the produce due to poor pre/postharvest practices, distribution losses, natural calamities, market fluctuations, and so on.

The researcher has observed that generally farmers prefer existing Supply Chain model either due to societal compulsions or need to conformity from peers.

The following diagram of a typical Indian farm produce supply chain is practices for most of the fresh produce that is cultivated and consumed domestically or exported to overseas destinations.

Among the issues that will be; the supply chain for fruits and vegetables mentions the existence of multiple parties that operate independently, with a very inadequate infrastructure linking them. Eight significant problems with the fruit and vegetable supply chain are listed below:

Problems With Cold Chain Management

Numerous issues affect the cold chain, such as inadequate cold chain capacity, a lack of cold chain networks, and a lack of cold chain infrastructure. This concern makes it difficult for farmers and business owners to manage their businesses effectively and to get fair payment for their produce.

Table 2. Consumption pattern and nutritional quotient of the local fruits

#	Fruit's Name & details	Consumption Pattern	Nutritional value
1.	**Jackfruit:** Botanically known as Artocarpus heterophyllus, a species of tree in the fig, mulberry, and breadfruit family (Moraceae). Largest tree fruit, measuring as much as 55 kg (120 pounds) in weight, 90 cm (35 inches) in length, and 50 cm (20 inches) in diameter. A mature jackfruit tree produces some 200 fruits per year, with older trees bearing up to 500 fruits in a year. The fruit matures during the rainy season from July to August. Predominant in Western Ghats of India.	Variety of dishes; custards, cakes, Idlis & Dosas. Leaves are used as a wrapping for steaming- Young leaves are tender enough to be used as a vegetable. Ripe jackfruit arils are sometimes seeded, fried, or freeze-dried and sold as jackfruit chips. The seeds from ripe fruits are edible once cooked/baked, commonly used in curry in the form of a traditional lentil and vegetable mix curry.	The edible pulp is 74% water, 23% carbohydrates, 2% protein, and 1% fat. The pulp is a source of dietary fiber. In a 100-gram portion, raw jackfruit provides 400 kJ (95 kcal), and is a rich source (20% or more of the Daily Value, DV) of vitamin B6 (25% DV). It contains moderate levels (10-19% DV) of vitamin C and potassium.
2.	**Guava:** Botanically known as Psidium guajava, they belong to family of berries (Myrtaceae). Guava fruits, usually measure 4 to 12 cm (1&1/2 to 4&1/2 in) long, are round or oval depending on the species. The fruit harvesting commences during rainy season continues through the winter months. Found in Bihar, Uttar Pradesh, Maharashtra, Karnataka, Orissa, West Bengal, Andhra Pradesh, and Tamil Nadu. Allahabad variety has global reputation.	Eaten raw with a pinch of salt and pepper, sold on many street corners as a popular snack.	Rich in dietary fiber and vitamin C, moderate levels of folic acid, a single common guava (P. guajava) fruit contains 257% of the Daily Value (DV) for vitamin C.) has 39% of the vitamin C in common varieties, its content in a 100 gram serving (90 mg) still provides 100% of the DV.
3.	**Papaya:** Botanically known as Carica papaya, belongs to the family Caricaceae. The fruit is a large berry about 15–45 cm (6–17+3/4 in) long and 10–30 cm (4–11+3/4 in) in diameter. The peak papaya season in India is from August – November. Orissa, West bengal, Kerala, Karnataka, Madhya Pradesh, Tamil Nadu, Gujarat and Goa.	The ripe fruit of the papaya is usually eaten raw, without skin or seeds. The black seeds of the papaya are edible and have a sharp, spicy taste.	Raw papaya pulp contains 88% water, 11% carbohydrates. It is a significant source of vitamin C (75% DV) and a moderate source of folate (10% DV).

continued on following page

Table 2. Continued

#	Fruit's Name & details	Consumption Pattern	Nutritional value
4.	**Fig:** Ficus carica, a species of small tree in the flowering plant family Moraceae. is tear-shaped, 3–5 cm (1–2 in) long, with a green skin that may ripen toward purple or brown, and sweet soft reddish flesh containing numerous crunchy seeds. Western Maharashtra, Gujarat, Uttar Pradesh (Lucknow & Saharanpur) Karnataka (Bellary, Chitradurga & Srirangapatna) and Tamilnadu (Coimbatore) are major clusters of the cultivation.	Eaten fresh or dried, or processed into jam, rolls, biscuits and other types of desserts. Since ripe fruit does not transport and keep well, most commercial production is in the dried and processed forms.	Raw figs are 79% water, 19% carbohydrates, 1% protein, and contain negligible fat (table). They are a moderate source (14% of the Daily Value, DV) of dietary fiber and 310 kilojoules (74 kcal) of food energy per 100-gram serving. dried figs are a rich source (more than 20% DV) of dietary fiber and the essential mineral manganese (26% DV), while calcium, iron, magnesium, potassium, and vitamin K are in moderate amounts.
5.	**Custard Apple:** Botanically known as Annona squamosa. It belongs to the family Annonaceae. the fruits are often scaly and succulent and are sometimes segmented. The medium-sized fruit of 250 gm to 500 gm with sweet pulp and pleasant aroma. The fruits have white flesh with custard-like consistency and dark brown seeds. The slightly acidic flavor is sometimes described as a cross between a strawberry and pineapple. The fruits are seen throughout the year, but peak season being winter and early summer. Cultivated in Andhra Pradesh, Maharashtra, Karnataka, Bihar, Orissa, Assam, and Tamil Nadu.	Custard apples have various culinary applications such as smoothies, fruit salads, or desserts (Sitaphal Rabdi).	Custard apple is relatively low in calories and fat while being a good source of dietary fiber, vitamin C, potassium, and magnesium. Calories: 98.94 kcal 5% Daily Value (DV) Carbohydrates: 20.38 grams 7% DV Dietary fiber: 5.1 grams 20% DV Protein: 1.62 grams 3% DV Fat: 0.67 grams 1% DV Vitamin C: 35.9 milligrams 60% DV Vitamin A: 22 micrograms 2% DV Potassium: 382 milligrams 8% DV Magnesium: 27 milligrams 6% DV Iron: 0.6 milligrams 3% DV

continued on following page

Problems With Infrastructure

In the F&V industry, supply chain infrastructure is crucial. Adequate and suitable infrastructure facilitates the smooth operation of agricultural businesses by farmers and agribusiness owners, as well as the timely and proper delivery of goods. The primary barrier in the agricultural product supply chain that results in significant losses is infrastructure.

Problems With Packaging

Given that F&V are extremely perishable items and that handling fresh produce requires appropriate packing, packaging is crucial. It is exceedingly difficult to sustain their shelf life without appropriate

Table 2. Continued

#	Fruit's Name & details	Consumption Pattern	Nutritional value
6.	**Phalsa:** Botanically known as Grewia asiatica, it belongs to the the mallow family Malvaceae. The fruit is an edible drupe 5–12 mm diameter, purple to black when ripe. Peak season during middle of June. Maharashtra, Gujarat, Bihar, Karnataka, Andhra Pradesh, and West Bengal cultivate the fruit.	A Sharbat or squash is prepared from the fruit pulp by mixing it with sugar and used as an astringent, stomachic and cooling agent. The root is used by Santhal tribals for rheumatisms. The stem bark is said to be used in refining sugar, for making ropes and its infusion is used as a demulcent. The leaves are used as an application to pustular eruptions. The buds are also prescribed by some physicians.	Carbohydrates 21.1 g Vitamin A 16.1 g Fibres 5.53 g Protein 1.57 g Fats 0.1 g Potassium 372 mg Calcium 136 mg Phosphorus 24.2 mg Sodium 17.3 mg Vitamin C 4.3 mg Iron 1.08 mg Vitamin B3 0.8 mg
7.	Ber: Scientifically called Ziziphus mauritiana. It belongs to the family Rhamnaceae. 1 The fruit is a soft, juicy, drupe that is 2.5 cm diameter, though in some cultivars the fruit size may reach up to 6.25 cm long and 4.5 cm wide. The form may be oval, obovate, round or oblong; the skin smooth or rough, glossy, thin but tough Some types ripen as early as October, others from mid-February to mid-March, others in March, or mid-March, to the end of April.	Eaten raw, pickled or used in beverages. They are sometimes stewed. Slightly under-ripe fruits are candied by a process of pricking, immersing in a salt solution. Ripe fruits are preserved by sun-drying and a powder is prepared for out-of-season purposes. Ber juice, or as ber butter is another way of consumption.	Energy 5.92 kcal Total fat 0.07 g Fiber 0.60 g Carbohydrate 17.00 g Protein 00.80 g Moisture 81.6-83 g Calcium 25.6 mg Phosphorus 26.8 mg Iron 0.76-1.8 mg Carotene 0.021 mg Thiamine 0.02-0.024 mg Riboflavin 0.02-0.038mg Niacin 0.7-0.873mg Citric acid 0.2-1.1 mg Ascorbic acid 65.8-76 mg Fluoride 0.1-0.2 mg Pectin 2.2 – 3.4 % dry basis

packaging. Cost is a critical component of this problem. Farmers find it challenging to package their products properly due to the high cost of packaging materials.

Problems With Technology

Numerous technical problems, including slow technological growth, ineffective technology, outmoded methods, and antiquated machinery, surround technology. Farmers and agribusiness owners find it challenging to employ the right technology and procedures to cut down on post-harvest losses and operational activity time as a result of these worries.

The Awareness and Knowledge of Farmers

To operate effectively and efficiently, farmers need be properly knowledgeable about how to employ the newest technology, strategies, etc. Occasionally, They lack expertise in the administration of post-harvesting goods, seed quality, etc. Since farmers are the primary source of fresh agricultural produce, the F&V supply chain cannot function effectively without the appropriate degree of knowledge and awareness among farmers.

Figure 1. Typical Indian farm produce supply chain
Source: Modi et all (2009)

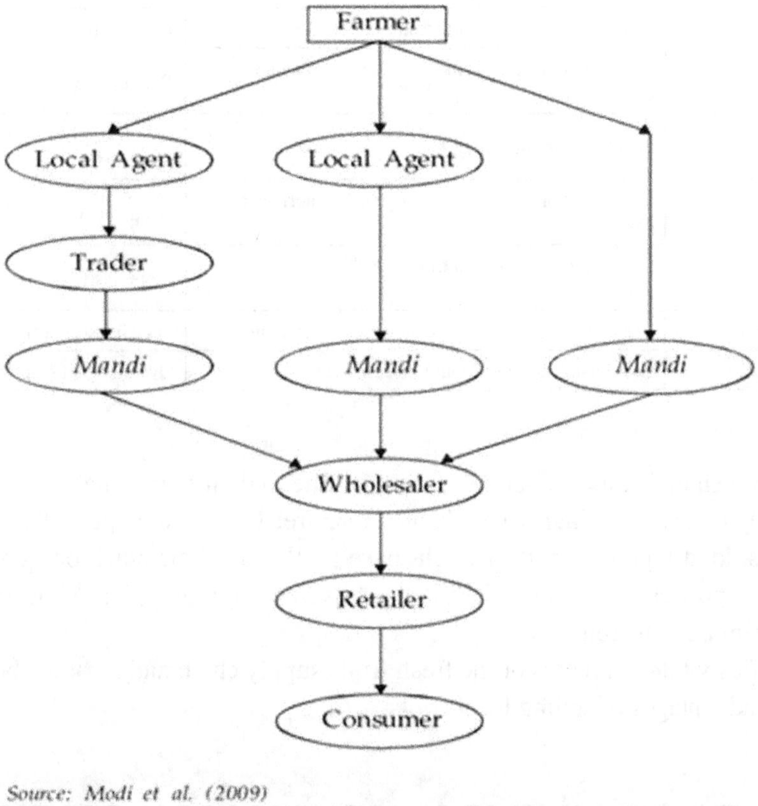

Problems With Quality

Since quality has a direct impact on people's health, it is a crucial component of the food industry. The timely and efficient delivery of fresh items with appropriate quality to the client is crucial for the supply chain. A well-managed supply network keeps product fresher for longer and keeps its quality from declining. Quality has a big influence on the supply chain, which makes it more efficient and reduces consumer rejection.

Problems With Transportation

Within the supply chain, transportation is crucial. The consumer cannot receive the items in a timely and satisfactory manner without adequate transportation. Due to their short shelf life, high perishability, and need for regulated temperature, perishable foods like fruits and vegetables require it even more.

Local Fruits Supply Side and Demand Side Advantages

It is always advantageous from either of the demand and supply side to support local fruits. Consumption of local fresh fruits not only benefits health of the consumers, but also generates positive economic,

Table 3. Advantages of processing local fruits

#	Parameter	Supply-side advantage	Demand-side advantage
1	Freshness	Visual appeal (texture and taste)	Filled with nutrition
2	Transportation Cost	Least (short supply chain with minimum fuel and energy)	Better prices
3	Accessibility	Local, consistent supply	Free from chemical ripening and preservatives
4	Packaging	No need of protective packaging due to short supply chain	Need not bear additional price for packaging
5	Processing	Can be processed in real time as pickles, juices, purees, jams.	Better taste, no preservatives
6	Social Responsibility	Preserves local varieties; supports local community	Socially Responsible Consumption
7	Environment	Eco-friendly as fewer polluting activities	Overall beneficiary of healthy ecosystem.

social and environmental. Fruits are nature's true gifts due to their nutritional value. However, most of them are extremely delicate and highly perishable in nature. Therefore, popular fruits and exotic fruits, even though are sold at a premium, they might have partly lost their nutrition quotient through long and cumbersome supply chain. Local fruits can be delivered through typical Short Food Supply Chain (SFSC), with minimum nutrition loss.

Table 3 identifies vital parameters of the fresh fruits supply chain and attribute both the supply side and demand side advantages of selling local fruits.

BEVERAGES: THE BEST WAY OF PROCESSING LOCAL FRESH FRUITS

Beverages have longer shelf life than raw fruits or juices. However, there are a number of useful factors that contribute to their production, processing, and rising popularity:

The softer, more fragile fruits tend to ripen before or at harvesting since they cannot be preserved for extended periods of time. Making juice is the sensible substitute.

- Fruit that is even more resilient could nevertheless have sections that are so flawed, ill-formed, or little that they cannot be sold as fresh entire fruit. The sound part can be juiced after thorough evaluation and cutting. It will be emphasised again and again in this work that rotting or almost spoiled fruit should never be juiced. Nonetheless, employing sound culls is a practical, technically sound, and financially sound utilisation approach.

Why it's more convenient to drink juices than whole fruits. Imagine a driver who is rushing and has a phone in her hand, or a mother with a fidgety toddler; imagine both of them trying to peel an orange instead of holding a juice container that is simple to open. For many, "dashboard dining" is a way of life, thus liquid products and creative packaging are essential.

- It can be difficult for the extremely young, old, and sick to eat, let alone peel some fruits. Juicing is a healthy, effective substitute. Recently identified ingredients in many fruit juices will increase the appeal of these goods in addition to their nutritional value and phytochemicals' extra health advantages.

Even flavorful juices can be combined or used as efficient carriers for additional natural or synthetic nutrients including vitamins, minerals, and phytochemicals, even if they might not be nutritionally balanced or contain phytochemicals.

- Compared to solid foods or fluids containing particles, fluid food products—including juices—are simpler to process, heat, cool, freeze, standardise, transport, etc. Processing efficiency, safety, and quality standards can therefore be more easily met.
- The ease with which fluids can be combined encourages the creation of novel juice blends with other goods and useful combos that aren't found in nature.

Juices with strong tastes serve as the foundation for a variety of juice by-products, including components for bakeries, smoothies, ice cream, and confectionary.

- Safe, stable, and aesthetically pleasing juice and beverage products are ensured by modern processing, packaging, ingredient technology, and distribution systems in a convenient, cost-effective form, even when the raw material source or season is far away.

Juices of all kinds and forms are vital for both food enjoyment and sustenance, according to a global survey of food markets (Table 1.1). The past five years have seen a noticeable acceleration of this trend. An expanding list of commercial wholesale juice goods available in international trade is provided in Table 1.2. Even if certain products or forms are now only produced on request in small quantities, this could all change in response to demand. Therefore, improving a product's value, safety, and quality while promoting its appeal is the aim of a food technologist. Figure 1.2 shows a comparison between an Indonesian traditional market and the juice section of a well-stocked American supermarket.

Processing Fresh Fruits Into Beverages: A Means to Achieve Nutritional Security

Premature deaths are being caused by non-communicable diseases (NCDs) such as diabetes, cancer, heart disease, stroke, and chronic lung disease. According to a study, NCDs are to blame for 74% of all deaths globally. Low- and middle-income nations account for more than 3/4 of all NCD mortality and 86% of the 17 million premature deaths—those that occur before the age of 70.

A person must eat at least 400 g (five servings) of fruit and vegetables each day, excluding potatoes, sweet potatoes, cassava, and other starchy roots, according to the WHO's Recommended Dietary Allowance (RDA). Similar to this, a child's healthy growth and cognitive development are enhanced during the first two years of life when they receive adequate nutrition. Additionally, it lowers the chance of gaining weight or becoming obese and eventually getting NCDs. As a result, it's wise to include plenty of hygienic fresh fruit eating.

The researcher observed during the research on consumption habits of fresh fruits that adults shy away from regular consumption of fresh fruits due to the hassles involved such as procuring quality fruits, storage, and cutting and cleaning them before consumption. Children are deprived of the fresh fruits either due to parental ignorance or children's unwillingness. Both these issues can be addressed by making fresh fruits juices and beverages readily available in the market. Apart from products derived from fresh fruit pulp, there is a need of R & D on whether seeds, skin of the fruits, leaves and other parts of the fresh fruit plants can be processed for healthy human consumption. Following possibilities may be explored within the framework of beverages industry as far as fresh fruits are concerned:

a. Instant Herbal tea preparations using kernels, dried leaves, etc. of fresh fruits having potential sources of flavonoids, vitamins and minerals.
b. Daily supply of freshly processed fruit juices early morning using packaged milk supply chain.
c. Encouraging Schools/Colleges to inspire their pupils consume fresh fruit based products rather than soft drinks.

This way, there will be increased demand for local fruit products, creating win-win situation for both local farmers and consumers.

Challenges of Processing Fresh Fruits into Beverages

Among all the processed and packaged food industries, fresh fruits processing is perhaps the most tricky and complicated in terms of meeting customer expectations..

A fresh fruit product has to maintain aesthetically decent presentation of the products; be it beverages, juices, candies, and so on. Often raw fresh fruit vendors encounter issues raised by their patrons about damaged or soiled produce, deterring the customers. Therefore, packaging of the product, ensuring safety and protection from external influences is critical. Besides appearance, the processor needs to ensure that taste and integrity are not negatively impacted and freshness is maintained. Hygiene and safety will play a major part here, as all products should be safe to consume with minimal risk of contamination. Following are the major challenges to be handled in this case:

Contamination

The risk of contamination is one of the biggest problems. Fruit is susceptible to dirt, pesticides, insects, and soil because of its origins. Customers are put in danger by any contamination, which can lead to complaints, unhappy customers, expensive product recalls, and even legal action against the company. It will have terrible effects on the company's reputation and make products unattractive.

Product Flow

Fruit products are frequently impacted by sticky residue. Because they readily become trapped along the production line and cause build-up and blockages, it makes them challenging to process. If ignored, it may lead to giveaway and excessive waste, as well as disturbance and equipment failures.

The processors must make an investment in appropriate machinery to ensure seamless produce flow. By doing this, the possibility of materials being harmed during production will also be decreased.

Environmental Conditions

Fruit frequently needs cooler temperatures to keep its constituents fresh and avoid rotting. Fruits that have been frozen must be processed at even lower temperatures in order to preserve the integrity of the product. Processing units must thus have highly functioning equipment that can operate at lower temperatures in order to meet quality standards and respect the plant's environment.

Delicate Handling

Fruit products are generally delicate. If handled recklessly, they are quickly bruised and damaged. Visible damage to a product could deter buyers from purchasing it. Products must be handled carefully to reduce the chance of damage, which frequently entails using manual procedures or locating equipment that permits meticulous processing.

Accuracy

Because portion management is crucial to keeping expenses down and meeting requirements, the processors have to make sure that the raw fruits under processing weigh correctly and stay within their predetermined bounds. Purchasing precise weighing apparatus is essential for separating resources into the exact amounts required for each product, resulting in more efficient procedures that reduces waste.

Handling Operations

The established processors of fresh fruits can handle large amounts of produce. Local fresh fruits may need customized equipment that can manage moderate loads without sacrificing speed or accuracy. Production costs must be checked while achieving higher turnaround times besides preserving output quality. This would need a manufacturing line that can handle just right amounts of materials.

Managing Product Format and Pack Size

Lastly, if a processor works with a variety of fruit items, it may require format modifications. For instance, Custard apples and Guavas differ greatly in terms of integrity; the processors need a production line that can manage different kinds of fruits. Besides, each product has different packing need, such as variable sizes and shapes, in addition to a range of formats. All products must be packaged effectively. The secret is to handle the changing needs of your products while coming up with robust and adaptable solutions—even if it means to have separate machinery or equipment.

DESIGNING A SHORT FOOD SUPPLY CHAIN FOR LOCAL FRESH FRUIT BASED BEVERAGES

It is frequently noted that rival supply chains pose a threat to the enterprises operating in the food supply chain context, as well as to agricultural systems in general. As a result, both academic academics and businesspeople are interested in the study of creating new models for food supply chains. The increasing

Figure 2. A typical short food supply chain proposed for local fresh fruit beverages

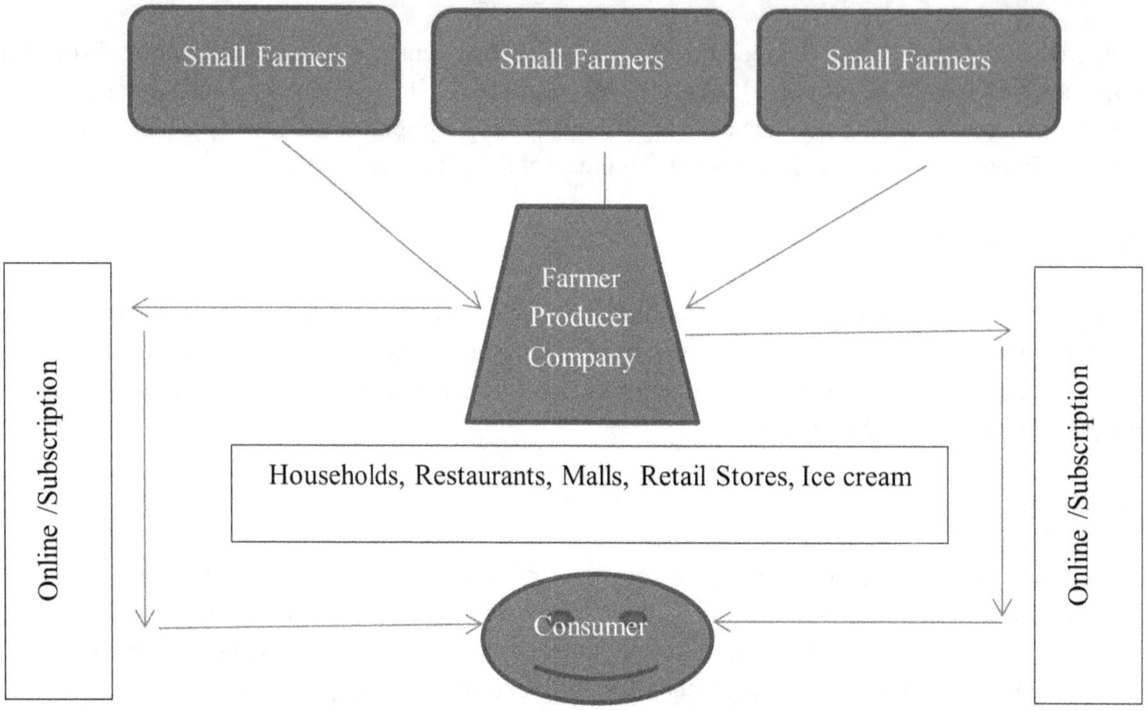

demands from consumers for a wider range of products, better packaging, and higher-quality services have only made matters more difficult.

Therefore, there is a great potential to build Short Food Supply Chains (SFSC) to supply Local Fresh Fruits. The author proposes a generic model of SFSC where Farmer Producer Companies (FPCs) will be formed involving 10 or more enthusiasts already into cultivation of the local fruits as covered in this study. Each FPC will carry out collection of the fruits, processing them into Juices or beverages and supply the same to Retail Stores, Ice cream parlors, restaurants, etc. Alternatively, online retailing directly to retail consumers can also be explored.

CONCLUSION

The article proposes a short food supply chain that will ensure sustainability for locally cultivated fresh fruits while safeguarding the environment, social cohesion, and local economy. In a Special Report on Climate Change and Land published a few years ago by the Intergovernmental Panel on Climate Change, it was stated that consuming food grown locally and that efficient food processing and transportation practices reduce food losses, increase food security, and reduce greenhouse gas (GHG) emissions. In this context, it is significant that an increasing percentage of consumers are looking for alternate food sources that are produced around where they live. These relatively new coordinated food distribution techniques are referred to as "short food supply chains" (SFSCs). The growing demand for high-quality products by consumers is the reason behind the popularity of SFSCs in recent years. Moreover, SFFCs may be seen as supporting healthy, sustainable farming methods and resilient farm-based livelihoods.

It has been demonstrated that SFSCs can increase farm income, promote sustainable farming methods, and aid in the development of local economies.

REFERENCES

Andrea, L. C., & Zavaglia, G. (2022). Sustainable Food Systems in Fruits and Vegetables Food Supply Chains. *Frontiers in Nutrition*, 9. PMID:35252306

Cirone, F., Masotti, M., Prosperi, P., Bosi, S., Dinelli, G., & Vittuari, M. (n.d.). *Business strategy pathways for short food supply chains: Sharing value between consumers and producers*. IEEE. doi:10.1016/j.spc.2023.07.017

Gokran, S., & Kuthambalayan, T. (2019). Creating sustainable fresh produce supply chains by managing uncertainties. *Journal of Cleaner Production*, *207*, 908–919. doi:10.1016/j.jclepro.2018.10.072

Guo, X., Tichar, T., Sikka, B., Agarwal, B., Gesh, K., Narula, S., Kumar, A., & Singh, K. (2023, December 26). *Scoping study on fruits and vegetables*. eDepot. https://edepot.wur.nl/552208

Jarzębowski, S., Bourlakis, M., & Bezat-Jarzębowska, A. (2020). Short Food Supply Chains (SFSC) as local and sustainable systems. *Sustainability (Basel)*, *12*(11), 4715. doi:10.3390/su12114715

Kshirsagar, P., P,, P., Y., B., & Marathe, V. R. (2012). Underutilized wild fruits of North Maharashtra. *Journal of Research in Plant Sciences, 1*(1), 071–076.

Meghwal, P. R., Singh, A., & Singh, D. (2021). Underutilized fruits and vegetables in hot arid regions of India: Status and prospects: A Review. *Agricultural Reviews*. doi:10.18805/ag.R-2087

Negi, S., & Anand, N. (2015). Issues and Challenges in the Supply Chain of Fruits & Vegetables Sector In India: A Review. *International Journal of Managing Value and Supply Chains*, *6*(2), 47–62. doi:10.5121/ijmvsc.2015.6205

Thulasiraman, V., Giri, M. S., Nandgopal, & Kothakota, A. (2020). *Need for a balance between short food supply chains and integrated food processing sectors: COVID 19 takeaways from India*. Springer. https://link.springer.com/article/10.1007/s13197-020-04942-0

Tort, Ö. Ö., Vayvay, Ö., & Çobanoğlu, E. (2022). *A Systematic Review of Sustainable Fresh Fruit and Vegetable Supply Chains*. MDPI. . doi:10.3390/su14031573

Chapter 14
Malaysian Oil Palm Industry:
A View on the Economic, Social, and Environmental Aspects

Muhammad Sallehudin Ali
https://orcid.org/0000-0003-1188-4553
Universiti Teknologi MARA, Malaysia

Selvakkumar Vaiappuri
https://orcid.org/0000-0002-8476-4424
Universiti Teknologi MARA, Malaysia

Sehrish Tariq
Universiti Teknologi MARA, Malaysia

ABSTRACT

Palm oil, renowned for its high yield per hectare, drives vast cultivation areas across major producing nations, notably Malaysia, a global leader in palm oil production. In 2020, Malaysia's palm oil sector contributed 2.7% to GDP, exporting 16.2 million metric tons valued at 73.3 billion Malaysian ringgit. Integral to the economy, it spurs rural development and generates substantial foreign exchange. However, its impact extends beyond economics, fostering intricate social dynamics, including labor abuses, land conflicts, and indigenous displacement. Environmental concerns, such as deforestation and biodiversity loss, necessitate sustainable practices and certification initiatives. This chapter delves into these issues, advocating for a balanced approach that prioritizes economic growth, social equity, and environmental stewardship in Malaysia's oil palm sector.

INTRODUCTION

Among vegetable oils, palm oil is the preferred option due to its high output per hectare reputation. The vast expanses of oil palm plantations, spanning millions of hectares in key producing nations, highlight the magnitude of production necessary to fulfil worldwide demand (Murphy, 2024). Although oil palm's

DOI: 10.4018/979-8-3693-2149-2.ch014

productivity and economic viability are largely due to its effective land use, same factors also give rise to environmental and sustainability concerns, which have sparked continuing discussions within the sector. Originating with pioneering initiatives in the early twentieth century, Malaysia's oil palm sector has evolved to the point of becoming a leading and vibrant industry. According to PEMANDU (2010), the objective of this industry is not only to develop the economic foundation but also to achieve the socioeconomic goal. Malaysia's oil palm history dates back more than a century, giving the country an advantage as one of the world's most successful providers of oils and fats. Dated back in 1917, Since the establishment of the commercialized plantation framework system, the planted area of oil palm expanded from 400 hectares in the 1920s to 3.4 million hectares in 2000 (Basiron & Weng, 2004) and reached 4.5 million hectares in 2009. In 1960, the entire planted area was just 54,700 hectares, and it was owned by huge estates, without any intervention from smallholders or government-owned plantations (Pletcher, 1991). Because of its swift expansion, oil palm has grown to be Malaysia's largest plantation crop, especially within the states of Sabah and Sarawak. Sabah has the most extensive plantation area, accounting for 1.432 million hectares, of the total oil palm planted area in 2011, while Sarawak possessed over 1.021 million hectares. In 2020, the Malaysian oil palm sector contributed 2.7 per cent to the nation's gross domestic product (GDP) (Shamsuddin et al., 2021). As the primary industry that have the ability to generate nation income, oil palm is one of Malaysia's finest products and contribute to main agricultural trade to the global market. According to Statista (2022), Malaysia exported approximately 16.2 million metric tons of palm oil and palm-derived products. These exports worth around 73.3 billion Malaysian ringgit. Overall, the oil palm business contributed around 36.9 billion ringgits to Malaysia's GDP.

OIL PALM PRODUCTION IN GLOBAL VIEW

Historically, the majority of the world's output of palm oil has been produced by Indonesia and Malaysia, who have been the leading producers of the oil (Hassan et al., 2024). These countries have become major players in the business, propelling the palm oil market with their vast plantations and effective production methods. Furthermore, Thailand, Nigeria, and Colombia stand out as prominent participants, making substantial contributions to the production of palm oil worldwide (Graham & Floering, 2024).

Table 1 shows the countries that are involved in oil palm cultivation and production. Indonesia is the largest oil palm producer in the world, with 45,300 Metric Tonnes (MT) contributing to 59.51% of the world's oil palm production. Malaysia is the second largest oil palm producer with 24.04% of global oil palm production. while other nations have the fewest, with just 6 223 (8.11%). Thailand produced 3,150 MT (4.14%), Colombia produced 1,747 MT (2.3%), and Nigeria produced 1,400 MT (1.88%), (Murphy, 2014; Murphy, 2015; Murphy, 2019). According to the Malaysian Department of Statistics, the growth rate of Malaysia's GDP in 2019 was 4.4%; however, in 2020, it dropped to -5.6%. The department provided this information. In 2020, agriculture contributed 7.8% of the overall contribution to the GDP; nevertheless, the percentage gain was somewhat lower than the year before. This was due to the fact that the commodities sub-sector, which includes oil palm, saw negative growth of 3.6%, which was worse than the 1.5% decrease it experienced in 2019.

Table 1. Global oil palm production in 2021

Rank	Country	Oil palm production	
		Mt (Million)	%
1	Indonesia	45300	59.51
2	Malaysia	18300	24.04
3	Thailand	3150	4.14
4	Colombia	1747	2.30
5	Nigeria	1400	1.84
6	Other	6223	8.18
	Total	**76120**	**100%**

Source: Department of statistic Malaysia (2021); Murphy (2019)

OVERVIEW OF THE OIL PALM INDUSTRY IN MALAYSIA

The oil palm sector in Malaysia has achieved significant growth. What began as an ornamental plant in Malaysia has become a big and significant industry towards the national income. The oil palm industry remains Malaysia's key commodity, delivering RM 48.31 billion to GDP in 2020, accounting for 56.8% of overall GDP contribution in agriculture sector (Siti, 2023). This number is the result of predictions. Oil palm, one of Malaysia's major industries, is also the country's primary agricultural export abroad. It was responsible for exporting over 16.2 million metric tonnes of oil palm and palm-based products. The projected value of these exports was around 73.35 billion Malaysian ringgit. Despites its excellency in bringing the prosperity in economic growth, concerns over the environmental impact of oil palm cultivation, as well as the rise of protectionism in the global economy, have posed a threat towards Malaysia's oil palm industry over the past few years. Although Malaysia's palm oil business has contributed to economic expansion and progress, it is inextricably linked to the environmental and social problems it raises (Hamid et al., 2020). The need for a more sustainable and ethical approach to palm oil production is highlighted by the concerns of deforestation, biodiversity loss, societal repercussions, and international condemnation. To ensure that the palm oil industry can coexist with the preservation of Malaysia's rich biodiversity and the well-being of its communities, governments, industry stakeholders, and consumers must work together to strike a balance between economic prosperity and environmental sustainability (Litja, 2020). A dedication to sustainable methods, ethical considerations, and shared responsibility for the future of our world are necessary for this delicate balancing act.

Malaysian oil palm industry also facing threshold of the production due to limited planting area and government policy that doesn't allowing the opening of new cultivation area but, Malaysia still able to maintain its position as the second largest oil palm producer after Indonesia for 5 consecutive years (MPOB, 2023). Regardless facing major challenges such as limited cultivation area, Malaysia is working hard to improve and increase the quality of local oil palm production to meet the demand. These can be seen through numerous government initiatives to enhance quality and quantity, as well as farming practices, in order to compete in the world market. The emergence of The Malaysian Sustainable Palm

Oil (MSPO) Certification Scheme which serve as the guidelines for Malaysian oil palm industry players throughout the supply chain shows that Malaysia is committed towards oil palm sector to meet the world standards. The sustainable farming practice also give advantages towards the farmers especially from small stake holders group as it can boost the yield with a limited cost and minimize the negative impact towards the environment (Mohd, 2023).

Oil palm is the product with the fastest growing global demand since it is used as an ingredient in foods, cosmetics, animal feed, bioenergy, and other products. However, due to a combination of natural and policy-level reasons, its contribution to the gross national product has been in a sluggish or declining phase over the past few years. The most significant natural barriers to the sector's progress are extreme weather, ageing trees, and plant diseases (Abu Bakar et al, 2023: Alam et al, 2015). The unfavorable weather that Malaysia's oil palm sector has to deal with highlights the critical necessity for adaptable tactics and resilience-building techniques. In order to guarantee the sustained development of one of Malaysia's most important economic sectors, the industry needs to manage the difficulties presented by climate fluctuation. The adoption of sustainable practices, research and development investments, and stakeholder collaboration, the oil palm business may enhance resilience, mitigate environmental effects, and promote the agricultural landscape's long-term sustainability in Malaysia. Building resilience in the face of climate change becomes not only necessary, but also vitally important for the oil palm sector's future and the communities it supports

On the other hand, the government's strict labour and immigration rules are not less responsible for the stagnation of business. The effects of a manpower shortage in Malaysia's oil palm sector are complex and have multiple dimensions. The primary outcome is a significant decline in the total productivity of oil palm crops. Lack of labour has a direct impact on crucial phases of planting, harvesting, and processing, leading to operational inefficiencies that affect the entire sector. The presence Covid-19 pandemic in early 2020 worsen the production of oil palm in Malaysia as this country relies heavily on foreign labour market (Shah, 2021). Concurrently, the sector struggles with an increase in production expenses while trying to draw and keep workers. The need for increased pay and the introduction of better working conditions both lead to an increase in operating costs. The financial sustainability of oil palm industries is significantly challenged by this economic strain, which is made worse by a lack of workers (Shah, 2021).

THE DYNAMIC OF INTERNATIONAL TRADE IN OIL PALM INDUSTRY.

At the convergence of geopolitical, economic, and environmental factors, the international trade in oil palm is essential to the global agribusiness landscape, particularly for producer nations. Unquestionably leading the world in oil palm growing and exporting are Indonesia and Malaysia. Together, these two countries produce a sizable majority of the palm oil produced worldwide. Their vast plantations and effective production methods place them in a prominent position, influencing the dynamics of global trade in the oil palm sector. Being a versatile commodity, and mainly used as the base of products such as cosmetics, biofuels and foods, palm oil demand across the globe have inclined for the past decades (Chew et al., 2022). Geopolitical concerns, consumer preferences, and economic variables all have an impact on trade patterns, which results in a dynamic and constantly shifting the international trade atmosphere entails intricately linked supply chains that connect global producers, traders, processors, and consumers.

The oil palm sector encounters various obstacles in the domain of global commerce. Import duties and tariffs levied by importing nations have the potential to impede palm oil's competitiveness and restrict its access to markets (Hassan et al., 2024). According to Hassan et al., (2024) international trade has become more complex due to the introduction of certification programs in response to sustainability concerns, such as deforestation and environmental repercussions. Furthermore, long-standing supply chains and commercial partnerships may be hampered by geopolitical unrest and changing trade policy among large economies.

Despite facing challenges, the oil palm industry has embraced innovation and adaptability in response to changing consumer needs and sustainability standards. The industry is constantly looking for methods to improve productivity, lessen its impact on the environment, and satisfy customer preferences. Examples of these efforts range from technology-driven processing and precision agriculture to sustainable practices and traceability programs.

Market diversification is a crucial tactic used by oil palm exporters to address trade issues (Giacomin, 2018). Aware of the risk involved in being dependent on a small number of important importing nations, producers actively work to increase their market share. Producers of palm oil seek to reduce the effects of trade restrictions imposed by particular countries and build a more resilient trade portfolio by diversifying the destinations for their exports. Oil palm industry players have made large investments in sustainable methods due to the increased focus on sustainability in global trade (Pacheco et al., 2018). The majority of industry players ranged from estate and small stake holder to the final manufacturer along the oil palm supply chain are dedicated in the adoption of sustainable method and innovation to respond towards sustainable development goals. This method includes initiatives like adopting zero-burning regulations, adhering to certification schemes like the Roundtable on Sustainable Palm Oil (RSPO), and practicing agroforestry. Producers understand that adhering to international sustainability standards improves market access and industry reputation while also reducing trade barriers.

The availability of advanced information technology such as Blockchain Technology, the challenges faced by the industry player regarding international trade can be minimised (Dutta et al., 2020). The ability of the producer firms to provide transparency and traceability of their product all across the globe provide a golden opportunity to gain trust among the consumers. Improving market traceability and transparency has become a proactive way to address sustainability and customer expectations-related issues. Industry players especially big companies are spending money on systems that offer comprehensive details about the source, manufacturing procedures, and supply chain of palm oil. This helps satisfy sustainability certification standards and fosters customer trust, which facilitates easier international trade.

In order to optimize their operation, Producers of oil palm are utilizing innovation and technology to streamline their processes and tackle obstacles in trade across borders. Innovations in processing technology, data-driven decision-making, and precision agriculture all boost productivity, lower environmental impact, and boost competitiveness (Hassan et al., 2024). These developments not only boost output but also show the sector as adaptable to the needs of international trade. In term of advocacy and diplomacy, oil palm industry players are actively engaging in advocacy efforts and diplomatic initiatives to address trade challenges. Engaging in diplomatic discussions with importing nations, taking part in global forums, and cooperating with industry associations facilitate the industry's expression of dedication to sustainable practices and ethical commerce. These initiatives help to cultivate a positive image throughout the world and may have an impact on trade laws that benefit the sector. Collaboration between the stakeholders including governments and industry players shows a dedicated commitment from the oil palm producer nation contribute to holistic approach in protecting the oil palm industry in international arena.

ISSUES AND CHALLENGES

Malaysia has been a world leader in the oil palm sector for the past 50 years, managing methodical, productive farms that produce a variety of palm oil-based goods. The results are the result of extensive, ongoing research and development efforts. Within thirty years, the oil palm business saw an average yearly growth rate of seven per cent (USDA, 2011). However, due to the advent of several barriers and problems, will impede or hinder the oil palm industry's performance. This will boost the expansion of an industry whose growth period may be drawing to a close. Malaysia has been the leading exporter and producer of oil palm since the 1960s until Indonesia's oil palm sector surpassed Malaysia's (Takata, 2008). The significant concerns and obstacles related to oil palm plantations have been ruled out based on past studies and scholars' views.

INTERNATIONAL TRADE BARRIERS IN OIL PALM INDUSTRY.

Malaysia's oil palm sector is confronted with multiple major trade obstacles that influence its international trade patterns. This section delves into two most important key aspects of trade barriers: tariffs and import restrictions, and sustainability certification requirements, examining their implications for Malaysian palm oil and the broader industry. According to Rodrik (2018), tariffs and import restrictions are frequently used by importing nations as regulatory tools to safeguard home industries or address other issues. Tariffs, which are basically taxes levied on imported commodities, tend to be a major factor influencing the competitiveness of oil palm is on global markets (Pacheco et al., 2017). Tariffs on palm oil are frequently imposed by importing nations for a variety of reasons, such as safeguarding homegrown businesses or resolving environmental issues related to the production of palm oil. Tariffs serve as economic obstacles for countries that export oil palm, such as Malaysia and Indonesia, raising the price of their goods and lowering the industry's competitiveness globally. Tariffs on oil palm have a variety of negative economic effects. Higher tariffs influence importers' purchasing decisions by making palm oil from Malaysia and Indonesia less appealing than oils from regions with lower or no tariffs (Adhikari, 2021). According to Adhikari (2021), this financial disincentive has an effect on exporting countries' trade balance, affecting their foreign exchange profits and possibly impeding economic growth. Since the oil palm business makes a substantial contribution to the GDP of exporting countries, tariffs have an adverse effect on the economy in numerous ways.

The international trade landscape for the oil palm sector is further complicated by restrictions on imports in addition to tariffs (Adhikari, 2021; Pacheco et al., 2017). These limitations can be in the shape of quality standards, licensing regulations, or quotas, among other things. Import limitations, which are frequently implemented in response to worries about ethical labour standards, deforestation, and environmental sustainability in the nations that produce palm oil, are intended to control the quantity and quality of imported palm oil. Global environmental problems related to palm oil production, such as deforestation and biodiversity loss, are often the driving force for import restrictions (Meijaard et al., 2021). Import restrictions often involve the requirement of adhering to sustainability certification systems, such the Roundtable on Sustainable Palm Oil (RSPO). Although the goal of these regulations is to encourage ethical behaviour, producers especially those with smaller operations may find challenging to comply with the strict guidelines, which might culminate in their expulsion from the market.

The oil palm business has a multifaceted issue due to the application of tariffs and import restrictions that impact economic, environmental, and geopolitical aspects. A complex strategy comprising international diplomatic endeavours, environmental measures, and stakeholder participation is needed to navigate these trade impediments. Securing the oil palm industry's future on the world scene requires striking a healthy balance between ecological practices and economic viability as it struggles with the complexities of global trade.

LACK OF AVAILABLE LAND FOR EXPANSION

Since 1960, Malaysia has been the top exporter and producer of oil palm, until neighbouring Indonesia surpassed it. The restricted availability of land for expansion hinders Malaysian oil palm sector from expanding its cultivation region resulting inability to boost production of oil palm (Asante, 2023). There is a worrying trend in Malaysia's accessible acreage for oil palm agriculture, according to recent data. The area available for oil palm plantations is decreasing due to the intensification of urbanization, infrastructure development, and conflicting land-use demands. The oil palm business faces obstacles from the spread of urban areas, conservation efforts, and regulatory measures intended to preserve trees for future generations.

The government's pledge to preserve at least 50 percent of forest area due to pressure from foreign NGOs on the issue of deforestation has slowed the spread of oil palm cultivation area. There are only 4.7 million acres of oil palm plantations, compared to 6.6 million hectares of agriculture gazetted area, resulting in a severe scarcity of agricultural land for the industry's further expansion. The industry, which has always depended on plantation growth to keep up with rising worldwide demand, is currently experiencing a bottleneck. The industry's ability to grow is limited by the scarcity of land, which affects its ability to take advantage of market opportunities and may impede economic progress.

The oil palm sector has no choice but to explore other option such as planting in unfavourable area which is increasingly centred in peripheral regions with poorer soils, less precipitation, and more challenging topography. This type of planting is more expensive to cultivate, less productive, and results in higher production costs (Sheng, 2023). Furthermore, this sort of terrain may increase environmental degradation resulting increase the concern among non-governmental organisations towards the industry. Therefore, the sector should investigate better options. Because it is essential to boost oil extraction yields without expanding cropland, the ideal solution is to implement a replanting program, paying special attention to palm trees held by smallholders (S. Chai, 2008). 25–30% of palm trees are expected to have finished their productive year. Given rising palm oil demand and the associated environmental and social issues associated with oil palm expansion, there is an urgent need for comprehensive understanding on how to increase average oil palm output per hectare while increasing overall oil palm production without increasing land usage.

The future of the Malaysian oil palm sector depends on strategic and sustainable approaches that ensure economic viability while protecting the country's natural resources for future generations. One of the biggest challenges facing the oil palm industry is the scarcity of available land for cultivation, which calls for a balanced and sustainable approach. Another is the industry's struggle to find innovative solutions, responsible land-use practices, and cooperative efforts between the government, industry, and environmental stakeholders.

HIGH COMPETITION FROM OTHER PRODUCERS

Malaysia, which has long dominated the global palm oil market, is up against fierce competition from its neighbours. Thailand, leveraging their expertise of agriculture, and Indonesia, with its huge tracts of oil palm plantations, have become formidable rivals. The growing competition between these countries in Southeast Asia changes the regional dynamics of the sector and puts Malaysia's established position in jeopardy. The oil palm sector is becoming increasingly competitive, particularly in terms of production costs. This intense rivalry comes from nearby nations like Thailand and Indonesia. In 2006, Indonesia surpassed Malaysia as the biggest producer of oil palm, a position it now holds. Due to changes in Indonesia's export tax regime, competition is anticipated to be stiffer this year. Indonesia reduced its export duty on oil palm products by more than half in October 2011, but Malaysia levies hefty taxes on crude oil palm shipments to preserve its indigenous refining sector. Many local downstream producers may be obliged to buy oil palm from that nation as a result of this legislation. Due to the abundance of inexpensive labour and adequate land, Indonesia is also able to manufacture oil palm at a low cost. Brazil has announced intentions to increase oil palm cultivation acreage in the Amazon Rainforest to more than 850 thousand hectares (Camargo et al., 2017). Incorporating the notion of sustainable development into its aims, Brazil wants to become a respectable producer as opposed to a huge producer. The ability of other producer in producing large volume of oil palm resulting lower cost of production and able to offer lower price in the market will risk Malaysian oil palm industry.

LOW PRODUCTIVITY AMONG SMALLHOLDERS

The annual data reveals a dynamic pattern in oil palm yields over the past decade. In 2013, the yield stood at 19.02 metric tons per hectare, marking a robust start to the period under consideration. However, subsequent years witnessed a gradual decline, reaching a low of 15.91 metric tons in 2016. The industry rebounded in the following years, experiencing some variability, ultimately settling at 15.49 metric tons in 2022. A few factors contribute to the decline fresh fruit bunch (FFB) production including climate condition, poor plantation management as well as the organisation of oil palm industry players along the supply chain.

Smallholder farmers in Malaysia make up a sizable portion of the oil palm sector and support the country's economy. But many encounter difficulties that lead to low yield of oil palm and low productivity among small holders is not a recent issue. According to Kushairi (2019), there are about 225,615 independent smallholders who owned less than 40.46ha of oil palm land which contributed to 17 percent of overall Malaysian oil palm area. Independent smallholders produce an average of 17 t/ha, whereas organised smallholders and plantations produce 21 t/ha and 23 t/ha, respectively (Mohd Suib et al, 2023). The average plot size per family averages out to 3.9 hectares, and these smallholders tend to have little exposure to the most recent developments of plantation technologies and efficient methods such as good agricultural practice that act as the catalyst to boost the yield. The critical problem faced by the small holder in Malaysia include limited access to resources, technological gaps, dependency on rainfed agriculture, and market access challenge.

According to Mohd Suib et al., the majority of oil palm smallholders in Malaysia are struggle with inadequate access to essential resources. Their capacity to purchase high-quality seeds, fertilizers, and cutting-edge farming technologies is hampered by a lack of financial resources. Insufficient financial

Figure 1. The average yield of oil palm fresh fruit bunch production per hectare from 2013 to 2022
Source: Statista, 2023

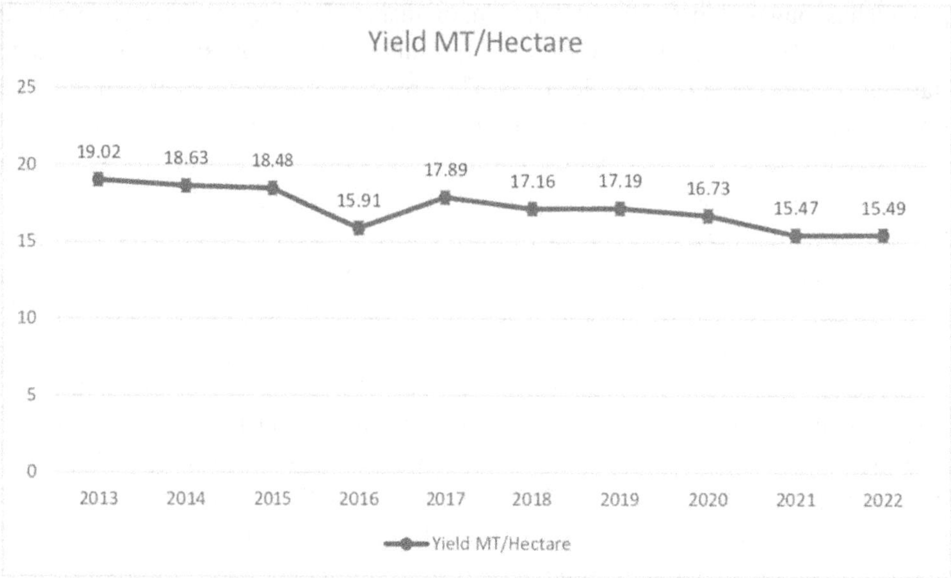

resources prevent smallholders from implementing optimal methods, hence impeding their ability to improve oil palm crops (Vamuloh et al., 2020). Modern agricultural technology that could greatly increase oil palm yield are frequently inaccessible to smallholders. However, in term of technological adoption, small holders are quite incapable to compete with other plantation as it incurs huge cost. Lower yields are a result of a lack of understanding regarding effective harvesting methods, pest and disease handling, and precision farming techniques. Technological adoption is also associated with the inadequate infrastructure in small holder farms (Mohd Suib et al, 2023; Pacheco et al., 2017). Poor roads, and limited access to transportation hinder small holder to reach their optimum operation efficiency. In term of market, it can be challenging for smallholders to secure their produce into marketplaces and to negotiate reasonable pricing. They are vulnerable to exploitation due to their lack of knowledge about market trends and their limited ability to negotiate. Smallholders can be empowered in the marketing element through increasing market links, disseminating market information, and encouraging collective bargaining.

As the smallholder group is a concerning group and have a significant contribution towards Malaysian FFB production, addressing the problem arise from these group becoming the main strategy to boost overall FFB production in Malaysia They are geographically spread, disorganised, and largely dependent on intermediaries to provide FFB to the closest mills (Khalid, 2018: Gutierrez, 2023). If these smallholders' group are not addressed properly, the prolonged problem will give a direct impact on the income of oil palm smallholders. They will likely abandon their farms, reducing the quantity and quality of oil palm produced in the country, resulting the diminishing of Malaysian oil palm industry's earnings. The involvement of intermediaries who influence prices at lower levels has worsened the issue. Small farmers do not obtain a fair price for their goods due to the decrease in oil prices. According to Mitchell (2011), the intermediary suppresses prices since the price paid by the middleman differs from the market price.

THE IMPACTS OF THE OIL PALM INDUSTRY IN MALAYSIA

Economic Perspectives

Malaysia's oil palm sector is the fourth greatest contributor to the national economy, accounting for approximately RM53 billion in gross national income. The decision made by the government which is by diversifying the economic dependence from the rubber and tin sector changed into the oil palm sector could influence the continuous achievement and resulting successful development of this sector from the beginning until the present day. The oil palm plantation was promoted by the government as one of the new agricultural commodities besides the rubber sector followed by the recommendation given by the world bank mission in 1995 (Rival, 2014). Those decision made was very important to expand further the narrow base of economic growth. Diversification strategy involved increasing the exports of oil palm by developing the manufacture through the establishment of industrial estates (Aljoghaiman, 2023).

The oil palm industry development opened a new dimension in the economic base to reduce the poverty among the poor by creating a high wealth for the nation as well as functioning as an appropriate tool for economic growth. The introduction of palm oil into the Malaysian economy in the late 1950s and early 1960s could not have arrived at a better time to help the country minimize income inequality, particularly in the most impoverished areas. (Bruno, 2023). Those countries that have rich natural resources are dependent on the agricultural sector as an important contributor to the economy. The productivity of agriculture is usually followed by rapid industrialization and thus has become one of the sources of long-term sustainable economic growth. The revenues generated by the agricultural commodity may have a positive impact on the manufacturing sector. However, the dependence on natural resources can be described as low economic diversification and greater industrialization. The prospects of industrialization will be increased when there is a strong link between agriculture and the domestic economy (Sadik et al., 2019) which encourages the downstream manufacturing activities in the oil palm industry.

Oil palm is a highly productive oil crop because it can produce yields up to ten times higher than other oilseed crops such as soybean, sunflower, and rapeseed, and has a productive life span that can reach over 20 years (Heimann et al., 2024). Oil palm can fulfil those demands followed by the growth of populations and the surge in renewable energy by increasing the yield production from the existing plantation areas. In addition, the productivity of oil palm will be increased by applying the innovation and development of scientific research into planting materials while ensuring sustainable practices. The cost competitiveness of oil palm will be the most affordable vegetable oil in the price-sensitive market, especially in developed countries which become suitable for animal fat replacement when oil palm becomes productive (Labys, & Pollak, 2024).

Besides that, according to Zakaria et al., (2024) the biomass production produced from mesocarp fibre, palm kernel shells, and empty fruit bunches is one of the renewable energy sources used to generate heat in plantation mills as an alternative to save the cost production, while palm oil-based biodiesel has been identified as alternative fuel due to its competitiveness price (Waters et al., 2024). The attribution in the technological innovations, quality improvement, and scientific development is depended on the utilization of oil palm in various sectors.

Furthermore, the uses of Palm Oil Mill Effluent (POME) have the potential to securitize the energy supply so that can reduce the carbon footprint while generating additional income based on the sale of surplus energy. Using POME which is an alternative energy source not only can save the costs of mill operation and waste treatment, but mills operator can get up to RM 3.8 million per year through the electricity generated (Kan et al., 2024). Income that is generated from POME has changed the perception of the by-product from waste to be transformed into a resource that can generate income or revenue. The unused electricity can be connected to the national grid under the Feed in Tariff (FIT) scheme which was introduced in the National Renewable Energy Act 2011 and as a support to the Fifth Fuel Policy target of achieving 5% of national grid-connected electricity.

The commodity crop becomes the development engine which is influenced by the good development of oil palm and the driver of development (Rival, 2014; Kurniaty, 2020). However, the rise of oil palm from the 1960s onwards has caused disruptions in the global market which is dominated by other types of oil products such as vegetable oils, notably soybean oils and the rapeseed oils industries. Hence, the introduction of tariff barriers and disguising non-tariff such as safety, societal and environmental concerns has given challenges to the oil palm industry to be expanded further because member countries of the EU want to protect their domestic oil industries. Other than that, they want to defend their local production of vegetable oil to monopoly back their market share by spreading negative information through the anti-palm oil campaigns as part of political issues. The response against oil palm is attributed to the competitiveness of oil palm in comparison with soybean oil and rapeseed oil as feedstock for biodiesel production. Those barriers were discrimination towards the oil palm industry as they can inhibit producing countries from exporting oil palm to the global market. When they are denying the growth of developing economies by enforcing natural-resource conservation might be seen as prejudice because, in western countries, they have abused their environment for economic advancement for decades.

SOCIAL PERSPECTIVES

This industry has been seen as a source of income and an effective method for alleviating poverty in developing countries. A sustainable oil palm plantation provides socioeconomic benefits such as long-term employment opportunities and poverty alleviation (Hassan et al., 2024). Depending on the roles played by the government and smallholder cooperatives, smallholders may greatly benefit from the development of oil palm industry due to its higher returns on land and labour than other commonly produced agricultural products (Hassan et al., 2024). For instance, oil palm might be an investment option for farmers seeking to increase their income. The oil palm industry in Malaysia has considerably contributed to the elimination of rural and small-scale farmer poverty (Hassan et al., 2024). Through palm oil cultivation, smallholder farmers who are essential to the Malaysian oil palm industry find ways to improve their standard of living. By engaging in the sector, these farmers may increase their income and support the health of rural communities. A key component of the industry's beneficial social impact is the empowerment of smallholders. Apart from that, infrastructure in rural areas is frequently improved as a result of investments made in the oil palm sector (Jelsma et al., 2024). The presence of industry can lead to improved roads, processing facilities, and community services, all of which can improve the general standard of living in areas that produce palm oil. This development enhances the social welfare of the local population. However, independent small farmers in this industry are considered inefficient and unproductive (Hamid et al., 2024). Independent smallholders are more subject to the volatile price of oil palm, which affects their daily fees, to be able to afford necessities such as food (Li, 2018). In order to mitigate the problems with small holders, Malaysian government has established government agency called Malaysian Palm Oil Board (MPOB) to facilitate and govern smallholders. MPOB is an extension agent that responsible to help and guide oil palm smallholder to improvise the quality of the farm and minimize the risk and problem faced in lower level. Enhancing advisory support networks and extension services makes it possible for smallholders to obtain timely information, technical assistance, and market intelligence. Smallholders can benefit from on-site coaching, workshops, and demonstrations from extension officers, agricultural experts, and industry professionals. These resources help smallholders adopt best practices, overcome obstacles, and grasp improvement potential.

This industry is naturally labour-intensive, requiring an average of five workers per hectare, whereas competing oils require only one person every 200 hectares. Due to the terrible working conditions and poor pay in oil palm fields, Malaysia mainly relies on foreign labour, especially from Indonesia (Jelsma et al., 2024). The Malaysian oil palm sector faces several issues related to labour rights, mistreatment of migrant workers, and insufficient social welfare support, all of which require immediate attention and coordinated efforts to address. Labour rights violations, including long working hours, poor pay, and limited access to healthcare and basic comforts, are a persistent concern within the business. A sizable percentage of the labour force in this sector is made up of migrant workers, who are frequently the targets of abuse and exploitation, including dishonest hiring practices, passport seizure, and subpar housing conditions. The Malaysian oil palm industry has taken several steps to address issues related to labour rights, migrant worker exploitation, and inadequate social welfare provisions. These efforts involve various stakeholders, including government agencies, industry associations, non-governmental organizations (NGOs), and international partners. The key initiatives of Malaysian oil palm industry players to protect the welfare of the labour includes establishing legislative and regulatory framework, certification and standards, and social welfare programs.

To safeguard workers' rights and stop exploitation, the Malaysian government has put laws and regulations into place. The Employment Act of 1955 establishes minimal requirements for pay, benefits, and working conditions for all workers, including those in the oil palm industry. To further protect migrant workers' rights and avoid abuse, the government has implemented particular legislation pertaining to their employment. The Malaysian Sustainable Palm Oil (MSPO) certification scheme incorporates social criteria aimed at promoting fair labour practices and protecting workers' rights. Companies certified under MSPO are required to comply with standards related to employment practices, occupational health and safety, and community engagement. Adherence to these standards is verified through audits conducted by accredited certification bodies. Social welfare program is also implemented to elevate the life condition of oil palm workers. This covers programs aimed at enhancing accessibility to housing, education, healthcare, and other necessities. Businesses may also carry out community development initiatives to improve the quality of life in the communities around them, particularly those impacted by the production of oil palm.

In addition, oil palm has had several detrimental social repercussions, including the expulsion of indigenous populations and those already affected by damage and land use changes. The key issues with this industry, which happened mostly during the launching phase of the new region, were housing and land rights issues, low salaries for plantation workers, and poor treatment. In isolated regions of Sabah and Sarawak, the woods and rivers represent a substantial component of certain indigenous populations' venues for vital subsistence activities and their primary source of income. Some of them still depend on the forest and river, as well as on subsistence activities like fishing and hunting. The conversion of forest areas in Sabah and Sarawak to oil palm plantations led to a decline in fish populations, the loss of connectedness to natural resources, and the demise of agriculture (Komarudin, et al., 2012). Pollution on rivers contributes to the decline of fish populations, while deforestation reduces forest resources such as wild fruits, rattan, and plant supplies resulting the shifting on rural population's source of income from relying on the forest into oil palm industry. The oil palm sector in Malaysia has a dynamic societal impact that includes both positive contributions and issues that need to be addressed. It is crucial to acknowledge and tackle these societal viewpoints in order to promote a viable and socially just industry. Through the adoption of global sustainability standards, participation in local communities, and the promotion of ethical practices, Malaysia's oil palm sector can effectively manage its social impact and maintain a balanced balance between social welfare and economic growth.

ENVIRONMENTAL PERSPECTIVES

The environment is one of the most essential factors for the survival of humans, animals, and plants. Everyone must take care of the environment so that it can be preserved for future generations. Environmental concerns are among the top priorities on plantations. Because large plantations can have a significant impact on the environment, Due to the vast scale of oil palm plantations, environmental degradation is one of the most significant challenges and always adds to the negative influence on the environment (Prasad et al., 2024). Deforestation is one of the environmental challenges caused by oil palm crops. The term "major deforestation" refers to large-scale logging activities that occur in certain locations (Gupta et al., 2024). Large-scale oil palm cultivation can result in severe deforestation. Significant deforestation may have devastating consequences for the ecosystem, leading to environmental problems.

The habitat of flora and wildlife is imperilled, which is one of the results of massive deforestation operations. Large tracts of tropical forests have been razed down to create land for oil palm plantations, which results in the loss of habitat for a variety of wildlife. Malaysia's great biodiversity is in danger simply because monoculture crops are replacing biodiverse habitats. Additionally, flora and wildlife serve as nourishment and supply sustenance for the tribe. The massive deforestation threatens both known and unknown species of flora and wildlife. The native communities that live within the area are also endangered as they heavily depend on the forest to make living due to the monoculture practice which exposes soil and destroys habitats for countless species. As concerns about environmental impacts grow, the oil palm industry is increasingly recognizing the need for sustainable practices. Numerous plantations strive to protect natural forests, vital habitats for a variety of plant and animal species, by following ethical principles including no deforestation commitments, high conservation value area protection, sustainable sourcing and certification as well as giving a full commitment on biodiversity monitoring and research (Nasution et al., 2024). The plantation communities are actively playing a role in the mitigate the risk, preservation of natural forests and important habitats through cooperation, appropriate practices, and continuous attempts to reduce ecological effect. To guarantee the industry's long-term beneficial contributions to both economic growth and environmental conservation, cooperation, innovation, and adherence to sustainability standards will be crucial.

Climate change is a consequence of greenhouse gases. The phrase "climate change" refers to the long-term changes in temperature and weather patterns. These alterations might be the result of natural processes, such as the solar cycle's oscillations. Human activities, particularly the combustion of fossil fuels such as coal, oil, and gas, have been the principal driver of climate change for a very long time (Trenberth, 2018). Climate change is a topic that frequently appears in the news nowadays. As a consequence of climate change, the polar ice is melting, and the sea level is rising. This occurs due to the extremely high temperature, which readily melts the ice block. This issue was extremely essential and harmful to the global human population. However, the recent research is able to prove that oil palm plantation is a potential carbon sink that sequestering carbon dioxide in the atmosphere. Carbon sequestering is the process of capturing and storing atmospheric carbon dioxide and it's recognized as one of the methods of reducing the amount of carbon dioxide that can lead to minimising the global climate change risk. According to Henson (2012), an oil palm plantation can absorb 161 tons of carbon dioxide annually on average per hectare. Another report made by Indonesian Palm Oil Association in 2022 An estimated 2.2 billion tons of carbon dioxide are absorbed annually by Indonesia's oil palm fields. The entire sequestration has an economic worth of approximately USD 44 billion showing the capability of oil palm industry in dampening the effect of carbon dioxide emission and minimize the impact towards the environment.

CONCLUSION

The production, trade, and impacts of the oil palm sector, a worldwide economic powerhouse, are intricately intertwined and dynamic, with Malaysia playing a crucial part in forming this complex environment. A thorough examination of oil palm production around the world demonstrates the crop's importance as a key supplier of vegetable oil, which is fuelled by rising production trends and always rising demand. This worldwide view prepares the reader for a deeper look at the dynamics of the industry in Malaysia, where a careful balance between environmental and economic considerations is required.

One of the main drivers of economic growth and a major contributor to the wealth of Malaysia is the oil palm sector. The industry's high yield per hectare, effective use of land, and abundance of job possibilities highlights its economic importance. But despite its economic contribution towards nation income, there are still challenges faced by this industry. The industry's responsiveness to environmental and social imperatives is demonstrated by Malaysia's dedication to sustainable practices and conservation initiatives, which stand out as critical aspects as the country navigates these problems.

The international trade dynamics of the oil palm industry add another layer of complexity. A robust global trade network connects major producers, with Indonesia and Malaysia taking the lead, and significant players such as Thailand, Nigeria, and Colombia contributing to the market. However, the industry encounters trade barriers that pose challenges to its seamless functioning. Tariffs, import restrictions, and sustainability certification requirements demand careful navigation. The need to address these barriers becomes paramount to ensuring the industry's continued growth and sustainability on the global stage.

International trade barriers, while posing challenges, also prompt reflection on the broader impacts of the oil palm industry. A comprehensive understanding of the industry's role in Malaysia's socio-environmental context is necessary due to the persistent threat of deforestation, biodiversity loss, and societal disputes. An emphasis on sustainable development, avoiding deforestation, and safeguarding regions with high conservation value demonstrates a dedication of Malaysian oil palm industry towards ethical behaviour. These programs support the narrative of environmental care and conservation inside the sector, together with open reporting, biodiversity monitoring, and cooperative collaborations.

To sum up, the worldwide perspective on oil palm cultivation paves the way for a sophisticated comprehension of Malaysia's position in this ever-evolving sector. An industry at the nexus of economic vitality and environmental responsibility is depicted in detail by the complex dance of international trade, initiatives to eliminate trade restrictions, and navigating social and environmental difficulties. The pursuit of sustainability, conservation, and ethical trade practices becomes not only necessary but also a beacon guiding the oil palm industry towards a harmonious coexistence of economic prosperity and environmental stewardship, as Malaysia aspires to maintain its position in the global oil palm landscape.

REFERENCES

Basiron, Y., Balu, N., & Chandramohan, D. (2004). Palm oil: the driving force of world oils and fats economy. *Oil palm industry economic journal, 4*(1), 1-10.

Camargo, F. A. O., Silva, L. S., Merten, G. H., Carlos, F. S., Baveye, P. C., & Triplett, E. W. (2017). Brazilian agriculture in perspective: Great expectations vs reality. *Advances in Agronomy*, *141*, 53–114. doi:10.1016/bs.agron.2016.10.003

Carlson, K. M., Heilmayr, R., Gibbs, H. K., Noojipady, P., Burns, D. N., Morton, D. C., Walker, N. F., Paoli, G. D., & Kremen, C. (2018). Effect of oil palm sustainability certification on deforestation and fire in Indonesia. *Proceedings of the National Academy of Sciences of the United States of America*, *115*(1), 121–126. doi:10.1073/pnas.1704728114 PMID:29229857

Chew, C. L., Low, L. E., Chia, W. Y., Chew, K. W., Liew, Z. K., Chan, E. S., & Show, P. L. (2022). Prospects of palm fruit extraction technology: Palm oil recovery processes and quality enhancement. *Food Reviews International, 38*(sup1), 893-920.

Dutta, P., Choi, T. M., Somani, S., & Butala, R. (2020). Blockchain technology in supply chain operations: Applications, challenges and research opportunities. *Transportation research part e: Logistics and transportation review, 142*, 102067.

Gelaye, Y., & Getahun, S. (2024). A review of the carbon sequestration potential of fruit trees and their implications for climate change mitigation: The case of Ethiopia. *Cogent Food & Agriculture*, *10*(1), 2294544. doi:10.1080/23311932.2023.2294544

Giacomin, V. (2018). The emergence of an export cluster: Traders and palm oil in early twentieth-century Southeast Asia. *Enterprise and Society*, *19*(2), 272–308. doi:10.1017/eso.2017.10

Graham, E., & Floering, I. (2024). *The modern plantation in the Third world* (Vol. 3). Taylor & Francis.

Gupta, S. S., Misra, S., & Ghosh, A. (2024). Biodiversity: goal and driver of agricultural sustainability. In Biodiversity and Bioeconomy (pp. 143-164). Elsevier. doi:10.1016/B978-0-323-95482-2.00007-9

Hamid, S. R., Arzaman, A. F. M., Razali, M. A., Yasin, N. I., Masrom, N. R., Sabri, N. A. A., & Margono, M. (2024). The deployment of the Malaysian sustainable palm oil standard in the agriculture sector. *Multidisciplinary Science Journal*, *6*(7), 2024115–2024115. doi:10.31893/multiscience.2024115

Hassan, M. A., Farid, M. A. A., Zakaria, M. R., Ariffin, H., Andou, Y., & Shirai, Y. (2024). Palm oil expansion in Malaysia and its countermeasures through policy window and biorefinery approach. *Environmental Science & Policy*, *153*, 103671. doi:10.1016/j.envsci.2024.103671

Heimann, T., Argueyrolles, R., Reinhardt, M., Schuenemann, F., Söder, M., & Delzeit, R. (2024). Phasing out palm and soy oil biodiesel in the EU: What is the benefit? *Global Change Biology. Bioenergy*, *16*(1), e13115. doi:10.1111/gcbb.13115

Henson, I. E., Ruiz, R. R., & Romero, H. M. (2012). The greenhouse gas balance of the oil palm industry in Colombia: A preliminary analysis. I. Carbon sequestration and carbon offsets. *Agronomia Colombiana*, *30*(3), 359–369.

Jelsma, I., Gay, F., Ollivier, J., & Rapidel, B. (2024). Collective action, replanting and resilience; Key lessons from 40 years of smallholder oil palm cultivation in the Ophir plantation, Indonesia. *Agricultural Systems*, *213*, 103801. doi:10.1016/j.agsy.2023.103801

Kan, K. W., Chan, Y. J., Tiong, T. J., & Lim, J. W. (2024). Maximizing biogas yield from palm oil mill effluent (POME) through advanced simulation and optimisation techniques on an industrial scale. *Chemical Engineering Science*, *285*, 119644. doi:10.1016/j.ces.2023.119644

Labys, W. C., & Pollak, P. K. (2024). *Commodity models for forecasting and policy analysis* (Vol. 4). Taylor & Francis.

Litja, D. (2020). *The implications of EU regulations to Malaysian palm oil exporting and its economic consequences.*

Meijaard, E., Brooks, T. M., Carlson, K. M., Slade, E. M., Garcia-Ulloa, J., Gaveau, D. L., Lee, J. S. H., Santika, T., Juffe-Bignoli, D., Struebig, M. J., Wich, S. A., Ancrenaz, M., Koh, L. P., Zamira, N., Abrams, J. F., Prins, H. H. T., Sendashonga, C. N., Murdiyarso, D., Furumo, P. R., & Sheil, D. (2020). The environmental impacts of palm oil in context. *Nature Plants*, *6*(12), 1418–1426. doi:10.1038/s41477-020-00813-w PMID:33299148

Murphy, D. (2018). *Oil palm value chain management.*

Murphy, D. J. (2014). The future of oil palm as a major global crop: Opportunities and challenges. *Journal of Oil Palm Research*, *26*(1), 1–24.

Murphy, D. J. (2015). What is the future for oil palm as a global crop. *World Agric*, *5*, 24–34.

Murphy, D. J. (2024). Sustainable vegetable oils. In *Functional Dietary Lipids* (pp. 31–47). Woodhead Publishing. doi:10.1016/B978-0-443-15327-3.00011-2

Nasution, E. D., Saidy, A. R., Priatmadi, B. J., Dasrial, M., Alfiana, H. U., & Jailani, R. (2024). Enhancing the sustainability of oil palm plantations through the application of principles and adaptive management of high conservation value areas in Central Kalimantan. *Plant Science Today*, *11*(1), 405–417.

Pacheco, P., Gnych, S., Dermawan, A., Komarudin, H., & Okarda, B. (2017). *The palm oil global value chain: Implications for economic growth and socialand environmental sustainability.*

Prasad, S., Yadav, K. K., Kumar, S., Pandita, P., Bhutto, J. K., Alreshidi, M. A., Balasubramani, R., Yaseen, Z. M., Osman, S. M., & Cabral-Pinto, M. M. (2024). Review on biofuel production: Sustainable development scenario, environment, and climate change perspectives-A sustainable approach. *Journal of Environmental Chemical Engineering*, 111996. doi:10.1016/j.jece.2024.111996

Rival, A., & Levang, P. (2014). *Palms of controversies: Oil palm and development challenges.* CIFOR.

Rodrik, D. (2018). What do trade agreements really do? *The Journal of Economic Perspectives*, *32*(2), 73–90. doi:10.1257/jep.32.2.73

Sadik-Zada, E. R., Loewenstein, W., & Hasanli, Y. (2019). Commodity revenues, agricultural sector and the magnitude of deindustrialization: A novel multisector perspective. *Economies*, *7*(4), 113. doi:10.3390/economies7040113

Shah, M. K. M. (2021). The Impact of Covid-19 Pandemic on Income and Employment in the Agriculture and Food Supply Industry. *Environment*, *6*(25), 171–188.

Shamsuddin, R., Singh, G., Kok, H. Y., Hakimi Rosli, M., Dawi Cahyono, N. A., Lam, M. K., & Low, A. (2021). Palm oil industry—processes, by-product treatment and value addition. *Sustainable Bioconversion of Waste to Value Added Products*, 121-143.

Shehu, S., Salleh, M. A., & Ahmad, A. A. (2020). The sustainable palm oil policies in Malaysia. *The Journal of Management Theory and Practice (JMTP)*, 56-60.

Siahaan, T. (2020). Indonesia environmental diplomacy in president Joko Widodo's era (2014-2019) of the issue rejection Indonesia's cpo by European Union. *Sociae Polites*, *21*(1), 73–94. doi:10.33541/sp.v21i1.1960

Statista Research Department. (2022, October 5). *Malaysia palm oil share of GDP*. SRD.

Vamuloh, V. V., Kozak, R. A., & Panwar, R. (2020). Voices unheard: Barriers to and opportunities for small farmers' participation in oil palm contract farming. *Journal of Cleaner Production*, *275*, 121955. doi:10.1016/j.jclepro.2020.121955

Waters, K., Altiparmak, S. O., Shutters, S. T., & Thies, C. (2024). The Green Mirage: The EU's Complex Relationship with Palm Oil Biodiesel in the Context of Environmental Narratives and Global Trade Dynamics. *Energies*, *17*(2), 343. doi:10.3390/en17020343

Zakaria, N. Z. J., Rozali, S., Mubarak, N. M., & Ibrahim, S. (2024). A review of the recent trend in the synthesis of carbon nanomaterials derived from oil palm by-product materials. *Biomass Conversion and Biorefinery*, *14*(1), 13–44. doi:10.1007/s13399-022-02430-3 PMID:35194538

Chapter 15
Navigating the Nexus: Economics and Environmental Responsibility in the Global Beverage Industry

Nitish Kumar Minz
https://orcid.org/0009-0000-4770-0336
School of Management and Commerce, K.R. Mangalam University, India

Deepika Chaudhary
School of Management and Commerce, K.R. Mangalam University, India

ABSTRACT

This research chapter delves into the intricate relationship between economics and environmental responsibility within the global beverage industry. The study seeks to understand how economic factors influence environmental practices and, conversely, how environmental responsibility impacts economic dynamics in this industry. Through an in-depth analysis of scholarly literature, case studies, and industry reports, the chapter explores the challenges, opportunities, and evolving strategies employed by beverage companies to balance economic objectives with environmental sustainability. The findings contribute to a nuanced understanding of the interconnected forces shaping the global beverage industry and provide insights for businesses, policymakers, and stakeholders striving for a harmonious integration of economic goals and environmental responsibility.

INTRODUCTION

The global beverage industry stands at the intersection of economic dynamics and environmental responsibility, presenting a complex interplay that significantly influences the industry's trajectory. As the world grapples with the challenges of sustainability and climate change, the beverage sector has become a focal point for examining how economic imperatives can align with environmental stewardship. This

DOI: 10.4018/979-8-3693-2149-2.ch015

introduction delves into the profound importance of understanding the intricate relationship between economics and environmental responsibility within the global beverage industry.

The beverage industry, encompassing sectors such as soft drinks, alcoholic beverages, and bottled water, plays a pivotal role in the global economy. According to Almeida et al. (2017), the industry's economic significance extends beyond its market value, encompassing supply chains, employment, and contributions to national GDPs. However, this economic prominence comes with inherent environmental challenges, including resource depletion, pollution, and carbon emissions (Weber & Saunders-Hogberg, 2018). Recognizing this, the industry faces a critical juncture where economic decisions must be harmonized with environmental responsibility.

At the heart of this study is the exploration of how economic factors shape environmental practices within the global beverage industry and, reciprocally, how environmental responsibility influences economic dynamics. The research question guiding this study is: How does the interplay between economics and environmental responsibility impact decision-making and practices in the global beverage industry? To address this question comprehensively, the study aims to achieve the following objectives:

1. Examine the economic forces influencing decision-making within the global beverage sector.
2. Explore the impact of economic strategies on environmental practices adopted by beverage companies.
3. Investigate the environmental responsibility initiatives implemented by leading beverage companies globally.
4. Analyze the motivations driving the incorporation of sustainable practices and their implications on business operations.
5. Identify challenges faced by the industry in balancing economic goals with environmental responsibility.
6. Highlight opportunities for innovation, efficiency, and positive environmental impact within the industry.

The significance of this study lies in its potential to provide a nuanced understanding of how the global beverage industry navigates the nexus between economic objectives and environmental responsibility. The outcomes of this research have implications for businesses, policymakers, and stakeholders invested in fostering a sustainable and responsible beverage industry.

This study aligns with the growing body of literature emphasizing the need for industries to address environmental challenges while pursuing economic goals. Boumediene and El Honda (2018) assert that corporate social responsibility (CSR) in the food and beverage industry is an essential aspect, reflecting a broader societal shift towards sustainable practices. Furthermore, studies by Akyelken and Keller (2014) and Rodriguez-Sanchez and Sellers-Rubio (2020) highlight the importance of sustainability and demand-side perspectives in shaping industry practices.

LITERATURE REVIEW

The literature review encompasses a comprehensive examination of pivotal research papers that contribute significantly to understanding the complex interplay between economics and environmental responsibility in the global beverage industry. The exploration begins with Adelodun et al.'s (2021) review of the impacts of the COVID-19 pandemiç on sustainable agri-food systems and agroecosystem decarbonization, shedding light on the interconnectedness of environmental sustainability and resilience during global crises.

Moving to the nexus of globalisation, logistics, and manufacturing, Akyelken and Keller (2014) frame the contextual elements influencing the beverage industry's operational dynamics. Almeida et al. (2017) further contribute by examining material selection for environmental responsibility, focusing on soft drinks packaging in Brazil. These studies provide a foundation for understanding the broader environmental implications of supply chain and manufacturing processes.

Al-Thani and Al-Ansari (2021) delve into industrial ecology, circular economy, and the energy-water-food nexus, offering insights into resource management objectives that shape sustainability practices in different sectors, including the beverage industry. Belyaeva et al. (2020) contribute by exploring sustainable business models in the food and beverage industry across Western and Central and Eastern European countries, providing a comparative perspective.

Examining the non-alcoholic beverage industry, Ben (2021) presents a case on sustainability as a business approach, showcasing the sector's evolving strategies. Boumediene and El Honda (2018) focus on corporate social responsibility in the soft drinks sector in Algeria, emphasizing the industry's social and ethical dimensions. Dri et al. (2015) offer best environmental management practices for the food and beverage manufacturing sector, guiding sustainable operational frameworks.

Fatunnisa et al. (2023) explore the relationship between corporate social responsibility and corporate sustainability within the food and beverage industry, offering insights into the broader implications of responsible business conduct. Giannarakis et al. (2020) investigate the effect of corporate governance characteristics on environmental performance, emphasizing governance's role in shaping sustainability practices.

Kapelko (2021) assesses corporate social responsibility efficiency for the international food and beverage manufacturing industry, contributing a quantitative perspective. Keulertz et al. (2016) focus on the water-energy-food nexus in arid regions, offering a lens into the unique challenges and opportunities faced by the beverage industry in specific geographical contexts.

Lyu et al. (2022) conduct a study on the energy investment and environmental sustainability nexus in China, providing valuable insights into the economic dimensions of energy consumption and environmental impact. Muller (2015) takes a step back towards a more coherent water resource management paradigm, addressing gaps in existing frameworks that can inform sustainable practices.

Nowotarska et al. (2021) present a case study of Carlsberg, examining corporate social responsibility in the beverage industry and offering a practical example of integrating sustainability into business operations. Pfitzer and Krishnaswamy (2007) emphasize the role of the food and beverage sector in expanding economic opportunity, highlighting the industry's potential for positive socioeconomic impact.

Podvorica and Ukaj (2019) investigate the role of consumers' behavior in applying green marketing in the non-alcoholic beverages industry in Kosovo, providing insights into consumer preferences and their impact on industry practices. Rodriguez-Sanchez and Sellers-Rubio (2020) outline a research agenda for sustainability in the beverage industry from the demand side, highlighting the importance of consumer-driven sustainability initiatives.

Steger et al. (2007) delve into the economic foundations of corporate sustainability, offering a theoretical perspective on how economic considerations intersect with sustainability goals. Weber and Saunders-Hogberg (2018) focus on water management and corporate social performance in the food and beverage industry, shedding light on the industry's responsibility in managing water resources.

The World Economic Forum Water Initiative (2012) contributes a seminal work on the water-food-energy-climate nexus, providing a foundational understanding of the interconnected challenges and opportunities in resource management. Finally, Xia and Yan (2022) offer a global production network perspective on the energy-food nexus, emphasizing the synergic impact of climate policy on sustainable production.

This literature review synthesizes key insights from diverse perspectives, offering a holistic understanding of the economic and environmental dimensions within the global beverage industry. The studies collectively illuminate the challenges, opportunities, and evolving strategies that shape the industry's sustainability practices. However, a research gap is identified concerning a comprehensive synthesis of these insights to inform a nuanced understanding of the nexus between economics and environmental responsibility in the beverage sector. The present study aims to bridge this gap by integrating and building upon the valuable contributions of existing research to advance the discourse on sustainable practices in the industry.

METHODOLOGY

The methodology involves a systematic literature review, utilizing selection criteria focused on relevance, credibility, and recentness. Major databases, including Google scholar, Research Gate and, Scopus, are employed to source scholarly articles, case studies, and industry reports. The data extraction process involves categorizing literature based on key themes, such as economic influences and environmental responsibility. The chosen approach ensures a comprehensive understanding of the nuanced nexus between economics and environmental practices in the global beverage industry. Synthesizing diverse literature contributes to addressing the research question by providing a holistic overview, identifying patterns, and highlighting gaps for further exploration.

ECONOMIC FACTORS SHAPING THE INDUSTRY

The global beverage industry operates within a dynamic economic landscape, where various forces shape decision-making processes. Market dynamics, characterized by supply and demand fluctuations, play a pivotal role in influencing the strategies adopted by beverage companies (Porter, 2008). As Porter suggests, a company's competitive advantage is influenced by its understanding of market forces and its ability to position itself effectively.

In the beverage sector, competition is fierce, with companies vying for market share and consumer loyalty. Economic factors, such as pricing strategies and product differentiation, become key determinants of success (Kotler et al., 2017). According to Kotler, marketing strategies are essential for companies to gain a competitive edge, especially in industries where choices abound.

Consumer behavior further amplifies the impact of economic forces. As consumers increasingly prioritize sustainability and environmental responsibility, beverage companies are compelled to align their economic strategies with these evolving preferences (Hassan et al., 2019). The demand for eco-friendly packaging, ethical sourcing of ingredients, and corporate social responsibility initiatives has grown substantially (Hassan et al., 2019).

The impact of economic strategies on environmental practices within the industry is evident in the choices made by beverage companies. For example, the adoption of circular economy principles, where resources are reused and recycled, is not just an environmental decision but a strategic economic move (Ellen MacArthur Foundation, 2013). This integration aligns with the idea that sustainable practices can be economically viable in the long run.

Moreover, economic factors also influence investment decisions in sustainable technologies and practices. As discussed by Porter and Kramer (2011), the concept of creating shared value suggests that economic success and societal progress are interlinked. Companies can achieve both economic benefits and contribute to environmental responsibility by strategically investing in initiatives that align with societal and environmental needs.

The economic forces shaping the global beverage industry encompass market dynamics, competitive strategies, and evolving consumer behaviors. The impact of these forces extends beyond traditional economic considerations, influencing the industry's approach to environmental responsibility.

ENVIRONMENTAL RESPONSIBILITY PRACTICES

Examining the environmental responsibility initiatives of leading beverage companies globally provides valuable insights into the evolving landscape of sustainable business practices. In recent years, several prominent companies have taken substantial steps to incorporate environmental responsibility into their core operations.

Coca-Cola, a beverage industry giant, has been at the forefront of adopting sustainable practices. Their commitment to replenishing water usage and promoting a circular economy showcases a multifaceted approach to environmental responsibility (The Coca-Cola Company, 2021). This initiative aligns with the understanding that responsible water management contributes not only to environmental conservation but also to the long-term resilience of the business.

Motivations behind incorporating sustainable practices vary but often include a combination of ethical considerations, regulatory compliance, and a desire to meet consumer expectations (Hassan et al., 2019). Ethical considerations involve a company's commitment to being a responsible corporate citizen, recognizing the impact of its operations on the environment and society (Hassan et al., 2019). Regulatory compliance, driven by increasingly stringent environmental regulations, encourages companies to adopt sustainable practices to avoid legal repercussions.

The implications of incorporating sustainable practices on business operations are multifaceted. In the short term, there may be costs associated with implementing eco-friendly technologies and transitioning to sustainable sourcing (Hassan et al., 2019). However, in the long run, these investments often result in operational efficiency, cost savings, and enhanced brand reputation (Delmas & Burbano, 2011). Additionally, as highlighted by Porter and Kramer (2011), integrating social and environmental considerations into business strategies can create shared value by addressing societal needs and generating economic value simultaneously.

The motivations and implications underscore the strategic importance of environmental responsibility for beverage companies. By examining the practices of industry leaders, a broader understanding of the challenges and opportunities associated with sustainable initiatives emerges.

CHALLENGES AND OPPORTUNITIES

Navigating the nexus between economic goals and environmental responsibility in the global beverage industry presents a myriad of challenges and opportunities. Identifying these factors is crucial for developing strategies that foster sustainable practices while maintaining economic viability.

Challenges

1. Cost Implications: One of the primary challenges is the immediate cost implications associated with adopting environmentally responsible practices. Initial investments in sustainable technologies, sourcing, and waste management can strain financial resources (Hitt et al., 2020).
2. Consumer Education and Perception: Shaping consumer behavior and perceptions is challenging. While there is a growing demand for sustainable products, educating consumers about the value and impact of environmentally responsible practices remains a hurdle (Luchs et al., 2010).
3. Regulatory Compliance: Adhering to evolving environmental regulations requires continuous adaptation. Navigating complex and dynamic regulatory landscapes poses challenges for companies, especially those operating in multiple regions (King & Lenox, 2000).

Opportunities

1. Innovation for Sustainability: The need for environmentally friendly practices fosters innovation. Companies can leverage research and development to create sustainable packaging, reduce energy consumption, and develop eco-friendly product lines (Hitt et al., 2020).
2. Operational Efficiency: Adopting sustainable practices often leads to increased operational efficiency. Resource optimization, waste reduction, and streamlined processes contribute to long-term cost savings (King & Lenox, 2000).
3. Positive Brand Image: Demonstrating a commitment to environmental responsibility enhances a company's brand image. Consumers are increasingly choosing brands with strong sustainability credentials, creating opportunities for market differentiation (Luchs et al., 2010).

Balancing these challenges and opportunities requires strategic alignment between economic and environmental objectives. Successful companies view challenges as opportunities for growth and innovation, ultimately contributing to both environmental sustainability and economic prosperity.

CASE STUDIES

This section of the study presents real-life case studies of select beverage companies that exemplify successful integration of economic objectives with environmental responsibility. These cases offer valuable insights into the strategies employed by industry leaders to navigate the nexus between profitability and sustainability.

Coca-Cola Company: "World Without Waste" Initiative

The Coca-Cola Company has embarked on a transformative journey with its "World Without Waste" initiative. Focused on addressing the global plastic waste challenge, Coca-Cola aims to collect and recycle the equivalent of every bottle or can it sell by 2030 (Coca-Cola, 2023). The initiative involves significant investments in sustainable packaging, recycling infrastructure, and public awareness campaigns. The company's commitment to circular economies showcases a holistic approach to environmental responsibility, demonstrating how industry giants can drive positive change.

Source: [Coca-Cola Sustainability] (https://www.coca-colacompany.com/sustainability)

Danone: B Corp Certification and Sustainable Practices

Danone, a multinational food-products corporation, has distinguished itself by obtaining B Corp certification, signaling its commitment to balancing purpose and profit. By prioritizing environmental and social responsibilities, Danone has implemented a range of sustainable practices, including responsible sourcing, carbon reduction efforts, and biodiversity conservation (Danone, 2023). This case study illustrates how a company can align economic success with a broader commitment to environmental and social stewardship.

Source: [Danone B Corp Certification] (https://www.danone.com/sustainability/)

Heineken: "Drop the C" Climate Action Program

Heineken's "Drop the C" program exemplifies a comprehensive approach to combatting climate change. The company has committed to significantly reducing carbon emissions across its value chain, with goals such as sourcing 100% renewable energy and transitioning to electric vehicles (Heineken, 2023). This case study showcases how a major player in the beverage industry can champion climate action while maintaining economic viability.

Source: [Heineken Sustainability] (https://www.theheinekencompany.com/sustainability)

Analyzing these case studies provides valuable insights into the diverse strategies employed by beverage companies to integrate economic goals with environmental responsibility. These real-life examples demonstrate that profitability and sustainability can be mutually reinforcing, offering lessons for industry peers and stakeholders.

RECOMMENDATIONS AND FUTURE DIRECTIONS

Recommendations for stakeholders in the beverage industry involve embracing circular economy principles, integrating sustainable supply chain practices, and investing in eco-friendly packaging technologies. Policymakers are urged to incentivize environmentally responsible practices, enforce stringent regulations, and collaborate with industry leaders to formulate comprehensive sustainability frameworks. Researchers should focus on developing standardized metrics for assessing environmental impact, conducting longitudinal studies on the efficacy of sustainable practices, and exploring the socio-economic implications of transitioning to greener business models.

Future research avenues should delve into the socio-economic impacts of consumer behavior on sustainable choices in the beverage industry, investigating how consumer awareness and preferences drive industry practices. Additionally, exploring the potential of emerging technologies, such as blockchain, in enhancing traceability and transparency in the supply chain, can be a promising avenue. Studying the effectiveness of collaborative initiatives among industry players to address common sustainability challenges and analyzing the role of financial incentives in promoting sustainable practices are crucial areas for further exploration. These recommendations and future directions aim to guide stakeholders, policymakers, and researchers towards fostering a more sustainable and responsible global beverage industry.

CONCLUSION

This research paper explored the intricate relationship between economics and environmental responsibility in the global beverage industry, aiming to understand their complex interplay. The synthesis of existing literature, case studies, and industry reports revealed several key findings that contribute to a nuanced understanding of this nexus.

Summary of Key Findings

1. Interconnected Forces: The global beverage industry operates within a web of interconnected forces, where economic decisions impact environmental practices and vice versa. The two dimensions are not mutually exclusive but are integral parts of a larger system.
2. Strategic Integration: Leading beverage companies, such as Coca-Cola, Danone, and Heineken, have demonstrated that economic success and environmental responsibility can be strategically integrated. Initiatives like the "World Without Waste," B Corp certification, and "Drop the C" program exemplify comprehensive approaches.
3. Challenges and Opportunities: Balancing economic goals with environmental responsibility presents challenges, including resource constraints and consumer behavior. However, these challenges also create opportunities for innovation, efficiency gains, and positive environmental impact.

Implications for the Global Beverage Industry:

The implications of this study extend to industry stakeholders, policymakers, and businesses aiming for a sustainable future. Recognizing the dual nature of economic and environmental considerations is essential for developing holistic strategies. The findings suggest:

1. Collaboration and Innovation: Industry collaboration and innovation are crucial for addressing challenges and capitalizing on opportunities. Shared initiatives and technological advancements can drive positive change.
2. Policy Support: Policymakers play a pivotal role in fostering an environment conducive to sustainable practices. Incentives, regulations, and frameworks supporting responsible business conduct can accelerate the industry's transition.

3. Consumer Awareness: Educating consumers about the environmental impact of their choices can drive demand for sustainable products. Increased awareness creates a market for eco-friendly innovations.

Harmonious Integration of Economics and Environment

The global beverage industry stands at a crossroads where economic success must align with environmental responsibility. The case studies and literature review illustrate that a harmonious integration of these aspects is not only possible but essential for long-term viability. This research serves as a call to action for industry players to embrace sustainable practices, contributing to a resilient and responsible global beverage sector.

As the industry evolves, continuous research, collaboration, and commitment will be imperative for navigating the complex interplay between economics and environmental responsibility.

REFERENCES

Adelodun, B., Kareem, K. Y., Kumar, P., Kumar, V., Choi, K. S., Yadav, K. K., Yadav, A., El-Denglawey, A., Cabral-Pinto, M., Son, C. T., Krishnan, S., & Khan, N. A. (2021). Understanding the impacts of the COVID-19 pandemic on sustainable agri-food system and agroecosystem decarbonization nexus: A review. *Journal of Cleaner Production*, *318*, 128451. doi:10.1016/j.jclepro.2021.128451 PMID:36570877

Akyelken, N., & Keller, H. (2014). Framing the nexus of globalisation, logistics and manufacturing in Europe. *Transport Reviews*, *34*(6), 674–690. doi:10.1080/01441647.2014.981885

Al-Thani, N. A., & Al-Ansari, T. (2021). Comparing the convergence and divergence within industrial ecology, circular economy, and the energy-water-food nexus based on resource management objectives. *Sustainable Production and Consumption*, *27*, 1743–1761. doi:10.1016/j.spc.2021.04.008

Almeida, C. M. V. B., Rodrigues, A. J. M., Agostinho, F., & Giannetti, B. F. (2017). Material selection for environmental responsibility: The case of soft drinks packaging in Brazil. *Journal of Cleaner Production*, *142*, 173–179. doi:10.1016/j.jclepro.2016.04.130

Belyaeva, Z., Rudawska, E. D., & Lopatkova, Y. (2020). Sustainable business model in food and beverage industry–a case of Western and Central and Eastern European countries. *British Food Journal*, *122*(5), 1573–1592. doi:10.1108/BFJ-08-2019-0660

Ben, B. (2021). *Sustainability a business approach case: the non-alcoholic beverage industry*.

Boumediene, O., & El Honda, Y. N. (2018). Corporate social responsibility in food and beverage industry: An analysis study of soft drinks sector in Algeria. *European Scientific Journal*, *14*(1), 1857–1881. doi:10.19044/esj.2018.v14n1p190

Dri, M., Antonopoulos, I. S., Canfora, P., & Gaudillat, P. (2015). *Best environmental management practice for the food and beverage manufacturing sector*. Final Draft.

Fatunnisa, H., Hamdani, N. A., & Permana, I. (2023, March). Exploring the Relationship Between Corporate Social Responsibility and Corporate Sustainability within the Food and Beverage Industry. In *Proceeding of International Conference on Business, Economics, Social Sciences, and Humanities* (Vol. 6, pp. 1085-1090). IEEE.

Giannarakis, G., Sariannidis, N., & Konteos, G. (2020). The effect of corporate governance characteristics on environmental performance: The case of food and beverage sector. *Open Journal of Business and Management*, *8*(05), 1988–2005. doi:10.4236/ojbm.2020.85122

Kapelko, M. (2021). Assessing Corporate Social Responsibility Efficiency for the International Food and Beverage Manufacturing Industry. *Proceedings in Food System Dynamics*, 56-63.

Keulertz, M., Sowers, J., Woertz, E., & Mohtar, R. (2016). The water-energy-food nexus in arid regions. In *The Oxford handbook of water politics and policy*. Oxford University Press.

Lin, J. (2007). *Sustainable supply chains in the food and beverage industry* [Doctoral dissertation].

Lyu, L., Khan, I., Zakari, A., & Bilal. (2022). A study of energy investment and environmental sustainability nexus in China: A bootstrap replications analysis. *Environmental Science and Pollution Research International*, *29*(6), 8464–8472. doi:10.1007/s11356-021-16254-7 PMID:34490557

Muller, M. (2015). The'nexus' as a step back towards a more coherent water resource management paradigm. *Water Alternatives*, *8*(1).

Nowotarska, A., Tomaszewska, M., Piotrowska, A., & Chłędzik, A. (2021). Corporate social responsibility in the beverage industry–a case study of Carlsberg. *International Business and Global Economy*, *40*, 9–18.

Pfitzer, M., & Krishnaswamy, R. (2007). *The Role of the Food & Beverage Sector in Expanding Economic Opportunity*. FSG.

Podvorica, G., & Ukaj, F. (2019). The role of consumers' behaviour in applying green marketing: An economic analysis of the non-alcoholic beverages industry in kosova. Wroclaw Review of Law. *The American Economist*, *9*(1), 1–25.

Rodriguez-Sanchez, C., & Sellers-Rubio, R. (2020). Sustainability in the beverage industry: A research agenda from the demand side. *Sustainability (Basel)*, *13*(1), 186. doi:10.3390/su13010186

Steger, U., Ionescu-Somers, A., & Salzmann, O. (2007). The economic foundations of corporate sustainability. *Corporate Governance: The international journal of business in society*, *7*(2), 162-177.

Weber, O., & Saunders-Hogberg, G. (2018). Water management and corporate social performance in the food and beverage industry. *Journal of Cleaner Production*, *195*, 963–977. doi:10.1016/j.jclepro.2018.05.269

World Economic Forum Water Initiative. (2012). *Water security: the water-food-energy-climate nexus*. Island Press.

Xia, Y., & Yan, B. (2022). Energy-food nexus scarcity risk and the synergic impact of climate policy: A global production network perspective. *Environmental Science & Policy*, *135*, 26–35. doi:10.1016/j.envsci.2022.04.008

Chapter 16
Review and Future Research Directions of Sustainability, Customer Values, Drivers, Attitudes, and Purchase Intention of Organic Products

Surbhi Sharma
https://orcid.org/0000-0002-2019-1823
Chandigarh University, India

ABSTRACT

This study evaluated 213 earlier works on organic products to accomplish this and put out a conceptual framework for additional research. This concept predicts that components including sustainability, drivers, customer values, demographics, and the socioeconomic environment that affect consumer attitude and intention. Further investigation may on indirect effects of sustainability, drivers, customer values, and the demographic and socio-economic background on inclinations to buy organic products is advised by the study. The research confirmed that protecting the environment, caring for animals, and preserving biodiversity are crucial aspects of sustainability. Price, willingness to pay and awareness are also the main motivators for buying organic personal care products, which are supported by customer values such as those related to the environment, health, and safety values. Age, marital status, and educational attainment of consumers are thought to be the main determinants.

INTRODUCTION

The organic personal care industry is anticipated to increase at a compound annual growth rate of 9.1% from 2022 to 2030, from a market size of USD 19.3 billion in 2021. (Grand view research, 2020). Growing customer demand for eco-friendly, sustainable products with more transparent product ingredients is a result of a growing consumer understanding of the advantages of organic products. The COVID-19

DOI: 10.4018/979-8-3693-2149-2.ch016

epidemic has greatly influenced the use of chemical-free personal care products as a result of rising consumer concern for their wellness, welfare, and sustainable development (Miftari et al., 2022). The rise in the popularity of products that are made with herbal ingredients has also pushed producers to introduce new commodities, as have rising investments in product research and development. For instance, Refresh Botanical increased its market share in India in April 2021 by introducing a line of products designed for sensitive, aged, and acne-prone skin types (Gebashe et al., 2022). The consumption of organic products has increased in the past few years as a result of economic growth, higher purchasing power, and growing interest in the potential health and wellness benefits of organic products. As a result, the market size of organic personal care products was estimated to be 64 billion Indian rupees in 2025 (Minhas, 2023). Moreover, In July 2021Unilever acquired Paula's Choice, a skincare brand which is known as for cruelty free products, high performing ingredients and science based innovation. And, in 2022 L'Oreal is become a part of K-beauty with its acquisition of Nanda co. Ltd which stylenanda and the cosmetics brand 3CE which is based on fashion, lifestyle and Beauty Company is situated in south Korea (Global market insights, 2023). The Food and Drug Administration of the USA and other companies have certain rules and policies for the manufacturing of personal care products in general (Carvalho et al., 2016), which has urged companies around the globe to produce more personal care products with simple extracts (Ghazali et al., 2017). The predictions estimate that by 2025, the economy for natural personal care products, which is currently estimated to be worth over USD 13 billion, will have grown by over 10% annually, witness to the rising demand for these products (Adroit Market Research, 2020). The use of science in the beauty industry is nothing new, but the current biotechnology trend is taking the science of beauty to a whole new level. However, the biotech movement is prompting researchers to find beauty ingredients that already exist in organisms in nature. Then they are able to replicate that natural process and mass produce ingredients in a lab.For instance, Skincare Company Algenist uses biotech methods to manufacture their patented ingredient, Alguronic Acid.The ingredient was originally found in microscopic algae. The algae use the compound to protect and regenerate their cells all while living in some of the harshest environments on the planet (Howarth, 2024).

With a revenue share of more than 43.5% in 2021, hypermarkets and supermarkets were the largest distribution channel sector. Many brands are extending their product lines to hypermarkets and supermarkets due to consumers' growing preference for organic beauty products (Grand view research, 2020). For instance, Thayers Natural Remedies, which L'Oréal purchased in 2020, increased the distribution of its product line to Walmart in February 2022, with more than 3,500 stores nationwide (Business wire, 2022). From 2022 to 2030, the fastest CAGR is projected for the e-commerce distribution channel sector. Generally, organic products categories cover skincare, hair products, creams, perfumes, body scrubs, cosmetics, lotions and body care. High prices frequently discourage demand, which has an impact on supply reliability even if the marketplace of organic products has seen significant expansion internationally (Malini et al., 2022). Existing literature clarifies the greatest prevalent problems in the supply chain for organic personal care products, and previous research has been done using qualitative techniques. Kottala, & Singh, (2015) asserts that qualitative research techniques assist in overcoming the shortcomings of qualitative techniques. Thus, more study is urgently needed to address the aspects of the supply chain of organic personal care products. Based on the foregoing discussion, we contend that the literature on the supply chain for organic personal care products has two obvious gaps: (a) there are few explanations for the varied consumer reactions to these products, and (b) there are few studies outlining the key elements influencing the expansion of the organic personal care industry. Due to the quantitative character of earlier papers on organic personal care goods, we suggested a qualitative study for future scholars to comprehend the complicated elements associated with the supply chain for organic personal care products. Consequently, the motive of this research is to analyze the literature on organic products and develop a suitable structure for a supply chain for sustainable organic personal care products.

OBJECTIVES AND RESEARCH METHODOLOGY

Objectives

The following are the objectives:

- To study the supply chain of organic personal care products in terms of sustainability.
- To review the values of customers
- To identify the different drivers and determinants of organic personal care products.
- To review the socioeconomic and demographic environment of organic personal care products.
- To determine market-level consumer attitudes about organic personal care products.

Research Methodology

Due to the qualitative character of this study, an effort was undertaken to review earlier research on the organic personal care products supply chain and usage that has been published in reputable and trusted publications. We identified 213 studies for this purpose using the following selection criteria:

- Keywords: organic personal care products, sustainability, values, drivers, attitude and purchase intention.
- Years procured: 2013-2023.
- Publishers: Elsevier, Emerald, Wiley, Springer, Interscience publisher, Taylor & Francis.
- Accessed from Scopus
- Filters applied: Subjects- business management & accounting; Document type-articles; Language- English.

The names of publishers evaluated for the literature analysis are highlighted in Figure 1. Emerald, which has established itself as a prominent publisher in the domain of organic personal care products, has published 77 of the 213 publications. Although many journals published articles under it, British Food was the top journal that published the most papers in it. Elsevier has published 59 papers, two of which were published in the "Journal of Cleaner Production" and "The Journal of Retailing and Consumer Services". The remaining papers were published in other Elsevier journals. Additionally, 23 papers were published in the Wiley Online Library and 30 papers were published in Taylor and Francis. In fact, springer releasing is the holder of 11 publications. According to Fig. 1, Sage and Inderscience each provided eight and five publications.

Figure 1. Publications in sources of Sage and Inderscience

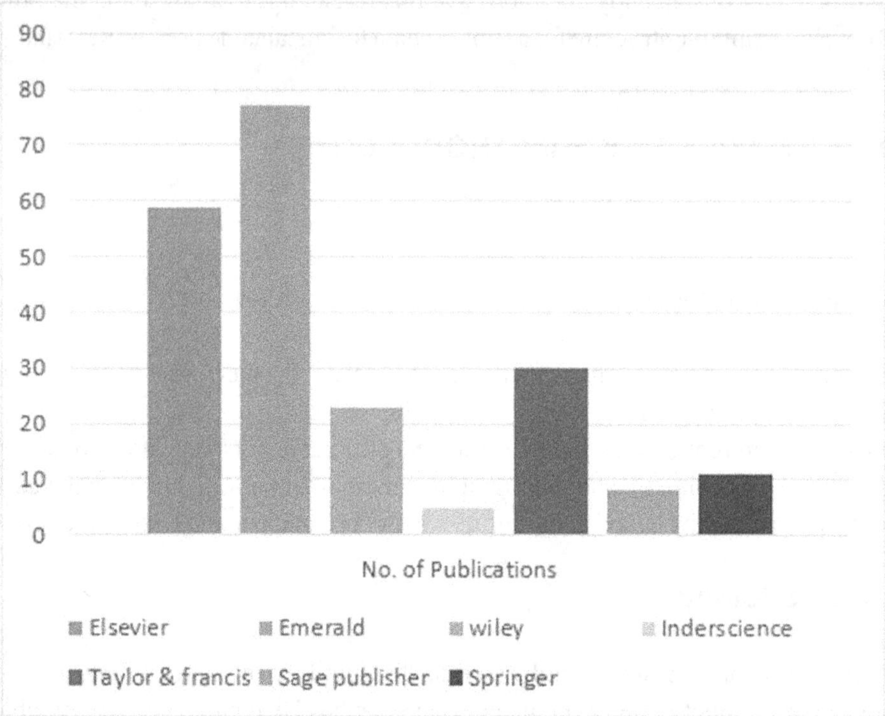

ORGANIC PERSONAL CARE PRODUCTS SUPPLY CHAIN

Supply Chain

The supply chain, a structure of interconnected enterprises, exists to satisfy the needs and desires of customers who have made known their preferences for particular goods and services. Businesses involved in this type of chain are involved in satisfying customers' wants (Treiblmaier & Garaus, 2023). That implies that various sorts of middlemen (retailers), transportation firms, warehouses, manufacturers, suppliers, and distributors are also covered. To increase the effectiveness of both individual entities and the chain as a whole, management in the aspect of the supply chain involves the coordination of conventional marketing duties and procedures used by the company and other chain members (Bag, & Rahman, 2023). Therefore, it involves coordinating production, storage, transportation, and supply chain location to maximize market flexibility and efficiency (Pal et al., 2023). In addition to all of the logistics-related activities, supply chain management also entails marketing, new product development, financing, and customer services. Production, inventory, location, transportation, and information can all be distinguished in the fundamental supply chain management model (Sinha et al., 2023). Each chain, however, faces a distinct set of market demands and operational difficulties. In the categories mentioned above, businesses must decide for themselves individually and collectively (Senna et al., 2023).

Supply Chain of Organic Personal Care Products

Eco-conscious items are more likely to be preferred by customers who are concerned about the environment and consumer behaviours (Han and Kim, 2010). The consumer consumption phenomena require strategic adjustments in the business environment. Requirements are increasingly being emphasized for product development, advertising initiatives, and law creation (Liobikiene et al., 2016). It is also regarded as a way for businesses to create new opportunities and gain a competitive edge (Moser, 2015). Businesses that reflect environmental consciousness are more likely to give customers a satisfying shopping experience, and their reputation encourages customers to purchase their products (Chen and Chai, 2010). Similarly to this, consumers prefer products which are natural products such as body and skin care items, pharmaceuticals, and dietary supplements when their awareness of their health increases (Ritter et al., 2015). (U.S. Food and Drug Administration, 2018). Supply chain management (SCM) does not only refer to efficient integrationbetween buyers and suppliers in planning and implementing all activities involved in sourcing, producing, and logistics management (Lummus & Vokurka, 1999; Petersen, Ragatz, & Monzca, 2005). It also includes coordination and collaboration among all chain actors, including customers.The collaborative role of the supply chain members is of leading importance when a sustainable competitive advantage has to be obtained for all members of the chain Members of organic food chains face several challenges in managing and linking profitability and the quality of the product (Zeithaml, 2000). The complex configuration of food chains and their actors complicates quality assurance on the one side and the equitable and efficient allocation of costs and returns to the supply chain actors on the other (King and Venturini, 2005). Additionally, organic personal care products have more sales than conventional products as buyers prefer to purchase environment concern items which also increased their interest in other aspects such as health and environmental values (Nielson et al., 2017). It is also reported in the literature that organic personal care products count as the second largest market in the United States, after organic eatery products (Kim and Chung, 2011). In particular, South Korea maintained its growth with a 2.4% market share, ranking ninth globally with $11.6 billion (Korea Cosmetics Association, 2019; Ha et al., 2021). Additionally, customer expectations are driving the personal care sector toward eco-friendly goods such as recyclable or plastic-free items, zero-waste packaging, and eco-friendly materials (Cosmetics Design-Asiab, 2020).

Although the market for green products may expand, most prior studies in this area have concentrated on organic food (Yadav and Pathak, 2017). Prior studies on environmental sustainability concentrated on topics including "attitude" (Chen, 2017), "decision-making factors" (Essoussi and Zahaf, 2008), "labeling" (Jonas and Roosen, 2005), and "trustworthiness" (Nuttavuthisit and Thgersen, 2017). These factors were mostly related to other organic product categories and studies from a marketing point of view. When Cho et al. (2015) investigated the relationship between organisational supply operations and behaviour, they focused only on organic foods. Because of the growing sustainability challenges, PCP also has significant growth potential (Kim and Chung, 2011). As far as we are concerned, no attempt has been made to look into customer behaviour concerning sustainable personal care products only (Kim and Chung, 2011; Liobikien and Bernatonien, 2017). To put it another way, prior studies focused on green products as a whole without taking into account variations in their qualities and traits (Liobikien et al., 2016).

Environmental and Health Benefits of Organic Personal Care Products

There are numerous health and environmental advantages of using organic personal care products. Non-organic skin care products contain synthetic, man-made chemicals such as sodium laurel, mineral oils, Laureth sulfate, and toxins that could be residues of pesticides. Studies have also found that they can contain mineral oil, petroleum, parabens, and other chemicals that, with long term use, can cause skin irritation, hormone imbalance, organ toxicity, and even cancer. Certified organic products are derived from plants and other naturally occurring ingredients. More importantly, those organic ingredients are grown without the use of pesticides, herbicides, synthetic fertilizers, genetically modified organisms (GMOs), and other additives or chemicals. With that, you can be sure your skin and body absorb only real, natural ingredients that aren't harmful. The beauty industry has received backlash for conducting animal testing for their products to ensure that they are safe for human use. Organic products don't need to, because, with natural ingredients, they're safe and harmless! Because organic products use naturally grown ingredients that are free from toxic pesticides and fertilizers, they don't leave a harmful footprint on the planet, particularly the soil, water, and air. Organic farming is also better for wildlife, causes lower pollution from pesticide and fertilizer sprays, and produces less carbon dioxide and less dangerous wastes. By using organic products, you're helping to minimize your environmental impact and support the sustainability of our environment.

Regulatory Frameworks and Certifications Related to Organic Personal Care Products

Organic cosmetics and personal care products shall be composed primarily of ingredients derived from plants, animals, or microorganisms and shall be manufactured, processed, and handled in conformity with the specifications set forth in these regulations. Natural and/or mineral ingredients must be utilized in accordance with these regulations. Synthetic ingredients (from petrochemical sources or synthetically manufactured through chemical reactions) shall not be used unless specifically approved under these criteria as an exception (Organic Cosmetics and Personal Care Products, 2019). As a general rule following ingredients and processes shall be prohibited:

Ingredients or raw materials produced using genetically modified organisms or their by-products, derivatives or catalysts. All forms of irradiation including gamma irradiation, X-rays etc. Testing of cosmetics products or their ingredients on animals by manufacturer or any third party associated with the manufacturing and processing of products or its ingredients. Nano-materials or ingredients made through nano-technology, except in cases where their inclusion is necessary to meet certain technological requirement, to be demonstrated by the producer and shall be subject to evaluation by accredited certification body. Ingredients from sources using applications of sewage sludge

In today's competitive beauty market, authenticity and credibility are two key aspects that separate successful brands from the rest. Obtaining cosmetics certifications is a crucial step towards achieving these objectives. These certifications validate that your products meet high-quality standards, are safe for use, and adhere to ethical practices.

APEDA- APEDA, or the Indian Agricultural Export Authority, regulates the Indian National Programme for Organic Production (NPOP) and the India Organic Logo. APEDA provides national standards for organic products through a National Accreditation Policy and Programme.

NPOP standards- Producer needs to obtain "India Organic" certification mark to export organic products. This mark signifies compliance with NPOP standards.

Organic cosmetics- Organic cosmetics must contain at least 95% organically produced ingredients, excluding water and salt. The remaining ingredients must consist of nonagricultural substances approved on the National List or non-organically produced agricultural products.

COSMOS- A COSMOS ORGANIC or COSMOS NATURAL signature means that a company has met a number of criteria to ensure consumers that their products are genuine organic or natural.

CDSCO- The Central Drug and Food Safety Authority of India (CDSCO) is the main authority responsible for regulating activities related to cosmetics.

Case Studies Highlighting Successful Sustainability Initiatives in the Organic Personal Care Industry

A study by Saira Atta et al., 2021 focuses on health, safety, the environment, hedonic and social value factors. By concentrating on such values, a marketer may better understand the customer's psychology for the personal care products and can develop an efficient market strategy to build brand value. This research demonstrates how certain particular values affect the re-buying intention of customers such as hedonic value, safety value, the environmental value and the health value. In this research the TBP theory is incorporated to understand the purpose of customers to buy organic foods. There is no support for each other for the outcome of environmental value with the aim to buy an organic product. The health value result with the desire to buy is not mutually supported. People are worried about the value of hedonics which are the reasons why it shows a good outcome with the buying intention. Also negative is the effect of security and social values with buying intent. There is no mediation between all factors according to our results. The results are distinct from prior studies and need additional action.

The study by Sniepiene, 2021, aimed to determine behavior of choice and consumption of organic cosmetic products according to the consumers' socio-demographic characteristics. Consumers indicated the reasons for choosing these products: health benefits, natural composition, and non-polluting environment during production, and recyclability of packaging. Most often, respondents do not use such cosmetics due to unclear labeling and the higher prices of these products. Sufficient and complete information on the label, a reliable and well-known producer are considered to be the most important identification criteria. In contrast, a special point of sale, clear and attractive promotional/visual information being the least important. From 2023 to 2030, the Natural & Organic Personal Care Products market displays a consistent and positive growth direction, indicating a favorable outlook for the industry. This growth is propelled by several key factors, including increasing consumer demand, advancements in technology, and shifting consumer preferences. A significant driver of the Natural & Organic Personal Care Products market is the growing consumer awareness of health and wellness. This heightened consciousness has resulted in a surge in demand for Natural & Organic Personal Care Products products that are perceived as healthier and more natural alternatives. Furthermore, technological advancements within the Natural & Organic Personal Care Products industry have led to the emergence of more efficient and sustainable production methods, further enhancing market growth.

Consumer Perceptions and Attitudes Towards Organic Personal Care Products

The socio-economic environment has dramatically changed the living standard of people in a developed manner in terms of occupation, income, education, spending pattern, purchasing power, health etc. This has led the people to get better things in life and fulfill their needs. In case of consuming organic products, people are becoming aware through media, campaign, seminars and conferences, health and nutritional education, doctor's advice and so on. Hence, in today's world peoples habits are rapidly changing. In the last few years the organic production and availability in the market has been increased and made a significant development in the economy. Several people have started to consider organic personal care products instead of conventional products because; it is healthier and less prone to chemicals. This kind of purchasing behavior plays an important role among the consumer perception towards buying organic personal care products. The purchase intention for organic products is understood as the preference of consumers to buy these products before conventional products. The environmental concerns of consumers lead them to show positive attitudes towards organic products as environmentally friendly, which leads consumers to buy them, due to the benefits they bring (Kim 2018). On the other hand, there is research that has linked attitudes with word-of-mouth (WOM) intentions (Shih et al. 2013; Lien and Cao 2014). Therefore, the pandemic caused by COVID-19 has changed the mindset of many consumers. They are increasingly aware of the risks of not caring for the planet. Before the pandemic, there was a perceived increase in collective environmental concern and sustainability, but COVID-19 has further accelerated this process and motivated more people to assume this responsibility. Thus, the health crisis could trigger the consumption of organic products, which are produced through environmentally friendly agricultural methods and that have not been artificially altered.

CONCEPTUAL MODEL

Sustainability

"Sustainability" is defined as "a progress that fulfils the needs of the present without compromising the ability of future generations to satisfy their own needs" in its official definition from 1987 by The World Commission on Environment and Development (WCED, 1987). Encouraging organic farming is a strategy that has the potential to expand sustainability in the food sector by influencing consumer attitudes and purchasing intentions (Bravo et al., 2013; Aschemann-Witzel and Zielke, 2015).

Drivers

The literature emphasized the earlier studies that might have affected the functioning of organic personal care products markets. Cost, distribution channels, belief, commitment, and good reputation are the discussed drivers described in the literature (Sadati et al., 2010; Kihlberg and Risvik, 2007; Bruschi et al., 2015; Lea & Worsley, 2005) that may affect the consumers' attitude when purchasing or using organic personal care products. Moreover, knowledge and trust are believed to affect consumer behaviour, according to earlier studies (Bamberg and Moser, 2007; Mkhize & Ellis, 2019; Vega-Zamora et al., 2019; Vitterso and Tangeland, 2015). Because that customers frequently cannot tell whether a product has been produced following organic standards, trust in labelling appears to be a crucial aspect

(Daugbjerg et al., 2014; Mkhize and Ellis, 2019). Hence, trust among consumers is a requirement for the commercial growth of sustainable products (Barney and Hansen, 1994), and it has been identified as a significant factor in decisions to buy organic produce (Konuk, 2018; Nuttavuthisit and Thogersen, 2017; Vega-Zamora et al., 2019).

Customers Values

Submitter et al., 2021 concluded that health, perceive value, environment, trust & involvement are the main determinants of consumer values related to organic products. As a result, existing academics have proposed several structures of a customer's perceived values, such as one study that found that consumer awareness, previous and current experience, and subjective standards all had a substantial impact on halal-labelled cosmetic and personal care items (Teng, 2018).In addition, one study examines the religious values of a consumer with purchase intention towards green products (Ghazali & Dilip, 2018). Hence, customer values play a vital role in making opinions& judgments of making decisions of a product (Butler et al., 2016; Varshneya & Das, 2017), which construct an affirmative attitude in consumers.

Demographic and Socioeconomic Variables

The utmost significant condition for predicting the purchasing behaviour of consumers in a given location or region are demographic and socioeconomic factors (Wier et al., 2003). Lockie et al., 2002 reported that women customers have high-income levels and levels of education. A different study from Janssen et al., 2009 found no differences in terms of income, age, or education levels. They concluded that there is no consensus on the social and demographic characteristics of the organic product customer. Also, Vergura et el., 2020 studied the six environmental concerns related to customer interactions that affected their attitude which had an impact on their purchasing behaviour of organic personal care products. Moreover, Matic & puh, 2016 concluded a study to investigate variables such as age, gender, and health consciousness that impact consumers' intentions related to an organic purchase (Persaud and Schillo, 2017). Also, Lavuri and Sreeramulu, 2019, looked into the relationship between purchasing personal care goods and demographical information about customers to determine the most important characteristics and their impact on decision-making. The significance of socioeconomic and demographic parameters is an ongoing discussion in the research (Shafie and Rennie, 2012). Hence, we anticipate that socioeconomic and demographic factors will have an impact on "attitude" and "intention".

Attitude

Ajzen & Fishbein (1980), said in one study if consumer attitude is positive towards any activities they are inclined towards a such particular behaviour. Existing research affirmed that if the attitude of a consumer is favourable towards any product ultimately his intention is positively influenced towards the such product (Van loo et al, 2013; Kim & Chung, 2011). Additionally, a study found a strong positive relationship between attitudes and buying behaviours for natural and organic products (Van Loo et al., 2013), but it also revealed that the high cost, limited variety, and scarcity of these products limit consumer attitudes and prevent them from becoming successful organic personal care product buyers (Yin et al., 2010). A discrepancy between consumers' attitudes and actual purchasing behaviour concerning organic products was also noted by Tarkiainen and Sundqvist (2005).

RESULTS

Table 1 illustrates that environmental protection was identified as the primary sustainability problem in all evaluated studies. Most studies revealed that consumers are largely unaware of how organic farming contributes to environmental conservation. This is a real indicator of how the organic market will develop in the future. Animal welfare, biodiversity preservation, free from chemicals and soil & water conservation have arisen as important sustainability elements of the organic product supply chain, with 60%, 55%, 55% and 45% literature support, respectively. This demonstrates that despite the unavoidable contribution organic agriculture makes to biodiversity preservation, this issue was not adequately addressed in earlier studies, and it must be investigated. Product safety and low-energy inputs received 40% of the literature's backing, demonstrating the need for low-energy inputs in the organic agricultural system. However, waste reduction is the least matter of sustainability according to previous research studies.

Environmental and health values are the most important customer values, according to table 2. 100% of the literature supported both variables. Customers are more likely to choose organic products when they are convinced of their environment, health and safety benefits. From the standpoint of organic market expansion, both received 50% literary support, which is excellent. However, only 10% were described in the previous studies, supposing that hedonic value was not significantly found in previous studies which indicates that less research work done on these values and consumers don't consider this value while purchasing organic personal care products.

Table 3 summarises the findings of the review of demographic and socioeconomic parameters and shows that, according to 70% of the literature, education is a significant factor in determining consumer purchasing behaviour. Marital status, age, and gender come next, with literature support of 40%, 35%, and 30%, respectively. With 15% support from the literature, income was found to be the least significant marker.

Consumer attitudes concerning organic products are favourable, according to studies listed in Table 4, and they have received 100% of the literature's recognition. Structural equation modelling is a commonly used statistical method for advising an innovative theory and building a body of knowledge about organic products. Every research from diverse nations and scholars employed various statistical approaches to produce generalizable results. However, the literature also shows that there is a disconnect between attitude and purchasing intentions in certain situations.

In fact, with 75% of the literature supporting it, premium price emerged as the key reason why consumers don't buy organic products. The high cost of organic goods, according to every study included in this analysis, has stifled market expansion. The inequity between supply and demand may be attributed to the low scale of manufacturing.

However, some studies also consider willingness to pay as a significant component, and this review found 55% of the literature to support this claim. This means that even though organic products are more expensive, people are still prepared to pay for them.

Furthermore, only 50% of the literature supports that consumers are adequately informed about the advantages of consuming organic personal care products. Customers who are generally aware of the possible benefits of products have optimistic attitudes and intents. Even though quality and trust are the next recognized factor in the literature, consumers do not always trust organic products, which lowers their perceived quality and product sales. The last criteria are loyalty & goodwill and the availability of products under literature gained 40% and 35% support. This states the role of other factors which cause the premium prices of organic products and demand for such products.

Table 1. Organic personal care product supply chain sustainability issues

S.no	Source	"Environmental protection"	"Animal welfare"	"Biodiversity preservation"	"Product safety"	"Low energy inputs"	"Soil & Water conservation"	"Waste reduction"	"Free from chemicals"
1	Lin et al.,2022	✓		✓	✓		✓	✓	
2	Chen et al., 2022	✓	✓	✓	✓	✓	✓		
3	Mansoor et al., 2022	✓	✓				✓	✓	✓
4	Sreen et L., 2022	✓		✓					✓
5	Hruba & Sadílek, 2022	✓		✓	✓	✓	✓		
6	Trivedi et al.,2022					✓			
7	Nguyen-Viet,2022	✓	✓	✓	✓				✓
8	Matharu et al.,2022	✓	✓	✓	✓			✓	✓
9	Shimul et al.,2022	✓	✓	✓				✓	✓
10	Segev & Liu, 2022	✓		✓		✓	✓		✓
11	Gaspar & Fernandes, 2022	✓	✓		✓		✓		✓
12	Odongo & Motari, 2022	✓	✓	✓		✓		✓	✓
13	Stojanova et al., 2021	✓	✓		✓		✓	✓	
14	Manchanda et al.,2021								
15	D'Souza et al., 2021								✓
16	Savelli et al., 2021		✓			✓			
17	Chung, 2020					✓			
18	Anetoh et al., 2020		✓		✓		✓		✓
19	Lo et al., 2020	✓	✓				✓		
20	Nguyen et al., 2019	✓	✓	✓		✓		✓	✓
Percentage support		70	60	55	40	40	45	35	55
Rank		1	2	3	5	5	4	6	3

Table 2. Customer values

S. NO	Study	Health value	Safety value	Social value	Hedonic value	Environmental value
1	Takaya,2018					✓
2	Yunus, 2018			✓		✓
3	Nagaraj,2021	✓	✓			
4	Krishnamohan & Kumar, 2021	✓				
5	Solis & Barska, 2021	✓	✓			✓
6	Alamsyah & Syarifuddin, 2016			✓		✓
7	Lyu & Choi, 2020				✓	
8	Balaji & Baskaran,2018		✓			
9	Kahraman, 2019					✓
10	Vergura, 2020				✓	✓
11	Kaur & Bhatia, 2018	✓	✓			
12	Mohammad & Baharun, 2017		✓			
13	Aste, 2017	✓				✓
14	photcharoen & chung, 2020	✓				
15	Teng et l., 2018		✓	✓		
16	pezua et al., 2016					✓
17	Afonso, 2017	✓				✓
18	Boon et al.,2020			✓		
19	Ahmad & Omar, 2020	✓				✓
20	Matic & puh, 2015	✓				✓
Percent support		45	30	20	10	55
Rank		2	3	4	5	1

DISCUSSION

Cultural, social, and economic issues, as well as significant environmental degradation, have put the sustainability of organic products in jeopardy. However, the supply chain for organic personal care products receives particular attention globally and is motivated by customer values and sustainability. Literature addressed that Funds for environmental protection encourage environmental performance. A company that produces a lot of pollution will be more eager to actively take on environmental protection duties the more government backing it receives. This is primarily due to the subsidies for environmental conservation having a specific policy-oriented direction. These subsidies can help businesses with their capital requirements and help cover some of the expenses associated with their environmental protection duties (Du et al., 2023). Results also indicated a beneficial relationship between organic produce, health consciousness, and environmental awareness. Additionally, consumers over 35 years old who care more about the environment than their health buy organic products (Afonso et al., 2017). Findings show that consumers' ignorance of the benefits of consuming organically has restricted market expansion, but producers' awareness of these benefits also acts as a hindrance because it encourages them to continue

Table 3. Demographic and socioeconomic factors

S.NO	Study	"Education"	"Income"	"Age"	"Gender"	"Marital status"
1	Kautish & Khare, 2022	✓				✓
2	Van et al., 2023		✓			
3	Ashrafi & Easmin, 2023	✓			✓	
4	Shah et al., 2023	✓		✓		✓
5	Tran et al., 2022		✓		✓	✓
6	Lou et al., 2022	✓				
7	Nketiah et al., 2022	✓			✓	
8	Mazharet al, 2022	✓		✓		
9	Ravi et al., 2022	✓		✓		✓
10	Leonidouet, 2022		✓		✓	
11	Mehraj & Qureshi, 2022	✓		✓		✓
12	Siraj et al., 2022	✓				✓
13	Kliem &Wolter, 2022	✓		✓		
14	Uliano et al., 2022			✓		
15	Sabat et al., 2022		✓			✓
16	Lavuri, 2022	✓				
17	Sousaet al., 2022				✓	
18	Alzaidi & Agag, 2022	✓				✓
19	Adil, 2022	✓		✓		
20	Robichaud, 2022	✓			✓	
Percentage Support		70	20	35	30	40
Rank		1	5	3	4	2

using traditional production methods. Or, to put it another way, most farmers manage their operations ineffectively. So it is important to develop research funds and take crucial initiatives for information technology and also to promote farm practices. Unorganized consumers typically have a limited understanding of the players in the supply chain for organic products because the global organic market is still tiny and underdeveloped. In order to combat the numerous market problems and maintain competitiveness, a strategic weapon might be the establishment of trust through effective marketing and providing customers with an unmatched value experience. Businesses can handle the complexity of the market if they combine their business partners from the supply chain of organic products. In order to reduce the level of inventory, expenses, and supply issues as well as to increase production, knowledge exchange, and dispersion, it is possible to consider both upstream and downstream consolidation of the organic production supply chain. Similarly to this, statements on the benefits of organic products for human health and the environment may persuade consumers to pay more for them. Products are transferred to those markets where there are more opportunities for large earnings since organic production is lower. Therefore, do past bad consumer experiences have an adverse effect on customer attitudes and choices? Additionally, over time, this can unquestionably reduce the initially observed gap between purchase intentions and attitude. The study's conclusions showed that socioeconomic and demographic factors

Table 4. Consumers' attitude towards organic products

S.N.	Study	Country	Data Collection	Techniques used	Positive	Negative
1	Zeng, 2022	Canada	Survey	Descriptive	✓	
2	Tekin & Coknaz, 2022	Turkey	Survey	Descriptive, SEM, AMOS	✓	
3	Chakraborty et al., 2022	India	Survey	Descriptive	✓	
4	Lin & Zhou, 2022	China	Survey	SEM	✓	
5	Kaur et al., 2022	Malaysia	Interview	Descriptive statistics (exploratory and confirmatory factor analysis)	✓	
6	Yakubu et al., 2022	Hungry	Survey	Delphi-ANP (Analytic Network Process)	✓	
7	Kutaula et al., 2022	United kingdom	Interview	Mixed method (Quantitative & Quanlitative)	✓	
8	Lim et al., 2022	Australia	Survey	Descriptive	✓	
9	Casalegno et al., 2022	Italy	Survey	Descriptive statistics	✓	
10	Nguyen et al., 2022	Germany	Survey	Server-based software	✓	
11	Graciano et al., 2022	Brazil	Survey	Exploratory factorial analysis & cluster analysis	✓	
12	Sultana et al., 2022	Bangladesh	Survey	Partial Least Square method	✓	
13	Al-Harbi & Badawi, 2022	Saudi Arabia	Interview	Statistical analysis (SEM)	✓	
14	Papadopoulou et al., 2022	Cyprus	Panel data	Mixed approach	✓	
15	Foroughi et al., 2022	Taiwan	Survey	partial least square technique	✓	
16	Volgger et al., 2022	Australia	Survey	subject experimental design	✓	
17	Luger et al., 2022	Austria	Survey	structural equation modelling	✓	
18	Zahra et al., 2022	Australia	Interview	a mixed-methods approach (Focus group & exploratory factor analysis)	✓	
19	Casais & Faria, 2022	Portugal	Survey	Descriptive statistics	✓	
20	Atal et al., 2022	Afghanistan	Survey	Partial least squares technique.	✓	
Percentage support					100	0

had an impact on attitude and intention. Education level, marital status and age group positively affect attitude and organic products purchase intention. And, Building a positive attitude across people of different ages, educational backgrounds, marital statuses, and socioeconomic statuses is one unexplored opportunity that can be addressed. Before creating and putting into action their goals, businesses must identify any hidden elements that might have an impact on their ability to grow. Therefore, the barrier for the organic industry is the greater cost of organic products. Due to the high level of consumer demand, increasing the production of organic personal care products and selling them in supermarkets would be an appropriate strategy for the industry to increase sales (Ogiemwonyi, 2022). Findings indicated that customer views towards organic personal care products were significantly influenced by relations between values and attitudes, environment, and health concerns. The findings also revealed a substantial correlation between purchase intention and the theory of planned behaviour variables. Further, variables like price, quality, willingness to pay and awareness, and product quality in organic production were all raised during the discussion about challenges to shopping. Previous studies cited cost as a key deterrent to buying organic products which is related to the findings from past studies.

Table 5. Drivers

S.NO	Study	Price	Awareness	Trust	Loyalty & Goodwill	Quality	Availability of products	Willingness to pay
1	Sheoran & Kumar, 2022	✓		✓				
2	Ghali, 2022	✓	✓			✓		✓
3	Colovic & Mitic, 2022	✓						
4	Purohit et al., 2022	✓	✓		✓			✓
5	Kumar et al., 2022	✓		✓	✓	✓		✓
6	Yun, 2022	✓	✓	✓				✓
7	Carranza et al., 2022	✓	✓				✓	
8	Qiao, 2022							
9	Rahman & Nguyen-Viet, 2022	✓	✓	✓		✓		✓
10	Nascimento & Loureiro, 2022	✓				✓	✓	
11	Chen et al., 2022			✓	✓		✓	✓
12	Alotaibi & Abbas, 2022	✓	✓		✓		✓	✓
13	Sharma et al., 2022					✓		
14	Mansoor et al., 2022		✓	✓				
15	Di Iorio et al., 2022	✓			✓	✓		✓
16	Coşkun et al., 2022	✓	✓	✓				
17	Fathima et al., 2022	✓		✓		✓		✓
18	Rathore et al., 2022	✓	✓		✓	✓	✓	✓
19	Mishra et al., 2022	✓			✓		✓	
20	Lin et al., 2022		✓	✓	✓	✓	✓	✓
	Percentage support	75	50	45	40	45	35	55
	Rank	1	3	4	5	4	6	2

RESEARCH IMPLICATIONS AND CONCLUSION

This is the first comprehensive qualitative study to take into account elements including customer values, demographic and socioeconomic factors, attitude towards the manufacture and consumption of organic products, and sustainability. A requirement for the building of a conceptual model for future study was taken to be an extensive review of the literature from various refereed publications. It would be intriguing to put structural equation modelling methods to the test using this conceptual model. According to survey findings, the market growth of organic personal care products worldwide was mostly driven by premium pricing, willingness to pay, and awareness. Major sustainability considerations included environmental protection, animal welfare, and biodiversity preservation. Additionally, two important customer values that people take into account while purchasing organic personal care products are the environment and health. Customer attitudes and buying intentions are influenced by education levels and marital status. The report makes three key recommendations for managerial ramifications that will shake up the demand and supply of organic products. The competitiveness in the supply chains of businesses has changed in the twenty-first century to favour value-added supply chains. Businesses would benefit from an understanding of the market environment and the development of the best marketing strategies to decrease lead times, waste rates, inventories, and costs while improving product quality, flavour, packaging and presentation. However, to accomplish this, businesses would need to integrate more supply chain partners for organic personal care products. To increase the overall sales of organic products, producers and retailers must collaborate with government agencies. As a result, environmental education delivered via internet media may alter consumers' perspectives and inspire them to live a healthy, sustainable lifestyle. Researchers, academics, and practitioners can all benefit from the current work. The fact that it covers all organic product categories means that one of its limits is the possibility of differences in drivers, customer values, and attitudes towards specific products. Therefore, it could be beneficial to explore the previously mentioned criteria concerning the various categories of organic products in future research.

REFERENCES

Aertsens, J., Verbeke, W., Mondelaers, K., & Van Huylenbroeck, G. (2009). Personal determinants of organic food consumption: A review. *British Food Journal*, *111*(10), 1140–1167. https://www.grandviewresearch.com/industry-analysis/organic-personal-care-market. doi:10.1108/00070700910992961

Afonso, C., Gavilán, D., Martins Gonçalves, H., & García de Madariaga, J. (2017). Why consumers purchase organic products? The role of environment, health and age. In *XXIX Congreso de Marketing AEMARK*. ESIC.

Aschemann-Witzel, J., & Zielke, S. (2015). Can't buy me green? A review of consumer perceptions of and behaviour toward the price of organic food. *J. Consum. Aff.* https://onlinelibrary.wiley.com/doi/10.1111/joca.12092/epdf

Atta, H. S., Abbas, B., & Syed, F. U. (2021). Study of Consumer Values for Organic Personal Care Products in the Fields of Health and Cosmetics. *International Journal of Innovative Science and Research Technology*, *6*(8).

Bag, S., & Rahman, M. S. (2023). The role of capabilities in shaping sustainable supply chain flexibility and enhancing circular economy-target performance: An empirical study. *Supply Chain Management*, *28*(1), 162–178. doi:10.1108/SCM-05-2021-0246

Bamberg, S., & Möser, G. (2007). Twenty years after Hines, Hungerford, and Tomera: A new meta-analysis of psycho-social determinants of pro-environmental behaviour. *Journal of Environmental Psychology*, *27*(1), 14–25. doi:10.1016/j.jenvp.2006.12.002

Barney, J. B., & Hansen, M. H. (1994). Trustworthiness as a source of competitive advantage. *Strategic Management Journal*, *15*(S1), 175–190. doi:10.1002/smj.4250150912

Bravo, C.P., Cordts, A., Schulze, B., & Spiller, A. (2013). Assessing determinants of organic food consumption using data from the German National Nutrition Survey II. *Food Qual. Prefer 28*, 60e70.

Bruschi, M. L. (2015). *Strategies to modify the drug release from pharmaceutical systems*. Woodhead Publishing.

Butler, K., Gordon, R., Roggeveen, K., Waitt, G., & Cooper, P. (2016). Social marketing and value in behaviour? Perceived value of using energy efficiently among low income older citizens. *Journal of Social Marketing*, *6*(2), 144–168. doi:10.1108/JSOCM-07-2015-0045

Carvalho, I. T., Estevinho, B. N., & Santos, L. (2016). Application of microencapsulated essential oils in cosmetic and personal healthcare products–a review. *International Journal of Cosmetic Science*, *38*(2), 109–119. doi:10.1111/ics.12232 PMID:25923295

Chen, C. T. A., & Borges, A. V. (2009). Reconciling opposing views on carbon cycling in the coastal ocean: Continental shelves as sinks and near-shore ecosystems as sources of atmospheric CO2. *Deep-sea Research. Part II, Topical Studies in Oceanography*, *56*(8-10), 578–590. doi:10.1016/j.dsr2.2009.01.001

Chen, T. B., & Chai, L. T. (2010). Attitude towards the environment and green products: Consumers' perspective. *Management Science and Engineering*, *4*(2), 27–39.

Cho, H., Jeong, S. H., Park, M. H., Kim, Y. H., Wolf, C., Lee, C. L., Heo, J. H., Sadhanala, A., Myoung, N. S., Yoo, S., Im, S. H., Friend, R. H., & Lee, T. W. (2015). Overcoming the electroluminescence efficiency limitations of perovskite light-emitting diodes. *Science*, *350*(6265), 1222–1225. doi:10.1126/science.aad1818 PMID:26785482

Daugbjerg, C., Smed, S., Andersen, L. M., & Schvartzman, Y. (2014). Improving eco-labelling as an environmental policy instrument: Knowledge, trust and organic consumption. *Journal of Environmental Policy and Planning*, *16*(4), 559–575. doi:10.1080/1523908X.2013.879038

Du, C., Zhang, Q., & Huang, D. (2023). Environmental protection subsidies, green technology innovation and environmental performance: Evidence from China's heavy-polluting listed firms. *PLoS One*, *18*(2), e0278629. doi:10.1371/journal.pone.0278629 PMID:36735660

Gebashe, F. C., Naidoo, D., Amoo, S. O., & Masondo, N. A. (2022). Cosmeceuticals: A newly expanding industry in South Africa. *Cosmetics*, *9*(4), 77. doi:10.3390/cosmetics9040077

Ghazali, E., Soon, P. C., Mutum, D. S., & Nguyen, B. (2017). Health and cosmetics: Investigating consumers' values for buying organic personal care products. *Journal of Retailing and Consumer Services*, *39*, 154–163. doi:10.1016/j.jretconser.2017.08.002

Ghazali, E. M., Mutum, D. S., & Ariswibowo, N. (2018). Impact of religious values and habit on an extended green purchase behaviour model. *International Journal of Consumer Studies*, *42*(6), 639–654. doi:10.1111/ijcs.12472

Ha, B. C., Lim, S. Y., & Lee, C. (2021). Impact of Organizations' Internal Green Supply Chain Management on Consumers' Purchasing Behavior for Personal Care Products. *Operations and Supply Chain Management: An International Journal*, *14*(3), 338–350. doi:10.31387/oscm0460306

Hamzaoui Essoussi, L., & Zahaf, M. (2008). Decision making process of community organic food consumers: An exploratory study. *Journal of Consumer Marketing*, *25*(2), 95–104. doi:10.1108/07363760810858837

Janssen, P. A., Saxell, L., Page, L. A., Klein, M. C., Liston, R. M., & Lee, S. K. (2009). Outcomes of planned home birth with registered midwife versus planned hospital birth with midwife or physician. *Canadian Medical Association Journal*, *181*(6-7), 377–383. doi:10.1503/cmaj.081869 PMID:19720688

Jonas, A., & Roosen, J. (2005). Private labels for premium products–the example of organic food. *international Journal of retail & Distribution Management, 33*(8), 636-653.

Kihlberg, I., & Risvik, E. (2007). Consumers of organic foods–value segments and liking of bread. *Food Quality and Preference, 18*(3), 471–481. doi:10.1016/j.foodqual.2006.03.023

Kim, Y., & Han, H. (2010). Intention to pay conventional-hotel prices at a green hotel–a modification of the theory of planned behavior. *Journal of Sustainable Tourism, 18*(8), 997–1014. doi:10.1080/09669582.2010.490300

Konuk, F. A. (2018). The role of store image, perceived quality, trust and perceived value in predicting consumers' purchase intentions towards organic private label food. *Journal of Retailing and Consumer Services, 43*, 304–310. doi:10.1016/j.jretconser.2018.04.011

Kottala, S. Y., & Singh, R. (2015). A review of sustainability, deterrents, personal values, attitudes and purchase intentions in the organic food supply chain. *Pacific Science Review B. Humanities and Social Sciences, 1*(3), 114–123.

Kottila, M. R., & Rönni, P. (2008). Collaboration and trust in two organic food chains. *British Food Journal, 110*(4/5), 376–394. doi:10.1108/00070700810868915

Lavuri, R., & Sreeramulu, D. (2019). Personal care products: A study on women consumer buying behaviour. *International Journal of Research & Review, 6*(6), 271–279.

Lea, E., & Worsley, T. (2005). Australians' organic food beliefs, demographics and values. *British Food Journal, 107*(11), 855–869. doi:10.1108/00070700510629797

Liobikienė, G., Mandravickaitė, J., & Bernatonienė, J. (2016). Theory of planned behavior approach to understand the green purchasing behavior in the EU: A cross-cultural study. *Ecological Economics, 125*, 38–46. doi:10.1016/j.ecolecon.2016.02.008

Lockie, S., Lyons, K., Lawrence, G., & Mummery, K. (2002). Eating 'green': Motivations behind organic food consumption in Australia. *Sociologia Ruralis, 42*(1), 23–40. doi:10.1111/1467-9523.00200

Malini, H., Yang, H., & Shin, H. (2022). *Halal and Cosmetics: Paving the Way for the Cosmetics Industries of Indonesia and Korea*. Insan Cendekia Mandiri.

Matić, M., & Puh, B. (2016). CONSUMERS'PURCHASE intentions towards natural cosmetics. *Ekonomski vjesnik/Econviews-Review of Contemporary Business. Entrepreneurship and Economic Issues, 29*(1), 53–64.

Miftari, I., Haas, R., Meixner, O., Imami, D., & Gjokaj, E. (2022). Factors Influencing consumer attitudes towards organic food products in a transition Economy—Insights from Kosovo. *Sustainability (Basel), 14*(10), 5873. doi:10.3390/su14105873

Moser, A. K. (2015). Thinking green, buying green? Drivers of pro-environmental purchasing behavior. *Journal of Consumer Marketing, 32*(3), 167–175. doi:10.1108/JCM-10-2014-1179

Nielson, C. B., Duethman, N. C., Howard, J. M., Moncure, M., & Wood, J. G. (2017). Burns: Pathophysiology of systemic complications and current management. *Journal of Burn Care & Research; Official Publication of the American Burn Association, 38*(1), e469–e481. doi:10.1097/BCR.0000000000000355 PMID:27183443

Nuttavuthisit, K., & Thøgersen, J. (2017). The importance of consumer trust for the emergence of a market for green products: The case of organic food. *Journal of Business Ethics, 140*(2), 323–337. doi:10.1007/s10551-015-2690-5

Ogiemwonyi, O. (2022). Factors influencing generation Y green behaviour on green products in Nigeria: An application of theory of planned behaviour. *Environmental and Sustainability Indicators, 13*, 100164. doi:10.1016/j.indic.2021.100164

Pal, B., Sarkar, A., & Sarkar, B. (2023). Optimal decisions in a dual-channel competitive green supply chain management under promotional effort. *Expert Systems with Applications, 211*, 118315. doi:10.1016/j.eswa.2022.118315

Persaud, A., & Schillo, S. R. (2017). Purchasing organic products: Role of social context and consumer innovativeness. *Marketing Intelligence & Planning, 35*(1), 130–146. doi:10.1108/MIP-01-2016-0011

Ritter, Á. M., Borchardt, M., Vaccaro, G. L., Pereira, G. M., & Almeida, F. (2015). Motivations for promoting the consumption of green products in an emerging country: Exploring attitudes of Brazilian consumers. *Journal of Cleaner Production, 106*, 507–520. doi:10.1016/j.jclepro.2014.11.066

Senna, P., Reis, A., Dias, A., Coelho, O., Guimaraes, J., & Eliana, S. (2023). Healthcare supply chain resilience framework: Antecedents, mediators, consequents. *Production Planning and Control, 34*(3), 295–309. doi:10.1080/09537287.2021.1913525

Shafie, F. A., & Rennie, D. (2012). Consumer perceptions towards organic food. *Procedia: Social and Behavioral Sciences, 49*, 360–367. doi:10.1016/j.sbspro.2012.07.034

Sinha, P., Kumar, S., & Chandra, C. (2023). Strategies for ensuring required service level for COVID-19 herd immunity in Indian vaccine supply chain. *European Journal of Operational Research, 304*(1), 339–352. doi:10.1016/j.ejor.2021.03.030 PMID:33776195

Šniepienė, G., & Jankauskienė, R. (2021). Organic personal care cosmetics: Behavior of choice and consumption. *Proceedings of CBU in Medicine and Pharmacy, 2*, 158–168. doi:10.12955/pmp.v2.190

Tarkiainen, A., & Sundqvist, S. (2005). Subjective norms, attitudes and intentions of Finnish consumers in buying organic food. *British Food Journal, 107*(11), 808–822. doi:10.1108/00070700510629760

Treiblmaier, H., & Garaus, M. (2023). Using blockchain to signal quality in the food supply chain: The impact on consumer purchase intentions and the moderating effect of brand familiarity. *International Journal of Information Management, 68*, 102514. doi:10.1016/j.ijinfomgt.2022.102514

Tsakiridou, E., Boutsouki, C., Zotos, Y., & Mattas, K. (2008). Attitudes and behaviour towards organic products: An exploratory study. *International Journal of Retail & Distribution Management, 36*(2), 158–175. doi:10.1108/09590550810853093

Van Loo, E. J., Diem, M. N. H., Pieniak, Z., & Verbeke, W. (2013). Consumer attitudes, knowledge, and consumption of organic yogurt. *Journal of Dairy Science*, *96*(4), 2118–2129. doi:10.3168/jds.2012-6262 PMID:23415537

Varshneya, G., & Das, G. (2017). Experiential value: Multi-item scale development and validation. *Journal of Retailing and Consumer Services*, *34*, 48–57. doi:10.1016/j.jretconser.2016.09.010

Vega-Zamora, M., Torres-Ruiz, F. J., & Parras-Rosa, M. (2019). Towards sustainable consumption: Keys to communication for improving trust in organic foods. *Journal of Cleaner Production*, *216*, 511–519. doi:10.1016/j.jclepro.2018.12.129

Vega-Zamora, M., Torres-Ruiz, F. J., & Parras-Rosa, M. (2019). Towards sustainable consumption: Keys to communication for improving trust in organic foods. *Journal of Cleaner Production*, *216*, 511–519. doi:10.1016/j.jclepro.2018.12.129

Vergura, D. T., Zerbini, C., & Luceri, B. (2020). Consumers' attitude and purchase intention towards organic personal care products. An application of the SOR model. *Sinergie Italian Journal of Management*, *38*(1), 121–137.

Vittersø, G., & Tangeland, T. (2015). The role of consumers in transitions towards sustainable food consumption. The case of organic food in Norway. *Journal of Cleaner Production*, *92*, 91–99. doi:10.1016/j.jclepro.2014.12.055

von Meyer-Hofer, M., Nitzko, S., & Spiller, A. (2015). Is there an expectation gap? Consumers' expectations towards organic: An exploratory survey in mature and emerging European organic food markets. *British Food Journal*, *117*(5), 1527–1546. doi:10.1108/BFJ-07-2014-0252

Wier, M., Hansen, L. G., Andersen, L. M., & Millock, K. (2003). Consumer preferences for organic foods. *Organic agriculture: Sustainability, markets and policies*, 257-271.

Yadav, R., & Pathak, G. S. (2017). Determinants of consumers' green purchase behavior in a developing nation: Applying and extending the theory of planned behavior. *Ecological Economics*, *134*, 114–122. doi:10.1016/j.ecolecon.2016.12.019

Yeon Kim, H., & Chung, J. E. (2011). Consumer purchase intention for organic personal care products. *Journal of Consumer Marketing*, *28*(1), 40–47. doi:10.1108/07363761111101930

Yin, Y. H., Sun, N., North, T. H., & Hu, S. S. (2010). Hook formation and mechanical properties in AZ31 friction stir spot welds. *Journal of Materials Processing Technology*, *210*(14), 2062–2070. doi:10.1016/j.jmatprotec.2010.07.029

Chapter 17
The Impact of Firmographics on Philanthropic Engagement in the Global Wine Industry

Rosana Fuentes-Fernández
University of Leon, Spain

Armand Gilinsky
https://orcid.org/0000-0001-8650-9825
Sonoma State University, USA

Joshua Aboah
https://orcid.org/0000-0003-1000-2109
The Commonwealth Scientific and Industrial Research Organisation, Australia

Sharon Forbes
Abertay University, UK

Coralie Haller
EM Strasbourg Business School, University of Strasbourg, France

Marc Dressler
University of Ludwigshafen, Germany

ABSTRACT

The pursuit of community engagement and support is commonly considered to be essential to the achievement of corporate social responsibility goals, irrespective of a firm's age, size, legal formation, or industry sector. Less well understood are the firmographic characteristics that may influence these philanthropic pursuits, namely, firm formation, firm closure, firm growth or decline, and firm relocation. This investigation into philanthropic engagement seeks to understand the impact of firmographics across the global wine industry. Data were collected via survey from 302 firms in the Old and New World wine sectors: Spain, France, Germany, New Zealand, and the United States. Ordinal logistic and multiple linear regressions were applied. Findings reveal that the cultural heritage of a wine business, and, to a lesser extent, its form of ownership, appear to be the two major determinants of philanthropic engagement.

DOI: 10.4018/979-8-3693-2149-2.ch017

INTRODUCTION

Wine businesses provide jobs and economic benefits for their communities via multiplier effects. Although wine businesses tend to respond to community concerns, many stakeholders remain uncertain about the other community benefits that these businesses may generate (McCuan & Hertz, 2015). With regards to the topics of corporate social responsibility (CSR) and sustainability in the wine industry, most focus at both a practical and academic level has been on environmental performance. For example, a plethora of literature has focused on environmental sustainability from either the wine production or wine consumption perspectives (see for example, Baiano, 2021; Dodds et al., 2013; Flores, 2018; Marshall et al., 2010).

Less focus has been applied to the topic of philanthropy, which is a subset of CSR and is also a practice aligned with the social dimension of sustainability (Aaltonen et al., 2015). Philanthropy has been described as the voluntary contribution by a business of money, goods, time or expertise to the public good (Schuyt, Bekkers & Smit, 2010). The topic of philanthropy has been examined in earlier literature, including identification of the types of philanthropic activities that busiensses engage in (Carroll & Buchholtz, 2003; Lee et al., 2009), the motivations for philanthropy (Forbes, Fuentes Fernandez & Gilinsky, 2018; Lahdesmaki & Takala, 2012; Liket & Maas, 2016), the common beneficiaries of philanthropy (Godfrey, 2005; Seifert et al., 2004), and the business benefits gained through philanthropy (Becker-Olsen et al., 2006; Brammer & Millington, 2005). However, one criticism of the philanthropic literature is that it has predominantly focused on studies of large corporations in the US (Schaper & Savery, 2004). This focus on corporations is problematic, given the importance of SMEs in terms of national economies (Lukacs, 2005; Rekkas, 2021; Stankovic et al., 2018), as well as in terms of their prevalence in the wine industry (Mora & Akhter, 2012; Duarte-Alonso et al., 2014). Previous research has also mostly examined philanthropy in a single nation and studies at an industry sector level are scarce.

Firmographics are variables which describe a business, including size, age, location, and number of employees (Altman & Vidaver-Cohen, 2000). Prior research has identified links betwen engagement in philanthropy and various firmographic variables. For instance, national differences in philanthropic practices and performance have been identified (Gjolberg, 2009; Palazzo, 2002), and differences relating to the indsutry sector are also suggested (Brammer & Millington, 2006b). Whilst relationships between philanthropy and some firmographic variables have been identified in prior research, there have been few studies which have explored this at an industry level, or in the wine industry specifically.

With its focus on wine businesses across five nations, this chapter addresses some of the aforementioned gaps in the philanthropy literature; specifically, it explores philanthropy in variously sized businesses, from a single industry, across multiple nations. The purpose of this study is to examine the influence of firmographics on philanthropy engagement across businesses in the global wine industry. Quantitative data was collected from wine businesses in five nations (i.e. United States, France, Spain, Germany and New Zealand) using a structured questionnaire.

This investigation presents the initial survey of firmographic variables that influence altruism in the global wine industry, via analysis of responses from wine executives representing both the Old and New World wine sectors. The findings of this study underscore the importance of considering the geographical context of wine businesses when assessing their philanthropic engagement. Understanding the influence of location, whether in the Old or New World wine sectors, can help businesses tailor their philanthropic initiatives to better align with local needs and preferences. This study contributes valuable insights into the relationship between firmographics and philanthropic behavior within the global wine industry. By identifying the significant impact of geographical location on philanthropic engagement, wine businesses can enhance their strategic decision-making processes and strengthen their relationships with stakeholders.

The intent is to provide greater guidance to researchers and industry practitioners to assess the efficacy of current and planned philanthropic initiatives. Philanthropy provides wine business owners and managers not only with a means to improve their communities, but also ameliorate relationships with individual stakeholders that sustain wine operations in the face of numerous external opportunities and challenges.

LITERATURE REVIEW

Firmographics

Firmographics, in simple terms, are descriptive attributes of businesses, such as size, industry sector, location, and firm age. Van Wissen (2000) suggests that firmographics encompasses the following processes: firm formation, firm closure, firm growth or decline, and firm relocation. He considered firmographics to be like demography because firms experience processes similar to those faced by human beings: birth and death, as well as ageing. Thus, essentially, firmographics is to businesses what demographics are to people.

Various firmographic variables have been examined in previous studies, often as a way to segment businesses or predict behaviour. For instance, research has explored the role of firmographics on the adoption of reverse logistics strategies in the food retailing sector; the variables of interest were firm location, years in business, anual sales, number of employees, and type of retail format (Vijayan et al., 2014). In another study, Zhang, Priestley and Ni (2018) examined the role of firmographic variables, such as industry, location, size and structure, as bankruptcy predictors. A recent study assessed how the firmographics of SMEs would affect the consideration of ESG factors when deciding to invest; the firmographic variables of interest in this study included location, firm age, gender and minority leadership (Arrieta, 2023). Indeed, firmographic variables can suit strategic assessments of wineries, especially when exploring environmental adaptation or in the context of sustainability (Carrillo-Higueras et al., 2018; Jaworski & Lurie, 2020).

Philanthropy

An old adage states that the primary responsibility of a business is to generate profits, but a more modern approach sees companies simultaneously contributing to social and environmental progress (Zerbini 2017; Porter & Kramer, 2002; Clarkson 1995; Davis 1960; Donaldson & Preston, 1995). This peripheral responsibility of a business is what is termed as Corporate Social Responsibility (CSR). The EU Commission defines CSR as a voluntary integration of social and environmental concerns in a business' operations in consultation with stakeholders (Zollo, 2004; Morsing & Schultz, 2006). CSR helps firms to enhance their competitiveness, enhance their reputation, and legitimize the firm (Maignan & Raltson, 2002; Surroca et al., 2010; Hill & Jones, 1992; Jo & Harjoto, 2011; Jones 1980).

In his seminal article, Carroll (1979), proposed the *"Pyramid of Corporate Social Responsibility"*. The CSR pyramid is divided into four dimensions: the economic, legal, ethical, and discretionary expectations. The latter, discretionary expectations, includes the concept of philanthropy. Corporate philanthropy consists of voluntary actions taken by a business to benefit society. Indeed, Seifert et al. (2004: 198) describe corporate philanthropy as "the most discretionary form of corporate social responsibility". More recently, Block et al. (2017) defined corporate philanthropy as the charitable transfer of corporate resources to recipients at below market prices in the form of direct giving of financial assets as well as in-kind gifts of employee time, goods or services. Similarly, Ricks and Williams (2005) describe philanthropy as an action whereby a corporation voluntarily donates a portion of its resources to a social cause.

Prior research has identified both altruistic (Tsang et al., 2009) and strategic motives (Liket & Maas, 2016; Morris et al, 2013) which drive business philanthropy. Other authors suggest that a hybrid of both self-interests together with societal interests drive philanthropic behaviour in a business (Brammer & Millington, 2005; Lahdesmaki & Takala, 2012). At a strategic level, philanthropic activities may provide businesses with differentiation advantages over competitors, improved brand image or reputation, and better relationships with stakeholders; these benefits can have an ultimate effect on financial performance (Bae et al., 2018; Lähdesmäki & Takala, 2012; Moratis, 2018).

Whilst the topic of philanthropy has received significant attention in academic publications, philanthropy in the wine industry is not well researched. One exception is a qualitative study of a small number of wine businesses in New Zealand, USA and Spain; altruistic motives were found to be the dominant driver of philanthropic engagement (Forbes, Fernández, & Gilinsky, 2018).

The Influence of Firmographics on Philanthropy

A plethora of studies have reported that the firmographics of organizations determine a firm's decision to engage in philanthropy. Some of the firmographics which have been found to stimulate philanthropic donations include the management of the organization (Degasperi & Mainardes, 2017), the age of the organization (Okten & Weisbrod, 2000), the government aid support (Mainardes et al., 2016), and the geographic range (Van Leeuwen & Wiepking, 2013). However, literature about the influence of firmographics on philanthropic engagement in the wine industry is scant.

The study considers the influence of four firmographics on philanthropy engagement by wine businesses across five nations. The firmographic variables of interest in this study are: (1) ownership structure, (2) firm size, (3) firm age, and (4) firm location.

Charitable donations are sometimes related to a business owner's personal values (Lähdesmäki & Takala, 2012; Schaper & Savery, 2004). Many business owners choose a cause for philanthropic giving because of experiences that have touched their lives. Generally, it would be expected that the processes involved in deciding on philanthropic engagement would be shorter for firms operated under sole proprietorship, than for firm's which require agreement between numerous stakeholders. Therefore, it is hypothesized that;

H_1: The ownership structure of a wine business will significantly influence its philanthropic engagement.

The firm size has been reported to influence business philanthropy. Generally, Amato and Amato (2007) observed that large firms engage in charitable giving more than medium and small-sized firms. Previous studies have used the number of employees as a proxy for categorising the size of a firm; this study also uses the number of employees as a measure of firm size. The second hypothesis *(H_2)* thus explores the influence that firm size has on a wine business's decision to engage in philanthropy.

H_2: The size of a wine business will significantly influence its philanthropic engagement.

Firm age is another important firmographic and has been examined in previous studies of philanthropy. For example, Amato and Amato (2012) found that business cycle had no effect on philanthropy in the retailer industry; this suggests that philanthropy engagement is not affected by whether a business is at a start-up or maturity stage in the business cycle. Similarly, Cha and Abebe (2016) also reported that firm age was not a predictor of corporate philanthropy. In contrast, a more recent study reported that older firms restricted the relationship between a CEO's characteristics and corporate philanthropy (Cha & Rew, 2021). The third hypothesis will thus explore the relationship between firm age and philanthropy:

H_3: The age of a wine business will significantly influence its philanthropic engagement.

Wine businesses located in the Old World rely on the historical origin of the grape as a competitive advantage, while those in the New World depend on their responsiveness to changing markets as a competitive advantage (Remaud & Couderc, 2006). Differences between wine businesses in Old World and New World nations are not just limited to marketing strategies, but encompass many aspects relating to grape growing and winemaking. Previous research has reported that the philanthropy practices implemented by wine business are different among Old World and New World countries (Fernández & Aboah, 2020). Therefore, it is hypothesized that;

H_4: The location of a wine business will significantly influence its philanthropic engagement.

METHODOLOGY

Data Collection

Data were collected from 302 wine firms across five countries – Spain, the US, New Zealand, France, and Germany via a survey using a structured questionnaire. The questionnaire was developed following a review of the literature and a qualitative phase in which a small number of wineries in New Zealand, the US and Spain were interviewed. The final questionnaire included seventeen multiple choice questions and one open-ended question. The four firmographics of interest were measured as follows:

(1) ownership structure – measured using listed categories (*OWN*)
(2) firm size – measured the number of full-time employees as a proxy (*FTE*)
(3) firm age – measured the number of years in operation (*YrsOp*)
(4) firm location – measured using Old World or New World as a proxy (*ECH*)

Each author was responsable for distributing the online questionnaire to wine businesses in his/her own nation, through the use of either Survey Monkey or Qualtrics. Authors were also responsible for sending follow-up messages to the surveyed wine businesses to encourage their participation in the research. The response rate varied across nations and was between 2-7% of total wine businesses.

The Sample

The surveyed businesses included both wineries and vineyards, and respondents were typically either an owner or a senior manager within the businesses. Over two-thirds (69%) of the wineries could be classified as small producers, with an annual production of under 180,000 litres.

For all the wine businesses that participated in the survey, the mean number of full-time employees is 29 and the mean years of operation for the wine firms is 37.8 years. The descriptive statistics on the ownership structure of participating wine businesses indicate that 47.5% are privately held companies, 20% are sole proprietors, 16.5% are partnerships, 5.9% are trusts, 5.6% are others (i.e. universities and research institutions), 3.3% are cooperatives, and 0.7% publicly listed company.

Data Analysis

Ordinal logistic and and multiple linear regression models were used to examine the effect of the various firmographics on wine business's philanthropic engagement. The regression model was expressed as in equation 1, where the dependent variable (y) represents each philanthropic issue under investigation.

$$y = \beta_0 + \beta_1 NatBus + \beta_2 FTE + \beta_3 OWN + \beta_4 YrsOp + \beta_5 ECH \quad (1)$$

The Ordinary Least Square (OLS) estimation was used for predicting the probability of a dependent variable occurring (P(y)) given the values of the firmographics in the multiple linear regression model. For the ordinal logistic regression models, the probability of predicting a dependent variable was estimated using the maximum likelihood estimation, expressed as:

$$P(y) = \frac{1}{1 + e^{-(\beta_0 + \beta_1 X_1 + \beta_{2X_2} + \ldots + \beta_n X_n}} \quad (2)$$

Where $e^{-(\beta 0 + \beta 1\, X1 + \beta 2\, X2 + \beta n\, xn)}$ is the natural log of the linear combination of predictors in the model and their respective coefficients, which are estimated using the maximum likelihood. The measurement of the independent variables is shown in Table 1, and the specifications of the type of regression model applied to each philanthropic issue are presented in Table 2.

Collinearity diagnostic tests were run to determine whether the multiple linear regression models suffer from multicollinearity. The average variance inflation factor (VIF) for the model (with strategic and altruistic motives as outcome variables) was 1.13 and 1.12 for the model with corporate and humanitarian benefits as outcome variables. These average VIF are closer to 1; hence, it is concluded that collinearity does not exist in the data. This conclusion is affirmed by the tolerance statistic, which is above 0.2 for all the models. Also, the assumption of proportional odd was tested for three philanthropic issues whose parameter estimations required the use of ordinal logistic regression model. Results of the test of parallel lines indicate that the chi-square tests are not statistically significant for the three philanthropic issues. Hence, the null hypothesis that the models' slope coefficients are equal for all response categories is not rejected, and that the assumption of proportional odds holds.

Table 1. Measurement of predictors in the model

Independent Variables	*Measure*
Nature of business activity	0 = Others 1 = Grape grower 2 = Winery 3 = Virtual winery 4 = Negociant 5 = Grape grower & wine producer 6 = Negociant & wine producer 7 = Fully integrated winery 8 = Cooperative 9 = Trade association
No. of Fulltime employees	Number of people
Type of firm ownership	0 = others 1 = Sole proprietor 2 = Partnership 3 = Privately held company 4 = Cooperative 5 = Trust 6 = Publicly listed company
No. of years in operation	Years
Enterprise cultural heritage (ECH)	1 =New wine world 2 = Old wine world

Table 2. Empirical models used for the respective philanthropic issues

<table>
<tr><th>Dependent Variables</th><th>Measure</th><th>Empirical model</th></tr>
<tr><td>Strategic motives</td><td rowspan="4">An index ranging from -3 to 3;
with -3 representing the least tendency/ inclination towards the philanthropic issue, and 3 represent the highest tendency/inclination .</td><td rowspan="4">Multiple linear regression</td></tr>
<tr><td>Altruistic motives</td></tr>
<tr><td>Corporate benefit</td></tr>
<tr><td>Humanitarian benefit</td></tr>
<tr><td>Mode of philanthropy engagement (planned philanthropy)</td><td>Likert scale from 1 to 5 representing least and highest tendencies respectively</td><td rowspan="2">Ordinal logistic regression</td></tr>
<tr><td>Perceived effectiveness of philanthropic practices</td><td>1= Most effective
2 = More effective
3 = Effective
4= Least effective</td></tr>
<tr><td>Level of philanthropic activity</td><td>1= Increasing each year
2 = Staying the same
3 = Decreasing each year
4 = None at all</td><td></td></tr>
</table>

RESULTS AND DISCUSSION

Results of the estimated regression models are presented and discussed in this section. First, the results on wine firm's motives for engaging in philanthropy are presented and discussed, followed by perceived benefits of philanthropy, the mode of philanthropy engagement, perceived effectiveness of philanthropy, and finally, the future level of philanthropic engagement.

Motive for Philanthropic Engagement

Results on the influence of firmographics on the tendency for wine firms to engage in philanthropy with a strategic and altruistic motive are shown in Table 3.

Results on the model parameters show that the number of full-time employees *(FTE)* and type of business ownership *(OWN)* are the firmographics that have statistically significant effects on a wine firm's tendency to engage in philanthropy with a strategic motive. The enterprise cultural heritage (ECH) and type of business ownership *(OWN)* have a statistically significant influence on the tendency for wine firms to engage in philanthropy with an altruistic motive.

Ceteris paribus, the tendency for a wine firm to engage in *strategic* philanthropy decreases by 0.14 when the firms are not operating as a sole proprietorship. Wine firms operating as partnerships have a lower tendency to engage in philanthropy with a strategic motive than those operating as a sole proprietorship, and a relatively higher tendency than those operating privately held wine companies.

Ceteris paribus, the tendency for a wine firm to engage in *altruistic* philanthropy increases by 0.108 when wine firms are not operating as sole proprietorships. Wine firms operating as a partnership have a higher tendency to engage in philanthropy with altruistic motives than those run by a sole proprietor. Publicly listed wine companies have the highest tendency to engage in philanthropy with an altruistic motive. The statistically significant results uphold the null hypothesis that the ownership structure of the wine firm influences the firm's philanthropic engagement. The findings corroborate those of Forbes et al. (2018), which indicated that wine firms predominantly engage in philanthropy for altruistic reasons.

Results indicate that compared with wine firms in the new wine world, wine firms in the old wine world have a lower tendency to engage in philanthropy with an altruistic motive. The findings affirm the asserted possible difference in philanthropic practice between the two wine worlds (Fernández &

Table 3. Coefficients: Motives for philanthropic engagement

	Coefficients [a]					*Coefficients* [b]				
Model	**Unstandardized Coefficients**		**Standardized Coefficients**	**t**	**Sig.**	**Unstandardized Coefficients**		**Standardized Coefficients**	**t**	**Sig.**
	B	**Std. Error**	**Beta**			**B**	**Std. Error**	**Beta**		
Constant	-.220	.277		-.797	.426	1.287	.228		5.645	.000
ECH	.236	.132	.116	1.790	.075	-1.181	.109	-.581	-10.855	**.000****
NatBus	.043	.025	.103	1.699	.090	.011	.021	.026	.523	.601
YrsOp	-.001	.001	-.072	-1.112	.267	.001	.001	.049	.913	.361
FTE	.001	.000	.156	2.644	**.009***	.001	.000	.071	1.454	.147
OWN	-.136	.051	-.162	-2.657	**.008***	.108	.042	.129	2.572	**.011***
a. Dependent Variable: Strategic motive *** Significant @ 1%* ** Significant @ 5%*										
b. Dependent Variable: Altruistic motive										

Table 4. Coefficients: Benefit for philanthropic engagement

Model	*Coefficients [a]*					*Coefficients [b]*				
	Unstandardized Coefficients		**Standardized Coefficients**	**t**	**Sig.**	**Unstandardized Coefficients**		**Standardized Coefficients**	**t**	**Sig.**
	B	**Std. Error**	**Beta**			**B**	**Std. Error**	**Beta**		
Constant	.061	.279		.218	.828	.937	.265		3.532	.000
ECH	-.146	.133	-.072	-1.099	.273	-.715	.127	-.352	-.5652	**.000[**]**
NatBus	.003	.026	.007	.117	.907	.008	.025	.019	.321	.749
YrsOp	-.002	.001	-.078	-1.184	.237	.000	.001	.014	.233	.816
FTE	.001	.000	.100	1.668	.096	.000	.000	.027	.481	.631
OWN	.066	.052	.079	1.278	.202	.005	.049	.006	.098	.922

[a] *Dependent Variable: People benefit*
[**] *significant @ 1%*
[*] *significant @ 5%*

[b] *Dependent Variable: Corporate benefit*

Aboah, 2020), and the hypothesis that the enterprise cultural heritage influences a wine firm's motive for philanthropic engagement. Ultimately, the findings affirm the assertion that firms can engage in philanthropy with a dual motive of helping society and gaining opportunities from their engagement (Gilinsky Jr, Forbes, & Fuentes-Fernández, 2018).

Perceived Benefits of Philanthropy

Results indicate that only the enterprise cultural heritage explains the variations in the perceived benefit for a wine firm to engage in philanthropy. The remaining firmographics do not have a statistically significant effect on a wine firm's perceived benefit for engaging in philanthropy. Wine firms in the new wine world perceive to gain both corporate benefit and humanitarian benefits for engaging in philanthropy than those in the old wine world. Indeed, the results resonate with the assertion made by Zollo (2004) that firms engaging in corporate philanthropy expect to gain revenue growth opportunities. The coefficient table presented in Table 4 provides detailed results on the effect of firmographics on perceived benefits of philanthropy in the wine industry.

Mode of Philanthropy Engagement

Responses to the question on the engagement of planned philanthropy were used to represent the mode of philanthropy engagement. Responses that demonstrate low tendencies to engage in planned philanthropy were regarded as ad hoc (unplanned) philanthropic engagement. The Nagelkerke R -square showedthat the model explains 17% of the variations in the planned engagement of philanthropy. Although statistically significant, the low Nagelkerke R – square suggests the possibility of other relevant predictors which are not captured in the model.

Results of the parameter estimates (in Table 5) show that out of the five firmographics, the enterprise cultural heritage *(ECH)* and the nature of business *(NatBus)* have a statistically significant influence on

Table 5. Parameter estimates: Mode of philanthropy engagement

		Estimate	Std. Error	Wald	df	Sig.	95% Confidence Interval	
							Lower Bound	Upper Bound
Threshold	Plan philanthropy = 0	-5.383	1.94	7.646	1	.006	-9.199	-1.568
	Plan philanthropy = 1	-3.052	1.90	2.577	1	.108	-6.778	.674
	Plan philanthropy= 2	-1.509	1.89	.633	1	.426	-5.226	2.209
	Plan philanthropy = 3	-.247	1.89	.017	1	.896	-3.961	3.466
	Plan philanthropy = 4	1.097	1.89	.335	1	.563	-2.617	4.811
Location	YrsOp	.001	.002	.137	1	.711	-.004	.006
	FTE	.002	.001	3.538	1	.060	-7.3E-005	.004
	ECH=1	1.206	.286	17.80	1	**.000****	.646	1.766
	ECH=2	0[a]	.	.	0	.	.	.
	NatBus=0	1.024	.76	1.797	1	.180	-.473	2.522
	NatBus=1	-.465	.69	.456	1	.499	-1.812	.883
	NatBus=2	-1.917	.61	9.813	1	**.002***	-3.117	-.718
	NatBus=3	-.727	.74	.959	1	.328	-2.182	.728
	NatBus=4	-1.305	1.02	1.628	1	.202	-3.310	.700
	NatBus=5	-1.274	.54	5.553	1	**.018***	-2.334	-.214
	NatBus=6	-2.467	1.22	4.109	1	**.043***	-4.852	-.082
	NatBus=7	-1.024	.54	3.647	1	.056	-2.076	.027
	NatBus=8	-.276	.92	.090	1	.765	-2.079	1.528
	NatBus=9	0[a]	.	.	0	.	.	.
	OWN=0	-1.573	1.90	.683	1	.408	-5.301	2.156
	OWN=1	-.246	1.83	.018	1	.893	-3.840	3.347
	OWN=2	-1.024	1.84	.311	1	.577	-4.620	2.572
	OWN=3	-.974	1.82	.285	1	.593	-4.548	2.600
	OWN=4	-1.712	2.02	.720	1	.396	-5.667	2.243
	OWN=5	-.286	1.88	.023	1	.879	-3.975	3.402
	OWN=6	0[a]	.	.	0	.	.	.

Link function: Logit.
*** significant @ 1%*
** significant @ 5%*

[a] *This parameter is set to zero because it is redundant.*

a wine firm's decision to engage in planned philanthropy. *Ceteris paribus*, the tendency for a wine firm located in the old wine world to engage in planned philanthropy increases by 1.2 more than those located in the new wine world. Results also show that compared to wine firms operating as trade associations, those that operate as a winery have 1.9 decreases in their tendency to engage in planned philanthropy while holding other variables constant. Trade associations are bigger than individual wineries. Therefore, the results appear to be consistent with those of Gilinsky, Forbes, and Fuentes-Fernández (2018), namely that smaller wine firms are less likely to plan their philanthropic engagement.

Wine firms operating as grape growers and wine producers have a decreased tendency to engage in planned philanthropy by 1.3 than those operating as a trade association. Similarly, wine firms operating as négociant and wine producers have a decreased tendency to engage in planned philanthropy by 2.5. The findings suggest that wine firms operating as trade associations have a higher tendency to engage in planned philanthropy than those operating as a winery, négociant and wine producers, and grape growers and wine producers. Hence, the null hypothesis that the nature of business influences a wine firm's philanthropic engagement is not rejected.

Perceived Effectiveness of Wine Donation

Based on the data analysis and summary of the characteristics of the wine firms surveyed in the six countries, the act of donating wine was the most commonly observed form of philanthropy among these firms. In other words, of all the philanthropic activities undertaken by the wine firms included in the study, donating wine emerged as the most prevalent practice across the six countries under investigation.

Results of the parameter estimates are presented in Table 6. The years of operation *(YrsOp),* the enterprise cultural heritage *(ECH),* and the nature of business *(NatBus)* have a statistically significant influence on a wine firm's perceived effectiveness of wine donation. The ordered log odds of perceiving wine donation as an effective philanthropic gesture increase by 1.67 for wine firms located in the new wine world than those located in the old wine world. The findings imply that wine firms in the new wine world tend to consider wine donation as more effective than those in the old wine world.

Results also show that compared to wine firms operating as trade associations, those that operate as both grape growers and wine producers have a 1.4 increase in their perceived effectiveness of wine donation as a philanthropic practice, while holding other variables constant.

Future Philanthropic Activity Levels

Results of the parameter estimates in Table 7 show that out of the five firmographics, only the type of business ownership (OWN) has a statistically significant influence on a wine firm's projected philanthropic activity. The ordered log odds of the future philanthropic activities increase by 18.4, 17.7, 17.7, 18.1, 16.9, and 19 for wine firms that are sole proprietors, partnerships, privately held companies, cooperatives, and trusts respectively than wine firms that are publicly listed companies while holding other variables constant.

The findings imply that wine firms operating as publicly listed companies have the highest tendency of increasing the levels of philanthropic activities in the future. Those operating under sole proprietorship have the second-highest tendency to increase their philanthropic activities in the future. Certainly, the future demand for philanthropic activities will stimulate philanthropic engagement for wine firms that do not strategically plan (Gilinsky Jr, Forbes & Fuentes-Fernández, 2018).

The summary of the discussed results is presented in Table 8.

Table 6. Parameter estimates: Effectiveness of wine donation

		Estimate	Std. Error	Wald	df	Sig.	95% Confidence Interval	
							Lower Bound	Upper Bound
Threshold	Effective Wine Donation = 1	-3.261	1.94	2.836	1	.092	-7.056	.534
	Effective Wine Donation = 2	-2.468	1.93	1.631	1	.202	-6.257	1.320
	Effective Wine Donation = 3	-1.835	1.93	.903	1	.342	-5.619	1.949
Location	YrsOp	-.007	.003	8.387	1	**.004***	-.012	-.002
	FTE	-.002	.002	1.286	1	.257	-.005	.001
	ECH=1	-1.617	.295	30.15	1	**.000****	-2.19	-1.040
	ECH=2	0[a]	.	.	0	.	.	.
	NatBus=0	-.480	.84	.328	1	.567	-2.12	1.163
	NatBus=1	-.312	.75	.174	1	.676	-1.78	1.152
	NatBus=2	-1.255	.67	3.518	1	.061	-2.57	.056
	NatBus=3	-.563	.79	.503	1	.478	-2.12	.992
	NatBus=4	-1.828	1.03	3.177	1	.075	-3.84	.182
	NatBus=5	-1.446	.603	5.752	1	**.016***	-2.63	-.264
	NatBus=6	-1.448	1.11	1.705	1	.192	-3.62	.725
	NatBus=7	-.812	.596	1.852	1	.174	-1.98	.357
	NatBus=8	.475	1.131	.177	1	.674	-1.74	2.692
	NatBus=9	0[a]	.	.	0	.	.	.
	OWN=0	-1.529	1.915	.637	1	.425	-5.28	2.225
	OWN=1	-.768	1.849	.173	1	.678	-4.39	2.855
	OWN=2	-.851	1.851	.211	1	.646	-4.48	2.776
	OWN=3	-.374	1.837	.041	1	.839	-3.97	3.226
	OWN=4	-2.280	2.098	1.182	1	.277	-6.39	1.831
	OWN=5	.675	1.909	.125	1	.724	-3.07	4.416
	OWN=6	0[a]	.	.	0	.	.	.

Link function: Logit.
*** significant @ 1%*
** significant @ 5%*

[a] *This parameter is set to zero because it is redundant.*

CONCLUSION AND SUGGESTIONS FOR FUTURE RESEARCH

This chapter purposely explored the influence that five firmographics have on the philanthropic behaviour of wine firms. Generally, although the models involving only the five firmographics are statistically significant, the low Nagelkerke R – square suggests that relevant predictors have been omitted in the

Table 7. Parameter estimates: Level of philanthropic activity

		Estimate	Std. Error	Wald	df	Sig.	95% Confidence Interval	
							Lower Bound	Upper Bound
Threshold	Level Phil Act = 0	-22.59	.965	547.92	1	.000	-24.48	-20.700
	Level Phil Act = 1	-21.73	.886	601.34	1	.000	-23.47	-19.995
	Level Phil Act = 2	-17.29	.853	411.52	1	.000	-18.97	-15.624
Location	YrsOp	-.003	.003	1.060	1	.303	-.010	.003
	FTE	-.001	.001	1.257	1	.262	-.003	.001
	ECH=1	.381	.331	1.321	1	.250	-.269	1.030
	ECH=2	0[a]	.	.	0	.	.	.
	NatBus=0	-.353	.937	.142	1	.706	-2.190	1.484
	NatBus=1	-.569	.849	.449	1	.503	-2.232	1.095
	NatBus=2	-.383	.718	.284	1	.594	-1.791	1.026
	NatBus=3	-.749	.885	.716	1	.397	-2.485	.986
	NatBus=4	-.364	1.227	.088	1	.767	-2.768	2.040
	NatBus=5	-.151	.634	.057	1	.812	-1.393	1.091
	NatBus=6	-.317	1.555	.041	1	.839	-3.365	2.732
	NatBus=7	-.077	.628	.015	1	.902	-1.308	1.153
	NatBus=8	-.111	1.202	.009	1	.926	-2.466	2.244
	NatuBus=9	0[a]	.	.	0	.	.	.
	OWN=0	-18.43	.938	386.12	1	.000**	-20.264	-16.588
	OWN=1	-17.74	.711	622.08	1	.000**	-19.135	-16.347
	OWN=2	-17.73	.712	620.26	1	.000**	-19.122	-16.332
	OWN=3	-18.11	.664	743.31	1	.000**	-19.413	-16.809
	OWN=4	-16.85	1.256	180.14	1	.000**	-19.312	-14.390
	OWN=5	-19.03	.000	.	1	.	-19.029	-19.029
	OWN=6	0[a]	.	.	0	.	.	.

Link function: Logit.

a. This parameter is set to zero because it is redundant.

Table 8. Summary results

Hypotheses	Findings
H_1: The ownership structure of a wine business will significantly influence its philanthropic engagement.	The ownership structure significantly influences the motives for philanthropic engagement.
H_2: The size of a wine business will significantly influence its philanthropic engagement.	The size of the wine business significantly influences the motives for philanthropic engagement.
H_3: The age of a wine business will significantly influence its philanthropic engagement.	The age of the wine business significantly influences the perceived effectiveness of wine donation as a philanthropic gesture.
H_4: The location of a wine business will significantly influence its philanthropic engagement.	The location of wince business significantly influences the perceived benefit of philanthropy, the mode of philanthropy engagement, and the perceived effectiveness of wine donation as a philanthropic gesture.

model. These predictors could be the demography of the wine firms. However, on average, only two of the firmographics explained the variations in five philanthropic activities.

Why do wine firms engage in philanthropy? In this study, the findings align with some previous research while also introducing nuances and areas for further investigation. The authors acknowledge the existing literature that suggests firms engage in philanthropy for various reasons, including strategic motives, altruism, and responding to public visibility (Campbell & Slack, 2006; Brammer, Millington & Pavelin, 2006b).

Moreover, the study identifies firmographics such as the number of full-time employees, ownership type, years of operation, cultural heritage, and nature of business as factors influencing philanthropic behavior among wine firms. While some of these factors have been explored in prior research, the specific context of wine firms adds a novel dimension to understanding corporate philanthropy

Furthermore, the authors note variations in philanthropic behavior between Old and New World sectors within the wine industry, indicating a need for further exploration into regional differences and the underlying rationales driving company altruism. This aspect introduces a fresh perspective that enriches the existing discourse on corporate social responsibility within the wine industry (Arco et al., 2020; Porter & Kramer, 2002).

Overall, while the study's findings support the broader understanding of corporate philanthropy and its motivations, they also contribute new insights specific to the wine industry. By identifying firmographics and regional differences, the study sets the stage for future research to delve deeper into the dynamics of philanthropic behavior within this sector and its implications for consumer preferences and societal impact (Cranenburgh & Arenas, 2014; Dennis, Buchholtz & Butts, 2009; Sánchez, 2000; Berman et al., 1999).

REFERENCES

Aaltonen, S., Heinze, A., Ielpa, G., & De Tommaso, D. (2015). Enterprise Cultural Heritage: The Source for Sustainable Competitive Advantage and Survival for Food Sector SMEs. *International Journal of Entrepreneurship and Innovation, 16*(2), 73–83. doi:10.5367/ijei.2015.0178

Altman, B. W., & Vidaver-Cohen, D. (2000). A framework for understanding corporate citizenship. *Business and Society Review, 105*(1), 1–7. doi:10.1111/0045-3609.00061

Amato, L., & Amato, C. (2007). The Effects of Firm Size and Industry on Corporate Giving. *Journal of Business Ethics, 72*(3), 229–241. doi:10.1007/s10551-006-9167-5

Amato, L., & Amato, C. H. (2012). Retail philanthropy: Firm size, industry, and business cycle. *Journal of Business Ethics, 107*(4), 435–448. doi:10.1007/s10551-011-1048-x

Arco, C. L., López, P. M. V., Pérez, L. M. C., & Rodríguez, A. L. (2020). How market value relates to corporate philanthropy and its assurance. The moderating effect of the business sector. *Business Ethics (Oxford, England), 29*(2), 266–281. doi:10.1111/beer.12264

Arrieta Paredes, M. P. (2023). ESG investing, reputation and government policies in British SMEs: why does firmographics matter? Bae, S., Masud, M., Kim, J. (2018). A cross-country investigation of corporate governance and corporate sustainability disclosure: A signalling theory perspective. *Sustainability*, *10*(8), 2611–2621.

Baiano, A. (2021). An overview on sustainability in the wine production chain. *Beverages*, *7*(1), 15. doi:10.3390/beverages7010015

Becker-Olsen, K. L., Cudmore, B. A., & Hill, R. P. (2006). The impact of perceived corporate social responsibility on consumer behaviour. *Journal of Business Research*, *59*(1), 46–53. doi:10.1016/j.jbusres.2005.01.001

Berman, S. L., Wicks, A. C., Kotha, S., & Jones, T. M. (1999). Does stakeholder orientation matter? The relationship between stakeholder management models and firm financial performance. *Academy of Management Journal*, *42*(5), 488–506. doi:10.2307/256972

Block, E. S., Glavas, A., Mannor, M. J., & Erskine, L. (2017). Business for good? An investigation into the strategy's firms use to maximize the impact of financial corporate philanthropy on employee attitudes. *Journal of Business Ethics*, *146*(1), 167–183. doi:10.1007/s10551-015-2930-8

Brammer, S., & Millington, A. (2005). Corporate Reputation and Philanthropy: An Empirical Analysis. *Journal of Business Ethics*, *61*(1), 29–44. doi:10.1007/s10551-005-7443-4

Brammer, S., & Millington, A. (2006b). Firm size, organizational visibility and corporate philanthropy: An empirical analysis. *Business Ethics (Oxford, England)*, *15*(1), 6–18. doi:10.1111/j.1467-8608.2006.00424.x

Brammer, S., Millington, A., & Pavelin, S. (2006a). Is philanthropy strategic? An analysis of the management of charitable giving in large UK companies. *Business Ethics (Oxford, England)*, *15*(3), 234–245. doi:10.1111/j.1467-8608.2006.00446.x

Campbell, D., & Slack, R. (2006). Public visibility as a determinant of the rate of corporate charitable donations. *Business Ethics (Oxford, England)*, *15*(1), 19–28. doi:10.1111/j.1467-8608.2006.00425.x

Carrillo-Higueras, F., Prajogo, D., & Smith, L. (2018). Environmental commitment and its drivers in the Australian wine industry: A behavioural approach. *Australasian Journal of Environmental Management*, *25*(4), 439–458. doi:10.1080/14486563.2018.1460630

Carroll, A. (1979). A Three Dimensional Conceptual Model of Corporate Performance. *Academy of Management Review*, *4*(4), 497–505. doi:10.2307/257850

Carroll, A. (2016). Carroll's Pyramid of CSR: Taking Another Look. International. *Journal of Corporate Social Responsibility*, *1*(1), 3. doi:10.1186/s40991-016-0004-6

Carroll, A., & Buchholtz, A. L. (2003). *Business and Society: Ethics, Sustainability and Stakeholder Management* (5th ed.). Thomson/South Western.

Cha, W., & Abebe, M. A. (2016). Board of directors and industry determinants of corporate philanthropy. *Leadership and Organization Development Journal*, *37*(5), 672–688. doi:10.1108/LODJ-09-2014-0189

Cha, W., & Rew, D. (2021). Cannot give you because of living on the top of a castle: CEOs, corporate philanthropy and firm age. *Society and Business Review*, *16*(3), 336–356. doi:10.1108/SBR-05-2020-0074

Clarkson, M. E. (1995). A stakeholder framework for analyzing and evaluating corporate social performance. *Academy of Management Review*, *20*(1), 92–117. doi:10.2307/258888

Cranenburgh, K. C. V., & Arenas, D. (2014). Strategic and Moral Dilemmas of Corporate Philanthropy in Developing Countries: Heineken in Sub-Saharan Africa. *Journal of Business Ethics*, *122*(3), 523–536. doi:10.1007/s10551-013-1776-1

Davis, K. (1960). Can business afford to ignore social responsibilities? *California Management Review*, *2*(3), 70–76. doi:10.2307/41166246

Degasperi, N. C., & Mainardes, E. W. (2017). What motivates money donation? A study on external motivators. *Revista de Administração (São Paulo)*, *52*(4), 363–373. doi:10.1016/j.rausp.2017.08.002

Dennis, B. S., Buchholtz, A. K., & Butts, M. M. (2009). The Nature of Giving: A Theory of Planned Behavior Examination of Corporate Philanthropy. *Business & Society*, *48*(3), 360–384. doi:10.1177/0007650307305368

Dodds, R., Graci, S., Ko, S., & Walker, L. (2013). What drives environmental sustainability in the New Zealand wine industry? An examination of driving factors and practices. *International Journal of Wine Business Research*, *25*(3), 164–184. doi:10.1108/IJWBR-2012-0015

Donaldson, T., & Preston, L. E. (1995). The stakeholder theory of the corporation: Concepts, evidence, and implications. *Academy of Management Review*, *20*(1), 65–91. doi:10.2307/258887

Duarte Alonso, A., Bressan, A., O'Shea, M., & Krajsic, V. (2014). Exporting wine in complex times: A study among small and medium wineries. *Journal of Small Business and Enterprise Development*, *21*(2), 345–364. doi:10.1108/JSBED-01-2014-0006

Flores, S. S. (2018). What is sustainability in the wine world? A cross-country analysis of wine sustainability frameworks. *Journal of Cleaner Production*, *172*, 2301–2312. doi:10.1016/j.jclepro.2017.11.181

Forbes, S. L., Fuentes-Fernández, R., & Gilinsky, A. (2018). An exploratory examination of philanthropy in the New Zealand, Spanish and US wine industries. *Wine Economics and Policy*, *7*(1), 35–44. doi:10.1016/j.wep.2018.01.002

Friedman, A. L., & Miles, S. (2006). *Stakeholders: Theory and Practice*. Oxford University Press. doi:10.1093/oso/9780199269860.001.0001

Frooman, J. (1999). Stakeholder influence strategies. *Academy of Management Review*, *24*(2), 191–205. doi:10.2307/259074

Fuentes-Fernández, R., & Aboah, J. (2020). Philanthropic Wine Firms and Their CSR Communication. In *Social Sustainability in the Global Wine Industry* (pp. 185–200). Springer. doi:10.1007/978-3-030-30413-3_13

Gilinsky, A. Jr, Forbes, S. L., & Fuentes-Fernández, R. (2018). An exploratory study of wine business philanthropy in the USA. *International Journal of Wine Business Research*, *30*(2), 201–217. doi:10.1108/IJWBR-01-2017-0006

Gjolberg, M. (2009). Measuring the immeasurable? Constructing an index of CSR practices and CSR performance in 20 countries. *Scandinavian Journal of Management*, *25*, 10–22.

Godfrey, P. C. (2005). The relationship between corporate philanthropy and shareholder wealth: A risk management perspective. *Academy of Management Review*, *30*(4), 777–798. doi:10.5465/amr.2005.18378878

Hill, C. W. L., & Jones, T. M. (1992). Stakeholder-agency theory. *Journal of Management Studies*, *29*(2), 131–154. doi:10.1111/j.1467-6486.1992.tb00657.x

Jaworski, B. J., & Lurie, R. S. (2020). *Second Principle: Use Propensity-Based Segmentation. The Organic Growth Playbook: Activate High-Yield Behaviors to Achieve Extraordinary Results*. Emerald. doi:10.1108/978-1-83982-684-920201006

Jensen, M. C. (2002). Value Maximization, Stakeholder Theory, and the Corporate Objective Function. *Business Ethics Quarterly*, *12*(2), 235–256. doi:10.2307/3857812

Jo, H., & Harjoto, M. A. (2011). Corporate governance and firm value: The impact of corporate social responsibility. *Journal of Business Ethics*, *103*(3), 351–383. doi:10.1007/s10551-011-0869-y

Jones, T. M. (1980). Corporate social responsibility revisited, redefined. *California Management Review*, *22*(3), 59–67. doi:10.2307/41164877

Lähdesmäki, M., & Takala, T. (2012). Altruism in business: An empirical study of philanthropy in the small business context. *Social Responsibility Journal*, *8*(3), 373–388. doi:10.1108/17471111211247947

Lee, J., Park, T., Moon, H. K., Yang, Y., & Kim, C. (2009). Corporate philanthropy, attitude towards corporations, and purchase intentions: A South Korea study. *Journal of Business Research*, *62*(10), 939–946. doi:10.1016/j.jbusres.2008.08.007

Liket, K., & Maas, K. (2016). Strategic philanthropy: Corporate measurement of philanthropic impacts as a requirement for a "happy marriage" of business and society. *Business & Society*, *55*(6), 889–921. doi:10.1177/0007650314565356

Maignan, I., & Ralston, D. A. (2002). Corporate social responsibility in Europe and the US: Insights from businesses' self-presentations. *Journal of International Business Studies*, *33*(3), 497–514. doi:10.1057/palgrave.jibs.8491028

Mainardes, E. W., Laurett, R., Degasperi, N. C. P., & Lasso, S. V. (2016). What motivates an individual to make donations of money and/or goods? *International Review on Public and Nonprofit Marketing*, *13*(1), 81–99. doi:10.1007/s12208-015-0145-4

Marshall, R. S., Akoorie, M. E. M., Hamann, R., & Sinha, P. (2010). Environmental practices in the wine industry: An empirical application of the theory of reasoned action and stakeholder theory in the United States and New Zealand. *Journal of World Business*, *45*(4), 405–414. doi:10.1016/j.jwb.2009.08.009

McCuan, D., & Hertz, R. (2015). *Preliminary Report Survey on Community Perceptions of Wine Businesses.* Sonoma State University Wine Business Institute.

Mora, P., & Manzoom, A. (2012). Why and how some wine SMEs resist to the crisis? *International Journal of Business and Globalisation, 8*(1), 95–111. doi:10.1504/IJBG.2012.043974

Moratis, L. (2018). Signaling responsibility? Applying signaling theory to the ISO 26000 standard for social responsibility. *Sustainability (Basel), 10*(11), 1–20. doi:10.3390/su10114172

Morris, S., Bartkus, B., Glassman, M., & Rhiel, G. (2013). Philanthropy and Corporate Reputation: An Empirical Investigation. *Corporate Reputation Review, 16*(4), 285–299. doi:10.1057/crr.2013.16

Morsing, M., & Schultz, M. (2006). Corporate social responsibility communication: Stakeholder information, response and involvement strategies. *Business Ethics (Oxford, England), 15*(4), 323–338. doi:10.1111/j.1467-8608.2006.00460.x

Okten, C., & Weisbrod, B. A. (2000). Determinants of donations in private nonprofit markets. *Journal of Public Economics, 75*(2), 255–272. doi:10.1016/S0047-2727(99)00066-3

Palazzo, B. (2002). US-German business ethics: An intercultural comparison. *Journal of Business Ethics, 41*(3), 195–216. doi:10.1023/A:1021239017049

Porter, M. E., & Kramer, M. (2002). The competitive advantage of corporate philanthropy. *Harvard Business Review*, (December), 5–16. PMID:12510538

Rekkas, T. (2021). Measuring the importance of SMEs to the national economy: The case of Greece. *Periodiko Epistimis & Technologias, 16*(2).

Remaud, H., & Couderc, J. P. (2006). Wine business practices: A new versus old wine world perspective. *Agribusiness, 22*(3), 405–416. doi:10.1002/agr.20094

Ricks, J. M. Jr, & Williams, J. A. (2005). Strategic corporate philanthropy: Addressing frontline talent needs through an educational giving program. *Journal of Business Ethics, 60*(2), 147–157. doi:10.1007/s10551-005-1175-3

Sánchez, C. M. (2000). Motives for Corporate Philanthropy in El Salvador: Altruism and Political Legitimacy. *Journal of Business Ethics, 27*(4), 363–375. doi:10.1023/A:1006169005234

Schaper, M. T., & Savery, L. K. (2004). Entrepreneurship and philanthropy: The case of small Australian firms. *Journal of Developmental Entrepreneurship, 9*(3), 239–250.

Schuyt, T., Bekkers, R., & Smit, J. (2010). The philanthropy scale: A sociological perspective in measuring new forms of pro social behaviour. *Social Work & Society, 8*(1), 121–135.

Seifert, B., Morris, S. A., & Bartkus, B. R. (2004). Having, giving, and getting: Slack resources, corporate philanthropy, and firm financial performance. *Business & Society, 43*(2), 135–161. doi:10.1177/0007650304263919

Stanković, M., Mrdak, G., & Stojanović, S. (2018). The importance of small and medium enterprises in modern economy. *KNOWLEDGE-International Journal, 28*(5), 1619–1624. doi:10.35120/kij28051619M

Sundaram, A. K., & Inkpen, A. C. (2004). Stakeholder Theory and 'The Corporate Objective Revisited': A Reply. *Organization Science*, *15*(3), 370–371. doi:10.1287/orsc.1040.0067

Surroca, J., Tribò, J. A., & Waddock, S. (2010). Corporate responsibility and financial performance: The role of intangible resources. *Strategic Management Journal*, *31*(5), 463–490. doi:10.1002/smj.820

Tsang, S., Welford, R., & Brown, M. (2009). Reporting on community investment. *Corporate Social Responsibility and Environmental Management*, *16*(3), 123–136. doi:10.1002/csr.178

Van Leeuwen, M. H., & Wiepking, P. (2013). National campaigns for charitable causes: A literature review. *Nonprofit and Voluntary Sector Quarterly*, *42*(2), 219–240. doi:10.1177/0899764012467084

Van Wissen, L. (2000). SIMFIRMS: Simulating the spatial demography of firms, with an application in the Netherlands. Proceedings from Computing in Economics and Finance 2000, Barcelona, Spain.

Vijayan, G., Kamarulzaman, N. H., Mohamed, Z. A., & Abdullah, A. M. (2014). Sustainability in food retail industry through reverse logistics. *International Journal of Supply Chain Management*, *3*(2), 11–23.

Zerbini, F. (2017). CSR initiatives as market signals: A review and research agenda. *Journal of Business Ethics*, *146*(1), 1–23. doi:10.1007/s10551-015-2922-8

Zhang, L., Priestley, J., & Ni, X. (2018). Influence of the event rate on discrimination abilities of bankruptcy prediction models. *arXiv preprint arXiv:1803.03756*.

Zollo, M. (2004). *Philanthropy or CSR: a strategic choice*. Paper presented at the London European Business Forum, London.

Chapter 18
The Music of Wine:
Resources for Wine Tourism and Wine's Immaterial Cultural Heritage Interpretation

Martín Gómez-Ullate
https://orcid.org/0000-0003-2180-4908
University of Extremadura, Spain & Polytechnic Institute of Castelo Branco, Portugal

Gerardo Vidal Gonçalves
Sabrosa History and Archaeology Association, Portugal & University of Evora, Portugal

ABSTRACT

In many regions of Spain and Portugal, wine is still not very profitable for winegrowers who barely recover the economic and human capital inputs dedicated throughout the year to each harvest. The economic logic of the market is rapidly transforming this landscape and heritage in more and more regions, promoting the mechanization of viticulture for the sake of productivity, giving priority above all to the volume of grapes obtained and the reduction of production costs. In this sense, goblet vines and low vines are giving way to trellising, and the latter to harvesting machinery. However, the value of vine cultivation and winemaking goes far beyond economic profitability as an inseparable part of the cultural landscape and Mediterranean cultures. This chapter delves into cases of good practices for wine tourism and the enormous wealth of the musical heritage and, in general, the intangible cultural heritage (sayings, customs, traditions, agrarian and culinary traditions) surrounding wine.

INTRODUCTION

In many regions of Spain and Portugal, wine is still not very profitable for winegrowers who barely recover the economic and human capital inputs dedicated throughout the year each harvest. However, the value of vine cultivation and winemaking goes far beyond economic profitability as an inseparable part of the cultural landscape and Mediterranean cultures. It is -like other cases of traditional economies- a "Mediterranean moral economy" (González Alcantud, 1995, 1998).

DOI: 10.4018/979-8-3693-2149-2.ch018

The economic logic of the market is rapidly transforming this landscape and heritage in more and more regions, promoting the mechanization of viticulture for the sake of productivity, giving priority above all to the volume of grapes obtained and the reduction of production costs. In this sense, goblet vines and low vines are giving way to trellising, and the latter to harvesting machinery.

While the benefits that technology brings to vineyard productivity are undeniable, there are inevitable impacts on the cultural dynamics of wine, such as the grape harvest, a tradition that today serves to reunite and reconnect family and social networks scattered throughout the national and international territory.

In order to safeguard this landscape and cultural heritage, it is necessary to promote it from the administration and private enterprise towards the diversification of economic activity, including activities that promote wine tourism. It is also necessary to raise awareness of the natural and cultural heritage surrounding wine, scattered among so many towns and people who have been able to safeguard it for hundreds and, in some cases, thousands of years.

This chapter delves into cases of good practices for wine heritage management, wine tourism and the enormous wealth of the musical heritage and, in general, the intangible cultural heritage (sayings, customs, traditions, agrarian and culinary traditions) surrounding wine.

For this purpose, we will use a bibliographic review of the vast cultural heritage around wine in Spain and Portugal and ethnographic insights from anthropological fieldwork.

MORAL ECONOMY

Following the Spanish anthropologist, González Alcantud, moral economy is a concept forged by J. Scott and P. Thompson, to refer to economic dynamics characterised (whether among the farmers of Southeast Asia or among the English peasants of the 14th century) by a negative entropic regulation, i.e. tending to establish the limits of self-subsistence or the "fair price" of agricultural products on the market. "Morality", in this sense, would be a regulating principle that prevents the emergence of positive entropy generating chaos (Scott, 1976: 157 ff. cited in González Alcantud, 1998).

Taking the example of economies of traditional agriculture as wine economy or pastoral economy, we would use the significant "moral economy" to to build on it, giving it a series of characteristics that would give it a new framework of meaning.

So we can talk of moral economy when an economic activity continues when the economic racionalism of profitability does not occur, nor are the risks of the activity fully covered by internal or external mechanisms. But we would add a new condition, when the activity is in itself a fundamental element of and for the cultural landscape or generates services that are not remunerated by the market or the administration, as is the case of the impact of grazing in the prevention and mitigation of losses caused by fires or of viticulture in providing essential elements to landscapes such as the Alto Douro Wine Region that has been declared a world heritage site by UNESCO in 2001.

In these cases, it is important for the administrations to support these economic environments when they fail to find the means in market logics to subsist, but not as a non-repayable subsidy, but as a remuneration for services and impacts on tourism or the environment that can nowadays be fairly accurately calculated.

Technology is raising productivity in agricultural and livestock activities. This naturally lower the prices of the products in origin and making unprofitable smallholder activities that have not transferred productivity gains via technology. At present days, while we write these lines, the tractors of many vine growers are blocking roads in many regions of Spain, in demonstrations because they are being paid 15 cents of an Euro per kilogram of grapes.

Whether or not they are publicly funded, it is fundamental for economic activities as viticulture or traditional extensive livestock management to diversify economic activity and sources of income in order to be able to generate resources that lead to living wages and do not lead to the disappearance or essential transformation of the activity. To this end, wine tourism or enotourism has been fundamental in wine economies for the preservation of the landscape and the revitalisation of less productive or commercial castes such as the Eva Beba in Badajoz or Brancellao in Orense (Spain).

WINE HERITAGE AND ARCHAEOLOGY

Archaeology has allowed us to know the antiquity of the use of wine among humans, the earliest traces of which have been dated to the early Neolithic period around 6000- 5800 BC in the Republic of Georgia by the Gadachrili Gora Regional Archaeological Project Expedition (GRAPE), a joint undertaking between the University of Toronto and the Georgian National Museum (McGovern et al., 2023). Dr. Patrick McGovern, the University of Pennsylvania Museum's Director of Biomolecular Archaeology has been searching and dating the oldest uses of wine among humans. He and his team have documented chemical evidence of fermented beverages on the insides of pottery jars in China discovering rests of a 9,000-year-old coction of a mix of rice, honey and fruit, comparing it with a modern aged Belgian ale or a barley wine.

Mcgovern has published valuable works of popular science on the prehistory of wine describing its cultural uses as "medicine, social lubricant, mind-altering substance, and highly valued commodity, focus of religious cults, pharmacopoeias, cuisines, economies, and society. As an evocative symbol of blood, it was used in temple ceremonies and occupies the heart of the Eucharist. Kings celebrated their victories with wine and made certain that they had plenty for the afterlife" (McGovern, 2007).

In classical societies, food meant much more than eating. According to the Greek philosopher Plutarch, who was born in Keroneia, in Bosnia, "We don't sit at the table to eat, but to eat together" (Montanari, 1998).

For the people of antiquity, including the Phoenicians, Greeks, Romans, Carthaginians and many others, wine played an important role, becoming part of the so-called nutritional triad of the Greeks: wheat, wine and olive oil (McGovern, 2003). In fact, through the influence of the Hellenes, the Romans acquired a taste for viticulture and wine. However, between the 1st and 2nd centuries AD, a Roman merchant, fond of cookery and exotic and expensive products, developed a "different" type of wine. The so-called "Conditium Paradoxum", or simply spiced wine, is one of the recipes of Marcus Gavius Apicius, the aforementioned Roman merchant and cook. In his recipe book, Apicius mentions other wines, liqueurs and digestives such as "wine for travellers", "Absintium Romanum", "Rosatum et Violacium" and "Conditium melizomum uiatorium", among others (Rodrigues, 2010).

In Roman times, wine was a very important product, so important that the effort to produce and distribute it was significant. Wine was transported in containers called amphorae, containers whose origin and etymology derive from ancient Greek civilisation. Amphorae were used to transport products such as wine, olive oil, garum or fish paste, among others. Lusitana, Pascual, Gauloise and Dressel amphorae, among others, were mainly used to transport wine. The amphora had a morphology that allowed the container to be transported by boat, on its own supports, over long distances. Wine was drunk socially,

Figure 1. Label, bottle, and marketing of Anphoras de Gallaecia

at events and by politicians and senators, in trade and business, wine in Roman times was a fundamental element in the daily life of society.

Wine Heritage, Archaeology, and Rural Development: Two Case Studies

Ancient Roman Wine Recreation

In 2017/2018, the Sabrosa History and Archaeology Association, in partnership with EROS Environment Research on Science Consulting, organised a small project to recreate one of Marcus Gavius Apicius' recipes, the "Conditium Paradoxum" or Roman spiced wine.

To this end, various translations of the famous work "De Re Culinária" were used, and it was possible to establish a grid for calculating and converting the data obtained from the documents consulted on the Conditium Paradoxum recipe.

A recipe was used from a medieval document acquired by private individuals in the centre of Europe, Belgium, which reproduced Marcus Gavius Apicius' recipe for the Conditium Paradoxum, in general and with minor changes.

By studying the data, calibrating it to current measurements and obtaining the products used by the merchant, an experimental archaeology session was carried out in the 1st century AD on the design of Marcus Gavius Apícius' Roman wine.

Once the activity was complete, a brand, a name and a graphic line were produced, inspired by the region of Northern Portugal and Galicia and some contributions from classical archaeology. The name of the prototype was Anphoras da Gallaecia: spiced Roman wine.

This experiment in experimental archaeology has been replicated in some places with a wine tradition around Europe. However, through other experiments and work carried out in the field of wine history, such as the study of some cave wine presses in the Douro region, Sabrosa, Mirandela, Vale de Telhas

(Gonçalves and Pereira, 2021), and Valpaços, a lot of information has been added about the history of wine in the region of Trás-os-Montes and Alto Douro and Alto Douro Vinhateiro.

"Amphoras da Gallaecia" is a spicy wine with a sweet and very aromatic flavour. The history of the recipe and the product itself takes us back to a past of flavours, aromas and trends, a past that AHAS has recreated for those consumers who are attentive to the common and Mediterranean past, a classic past full of stories and histories.

"Amphoras da Gallaecia" should be consumed slightly warmed in a balloon glass, over a container with a concentrate of sugar, ethyl alcohol and lemon and orange peels, at a temperature of between 12° and 16° centigrade. The spiced wine was usually consumed slightly warm, enjoyed on a triclinium (Roman couch), in the company of friends, family, businessmen or senators and politicians,

The Alto Douro Wine Region is, as we know, the first demarcated and regulated wine region in the world (Andresen, Aguiar and Curado, 2004; Brochado de Almeida, Antunes and Faria, 1999; Fonseca, 1949). Ancient Romans would have discovered the benefits of a sweet, spicy wine produced on the slopes of the Douro more than 1800 years before the Pombaline demarcations.

Spiced and sweet wine, especially warmed wine, has survived since Roman times in various communities in central Europe, northern Europe and parts of the Middle East. However, the purity of the original flavours can only be achieved by using historical and documentary information and the best products. The Anphoras da Gallaécia project also had a very important source of inspiration in the ancient landscapes of the Alto Douro Wine Region, its surroundings and its historical legacy and the sights and sounds of the region.

Ancient Roman Rural Tourism Recreation

Another case study of archaeological recreation also based on the Apicius' "De Re Culinária" and other recipies authors (Marcial, Columela, Plinio, Catón, Virgilio) is the prize awarded rural tourism Aqua Libera, in the little village of Aljucen (245 inhabitants) in the province of Badajoz (Spain), close to Mérida, the Ancient Roman important city of Emerita Augusta.

A unique place in Spain and Europe, Aqua Libera is the recreation of a Roman Vila or Domus, were the tourism experience starts by dressing the guests as ancient Romans. The food is served in a triclinium or biclinium under the light of "lucernae" (olive oil lamps) comprising 7 or 8 disses, and spiced wine diluted with water. A wreath of flowers on the heads of the guests, as believed in ancient Rome, is placed to prevent the wine from rising too quickly to the head.

We have considered this rural tourism a best practices case, not only because of their accurate reconstruction of a Roman Domus and recipes but for their social inclusive perspective that retains affordable prices for its services for a good part of the population and offers discounts to pilgrims who pass through Aljucen on the Via de la Plata to Santiago de Compostela.

WINE AND MUSIC

Wine, Philosophy, Poetry, and Music

If archaeology can provide the wine economy with elements that give it added value, the same is true of historiography and anthropology, which have documented the human conception and poetic and lyrical expression of wine since the appearance of writing in Eurasian and Mediterranean cultures and civilisations.

In this work we have focused on the special relationship between wine and music, analysing the anonymous popular expressions and authored that have transcended and have been recorded, safeguarded and transmitted over generations.

Another line that is emerging today as a business idea and added value in the wine market, but which has been around for centuries, is that which links drinking certain types of wine while listening to certain types of music, or how a particular music can affect the wines taste in what has been called "wine acoustics" (Cadó Martínez, 2016). This peculiar type of wine and music pairing was already dealt with in Romanticism by authors such as Hoffman and Baudelaire. In his classic book, Wine and Hashish, Baudelaire (1851/2020) quotes Hoffman:

"The conscientious musician must use Champagne to compose a comic opera. In it he will find the sparkling, light-hearted joy that the genre demands. Religious music demands wine from the Rhine or the Jurançon. As in the depths of profound ideas, there is a heady bitterness in them. But heroic music cannot do without Burgundy wine, it possesses the stern impetus and seduction of patriotism".

Focusing on the lyric of wine and the poetic and philosophical expressions, we can discover to what extent it has been an element of vital and cultural structuring in all civilisations and how drunkenness has been extolled as a vehicle of ascesis and transcendence.

Octavio Paz published the thoughts of the Chinese philosopher Lieu Lin, one of the seven great poets of his century, the third B.C., and a member of the "Bamboo Grove" group, made up of the seven poets and seven drinkers. Wine among these men provoked a state of blissful accord with the world, a momentary reconciliation with the flow of life. In the words of Lieu Lin:

"A friend of mine, a superior man, considers eternity to be a morning; and ten thousand years, a mere blink of an eye. The sun and the rain are the windows of his house. The eight confines, his avenues. He walks, light and without destination, leaving no trace: the sky for a roof, the earth for a bed. When he stops, he holds a bottle and a glass: when he travels, he carries a wineskin and a decanter at his side. His only thought is of wine: nothing beyond or here concerns him".

In Mediterranean cultures, wine has been associated with music and festivity since the most ancient representations of the god Dionysus, accompanied by fauns always represented playing a flute. The Dionysian attitude entails the symposiacal or convivial carpe diem, which according to Sariego (2019) can take two forms: the anacreontic, which emphasises the consoling power of unbridled devotion to drink; and the Horatian, which advises a moderate use of wine in conjunction with more sophisticated pleasures, such as conversation, books, music and withdrawal from the worries of the world.

In Catholic cultures, wine being an element of the liturgical-sacred and profane orb, it has been specialy controlled. In the 7th century, an attempt was made to prevent them "from invoking the name of the execrable Bacchus when pressing grapes in the wine presses, or pouring wine into the jars, and making noise and laughing... " (Tejada y Ramiro, 1849 cited in Samaniego Campos, 2020). This is also found in some of the expressions collected by ethnomusicologists that mix Spanish and Latin. There is one that referring to the "porrón" (a specific wine bottle):

Figure 2. 15th-century Porrón from Valencia (Collections of the Museo Nacional de Cerámica y de las Artes Suntuarias González Martí) Jerónimo Roure Pérez, Dorieo, Wikimedia Commons (License CC-BY-SA 4.0).

No te vayas, Catalina

y si te vas poco a poco,

que me has costao treinta reales

"Per Christum Dominum Nostrum"[1].

(Conde and Fernández, 2002)

This other, collected in Elizondo, in the Baztan Valley, expresses the last wishes of a good drinker interspersed with the emblematic words of the first response at funerals and anniversaries. The devotee of Bacchus represents his own funeral in advance, and asks the priest not to dip the hyssop in the pure holy water, but mixed with red wine. And when he arrives at the pater noster, he asks a neighbour to bring a jug of good wine for all the others to drink to his health around the box:

"Libera me Domine" kantatzean, ez busti ixaporik urean, arnoan busti zazu han ongi sartu zazu; hori da nahiko dudana; hilean bizian bezala. "Pater noster" aphezak kantatzean dariliarák islean arno saltzale bati pinta bai khararazi; zeraldo beltzaren ondoan nere osagariariari edan.

Figure 3. The Gate of Wine in the Alhambra of Granada
Source: Wikimedia Commons

(Conde and Fernández, 2002)

In our ethnogrphic fieldwork we have also registered in Sierra de Francia's region, a expression in latin to refer to the vineyards that are poor and do not produce a lot "Mísere", as miserable, and it is associated with a wine of good taste.

Another curious use of the catholic liturgic dimension for wine is the term "baptised wine", for the wine that have been mixed with water, a custom practiced by some winemakers to lower the grade and by others to obtain higher profits. This is referred in an ancient Spanish proverb: "Vino bautizado no vale un cornado; vino moro, plata y oro" ("Baptised wine is not worth a dime; Moorish wine is worth silver and gold"). (Diaz)

The playful use and philosophical expression of wine is also characteristic of Islamic cultures. In Granada's Alhambra one of the main entrances it was called The Gate of Wine (see Figure 2).

During the 11th century the Sevillian court was noted for its gaiety, its poetry and its music. Seville was "the city of joyful and laughing poetry, the city of music". One of the most exciting Hispano-Arabic popular poets of the 12th century was Ibn Quzman or Abenguzmán, from Córdoba (1086-1160), author of a songbook of 149 zéjeles, intended to be sung by minstrels, street beggars, rogues and women, in festive and jesters' dances (Salinas Santos, 2000). We reproduce one of them that has been a thematic recurrence in Spanish popular music.

"When I die, these are my burial instructions:
I shall sleep with a vine between my eyelids;

let them wrap me in its leaves as a shroud
and put a turban of vine branches on my head"

In hispanic cultures, this hyperbolic love expression for wine has found its way in many variations. In Don Quixote de la Mancha, Cervantes puts the following into Sancho Panza's mouth:

"Cuándo yo me muera
no me lloren los parientes
llórenme los alambiques
donde sacan aguardiente[2]."

We can find variants in the first and -more depersonalised- in the third person in Spanish popular music songbooks in several regions.

"Un borracho se murió
y dejó en el testamento
que lo enterraren en viña
para chupar los sarmientos[3]"
(Salinas Santos, 2000).

Or this variation extended in the wine folklore in the north, south and center of Spain:

El Tio Pimiento ha "dejao" dispuesto
en el testamento que le han de enterrar,
que le han de enterrar,
en una bodega dentro de una cuba
con un ramo de uvas en el paladar,
en el paladar.
A mi gusta el pin piripinpinpin
con la bota empiná parapampampan.
Con el pin piripinpinpin,
con el pan parapampampan,
al que no le gusta el vino es un animal,
es un animal o no tiene ni un real.
Todos los borrachos van a la taberna,
se beben el vino, se gastan las perras,
se gastan las perras.
Luego van casa con una merluza
y todo lo paga la pobre Maruja.
A mi gusta el pin piripinpinpin
con la bota empiná parapampampan.
Con el pin piripinpinpin,
con el pan parapampampan,
al que no le gusta el vino es un animal,

es un animal o no tiene ni un real
(que es lo más normal)[4].

In addition to repeating the funeral elegy to wine, this song introduces an important dimension of the anthropology of wine, its role in domestic violence and in the disintegration of families.

In Portugal, we can find the same apology of wine in the song "Era o vinho", that recreates it in a superlative way:

Era o vinho meu Deus era o vinho,
Era o vinho que eu mais adorava.
Só por morte meu Deus só por morte,
Só por morte o vinho deixava.
Ai eu hei-de morrer na adega,
Ai o tonel é o meu caixão.
Ai hei-de levar de mortalha,
Ai um copo cheio na mão.
Ai rapazes quando eu morrer,
Ai enterrai-me numa vinha.
Ai façam a cova bem funda,
Ai deitem-lhe vinho por cima.
Ai rapazes quando morrer,
Ai não quero choros nem gritos.
Ai só quero à minha beira,
um garrafão de cinco litros[5].

If cultural projects and institutions are essential for the safeguarding of the musical heritage of wine, individuals themselves are also finding the means to make their versions of songs and sayings available. In the case of "Era o vinho", the version of Maria Soares, a 90-year-old lady who has published her own songs, is longer and probably more faithful to the original than the one collected by the project "A musica portuguesa a gostar de ela propria[6]".

Following this single element in wine immaterial heritage we have immersed ourselves in the Spanish-Arabic literature of 12th century Al Andalus, we have captured the theme in Cervantes' universal Don Quixote, we have seen how it has travelled to the wine regions of America (Chile), and how it continues to live on in traditional Spanish music to this day, hand in hand with other fundamental social dimensions of wine. Therefore, searching for wine themes and resources, we can build a database full of cultural key themes and resources which are an inexhaustible source for the interpretation and education of the cultural heritage around wine for that complex diversity of agents that we can call wine cultural mediators.

WINE HERITAGE RESOURCES

The tangible and intangible cultural heritage composing the cultural universe of wine is interpreted, safeguarded, enhanced, displayed and managed by public and private entities through various mechanisms, mainly a) public museums and private collections and b) wine routes. Beyond the museums, many songs, sayings, customs and traditions about wine are still alive in the cultures of the Iberian Peninsula.

In the enormous collection of the Ethnographic Centre Joaquín Díaz Foundation, which is open and free to the public, we can find a multitude of references to toasts, songs, stories in cartoons and comic strips, ethnomusicological recordings, string-sheets, etc.

Toasts for example, are considered as a genre. Joaquín Diaz introduces us to this genre:

From the German "ich bringe dir es" - is, in oral culture, more than just a friendly term used to invite people to drink. It is a genre. There are hundreds of different examples that could support this thesis and demonstrate the existence of several characteristic types within the same model. Its use is very ancient and Cobarruvias, in his Tesoro de la Lengua Castellana o Española, alludes to a mention by Cornelius and Tacitus of this way of celebrating of the Tudescos in their convites, weddings and meetings. According to him (1611) it is said "brindez", although Quevedo already clearly uses "brindis".

Diaz classify the toasts into three categories:

1. Those that invite to drink and serve as justification for the meeting, friendship or the simple drink; "Bienvenido seas, vino/ hijo de la cepa tuerta./Tú que te quieres meter/y yo que te abro la puerta" (Welcome, wine/ son of the one-eyed vine/you who want to get in/and I who open the door for you). Or "Un gato subió a una parra/y la parra abajo vino/y vino sobre nosotros/y sobre nosotros, vino».''a cat climbed a vine/and the vine tumbled down/and it came upon us/and upon us, Wine!".
2. Those which serve to express a wish (for happiness, unhappiness, oblivion, free drink, etc.); «El cuco canta en la tierra/y la gaviota en el mar/y yo canto en la taberna/pa beber y no pagar»"The cuckoo sings in the earth/and the seagull in the sea/and I sing in the tavern/to drink and not pay". Or "Brindo y bebo/y al que no beba que se le sequen los huevos" ("I Toast and drink, and that who do not do it, may his balls dry").
3. Those that praise the properties of wine, talk about its lineage or warn what can happen to those who drink too much of it. «Oh vino, rico licor / criado entre verdes matas / a cuántos hombres de bien/les haces andar a gatas» ("Oh wine, rich liquor / bred among green bushes / to how many good men / you make them crawl").

This theme and this expression - "to crawl on all fours" - is also part of the Portuguese musical tradition, which always inspires works by authors who know how to make the best of the tradition, such as Federico García Lorca or the author of the fado "Oiça lá oh, senhor vinho", Alberto Janes, who composed both its gayly music and its poetic lyrics. It was masterfully sung by Amalia Rodrigues and, years later, by Mariza, among dozens of fadists that have shorten the lyrics leaving two parts aside (Mendes and Gouveia, 2014) tell us in their book Poetas Populares do Fado Tradicional.

Oiça lá ó senhor vinho[7]
Vai responder-me, mas com franqueza
Porque é que tira toda a firmeza
A quem encontra no seu caminho;
Lá por beber um copinho a mais
Até pessoas pacatas

Amigo vinho em desalinho
Vossa mercê faz andar de gatas
É mau procedimento
E há intenção naquilo que faz
Entra-se em desequilíbrio
Não há equilíbrio que seja capaz;
As leis da física falham
E a vertical em qualquer lugar
Oscila sem se deter
E deixa de ser perpendicular
Eu já fui, responde o vinho:
A folha solta a gritar ao vento
Fui raio de sol sobre o firmamento
E trouxe á uva doce carinho;
Ainda guardo o calor do sol
E assim eu até dou vida
Aumento o valor seja de quem for
Na boa conta, peso e medida
E só faço mal a quem me julga
ninguém faz pouco de mim
Quem me trata como água
É ofensa!... paga-a!... eu cá sou assim;
Vossa mercê tem razão
É ingratidão falar mal do vinho
E a provar o que digo
Vamos meu amigo a mais um copinho
Injustiça, respondeu o vinho
Eu pago tudo sozinho
Tantos perdidos pela bebida
Sem ter na vida provado vinho
Tomam bebidas estrangeiras
E mais ruins que ninguém as traga
A coisa aquece e fica afinada
Mas se há trapalhada o vinho é que paga
Isto está mais do que errado
Eu sou difamado, é mais que certinho
Até calda de tomate
Se der disparate, dizem: foi o vinho
E ninguém pensa nas penas
De quem nesta vida já não tem carinho
E que eu torno mais pequenas
Ao fazer apenas esquecer no vinho

Table 1. Material and immaterial expressions an manifestations of wine heritage

1. Utensils for the manufacture and consumption of wine (i.e. Anphorae, crown of flowers, glasses and cups, "porrones")
2. Recipes
3. Iconography of wine (i.e. gods of wine)
4. Customs surrounding the making, selling and consumption of wine (i.e. Toasts)
5. Authored poetry and music on wine
6. Popular poetry and music on wine (songs, romances, proverbs, proclamations, riddles)

This brilliant dialogue between the wine and the drinker, which has become one of the most classic fados in the modern history of the genre, covers a variety of themes that are part of the history of wine (the negative effects of drunkenness, the positive effects of wine consumption in its right measure, the socio-cultural competition of wine with other foreign drinks in Portugal and Spain, especially since the second half of the 20th century).

To conclude this work on the heritage surrounding wine, mainly the intangible heritage, we summarise in table 1 the sources and resources that we can currently find on wine and its cultural dimension.

It is important to carry out comparative studies, at least in Mediterranean cultures, based on careful translations in order to offer all this international heritage to wine mediators, especially important for wineries offering guided tours, museums, wine guides, cultural managers.

The enhancement of the cultural heritage of the wine-growing and winemaking industry has the effect of enhancing the value of the wine itself, especially traditional wines, from small commercial wineries and artisanal wineries.

The valorization of the wine cultural heritage results in the valorization of the wine itself, especially of traditional wines, from small commercial wineries and artisanal wineries, normally, in the case of the Iberian Peninsula, located in peripheral and disadvantaged rural areas.

Their economic undervaluation by the market contrasts enormously with the importance of these moral economies for the cultural landscape and the structuring of tradition and identity. An essential importance although difficult to quantify economically.

For this reason, these small economies must survive supported by the public administrations; not so much to compensate for the loss of profitability of these activities in the face of large mechanized wineries, but to recognize this added value that they bring to the cultural landscape and to the natural and cultural heritage.

On the other hand, these small economies must do their utmost to revalue their products and, to this end, make use of all available resources to understand and transmit the enormous cultural value of wine.

REFERENCES

Baudelaire, C. (1851/2020). Du vin et du Haschisch. Editorial. Mille Et Une Nuits. La petite collection. Paris.

Cadó Martínez, J. L. R. (2016). *Concert Wine.* Acústica del vino.

Conde, A. L., & Fernández, A. T. (2002). Entre el Vino Sacro y el Profano: Caminos de la Música. In Caminería hispánica: actas del V Congreso Internacional de Caminería Hispánica. Celebrado en Valencia *(España),* (pp. 499-518). Aache.

Díaz, J. (2001) Los brindis. *Revista de Folklore*. https://funjdiaz.net/joaquin-diaz-articulos-ficha.php?id=761&qry=vino+

Díaz, J. (2001). *Pregón de cigales. Ensalzando el vino joven. Obra completa*. Fundación Joaquín Díaz. https://funjdiaz.net/joaquin-diaz-articulos-ficha.php?id=20192&qry=vino+

Garrido Domené, F., Laguna Mariscal, G., & Aguirre Quintero, F. (2019). Dioniso, el vino y la música. Divino frenesí, de ayer a hoy, Córdoba: Ed.Publicaciones de la Universidad de Córdoba.

González Alcantud, J. A. (1995). *Cultivos y herramientas. Antropografías de la economía moral mediterránea. Revista de Antropología Social, ni 4*. Servicio de Publicaciones. Universidad Complutense.

Iovino, R., & Mattion, I. (2009). *Sinfonía gastronómica:(música, eros y cocina)* (Vol. 43). Siruela.

McGovern, P. (2007). *Ancient Wine: The Search for the Origins of Viniculture*. Princeton Science Library.

McGovern, P., Jalabadze, M., Batiuk, S., Callahan, M., Smith, K., Hall, G., Kvavadze, E., Maghradze, D., Rusishvili, N., Bouby, L., Failla, O., Cola, G., Mariani, L., Boaretto, E., Bacilieri, R., This, P., Wales, N., & Lordkipanidze, D. (2017). Early Neolithic wine of Georgia in the South Caucasus. *Proceedings of the National Academy of Sciences of the United States of America*, *114*(48), 201714728. doi:10.1073/pnas.1714728114 PMID:29133421

Mendes, F., & Gouveia, D. (2014). Poetas Populares do Fado Tradicional INCM – Imprensa Nacional Casa da Moeda Salinas Campos, Maximiliano. (2000). ¡Toquen flautas y tambores!: Una historia social de la música desde las culturas populares en Chile, siglos XVI-XX. *Revista Musical Chilena*, *54*(193), 45–82. doi:10.4067/S0716-27902000019300003

Sariego, M. M. M. (2019). Días de vino y rosas: el" carpe diem" convival y sus realizaciones literarias. In *Dionisio, el vino y la música: divino frenesí de ayer a hoy* (pp. 145–159). Editorial Cérix.

ADDITIONAL READING

Baudelaire, C. (1851/2020). Du vin et du Haschisch. Mille Et Une Nuits. La petite collection. Paris.

Campos, S. (2000). ¡Toquen flautas y tambores!: Una historia social de la música desde las culturas populares en Chile, siglos XVI-XX. *Revista Musical Chilena*, *54*(193), 45–82. doi:10.4067/S0716-27902000019300003

McGovern, P. (2007). *Ancient Wine: The Search for the Origins of Viniculture*. Princeton Science Library.

KEY TERMS AND DEFINITIONS

Baptised Wine: Wine that has been diluted with water to lower its alcoholic strength or increase its profitability.

Cultural Heritage: Set of tangible and intangible cultural elements that are transmitted from generation to generation and recognised by the members of a culture as well as by outsiders as fundamental to its expression of identity.

Merluza: (In Spanish) Hake. Figuratively drunkenness.

Moral Economy: An economic activity that is still carried out when it is no longer profitable, and which the public administration has a duty to safeguard because of its important contribution to heritage and the cultural landscape.

Porrón: (In Spanish) Wine drinking vessel, usually made of glass or ceramic, with two holes, the one that is directed to the drinker's mouth of small diameter to allow the wine to fall in a fine stream.

Wine Heritage: Tangible and intangible cultural heritage arising from the production, consumption and ideation of wine.

Zejel: A strophic composition of Spanish metric, of Arabic origin, commonly used by popular poets in Al Andalus.

ENDNOTES

1 Don't go, Catalina/ and if you go little by little / you have cost me thirty reals / "Per Christum Dominum Nostrum.

2 "When I die/ may not my relatives mourn me / let the stills mourn me /where they make eau-de-vie".

3 . "A drunkard died / and left in his will / to be buried in a vineyard / to suck the vine shoots".

4 "Uncle Pepper has disposed/ in his will that he is to be buried,/ that he is to be buried/ in a cellar inside a vat/ with a bunch of grapes/ in the roof of his mouth/in the roof of his mouth./I like the pin piripinpinpinpin/from the boot steeped,/parapampampan./With the pin piripinpinpin,/with the parapampampan,/who doesn't like wine is an animal,/is an animal or doesn't even have a niquel./ All the drunks go to the tavern,/they drink the wine, they spend their money,/they spend their money./ Then they go home/ with a hake (drunkness)/and it's all on poor Maruja (their wives)./ I like the pin piripinpinpin pin/With the boot steeped for the pampampan./With the pin piripinpinpin,/with the parapampampan,/who doesn't like wine is an animal,/is an animal or doesn't even have a niquel/ (which is the most normal thing)."

5 It was the wine, my God, it was the wine,/ It was the wine that I loved the most./ Only by death, my God, only by death,/ Only death I would leave the wine./ Oh, I'll die in the cellar,/ The vat is my coffin/ Oh, I'll wear a shroud,/ A full glass in my hand./ Oh boys when I die,/ Bury me in a vineyard./ Make the grave deep,/ Pour wine over it./ Oh boys, when I die,/ I don't want any crying or screaming./ I just want you by my side,/ a five-litre jug.

6 For comparing them: Maria Soares' Version (https://asminhascantigas.blogspot.com/2013/09/era-o-vinho.html) vs. Women from Alpendorada e Matos, Marco de Canaveses, Porto (https://amusicaportuguesaagostardelapropria.org/videos/era-o-vinho/)

7 Listen, Mr Wine / You're going to answer me, but frankly/ Why do you take away all firmness/ Whoever you meet on your way;/ Just for having one glass too many/ Even quiet people/ My friend, wine, when not in order / You're the one who makes to crawl on all fours./ It's bad behaviour/And there's intention in what you do/ You become unbalanced/ There's no balance that can do it;/ The laws of physics fail / And the vertical everywhere / Oscillates without stopping/ And ceases to be

perpendicular./ I've been, replies the wine: /A loose leaf screaming in the wind/ I was a sunbeam in the firmament / And brought sweet affection to the grape; / I still keep the warmth of the sun / And so I even give life / I increase the value of whoever drinks me/ In good account, weight and measure. / And I only hurt those who judge me nobody and makes fun of me/ Who treats me like water/ It's an offence... and pays for it... I'm like that;/ Your Honour is right/ It's ingratitude to speak ill of wine/ And to prove my point/ Let's have another glass, my friend. /Injustice, replied the wine /I pay for everything myself/ So many lost to drink/ Without having tasted wine in their lives / They drink foreign drinks/ And it's bad enough that nobody can stand them/ The thing gets hot and tuned/ But if there's a mix-up, it's the wine that pays./ This is more than wrong/ I'm slandered, it's more than true/ Even tomato syrup/ If it goes wrong, they say: it was the wine/ And nobody thinks about the sorrows/ Of those who no longer have affection in this life/ And that I make smaller/ By making them forget in the wine

Chapter 19
The Rise of the Functional Beverages Market:
Indicators Post COVID-19 Pandemic

Seda Yildirim
https://orcid.org/0000-0003-4367-6652
Tekirdag Namık Kemal University, Turkey

Durmus Cagri Yildirim
Tekirdag Namık Kemal University, Turkey

Ömer Esen
https://orcid.org/0000-0002-4762-9282
Tekirdag Namık Kemal University, Turkey

ABSTRACT

The COVID-19 pandemic has brought significant changes to people's lifestyles all over the world. Even after the pandemic, many people continue to maintain a healthy lifestyle. As a result, healthy food and drinks have become more popular and are driving consumer preferences in the food and beverage market. It is essential for a healthy lifestyle to consume healthy drinks that are affordable for everyone. In this point, functional foods and beverages have gained significant value. This study investigates the global functional beverage market trends before and after the pandemic. In addition, the study aims to provide a comprehensive analysis of how consumer preferences are changing in response to the trend of functional beverages. It is aimed to give an economic and marketing approach for the rise of functional beverage market.

INTRODUCTION

The COVID-19 has changed everything about human life, affecting their daily routines and hygiene (Öncü et al., 2021; Yıldırım et al., 2021; Bostanci et al., 2022; Aydın et al., 2023). People nowadays

DOI: 10.4018/979-8-3693-2149-2.ch019

Figure 1. Traditional functional food
Source: created by the authors based on Türk Sağlık Vakfı, (n.d.)

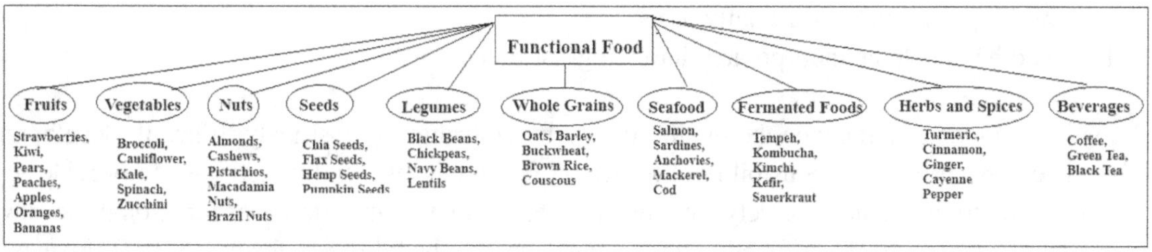

are becoming more health-conscious and are adopting various measures to maintain good health. This includes the use of vitamins and food supplements, as well as self-diagnosis. Additionally, people are increasingly making choices that promote a longer and healthier life (Yıldırım, 2023). Functional foods and beverages are gaining popularity as more people seek to improve their health and wellbeing. The food industry has been revolutionized due to the need for solutions to health problems caused by food and consumers' desire for good nutrition, longer life expectancy, and reduced treatment costs. Consequently, there has been a gradual increase in demand for functional foods (NovaNutrica, 2018). Functional foods have become increasingly popular in health and wellness communities in recent years. These foods are highly nutritious and have been linked to numerous health benefits. For instance, they may guard against diseases, prevent nutrient deficiencies, and promote growth and development (Türk Sağlık Vakfı, n.d.). Over time, researchers have discovered the beneficial substances contained in the structures of traditionally consumed foods. By enriching these beneficial ingredients, new foods have been produced. The term 'Functional foods' was first researched and used in Japan during the 1980s and has since become widespread in Europe and America (Gıda Takviyesi ve Beslenme Derneği, 2017). Functional foods are defined as foods that can reduce the risk of disease, improve existing health conditions, or help maintain good health. It is important to note that functional food and organic food are not the same. Organic food is produced according to the organic farming method, while functional foods are foods that naturally contain bioactive components in their composition. It is also important to note that functional foods are not a type of food supplement (Özel Beslenme, 2022). Functional foods are not in the form of medicine, capsules or nutritional supplements. They are part of our daily diet and include fruits and vegetables, grains, beverages, fortified and enhanced foods. It is important to note that the concepts of supplementary foods and functional foods are often confused. The main difference between the two is that functional foods are consumed as part of normal nutrition, while supplementary foods come in the form of capsules, powders, or other beverages that are not in the classical food form. Although supplementary foods may have a supportive effect on functional health, they cannot be used instead of medication (Koçak, 2019). Nowadays, some foods are fortified with additional nutrients, such as vitamins, minerals, probiotics, or fiber, to enhance their health benefits (Türk Sağlık Vakfı, n.d.). Figure 1 shows some traditional functional food as below:

For a food to be classified as "functional", it must meet certain criteria (NBLTürkiye, n.d.):

- It should not be in capsule or drug form.
- Its effects should be approved by experts.
- It should provide sufficient nutrition.

- It should have a positive impact on one or more bodily functions.
- It should reduce the risk of disease.
- It should be consumable on a daily basis.
- It should be able to be incorporated into a regular diet.

Functional foods can enhance the quality of life by contributing positively to health development and improvement. It is the responsibility of health professionals, especially dietitians, to provide accurate information to individuals, society, and industry regarding the importance of functional foods with proven effects (Özkaya,2021). A functional food can appear in the following forms: (NBLTürkiye, n.d.):

1. Whole foods that are found in nature,
2. Foods that have some ingredients added to them,
3. Foods that have some ingredients removed from them,
4. Foods that have one or more of their ingredients modified,
5. Foods that include any of the above four categories.,

The Functional Beverage market is a rapidly growing industry with strong economic value. The target audience of the functional beverage market includes different groups such as "*children, elderly, athletes, people with weak communication systems, fitness enthusiasts*"(Gupta et al., 2023). According to researchers, the functional food sector is experiencing the highest growth rate in the food industry, followed by natural products. Studies have shown that consuming fruits and vegetables can protect against various diseases and promote a healthy lifestyle (The Snack Haus, n.d.). In this context, this chapter aims to give a brief review for functional and healthy beverage market and industry. Accordingly, some economic indicators and reports will be reviewed and concluded. This chapter focuses on examining the rise of functional beverage market-industry and also showing the comparison of economic and statistical developments before and after COVID-19. It is thought to give an useful information for the academicians, students and professionals. The importance of this study is to giving recent information about functional beverage consumption globally for post-COVID-19 pandemic. It is a rising beverage market and the future of this market also seems to get bigger. Accordingly, it is thought to be useful source for scholars, students and marketers. This section provides an overview of the functional beverage market for compilation purposes. The information that the chapter will provide to readers can be summarized as follows:

- What exactly is a functional drink and what are its different types?
- How big is the functional beverage market in terms of size?
- What are the future predictions for the functional beverage market?
- Can you provide information on the consumption of functional beverages by country or region?
- Is there any relationship between the COVID-19 pandemic and functional beverage consumption?

FUNCTIONAL BEVERAGE INDUSTRY

Functional beverage market should be determined differently from functional drinks in general. Functional beverage refers to healthy beverages including drinks with vitamins, minerals, herbs etc. On the

Table 1. Indicators of functional beverages market (2022-2023)

Indicators	Sub-factors	Economic Details
Economic growth	Market size	USD 261.56 Billion
	Growth rate	6.50%
Products	Energy Drink	It is a rising trend in the recent years. Especially, the COVID-19 pandemic spurred the demand of energy drinks.
	Caffeinated Beverages	It is estimated to reach USD 368.60 billion by 2032.
	Probiotic Drinks	By the COVID-10, the importance of probiotics has been increased.
	Vegetable and Fruit Beverages	These beverages is healthier and the COVID-19 spurred the demand of Vegetable and Fruit Beverages
	Dairy-based beverages	Dairy-based beverages are a great source of energy and nutrition for everybody (including all ages)
Trends	Health and Wellness	Consumers increasingly choose healthy drinks with extra benefits.
	Weight Loss	Weight loss benefits come in various flavors, such as time-saving, low-calorie snacks that can be used as a substitute for parties or as part of a regular diet for weight loss. The most popular type of these snacks are meal replacement shakes, which provide protein to support muscle growth, carbohydrates to fuel workouts, and essential nutrients and minerals.
Distribution Channel Insights		Throughout the assumed period, the grocery/hypermarket class is expected to dominate the market, as customers increasingly rely on them for their food and beverage purchases.
Geography Insights		Zero-calorie, zero-sugar, and low-carb drinks are increasingly popular in the US. Beverages contribute to nutrition and water intake.

Source: created by the authors based on Precedence Research (2023)

other side, functional drinks refer to broader drink category in the related industry (Gupta et al., 2023). Experts seeking treatment in the field of health emphasize the importance of nutrients as supplements along with medications. Functional foods and beverages have become popular as a result of the rise of healthy lifestyles, sustainability and the effects of the COVID-19 pandemic in recent years (Precedence Research, 2023). According to Precedence Research (2023)'s report on Food and Beverages, there are useful information about functional beverages in recent years. In Table 1, some indicators and economic details are shown as below:

According to the report of Euromonitor International (2023), Table 2 shows some key points as below:

Consumers make their choices when using functional foods based on the benefits they provide. In this way, an option corresponding to all kinds of hygiene will be followed in the consumption of functional drinks. According to Glanbia nutritional, (2022), consumers' expectations from functional beverage consumption can be summarized as Table 3:

It is very difficult to find a single definition of functional food and beverage that is accepted world-wide. Because in every country, it is possible to come across functional foods or beverages in different categories as a result of some tastes, food cultures and eating habits (Nazir et al., 2019). When considering different definitions and categories for functional beverages, some main categories for functional beverages are shown in Figure 2:

When the current indicators of the Functional Beverage market are examined, it is seen that it is one of the fastest-growing Functional Beverage market is currently one of the fastest growing markets. Its target audience includes the elderly, children, athletes, and those with low immunity. Functional bever-

Table 2. Key points for functional beverages

Key Points	Situation
Future predictions for the functional beverage market	Consumers do not hesitate to look for the functional beverage that best suits them. At this point, it would be useful for the future to classify consumers according to market segments and identify the segments of the functional beverage market.
Making yourself better:	It is seen that people have attitudes based on their own knowledge rather than institutions. People choose what is best for their own health.
Stress:	We live in a stressful world and people need more energy when dealing with stress.
Digitalization:	With digitalization, consumers can see new and alternative products more easily.
Medicine food:	People want to maintain their health and well-being with the help of healthy foods instead of chemical drugs.

Source: created by the authors based on Euromonitor International (2023).

ages are distributed among the target audience based on their specific types. The target market includes the elderly, children, athletes, and those with low immunity. Functional beverages are distributed in the target market according to their types (Gupta et al., 2023).

In the below part, current indicators about functional beverage market will be reviewed as it is purposed.

ECONOMIC TRENDS IN FUNCTIONAL BEVERAGE INDUSTRY: GLOBAL INDICATORS

Functional foods have gained popularity due to changes in lifestyle, interest in healthy living, quality aging, and stress management (Corbo et al., 2014). According to Euromonitor, the global functional beverage market is expected to grow (6.4%) between 2021 and 2026. The functional beverage market is large in the Asia Pacific region, and then the functional beverage markets can be listed according to their size, such as North America, Latin America and Eastern Europe (Glanbia nutritional, 2023). The

Table 3. Consumers' expectations from a functional beverage consumption

Expectations That Support Well-Being	Expectation for Direct Health Protection Purposes
Energy Output	Limiting security protection
Relaxation creates home comfort	Immune support and immunity strengthening
Increasing focus	Helping healthy aging
Helping with the need for healthy sleep	Supporting weight management
Stress relief or reduction	Supporting muscle recordings
	Registering the joint helps
	Providing bone support
	Support cholesterol management
	Helping eye health
	Providing healthy skin and hair

Source: created by the authors based on data from Glanbia nutritional, (2022).

Figure 2. Main categories for functional beverages
Source: created by the authors

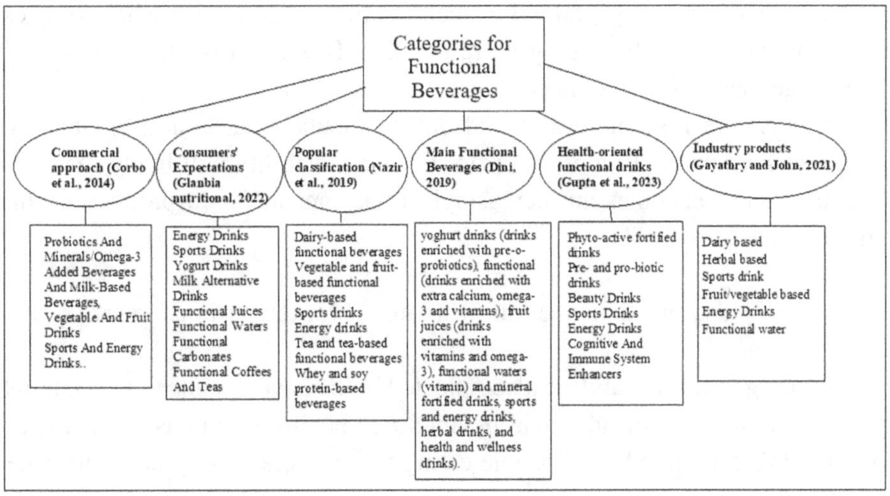

consumption of functional beverages varies according to gender and age, which is determined by several variables. Moreover, people prefer different functional drinks based on their gender and age. For instance, men tend to prefer drinks with high protein, nootropics, and omega-3 while women tend to go for products containing collagen, extra vitamins, and probiotics. As for the age factor, people aged 65 and over lean towards functional drinks that contain electrolytes and vitamins, whereas younger people prefer protein-based drinks (Mintel, 2023).

The COVID-19 pandemic has created a global shock. This shock deeply affected the economy as well as the health sector. Some changes have occurred in consumers' behavior and preferences in purchasing goods and services. Consumers are opting for healthier food choices amidst the economic crisis. Consumers are choosing healthier food and drink options due to the economic crisis. Finlays (2022) trend research on the beverage market shows both differences between generations' beverage preferences and changes after COVID-19. Finlays (2022)'s findings regarding trends in the beverage industry can be summarized as follows:

- When we look at the beverage consumption habits of Millennials and Gen Z groups, it is seen that they consume less alcoholic beverages than other groups. It seems that consumers have a tendency to reduce sugar and alcohol-containing foods that affect the body and mind. At this point, healthier, less sugary, calorie-controlled drinks come to the fore in beverage preferences.
- As a result of the crises caused by COVID-19, both health and financial difficulties have made people more stressed. Therefore, drinks that reduce stress and make people feel better have come to the fore. It can be said that there has been a significant growth in tea and relaxing tea varieties.
- Considering the importance that consumers attach to environmental values, it is seen that environmentally friendly brands, those with natural ingredients, those that give importance to recycling and low carbon absorption are at the forefront among the brands in the beverage market.

Georgie (2023) predicts some future trends in the beverage industry, which are as follows:

- Firstly, due to the high competition in the beverage market, brands must continually adapt to new innovations in order to keep up with changing consumer trends.
- Secondly, people are increasingly adopting healthier lifestyles, and as such, beverages with natural and healthy ingredients are becoming more popular. This trend is likely to drive the growth of brewed beverages and teas in the market.
- Finally, consumers are now more aware of environmental issues and sustainability, which has become a permanent value. Brands that prioritize sustainability will likely see growth in the future, as sustainability becomes an increasingly important factor in production, marketing, and consumption trends.

Foragekitchen (2023) also mentions the following trends for the beverage market:

- The increase in vegan eating habits is also reflected in the beverage market. The number of people choosing a vegan diet for ethical, environmental and health reasons is increasing. For example, it was observed that the number of people eating vegan increased by 600% in America between 2014 and 2017.
- Within the scope of sustainability concerns, consumers are more interested in beverage brands' packaging containing elements such as recycling, zero waste and sustainable agricultural products.
- As mental health has become important, consumers are starting to look for foods that can increase their cognitive functions and mood in their eating habits.
- Conscious eating habits direct consumers to be more careful when choosing food and beverages.
- While the soft drink market is growing, the use of robot assistants in the food industry is also increasing.

Kerschbaumer (2023) has summarized the new trends in the beverage market as follows:

- Brands in the food and beverage market are expected to focus on not only flavor but also health.
- Consumers are now looking for foods that can strengthen their immune systems.
- The market for products with natural ingredients has been growing, as consumers prefer healthier options. In the future, brands with natural ingredients in their beverages will be more competitive.
- Beverages that offer proactive health benefits are also gaining importance in the beverage market.

As a result of the harm that sugar consumption causes to human health, consumers have begun to follow measures to reduce sugar consumption. Sugar-free foods and beverages have come to the fore in eating habits. The market for products such as "soda, energy drinks and tea", especially low-sugar or sugar-free drinks, has experienced great growth. Conscious consumers continue to turn to drinks that do not cause gas and bloating in order to protect their digestive health and intestinal health. On the other hand, probiotic-containing beverages are expected to grow significantly in the future (Patsnap, 2023).

NIQ (2023) determined there were several prominent beverage trends for the summer season. These include a growing trend in the soft drinks market, which is likely due to lifestyle changes and COVID-19 driving people to non-alcoholic drinks. Another trend is the emergence of fusion drinks, which involve adding fresh fruit to non-alcoholic drinks like water and tea. Cold brewed coffee has also become increasingly popular due to its smooth taste and lower caffeine content. Additionally, there is an increase

Table 4. Prebiotics usage by 2022

Regions	Percent (%)
South America	53
North America	59
Europe	48
Asia-Pacific	63
Global	54

Source: created by the authors based on data from DPO, (2023).

in demand for sports drinks as people become more health-conscious. Finally, beverages containing products made with sustainable agricultural practices are also gaining popularity (NIQ, 2023).

The most noticeable change in the beverage market is that the products leading the way are herbal drinks that strengthen immunity, drinks that help detox and energy drinks (Newsroom, 2023). As per the report by EHL in 2023, functional beverages such as Taiwan tea, organic soy milk, and green tea are gaining popularity among consumers. Fermented drinks that promote good health are also in high demand. Energy drinks with celebrity endorsements are continuing to grow in popularity. Non-alcoholic soda, non-alcoholic beer, and other similar beverages are also preferred by consumers. Healthy drinks are considered to be the most promising and rapidly growing market segment (EHL, 2023). Innova Market Insights (2023) said that consumers care more about their health. In addition, food and beverages prepared with products produced from sustainable agriculture are in the trends of the future (Innova Market Insights, 2023).

Doehler (2023) determined a healthy lifestyle reduced sugary drink consumption. Consumers with increasing health concerns have turned to low-sugar or sugar-free alternative drinks. While natural vitamin or herbal beverages come to the fore; Functional energy drinks, sports drinks and beauty drinks also emerge as growing markets (Doehler, 2023).

As consumers become more aware of the benefits of prebiotics on overall health, the prebiotic industry is expected to develop more new products. Consumers prefer to have prebiotics in a variety of categories, as they often look for functional products (DPO, 2023). As seen in Table 4, the usage of prebiotics is shown by region in 2022. According to 2022 data (see table 4) in South America, 53 percent of consumers use prebiotics. According to 2022 data in North America, 59 percent of consumers use prebiotics. 48 percent of consumers in Europe; 63 percent of consumers in the Asia-Pacific region and 44 percent of consumers globally will use prebiotics in 2022.

It is a preferred type of beverage to save energy and keep it personal and lively in terms of its intended use. It is preferred primarily by athletes (Elad, 2023). According to Elad (2023), some global data regarding the consumption of Energy Drinks can be summarized as follows:

- Research on energy consumption shows that 13 percent of consumers drank natural energy drinks in the last 3 months.
- Globally, 52 percent consume energy drinks three or three times a week.
- Caffeine amount, price and taste are important factors when choosing energy drinks.
- Generation Y constitutes a large target group in terms of energy consumption.
- Globally, it is stated that the energy drink market will be around 98.8 billion dollars in 2032.

Table 5. Global sales of energy drinks, 2022

Country	Sales (average per capita volume)
United States	28.4
United Kingdom	11.97
Japan	10.51
Spain	8.84
Germany	7.40
Indonesia	5.12
Mexico	2.30
France	2.15
China	1.57
Russia	0.23

Source: created by the authors based on data from Elad, B. (2023)

Table 6. Distribution of energy drink consumers by age group in America (September 2023)

Age	Percent (%)
18-29 years	33%
30-49 years	35%
50-64 years	14%

Source: created by the authors based on data from Statista, (2023).

When Energy Beverage consumption is examined for 2022, it is possible to see the highest sales in the world in America as seen in Table 5.

As seen in table 6, most of young American drinks energy drinks. Also, sports drinks are beverages consumed by athletes before or during training. People who engage in intense physical activity also frequently consume sports drinks. Although the largest energy drink market in the world is in America; There is also a large market for sports drinks. The global sports drink market size calculated in 2018 was recorded as 22.37 billion dollars (Grand view research, (2018).

When we look at the statistics, the most consumed beverage after water is tea. According to FAO, around 7 billion metric tons of tea were consumed globally in 2020. According to the results of Statista's research, Turkey is the country where tea is consumed the most. Table 7 shows percent of consumers who consumed tea in their daily routine.

Studies show that Americans drink tea to reduce stress, relax and calm down. For example, American consumers consumed more than 3.9 billion gallons of tea in 2021 (Tea Association of the USA Inc., (2022). As seen in Figure 3, it was determined that people in Turkey consume a lot of tea and that it is the country that consumes the most tea in the world . In search of alternative beverages, people have become more interested in tea and brewed tea products. When tea consumption indicators are examined, it can be said that the tea market is an important competitive market (Gaille, 2017).

In recent years, the tea industry has been expanding its range of varieties by producing traditional blends in various parts of the world and encouraging consumers to consume more tea. Although the

Table 7. Tea drink, 2022

Country	Percent (%)
Turkey	90%
Kenya	83%
Pakistan	83%
Morocco	80%
India	72%
Irland	69%
United Kingdom	59%
Germany	56%
USA	49%
China	45%
Spain	39%

Source: created by the authors based on data from Fleck, A. (2023).

tea sector faced difficulties in 2015 due to global changes in the world tea industry, including changes in producing countries, there was an increase in promotional fairs and festivals. Despite a significant decrease in tea production in 2015 due to climatic conditions, the global tea market is expected to maintain its dominant position in the following period (Kar, 2016). According to the information compiled from the Eastern Black Sea Exporters Association (DKİB) data, 568 tons of tea were exported from the country to 53 countries in January. A profit of 1 million 451 thousand 816 dollars was made from the export in question. Germany, England and the Netherlands were the countries with the most exports. In the first month of 2022, tea worth 277 thousand 298 dollars was sold to Germany, 234 thousand 240 dollars to England and 174 thousand 293 dollars to the Netherlands in the first month of 2022. (İstanbul Ticaret Gazetesi, 2022).

According to records in 2019, China ranks first in world tea production with 2.5 million tons. While China's production decreased by 11.4% compared to the previous year, its production areas increased by 6.3% compared to the previous year, with a production area of 3.2 million hectares. India ranks second with 628 thousand tons of production, and Kenya ranks third with 269 thousand tons of production. In

Figure 3. Tea market profile, 2016
Source: created by the authors based on data from Gaille, 2017

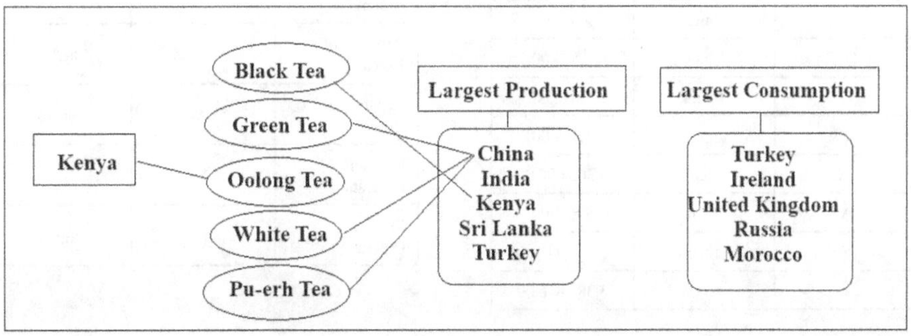

Table 8. Tea statistics 2023

Country	Element	Unit	Value
Africa	Area harvested (A)	ha	444,875.00
Africa	Yield (Y)	hg/ha	18,825.00
Africa	Production (P)	tonnes	837,492.00
Americas	A	ha	37,729.00
Americas	Y	hg/ha	90,448.00
Americas	P	tonnes	341,251.00
Argentina	A	ha	32,980.00
Argentina	Y	hg/ha	101,645.00
Argentina	P	tonnes	335,225.00
Asia	A	ha	4,823,033.00
Asia	Y	hg/ha	12,107.00
Asia	P	tonnes	5,839,104.00
Azerbaijan	A	ha	620.00
Azerbaijan	Y	hg/ha	15,032.00
Azerbaijan	P	tonnes	932.00
Bangladesh	A	ha	59,364.00
Bangladesh	Y	hg/ha	15,149.00
Bangladesh	P	tonnes	89,931.00
Bolivia (Plurinational State of)	A	ha	279.00
Bolivia (Plurinational State of)	Y	hg/ha	43,441.00
Bolivia (Plurinational State of)	P	tonnes	1,212.00
Brazil	A	ha	207.00
Brazil	Y	hg/ha	22,560.00
Brazil	P	tonnes	467.00
Burundi	A	ha	11,603.00
Burundi	Y	hg/ha	14,080.00
Burundi	P	tonnes	16,337.00
Cameroon	A	ha	2,097.00
Cameroon	Y	hg/ha	26,853.00
Cameroon	P	tonnes	5,631.00
Central America	A	ha	1,524.00
Central America	Y	hg/ha	7,822.00
Central America	P	tonnes	1,192.00
China	A	ha	3,365,697.00
China	Y	hg/ha	8,867.00
China	P	tonnes	2,984,341.00
China, mainland	A	ha	3,353,846.00
China, mainland	Y	hg/ha	8,856.00
China, mainland	P	tonnes	2,970,000.00
Colombia	A	ha	63.00
Colombia	Y	hg/ha	24,921.00
Colombia	P	tonnes	157.00
Democratic Republic of the Congo	A	ha	9,821.00
Democratic Republic of the Congo	Y	hg/ha	2,799.00
Democratic Republic of the Congo	P	tonnes	2,749.00
Ecuador	A	ha	625.00
Ecuador	Y	hg/ha	21,632.00
Ecuador	P	tonnes	1,352.00
El Salvador	A	ha	350.00
El Salvador	Y	hg/ha	18,686.00
Myanmar	P	hg/ha	14,050.00
Myanmar	A	tonnes	126,486.00
Nepal	Y	ha	28,157.00
Nepal	P	hg/ha	8,620.00
Nepal	A	tonnes	24,270.00
Oceania	Y	ha	4,093.00
Oceania	P	hg/ha	14,056.00
Oceania	A	tonnes	5,753.00
Papua New Guinea	Y	ha	4,093.00
Papua New Guinea	P	hg/ha	14,056.00
Papua New Guinea	A	tonnes	5,753.00
Peru	Y	ha	2,051.00
Peru	P	hg/ha	8,025.00
Peru	A	tonnes	1,646.00
Republic of Korea	Y	ha	2,286.00
Republic of Korea	P	hg/ha	10,770.00
Republic of Korea	A	tonnes	2,462.00
Russian Federation	Y	ha	488.00
Russian Federation	P	hg/ha	7,008.00

continued on following page

Table 8. Continued

Country	Element	Unit	Value
Russian Federation	A	tonnes	342.00
Rwanda	Y	ha	21,128.00
Rwanda	P	hg/ha	15,924.00
Rwanda	A	tonnes	33,645.00
Southern Europe	Y	ha	124.00
Southern Europe	P	hg/ha	8,065.00
Southern Europe	A	tonnes	100.00
Sri Lanka	Y	ha	264,688.00
Sri Lanka	P	hg/ha	10,521.00
Sri Lanka	A	tonnes	278,489.00
Thailand	Y	ha	19,532.00
Thailand	P	hg/ha	50,019.00
Thailand	A	tonnes	97,697.00
Turkey	Y	ha	83,451.00
Turkey	P	hg/ha	30,579.00
Turkey	A	tonnes	255,183.00
Uganda	Y	ha	29,573.00
Uganda	P	hg/ha	21,442.00
Uganda	A	tonnes	63,411.00
United Republic of Tanzania	Y	ha	21,813.00
United Republic of Tanzania	P	hg/ha	21,115.00
United Republic of Tanzania	A	tonnes	46,058.00
Viet Nam	Y	ha	107,366.00
Viet Nam	P	hg/ha	22,399.00
Viet Nam	A	tonnes	240,493.00
Zambia	Y	ha	676.00
Zambia	P	hg/ha	13,876.00
Zambia	A	tonnes	938.00
Zimbabwe	Y	ha	2,460.00
Zimbabwe	P	hg/ha	15,110.00
Zimbabwe	A	tonnes	3,717.00
El Salvador	Y	tonnes	654.00
Ethiopia	P	ha	9,861.00
Ethiopia	A	hg/ha	10,482.00
Ethiopia	Y	tonnes	10,336.00
Georgia	P	ha	2,274.00
Georgia	A	hg/ha	10,554.00
Georgia	Y	tonnes	2,400.00
Guatemala	P	ha	1,174.00
Guatemala	A	hg/ha	4,583.00

Country	Element	Unit	Value
Guatemala	Y	tonnes	538.00
India	P	ha	629,778.00
India	A	hg/ha	22,622.00
India	Y	tonnes	1,424,662.00
Indonesia	P	ha	107,905.00
Indonesia	A	hg/ha	12,819.00
Indonesia	Y	tonnes	138,323.00
Iran (Islamic Republic of)	P	ha	15,073.00
Iran (Islamic Republic of)	A	hg/ha	56,182.00
Iran (Islamic Republic of)	Y	tonnes	84,683.00
Japan	P	ha	39,100.00
Japan	A	hg/ha	17,852.00
Japan	Y	tonnes	69,800.00
Kenya	P	ha	269,400.00
Kenya	A	hg/ha	21,140.00
Kenya	Y	tonnes	569,500.00
Madagascar	P	ha	1,729.00
Madagascar	A	hg/ha	2,209.00
Madagascar	Y	tonnes	382.00
Malawi	P	ha	18,108.00
Malawi	A	hg/ha	26,433.00
Malawi	Y	tonnes	47,865.00
Malaysia	P	ha	1,869.00
Malaysia	A	hg/ha	50,268.00
Malaysia	Y	tonnes	9,395.00
Mali	P	ha	91.00
Mali	A	hg/ha	9,451.00
Mali	Y	tonnes	86.00
Mauritius	P	ha	685.00
Mauritius	A	hg/ha	15,810.00
Mauritius	Y	tonnes	1,083.00
Melanesia	P	ha	4,093.00
Melanesia	A	hg/ha	14,056.00
Melanesia	Y	tonnes	5,753.00
Montenegro	P	ha	124.00
Montenegro	A	hg/ha	8,065.00
Montenegro	Y	tonnes	100.00
Mozambique	P	ha	44,746.00
Mozambique	A	hg/ha	7,507.00
Mozambique	Y	tonnes	33,592.00
Myanmar	P	ha	90,023.00

Source: adapted from open access data from UN data (2021)

Kenya, while production areas increased by 14.1% compared to the previous year, there was a decrease in production by 6.9%. In 2019, 1.7% of the world's tea planting areas and 4.0% of the production took place in Turkey (Strateji Geliştirme Başkanlığı, (2021).

In 2020, 57% of the world's tea exports were made by Kenya, China and India. While Kenya is the leader in exports with 452 thousand tons, the second largest country is China with 351 thousand tons. Pakistan, Russian Federation and England are important countries in imports. While Pakistan ranks first with 254 thousand tons of imports, the Russian Federation ranks second with 151 thousand tons and the United Kingdom ranks third with 130 thousand tons (Strateji Geliştirme Başkanlığı, (2021).

Table 8 shows "Area harvested (A), Yield (Y), Production (P)" indicators for tea in 2021. In addition, the total area of tea cultivation in the world in 2021 is 5.2 million hectares. Approximately 64% of the total area is located in China and 10% in India. The world tea area, which was 4.7 million hectares in 2017, increased by approximately 10.6% in the last 5 years and reached 5.2 million hectares in 2021 (Erkal, 2023).

One product that stands out among functional and healthy drinks is kefir. Kefir, whose homeland is the Caucasus, is a fermented dairy product. It is obtained by fermenting cow, goat and sheep milk. Kefir is similar in appearance to buttermilk and has a sour taste. Its sourness increases with the length of fermentation time. As with many fermented products, it is important for the health of the digestive system. It strengthens and protects the immune system with its rich vitamin, mineral and probiotic content. To benefit from the benefits of kefir, it must be consumed regularly. (Memorial Tıbbi Yayın Kurulu, (2023). Kefir is a probiotic drink that differs from prebiotic yoghurt as it contains substances that increase the growth of beneficial microorganisms. It has been consumed by the people of the Caucasus as a health drink for centuries and is now enjoyed worldwide. Its positive effects on health were discovered in the early 8th century and its fame soon spread beyond the borders of the Caucasus to Russia, Europe, the USA and Australia in the early 19th century (Ovalı, 2020:8).

SOLUTIONS AND RECOMMENDATIONS

In this study, an overview of the functional beverage market is given. The following situations can be stated for the functional beverage market examined with an economic and market-based approach:

- Export of products in the functional beverage market will be beneficial in order to open up to new markets.
- Necessary R&D studies should be carried out to develop alternative functional beverage products.
- Since it is a rising and competitive market, the distribution channel, positioning strategy and target audience that will be most advantageous for the countries can be determined,
- Focusing on a specific functional beverage category rather than the entire product range can provide competitive advantage.
- Countries must continue to produce functional beverages in accordance with the necessary principles in terms of food safety and sustainability.
- Continuity is important in the production of functional and healthy beverages in terms of both food and health.

FUTURE RESEARCH DIRECTIONS

The aim of this research is to give a brief outline of functional drinks, globally, by utilizing current, publicly available data, reports, and other resources. It's important to mention that this study is limited to secondary data sources. In the future, research can focus on empirical methods to investigate market statistics for specific countries during specific periods. It's worth noting that the size of the market and the future of functional beverages may vary from country to country around the world. It can be give following directions for future studies as below:

- For future research, analysts can estimate the market size of functional beverages by studying specific brands.
- In upcoming studies, researchers may investigate the global or regional market size of functional beverages.
- In future research, econometric analysis and time series can provide more empirical evidence regarding the size of the functional beverage market.

CONCLUSION

Functional food products and markets have gained a lot of attention in recent years due to their rising economic value. This study specifically focuses on the functional beverage industry within the functional food category. The aim of the study is to provide readers with an overview of the industry from an economic and market-based perspective. The book chapter provides basic information on functional foods and highlights the latest market indicators. To ensure accuracy, the study relies on the most up-to-date and reliable secondary sources available. In recent years, the functional food and beverage industry has experienced remarkable growth. This is due to increasing awareness about the importance of maintaining a healthy lifestyle, the ease of accessing information through digital technologies, and the impact of the COVID-19 pandemic (Nazir et al., 2019; Corbo et al., 2014; Tireki, 2021; Gupta, 2023). While human life is changing in every aspect with the COVID-19 pandemic (Öncü et al., 2021; Bostanci et al., 2022); It can be said that people's personal efforts to be healthier have also increased. In this respect, although there are undesirable situations such as self-diagnosis and excessive vitamin use (Yıldırım, 2023), the increase in the use of healthy foods and beverages through nutrition instead of drugs and chemical-containing products is a very positive situation.

Sustainable health for societies is so important issue in the context of sustainable development (Yıldırım et al., 2020). When considering 2030 SDGs, achieving sustainable health system in a society should be ensured in the long term. During the COVID-19 pandemic, both of developing and developed countries challenged by health crises and they saw how it was hard to achieve sustainable well-being of society in the long term. In some situations, people might not have access to the necessary medication or vaccines when urgent treatment is required. Additionally, some diseases might not be adequately treatable with medicine. In such cases, maintaining a healthy lifestyle and eating habits can help build resistance to illnesses. Consuming functional foods and beverages can also be beneficial to improve overall health and resilience during sudden health crises. The popularity of functional foods and beverages, which are associated with a healthy lifestyle, has increased during the COVID-19 pandemic. These products are being viewed as an alternative means of supporting global health, and to combat various viruses and infectious diseases that may arise in the future. However, it is important to conduct the necessary toxicological tests, determine the optimal usage rates, and promote healthy exercise habits to effectively fight against diseases such as COVID-19. The misuse of functional foods and beverages can potentially lead to other health issues, and therefore, proper caution and moderation must be exercised in their use (Farzana et al., 2022; Gouvarchinghaleh et al., 2023; Thakur and Thakur, 2021; Han and Hoang, 2020; Yang et al., 2020). Among functional drinks, it may be more beneficial for a sustainable society for the future if businesses continue to produce sustainable foods and beverages that positively support aging, strengthen immunity and have healthy ingredients.

ACKNOWLEDGMENT

Turkish references are translated into English. The author(s) gives keywords and definitions based on this study as a result of the review.

REFERENCES

Aydın, K., Yıldırım, S., & Çizer, E. Ö. (2023). Big Dilemma In Face Mask Consumption: Environmental Sensitivity Versus The Fear Of COVID-19. *International Journal of Global Warming*, *29*(3), 207–226. doi:10.1504/IJGW.2023.129490

Bostanci, S., Yildirim, S., & Erdoğan, F. (2022). A review on e-Government Portal's services within Hospital Information System during Covid-19 pandemic. *Konuralp Tip Dergisi*, *14*(S1), 271–279. doi:10.18521/ktd.1036010

Corbo, M. R., Bevilacqua, A., Petruzzi, L., Casanova, F. P., & Sinigaglia, M. (2014). Functional Beverages: The Emerging Side of Functional Foods. *Comprehensive Reviews in Food Science and Food Safety*, *13*(6), 1192–1206. doi:10.1111/1541-4337.12109

Dini, I. (2019). 1 - An Overview of Functional Beverages. Academic Press. doi:10.1016/B978-0-12-816397-9.00001-7

Doehler. (2023). *Trends and developments in the beverage industry in 2023.* Doehler. https://www.doehler.com/en/news-media/details/trends-and-developments-in-the-beverage-industry-in-2023.html

DPO. (2023). *Global Market Trends 2023: Beverages*. DPO. https://dpointernational.com/wp-content/uploads/2023/03/GLOBAL-MARKET-TRENDS-2023-BEVERAGES.pdf

EHL. (2023). *Drink trends in 2023: 8 beverages you've got to try this year.* EHL. https://www.hospitalitynet.org/news/4115081.html

Elad, B. (2023). *Energy Drink Statistics – By Demographic, Distribution, Country, Consumers and Region*. Enterprise Apps Today. https://www.enterpriseappstoday.com/stats/energy-drink-statistics.html

Erkal, H. (2023). *Ürün Raporu ÇAY 2023 (Product Report Tea 2023)*, https://arastirma.tarimorman.gov.tr/tepge/Belgeler/PDF%20%C3%9Cr%C3%BCn%20Raporlar%C4%B1/2023%20%C3%9Cr%C3%BCn%20Raporlar%C4%B1/%C3%87ay%20%C3%9Cr%C3%BCn%20Raporu%202023-383%20TEPGE.pdf

Euromonitor International. (2023). *Need States: Understanding the Future of Functional Beverages, Overview*. Euromonitor International. https://www.euromonitor.com/need-states-understanding-the-future-of-functional-beverages/report

Farzana, M., Shahriar, S., Jeba, F. R., Tabassum, T., Araf, Y., Ullah, M. A., Tasnim, J., Chakraborty, A., Naima, T. A., Marma, K. K. S., Rahaman, T. I., & Hosen, M. J. (2022). Functional food: Complementary to fight against COVID-19. *Beni-Suef University Journal of Basic and Applied Sciences*, *11*(1), 33. doi:10.1186/s43088-022-00217-z PMID:35284580

Finlays. (2022). *Global Beverage Trends 2023*. Finlays. https://www.finlays.net/wp-content/uploads/2022/11/Global-Beverage-Trends-2023.pdf

Fleck, A. (2023). *Who Drinks Tea?* Statista. https://www.statista.com/chart/29582/share-of-people-that-drink-tea-in-selected-countries/

Foragekitchen. (2023). *13 Food and Beverage Industry Trends in 2023*. Foragekitchen. https://www.foragekitchen.com/resources/2023/7/25/13-food-and-beverage-industry-trends-in-2023

Gaille, B. (2017). *19 Shocking Tea Consumption Statistics*. Brandon Gaille. https://brandongaille.com/18-shocking-tea-consumption-statistics/

Gayathry, K. S., & John, J. A. (2021). Functional beverages: Special focus on anti-diabetic potential. *Journal of Food Processing and Preservation*, *45*, e15974. doi:10.1111/jfpp.15974

Georgie, N. (2023). *Food and Beverage Industry: Beverage Industry Trends in 2023*. Blue Cart. https://www.bluecart.com/blog/beverage-industry-trends#:~:text=The%202023%20beverage%20industry%20trends%20include%3A&text=and%20mocktail%20drinks-,Hybrid%20beverages,Sugar%20reduction

Gouvarchinghaleh, H. E., Kiany, F., Parastouei, K., Alishir, G., Jafari, N. J., Fooladi, A. A. I., Pargar, A., Ghazvini, A., Mirnejad, R., Raei, M., Olounabadi, A. S., Babaei, M., Heydari, S., Rostami, H., Shahriary, A., Farnoosh, G., Sobhani, V., & Mazhari, M. M. (2023). The effects of functional foods mixture on inflammatory cytokines and biochemical findings in hospitalized patients with COVID-19: A randomized double-blind controlled trial. *Trials*, *24*(1), 442. doi:10.1186/s13063-023-07481-z PMID:37408032

Grand view research. (2018). *Sports Drink Market Size, Share & Trends Analysis Report By Product (Isotonic, Hypertonic, Hypotonic)*. Grand View Research. https://www.grandviewresearch.com/industry-analysis/sports-drink-market

Gupta, A., Sanwal, N., Bareen, M. A., Barua, S., Sharma, N., Olatunji, O. J., Nirmal, N. P., & Jatindra, K. (2023). Sahu, (2023). Trends in functional beverages: Functional ingredients, processing technologies, stability, health benefits, and consumer perspective. *Food Research International*, *170*, 113046. doi:10.1016/j.foodres.2023.113046 PMID:37316029

Han, B., & Hoang, B. X. (2020). Opinions on the current pandemic of COVID-19: Use functional food to boost our immune functions. *Journal of Infection and Public Health*, *13*(12), 1811–1817. doi:10.1016/j.jiph.2020.08.014 PMID:32948484

Innova Market Insights. (2023). *Top Ten Trends for 2023*. Innova Market Insights. https://www.innovamarketinsights.com/trends/top-ten-trends-for-2023-redefining-value-in-a-volatile-world/

İstanbul Ticaret Gazetesi. (2022). *Çay İhracatı 2022 yılının ilk ayında 1. Milyon dolar kazandırdı (Tea Exports brought 1. Million dollars in the first month of 2022).* Istanbul Ticaret Gazetesi. https://istanbulticaretgazetesi.com/tr/cay-ihracati-2022-yilinin-ilk-ayinda-14-milyon-dolar-kazandirdi

Kar, M. Y. (2016). *2030 Yilinda Çay Sektörümüz Raporu (Our Tea Industry Report In 2030).* Caysiad. https://www.caysiad.org.tr/index.php?sayfa=203.90&d=tr

Kerschbaumer, C. (2023). *The top trends 2023 on the beverage market.* Austria Juice. https://www.austriajuice.com/news-blog/the-top-trends-on-the-beverage-market

Koçak, D. (2019). *Fonksiyonel Besin Nedir? (What Is Functional Food?).* Milliyet. https://www.milliyet.com.tr/cadde/dilara-kocak/fonksiyonel-besin-nedir-2902052

Kunst, A. (2023). *Consumers of energy drinks in the United States as of September 2023, by age, November 2023.* Statista. https://www.statista.com/forecasts/228168/energy-drinks-consumption-usa

Memorial Tıbbi Yayın Kurulu. (2023). *Kefirin faydaları nelerdir? (What are the benefits of kefir?).* Memorial. https://www.memorial.com.tr/saglik-rehberi/kefirin-faydalari-nelerdir

Mintel. (2023). *The Future of Global Functional Drinks Trends.* Mintel. https://www.mintel.com/food-and-drink-market-news/the-future-of-global-functional-drinks-trends/#:~:text=Drinks%20that%20offer%20health%20benefits,market%20is%20expanding%20and%20diversifying

Nazir, M., Arif, S., Khan, R. S., Nazir, W., Khalid, N., & Maqsood, S. (2019). Opportunities and challenges for functional and medicinal beverages: Current and future trends. *Trends in Food Science & Technology*, *88*, 513–526. doi:10.1016/j.tifs.2019.04.011

NBLTürkiye. (n.d.). *Fonksiyonel Beslenme Nedir? Fonksiyonel Beslenme Hakkında Her Şey (What is Functional Nutrition?)* All About Functional Nutrition. https://nblturkiye.com/fonksiyonel-beslenme-nedir-fonksiyonel-beslenme-hakkinda-her-sey/

NovaNutrica. (2018). *Modern Çağda Yeni Bir Beslenme Alışkanlığı: Fonksiyonel Gıdalar (A New Nutrition Habit in the Modern Age: Functional Foods).* NovaNutrica. https://www.novanutrica.com/modern-cagda-yeni-bir-beslenme-aliskanligi-fonksiyonel-gidalar

Öncü, M. A., Yildirim, S., Bostanci, S., & Erdoğan, F. (2021). The Effect of COVID-19 Pandemic on Health Management and Health Services: A Case of Turkey. *Duzce Medical Journal*, *23*(Special Issue), 61–70. doi:10.18678/dtfd.860733

Ovalı, B. B. (2020). Fonksiyonel Probiyotik: Kefir. *Bursa Gıda Bülten*, Ocak-Şubat-Mart 2020, Bülten Sayısı, 47 https://arastirma.tarimorman.gov.tr/bursagida/Belgeler/e-B%C3%BClten/2020%20SAYI%2047.pdf

Özel Beslenme. (2022). *Fonksiyonel Gıda Nedir? (What is Functional Food?).* Ozel Beslenme. https://www.ozelbeslenme.com/blogs/blog/fonksiyonel-gida-nedir

Özkaya, Ş. Ö. (2021). Quality of Life and Functional Foods, Fenerbahce University. *Journal of Health Sciences*, *1*(1), 62–68.

Patsnap, (2023). *7 Key Beverage Industry Trends to Watch Out For in 2023.* Patsnap. https://www.patsnap.com/resources/blog/7-key-beverage-industry-trends-to-watch-out-for-in-2023/

Precedence Research. (2023). *Functional Beverages Market (By Type: Energy Drink, Caffeinated Beverages, Probiotic Drinks, Vegetable and fruit beverages, Others; By Application: Health and Wellness, Weight Loss; By Ingredient: Antioxidants, Minerals, Amino acids, Probiotics, Prebiotics, Vitamins, Others; By End User: Athletes, Fitness Lifestyle Users, Others; By Distribution Channel).* Precedence Research. https://www.precedenceresearch.com/functional-beverages-market

Strateji Geliştirme Başkanlığı. (2021).*Tarım Ürünleri Piyasaları, ÇAY, (Agricultural Products Markets, TEA).* Arastirma. https://arastirma.tarimorman.gov.tr/tepge/Belgeler/PDF%20Tar%C4%B1m%20%C3%9Cr%C3%BCnleri%20Piyasalar%C4%B1/2021-Haziran%20Tar%C4%B1m%20%C3%9Cr%C3%BCnleri%20Raporu/%C3%87ay,%20Haziran-2021,%20Tar%C4%B1m%20%C3%9Cr%C3%BCnleri%20Piyasa%20Raporu,%20TEPGE.pdf

Tea Association of the USA Inc. (2022). *Tea Fact Sheet – 2022.* Tea USA. https://www.teausa.com/teausa/images/Tea_Fact_2021.pdf

Thakur, H.A. & N.S. Thakur, N.S.,(2021). Role of functional food components in COVID-19 pandemic: A review, *Annals of Phytomedicine*, Volume10, Special Issue1 (COVID-19): S240-S250, 2021

The Snack Haus. (n.d.). *Geleceğin Gidalari: Fonksiyonel Gidalar, (Foods of the Future: Functional Foods).* The Snack Haus. https://thesnackhaus.com/blog/fonksiyonel-gidalar/

(2021). Tireki, s. (2021). A review on packed non-alcoholic beverages: Ingredients, production, trends and future opportunities for functional product development. *Trends in Food Science & Technology, 112*(June), 442–454.

Yang, F., Zhang, Y., Tariq, A., Jiang, X., Ahmed, Z., Zhihao, Z., Idrees, M., Azizullah, A., Adnan, M., & Bussmann, R. W. (2020). Food as medicine: A possible preventive measure against coronavirus disease (COVID-19). *Phytotherapy Research, 34*(12), 3124–3136. doi:10.1002/ptr.6770 PMID:32468635

Yıldırım, S. (2023). The Challenge of Self-diagnosis on Mental Health Through Social Media: A Qualitative Study. In G. Battineni, M. Mittal, & N. Chintalapudi (Eds.), *Computational Methods in Psychiatry*. Springer. doi:10.1007/978-981-99-6637-0_10

Yıldırım, S., Bostancı, S. H., Yıldırım, D. Ç., & Erdoğan, F. (2021). Rethinking mobility of international university students during COVID-19 pandemic. *Higher Education Evaluation and Development, 15*(2), 98–113. doi:10.1108/HEED-01-2021-0014

Yıldırım, S., Yildirim, D. C., & Calıskan, H. (2020). The influence of health on economic growth from the perspective of sustainable development: A case of OECD countries. *World Journal of Entrepreneurship, Management and Sustainable Development, 16*(3), 181–194. doi:10.1108/WJEMSD-09-2019-0071

ADDITIONAL READING

Sevik, N., & Yıldırım, S. (2023). Sustainable Enterprises Post COVID-19 Pandemic: The Rise of Sustainable Fashion Enterprises. In R. Castanho (Ed.), *Handbook of Research on Current Advances and Challenges of Borderlands, Migration, and Geopolitics* (pp. 343–359). IGI Global. doi:10.4018/978-1-6684-7020-6.ch017

Yıldırım, S. (2021). Do green women influencers spur sustainable consumption patterns? Descriptive evidences from social media influencers. *Ecofeminism and Climate Change*, *2*(4), 198–210. doi:10.1108/EFCC-02-2021-0003

Yıldırım, S. (2023). The Challenge of Self-diagnosis on Mental Health Through Social Media: A Qualitative Study. In G. Battineni, M. Mittal, & N. Chintalapudi (Eds.), *Computational Methods in Psychiatry*. Springer. doi:10.1007/978-981-99-6637-0_10

Yıldırım, S., & Bostancı, S. H. (2021). The efficiency of e-government portal management from a citizen perspective: Evidences from Turkey, *World Journal of Science. Technology and Sustainable Development*, *18*(3), 259–273. doi:10.1108/WJSTSD-04-2021-0049

Yıldırım, S., Bostancı, S. H., Yıldırım, D. Ç., & Erdoğan, F. (2021). Rethinking mobility of international university students during COVID-19 pandemic. *Higher Education Evaluation and Development*, *15*(2), 98–113. doi:10.1108/HEED-01-2021-0014

Yıldırım, S., & Yıldırım, D. Ç. (2020). Achieving Sustainable Development Through a Green Economy Approach. In S. Patti & G. Trizzino (Eds.), *Advanced Integrated Approaches to Environmental Economics and Policy: Emerging Research and Opportunities* (pp. 1–22). IGI Global. doi:10.4018/978-1-5225-9562-5.ch001

Yıldırım, S., Yildirim, D. C., & Calıskan, H. (2020). The influence of health on economic growth from the perspective of sustainable development: A case of OECD countries. *World Journal of Entrepreneurship, Management and Sustainable Development*, *16*(3), 181–194. doi:10.1108/WJEMSD-09-2019-0071

KEY TERMS AND DEFINITIONS

Beverage Market: A market includes various drinks and beverages.

Functional Beverages: A beverage or drink that provides some benefits such as well-being, relaxation, aging-support, energy-support for consumer.

Healthy Beverages: A beverage or drink that provides health outcomes for consumer.

Compilation of References

(2021). Tireki, s. (2021). A review on packed non-alcoholic beverages: Ingredients, production, trends and future opportunities for functional product development. *Trends in Food Science & Technology*, *112*(June), 442–454.

Aaltonen, S., Heinze, A., Ielpa, G., & De Tommaso, D. (2015). Enterprise Cultural Heritage: The Source for Sustainable Competitive Advantage and Survival for Food Sector SMEs. *International Journal of Entrepreneurship and Innovation*, *16*(2), 73–83. doi:10.5367/ijei.2015.0178

Ab Rashid, N., & Bojei, J. (2020). The relationship between halal traceability system adoption and environmental factors on halal food supply chain integrity in Malaysia. *Journal of Islamic Marketing*, *11*(1), 117–142. doi:10.1108/JIMA-01-2018-0016

Ab Talib, M. S., & Zulfakar, M. H. (2023). Sustainable halal food supply chain management in a small rentier halal market. *Arab Gulf Journal of Scientific Research*. doi:10.1108/AGJSR-11-2022-0251

Abbas, J. (2020). Impact of total quality management on corporate sustainability through the mediating effect of knowledge management. *Journal of Cleaner Production*, *244*, 118806. doi:10.1016/j.jclepro.2019.118806

Abbas, J., & Sagsan, M. (2019). Impact of knowledge management practices on green innovation and corporate sustainable development: A structural analysis. *Journal of Cleaner Production*, *229*, 611–620. doi:10.1016/j.jclepro.2019.05.024

Abdul Rahim, N. R., Abdullah, I., Yahya, N. A., Awang, M. N., Muhammad, S. Z., Ahmad Sabri, S., & Ahmad, N. N. (2022). Negotiation of needs towards halal talents sustainability. *Journal of Islamic Marketing*, *13*(1), 20–44. doi:10.1108/JIMA-11-2019-0245

Abdullah, M. A., & Azam, M. S. E. (2020). Halal entrepreneurship from maqasid-al-sharia'h perspective: Inseparable concept for halalpreneurs. *Food Research*, *4*(S1), 34–42. doi:10.26656/fr.2017.4(S1).S07

Abdullah, R., Sabar, R., & Mustafar, M. (2018). Green Halal supply chain in Malaysian halal food companies: A conceptual framework. *International Journal of Supply Chain Management*, *7*(5), 502–510. https://www.scopus.com/inward/record.uri?eid=2-s2.0-85060870564&partnerID=40&md5=04ca49f07d21949606b68e3ce6c0a3c1

Acuti, D., Mazzoli, V., Grazzini, L., & Rinaldi, R. (2019). New patterns in wine consumption: The wine by the glass trend. *British Food Journal*, *122*(8), 2655–2669. doi:10.1108/BFJ-04-2019-0299

Adelodun, B., Kareem, K. Y., Kumar, P., Kumar, V., Choi, K. S., Yadav, K. K., Yadav, A., El-Denglawey, A., Cabral-Pinto, M., Son, C. T., Krishnan, S., & Khan, N. A. (2021). Understanding the impacts of the COVID-19 pandemic on sustainable agri-food system and agroecosystem decarbonization nexus: A review. *Journal of Cleaner Production*, *318*, 128451. doi:10.1016/j.jclepro.2021.128451 PMID:36570877

Adham, K. A., Muhamad, N. S., & Said, M. F. (2020). Diagnosing the Halal Industry of Taiwan: A viable system model approach. *Jurnal Pengurusan*, *58*, 169–179. doi:10.17576/pengurusan-2020-58-14

Aertsens, J., Verbeke, W., Mondelaers, K., & Van Huylenbroeck, G. (2009). Personal determinants of organic food consumption: A review. *British Food Journal*, *111*(10), 1140–1167. https://www.grandviewresearch.com/industry-analysis/organic-personal-care-market. doi:10.1108/00070700910992961

Afonso, C., Gavilán, D., Martins Gonçalves, H., & García de Madariaga, J. (2017). Why consumers purchase organic products? The role of environment, health and age. In *XXIX Congreso de Marketing AEMARK*. ESIC.

Afshari, H., Searcy, C., & Jaber, M. Y. (2020). The role of eco-innovation drivers in promoting additive manufacturing in supply chains. *International Journal of Production Economics*, *223*, 107538. doi:10.1016/j.ijpe.2019.107538

Aftab, J., Abid, N., Sarwar, H., & Veneziani, M. (2022). Environmental ethics, green innovation, and sustainable performance: Exploring the role of environmental leadership and environmental strategy. *Journal of Cleaner Production*, *378*, 134639. doi:10.1016/j.jclepro.2022.134639

Agro, E. F. E. (2024). *Las bebidas espirituosas amplían su autorregulación con normas para 'influencers' y las 0,0.* EFE:Agro https://efeagro.com/bebidas-espirituosas-amplian-autorregulacion/

Aguilar, R. (2014). *Innovación Abierta vs Innovación Cerrada I+DEA*. I+DEA. https://www.imasdea.com.mx/innovacion-abierta-vs-innovacion-cerrada/

Ahmad Tarmizi, H., Kamarulzaman, N. H., Abd Rahman, A., & Atan, R. (2020). Adoption of internet of things among Malaysian halal agro-food smes and its challenges. *Food Research*, *4*(S1), 256–265. doi:10.26656/fr.2017.4(S1).S26

Ahmad, N., Ghazali, N., Abdullah, M. F., Nordin, R., Nasir, I. N. M., & Farid, N. A. M. (2020). Green marketing and its effect on consumers' purchase behaviour: An empirical analysis. *Journal of International Business. Economics and Entrepreneurship*, *5*(2), 46–55.

Akyelken, N., & Keller, H. (2014). Framing the nexus of globalisation, logistics and manufacturing in Europe. *Transport Reviews*, *34*(6), 674–690. doi:10.1080/01441647.2014.981885

Alam, M. Z. (2023). A Study on The Selection Motives and Challenges Faced by Consumers Concerning Green Packaged Products. *TEM Journal*, *12*(4), 2273. doi:10.18421/TEM124-38

Alant, K., & Bruwer, J. (2004). Wine tourism behaviour in the context of a motivational framework for wine regions and cellar doors. *Journal of Wine Research*, *15*(1), 27–37. doi:10.1080/0957126042000300308

Albino, V., Balice, A., & Dangelico, R. M. (2009). Environmental strategies and green product development: An overview on sustainability-driven companies. *Business Strategy and the Environment*, *18*(2), 83–96. doi:10.1002/bse.638

Albort-Morant, G., Henseler, J., Leal-Millán, A., & Cepeda-Carrión, G. (2017). Mapping the field: A bibliometric analysis of green innovation. *Sustainability (Basel)*, *9*(6), 1011. doi:10.3390/su9061011

Albort-Morant, G., Leal-Millán, A., & Cepeda-Carrión, G. (2016). The antecedents of green innovation performance: A model of learning and capabilities. *Journal of Business Research*, *69*(11), 4912–4917. doi:10.1016/j.jbusres.2016.04.052

Albort-Morant, G., Leal-Rodríguez, A. L., & De Marchi, V. (2018). Absorptive capacity and relationship learning mechanisms as complementary drivers of green innovation performance. *Journal of Knowledge Management*, *22*(2), 432–452. doi:10.1108/JKM-07-2017-0310

Aldrich, H. E., & Cliff, J. E. (2003). The pervasive effects of family on entrepreneurship: Toward a family embeddedness perspective. *Journal of Business Venturing*, *18*(5), 573–596. doi:10.1016/S0883-9026(03)00011-9

Ali, M. H., Chung, L., Kumar, A., Zailani, S., & Tan, K. H. (2021). A sustainable Blockchain framework for the halal food supply chain: Lessons from Malaysia. *Technological Forecasting and Social Change*, *170*, 120870. Advance online publication. doi:10.1016/j.techfore.2021.120870

Ali, M. H., & Suleiman, N. (2018). Eleven shades of food integrity: A halal supply chain perspective. *Trends in Food Science & Technology*, *71*, 216–224. doi:10.1016/j.tifs.2017.11.016

Allam, Z., & Dhunny, Z. A. (2019). On big data, artificial intelligence and smart cities. *Cities (London, England)*, *89*, 80–91. doi:10.1016/j.cities.2019.01.032

Almeida, C. M. V. B., Rodrigues, A. J. M., Agostinho, F., & Giannetti, B. F. (2017). Material selection for environmental responsibility: The case of soft drinks packaging in Brazil. *Journal of Cleaner Production*, *142*, 173–179. doi:10.1016/j.jclepro.2016.04.130

Alonso, A., & Bressan, A. (2016). Micro and small business innovation in a traditional industry. *International Journal of Innovation Science*, *8*(4), 311–330. doi:10.1108/IJIS-06-2016-0013

Alonso, A., Bressan, A., Kim, O., Kok, S., & Atay, E. (2022). Integrating tradition and innovation within a wine tourism and hospitality experience. *International Journal of Tourism Research*, *25*(1), 169–182. doi:10.1002/jtr.2561

Alonso, A., & Kok, S. (2020). Identifying key wine product and wine tourism attributes in an ultra-peripheral wine region: Implications for wine consumers and wine tourism. *Tourism Recreation Research*, *45*(4), 469–484. doi:10.1080/02508281.2020.1746999

Alonso, A., Kok, S., & O'brien, S. (2019). Understanding approaches to innovation through the dynamic capabilities lens: A multi-country study of the wine industry. *International Journal of Innovation Management*, *23*(6), 1950054. doi:10.1142/S1363919619500543

Alonso, A., & O'Neill, M. (2010). Wine tourismin Spain: The case of three wine regions. *Tourism: An International Interdisciplinary Journal*, *57*(4), 405–420.

Al-Tayyar, N. A., Youssef, A. M., & Al-hindi, R. (2020). Antimicrobial food packaging based on sustainable Bio-based materials for reducing foodborne Pathogens: A review. *Food Chemistry*, *310*, 125915. doi:10.1016/j.foodchem.2019.125915 PMID:31841936

Al-Thani, N. A., & Al-Ansari, T. (2021). Comparing the convergence and divergence within industrial ecology, circular economy, and the energy-water-food nexus based on resource management objectives. *Sustainable Production and Consumption*, *27*, 1743–1761. doi:10.1016/j.spc.2021.04.008

Altman, B. W., & Vidaver-Cohen, D. (2000). A framework for understanding corporate citizenship. *Business and Society Review*, *105*(1), 1–7. doi:10.1111/0045-3609.00061

Alves, H. M., Sousa, B., Carvalho, A., Santos, V., Lopes Dias, Á., & Valeri, M. (2022). Encouraging brand attachment on consumer behaviour: Pet-friendly tourism segment. [JTHSM]. *Journal of Tourism, Heritage & Services Mar-keting*, *8*(2), 16–24.

Amankwah-Amoah, J., Danso, A., & Adomako, S. (2019). Entrepreneurial orientation, environmental sustainability and new venture performance: Does stakeholder integration matter? *Business Strategy and the Environment*, *28*(1), 79–87. doi:10.1002/bse.2191

Amarando, M., Assenov, I., & Visuthismajarn, P. (2019). A systematic review of sustainable wine tourism research in asia 2000-2018. *African Journal of Hospitality, Tourism and Leisure*, *8*(4), 2223–814X.

Amato, L., & Amato, C. (2007). The Effects of Firm Size and Industry on Corporate Giving. *Journal of Business Ethics*, *72*(3), 229–241. doi:10.1007/s10551-006-9167-5

Amato, L., & Amato, C. H. (2012). Retail philanthropy: Firm size, industry, and business cycle. *Journal of Business Ethics*, *107*(4), 435–448. doi:10.1007/s10551-011-1048-x

American Marketing Association. (2017). *What is Marketing? —The Definition of Marketing*. AMA. https://www.ama.org/the-definition-of-marketing-what-is-marketing/

Amore, M. D., & Bennedsen, M. (2016). Corporate governance and green innovation. *Journal of Environmental Economics and Management*, *75*, 54–72. doi:10.1016/j.jeem.2015.11.003

Anderson, K. (2013). Is Georgia the next "new" wine-exporting country? *Journal of Wine Economics*, *8*(1), 1–28. doi:10.1017/jwe.2013.7

Anderson, P. (2009). Is it time to ban alcohol advertising? *Clinical Medicine*, *9*(2), 121–124. doi:10.7861/clinmedicine.9-2-121 PMID:19435114

Andoni, M., Robu, V., Flynn, D., Abram, S., Geach, D., Jenkins, D., McCallum, P., & Peacock, A. (2019). Blockchain technology in the energy sector: A systematic review of challenges and opportunities. *Renewable & Sustainable Energy Reviews*, *100*, 143–174. doi:10.1016/j.rser.2018.10.014

Andrade, D. M., De Lima, J. B., Antonialli, L. M., & De Muylder, C. F. (2011). The family social capital impact in practices of learning, change and innovation in entrepreneurial family businesses. *African Journal of Business Management*, *5*, 12819–12828.

Andrade-Suárez, M., & Caamaño-Franco, I. (2020). The Relationship between industrial heritage, wine tourism, and sustainability: A case of local community perspective. *Sustainability (Basel)*, *12*(18), 7453. doi:10.3390/su12187453

Andrea, L. C., & Zavaglia, G. (2022). Sustainable Food Systems in Fruits and Vegetables Food Supply Chains. *Frontiers in Nutrition*, 9. PMID:35252306

Angelova, M., & Pastarmadzhieva, D. (2020). Development of bio-based economy: Entrepreneurial endeavors and innovation across Bulgarian wine industry. *Journal of International Students*, *13*(2), 149–162. doi:10.14254/2071-8330.2020/13-2/11

Annunziata, E., Pucci, T., Frey, M., & Zanni, L. (2018). The role of organizational capabilities in attaining corporate sustainability practices and economic performance: Evidence from Italian wine industry. *Journal of Cleaner Production*, *171*, 1300–1311. doi:10.1016/j.jclepro.2017.10.035

Anssari, O. M., Alkaldy, E. A., Almudhaffar, N., AlTaee, A. N., & Ali, N. S. (2020). A feasibility study of electrical energy generation from municipal solid waste in Iraq: Najaf case study. *Iranian Journal of Electrical and Computer Engineering*, *10*(4), 3403–3411. doi:10.11591/ijece.v10i4.pp3403-3411

Aragón-Correa, J. A. (1998). Strategic proactivity and firm aroach to the natural environment. *Academy of Management Journal*, *41*(5), 556–567. doi:10.2307/256942

Arco, C. L., López, P. M. V., Pérez, L. M. C., & Rodríguez, A. L. (2020). How market value relates to corporate philanthropy and its assurance. The moderating effect of the business sector. *Business Ethics (Oxford, England)*, *29*(2), 266–281. doi:10.1111/beer.12264

Arfi, W. B., Hikkerova, L., & Sahut, J. M. (2018). External knowledge sources, green innovation and performance. *Technological Forecasting and Social Change*, *129*, 210–220. doi:10.1016/j.techfore.2017.09.017

Ar, I. M. (2012). The impact of green product innovation on firm performance and competitive capability: The moderating role of managerial environmental concern. *Procedia: Social and Behavioral Sciences*, *62*, 854–864. doi:10.1016/j.sbspro.2012.09.144

Arici, H., & Uysal, M. (2022). Leadership, green innovation, and green creativity: A systematic review. *Service Industries Journal*, *42*(6), 280–320. doi:10.1080/02642069.2021.1964482

Arieftiara, D., Nawir, J., & Julianisa, I. A. (2022). Halal Food Certification, Financial Performance, and Sustainability Reporting: Comparative Study of Food and Beverage Firms in Malaysia and Indonesia. *AgBioForum*, *24*(2), 12–22. https://www.scopus.com/inward/record.uri?eid=2-s2.0-85144748584&partnerID=40&md5=a70dde874837ebf5eaf159d6bbcf378c

Ariffin, M. F. M., & Hamid, M. F. A. (2021). Negotiating Halal Crimes: The Use Of Block-Chain Technology. *Global Journal Al-Thaqafah*, *11*(1), 41–48. https://www.scopus.com/inward/record.uri?eid=2-s2.0-85114418195&partnerID=40&md5=2a7ff7dcf4aa9c4c66ec2d6dfb550f8e

Arifin, A., Wyman, F., & Hendijani, R. B. (2021). An investigation of the aspects affecting non-Muslim customers' purchase intention of halal food products in Jakarta, indonesia. *Future of Food: Journal on Food, Agriculture and Society*, *9*(2), 1–13. doi:10.17170/kobra-202102163257

Arregle, J.-L., Hitt, M. A., Sirmon, D. G., & Very, P. (2007). The development of organizational social capital: Attributes of family firms. *Journal of Management Studies*, *44*(1), 72–95. doi:10.1111/j.1467-6486.2007.00665.x

Arrieta Paredes, M. P. (2023). ESG investing, reputation and government policies in British SMEs: why does firmographics matter? Bae, S., Masud, M., Kim, J. (2018). A cross-country investigation of corporate governance and corporate sustainability disclosure: A signalling theory perspective. *Sustainability*, *10*(8), 2611–2621.

Asadi, S., Pourhashemi, S., Nilashi, M., Abdullah, R., Samad, S., Yadegaridehkordi, E., & Razali, N. (2020). Investigating influence of green innovation on sustainability performance: A case on Malaysian hotel industry. *Journal of Cleaner Production*, *258*, 120860. doi:10.1016/j.jclepro.2020.120860

Aschemann-Witzel, J., & Zielke, S. (2015). Can't buy me green? A review of consumer perceptions of and behaviour toward the price of organic food. *J. Consum. Aff.* https://onlinelibrary.wiley.com/doi/10.1111/joca.12092/epdf

Asiaei, K., & Bontis, N. (2019). Translating knowledge management into performance: The role of performance measurement systems. *Management Research Review*, *43*(1), 113–132. doi:10.1108/MRR-10-2018-0395

Asociación Española de Ciudades del Vino. (2022). *Guía práctica de turismo sostenible Rutas del Vino de España* [PDF File]. ACEVIN. https://rutadelvinosierradefrancia.files.wordpress.com/2023/02/guia-practica-turismo-sostenible.-rutas-del-vino-de-espana-1.pdf

Asociación Española de Ciudades del Vino. (2022). *Informe de visitantes a bodegas y museos del vino* [PDF File]. ACEVIN. https://wineroutesofspain.com/wp-content/uploads/2023/06/informe-visitas-a-bodegas-y-museos-rve-2022.pdf

Astrachan, J. H., & Shanker, M. C. (2003). Family businesses' contribution to the US economy: A closer look. *Family Business Review*, *16*(3), 211–219. doi:10.1177/08944865030160030601

Atapattu, A., & Jayakody, J. (2014). The interaction effect of organizational practices and employee values on knowledge management (KM) success. *Journal of Knowledge Management*, *18*(2), 307–328. doi:10.1108/JKM-07-2013-0276

Atkin, T., Gilinsky, A. Jr, & Newton, S. K. (2012). Environmental strategy: Does it lead to competitive advantage in the US wine industry? *International Journal of Wine Business Research*, *24*(2), 115–133. doi:10.1108/17511061211238911

Atta, H. S., Abbas, B., & Syed, F. U. (2021). Study of Consumer Values for Organic Personal Care Products in the Fields of Health and Cosmetics. *International Journal of Innovative Science and Research Technology*, *6*(8).

Awan, U., Nauman, S., & Sroufe, R. (2021). Exploring the effect of buyer engagement on green product innovation: Empirical evidence from manufacturers. *Business Strategy and the Environment*, *30*(1), 463–477. doi:10.1002/bse.2631

Aydın, K., Yıldırım, S., & Çizer, E. Ö. (2023). Big Dilemma In Face Mask Consumption: Environmental Sensitivity Versus The Fear Of COVID-19. *International Journal of Global Warming*, *29*(3), 207–226. doi:10.1504/IJGW.2023.129490

Azhar, A., & Tu, Y. T. (2021). The investigation of key factors for successful implementation of sustainable halal food supply chain management. *Food Research*, *5*(6), 221–228. doi:10.26656/fr.2017.5(6).235

Azmi, F. R., Abdullah, A., Bakri, M. H., Musa, H., & Jayakrishnan, M. (2018). The adoption of halal food supply chain towards the performance of food manufacturing in Malaysia. *Management Science Letters*, *8*(7), 755–766. doi:10.5267/j.msl.2018.5.0010

Azmi, F. R., Abdullah, A., Musa, H., & Wan Mahmood, W. H. (2020). Perception of food manufacturers towards adoption of halal food supply chain in Malaysia: Exploratory factor analysis. *Journal of Islamic Marketing*, *11*(3), 571–589. doi:10.1108/JIMA-12-2018-0236

Bag, S., Dhamija, P., Bryde, D. J., & Singh, R. K. (2022). Effect of eco-innovation on green supply chain management, circular economy capability, and performance of small and medium enterprises. *Journal of Business Research*, *141*, 60–72. doi:10.1016/j.jbusres.2021.12.011

Bag, S., & Rahman, M. S. (2023). The role of capabilities in shaping sustainable supply chain flexibility and enhancing circular economy-target performance: An empirical study. *Supply Chain Management*, *28*(1), 162–178. doi:10.1108/SCM-05-2021-0246

Baiano, A. (2021). An overview on sustainability in the wine production chain. *Beverages*, *7*(1), 15. doi:10.3390/beverages7010015

Bai, C., Dallasega, P., Orzes, G., & Sarkis, J. (2020). Industry 4.0 technologies assessment: A sustainability perspective. *International Journal of Production Economics*, *229*, 107776. doi:10.1016/j.ijpe.2020.107776

Bain & Company. (2023, November 24). *El 68% de los millenials en el mundo están preocupados por la sostenibilidad ambiental*. BAIN. https://www.bain.com/es/about/media-center/press-releases/south-america/2023/el-68-de-los-millennials-en-el-mundo-estan-preocupados-por-la-sostenibilidad-ambiental2/

Baird, T., Hall, C., & Castka, P. (2018). New Zealand winegrowers attitudes and behaviours towards wine tourism and sustainable winegrowing. *Sustainability (Basel)*, *10*(3), 797. doi:10.3390/su10030797

Baird, T., Hall, C., Castka, P., & Ramkissoon, H. (2022). Innovation, wine tourism, and sustainable winegrowing in cool climate regions: A longitudinal international comparative analysis. In *Handbook of innovation for sustainable tourism* (pp. 167–191). Edward Elgar Publishing.

Bamberg, S., & Möser, G. (2007). Twenty years after Hines, Hungerford, and Tomera: A new meta-analysis of psycho-social determinants of pro-environmental behaviour. *Journal of Environmental Psychology*, *27*(1), 14–25. doi:10.1016/j.jenvp.2006.12.002

Bandinelli, R., Acuti, D., Fani, V., Bindi, B., & Aiello, G. (2020). Environmental practices in the wine industry: An overview of the Italian market. *British Food Journal*, *122*(5), 1625–1646. doi:10.1108/BFJ-08-2019-0653

Barba-Sánchez, V., & Atienza-Sahuquillo, C. (2016). Environmental proactivity and environmental and economic performance: Evidence from the winery sector *Sustainability*, *8*.

Barber, N., Taylor, C., & Strick, S. (2009). Wine consumers' environmental knowledge and attitudes: Influence on willingness to purchase. *International Journal of Wine Research, 1*(null), 59-72. doi:10.2147/IJWR.S4649

Barbieri, N., Ghisetti, C., Gilli, M., Marin, G., & Nicolli, F. (2016). A survey of the literature on environmental innovation based on main path analysis. *Journal of Economic Surveys*, *30*(3), 596–623. doi:10.1111/joes.12149

Barney, J. B., & Hansen, M. H. (1994). Trustworthiness as a source of competitive advantage. *Strategic Management Journal*, *15*(S1), 175–190. doi:10.1002/smj.4250150912

Barney, J., Ketchen, D. Jr, & Wright, M. (2011). The future of resource-based theory: Revitalization or decline? *Journal of Management*, *37*(5), 1299–1315. doi:10.1177/0149206310391805

Basiron, Y., Balu, N., & Chandramohan, D. (2004). Palm oil: the driving force of world oils and fats economy. *Oil palm industry economic journal, 4*(1), 1-10.

Baudelaire, C. (1851/2020). Du vin et du Haschisch. Editorial. Mille Et Une Nuits. La petite collection. Paris.

Baumane-Vītoliņa, I., Woschank, M., Apsalone, M., Šumilo, Ē., & Pacher, C. (2022). Organizational Innovation Implications for Manufacturing SMEs: Findings from an Empirical Study. *Procedia Computer Science*, *200*, 738–747. doi:10.1016/j.procs.2022.01.272

Beber, C. L., Lecomte, L., Rodrigo, I., Canali, M., Pinto, A. S., Pomarici, E., ... Malorgio, G. (2023). The Agroecological Challenges in the Wine Sector: Perceptions from European Stakeholders. *Wine Economics and Policy*, *12*(2), 1–32. doi:10.36253/wep-15244

Beck, U. (1998). *La sociedad del riesgo: Hacia una nueva modernidad.* Paidós. https://www.gub.uy/sistema-nacional-emergencias/sites/sistema-nacional-emergencias/files/documentos/publicaciones/La%2Bsociedad%2Bdel%2Briesgo%2Bhacia%2Buna%2Bnueva%2Bmodernidad%20-BECK.pdf

Becker-Olsen, K. L., Cudmore, B. A., & Hill, R. P. (2006). The impact of perceived corporate social responsibility on consumer behaviour. *Journal of Business Research*, *59*(1), 46–53. doi:10.1016/j.jbusres.2005.01.001

Beiro, R. (2023, April 13). *La apuesta española por la sostenibilidad en la industria del vino.* Vinetur. https://www.vinetur.com/2023041372919/la-apuesta-espanola-por-la-sostenibilidad-en-la-industria-del-vino.html

Belyaeva, Z., Rudawska, E. D., & Lopatkova, Y. (2020). Sustainable business model in food and beverage industry–a case of Western and Central and Eastern European countries. *British Food Journal*, *122*(5), 1573–1592. doi:10.1108/BFJ-08-2019-0660

Ben, B. (2021). *Sustainability a business approach case: the non-alcoholic beverage industry.*

Bendímez Patterson, J. (1987, September – December). Antecedentes históricos de los indígenas de Baja California. *Estudios Fronterizos (México)*, *5*(14), 11–46. doi:10.21670/ref.1987.14.a01

Berman, S. L., Wicks, A. C., Kotha, S., & Jones, T. M. (1999). Does stakeholder orientation matter? The relationship between stakeholder management models and firm financial performance. *Academy of Management Journal*, *42*(5), 488–506. doi:10.2307/256972

Berrone, P., Cruz, C., & Gomez-Mejia, L. (2012). Socioemotional wealth in family firms: Theoretical dimensions, assessment aroaches, and agenda for future research. *Family Business Review*, *25*(3), 258–279. doi:10.1177/0894486511435355

Berrone, P., Fosfuri, A., Gelabert, L., & Gomez-Mejia, L. R. (2013). Necessity as the mother of 'green' inventions: Institutional pressures and environmental innovations. *Strategic Management Journal*, *34*(8), 891–909. doi:10.1002/smj.2041

Bhargava, N., Sharanagat, V. S., Mor, R. S., & Kumar, K. (2020). Active and intelligent biodegradable packaging films using food and food waste-derived bioactive compounds: A review. *Trends in Food Science & Technology*, *105*, 385–401. doi:10.1016/j.tifs.2020.09.015

Bhat, V. N. (1993). Green marketing begins with green design. *Journal of Business and Industrial Marketing*, *8*(4), 26–31. doi:10.1108/08858629310047243

Bhutta, M. K. S., Muzaffar, A., Egilmez, G., Huq, F., Malik, M. N., & Warraich, M. A. (2021). Environmental sustainability, innovation capacity, and supply chain management practices nexus: A mixed methods research approach. *Sustainable Production and Consumption*, *28*, 1508–1521. doi:10.1016/j.spc.2021.08.015

Bigliardi, B., & Galati, F. (2017). Family firms and collaborative innovation: Present debates and future research. *European Journal of Innovation Management*. doi:10.1108/EJIM-05-2017-0054

Bigné, J., Sanchez, I., & Sanchez, J. (2001). Tourism Image, Evaluation Vari-ables and After Purchase Behaviour: Inter-Relationships. *Tourism Management*, *22*(6), 607–616. doi:10.1016/S0261-5177(01)00035-8

Bjork, S., Offer, A., & Söderberg, G. (2014). Time series citation data: The Nobel Prize in economics. *Scientometrics*, *98*(1), 185–196. doi:10.1007/s11192-013-0989-5

Block, E. S., Glavas, A., Mannor, M. J., & Erskine, L. (2017). Business for good? An investigation into the strategy's firms use to maximize the impact of financial corporate philanthropy on employee attitudes. *Journal of Business Ethics*, *146*(1), 167–183. doi:10.1007/s10551-015-2930-8

Block, J. H. (2012). R&D investments in family and founder firms: An agency perspective. *Journal of Business Venturing*, *27*(2), 248–265. doi:10.1016/j.jbusvent.2010.09.003

Block, J. H., & Wagner, M. (2014). The effect of family ownership on different dimensions of corporate social responsibility: Evidence from large U.S. firms. *Business Strategy and the Environment*, *23*(7), 475–492. doi:10.1002/bse.1798

Block, J., Miller, D., Jaskiewicz, P., & Spiegel, F. (2013). Economic and technological importance of innovations in large family and founder firms: An analysis of patent data. *Family Business Review*, *26*(2), 180–199. doi:10.1177/0894486513477454

Blome, C., Schoenherr, T., & Eckstein, D. (2014). The impact of knowledge transfer and complexity on supply chain flexibility: A knowledge-based view. *International Journal of Production Economics*, *147*, 307–316. doi:10.1016/j.ijpe.2013.02.028

Bonilla, S. H., Silva, H. R. O., da Silva, M. T., Gonçalves, R. F., & Sacomano, J. B. (2018). Industry 4.0 and sustainability implications: A scenario-based analysis of the impacts and challenges. *Sustainability (Basel)*, *10*(10), 3740. doi:10.3390/su10103740

Bonn, M., Cho, M., & Um, H. (2018). The evolution of wine research: A 26-year historical examination of topics, trends and future direction. *International Journal of Contemporary Hospitality Management*, *30*(1), 286–312. doi:10.1108/IJCHM-09-2016-0521

Boons, F., Montalvo, C., Quist, J., & Wagner, M. (2013). Sustainable innovation, business models and economic performance: An overview. *Journal of Cleaner Production*, *45*, 1–8. doi:10.1016/j.jclepro.2012.08.013

Booyens, I. (2020). Tourism innovation in the Western Cape, South Africa: Evidence from wine tourism. In *New directions in South African tourism geographies* (pp. 183–202). Springer. doi:10.1007/978-3-030-29377-2_11

Borsatto, J., & Bazani, C. (2021). Green innovation and environmental regulations: A systematic review of international academic works. *Environmental Science and Pollution Research International*, *28*(45), 63751–63768. doi:10.1007/s11356-020-11379-7 PMID:33141379

Bossle, M. B., de Barcellos, M. D., Vieira, L. M., & Sauvée, L. (2016). The drivers for adoption of eco-innovation. *Journal of Cleaner Production, 113*, 861–872. doi:10.1016/j.jclepro.2015.11.033

Bostanci, S., Yildirim, S., & Erdoğan, F. (2022). A review on e-Government Portal's services within Hospital Information System during Covid-19 pandemic. *Konuralp Tip Dergisi, 14*(S1), 271–279. doi:10.18521/ktd.1036010

Boumediene, O., & El Honda, Y. N. (2018). Corporate social responsibility in food and beverage industry: An analysis study of soft drinks sector in Algeria. *European Scientific Journal, 14*(1), 1857–1881. doi:10.19044/esj.2018.v14n1p190

BOUNCE. (2023). *Wine lovers index 2023*. BOUNCE. https://usebounce.com/blog/wine-lovers-index-2023

Boz, Z., Korhonen, V., & Koelsch Sand, C. (2020). Consumer considerations for the implementation of sustainable packaging: A review. *Sustainability (Basel), 12*(6), 2192. doi:10.3390/su12062192

Brammer, S., & Millington, A. (2005). Corporate Reputation and Philanthropy: An Empirical Analysis. *Journal of Business Ethics, 61*(1), 29–44. doi:10.1007/s10551-005-7443-4

Brammer, S., & Millington, A. (2006b). Firm size, organizational visibility and corporate philanthropy: An empirical analysis. *Business Ethics (Oxford, England), 15*(1), 6–18. doi:10.1111/j.1467-8608.2006.00424.x

Brammer, S., Millington, A., & Pavelin, S. (2006a). Is philanthropy strategic? An analysis of the management of charitable giving in large UK companies. *Business Ethics (Oxford, England), 15*(3), 234–245. doi:10.1111/j.1467-8608.2006.00446.x

Bravo, C.P., Cordts, A., Schulze, B., & Spiller, A. (2013). Assessing determinants of organic food consumption using data from the German National Nutrition Survey II. *Food Qual. Prefer 28*, 60e70.

Breiby, M. A., Duedahl, E., Øian, H., & Ericsson, B. (2020). Exploring sustainable experiences in tourism. *Scandinavian Journal of Hospitality and Tourism, 20*(4), 335–351. doi:10.1080/15022250.2020.1748706

Breznik, K. (2018). Knowledge management–from its inception to the innovation linkage. *Procedia: Social and Behavioral Sciences, 238*, 141–148. doi:10.1016/j.sbspro.2018.03.017

Broc, Ò. (2019). Cerveza sin alcohol para vender más alcohol. *El Comidista*. https://elcomidista.elpais.com/elcomidista/2019/10/10/articulo/1570720904_131455.html

Broccardo, L., & Zicari, A. (2020). Sustainability as a driver for value creation: A business model analysis of small and medium entreprises in the Italian wine sector. *Journal of Cleaner Production, 259*, 120852. doi:10.1016/j.jclepro.2020.120852

Brochado, A., Stoleriu, O., & Lupu, C. (2021). Wine tourism: A multisensory experience. *Current Issues in Tourism, 24*(5), 597–615. doi:10.1080/13683500.2019.1649373

Brunner-Sperdin, A., & Peters, M. (2009). What influences guests' emotions? The case of high-quality hotels. *International Journal of Tourism Research, 11*(2), 171–183. doi:10.1002/jtr.718

Bruschi, M. L. (2015). *Strategies to modify the drug release from pharmaceutical systems*. Woodhead Publishing.

Bruwer, J. (2003). South African wine routes: Some perspectives on the wine tourism industry's structural dimensions and wine tourism product. *Tourism Management, 24*(4), 423–435. doi:10.1016/S0261-5177(02)00105-X

Bruwer, J., & Alant, K. (2009). The hedonic nature of wine tourism consumption: An experiential view. *International Journal of Wine Business Research, 21*(3), 235–257. doi:10.1108/17511060910985962

Bruwer, J., & Rueger-Muck, E. (2019). Wine tourism and hedonic experience: A motivation-based experiential view. *Tourism and Hospitality Research, 19*(4), 488–502. doi:10.1177/1467358418781444

Bucci, M., & El-Diraby, T. (2018). The functions of knowledge management processes in urban impact assessment: The case of Ontario. *Impact Assessment and Project Appraisal*, *36*(3), 265–280. doi:10.1080/14615517.2018.1445179

Bujok, P., Kempla, M., Porzer, M., Jelinek, J., & Janeckova, N. (2016). Example of the development and changes in tourism presented on historical growth of the city of hodonn. *Ecology, Economics, Education and Legislation*, *1*, 345–352.

Butler, K., Gordon, R., Roggeveen, K., Waitt, G., & Cooper, P. (2016). Social marketing and value in behaviour? Perceived value of using energy efficiently among low income older citizens. *Journal of Social Marketing*, *6*(2), 144–168. doi:10.1108/JSOCM-07-2015-0045

Butt, A., Khan, S. N., Zakir, M. M., Rana, W., & Laila, A. (2021). Firms greenwashing practices and consumers' perception: Role of marketing and non-marketing external stake holders in firms greenwashing practices. *Indian Journal of Economics and Business*, *20*(3), 689–706.

Bux, C., Varese, E., Amicarelli, V., & Lombardi, M. (2022). Halal Food Sustainability between Certification and Blockchain: A Review. *Sustainability (Basel)*, *14*(4), 2152. doi:10.3390/su14042152

Byrne, B. (2008). *Structural Equation Modeling with EQS: Basic Concepts, Applications, and Programming*. Psychology Press.

Cabrera-Flores, M., Cota-Cota, C., Mellink-Mendez, S., & León-Pozo, A. (2024). Wine and craft beer in Baja California: An approach to innovation through label design. *International Journal of Entrepreneurship and Small Business*, *51*(1), 10060584. doi:10.1504/IJESB.2024.10060584

Cadó Martínez, J. L. R. (2016). *Concert Wine.* Acústica del vino.

Cainelli, G., Mazzanti, M., & Montresor, S. (2012). Environmental innovations, local networks and internationalization. *Industry and Innovation*, *19*(8), 697–734. doi:10.1080/13662716.2012.739782

Calabrò, A., Vecchiarini, M., Gast, J., Campopiano, G., De Massis, A., & Kraus, S. (2019). Innovation in family firms: A systematic literature review and guidance for future research. *International Journal of Management Reviews*, *21*(3), 317–355. doi:10.1111/ijmr.12192

Calvo-Porral, Orosa-González, J., & Blazquez-Lozano, F. (2018). A clustered-based segmentation of beer consumers: From "beer lovers" to "beer to fuddle". *British Food Journal*, *120*(6), 1280–1294. doi:10.1108/BFJ-11-2017-0628

Camargo, F. A. O., Silva, L. S., Merten, G. H., Carlos, F. S., Baveye, P. C., & Triplett, E. W. (2017). Brazilian agriculture in perspective: Great expectations vs reality. *Advances in Agronomy*, *141*, 53–114. doi:10.1016/bs.agron.2016.10.003

Campbell, B., Khachatryan, H., Behe, B., Dennis, J., & Hall, C. (2015). Consumer perceptions of eco-friendly and sustainable terms. *Agricultural and Resource Economics Review*, *44*(1), 21–34. doi:10.1017/S1068280500004603

Campbell, D., & Slack, R. (2006). Public visibility as a determinant of the rate of corporate charitable donations. *Business Ethics (Oxford, England)*, *15*(1), 19–28. doi:10.1111/j.1467-8608.2006.00425.x

Caniglia, G., Luederitz, C., von Wirth, T., Fazey, I., Martin-López, B., Hondrila, K., & Lang, D. J. (2021). A pluralistic and integrated approach to action-oriented knowledge for sustainability. *Nature Sustainability*, *4*(2), 93–100. doi:10.1038/s41893-020-00616-z

Cañizares-Ruiz, M. C. C., & Ruiz-Pulpón, Á. R. R. (2020). Paisajes del viñedo, turismo y sostenibilidad: Interrelaciones teóricas y aplicadas. *Investigaciones Geográficas*, (74), 9–28. doi:10.14198/INGEO2020.CRRP

Cantino, V., Giacosa, E., & Cortese, D. (2019). A sustainable perspective in wine production for common-good management: The case of Fontanafredda biological "reserve. *British Food Journal*, *121*(2), 259–274. doi:10.1108/BFJ-06-2018-0351

Cantó-Gómez, A., & Mantecón, A. (2020). El "tardeo" en Alicante: la mercantilización del espacio en una ciudad turística. *Ciudad y terriorio. Estudios territoriales, 52*(2006), 2659-3254. doi:10.37230/CyTET.2020.206.06

Canziani, B., & Byrd, E. (2017). Exploring the influence of regional brand equity in an emerging wine sector. *Journal of Wine Economics, 12*(4), 370–377. doi:10.1017/jwe.2017.30

Caputo, F., Garcia-Perez, A., Cillo, V., & Giacosa, E. (2019). A knowledge-based view of people and technology: Directions for a value co-creation-based learning organization. *Journal of Knowledge Management, 23*(7), 1314–1334. doi:10.1108/JKM-10-2018-0645

Carchano, M., Carrasco, I., & González, Á. (2023). Eco-innovation and environmental performance: Insights from Spanish wine companies. *Annals of Public and Cooperative Economics, n/a*(n/a). doi:https://doi.org/ doi:10.1111/apce.12421

Carchano, M., Carrasco, I., & González, A. (2023). Examining environmental proactivity in the Spanish wine industry: The moderating role of size. *Agribusiness, n/a*(n/a). doi:https://doi.org/ doi:10.1002/agr.21882

Carlsen, P. (2004). A review of global wine tourism research. *Journal of Wine Research, 15*(1), 5–13. doi:10.1080/0957126042000300281

Carlson, K. M., Heilmayr, R., Gibbs, H. K., Noojipady, P., Burns, D. N., Morton, D. C., Walker, N. F., Paoli, G. D., & Kremen, C. (2018). Effect of oil palm sustainability certification on deforestation and fire in Indonesia. *Proceedings of the National Academy of Sciences of the United States of America, 115*(1), 121–126. doi:10.1073/pnas.1704728114 PMID:29229857

Carmines, E., & Zeller, R. (1979). *Reliability and validity assessment* (Vol. 17). Sage Publications. doi:10.4135/9781412985642

Carnes, C. M., & Ireland, R. D. (2013). Familiness and innovation: Resource bundling as the missing link. *Entrepreneurship Theory and Practice, 37*(6), 1399–1419. doi:10.1111/etap.12073

Carrillo-Hermosilla, J., Del Río, P., & Könnölä, T. (2010). Diversity of eco-innovations: Reflections from selected case studies. *Journal of Cleaner Production, 18*(10), 1073–1083. doi:10.1016/j.jclepro.2010.02.014

Carrillo-Higueras, F., Prajogo, D., & Smith, L. (2018). Environmental commitment and its drivers in the Australian wine industry: A behavioural approach. *Australasian Journal of Environmental Management, 25*(4), 439–458. doi:10.1080/14486563.2018.1460630

Carroll, A. (1979). A Three Dimensional Conceptual Model of Corporate Performance. *Academy of Management Review, 4*(4), 497–505. doi:10.2307/257850

Carroll, A. (2016). Carroll's Pyramid of CSR: Taking Another Look. International. *Journal of Corporate Social Responsibility, 1*(1), 3. doi:10.1186/s40991-016-0004-6

Carroll, A., & Buchholtz, A. L. (2003). *Business and Society: Ethics, Sustainability and Stakeholder Management* (5th ed.). Thomson/South Western.

Carvalho, I. T., Estevinho, B. N., & Santos, L. (2016). Application of microencapsulated essential oils in cosmetic and personal healthcare products–a review. *International Journal of Cosmetic Science, 38*(2), 109–119. doi:10.1111/ics.12232 PMID:25923295

Carvalho, M., Kastenholz, E., & Carneiro, M. (2021). Co-creative tourism experiences–a conceptual framework and its application to food & wine tourism. *Tourism Recreation Research*, 1–25.

Cassia, L., De Massis, A., & Pizzurno, E. (2011). An exploratory investigation on NPD in small family businesses from Northern Italy, *International Journal of Business, Management, and social sciences, 2*, 1-14.

Castaneda, M. G., Martinez, C. P., Marte, R., & Roxas, B. (2015). Explaining the environmentally-sustainable consumer behavior: A social capital perspective. *Social Responsibility Journal, 11*(4), 658–676. doi:10.1108/SRJ-02-2014-0019

Cennamo, C., Berrone, P., Cruz, C., & Gomez-Mejia, L. R. (2012). Socio-emotional wealth and proactive stakeholder engagement: Why family-controlled firms care more about their stakeholders. *Entrepreneurship Theory and Practice, 36*(6), 1153–1173. doi:10.1111/j.1540-6520.2012.00543.x

Cepeda-Carrion, G., Cegarra-Navarro, J., & Cillo, V. (2019). Tips to use partial least squares structural equation modelling (PLS-SEM) in knowledge management. *Journal of Knowledge Management, 23*(1), 67–89. doi:10.1108/JKM-05-2018-0322

Cerveceros de España. (2003). Código de Autorregulación Publicitaria de Cerveceros de España. *Cerveceros de España*. https://cerveceros.org/uploads/60ad057cdcd31__CAP _CE_envigor.pdf

Chain, M. M., Vermeulen, W. J., Meeus, M. T., & Hekkert, M. P. (2009). Enhancing our understanding of the role of environmental policy in environmental innovation: Adoption explained by the accumulation of policy instruments and agent-based factors. *Environmental Science & Policy, 12*(7), 934–947. doi:10.1016/j.envsci.2009.06.001

Chamorro-Fernández, A., Alonso Sardón, M., & Mirón Canelo, J. (2005). Valoración de la producción científica y epidemiológica sobre alcoholismo en España (1996-2002). *A tu. Salud (Barranquilla), 49*, 16–19.

Chang, C., & Chen, Y. (2013). Green organizational identity and green innovation. *Management Decision, 51*(5), 1056–1070. doi:10.1108/MD-09-2011-0314

Chang, C., & Lin, T. (2015). The role of organizational culture in the knowledge management process. *Journal of Knowledge Management, 19*(3), 433–455. doi:10.1108/JKM-08-2014-0353

Charters, S., & Ali-Knight, J. (2002). Who is the wine tourist? *Tourism Management, 23*(3), 311–319. doi:10.1016/S0261-5177(01)00079-6

Chauhan, V. Z. (2020). Value-Action Gap Towards Green Consumer Behavior: A Theoretical Review and Analysis. [IJCRT]. *International Journal of Creative Research Thoughts, 8*(4), 497–505.

Cha, W., & Abebe, M. A. (2016). Board of directors and industry determinants of corporate philanthropy. *Leadership and Organization Development Journal, 37*(5), 672–688. doi:10.1108/LODJ-09-2014-0189

Cha, W., & Rew, D. (2021). Cannot give you because of living on the top of a castle: CEOs, corporate philanthropy and firm age. *Society and Business Review, 16*(3), 336–356. doi:10.1108/SBR-05-2020-0074

Chen, C. C., Sujanto, R. Y., Bui, T. D., & Tseng, M. L. (2023). Sustainable recyclate packaging in Indonesian food and beverage industry: A hybrid decision-making analysis in consumption stages. *Quality & Quantity, 57*(3), 2053–2089. doi:10.1007/s11135-022-01458-x

Chen, C. T. A., & Borges, A. V. (2009). Reconciling opposing views on carbon cycling in the coastal ocean: Continental shelves as sinks and near-shore ecosystems as sources of atmospheric CO2. *Deep-sea Research. Part II, Topical Studies in Oceanography, 56*(8-10), 578–590. doi:10.1016/j.dsr2.2009.01.001

Cheng, H., Chen, C., Wu, S., Mirza, Z. A., & Liu, Z. (2017). Emergy evaluation of cropping, poultry rearing, and fish raising systems in the drawdown zone of Three Gorges Reservoir of China. *Journal of Cleaner Production, 144*, 559–571. doi:10.1016/j.jclepro.2016.12.053

Chen, M. J., Grube, J. W., Bersamin, M., Waiters, E., & Keefe, D. B. (2005). Alcohol advertising: What makes it attractive to youth? *Journal of Health Communication, 10*(6), 553–565. doi:10.1080/10810730500228904 PMID:16203633

Chen, T. B., & Chai, L. T. (2010). Attitude towards the environment and green products: Consumers' perspective. *Management Science and Engineering*, *4*(2), 27–39.

Chen, Y. (2008). The driver of green innovation and green image – green core competence. *Journal of Business Ethics*, *81*(3), 531–543. doi:10.1007/s10551-007-9522-1

Chen, Y., Chang, C., & Wu, F. (2012). Origins of green innovations: The differences between proactive and reactive green innovations. *Management Decision*, *50*(3), 368–398. doi:10.1108/00251741211216197

Chew, C. L., Low, L. E., Chia, W. Y., Chew, K. W., Liew, Z. K., Chan, E. S., & Show, P. L. (2022). Prospects of palm fruit extraction technology: Palm oil recovery processes and quality enhancement. *Food Reviews International, 38*(sup1), 893-920.

Chieco, C., Morrone, L., Magli, M., Gelmetti, A., Pedo, S., Roman Villegas, T., & Eccel, E. (2023). Italian winegrowers' and wine makers' attitudes toward climate hazards and their strategy of adaptation to the change. *Italian Journal of Agrometeorology*, (1), 47–65. doi:10.36253/ijam-1874

Chin, W. W. (1998). Issues and Opinion on Structural Equation Modeling. *Management Information Systems Quarterly*, *22*, 1, 7–15.

Chiou, T. Y., Chan, H. K., Lettice, F., & Chung, S. H. (2011). The influence of greening the suliers and green innovation on environmental performance and competitive advantage in Taiwan. *Transportation Research Part E, Logistics and Transportation Review*, *47*(6), 822–836. doi:10.1016/j.tre.2011.05.016

Chirilli, C., Molino, M., & Torri, L. (2022). Consumers' awareness, behavior and expectations for food packaging environmental sustainability: Influence of socio-demographic characteristics. *Foods*, *11*(16), 2388. doi:10.3390/foods11162388 PMID:36010389

Cho, H., Jeong, S. H., Park, M. H., Kim, Y. H., Wolf, C., Lee, C. L., Heo, J. H., Sadhanala, A., Myoung, N. S., Yoo, S., Im, S. H., Friend, R. H., & Lee, T. W. (2015). Overcoming the electroluminescence efficiency limitations of perovskite light-emitting diodes. *Science*, *350*(6265), 1222–1225. doi:10.1126/science.aad1818 PMID:26785482

Choi, S., & Lee, S. (2020). Eco-Packaging and its Market Performance: UPC-level Sales, Brand Spillover Effects, and Curvilinearity. *Sustainability (Basel)*, *12*(21), 9061. doi:10.3390/su12219061

Chrisman, J., Chua, J., De Massis, A., Frattini, F., & Wright, M. (2015). The ability and willingness paradox in family firm innovation. *Journal of Product Innovation Management*, *32*(3), 310–318. doi:10.1111/jpim.12207

Chrisman, J., & Patel, P. (2012). Variations in R&D investments of family and nonfamily firms: Behavioral agency and myopic loss aversion perspectives. *Academy of Management Journal*, *55*(4), 976–997. doi:10.5465/amj.2011.0211

Christ, K. L., & Burritt, R. L. (2013). Critical environmental concerns in wine production: An integrative review. *Journal of Cleaner Production*, *53*, 232–242. doi:10.1016/j.jclepro.2013.04.007

Chua, J. H., Chrisman, J. J., & Sharma, P. (1999). Defining the family business by behavior. *Entrepreneurship Theory and Practice*, *23*(4), 19–39. doi:10.1177/104225879902300402

Chua, J. H., Chrisman, J. J., Steier, L. P., & Rau, S. B. (2012). Sources of heterogeneity in family firms: An introduction. *Entrepreneurship Theory and Practice*, *44*(6), 1, 3–19. doi:10.1111/j.1540-6520.2012.00540.x

Chu, Z., Wang, L., & Lai, F. (2018). Customer pressure and green innovations at third party logistics providers in China: The moderation effect of organizational culture. *International Journal of Logistics Management*, *30*(1), 57–75. doi:10.1108/IJLM-11-2017-0294

Cillo, V., Garcia-Perez, A., Del Giudice, M., & Vicentini, F. (2019). Blue-collar workers, career success and innovation in manufacturing. *Career Development International*, *24*(6), 529–544. doi:10.1108/CDI-11-2018-0276

Cillo, V., Rialti, R., Bertoldi, B., & Ciampi, F. (2019). Knowledge management and open innovation in agri-food crowdfunding. *British Food Journal*, *121*(2), 242–258. doi:10.1108/BFJ-07-2018-0472

Cirone, F., Masotti, M., Prosperi, P., Bosi, S., Dinelli, G., & Vittuari, M. (n.d.). *Business strategy pathways for short food supply chains: Sharing value between consumers and producers*. IEEE. doi:10.1016/j.spc.2023.07.017

Clarkson, M. E. (1995). A stakeholder framework for analyzing and evaluating corporate social performance. *Academy of Management Review*, *20*(1), 92–117. doi:10.2307/258888

Classen, N., Carree, M., Van Gils, A., & Peters, B. (2014). Innovation in family and non-family SMEs: An exploratory analysis. *Small Business Economics*, *42*(3), 595–609. doi:10.1007/s11187-013-9490-z

Coddington, W. (1993). *Environmental marketing: positive strategies for reaching the green consumer*. McGraw - Hill Companies.

Código 84. (2023 December). *Lo importante para 2024.* AECOC. https://www.aecoc.es/revistas/codigo-84/

Código 84. (2023). *Impacto de la sostenibilidad en la cesta de la compra.* AECOC. https://www.aecoc.es/revistas/codigo-84/

Collins, R. L., Martino, S. C., Kovalchik, S. A., D'Amico, E. J., Shadel, W. G., Becker, K. M., & Tolpadi, A. (2017). Exposure to alcohol advertising and adolescents' drinking beliefs: Role of message interpretation. [h]. *Health Psychology*, *36*(9), 890–897. doi:10.1037/hea0000521 PMID:28639822

Conde, A. L., & Fernández, A. T. (2002). Entre el Vino Sacro y el Profano: Caminos de la Música. In Caminería hispánica: actas del V Congreso Internacional de Caminería Hispánica. Celebrado en Valencia (*España),* (pp. 499-518). Aache.

Consejo Mexicano Vitivinícola. (2018). *Plan Rector 2018.* UVAY Vino. https://uvayvino.org.mx/html/docs/plan_rector_2018.pdf

Coppola, G., Gaudio, M. T., Lopresto, C. G., Calabro, V., Curcio, S., & Chakraborty, S. (2021). Bioplastic from Renewable Biomass: A Facile Solution for a Greener Environment. *Earth Systems and Environment*, *5*(2), 231–251. doi:10.1007/s41748-021-00208-7

Corbetta, G., & Salvato, C. (2004). Self-serving or self-actualizing? Models of man and agency costs in different types of family firms: A commentary on Comparing the agency costs of family and non-family firms: Conceptual Issues and Exploratory Evidence. *Entrepreneurship Theory and Practice*, *28*(4), 355–362. doi:10.1111/j.1540-6520.2004.00050.x

Corbo, M. R., Bevilacqua, A., Petruzzi, L., Casanova, F. P., & Sinigaglia, M. (2014). Functional Beverages: The Emerging Side of Functional Foods. *Comprehensive Reviews in Food Science and Food Safety*, *13*(6), 1192–1206. doi:10.1111/1541-4337.12109

Correia, A., Melo, C., & Carvalho, C. (2022). Wine Tourism Experiences: An Exploratory Approach to Innovation Potential in the Douro Valley, Portugal. In *Advances in Tourism, Technology and Systems* (pp. 243–253). Springer. doi:10.1007/978-981-16-9701-2_20

Cortés Palacios, H. A. (2016). *Influencia del financiamiento y de la innovación en el desempeño de las PyMEs manufacturas en el estado de Aguascalientes.* Universidad Autónoma de Aguascalientes. http://bdigital.dgse.uaa.mx:8080/xmlui/bitstream/handle/11317/1225/416148.pdf?sequence=1&isAllowed=y

Costa, J. M., Catarino, S., Escalona, J. M., & Comuzzo, P. (2022). Achieving a more sustainable wine supply chain—Environmental and socioeconomic issues of the industry. In J. M. Costa, S. Catarino, J. M. Escalona, & P. Comuzzo (Eds.), *Improving Sustainable Viticulture and Winemaking Practices* (pp. 1–24). Academic Press. doi:10.1016/B978-0-323-85150-3.00009-8

Covarrubias, J., & Thach, L. (2015). Wines of Baja Mexico: A qualitative study examining viticulture, enology, and marketing practices. *Wine Economics and Policy*, *4*(2), 110–115. doi:10.1016/j.wep.2015.11.001

Craig, J. B. L., & Moores, K. (2006). A 10 year longitudinal investigation of strategy, systems, and environment on innovation in family firms. *Family Business Review*, *19*(1), 1–10. doi:10.1111/j.1741-6248.2006.00056.x

Craig, J. B., & Dibrell, C. (2006). The natural environment, innovation, and firm performance: A comparative study. *Family Business Review*, *19*(4), 275–288. doi:10.1111/j.1741-6248.2006.00075.x

Cranenburgh, K. C. V., & Arenas, D. (2014). Strategic and Moral Dilemmas of Corporate Philanthropy in Developing Countries: Heineken in Sub-Saharan Africa. *Journal of Business Ethics*, *122*(3), 523–536. doi:10.1007/s10551-013-1776-1

Crespi-Vallbona, M., & Mascarilla-Miró, O. (2020). Wine lovers: Their interests in tourist experiences. *International Journal of Culture, Tourism and Hospitality Research*, *14*(2), 239–258. doi:10.1108/IJCTHR-05-2019-0095

Crippa, M., Solazzo, E., Guizzardi, D., Monforti-Ferrario, F., Tubiello, F. N., & Leip, A. (2021). Food systems are responsible for a third of global anthropogenic GHG emissions. *Nature Food*, *2*(3), 198–209. doi:10.1038/s43016-021-00225-9 PMID:37117443

Cuevas-Vargas, H., Parga-Montoya, N., & Estrada, S. (2020). Incidencia de la innovación en marketing en el rendimiento empresarial: Una aplicación basada en modelamiento con ecuaciones estructurales. *Estudios Gerenciales*, 66–79. doi:10.18046/j.estger.2020.154.3475

Cui, R., Wang, J., Xue, Y., & Liang, H. (2021). Interorganizational learning, green knowledge integration capability and green innovation. *European Journal of Innovation Management*, *24*(4), 1292–1314. doi:10.1108/EJIM-11-2019-0325

Dangelico, R. M. (2016). Green product innovation: Where we are and where we are going. *Business Strategy and the Environment*, *25*(8), 560–576. doi:10.1002/bse.1886

Darnay, S. (2016). Quality of landscape and sustainability benefit to wine tourism: Contexts and commitments. In *Wine and Tourism* (pp. 15–25). Springer. doi:10.1007/978-3-319-18857-7_2

Dascalu, I., Manescu, C., & Sirb, N. M. (2019). The impact of the wine sector on economy. *Journal of Biotechnology*, *305*, S86. doi:10.1016/j.jbiotec.2019.05.296

Daugbjerg, C., Smed, S., Andersen, L. M., & Schvartzman, Y. (2014). Improving eco-labelling as an environmental policy instrument: Knowledge, trust and organic consumption. *Journal of Environmental Policy and Planning*, *16*(4), 559–575. doi:10.1080/1523908X.2013.879038

David Lee, J., Bahl, A., Black, G. S., Duber-Smith, D. C., & Vowles, N. S. (2016). Sustainable and non-sustainable consumer behavior in young adults. *Young Consumers*, *17*(1), 78–93. doi:10.1108/YC-08-2015-00548

Davis, K. (1960). Can business afford to ignore social responsibilities? *California Management Review*, *2*(3), 70–76. doi:10.2307/41166246

De Aza Payano, E. K. (2012). *Innovación Incremental y Innovación Radical/ Disruptiva*. EOI. https://www.eoi.es/blogs/estefanykaryelindeaza/2012/03/07/innovacion-incremental-y-innovacion-radical-disruptiva/

de Jesus, A., Antunes, P., Santos, R., & Mendonça, S. (2019). Eco-innovation pathways to a circular economy: Envisioning priorities through a Delphi approach. *Journal of Cleaner Production*, *228*, 1494–1513. doi:10.1016/j.jclepro.2019.04.049

De Marchi, V. (2012). Environmental innovation and R&D cooperation: Empirical evidence from Spanish manufacturing firms. *Research Policy*, *41*(3), 614–623. doi:10.1016/j.respol.2011.10.002

De Massis, A., Frattini, F., & Lichtenthaler, U. (2013). Research on technological innovation in family firms: Present debates and future directions. *Family Business Review*, *26*(1), 10–31. doi:10.1177/0894486512466258

De Massis, A., Kotlar, J., Wright, M., & Kellermanns, F. W. (2018). Sector-based entrepreneurial capabilities and the promise of sector studies in entrepreneurship. *Entrepreneurship Theory and Practice*, *42*(1), 1, 3–23. doi:10.1177/1042258717740548

De Steur, H., Temmerman, H., Gellynck, X., & Canavari, M. (2020). Drivers, adoption, and evaluation of sustainability practices in Italian wine SMEs. *Business Strategy and the Environment*, *29*(2), 744–762. doi:10.1002/bse.2436

Debicki, B. J., Matherne, C. F. III, Kellermanns, F. W., & Chrisman, J. J. (2009). Family business research in the new millennium: An overview of the who, the where, the what, and the why. *Family Business Review*, *22*(2), 151–166. doi:10.1177/0894486509333598

Degasperi, N. C., & Mainardes, E. W. (2017). What motivates money donation? A study on external motivators. *Revista de Administração (São Paulo)*, *52*(4), 363–373. doi:10.1016/j.rausp.2017.08.002

Deku, W. A., Wang, J., & Das, N. (2023). Innovations in entrepreneurial marketing dimensions: Evidence of Halal food SMES in Ghana. *Journal of Islamic Marketing*, *14*(3), 680–713. doi:10.1108/JIMA-03-2021-0098

Del Brío González, J., & Barba-Sanchez, V. (2020). The Mediating Effect of Environmental Proactivity on the Influence of Stakeholder Pressure and Environmental Strategy of Wineries in Spain. *International Journal of Environmental Research*, *14*(6), 771–783. doi:10.1007/s41742-020-00281-2

Del Río González, P. (2009). The empirical analysis of the determinants for environmental technological change: A research agenda. *Ecological Economics*, *68*(3), 861–878. doi:10.1016/j.ecolecon.2008.07.004

Del Río, P., Carrillo-Hermosilla, J., Könnölä, T., & Bleda, M. (2011). *Business strategies and capacities for eco-innovation*. Instituto de Empresa Business School Working Paper, EC8-124-I.

Del Río, P., Peñasco, C., & Romero-Jordán, D. (2015). Distinctive features of environmental innovators: An econometric analysis. *Business Strategy and the Environment*, *24*(6), 361–385. doi:10.1002/bse.1822

Delmas, M. A., & Gergaud, O. (2014). Sustainable certification for future generation: The case of family business. *Family Business Review*, *27*, 228–243. doi:10.1177/0894486514538651

Demir, A., Budur, T., Omer, H., & Heshmati, A. (2021). Links between knowledge management and organisational sustainability: Does the ISO 9001 certification have an effect? *Knowledge Management Research and Practice*, 1–14. doi:10.1080/14778238.2020.1860663

Dennis, B. S., Buchholtz, A. K., & Butts, M. M. (2009). The Nature of Giving: A Theory of Planned Behavior Examination of Corporate Philanthropy. *Business & Society*, *48*(3), 360–384. doi:10.1177/0007650307305368

Dharmadhikari, S. (2012). Eco-friendly packaging in supply chain. *IUP Journal of Supply Chain Management*, *9*(2), 7.

Di Vaio, A., & Varriale, L. (2020). Blockchain technology in supply chain management for sustainable performance: Evidence from the airport industry. *International Journal of Information Management, 52*, 102014. doi:10.1016/j.ijinfomgt.2019.09.010

Diamantopoulos, A., Riefler, P., & Roth, K. P. (2008). Advancing formative measurement models. *Journal of Business Research, 61*(12), 1203–1218. doi:10.1016/j.jbusres.2008.01.009

Dias, A., Sousa, B., Santos, V., Ramos, P., & Madeira, A. (2023). Wine Tourism and Sustainability Awareness: A Consumer Behavior Perspective. *Sustainability (Basel), 15*(6), 6. doi:10.3390/su15065182

Díaz, J. (2001) Los brindis. *Revista de Folklore*. https://funjdiaz.net/joaquin-diaz-articulos-ficha.php?id=761&qry=vino+

Díaz, J. (2001). *Pregón de cigales. Ensalzando el vino joven. Obra completa.* Fundación Joaquín Díaz. https://funjdiaz.net/joaquin-diaz-articulos-ficha.php?id=20192&qry=vino+

Díaz-García, C., González-Moreno, Á., & Sáez-Martínez, F. J. (2015). Eco-innovation: Insights from a literature review. *Innovation (North Sydney, N.S.W.), 17*(1), 6–23. doi:10.1080/14479338.2015.1011060

Ding, Q., Khattak, S. I., & Ahmad, M. (2021). Towards sustainable production and consumption: Assessing the impact of energy productivity and eco-innovation on consumption-based carbon dioxide emissions (CCO2) in G-7 nations. *Sustainable Production and Consumption, 27*, 254–268. doi:10.1016/j.spc.2020.11.004

Dinh, M. T. T., Su, D. N., Tran, K. T., Luu, T. T., Duong, T. H., & Johnson, L. W. (2022). Eco-designed retail packaging: The empirical conceptualization and measurement. *Journal of Cleaner Production, 379*, 134717. doi:10.1016/j.jclepro.2022.134717

Dini, I. (2019). 1 - An Overview of Functional Beverages. Academic Press. doi:10.1016/B978-0-12-816397-9.00001-7

Dodds, R., Graci, S., Ko, S., & Walker, L. (2013). What drives environmental sustainability in the New Zealand wine industry? An examination of driving factors and practices. *International Journal of Wine Business Research, 25*(3), 164–184. doi:10.1108/IJWBR-2012-0015

Doehler. (2023). *Trends and developments in the beverage industry in 2023.* Doehler. https://www.doehler.com/en/news-media/details/trends-and-developments-in-the-beverage-industry-in-2023.html

Dolan, R., & Goodman, S. (2017). Succeeding on social media: Exploring communication strategies for wine marketing. *Journal of Hospitality and Tourism Management, 33*, 23–30. doi:10.1016/j.jhtm.2017.09.001

Doloreux, D., & Kraft, L. (2019). A Taxonomy of Eco-Innovation Types in SMEs: Exploring Different Firm Profiles in the Canadian Wine Industry. *Sustainability (Basel), 11*(20), 5776. doi:10.3390/su11205776

Doluca, H., Wagner, M., & Block, J. (2018). Sustainability and environmental behavior in family firms: A longitudinal analysis of environment-related activities, innovation and performance. *Business Strategy and the Environment, 27*(1), 152–172. doi:10.1002/bse.1998

Donaldson, T., & Preston, L. E. (1995). The stakeholder theory of the corporation: Concepts, evidence, and implications. *Academy of Management Review, 20*(1), 65–91. doi:10.2307/258887

Donner, M., Gohier, R., & de Vries, H. (2020). A new circular business model typology for creating value from agro-waste. *The Science of the Total Environment, 716*, 137065. Advance online publication. doi:10.1016/j.scitotenv.2020.137065 PMID:32044489

Donthu, N., Kumar, S., Mukherjee, D., Pandey, N., & Lim, W. M. (2021). How to conduct a bibliometric analysis: An overview and guidelines. *Journal of Business Research, 133*, 285–296. doi:10.1016/j.jbusres.2021.04.070

Dosi, G. (1992). Fuentes, métodos y efectos microeconómicos de la innovación. *Ekonomiaz: Revista vasca de economía, 22*, 269–332.

DPO. (2023). *Global Market Trends 2023: Beverages*. DPO. https://dpointernational.com/wp-content/uploads/2023/03/GLOBAL-MARKET-TRENDS-2023-BEVERAGES.pdf

Dressler, M. (2023). Sustainable Business Model Design: A Multi-Case Approach Exploring Generic Strategies and Dynamic Capabilities on the Example of German Wine Estates. *Sustainability (Basel), 15*(5), 3880. doi:10.3390/su15053880

Dri, M., Antonopoulos, I. S., Canfora, P., & Gaudillat, P. (2015). *Best environmental management practice for the food and beverage manufacturing sector*. Final Draft.

Drucker, P. F. (2004). *The effective executive: The definitive guide to getting the right things done*. Harper Business.

Duarte Alonso, A., Bressan, A., Kiat Kok, S., & O'Brien, S. (2021). Filling up the sustainability glass: Wineries' initiatives towards sustainable wine tourism. *Tourism Recreation Research*, 1–15. doi:10.1080/02508281.2021.1885801

Duarte Alonso, A., Bressan, A., O'Shea, M., & Krajsic, V. (2014). Exporting wine in complex times: A study among small and medium wineries. *Journal of Small Business and Enterprise Development, 21*(2), 345–364. doi:10.1108/JSBED-01-2014-0006

Duarte, M., Dias, Á., Sousa, B., & Pereira, L. (2023). Lifestyle entrepreneur-ship as a vehicle for leisure and sustainable tourism. *International Journal of Environmental Research and Public Health, 20*(4), 3241. doi:10.3390/ijerph20043241 PMID:36833935

Du, C., Zhang, Q., & Huang, D. (2023). Environmental protection subsidies, green technology innovation and environmental performance: Evidence from China's heavy-polluting listed firms. *PLoS One, 18*(2), e0278629. doi:10.1371/journal.pone.0278629 PMID:36735660

Dudaroğlu, M., Öner, M. A., & Önday, Ö. (2018). Impact of family influence on top management team in family businesses: A path-analytic study on automotive parts industry in Turkey. *International Journal of Contemporary Alied Researches, 5*(3), 123–161.

Duran, P., Kammerlander, N., Van Essen, M., & Zellweger, T. (2016). Doing more with less: Innovation input and output in family firms. *Academy of Management Journal, 59*(4), 1224–1264. doi:10.5465/amj.2014.0424

Dutta, P., Choi, T. M., Somani, S., & Butala, R. (2020). Blockchain technology in supply chain operations: Applications, challenges and research opportunities. *Transportation research part e: Logistics and transportation review, 142*, 102067.

Dwipamurti, I. G. A. N., Mawardi, M. K., & Nuralam, I. P. (2018). The ef-fect of green marketing on brand image and purchase decision (Study on consumer of Starbucks Café Ubud, Gianyar Bali). *Jurnal Administrasi Bisnis, 61*(3).

Dyer, W. G. (2018). Are family firms really better? Reexamining examining the 'family effect'on firm performance. *Family Business Review, 31*(2), 240–248. doi:10.1177/0894486518776516

EHL. (2023). *Drink trends in 2023: 8 beverages you've got to try this year.* EHL. https://www.hospitalitynet.org/news/4115081.html

Elad, B. (2023). *Energy Drink Statistics – By Demographic, Distribution, Country, Consumers and Region*. Enterprise Apps Today. https://www.enterpriseappstoday.com/stats/energy-drink-statistics.html

ElHaffar, G., Durif, F., & Dubé, L. (2020). Towards closing the attitude-intention-behavior gap in green consumption: A narrative review of the literature and an overview of future research directions. *Journal of Cleaner Production, 275*, 122556. doi:10.1016/j.jclepro.2020.122556

Elías, L. (2008). Paisaje del viñedo: Patrimonio y recurso. *Pasos (El Sauzal), 6*(2), 137–158. doi:10.25145/j.pasos.2008.06.012

Elkington, J. (1997). *The triple bottom line sustainability's accountants.*

Elseidi, R. I. (2018). Determinants of halal purchasing intentions: Evidences from UK. *Journal of Islamic Marketing, 9*(1), 167–190. doi:10.1108/JIMA-02-2016-0013

Endri, E., Syafarudin, A., Santoso, S., Imaningsih, E. S., Suharti, T., & Rinda, R. T. (2020). Consumption behavior patterns of generations Y Halal products in Indonesia. *Academy of Entrepreneurship Journal, 26*(2), 1–10. https://www.scopus.com/inward/record.uri?eid=2-s2.0-85087295237&partnerID=40&md5=c9cf2090de2186839b0aef47463b286a

Erkal, H. (2023). *Ürün Raporu ÇAY 2023 (Product Report Tea 2023),* https://arastirma.tarimorman.gov.tr/tepge/Belgeler/PDF%20%C3%9Cr%C3%BCn%20Raporlar%C4%B1/2023%20%C3%9Cr%C3%BCn%20Raporlar%C4%B1/%C3%87ay%20%C3%9Cr%C3%BCn%20Raporu%202023-383%20TEPGE.pdf

Eryigit, N., & Özcüre, G. (2015). Eco-Innovation as Modern Era Strategy of Companies in Developing Countries: Comparison Between Turkey and European Union. *Procedia: Social and Behavioral Sciences, 195*, 1216–1225. doi:10.1016/j.sbspro.2015.06.246

Espejel, M. I., & Ferrer, Á. Leyva, uana C., & Santos, M. (2014). Turismo en el valle de Guadalupe: ¡Tanto qué hacer! In J. C. Leyva & M. I. Espejel (Eds.), *El Valle de Guadalupe* (pp. 94–101). ENS. http://webfc.ens.uabc.mx/documentos/El%20Valle%20de%20Guadalupe.pdf

Esvandiari, M. (2023). The Effect of Eco-Friendly Packaging on Purchase Intention with Consumer Perception as an Intervening Variable. *International Journal of Entrepreneurship and Sustainability Studies, 3*(2), 62–80. doi:10.31098/ijeass.v3i2.1818

Euromonitor International. (2023). *Need States: Understanding the Future of Functional Beverages, Overview.* Euromonitor International. https://www.euromonitor.com/need-states-understanding-the-future-of-functional-beverages/report

European Commision. (2019). *Agricultural Policy: COP21 United for climate.* EC. https://agriculture.ec.europa.eu/document/download/7c24c51f-55d1-4015-90d9-0fd8e974b525_en?filename=cop21-what-eu-agricultural-policy-does-for-climate_en.pdf&prefLang=es

European Commission. (2017). *Special Eurobarometer 459: Climate change.* EC. https://ec.europa.eu/clima/sites/clima/files/suort/docs/report_2017_en.pdf

Faccio, M., & Lang, L. H. P. (2002). The ultimate ownership of Western European corporations. *Journal of Financial Economics, 65*(3), 365–395. doi:10.1016/S0304-405X(02)00146-0

Fagerberg, J., Mowery, D. C., & Nelson, R. R. (Eds.). (2005). *The Oxford handbook of innovation.* Oxford university press.

Falcó, J. M., Marco-Lajara, B., García, E. S., & Falcó, J. M. (2023). El enoturismo como catalizador de los objetivos de desarrollo sostenible: Un análisis aplicado a la industria vinícola española. *GeoGraphos: Revista Digital para Estudiantes de Geografía y Ciencias Sociales, 14*(152), 121–140. doi:10.14198/GEOGRA2023.14.156

Falk, R., & Miller, N. (1992). *A primer for soft modeling.* University of Akron Press.

Farrukh, M., Javed, S., Raza, A., & Lee, J. W. C. (2021). Twenty years of green innovation research: Trends and way forward. *World Journal of Entrepreneurship, Management and Sustainable Development, 17*(3), 488–501. doi:10.1108/WJEMSD-06-2020-0068

Farzana, M., Shahriar, S., Jeba, F. R., Tabassum, T., Araf, Y., Ullah, M. A., Tasnim, J., Chakraborty, A., Naima, T. A., Marma, K. K. S., Rahaman, T. I., & Hosen, M. J. (2022). Functional food: Complementary to fight against COVID-19. *Beni-Suef University Journal of Basic and Applied Sciences*, *11*(1), 33. doi:10.1186/s43088-022-00217-z PMID:35284580

Fatunnisa, H., Hamdani, N. A., & Permana, I. (2023, March). Exploring the Relationship Between Corporate Social Responsibility and Corporate Sustainability within the Food and Beverage Industry. In *Proceeding of International Conference on Business, Economics, Social Sciences, and Humanities* (Vol. 6, pp. 1085-1090). IEEE.

Fawzy, S., Osman, A. I., Doran, J., & Rooney, D. W. (2020). Strategies for mitigation of climate change: A review. *Environmental Chemistry Letters*, *18*(6), 2069–2094. doi:10.1007/s10311-020-01059-w

Federación Española de Industrias de Alimentación y Bebidas (FIAB). (2023). Volumen de bebida consumido por persona en el hogar en 2021, desglosado por grupos de productos (en litros). *Statista*. https://es.statista.com/estadisticas/475374/consumo-per-capita-de-bebida-en-el-hogar-en-espana-por-producto/

Federación Española de Industrias de Alimentación y Bebidas. (2020). *Guía al consumidor sobre sostenibilidad* [PDF File]. FIAB. https://fiab.es/wp-content/uploads/2017/11/2017_GUIA-AL-CONSUMIDOR-DE-SOSTENIBILIDAD.pdf

Federación Española del Vino. (2023). *El sector en cifras*. FEV. https://www.fev.es/sector-cifras/

Felix, R., Gonzalez, E. M., Castano, R., Carrete, L., & Gretz, R. T. (2022). When the green in green packaging backfires: Gender effects and perceived masculinity of environmentally friendly products. *International Journal of Consumer Studies*, *46*(3), 925–943. doi:10.1111/ijcs.12738

Fernandes, S., Ferreira, D., Alves, T., & de Sousa, B. M. B. (2021). Glamp-ing and the development of sustainable tourism: a Portuguese case study. Handbook of Sustainable Development and Leisure Services, 201-222.

Fernández-Olmos, M., Gargallo-Castel, A., & Malorgio, G. (2021). Do institutional networks affect winery survival? *British Food Journal*, *123*(7), 2478–2491. doi:10.1108/BFJ-09-2020-0836

Fernando, R. L. S. (2019). Solid waste management of local governments in the Western Province of Sri Lanka: An implementation analysis. *Waste Management (New York, N.Y.)*, *84*, 194–203. doi:10.1016/j.wasman.2018.11.030 PMID:30691892

Fernando, Y., Jabbour, C., & Wah, W. (2019). Pursuing green growth in technology firms through the connections between environmental innovation and sustainable business performance: Does service capability matter? *Resources, Conservation and Recycling*, *141*, 8–20. doi:10.1016/j.resconrec.2018.09.031

Fernando, Y., Tseng, M. L., Sroufe, R., Abideen, A. Z., Shaharudin, M. S., & Jose, R. (2021). Eco-innovation impacts on recycled product performance and competitiveness: Malaysian automotive industry. *Sustainable Production and Consumption*, *28*, 1677–1686. doi:10.1016/j.spc.2021.09.010

Ferrer, J. R., García-Cortijo, M. C., Pinilla, V., & Castillo-Valero, J. S. (2022). The business model and sustainability in the Spanish wine sector. *Journal of Cleaner Production*, *330*, 129810. doi:10.1016/j.jclepro.2021.129810

Ferrer, J. R., García-Cortijo, M.-C., Pinilla, V., Castillo-Valero, J.-S., & Serrano, R. (2023). Sustainability and growth: Evidence from Spanish wine industry. *Spanish Journal of Agricultural Research*, *21*(2), e0104. doi:10.5424/sjar/2023212-20241

Festa, G., Shams, S., Metallo, G., & Cuomo, M. T. (2020). Opportunities and challenges in the contribution of wine routes to wine tourism in Italy–A stakeholders' perspective of development. *Tourism Management Perspectives*, *33*, 100585. doi:10.1016/j.tmp.2019.100585

Filopoulos, S., & Frittella, N. (2019). Designing sustainable and responsible wine tourism experiences *BIO Web of Conferences*. IEEE. 10.1051/bioconf/20191203006

Finlays. (2022). *Global Beverage Trends 2023*. Finlays. https://www.finlays.net/wp-content/uploads/2022/11/Global-Beverage-Trends-2023.pdf

Fiore, M., Silvestri, R., Contò, F., & Pellegrini, G. (2017). Understanding the relationship between green approach and marketing innovations tools in the wine sector. *Journal of Cleaner Production*, *142*, 4085–4091. doi:10.1016/j.jclepro.2016.10.026

Fleck, A. (2023). *Who Drinks Tea?* Statista. https://www.statista.com/chart/29582/share-of-people-that-drink-tea-in-selected-countries/

Flores, S., & Medeiros, R. (2016). Wine tourism moving towards sustainable viticulture? Challenges, opportunities and tools to internalize sustainable principles in the wine sector. In: Peris-Ortiz, M., Del Río Rama, M., Rueda-Armengot, C. (eds) Wine and Tourism. Springer, Cham. doi:10.1007/978-3-319-18857-7_16

Flores, S. S. (2018). What is sustainability in the wine world? A cross-country analysis of wine sustainability frameworks. *Journal of Cleaner Production*, *172*, 2301–2312. doi:10.1016/j.jclepro.2017.11.181

FoodDrink Europe. (2017). *Visión de sostenibilidad ambiental para 2030. Logros, Desafíos y Oportunidades* [PDF File]. FIAB. https://fiab.es/wp-content/uploads/2017/11/2012_VISIO%CC%81N-DE-SOSTENIBILIDAD-MEDIOAMBIENTAL-PARA-2030-FDE.pdf

Foragekitchen. (2023). *13 Food and Beverage Industry Trends in 2023*. Foragekitchen. https://www.foragekitchen.com/resources/2023/7/25/13-food-and-beverage-industry-trends-in-2023

Forbes, S. L., Cohen, D. A., Cullen, R., Wratten, S. D., & Fountain, J. (2009). Consumer attitudes regarding environmentally sustainable wine: An exploratory study of the New Zealand marketplace. *Journal of Cleaner Production*, *17*(13), 1195–1199. doi:10.1016/j.jclepro.2009.04.008

Forbes, S. L., Fuentes-Fernández, R., & Gilinsky, A. (2018). An exploratory examination of philanthropy in the New Zealand, Spanish and US wine industries. *Wine Economics and Policy*, *7*(1), 35–44. doi:10.1016/j.wep.2018.01.002

Fornell, C., & Larcker, D. (1981). Evaluating structural equation models with unobservable variables and measurement error. *JMR, Journal of Marketing Research*, *18*(1), 39–50. doi:10.1177/002224378101800104

Fortes, A., Carvalho, A., & Sousa, B. (2023). Determinants of Green Con-sumer Behavior in Tourism and Hotel Management Contexts: A Study Applied to the Côa Region. In Advances in Tourism, Technology and Sys-tems: Selected Papers from ICOTTS 2022, Volume 2 (pp. 323-332). Sin-gapore: Springer Nature Singapore.

Fouziya, R., & Gracious, J. (2018). Awareness of green marketing and its influence on consumer perception: An exploratory study. *Sumedha Journal of Management*, *7*(2), 62–68.

Fraga, H., García de Cortázar Atauri, I., & Santos, J. A. (2018). Viticultural irrigation demands under climate change scenarios in Portugal. *Agricultural Water Management*, *196*, 66–74. doi:10.1016/j.agwat.2017.10.023

Frank, H., Lueger, M., Nosé, L., & Suchy, D. (2010). The concept of Familiness: Literature review and systems theory-based reflections. *Journal of Family Business Strategy*, *1*(3), 119–130. doi:10.1016/j.jfbs.2010.08.001

Friedman, A. L., & Miles, S. (2006). *Stakeholders: Theory and Practice*. Oxford University Press. doi:10.1093/oso/9780199269860.001.0001

Frigon, A., Doloreux, D., & Shearmur, R. (2020). Drivers of eco-innovation and conventional innovation in the Canadian wine industry. *Journal of Cleaner Production*, *275*, 124115. doi:10.1016/j.jclepro.2020.124115

Fritzsche, D., & Oz, E. (2007). Personal values' influence on the ethical dimension of decision making. *Journal of Business Ethics*, *75*(4), 335–343. doi:10.1007/s10551-006-9256-5

Frooman, J. (1999). Stakeholder influence strategies. *Academy of Management Review*, *24*(2), 191–205. doi:10.2307/259074

Frost, W., Frost, J., Strickland, P., & Maguire, J. (2020). Seeking a competitive advantage in wine tourism: Heritage and storytelling at the cellar-door. *International Journal of Hospitality Management*, *87*, 102460. doi:10.1016/j.ijhm.2020.102460

Fuentes-Fernández, R., & Aboah, J. (2020). Philanthropic Wine Firms and Their CSR Communication. In *Social Sustainability in the Global Wine Industry* (pp. 185–200). Springer. doi:10.1007/978-3-030-30413-3_13

Fuentes-Fernández, R., Martínez-Falcó, J., Sánchez-García, E., & Marco-Lajara, B. (2022). Does ecological agriculture moderate the relationship between wine tourism and economic performance? A structural equation analysis applied to the ribera del duero wine context. *Agriculture*, *12*(12), 2143. doi:10.3390/agriculture12122143

Fuller, D. A. (1999). *Sustainable marketing: Managerial - ecological issues*. Sage Publications. doi:10.4135/9781452220611

Gaille, B. (2017). *19 Shocking Tea Consumption Statistics.* Brandon Gaille. https://brandongaille.com/18-shocking-tea-consumption-statistics/

Galán, I., González, M., & Valencia-Martín, J. (2014). Patrones de consumo de alcohol en España: Un país en transición. *Revista Española de Salud Pública*, *88*(4), 529–540. doi:10.4321/S1135-57272014000400007 PMID:25090408

Galati, A., Crescimanno, M., Tinervia, S., & Fagnani, F. (2017). Social media as a strategic marketing tool in the Sicilian wine industry: Evidence from Facebook. *Wine Economics and Policy*, *6*(1), 40–47. doi:10.1016/j.wep.2017.03.003

Galati, A., Schifani, G., Crescimanno, M., & Migliore, G. (2019). "Natural wine" consumers and interest in label information: An analysis of willingness to pay in a new Italian wine market segment. *Journal of Cleaner Production*, *227*, 405–413. doi:10.1016/j.jclepro.2019.04.219

Galbreath, J. (2019). Drivers of Green Innovations: The Impact of Export Intensity, Women Leaders, and Absorptive Capacity. *Journal of Business Ethics*, *158*(1), 47–61. doi:10.1007/s10551-017-3715-z

Galbreath, J., Charles, D., & Oczkowski, E. (2016). The Drivers of Climate Change Innovations: Evidence from the Australian Wine Industry. *Journal of Business Ethics*, *135*(2), 217–231. doi:10.1007/s10551-014-2461-8

Gallarotti, G. (1995). It pays to be green: The managerial incentive structure and environmentally sound strategies. *The Columbia Journal of World Business*, *30*(4), 38–57. doi:10.1016/0022-5428(95)90004-7

Gámez, M., & Núñez Tapia, F. A. (2020). Investigaciones, enfoques interdisciplinarios y perspectivas sobre el patrimonio industrial. In *M. Gámez y F.A. Núñez (Coords.), Y se detuvieron las máquinas. Lenguajes, reconversión y espacios simbólicos sobre el Patrimonio Industrial.* El Colegio de San Luis.

García, A., Meraz-Ruiz, L., & Díaz, E. R. (2018). Wine Tourism and Wine Marketing in Family-Owned Micro Wineries in Guadalupe Valley, Mexico. *Rosa dos Ventos, 10*(4), 690–711.

García, G. (2022, October 26). *Producción sostenible, clave en la industria de alimentos y bebidas*. The Food Tech. https://thefoodtech.com/seguridad-alimentaria/produccion-sostenible-clave-en-la-industria-de-alimentos-y-bebidas/

García-Casarejos, N., Gargallo, P., & Cabanes, B. (2018). Un marco teórico para delimitar el concepto de enoturismo sostenible desde un enfoque multi-nivel. In *E3S Web of Conferences* (Vol. 50, p. 03002). EDP Sciences. doi:10.1051/e3sconf/20185003002

Garduño, E., (2015). *Pueblos Indígenas de México en el Siglo XXI; Yumanos, cucapá, kiliwa, pa ipai, kumiai*, México, Comisión Nacional para el Desarrollo de los Pueblos Indígenas.

Garrido Domené, F., Laguna Mariscal, G., & Aguirre Quintero, F. (2019). Dioniso, el vino y la música. Divino frenesí, de ayer a hoy, Córdoba: Ed.Publicaciones de la Universidad de Córdoba.

Gauthier, J., & Wooldridge, B. (2012). Influences on sustainable innovation adoption: Evidence from leadership in energy and environmental design. *Business Strategy and the Environment*, *21*(2), 98–110. doi:10.1002/bse.716

Gayathry, K. S., & John, J. A. (2021). Functional beverages: Special focus on anti-diabetic potential. *Journal of Food Processing and Preservation*, *45*, e15974. doi:10.1111/jfpp.15974

Gebashe, F. C., Naidoo, D., Amoo, S. O., & Masondo, N. A. (2022). Cosmeceuticals: A newly expanding industry in South Africa. *Cosmetics*, *9*(4), 77. doi:10.3390/cosmetics9040077

Gedajlovic, E., Carney, M., Chrisman, J. J., & Kellermanns, F. W. (2012). The adolescence of family firm research: Taking stock and planning for the future. *Journal of Management*, *38*(4), 1010–1037. doi:10.1177/0149206311429990

Gelaye, Y., & Getahun, S. (2024). A review of the carbon sequestration potential of fruit trees and their implications for climate change mitigation: The case of Ethiopia. *Cogent Food & Agriculture*, *10*(1), 2294544. doi:10.1080/23311932.2023.2294544

Geldes, C., & Felzensztein, C. (2013). Marketing innovations in the agribusiness sector. *Academia (Caracas)*, *26*(1), 108–138. doi:10.1108/ARLA-05-2013-0042

Georgie, N. (2023). *Food and Beverage Industry: Beverage Industry Trends in 2023*. Blue Cart. https://www.bluecart.com/blog/beverage-industry-trends#:~:text=The%202023%20beverage%20industry%20trends%20include%3A&text=and%20mocktail%20drinks-,Hybrid%20beverages,Sugar%20reduction

Getz, D. (2000). *Explore wine tourism: Management, development and destinations*. Cognizant.

Getz, D., & Brown, G. (2006). Critical success factors for wine tourism regions: A demand analysis. *Tourism Management*, *27*(1), 146–158. doi:10.1016/j.tourman.2004.08.002

Ghazali, E. M., Mutum, D. S., & Ariswibowo, N. (2018). Impact of religious values and habit on an extended green purchase behaviour model. *International Journal of Consumer Studies*, *42*(6), 639–654. doi:10.1111/ijcs.12472

Ghazali, E., Soon, P. C., Mutum, D. S., & Nguyen, B. (2017). Health and cosmetics: Investigating consumers' values for buying organic personal care products. *Journal of Retailing and Consumer Services*, *39*, 154–163. doi:10.1016/j.jretconser.2017.08.002

Giacomarra, M., Galati, A., Crescimanno, M., & Vrontis, D. (2020). Geographical cues: Evidences from New and Old World countries' wine consumers. *British Food Journal*, *122*(4), 1252–1267. doi:10.1108/BFJ-08-2019-0580

Giacomin, V. (2018). The emergence of an export cluster: Traders and palm oil in early twentieth-century Southeast Asia. *Enterprise and Society*, *19*(2), 272–308. doi:10.1017/eso.2017.10

Giannarakis, G., Sariannidis, N., & Konteos, G. (2020). The effect of corporate governance characteristics on environmental performance: The case of food and beverage sector. *Open Journal of Business and Management*, *8*(05), 1988–2005. doi:10.4236/ojbm.2020.85122

Gil, A., & Carrillo, F. (2016). Knowledge transfer and the learning process in Spanish wineries. *Knowledge Management Research and Practice*, *14*(1), 60–68. doi:10.1057/kmrp.2014.12

Gilinsky, A. Jr, Forbes, S. L., & Fuentes-Fernández, R. (2018). An exploratory study of wine business philanthropy in the USA. *International Journal of Wine Business Research, 30*(2), 201–217. doi:10.1108/IJWBR-01-2017-0006

Gilinsky, A. Jr, Newton, S. K., & Vega, R. F. (2016). Sustainability in the Global Wine Industry: Concepts and Cases. *Agriculture and Agricultural Science Procedia, 8*, 37–49. doi:10.1016/j.aaspro.2016.02.006

Gjerding, A. N. (2003). The Flexible Firm: New Concepts and Differences Between the Nordic Systems of Innovation. In M. C.; L. Heitor B. Å. (eds), null (Ed.), Innovation, Competence Building, and Social Cohesion in Europe (pp. 122–143). Jessica Kingsley Publishers.

Gjolberg, M. (2009). Measuring the immeasurable? Constructing an index of CSR practices and CSR performance in 20 countries. *Scandinavian Journal of Management, 25*, 10–22.

Godfrey, P. C. (2005). The relationship between corporate philanthropy and shareholder wealth: A risk management perspective. *Academy of Management Review, 30*(4), 777–798. doi:10.5465/amr.2005.18378878

Gokran, S., & Kuthambalayan, T. (2019). Creating sustainable fresh produce supply chains by managing uncertainties. *Journal of Cleaner Production, 207*, 908–919. doi:10.1016/j.jclepro.2018.10.072

Golicic, S. L. (2022). Changes in sustainability in the global wine industry. *International Journal of Wine Business Research, 34*(3), 392–409. doi:10.1108/IJWBR-03-2021-0021

Golicic, S. L., Flint, D. J., & Signori, P. (2017). Building business sustainability through resilience in the wine industry. *International Journal of Wine Business Research, 29*(1), 74–97. doi:10.1108/IJWBR-02-2016-0005

Gómez-Fraguela, J. A., Fernández Pérez, N., Romero Tríñanes, E., & Luengo Martín, A. (2008). El botellón y el consumo de alcohol y otras drogas en la juventud. *Psicothema, 20*(2), 211–217. PMID:18413080

Gómez, M., Pratt, M., & Molina, A. (2019). Wine tourism research: A systematic review of 20 vintages from 1995 to 2014. *Current Issues in Tourism, 22*(18), 2211–2249. doi:10.1080/13683500.2018.1441267

Gómez-Mejia, L. R., Hynes, K. T., Nunez-Nickel, M., & Moyano-Fuentes, H. (2007). Socioemotional wealth and business risk in family-controlled firms: Evidence from Spanish olive oil mills. *Administrative Science Quarterly, 52*(1), 106–137. doi:10.2189/asqu.52.1.106

Gomez-Mejia, L., Campbell, J., Martin, G., Hoskisson, R., Makri, M., & Sirmon, D. (2014). Socioemotional wealth as a mixed gamble: Revisiting family firm RandD investments with the behavioral agency model. *Entrepreneurship Theory and Practice, 38*(6), 1351–1374. doi:10.1111/etap.12083

Góngora-Rosado, M. A. (2017). *Baja California, México: Puerta norte del vino latinoamericano.* Retos y Oportunidades socioambientales.

González Alcantud, J. A. (1995). *Cultivos y herramientas. Antropografías de la economía moral mediterránea. Revista de Antropología Social, ni 4.* Servicio de Publicaciones. Universidad Complutense.

Gonzalez-SanJose, M. Gómez-Miguel, V. & Sotés, V. (2017). The wine culture, a driver of the sustainable development of wine regions. *BIO web of conferences, 40th World Congress of Vine and Wine.* IEEE.

González-SanJosé, M. L., Gómez-Miguel, V., & Sotés, V. (2017). La Cultura del Vino, motor del desarrollo sostenible de las regiones vitivinícolas. In *BIO Web of Conferences* (*Vol. 9*, p. 04003). EDP Sciences.

Goodwin, I. (2022). Programmatic alcohol advertising, social media and public health: Algorithms, automated challenges to regulation, and the failure of public oversight. *The International Journal on Drug Policy, 109*, 103826. doi:10.1016/j.drugpo.2022.103826 PMID:35994939

Gouvarchinghaleh, H. E., Kiany, F., Parastouei, K., Alishir, G., Jafari, N. J., Fooladi, A. A. I., Pargar, A., Ghazvini, A., Mirnejad, R., Raei, M., Olounabadi, A. S., Babaei, M., Heydari, S., Rostami, H., Shahriary, A., Farnoosh, G., Sobhani, V., & Mazhari, M. M. (2023). The effects of functional foods mixture on inflammatory cytokines and biochemical findings in hospitalized patients with COVID-19: A randomized double-blind controlled trial. *Trials, 24*(1), 442. doi:10.1186/s13063-023-07481-z PMID:37408032

Graham, E., & Floering, I. (2024). *The modern plantation in the Third world* (Vol. 3). Taylor & Francis.

Grand view research. (2018). *Sports Drink Market Size, Share & Trends Analysis Report By Product (Isotonic, Hypertonic, Hypotonic)*. Grand View Research. https://www.grandviewresearch.com/industry-analysis/sports-drink-market

Grant, R. (1997). The knowledge-based view of the firm: Implications for management practice. *Long Range Planning, 30*(3), 450–454. doi:10.1016/S0024-6301(97)00025-3

Grebmer, C., & Diefenbach, S. (2022). Perceiving and believing? The subjective persuasiveness of graphic design elements and eco-friendly packaging materials on consumers' environmental consciousness. *International Journal of Sustainable Development, 4*(3-4), 234–252.

Grimstad, S. (2011). Developing a framework for examining business-driven sustainability initiatives with relevance to wine tourism clusters. *International Journal of Wine Business Research, 23*(1), 62–82. doi:10.1108/17511061111121416

Guo, X., Tichar, T., Sikka, B., Agarwal, B., Gesh, K., Narula, S., Kumar, A., & Singh, K. (2023, December 26). *Scoping study on fruits and vegetables*. eDepot. https://edepot.wur.nl/552208

Gupta, S. S., Misra, S., & Ghosh, A. (2024). Biodiversity: goal and driver of agricultural sustainability. In Biodiversity and Bioeconomy (pp. 143-164). Elsevier. doi:10.1016/B978-0-323-95482-2.00007-9

Gupta, A., Sanwal, N., Bareen, M. A., Barua, S., Sharma, N., Olatunji, O. J., Nirmal, N. P., & Jatindra, K. (2023). Sahu, (2023). Trends in functional beverages: Functional ingredients, processing technologies, stability, health benefits, and consumer perspective. *Food Research International, 170*, 113046. doi:10.1016/j.foodres.2023.113046 PMID:37316029

Gu, Q., Qiu, H., King, B., & Huang, S. (2020). Understanding the wine tourism experience: The roles of facilitators, constraints, and involvement. *Journal of Vacation Marketing, 26*(2), 211–229. doi:10.1177/1356766719880253

Ha, B. C., Lim, S. Y., & Lee, C. (2021). Impact of Organizations' Internal Green Supply Chain Management on Consumers' Purchasing Behavior for Personal Care Products. *Operations and Supply Chain Management: An International Journal, 14*(3), 338–350. doi:10.31387/oscm0460306

Habbershon, T. G., & Williams, M. L. (1999). A resource-based framework for assessing the strategic advantages of family firms. *Family Business Review, 12*(1), 1–25. doi:10.1111/j.1741-6248.1999.00001.x

Habbershon, T. G., Williams, M., & MacMillan, I. C. (2003). A unified systems perspective of family firm performance. *Journal of Business Venturing, 18*(4), 451–465. doi:10.1016/S0883-9026(03)00053-3

Haile, E. A., & Tüzüner, V. L. (2022). Organizational learning capability and its impact on organizational innovation. *Asia Pacific Journal of Innovation and Entrepreneurship, 16*(1), 69–85. doi:10.1108/APJIE-03-2022-0015

Hair, J. F. Jr, Ringle, C. M., & Sarstedt, M. (2013). Partial least squares structural equation modeling: Rigorous alications, better results, and higher acceptance. *Long Range Planning, 46*(1-2), 1–12. doi:10.1016/j.lrp.2013.01.001

Hair, J. F., Risher, J. J., Sarstedt, M., & Ringle, C. M. (2019). When to use and how to report the results of PLS-SEM. *European Business Review, 31*(1), 1, 2–24. doi:10.1108/EBR-11-2018-0203

Hair, J. F., Sarstedt, M., Pieper, T. M., & Ringle, C. M. (2012). The use of partial least squares structural equation modeling in strategic management research: A review of past practices and recommendations for future alications. *Long Range Planning*, *45*(5-6), 5–6, 320–340. doi:10.1016/j.lrp.2012.09.008

Hair, J. F., Sarstedt, M., & Ringle, C. (2019). Rethinking some of the rethinking of partial least squares. *European Journal of Marketing*, *53*(4), 566–584. doi:10.1108/EJM-10-2018-0665

Hair, J., Hult, G., Ringle, C., & Sarstedt, M. (2016). *A primer on partial least squares structural equation modeling (PLS-SEM)*. SAGE Publications.

Hair, J., Hult, G., Ringle, C., Sarstedt, M., Castillo-Apraiz, J., Cepeda Carrion, G., & Roldán, J. (2019). *Manual de Partial Least Squares Structural Equation Modeling (PLS-SEM) (2ª Edición)*. OmniaScience Scholar. doi:10.3926/oss.37

Haleem, A., Khan, M. I., & Khan, S. (2021). Conceptualising a framework linking halal supply chain management with sustainability: An India centric study. *Journal of Islamic Marketing*, *12*(8), 1535–1552. doi:10.1108/JIMA-07-2019-0149

Hall, C. (1996). Wine tourism in New Zealand. Proceedings of tourism down under II: A research conference (pp. 109-119). Donedin: Universidad de Otago.

Hall, C., Johnson, G., Cambourne, B., Macionis, N., Mitchell, R., & Sharples, L. (2009). Wine tourism: an introduction. In *Wine tourism around the world* (pp. 1–23). Routledge. doi:10.4324/9780080521145-1

Hall, C., & Macionis, N. (1998). Wine tourism in Australia and New Zealand. In R. Butler, (Eds.), *Tourism and recreation in rural areas* (pp. 267–298). Wiley.

Hall, C., Sharples, L., Cambourne, B., & Macionis, N. (2000). *Wine tourism around the world: development, management and markets*. Editorial Elsevier.

Hamann, P. A. (2013). *El marketing verde. Un compromiso de todos. Tiem-po de Opinión. Pág*. Universidad ESAN.

Hamid, S. R., Arzaman, A. F. M., Razali, M. A., Yasin, N. I., Masrom, N. R., Sabri, N. A. A., & Margono, M. (2024). The deployment of the Malaysian sustainable palm oil standard in the agriculture sector. *Multidisciplinary Science Journal*, *6*(7), 2024115–2024115. doi:10.31893/multiscience.2024115

Hamzaoui Essoussi, L., & Zahaf, M. (2008). Decision making process of community organic food consumers: An exploratory study. *Journal of Consumer Marketing*, *25*(2), 95–104. doi:10.1108/07363760810858837

Hanaysha, J. R. (2022). Impact of social media marketing features on consumer's purchase decision in the fast-food industry: Brand trust as a mediator. *International Journal of Information Management Data Insights*, *2*(2), 100102. doi:10.1016/j.jjimei.2022.100102

Han, B., & Hoang, B. X. (2020). Opinions on the current pandemic of COVID-19: Use functional food to boost our immune functions. *Journal of Infection and Public Health*, *13*(12), 1811–1817. doi:10.1016/j.jiph.2020.08.014 PMID:32948484

Han, H. (2021). Consumer behavior and environmental sustainability in tourism and hospitality: A review of theories, concepts, and latest research. *Journal of Sustainable Tourism*, *29*(7), 1021–1042. doi:10.1080/09669582.2021.1903019

Hannan, M. A., Hoque, M. M., Hussain, A., Yusof, Y., & Ker, P. J. (2018). State-of-the-Art and Energy Management System of Lithium-Ion Batteries in Electric Vehicle Applications: Issues and Recommendations. *IEEE Access : Practical Innovations, Open Solutions*, *6*, 19362–19378. doi:10.1109/ACCESS.2018.2817655

Hassan, M. A., Farid, M. A. A., Zakaria, M. R., Ariffin, H., Andou, Y., & Shirai, Y. (2024). Palm oil expansion in Malaysia and its countermeasures through policy window and biorefinery approach. *Environmental Science & Policy*, *153*, 103671. doi:10.1016/j.envsci.2024.103671

He, F., Miao, X., Wong, C. W., & Lee, S. (2018). Contemporary corporate eco-innovation research: A systematic review. *Journal of Cleaner Production*, *174*, 502–526. doi:10.1016/j.jclepro.2017.10.314

Heimann, T., Argueyrolles, R., Reinhardt, M., Schuenemann, F., Söder, M., & Delzeit, R. (2024). Phasing out palm and soy oil biodiesel in the EU: What is the benefit? *Global Change Biology. Bioenergy*, *16*(1), e13115. doi:10.1111/gcbb.13115

Henseler, J., Hubona, G., & Ray, P. (2016). Using PLS path modeling in new technology research: Updated guidelines. *Industrial Management & Data Systems*, *116*(1), 2–20. doi:10.1108/IMDS-09-2015-0382

Henseler, J., Ringle, C. M., & Sarstedt, M. (2015). A new criterion for assessing discriminant validity in variance-based structural equation modeling. *Journal of the Academy of Marketing Science*, *43*(1), 115–135. doi:10.1007/s11747-014-0403-8

Henseler, J., Ringle, C. M., & Sinkovics, R. R. (2009). The use de partial least squares path modeling in international marketing. *Advances in International Marketing*, *20*, 277–320. doi:10.1108/S1474-7979(2009)0000020014

Henson, I. E., Ruiz, R. R., & Romero, H. M. (2012). The greenhouse gas balance of the oil palm industry in Colombia: A preliminary analysis. I. Carbon sequestration and carbon offsets. *Agronomia Colombiana*, *30*(3), 359–369.

Hew, J.-J., Wong, L.-W., Tan, G. W.-H., Ooi, K.-B., & Lin, B. (2020). The blockchain-based Halal traceability systems: A hype or reality? *Supply Chain Management*, *25*(6), 863–879. doi:10.1108/SCM-01-2020-0044

Hicks, C., & Dietmar, R. (2007). Improving cleaner production through the alication of environmental management tools in China. *Journal of Cleaner Production*, *15*(5), 395–408. doi:10.1016/j.jclepro.2005.11.008

Hill, C. W. L., & Jones, T. M. (1992). Stakeholder-agency theory. *Journal of Management Studies*, *29*(2), 131–154. doi:10.1111/j.1467-6486.1992.tb00657.x

Hizarci-Payne, A. K., İpek, İ., & Kurt Gümüş, G. (2021). How environmental innovation influences firm performance: A meta-analytic review. *Business Strategy and the Environment*, *30*(2), 1174–1190. doi:10.1002/bse.2678

Hojnik, J., Ruzzier, M., & Manolova, T. S. (2018). Internationalization and economic performance: The mediating role of eco-innovation. *Journal of Cleaner Production*, *171*, 1312–1323. doi:10.1016/j.jclepro.2017.10.111

Hopfenbeck, W. (1993). *The green management revolution: Lessons in envi-ronmental excellence*. Prentice Hall.

Horbach, J. (2008). Determinants of environmental innovation—New evidence from German panel data sources. *Research Policy*, *37*(1), 163–173. doi:10.1016/j.respol.2007.08.006

Horbach, J., Oltra, V., & Belin, J. (2013). Determinants and specificities of eco-innovations compared to other innovations—An econometric analysis for the French and German industry based on the community innovation survey. *Industry and Innovation*, *20*(6), 523–543. doi:10.1080/13662716.2013.833375

Horbach, J., Rammer, C., & Rennings, K. (2012). Determinants of eco-innovations by type of environmental impact—The role of regulatory push/pull, technology push, and market pull. *Ecological Economics*, *78*, 112–122. doi:10.1016/j.ecolecon.2012.04.005

Horváthová, E. (2012). The impact of environmental performance on firm performance: Short-term costs and long-term benefits? *Ecological Economics*, *84*, 91–97. doi:10.1016/j.ecolecon.2012.10.001

Huang, B., Pan, Z., Su, X., & An, L. (2018). Recycling of lithium-ion batteries: Recent advances and perspectives. *Journal of Power Sources*, *399*, 274–286. doi:10.1016/j.jpowsour.2018.07.116

Huang, Y. C., Ding, H. B., & Kao, M. R. (2009). Salient stakeholder voices: Family business and green innovation adoption. *Journal of Management & Organization*, *15*(3), 309–326. doi:10.5172/jmo.2009.15.3.309

Hu, L., & Bentler, P. (1998). Fit indices in covariance structure modeling: Sensitivity to underparameterized model misspecification. *Psychological Methods*, *3*(4), 424–453. doi:10.1037/1082-989X.3.4.424

Huriah, T., Permana, I., Octavia, M., & Abdul Hamid, S. H. B. (2022). Understanding the purchasing behaviors of halal cosmetics of teenagers in Indonesia using the theory of planned behavior and theory of consumption value. *Bali Medical Journal*, *11*(3), 1608–1613. doi:10.15562/bmj.v11i3.3704

Iannone, B. (2015). Sustainability to Improve Knowledge Values and Intangible Capital: A Case Study in Wine Sector. In *European Conference on Knowledge Management* (p. 367). Academic Conferences International Limited.

Innova Market Insights. (2023). *Top Ten Trends for 2023*. Innova Market Insights. https://www.innovamarketinsights.com/trends/top-ten-trends-for-2023-redefining-value-in-a-volatile-world/

Interprofesional del Vino de España. (2022 July 20). *Estrategia del sector vitivinícola español 2022-2027* [PDF File]. Interprofesional del Vino. https://interprofesionaldelvino.es/wp-content/uploads/2023/11/20072022_Presentacion-Publica_Plan-Estrategico-OIVEE_web-3.pdf

Interprofesional del Vino de España. (2023). *La relevancia económica y social del sector vitivinícola en España* [PDF file]. https://interprofesionaldelvino.es/wp-content/uploads/2023/11/Informe_relevancia_economica_y_social_del_sector_vitivinicola-_en-_Espana_2023_OIVEE_vf.pdf

Iovino, R., & Mattion, I. (2009). *Sinfonía gastronómica:(música, eros y cocina)* (Vol. 43). Siruela.

Iranmanesh, M., Mirzaei, M., Parvin Hosseini, S. M., & Zailani, S. (2020). Muslims' willingness to pay for certified halal food: An extension of the theory of planned behaviour. *Journal of Islamic Marketing*, *11*(1), 14–30. doi:10.1108/JIMA-03-2018-0049

Islam, M. M., Ab Talib, M. S., & Muhamad, N. (2023). Developing theoretical lenses for upstream halal businesses. *Journal of Islamic Marketing*. doi:10.1108/JIMA-05-2022-0156

Ismail, M. B., Mohamad, N. B., & Ahamat, A. (2023). Learning Orientation as Mediator between International Entrepreneurial Orientation and International Firm Performance in Global Halal Industry. *Global Journal Al-Thaqafah*, *SI*(Special Issue), 53–64. doi:10.7187/GJATSI072023-5

İstanbul Ticaret Gazetesi. (2022). *Çay İhracatı 2022 yılının ilk ayında 1. Milyon dolar kazandırdı (Tea Exports brought 1. Million dollars in the first month of 2022)*. Istanbul Ticaret Gazetesi. https://istanbulticaretgazetesi.com/tr/cay-ihracati-2022-yilinin-ilk-ayinda-14-milyon-dolar-kazandirdi

Jabbour, C. J. C., Jugend, D., de Sousa Jabbour, A. B., Gunasekaran, A., & Latan, H. (2015). Green product development and performance of Brazilian firms: Measuring the role of human and technical aspects. *Journal of Cleaner Production*, *87*, 442–451. doi:10.1016/j.jclepro.2014.09.036

Janssen, P. A., Saxell, L., Page, L. A., Klein, M. C., Liston, R. M., & Lee, S. K. (2009). Outcomes of planned home birth with registered midwife versus planned hospital birth with midwife or physician. *Canadian Medical Association Journal*, *181*(6-7), 377–383. doi:10.1503/cmaj.081869 PMID:19720688

Japutra, A., Ekinci, Y., & Simkin, L. (2014). Exploring brand attachment, its determinants and outcomes. *Journal of Strategic Marketing*, *22*(7), 616–630. doi:10.1080/0965254X.2014.914062

Jarzębowski, S., Bourlakis, M., & Bezat-Jarzębowska, A. (2020). Short Food Supply Chains (SFSC) as local and sustainable systems. *Sustainability (Basel)*, *12*(11), 4715. doi:10.3390/su12114715

Jaskiewicz, P., & Dyer, W. G. (2017). Addressing the elephant in the room: Disentangling family heterogeneity to advance family business research. *Family Business Review*, *30*(2), 111–118. doi:10.1177/0894486517700469

Jaworski, B. J., & Lurie, R. S. (2020). *Second Principle: Use Propensity-Based Segmentation. The Organic Growth Playbook: Activate High-Yield Behaviors to Achieve Extraordinary Results*. Emerald. doi:10.1108/978-1-83982-684-920201006

Jelsma, I., Gay, F., Ollivier, J., & Rapidel, B. (2024). Collective action, replanting and resilience; Key lessons from 40 years of smallholder oil palm cultivation in the Ophir plantation, Indonesia. *Agricultural Systems*, *213*, 103801. doi:10.1016/j.agsy.2023.103801

Jensen, M. C. (2002). Value Maximization, Stakeholder Theory, and the Corporate Objective Function. *Business Ethics Quarterly*, *12*(2), 235–256. doi:10.2307/3857812

Jo, H., & Harjoto, M. A. (2011). Corporate governance and firm value: The impact of corporate social responsibility. *Journal of Business Ethics*, *103*(3), 351–383. doi:10.1007/s10551-011-0869-y

Jonas, A., & Roosen, J. (2005). Private labels for premium products–the example of organic food. *international Journal of retail & Distribution Management, 33*(8), 636-653.

Jones, T. M. (1980). Corporate social responsibility revisited, redefined. *California Management Review*, *22*(3), 59–67. doi:10.2307/41164877

Kahraman, A., & Kazançoğlu, İ. (2019). Understanding consumers' purchase intentions toward natural-claimed products: A qualitative research in personal care products. *Business Strategy and the Environment*, *28*(6), 1218–1233. doi:10.1002/bse.2312

Kakani, V., Nguyen, V. H., Kumar, B. P., Kim, H., & Pasupuleti, V. R. (2020). A critical review on computer vision and artificial intelligence in food industry. *Journal of Agriculture and Food Research*, *2*, 100033. Advance online publication. doi:10.1016/j.jafr.2020.100033

Kalafatis, S. P., Pollard, M., East, R., & Tsogas, M. H. (1999). Green mar-keting and Ajzen's theory of planned behavior: A cross - market examina-tion. *Journal of Consumer Marketing*, *16*(5), 441–460. doi:10.1108/07363769910289550

Kamble, S. S., Gunasekaran, A., & Gawankar, S. A. (2018). Sustainable Industry 4.0 framework: A systematic literature review identifying the current trends and future perspectives. *Process Safety and Environmental Protection*, *117*, 408–425. doi:10.1016/j.psep.2018.05.009

Kammerer, D. (2009). The effects of customer benefit and regulation on environmental product innovation., Empirical evidence from aliance manufacturers in Germany. *Ecological Economics*, *68*(8-9), 2285–2295. doi:10.1016/j.ecolecon.2009.02.016

Kammerlander, N., & Ganter, M. (2015). An attention-based view of family firm adaptation to discontinuous technological change: Exploring the role of family CEOs' noneconomic goals. *Journal of Product Innovation Management*, *32*(3), 361–383. doi:10.1111/jpim.12205

Kan, K. W., Chan, Y. J., Tiong, T. J., & Lim, J. W. (2024). Maximizing biogas yield from palm oil mill effluent (POME) through advanced simulation and optimisation techniques on an industrial scale. *Chemical Engineering Science*, *285*, 119644. doi:10.1016/j.ces.2023.119644

Kapelko, M. (2021). Assessing Corporate Social Responsibility Efficiency for the International Food and Beverage Manufacturing Industry. *Proceedings in Food System Dynamics*, 56-63.

Kar, M. Y. (2016). *2030 Yilinda Çay Sektörümüz Raporu (Our Tea Industry Report In 2030)*. Caysiad. https://www.caysiad.org.tr/index.php?sayfa=203.90&d=tr

Karagiannis, D., & Metaxas, T. (2020). Sustainable wine tourism development: Case studies from the Greek region of Peloponnese. *Sustainability (Basel), 12*(12), 5223. doi:10.3390/su12125223

Karakaya, E., Hidalgo, A., & Nuur, C. (2014). Diffusion of eco-innovations: A review. *Renewable & Sustainable Energy Reviews, 33*, 392–399. doi:10.1016/j.rser.2014.01.083

Kassarjian, H. H. (1971). Personality and consumer behavior: A review. *JMR, Journal of Marketing Research, 8*(4), 409–418. doi:10.1177/002224377100800401

Katuk, N. (2019). The application of blockchain for halal product assurance: A systematic review of the current developments and future directions. *International Journal of Advanced Trends in Computer Science and Engineering, 8*(5), 1893–1902. doi:10.30534/ijatcse/2019/13852019

Kemp, R. (2010). Eco-Innovation: Definition, measurement, and open research issues. *Economics and Politics, 27*(3), 397–420.

Kemp, R., & Pearson, P. (2007). Final report MEI project about measuring eco-innovation. *UM Merit, Maastricht, 10*(2), 1–120.

Kerschbaumer, C. (2023). *The top trends 2023 on the beverage market*. Austria Juice. https://www.austriajuice.com/news-blog/the-top-trends-on-the-beverage-market

Kesidou, E., & Demirel, P. (2012). On the drivers of eco-innovations: Empirical evidence from the UK. *Research Policy, 41*(5), 862–870. doi:10.1016/j.respol.2012.01.005

Ketelsen, M., Janssen, M., & Hamm, U. (2020). Consumers' response to environmentally-friendly food packaging-A systematic review. *Journal of Cleaner Production, 254*, 120123. doi:10.1016/j.jclepro.2020.120123

Keulertz, M., Sowers, J., Woertz, E., & Mohtar, R. (2016). The water-energy-food nexus in arid regions. In *The Oxford handbook of water politics and policy*. Oxford University Press.

Khan, M. I., Khalid, S., Zaman, U., José, A. E., & Ferreira, P. (2021). Green paradox in emerging tourism supply chains: Achieving green consumption behavior through strategic green marketing orientation, brand social re-sponsibility, and green image. *International Journal of Environmental Research and Public Health, 18*(18), 9626. doi:10.3390/ijerph18189626 PMID:34574552

Khan, M. I., Khan, S., & Haleem, A. (2022). Analysing barriers towards management of Halal supply chain: A BWM approach. *Journal of Islamic Marketing, 13*(1), 66–80. doi:10.1108/JIMA-09-2018-0178

Khan, M. I., Shin, J. H., & Kim, J. D. (2018). The promising future of microalgae: Current status, challenges, and optimization of a sustainable and renewable industry for biofuels, feed, and other products. *Microbial Cell Factories, 17*(1), 36. doi:10.1186/s12934-018-0879-x PMID:29506528

Khanna, M., Deltas, G., & Harrington, D. R. (2009). Adoption of pollution prevention techniques: The role of management systems and regulatory pressures. *Environmental and Resource Economics, 44*(1), 85–106. doi:10.1007/s10640-009-9263-y

Khan, S., Khan, M. I., Haleem, A., & Jami, A. R. (2022). Prioritising the risks in Halal food supply chain: An MCDM approach. *Journal of Islamic Marketing, 13*(1), 45–65. doi:10.1108/JIMA-10-2018-0206

Kianto, A., Sáenz, J., & Aramburu, N. (2017). Knowledge-based human resource management practices, intellectual capital and innovation. *Journal of Business Research, 81*, 11–20. doi:10.1016/j.jbusres.2017.07.018

Kihlberg, I., & Risvik, E. (2007). Consumers of organic foods–value segments and liking of bread. *Food Quality and Preference, 18*(3), 471–481. doi:10.1016/j.foodqual.2006.03.023

Kim, Y., & Han, H. (2010). Intention to pay conventional-hotel prices at a green hotel–a modification of the theory of planned behavior. *Journal of Sustainable Tourism*, *18*(8), 997–1014. doi:10.1080/09669582.2010.490300

Kinnear, T. C., Taylor, J. R., & Ahmed, S. A. (1974). Ecologically con-cerned consumers: Who are they. *Journal of Marketing*, 20–24.

Kiranantawat, B. & Ahmad, S. (2022). Conceptualising the relationship between green dynamic capability and SME sustainability performance: the role of green innovation, organisational creativity and agility. *International Journal of Organizational Analysis*. doi:10.1108/IJOA-04-2022-3246

Kiran, K. U. (2012). Opportunity and Challenges of Green Marketing with special references to Pune. *International Journal of Management and So-cial Sciences Research*, *1*(1), 18–24.

Kirk, D. (1996). *Environmental management for hotels: A student's hand-book*. Butterworth-Heinemann.

Kismawadi, E. R. (2023). Improving Islamic bank performance through agency cost and dual board governance. *Journal of Islamic Accounting and Business Research*. doi:10.1108/JIABR-01-2023-0035

Kismawadi, E. R. (2024). Contribution of Islamic banks and macroeconomic variables to economic growth in developing countries: Vector error correction model approach (VECM). *Journal of Islamic Accounting and Business Research*, *15*(2), 306–326. doi:10.1108/JIABR-03-2022-0090

Kismawadi, E. R., Irfan, M., Al Muddatstsir, U. D., & Abdulkarim, F. M. (2023). Fintech innovations: Risk mitigation strategies in Islamic finance. In *Fintech Applications in Islamic Finance* (pp. 35–58). AI, Machine Learning, and Blockchain Techniques. doi:10.4018/979-8-3693-1038-0.ch003

Kline, R. (2011). *Principles and practice of structural equation modeling*.

Kline, R. (2011). *Principles and practice of structural equation modelling*. Guilford Press.

Knight, H., Megicks, P., Agarwal, S., & Leenders, M. (2019). Firm resources and the development of environmental sustainability among small and medium-sized enterprises: Evidence from the Australian wine industry. *Business Strategy and the Environment*, *28*(1), 25–39. doi:10.1002/bse.2178

Knowles, T., Diamantis, D., & El-Mourhabi, J. B. (2004). *The Globalization of Tourism and Hospitality. A Strategic Perspective*. Cengage Learning.

Koçak, D. (2019). *Fonksiyonel Besin Nedir? (What Is Functional Food?)*. Milliyet. https://www.milliyet.com.tr/cadde/dilara-kocak/fonksiyonel-besin-nedir-2902052

Konuk, F. A. (2018). The role of store image, perceived quality, trust and perceived value in predicting consumers' purchase intentions towards organic private label food. *Journal of Retailing and Consumer Services*, *43*, 304–310. doi:10.1016/j.jretconser.2018.04.011

Kotler, P., Armstrong, G., Araujo, L. A., & Ayala, L. E. P. (2017). *Fundamentos de Marketing*. Pearson Educación de México. https://dialnet.unirioja.es/servlet/libro?codigo=822679

Kottala, S. Y., & Singh, R. (2015). A review of sustainability, deterrents, personal values, attitudes and purchase intentions in the organic food supply chain. *Pacific Science Review B. Humanities and Social Sciences*, *1*(3), 114–123.

Kottila, M. R., & Rönni, P. (2008). Collaboration and trust in two organic food chains. *British Food Journal*, *110*(4/5), 376–394. doi:10.1108/00070700810868915

Kotur, A. (2023). A bibliometric review of research in wine tourism experiences: insights and future research directions. *International Journal of Wine Business Research*.

Kouhizadeh, M., Saberi, S., & Sarkis, J. (2021). Blockchain technology and the sustainable supply chain: Theoretically exploring adoption barriers. *International Journal of Production Economics*, *231*, 107831. doi:10.1016/j.ijpe.2020.107831

Krae, A., Goutas, L., & von Schlie, A. (2011). The family business brand: An inquiry into the construction of the image of family businesses. *Journal of Family Business Management*, *1*(1), 37–46.

Kraus, S., Rehman, S. U., & García, F. J. S. (2020). Corporate social responsibility and environmental performance: The mediating role of environmental strategy and green innovation. *Technological Forecasting and Social Change*, *160*, 120262. doi:10.1016/j.techfore.2020.120262

Kreamer, L., Albritton, B., Tonidandel, S., & Rogelberg, S. G. (2021). The use and misuse of organizational research methods 'best practice' articles. *Organizational Research Methods*, *1*(1), 1–19. 10944281211060706

Krisharyanto, E., Retnowati, E., & Hastuti, N. T. (2019). Regulation and provisions for supervision of halal products in Indonesia. *Journal of Legal, Ethical and Regulatory Issues, 22*(1). https://www.scopus.com/inward/record.uri?eid=2-s2.0-85063267345&partnerID=40&md5=65f177af5906f2dab2f098ca6562db8a

Kshirsagar, P., P,, P., Y., B., & Marathe, V. R. (2012). Underutilized wild fruits of North Maharashtra. *Journal of Research in Plant Sciences, 1*(1), 071–076.

Kumar, Y., Shukla, P., Singh, P., Prabhakaran, P. P., Tanwar, V. K., & Kumar, Y. (2014). Bio-plastics. A perfect tool for eco-friendly food packaging: A Review. *Journal of Food Product Development and Packaging, 1*(1), 01-06.

Kumar, G., Meena, P., & Difrancesco, R. (2021). How do collaborative culture and capability improve sustainability? *Journal of Cleaner Production, 291*, 125824. doi:10.1016/j.jclepro.2021.125824

Kumar, S., Mukherjee, A., & Dutta, J. (2020). Chitosan based nanocomposite films and coatings: Emerging antimicrobial food packaging alternatives. *Trends in Food Science & Technology*, *97*, 196–209. doi:10.1016/j.tifs.2020.01.002

Kunst, A. (2023). *Consumers of energy drinks in the United States as of September 2023, by age, November 2023*. Statista. https://www.statista.com/forecasts/228168/energy-drinks-consumption-usa

Kusiak, A. (2018). Smart manufacturing. *International Journal of Production Research*, *56*(1–2), 508–517. doi:10.1080/00207543.2017.1351644

Kutateladze, R., Koblianidze, T., & Kochlamazashvili, L. (2021). Wine tourism as a mechanism for rural and regional development of Georgia. *Agricultural Economics and Rural Development*, *8*(1), 17–29.

La Porta, R., Lopez-de-Silanes, F., & Shleifer, A. (1999). Corporate ownership around the world. *The Journal of Finance*, *54*(2), 471–517. doi:10.1111/0022-1082.00115

Labys, W. C., & Pollak, P. K. (2024). *Commodity models for forecasting and policy analysis* (Vol. 4). Taylor & Francis.

Laguir, I., Laguir, L., & Elbaz, J. (2016). Are family small and medium sized enterprises more socially responsible than nonfamily small and medium sized enterprises? *Corporate Social Responsibility and Environmental Management*, *23*(6), 386–398. doi:10.1002/csr.1384

Lähdesmäki, M., & Takala, T. (2012). Altruism in business: An empirical study of philanthropy in the small business context. *Social Responsibility Journal*, *8*(3), 373–388. doi:10.1108/17471111211247947

Laila, N., Ratnasari, R. T., Ismail, S., Mohd Hidzir, P. A., & Mahphoth, M. H. (2023). The intention of small and medium enterprises' owners to participate in waqf: The case of Malaysia and Indonesia. *International Journal of Islamic and Middle Eastern Finance and Management*, *16*(3), 429–447. doi:10.1108/IMEFM-01-2022-0014

Lam, L., Nguyen, P., Le, N., & Tran, K. (2021). The relation among organizational culture, knowledge management, and innovation capability: Its implication for open innovation. *Journal of Open Innovation*, *7*(1), 66. doi:10.3390/joitmc7010066

Lan, B. T. H., Phuong, T. T. L., Dat, T. T., & Truong, D. D. (2023). Factors affecting the purchase intention of products with environmentally friendly packaging of urban residents in Ho Chi Minh City, Vietnam. *Sustainability (Basel)*, *15*(9), 7726. doi:10.3390/su15097726

Lavandoski, J., Vargas-Sánchez, A., Pinto, P., & Silva, J. A. (2018). Causes and effects of wine tourism development in organizational context: The case of Alentejo, Portugal. *Tourism and Hospitality Research*, *18*(1), 107–122. doi:10.1177/1467358416634159

Lavuri, R., & Sreeramulu, D. (2019). Personal care products: A study on women consumer buying behaviour. *International Journal of Research & Review*, *6*(6), 271–279.

Le Breton-Miller, I., & Miller, D. (2006). Why do some family businesses out-compete? Governance, long-term orientation, and sustainable capability. *Entrepreneurship Theory and Practice*, *30*(6), 731–746. doi:10.1111/j.1540-6520.2006.00147.x

Lea, E., & Worsley, T. (2005). Australians' organic food beliefs, demographics and values. *British Food Journal*, *107*(11), 855–869. doi:10.1108/00070700510629797

Lee, J., Park, T., Moon, H. K., Yang, Y., & Kim, C. (2009). Corporate philanthropy, attitude towards corporations, and purchase intentions: A South Korea study. *Journal of Business Research*, *62*(10), 939–946. doi:10.1016/j.jbusres.2008.08.007

Leenders, M. A. A. M., & Chandra, Y. (2013). Antecedents and consequences of green innovation in the wine industry: The role of channel structure. *Technology Analysis and Strategic Management*, *25*(2), 203–218. doi:10.1080/09537325.2012.759203

Lee, S., Kim, B., & Kim, H. (2012). An integrated view of knowledge management for performance. *Journal of Knowledge Management*, *16*(2), 183–203. doi:10.1108/13673271211218807

Lekics, V. (2021). Sustainable Innovation in Wine Industry. *Systematic Reviews*, *13*(1), 55–73. PMID:33573701

León-Pozo, A., Robinson Trápaga, D. G., Cabrera-Flores, M. R., & Collins García, R. (2022). *La industria vitivinícola mexicana en el siglo xxi: Retos económicos, sociales y ambientales*. Acento Editores. https://repositorio.cetys.mx/handle/60000/1488

Le, P., Lei, H., Le, T., Gong, J., & Ha, A. (2020). Developing a collaborative culture for radical and incremental innovation: The mediating roles of tacit and explicit knowledge sharing. *Chinese Management Studies*, *14*(4), 957–975. doi:10.1108/CMS-04-2019-0151

Lichy, J., Kachour, M., & Stokes, P. (2023). Questioning the business model of sustainable wine production: The case of French "Vallée du Rhône" wine growers. *Journal of Cleaner Production*, *417*, 137891. doi:10.1016/j.jclepro.2023.137891

Liket, K., & Maas, K. (2016). Strategic philanthropy: Corporate measurement of philanthropic impacts as a requirement for a "happy marriage" of business and society. *Business & Society*, *55*(6), 889–921. doi:10.1177/0007650314565356

Li, M., Tian, Z., Liu, Q., & Lu, Y. (2022). Literature review and research prospect on the drivers and effects of green innovation. *Sustainability (Basel)*, *14*(16), 9858. doi:10.3390/su14169858

Lin, J. (2007). *Sustainable supply chains in the food and beverage industry* [Doctoral dissertation].

Lin, R. J., Tan, K. H., & Geng, Y. (2013). Market demand, green product innovation, and firm performance: Evidence from Vietnam motorcycle industry. *Journal of Cleaner Production*, *40*, 101–107. doi:10.1016/j.jclepro.2012.01.001

Liobikienė, G., Mandravickaitė, J., & Bernatonienė, J. (2016). Theory of planned behavior approach to understand the green purchasing behavior in the EU: A cross-cultural study. *Ecological Economics, 125*, 38–46. doi:10.1016/j.ecolecon.2016.02.008

Litja, D. (2020). *The implications of EU regulations to Malaysian palm oil exporting and its economic consequences.*

Llach, J., & Nordquist, M. (2010). Innovation in family and non-family businesses: A resource perspective. *International Journal of Entrepreneurial Venturing, 2*(3/4), 381–399. doi:10.1504/IJEV.2010.037119

Lockie, S., Lyons, K., Lawrence, G., & Mummery, K. (2002). Eating 'green': Motivations behind organic food consumption in Australia. *Sociologia Ruralis, 42*(1), 23–40. doi:10.1111/1467-9523.00200

Londhe, B. R. (2014). Marketing Mix for Next Generation Marketing. *Procedia Economics and Finance, 11*, 335–340. doi:10.1016/S2212-5671(14)00201-9

López Pérez, G., García Sánchez, I. M., & Zafra Gómez, J. L. (2023). A systematic literature review and bibliometric analysis of eco-innovation on financial performance: Identifying barriers and drivers. *Business Strategy and the Environment, n/a*(n/a). doi:10.1002/bse.3550

López-Torres, G., Garza-Reyes, J., Maldonado-Guzmán, G., Kumar, V., Rocha-Lona, L., & Cherrafi, A. (2019). Knowledge management for sustainability in operations. *Production Planning and Control, 30*(10), 813–826. doi:10.1080/09537287.2019.1582091

Lubowiecki-Vikuk, A., de Sousa, B. M. B., Đerčan, B. M., & Leal Filho, W. (Eds.). (2021). *Handbook of Sustainable Development and Leisure Ser-vices*. Springer. doi:10.1007/978-3-030-59820-4

Lumpkin, G. T., Brigham, K. H., & Moss, T. W. (2010). Long-term orientation: Implications for the entrepreneurial orientation and performance of family businesses. *Entrepreneurship and Regional Development, 22*(3-4), 3–4, 241–264. doi:10.1080/08985621003726218

Lyu, L., Khan, I., Zakari, A., & Bilal. (2022). A study of energy investment and environmental sustainability nexus in China: A bootstrap replications analysis. *Environmental Science and Pollution Research International, 29*(6), 8464–8472. doi:10.1007/s11356-021-16254-7 PMID:34490557

Mac Kay Tepper, C. (2013). Hilando fino con el agua y el vino. In J. Leyva & M. Espejel (Eds.), *El Valle de Guadalupe. Conjugando tiempos* (pp. 37–47). Universidad Autónoma de Baja California., http://webfc.ens.uabc.mx/documentos/El Valle de Guadalupe.pdf

Machado, A., Vareiro, L., Sousa, B., Figueira, V., & Lavandoski, J. (2022). Green marketing trends in specific contexts of tourism and music festivals: preliminary insights. In *Advances in Tourism, Technology and Systems: Selected Papers from ICOTTS 2021* (Vol. 2, pp. 87–96). Springer Nature Singapore. doi:10.1007/978-981-16-9701-2_8

Macías, A. B. (2005). Una conceptualización comprehensiva de la innovación educativa. *Innovación Educativa (México, D.F.), 5*(28), 19–31.

Magoni, C. (2009). *Historia de la Vid y el Vino en Baja California*. Universidad Iberoamericana.

Maignan, I., & Ralston, D. A. (2002). Corporate social responsibility in Europe and the US: Insights from businesses' self-presentations. *Journal of International Business Studies, 33*(3), 497–514. doi:10.1057/palgrave.jibs.8491028

Mainardes, E. W., Laurett, R., Degasperi, N. C. P., & Lasso, S. V. (2016). What motivates an individual to make donations of money and/or goods? *International Review on Public and Nonprofit Marketing, 13*(1), 81–99. doi:10.1007/s12208-015-0145-4

Malaina, A. (2011). *Niños y vino, se rompe el tabú* [PDF File]. Interprofesional del Vino. https://www.riojatrek.com/wp-content/uploads/2011/02/VV104_22-25_vinos_y_ninos.pdf

Malini, H., Yang, H., & Shin, H. (2022). *Halal and Cosmetics: Paving the Way for the Cosmetics Industries of Indonesia and Korea*. Insan Cendekia Mandiri.

Manthiram, A. (2020). A reflection on lithium-ion battery cathode chemistry. *Nature Communications*, *11*(1), 1550. doi:10.1038/s41467-020-15355-0 PMID:32214093

March Cerdá, J. C., Martín Barato, A., López Doblas, M., Luque Martín, N., Prieto Rodríguez, M. A., & Danet Danet, A. (2014). La publicidad de bebidas alcohólicas en España y su repercusión en la población adolescente. *Revista Española de Drogodependencias*, *39*(4), 59–76.

Marco-Lajara, B., Zaragoza-Saez, P., & Martínez-Falcó, J. (2022b). Green Innovation: Balancing Economic Efficiency With Environmental Protection. In Frameworks for Sustainable Development Goals to Manage Economic, Social, and Environmental Shocks and Disasters (pp. 239-254). IGI Global.

Marco-Lajara, B., Zaragoza-Sáez, P., Martínez-Falcó, J., & Sánchez-García, E. (2022d). Las rutas del vino de España: el impacto económico derivado de las visitas a bodegas y museos [Spain's wine routes: the economic impact of visits to wineries and museums] In Investigación y transferencia de las ciencias sociales frente a un mundo en crisis [Social science research and transfer in the face of a world in crisis](pp. 1774–1800).

Marco-Lajara, B., García, E. S., Larrosa, P. S., & Martínez-Falcó, J. (2022a). Knowledge creation and diffusion inspecialized environments: What are the factors involved? In *Empresa, economía y derecho. Oportunidades ante un entorno global y disruptivo* (pp. 432–459). Dykinson.

Marco-Lajara, B., Martínez-Falcó, J., Millan-Tudela, L. A., & Sánchez-García, E. (2023a). Analysis of the structure of scientific knowledge on wine tourism: A bibliometric analysis. *Heliyon*, *9*(2), e13363. doi:10.1016/j.heliyon.2023.e13363 PMID:36816306

Marco-Lajara, B., Martínez-Falcó, J., Sánchez-García, E., & Millan-Tudela, L. A. (2023b). Analyzing the Role of Renewable Energy in Meeting the Sustainable Development Goals: A Bibliometric Analysis. *Energies*, *16*(7), 3137. doi:10.3390/en16073137

Marco-Lajara, B., Úbeda-García, M., Zaragoza-Sáez, P., Poveda-Pareja, E., & Martínez Falcó, J. (2023). Enoturismo y sostenibilidad: Estudio de casos en la Ruta del Vino de Alicante (España). *Pasos (El Sauzal)*, *21*(2), 307–320. doi:10.25145/j.pasos.2023.21.020

Marco-Lajara, B., Zaragoza-Sáez, P. C., Martínez-Falcó, J., & Sánchez-García, E. (2023d). Does green intellectual capital affect green innovation performance? Evidence from the Spanish wine industry. *British Food Journal*, *125*(4), 1469–1487. doi:10.1108/BFJ-03-2022-0298

Marco-Lajara, B., Zaragoza-Sáez, P., Martínez-Falcó, J., & Ruiz-Fernández, L. (2022c). The effect of green intellectual capital on green performance in the Spanish wine industry: A structural equation modeling approach. *Complexity*, *2022*, 2022. doi:10.1155/2022/6024077

Marcus, A., & Fremeth, A. (2009). Green management matters regardless. *The Academy of Management Perspectives*, *23*(3), 17–26. doi:10.5465/amp.2009.43479261

Marín, D., Armengol, J., Carbonell-Bejerano, P., Escalona, J. M., Gramaje, D., Hernández-Montes, E., Intrigliolo, D. S., Martínez-Zapater, J. M., Medrano, H., Mirás-Avalos, J. M., Palomares-Rius, J. E., Romero-Azorín, P., Savé, R., Santesteban, L. G., & de Herralde, F. (2021). Challenges of viticulture adaptation to global change: Tackling the issue from the roots. *Australian Journal of Grape and Wine Research*, *27*(1), 8–25. doi:10.1111/ajgw.12463

Marshall, R. S., Akoorie, M. E. M., Hamann, R., & Sinha, P. (2010). Environmental practices in the wine industry: An empirical application of the theory of reasoned action and stakeholder theory in the United States and New Zealand. *Journal of World Business*, *45*(4), 405–414. doi:10.1016/j.jwb.2009.08.009

Martínez Falcó, J., Marco-Lajara, B., Zaragoza-Sáez, P., & Sánchez-García, E. (2023). Vino, Turismo y COVID-19: El impacto de la COVID-19 en las Rutas del Vino de España. *Pasos (El Sauzal)*, *21*(1), 83–97. doi:10.25145/j.pasos.2023.21.006

Martínez-Falcó, J. M., Marco-Lajara, B., & Zaragoza-Saez, P. (2023a). Corporate Social Responsibility vs. Corporate Sustainability: Different Concepts for a Common Goal. In Positive and Constructive Contributions for Sustainable Development Goals (pp. 76-87). IGI Global.

Mártínez-Falcó, J., Marco-Lajara, B., & Zaragoza-Sáez, P. (2023b). Corporate Social Responsibility: A Comprehensive Analysis. In Positive and Constructive Contributions for Sustainable Development Goals (pp. 131-160). IGI Global.

Martínez-Falcó, J., Marco-Lajara, B., Sánchez-García, E., & Millan-Tudela, L. A. (2023c). Sustainable Development Goals in the Business Sphere: A Bibliometric Review. *Sustainability (Basel)*, *15*(6), 5075. doi:10.3390/su15065075

Martínez-Falcó, J., Marco-Lajara, B., Zaragoza Sáez, P. D. C., & Sánchez-García, E. (2023d). Wine tourism in Spain: The economic impact derived from visits to wineries and museums on wine routes. *Investigaciones Turísticas*, *25*(25), 168–195. doi:10.14198/INTURI.21219

Martínez-Falcó, J., Marco-Lajara, B., Zaragoza-Sáez, P. D. C., & Millan-Tudela, L. A. (2023e). Wine tourism as a catalyst for green innovation: Evidence from the Spanish wine industry. *British Food Journal*. doi:10.1108/BFJ-08-2022-0690

Martínez-Falcó, J., Marco-Lajara, B., Zaragoza-Sáez, P., & Gilinsky, A. (2024b). Wine Tourism in the Valencian Community: A Comparative Analysis. *Investigaciones Turísticas*, (27), 29–52.

Martínez-Falcó, J., Marco-Lajara, B., Zaragoza-Sáez, P., & Millán-Tudela, L. A. (2023f). Analyzing the effect of Corporate Social Responsibility on Green Innovation Performance in the Spanish wine industry: A structural equation modeling analysis. *Agribusiness*, *39*(4), 985–1006. doi:10.1002/agr.21820

Martínez-Falcó, J., Marco-Lajara, B., Zaragoza-Sáez, P., & Sánchez-García, E. (2023g). The effect of knowledge management on sustainable performance: Evidence from the Spanish wine industry. *Knowledge Management Research and Practice*, 1–16. doi:10.1080/14778238.2023.2218045

Martínez-Falcó, J., Martínez-Falcó, J., Marco-Lajara, B., Sánchez-García, E., & Visser, G. (2023i). Aligning the Sustainable Development Goals in the Wine Industry: A Bibliometric Analysis. *Sustainability (Basel)*, *15*(10), 8172. doi:10.3390/su15108172

Martínez-Falcó, J., Sánchez-García, E., Marco-Lajara, B., & Georgantzis, N. (2024a). The interplay between competitive advantage and sustainability in the wine industry: A bibliometric and systematic review. *Discover Sustainability*, *5*(1), 13. doi:10.1007/s43621-024-00196-4

Martínez-Falcó, J., Sánchez-García, E., Marco-Lajara, B., & Millan-Tudela, L. A. (2023j). Do organizational commitment and consumer satisfaction mediate the relationship corporate social responsibility-sustainable performance? Assessing happiness management in Spanish wineries. *Management Decision*. doi:10.1108/MD-02-2023-0217

Martínez, M. P., Cremasco, C. P., Gabriel Filho, L. R. A., Junior, S. S. B., Bednaski, A. V., Quevedo-Silva, F., & Padgett, R. C. M. L. (2020). Fuzzy inference system to study the behavior of the green consumer facing the perception of greenwashing. *Journal of Cleaner Production*, *242*, 116064. doi:10.1016/j.jclepro.2019.03.060

Martin, H., Hernández, B., & Herrero, A. (2020). Social consciousness and perceived risk as drivers of crowdfunding as a socially responsible investment in tourism. *Journal of Travel Research*, *60*(1), 16–30. doi:10.1177/0047287519896017

Martinho, G., Pires, A., Portela, G., & Fonseca, M. (2015). Factors affecting consumers' choices concerning sustainable packaging during product purchase and recycling. *Resources, Conservation and Recycling*, *103*, 58–68. doi:10.1016/j.resconrec.2015.07.012

Martinho, V. J. P. D. (2021). Contributions from Literature for Understanding Wine Marketing. *Sustainability (Basel)*, *13*(13), 13. Advance online publication. doi:10.3390/su13137468

Martins, V., Rampasso, I., Anholon, R., Quelhas, O., & Leal Filho, W. (2019). Knowledge management in the context of sustainability: Literature review and opportunities for future research. *Journal of Cleaner Production*, *229*, 489–500. doi:10.1016/j.jclepro.2019.04.354

Marx, W., Haunschild, R., & Bornmann, L. (2017). Climate change and viticulture-a quantitative analysis of a highly dynamic research field. *Vitis*, *56*(1).

Masudin, I., Jie, F., Djajadikerta, H., & Widayat, W. (2021). The effect of halal retail and manufacturing technology readiness on halal meat logistics performance. *International Journal of Logistics Systems and Management*, *40*(1), 1–27. doi:10.1504/IJLSM.2021.117688

Mat Aron, N. S., Khoo, K. S., Chew, K. W., Show, P. L., Chen, W.-H., & Nguyen, T. H. P. (2020). Sustainability of the four generations of biofuels – A review. *International Journal of Energy Research*, *44*(12), 9266–9282. doi:10.1002/er.5557

Matić, M., & Puh, B. (2016). CONSUMERS'PURCHASE intentions towards natural cosmetics. *Ekonomski vjesnik/Econviews-Review of Contemporary Business. Entrepreneurship and Economic Issues*, *29*(1), 53–64.

Mat, N. K. N., Sulaiman, Y., Abdghani, N. H., & Mohamad, M. (2020). Halal consumption determinants: The mediating role of risk perception and muslim lifestyle. *Malaysian Journal of Consumer and Family Economics*, *24*, 63–78. https://www.scopus.com/inward/record.uri?eid=2-s2.0-85094201810&partnerID=40&md5=57285140ec6a05c8f5b9da0479241126

Matzler, K., Veider, V., Hautz, J., & Stadler, C. (2015). The impact of family ownership, management, and governance on innovation. *Journal of Product Innovation Management*, *32*(3), 319–333. doi:10.1111/jpim.12202

Mazzi, C. (2011). Family business and financial performance: Current state of knowledge and future research challenges. *Journal of Family Business Strategy*, *2*(3), 166–181. doi:10.1016/j.jfbs.2011.07.001

McCuan, D., & Hertz, R. (2015). *Preliminary Report Survey on Community Perceptions of Wine Businesses.* Sonoma State University Wine Business Institute.

McGovern, P. (2007). *Ancient Wine: The Search for the Origins of Viniculture*. Princeton Science Library.

McGovern, P., Jalabadze, M., Batiuk, S., Callahan, M., Smith, K., Hall, G., Kvavadze, E., Maghradze, D., Rusishvili, N., Bouby, L., Failla, O., Cola, G., Mariani, L., Boaretto, E., Bacilieri, R., This, P., Wales, N., & Lordkipanidze, D. (2017). Early Neolithic wine of Georgia in the South Caucasus. *Proceedings of the National Academy of Sciences of the United States of America*, *114*(48), 201714728. doi:10.1073/pnas.1714728114 PMID:29133421

Meena, R. S., Kumar, S., Datta, R., Lal, R., Vijayakumar, V., Brtnicky, M., Sharma, M. P., Yadav, G. S., Jhariya, M. K., Jangir, C. K., Pathan, S. I., Dokulilova, T., Pecina, V., & Marfo, T. D. (2020). Impact of agrochemicals on soil microbiota and management: A review. *Land (Basel)*, *9*(2), 34. doi:10.3390/land9020034

Meghwal, P. R., Singh, A., & Singh, D. (2021). Underutilized fruits and vegetables in hot arid regions of India: Status and prospects: A Review. *Agricultural Reviews*. doi:10.18805/ag.R-2087

Mehta, K., & Chugan, P. (2015). Green HRM in pursuit of environmentally sustainable business. Pursuit of Environmentally Sustainable Business. *Universal Journal of Industrial and Business Management, 3*(3), 74–81. doi:10.13189/ujibm.2015.030302

Mehta, R., & Bhanja, N. (2017). Consumer preferences for wine attributes in an emerging market. *International Journal of Retail & Distribution Management, 46*(1), 34–48. doi:10.1108/IJRDM-04-2017-0073

Meijaard, E., Brooks, T. M., Carlson, K. M., Slade, E. M., Garcia-Ulloa, J., Gaveau, D. L., Lee, J. S. H., Santika, T., Juffe-Bignoli, D., Struebig, M. J., Wich, S. A., Ancrenaz, M., Koh, L. P., Zamira, N., Abrams, J. F., Prins, H. H. T., Sendashonga, C. N., Murdiyarso, D., Furumo, P. R., & Sheil, D. (2020). The environmental impacts of palm oil in context. *Nature Plants, 6*(12), 1418–1426. doi:10.1038/s41477-020-00813-w PMID:33299148

Meler, M., & Ham, M. (2012). Green marketing for green tourism. In *Facul-ty of tourism and hospitality management in opatija. Biennial In-ternational congress. tourism & hospitality industry* (p. 130). University of Rijeka, Faculty of Tourism & Hospitality Management.

Meloni, G., Anderson, K., Deconinck, K., & Swinnen, J. (2019). Wine Regulations. *Applied Economic Perspectives and Policy, 41*(4), 620–649. doi:10.1093/aepp/ppz025

Memorial Tıbbi Yayın Kurulu. (2023). *Kefirin faydaları nelerdir? (What are the benefits of kefir?).* Memorial. https://www.memorial.com.tr/saglik-rehberi/kefirin-faydalari-nelerdir

Mendes, F., & Gouveia, D. (2014). Poetas Populares do Fado Tradicional INCM – Imprensa Nacional Casa da Moeda Salinas Campos, Maximiliano. (2000). ¡Toquen flautas y tambores!: Una historia social de la música desde las culturas populares en Chile, siglos XVI-XX. *Revista Musical Chilena, 54*(193), 45–82. doi:10.4067/S0716-27902000019300003

Meraz Ruiz, L. (2013). La trascendencia histórica de la zona vitivinícola de Baja California. *Multidisciplinaria, 16,* 66–87. http://www.revistas.unam.mx/index.php/multidisciplina/article/view/50080

Merigó, J. M., Mas-Tur, A., Roig-Tierno, N., & Ribeiro-Soriano, D. (2015). A bibliometric overview of the Journal of Business Research between 1973 and 2014. *Journal of Business Research, 68*(12), 2645–2653. doi:10.1016/j.jbusres.2015.04.006

Micheaux, H., & Aggeri, F. (2021). Eco-modulation as a driver for eco-design: A dynamic view of the French collective EPR scheme. *Journal of Cleaner Production, 289*, 125714. doi:10.1016/j.jclepro.2020.125714

Miftari, I., Haas, R., Meixner, O., Imami, D., & Gjokaj, E. (2022). Factors Influencing consumer attitudes towards organic food products in a transition Economy—Insights from Kosovo. *Sustainability (Basel), 14*(10), 5873. doi:10.3390/su14105873

Migdadi, M. (2021). Knowledge management, customer relationship management and innovation capabilities. *Journal of Business and Industrial Marketing, 36*(1), 111–124. doi:10.1108/JBIM-12-2019-0504

Milfont, T. L., & Markowitz, E. (2016). Sustainable consumer behavior: A multilevel perspective. *Current Opinion in Psychology, 10*, 112–117. doi:10.1016/j.copsyc.2015.12.016

Miller, D., & Le Breton-Miller, I. (2005). *Managing for the Long Run: Lessons in Competitive Advantage from Great Family Businesses.* Harvard Business School Press.

Miller, D., Le Breton-Miller, I., & Lester, R. H. (2013). Family firm governance, strategic conformity and performance: Institutional versus strategic perspectives. *Organization Science, 24*(1), 189–209. doi:10.1287/orsc.1110.0728

Ministerio de Agricultura, P. y A. (MAPA). (2023). Volumen de cerveza consumida con y sin alcohol en los hogares españoles entre 2011 y 2021 (en miles de kilos). *Statista*. https://es.statista.com/estadisticas/487254/consumo-de-cerveza-de-los-hogares-por-tipo-en-espana/

Ministerio de Sanidad. (2022). *Informe del Plan Nacional sobre Drogas*. PNSD. https://pnsd.sanidad.gob.es/home.htm

Mintel. (2023). *The Future of Global Functional Drinks Trends*. Mintel. https://www.mintel.com/food-and-drink-market-news/the-future-of-global-functional-drinks-trends/#:~:text=Drinks%20that%20offer%20health%20benefits,market%20is%20expanding%20and%20diversifying

Mishra, P., & Sharma, P. (2014). Green marketing: Challenges and opportu-nities for business. *BVIMR Management Edge, 7*(1).

Mohamed, Y. H., Abdul Rahim, A. R., & Ma'aram, A. (2020). The effect of halal supply chain management on halal integrity assurance for the food industry in Malaysia. *Journal of Islamic Marketing*, *12*(9), 1734–1750. doi:10.1108/JIMA-12-2018-0240

Mohsin, M., Kamran, H. W., Atif Nawaz, M., Sajjad Hussain, M., & Dahri, A. S. (2021). Assessing the impact of transition from nonrenewable to renewable energy consumption on economic growth-environmental nexus from developing Asian economies. *Journal of Environmental Management*, *284*, 111999. doi:10.1016/j.jenvman.2021.111999 PMID:33556829

Montalvo-Falcón, J. V., Sánchez-García, E., Marco-Lajara, B., & Martínez-Falcó, J. (2023). Green human resource management and economic, social and environmental performance: Evidence from the Spanish wine industry. *Heliyon*, *9*(10), e20826. doi:10.1016/j.heliyon.2023.e20826 PMID:37860533

Montalvo-Falcón, J. V., Sánchez-García, E., Marco-Lajara, B., & Martínez-Falcó, J. (2023). Sustainability Research in the Wine Industry: A Bibliometric Approach. *Agronomy (Basel)*, *13*(3), 871. doi:10.3390/agronomy13030871

Monteiro, J., Silva, F. J. G., Ramos, S. F., Campilho, R. D. S. G., & Fonseca, A. M. (2019). Eco-design and sustainability in packaging: A survey. *Procedia Manufacturing*, *38*, 1741–1749. doi:10.1016/j.promfg.2020.01.097

Mora, P., & Manzoom, A. (2012). Why and how some wine SMEs resist to the crisis? *International Journal of Business and Globalisation*, *8*(1), 95–111. doi:10.1504/IJBG.2012.043974

Moratis, L. (2018). Signaling responsibility? Applying signaling theory to the ISO 26000 standard for social responsibility. *Sustainability (Basel)*, *10*(11), 1–20. doi:10.3390/su10114172

Morck, R., & Bernard, Y. (2004). Family control and the rent–seeking society. *Entrepreneurship Theory and Practice*, *28*(4), 391–409. doi:10.1111/j.1540-6520.2004.00053.x

Morgan, J., Cuamea, O., & Minaverry, C. (2016). El enoturismo en México: comportamiento de viaje y patrones de consumo en la ruta del vino, Baja California. *RED Sociales, 3*(6), 73–98. http://www.redsocialesunlu.net/wp-content/uploads/2016/10/RSOC017-004-Morgan-Medina-J.-

Morris, S., Bartkus, B., Glassman, M., & Rhiel, G. (2013). Philanthropy and Corporate Reputation: An Empirical Investigation. *Corporate Reputation Review*, *16*(4), 285–299. doi:10.1057/crr.2013.16

Mor, S., & Ravindra, K. (2023). Municipal solid waste landfills in lower- and middle-income countries: Environmental impacts, challenges and sustainable management practices. *Process Safety and Environmental Protection*, *174*, 510–530. doi:10.1016/j.psep.2023.04.014

Morsing, M., & Schultz, M. (2006). Corporate social responsibility communication: Stakeholder information, response and involvement strategies. *Business Ethics (Oxford, England)*, *15*(4), 323–338. doi:10.1111/j.1467-8608.2006.00460.x

Moscovici, D., Gow, J., Alonso Ugaglia, A., Rezwanul, R., Valenzuela, L., & Mihailescu, R. (2022). Consumer preferences for organic wine - Global analysis of people and place. *Journal of Cleaner Production, 368*, 133215. doi:10.1016/j.jclepro.2022.133215

Moser, A. K. (2015). Thinking green, buying green? Drivers of pro-environmental purchasing behavior. *Journal of Consumer Marketing, 32*(3), 167–175. doi:10.1108/JCM-10-2014-1179

Moyano-Fuentes, J., Maqueira-Marín, J. M., & Bruque-Cámara, S. (2018). Process innovation and environmental sustainability engagement: An application on technological firms. *Journal of Cleaner Production, 171*, 844–856. doi:10.1016/j.jclepro.2017.10.067

Mozell, M. R., & Thach, L. (2014). The impact of climate change on the global wine industry: Challenges & solutions. *Wine Economics and Policy, 3*(2), 81–89. doi:10.1016/j.wep.2014.08.001

Muller, M. (2015). The'nexus' as a step back towards a more coherent water resource management paradigm. *Water Alternatives, 8*(1).

Munasinghe, M., Jayasinghe, P., Deraniyagala, Y., Matlaba, V. J., Santos, J. F. D., Maneschy, M. C., & Mota, J. A. (2019). Value–Supply Chain Analysis (VSCA) of crude palm oil production in Brazil, focusing on economic, environmental and social sustainability. *Sustainable Production and Consumption, 17*, 161–175. doi:10.1016/j.spc.2018.10.001

Muñoz-Pascual, L., Galende, J., & Curado, C. (2019). Human resource management contributions to knowledge sharing for a sustainability-oriented performance: A mixed methods approach. *Sustainability (Basel), 12*(1), 161. doi:10.3390/su12010161

Murphy, D. (2018). *Oil palm value chain management.*

Murphy, D. J. (2014). The future of oil palm as a major global crop: Opportunities and challenges. *Journal of Oil Palm Research, 26*(1), 1–24.

Murphy, D. J. (2015). What is the future for oil palm as a global crop. *World Agric, 5*, 24–34.

Murphy, D. J. (2024). Sustainable vegetable oils. In *Functional Dietary Lipids* (pp. 31–47). Woodhead Publishing. doi:10.1016/B978-0-443-15327-3.00011-2

Muscio, A., Nardone, G., & Stasi, A. (2017). How does the search for knowledge drive firms' eco-innovation? Evidence from the wine industry. *Industry and Innovation, 24*(3), 298–320. doi:10.1080/13662716.2016.1224707

Nasution, E. D., Saidy, A. R., Priatmadi, B. J., Dasrial, M., Alfiana, H. U., & Jailani, R. (2024). Enhancing the sustainability of oil palm plantations through the application of principles and adaptive management of high conservation value areas in Central Kalimantan. *Plant Science Today, 11*(1), 405–417.

Nave, A., do Paço, A., & Duarte, P. (2021). A systematic literature review on sustainability in the wine tourism industry: Insights and perspectives. *International Journal of Wine Business Research, 33*(4), 457–480.

Naylor, R. L., Hardy, R. W., Buschmann, A. H., Bush, S. R., Cao, L., Klinger, D. H., Little, D. C., Lubchenco, J., Shumway, S. E., & Troell, M. (2021). A 20-year retrospective review of global aquaculture. *Nature, 591*(7851), 551–563. doi:10.1038/s41586-021-03308-6 PMID:33762770

Nazir, M., Arif, S., Khan, R. S., Nazir, W., Khalid, N., & Maqsood, S. (2019). Opportunities and challenges for functional and medicinal beverages: Current and future trends. *Trends in Food Science & Technology, 88*, 513–526. doi:10.1016/j.tifs.2019.04.011

NBLTürkiye. (n.d.). *Fonksiyonel Beslenme Nedir? Fonksiyonel Beslenme Hakkında Her Şey (What is Functional Nutrition?)* All About Functional Nutrition. https://nblturkiye.com/fonksiyonel-beslenme-nedir-fonksiyonel-beslenme-hakkinda-her-sey/

Neethling, E., Barbeau, G., Coulon-Leroy, C., & Quénol, H. (2019). Spatial complexity and temporal dynamics in viticulture: A review of climate-driven scales. *Agricultural and Forest Meteorology*, *276-277*, 107618. doi:10.1016/j.agrformet.2019.107618

Negi, S., & Anand, N. (2015). Issues and Challenges in the Supply Chain of Fruits & Vegetables Sector In India: A Review. *International Journal of Managing Value and Supply Chains*, *6*(2), 47–62. doi:10.5121/ijmvsc.2015.6205

Netemeyer, R. G., Krishnan, B., Pullig, C., Wang, G., Yagci, M., Dean, D., Ricks, J., & Wirth, F. (2004). Developing and validating measures of facets of customer-based brand equity. *Journal of Business Research*, *57*(2), 209–224. doi:10.1016/S0148-2963(01)00303-4

Ngah, A. H., Gabarre, S., Han, H., Rahi, S., Al-Gasawneh, J. A., & Park, S.-H. (2021). Intention to purchase halal cosmetics: Do males and females differ? a multigroup analysis. *Cosmetics*, *8*(1), 1–14. doi:10.3390/cosmetics8010019

Nguyen, A. T., Yến-Khanh, N., & Thuan, N. H. (2021). Consumers' purchase intention and willingness to pay for eco-friendly packaging in Vietnam. *Sustainable Packaging*, 289-323.

Nguyen, A. T., Parker, L., Brennan, L., & Lockrey, S. (2020). A consumer definition of eco-friendly packaging. *Journal of Cleaner Production*, *252*, 119792. doi:10.1016/j.jclepro.2019.119792

Nguyen, N. T., Nguyen, L. H. A., & Tran, T. T. (2021). Purchase behavior of young consumers toward green packaged products in Vietnam. *The Journal of Asian Finance. Economics and Business*, *8*(1), 985–996.

Nielson, C. B., Duethman, N. C., Howard, J. M., Moncure, M., & Wood, J. G. (2017). Burns: Pathophysiology of systemic complications and current management. *Journal of Burn Care & Research; Official Publication of the American Burn Association*, *38*(1), e469–e481. doi:10.1097/BCR.0000000000000355 PMID:27183443

Nieto, M. J., Santamaria, L., & Fernandez, Z. (2015). Understanding the innovation behavior of family firms. *Journal of Small Business Management*, *53*(2), 382–399. doi:10.1111/jsbm.12075

Noel, J. K., Sammartino, C. J., & Rosenthal, S. R. (2020). Exposure to Digital Alcohol Marketing and Alcohol Use: A Systematic Review. *Journal of Studies on Alcohol and Drugs*, *19*(s19), 57–67. doi:10.15288/jsads.2020.s19.57 PMID:32079562

Nor Zaidi, F. L. A., Jamaludin, M. A., & Tukiran, N. A. (2022). MUSLIM CONSUMERS' PERCEPTIONS ON COUNTERFEIT COSMETICS. *Malaysian Journal of Syariah and Law*, *10*(1), 76–82. doi:10.33102/mjsl.vol10no1.385

Nordqvist, M., Sharma, P., & Chirico, F. (2014). Family firm heterogeneity and governance: A configuration aroach. *Journal of Small Business Management*, *52*(2), 192–209. doi:10.1111/jsbm.12096

Norton, V., Waters, C., Oloyede, O. O., & Lignou, S. (2022). Exploring consumers' understanding and perception of sustainable food packaging in the UK. *Foods*, *11*(21), 3424. doi:10.3390/foods11213424 PMID:36360036

NovaNutrica. (2018). *Modern Çağda Yeni Bir Beslenme Alışkanlığı: Fonksiyonel Gıdalar (A New Nutrition Habit in the Modern Age: Functional Foods)*. NovaNutrica. https://www.novanutrica.com/modern-cagda-yeni-bir-beslenme-aliskanligi-fonksiyonel-gidalar

Nowotarska, A., Tomaszewska, M., Piotrowska, A., & Chłędzik, A. (2021). Corporate social responsibility in the beverage industry–a case study of Carlsberg. *International Business and Global Economy*, *40*, 9–18.

Nugroho, A. J. S., Ihalauw, J. J. O. I., & Kristian, N. A. N. A. (2022). The Moderating Effect of Trust and Product Involvement on Antecedents of Halal Brands to Purchase Intention towards the Competitiveness of the Sharia Economic System in Indonesia. *Journal of System and Management Sciences*, *12*(5), 374–396. doi:10.33168/JSMS.2022.0522

Núñez Tapia, F. A. (2017). Jack Dempsey's Hotel in Baja California: The Playa Ensenada. *The Journal of San Diego History*, *63*, 147–170. https://sandiegohistory.org/journal/2018/march/summer-2017-2/

Núñez Tapia, F. A., Cabrera-Flores, M., Sánchez López, J., & Collins García, R. (2022). Ruta del vino y fiestas de la vendimia: expresiones de la vocación enoturística, el patrimonio cultural y la identidad bajacaliforniana. In A. Vázquez, N. Borrego, A. Herrera, & E. Sánchez (Eds.), *La industria vitivinícola mexicana en el siglo XXI: retos económicos, sociales y ambientales* (pp. 509–536). Centro de Investigación y Asistencia en Tecnología y Diseño del Estado de Jalisco A.C.

Nuttavuthisit, K., & Thøgersen, J. (2017). The importance of consumer trust for the emergence of a market for green products: The case of organic food. *Journal of Business Ethics*, *140*(2), 323–337. doi:10.1007/s10551-015-2690-5

Observatorio Español de las Drogas y las Adicciones. (2021). INFORME 2021: Alcohol, tabaco y drogas ilegales en España. *Ministerio de Sanidad. Delegación del Gobierno para el Plan Nacional sobre Drogas*, 52-65.

OECD. (2005). *Eco-innovation in industry: enabling green growth*. OECD.

OECD. (2005). *Oslo Manual: A Guide to Collecting and Interpreting Innovation Data*. OECD. http://www.itq.edu.mx/convocatorias/manualdeoslo.pdf

OECD. (2005). Oslo manual: Guidelines for collecting and interpreting innovation data (3rd ed). Organisation for Economic Co-operation and Development : Statistical Office of the European Communities.

OECD. (2012). *The future of eco-innovation: The role of business models in green transformation*. OECD. https://www.oecd.org/innovation/inno/49537036.pdf

Ogiemwonyi, O. (2022). Factors influencing generation Y green behaviour on green products in Nigeria: An application of theory of planned behaviour. *Environmental and Sustainability Indicators*, *13*, 100164. doi:10.1016/j.indic.2021.100164

Okten, C., & Weisbrod, B. A. (2000). Determinants of donations in private nonprofit markets. *Journal of Public Economics*, *75*(2), 255–272. doi:10.1016/S0047-2727(99)00066-3

Oliveira, C. P., & Sousa, B. M. (2020). Green consumer behavior and its implications on brand marketing strategy. In *Green marketing as a posi-tive driver toward business sustainability* (pp. 69–95). IGI Global. doi:10.4018/978-1-5225-9558-8.ch004

Oliver, R. L. (1999). Whence consumer loyalty? *Journal of Marketing*, *63*(4, suppl1), 33–44. doi:10.1177/00222429990634s105

Oltean, F., & Gabor, M. R. (2022). Wine Tourism—A Sustainable Management Tool for Rural Development and Vineyards: Cross-Cultural Analysis of the Consumer Profile from Romania and Moldova. *Agriculture*, *12*(10), 1614. doi:10.3390/agriculture12101614

Öncü, M. A., Yildirim, S., Bostanci, S., & Erdoğan, F. (2021). The Effect of COVID-19 Pandemic on Health Management and Health Services: A Case of Turkey. *Duzce Medical Journal*, *23*(Special Issue), 61–70. doi:10.18678/dtfd.860733

Organización de Consumidores y Usuarios. (2023). Cervezas sin y 0,0%, ¿la alternativa? *OCU.org*. https://www.ocu.org/alimentacion/alimentos/noticias/cervezas-sin-y-00

Organización Internacional de la Viña y el Vino. (2020). *Plan Estratégico de la OIVE 2020-2024* [PDF file]. OIVE. https://www.OIVE.int/public/medias/7220/es-OIVE-strategic-plan-2020-2024-web.pdf

Organización Internacional de la Viña y el Vino. (2023). *Aspectos de la coyuntura mundial: Situación del sector en 2022.* OIV. https://www.oiv.int/public/medias/7903/actualidad-oiv-de-la-coyuntura-del-sector-vitivin-cola-mundi.pdf

Oricain, N. D., Olmos, M. F., & Castel, A. G. (2022). Determinants of organic wine production: An application in the DOC Rioja wine industry. *Spanish Journal of Agricultural Research, 20*(3), 18.

Orzan, G., Cruceru, A. F., Bălăceanu, C. T., & Chivu, R. G. (2018). Consumers' behavior concerning sustainable packaging: An exploratory study on Romanian consumers. *Sustainability (Basel), 10*(6), 1787. doi:10.3390/su10061787

Osman, S., Ab. Rahman, S., & Jalil, A. (2020). Issues in halal food product labelling: A conceptual paper. *Food Research, 4*, 214–219. doi:10.26656/fr.2017.4(S1).S15

OTRVE. (2021). *Informe de visitantes a bodegas y museos de las rutas del vino de España. Año 2021 [Report on visitors to wineries and museums on the Wine Routes of Spain. Year 2021].* OTRVE. https://wineroutesofspain.com/wp-content/uploads/2022/06/informe-visitas-a-bodegas-y-museos-rve-2021.pdf

Ouakouak, M., & Ouedraogo, N. (2019). Fostering knowledge sharing and knowledge utilization: The impact of organizational commitment and trust. *Business Process Management Journal, 25*(4), 757–779. doi:10.1108/BPMJ-05-2017-0107

Ouvrard, S., Jasimuddin, S. M., & Spiga, A. (2020). Does sustainability push to reshape business models? Evidence from the European wine industry. *Sustainability (Basel), 12*(6), 2561. doi:10.3390/su12062561

Ovalı, B. B. (2020). Fonksiyonel Probiyotik: Kefir. *Bursa Gıda Bülten*, Ocak-Şubat-Mart 2020, Bülten Sayısı, 47 https://arastirma.tarimorman.gov.tr/bursagida/Belgeler/e-B%C3%BClten/2020%20SAYI%2047.pdf

Özel Beslenme. (2022). *Fonksiyonel Gıda Nedir? (What is Functional Food?).* Ozel Beslenme. https://www.ozelbeslenme.com/blogs/blog/fonksiyonel-gida-nedir

Özkaya, Ş. Ö. (2021). Quality of Life and Functional Foods, Fenerbahce University. *Journal of Health Sciences, 1*(1), 62–68.

Pacheco, P., Gnych, S., Dermawan, A., Komarudin, H., & Okarda, B. (2017). *The palm oil global value chain: Implications for economic growth and socialand environmental sustainability.*

Paço, A., Raposo, M., & Filho, W. L. (2009). "Green" segmentation: An application to the Portuguese consumer market. Journal of Targeting. *Measurement and Analysis for Marketing, 17*(1), 17–25.

Paidari, S., Ahari, H., Pasqualone, A., Anvar, A., Allah Yari Beyk, S., & Moradi, S. (2023). Bio-nanocomposites and their potential applications in physiochemical properties of cheese: An updated review. *Journal of Food Measurement and Characterization, 17*(3), 1–12. doi:10.1007/s11694-022-01800-9

Paillé, P., Chen, Y., Boiral, O., & Jin, J. (2014). The impact of human resource management on environmental performance: An employee-level study. *Journal of Business Ethics, 121*(3), 451–466. doi:10.1007/s10551-013-1732-0

Palazzo, B. (2002). US-German business ethics: An intercultural comparison. *Journal of Business Ethics, 41*(3), 195–216. doi:10.1023/A:1021239017049

Pal, B., Sarkar, A., & Sarkar, B. (2023). Optimal decisions in a dual-channel competitive green supply chain management under promotional effort. *Expert Systems with Applications, 211*, 118315. doi:10.1016/j.eswa.2022.118315

Palmié, M., Miehé, L., Oghazi, P., Parida, V., & Wincent, J. (2022). The evolution of the digital service ecosystem and digital business model innovation in retail: The emergence of meta-ecosystems and the value of physical interactions. *Technological Forecasting and Social Change, 177*, 121496. doi:10.1016/j.techfore.2022.121496

Paniagua-Repetto, H. (2007). Vacaciones y ausencia de publicidad de alcohol alrededor de los centros educativos: ¿una casualidad? *Anales de Pediatría (Barcelona, Spain)*, *66*(2), 224. doi:10.1016/S1695-4033(07)70383-1

Park, C. W., Macinnis, D. J., Priester, J., Eisingerich, A. B., & Iacobucci, D. (2010). Brand attachment and brand attitude strenght: Conceptual and empirical differentiation of two critical brand equity drivers. *Journal of Marketing*, *74*(6), 1–17. doi:10.1509/jmkg.74.6.1

Parvin Hosseini, S. M., Mirzaei, M., & Iranmanesh, M. (2020). Determinants of Muslims' willingness to pay for halal certified food: Does religious commitment act as a moderator in the relationships? *Journal of Islamic Marketing*, *11*(6), 1225–1243. doi:10.1108/JIMA-02-2018-0043

Passaro, R., Quinto, I., Scandurra, G., & Thomas, A. (2023). The drivers of eco-innovations in small and medium-sized enterprises: A systematic literature review and research directions. *Business Strategy and the Environment*, *32*(4), 1432–1450. doi:10.1002/bse.3197

Patel, R. (2016). Green Marketing: As Tool for Sustainable Development. *Journal of Business and Management*, *18*(8), 139–142. doi:10.9790/487X-180803139142

Patsnap, (2023). *7 Key Beverage Industry Trends to Watch Out For in 2023.* Patsnap. https://www.patsnap.com/resources/blog/7-key-beverage-industry-trends-to-watch-out-for-in-2023/

Paulraj, A. (2012). Understanding the relationships between internal resources and capabilities, sustainable supply management and organizational sustainability. *The Journal of Supply Chain Management*, *47*(1), 19–37. doi:10.1111/j.1745-493X.2010.03212.x

Pearson, A. W., Carr, J. C., & Shaw, J. C. (2008). Toward a theory of familiness: A social capital perspective. *Entrepreneurship Theory and Practice*, *32*(6), 949–969. doi:10.1111/j.1540-6520.2008.00265.x

Peattie, K. (1995). Environmental marketing management: Meeting the green challenge. *Financial Times Management.*

Peattie, K., & Crane, A. (2005). Green marketing: Legend, myth, farce or prophesy. *Qualitative Market Research*, *8*(4), 357–370. doi:10.1108/13522750510619733

Peloza, J., Ye, C., & Montford, W. J. (2015). When companies do good, are their products good for you? How corporate social responsibility creates a health halo. *Journal of Public Policy & Marketing*, *34*(1), 19–31. doi:10.1509/jppm.13.037

Pereira, A., & Vence, X. (2012). Key business factors for Eco-innovation: An overview of recent firm-level empirical studies. *Cuadernos de Gestión*, *12*(Especial - Innovación), 73–103. doi:10.5295/cdg.110308ap

Pérez-López, S., & Alegre, J. (2012). Information technology competency, knowledge processes and firm performance. *Industrial Management & Data Systems*, *112*(4), 644–662. doi:10.1108/02635571211225521

Pérez-Luño, A., Alegre, J., & Valle-Cabrera, R. (2019). The role of tacit knowledge in connecting knowledge exchange and combination with innovation. *Technology Analysis and Strategic Management*, *31*(2), 186–198. doi:10.1080/09537325.2018.1492712

Perri, A., & Peruffo, E. (2017). *Family business and technological innovation. Empirical insights from the Italian pharmaceutical industry.* Palgrave Macmillan., doi:10.1007/978-3-319-61596-7

Persaud, A., & Schillo, S. R. (2017). Purchasing organic products: Role of social context and consumer innovativeness. *Marketing Intelligence & Planning*, *35*(1), 130–146. doi:10.1108/MIP-01-2016-0011

Petljak, K., Naletina, D., & Bilogrević, K. (2019). Considering ecologically sustainable packaging during decision-making while buying food products. *Ekonomika Poljoprivrede*, *66*(1), 107–126. doi:10.5937/ekoPolj1901107P

Petriashvili, A., Mach, J., Štěbeták, M., Prášilová, M., Svoboda, R., Navrátilová, M., Beranová, M., Veselá, K., Hofman, V., & Němec, O. (2023). The impact of climate change on the sustainability of wine production and the structure of its consumption in Czechia. *Heliyon*, *9*(7), e17882. doi:10.1016/j.heliyon.2023.e17882 PMID:37539305

Pfitzer, M., & Krishnaswamy, R. (2007). *The Role of the Food & Beverage Sector in Expanding Economic Opportunity*. FSG.

Piñeiro, M. V., de Salvo, P., & Giommi, F. (2019). Rural tourism and territorial development in Italy. In *Sustainability Assessment at the 21st century*. IntechOpen.

Pinto, L. G., Cavique, L., & Santos, J. M. A. (2022). Marketing Mix and New Product Diffusion Models. *Procedia Computer Science*, *204*, 885–890. doi:10.1016/j.procs.2022.08.107

Plan de Sostenibilidad Turística de Campo de Criptana. (2023). *About*. Plan de Sostenibilidad Truistica de Camap de Criptata. https://pstdcampodecriptana.es/

Plaza, A. (2021). ¿Anuncios de whisky y ginebra en TV? Llevan décadas prohibidos pero cuelan con versiones «light». *eldiario.es*. https://www.eldiario.es/economia/anuncios-whisky-ginebra-tv-llevan-decadas-prohibidos-cuelan-versiones-light_1_7946458.html

Podvorica, G., & Ukaj, F. (2019). The role of consumers' behaviour in applying green marketing: An economic analysis of the non-alcoholic beverages industry in kosova. Wroclaw Review of Law. *The American Economist*, *9*(1), 1–25.

Poitras, L., & Donald, G. (2006). Sustainable wine tourism: The host community perspective. *Journal of Sustainable Tourism*, *14*(5), 425–448. doi:10.2167/jost587.0

Polas, M., Tabash, M., Bhattacharjee, A. & Dávila, G. A. (2021). Knowledge management practices and green innovation in SMES: The role of environmental awareness towards environmental sustainability. *International Journal of Organizational Analysis*. doi:10.1108/IJOA-03-2021-2671

Polonsky, M. (2011). Transformative green marketing: Impediments and o:ortunities. *Journal of Business Research*, *64*(12), 1311–1319. doi:10.1016/j.jbusres.2011.01.016

Polonsky, M. J. (1994). An Introduction to Green Marketing. *Electronic Green Journal*, *1*(2). Advance online publication. doi:10.5070/G31210177

Polonsky, M. J. (1995). A stakeholder theory approach to designing envi-ronmental marketing strategy. *Journal of Business and Industrial Marketing*, *10*(3), 29–46. doi:10.1108/08858629510096201

Pomarici, E., Asioli, D., Vecchio, R., & Næs, T. (2018). Young consumers' preferences for water-saving wines: An experimental study. *Wine Economics and Policy*, *7*(1), 65–76. doi:10.1016/j.wep.2018.02.002

Pomarici, E., Corsi, A., Mazzarino, S., & Sardone, R. (2021). The Italian wine sector: Evolution, structure, competitiveness and future challenges of an enduring leader. *Italian Economic Journal*, *7*(2), 259–295. doi:10.1007/s40797-021-00144-5

Pomarici, E., & Vecchio, R. (2019). Will sustainability shape the future wine market? *Wine Economics and Policy*, *8*(1), 1–4. doi:10.1016/j.wep.2019.05.001

Popovic, I., Bossink, B. A., & van der Sijde, P. C. (2019). Factors influencing consumers' decision to purchase food in environmentally friendly packaging: What do we know and where do we go from here? *Sustainability (Basel)*, *11*(24), 7197. doi:10.3390/su11247197

Portela, J., & Domínguez, M. (2020). Las rutas del vino como motores de dinamización socio-territorial: El caso de Castilla y León. *Boletín de la Asociación de Geógrafos Españoles*, *84*(2789), 1–36.

Porter, M. E., & Kramer, M. (2002). The competitive advantage of corporate philanthropy. *Harvard Business Review*, (December), 5–16. PMID:12510538

Porter, M., & Van der Linde, C. (1995). Green and competitive: Ending the stalemate. *Harvard Business Review*, *73*, 120–134.

Poza, E. J. (2013). *Family business*. Cengage Learning.

Prabhakar, G., Reddy, P., Savinkina, L., Gantasala, S., & Ankireddy, S. (2018). Influence of organisational culture dimensions on knowledge management processes in higher educational institutions. *International Journal of Knowledge Management Studies*, *9*(1), 51–71. doi:10.1504/IJKMS.2018.089693

Pradana, M., Pérez-Luño, A., & Fuentes-Blasco, M. (2019). Revisiting measure of absorptive capacity: Applying the scales in Spanish wine industry. *Journal of Management Information and Decision Sciences*, *22*(4), 515–526.

Prasad, S., Yadav, K. K., Kumar, S., Pandita, P., Bhutto, J. K., Alreshidi, M. A., Balasubramani, R., Yaseen, Z. M., Osman, S. M., & Cabral-Pinto, M. M. (2024). Review on biofuel production: Sustainable development scenario, environment, and climate change perspectives-A sustainable approach. *Journal of Environmental Chemical Engineering*, 111996. doi:10.1016/j.jece.2024.111996

Prayag, G., & Ryan, C. (2012). Antecedents of tourists' loyalty to Mauritius: The role and influence of destination image, place attachment, personal involvement, and satisfaction. *Journal of Travel Research*, *51*(3), 342–356. doi:10.1177/0047287511410321

Prayuti, Y. (2020). MUSLIM FOOD CONSUMER PROTECTION THROUGH THE REGULATION OF HALAL LABELS IN INDONESIA. *Jurnal IUS Kajian Hukum Dan Keadilan*, *8*(1), 17–25. doi:10.29303/ius.v8i1.716

Precedence Research. (2023). *Functional Beverages Market (By Type: Energy Drink, Caffeinated Beverages, Probiotic Drinks, Vegetable and fruit beverages, Others; By Application: Health and Wellness, Weight Loss; By Ingredient: Antioxidants, Minerals, Amino acids, Probiotics, Prebiotics, Vitamins, Others; By End User: Athletes, Fitness Lifestyle Users, Others; By Distribution Channel)*. Precedence Research. https://www.precedenceresearch.com/functional-beverages-market

Pucci, T., Casprini, E., Galati, A., & Zanni, L. (2020). The virtuous cycle of stakeholder engagement in developing a sustainability culture: Salcheto winery. *Journal of Business Research*, *119*, 364–376. doi:10.1016/j.jbusres.2018.11.009

Pulpón, A. & Ruiz, M. (2019). *Potential of vineyard landscapes for sustainable tourism.*

Qayyum, A., Jamil, R. A., & Sehar, A. (2023). Impact of green marketing, greenwashing and green confusion on green brand equity. *Spanish Journal of Marketing-ESIC*, *27*(3), 286–305. doi:10.1108/SJME-03-2022-0032

Qing, L., Chun, D., Ock, Y.-S., Dagestani, A. A., & Ma, X. (2022). What Myths about Green Technology Innovation and Financial Performance’s Relationship? A Bibliometric Analysis Review. *Economies*, *10*(4), 92. doi:10.3390/economies10040092

Quiles-Soler, M. (2005). *Análisis de la publicidad de bebidas al- cohólicas: valores percibidos y consumo en población universitaria*. Universitat d'Alacant.

Quivy. R., & Campenhoudt, L. (2005). Manual de Investigação em Ciências Sociais, Gradiva Publicações Lda., 4.

Rabadán, A., & Bernabéu, R. (2021). An approach to eco-innovation in wine production from a consumer's perspective. *Journal of Cleaner Production*, *310*, 127479. doi:10.1016/j.jclepro.2021.127479

Rabadán, A., González-Moreno, Á., & Sáez-Martínez, F. (2019). Improving firms' performance and sustainability: The case of eco-innovation in the agri-food industry. *Sustainability (Basel)*, *11*(20), 5590. doi:10.3390/su11205590

Rachao, S., Breda, Z., Fernandes, C., & Joukes, V. (2020). Cocreation of tourism experiences: Are food-related activities being explored? *British Food Journal*, *122*(3), 910–928. doi:10.1108/BFJ-10-2019-0769

Rachmawati, E., & Suroso, A. (2022). A moderating role of halal brand awareness to purchase decision making. *Journal of Islamic Marketing*, *13*(2), 542–563. doi:10.1108/JIMA-05-2020-0145

Rahman, M., Moonesar, I., Hossain, M., & Islam, M. (2018). Influence of organizational culture on knowledge transfer: Evidence from the Government of Dubai. *Journal of Public Affairs*, *18*(1), 1696. doi:10.1002/pa.1696

Rajapathirana, R. P. J., & Hui, Y. (2018). Relationship between innovation capability, innovation type, and firm performance. *Journal of Innovation & Knowledge*, *3*(1), 44–55. doi:10.1016/j.jik.2017.06.002

Ramesh, M. (2020). Impact Of Packaging On The Purchase Decision Of Consumers: A Special Reference To The Online Purchase Of Green Products. *Journal of Engineering Sciences, 11*(1).

Ramírez, L., & García, I. (2013). Los paisajes de la vid en Ribera del Guadiana como recurso turístico. In S. Pérez & J. Blánquez (Eds.), *Patrimonio cultural de la vid y el vino* (pp. 307–3017). Universidad Autónoma de Madrid.

Rana, R. L., Tricase, C., & De Cesare, L. (2021). Blockchain technology for a sustainable agri-food supply chain. *British Food Journal*, *123*(11), 3471–3485. doi:10.1108/BFJ-09-2020-0832

Ratten, V. (2018). Eco-innovation and competitiveness in the Barossa Valley wine region. *Competitiveness Review*, *28*(3), 318–331. doi:10.1108/CR-01-2017-0002

Rehman, S. U., Kraus, S., Shah, S. A., Khanin, D., & Mahto, R. (2021). Analyzing the relationship between green innovation and environmental performance in large manufacturing firms. *Technological Forecasting and Social Change*, *163*, 120481. doi:10.1016/j.techfore.2020.120481

Reinartz, W., Haenlein, M., & Henseler, J. (2009). An empirical comparison of the efficacy of covariance-based and variance-based SEM. *International Journal of Research in Marketing*, *26*(4), 332–344. doi:10.1016/j.ijresmar.2009.08.001

Rejeb, A., Keogh, J. G., Rejeb, K., & Dean, K. (2021). Halal food supply chains: A literature review of sustainable measures and future research directions. *Foods and Raw Materials*, *9*(1), 106–116. doi:10.21603/2308-4057-2021-1-106-116

Rejeb, A., Rejeb, K., & Zailani, S. (2021). Are Halal Food Supply Chains Sustainable: A Review And Bibliometric Analysis. *Journal of Foodservice Business Research*, *24*(5), 554–595. doi:10.1080/15378020.2021.1883214

Rekkas, T. (2021). Measuring the importance of SMEs to the national economy: The case of Greece. *Periodiko Epistimis & Technologias*, *16*(2).

Remaud, H., & Couderc, J. P. (2006). Wine business practices: A new versus old wine world perspective. *Agribusiness*, *22*(3), 405–416. doi:10.1002/agr.20094

Ricks, J. M. Jr, & Williams, J. A. (2005). Strategic corporate philanthropy: Addressing frontline talent needs through an educational giving program. *Journal of Business Ethics*, *60*(2), 147–157. doi:10.1007/s10551-005-1175-3

Ridho Kismawadi, E., Irfan, M., & Shah, S. M. A. R. (2023). Revolutionizing islamic finance: Artificial intelligence's role in the future of industry. In The Impact of AI Innovation on Financial Sectors in the Era of Industry 5.0 (pp. 184–207). doi:10.4018/979-8-3693-0082-4.ch011

Rigdon, E. E., Sarstedt, M., & Ringle, C. M. (2017). On comparing results from CB-SEM and PLS-SEM: Five perspectives and five recommendations, *Marketing: ZFP–Journal of Research and Management, 39*, 4-16.

Ringle, C. M., Wende, S., & Becker, J. M. (2015). *SmartPLS 3*. SmartPLS 3. http://www.smartpls.com (2015)

Ringle, C. M., Sarstedt, M., Mitchell, R., & Gudergan, S. P. (2018). Partial least squares structural equation modeling in HRM research. *International Journal of Human Resource Management*, *31*(12), 1617–1643. doi:10.1080/09585192.2017.1416655

Ringle, C. M., Sarstedt, M., & Straub, D. W. (2012). A critical look at the use of PLS-SEM in MIS quarterly. *Management Information Systems Quarterly*, *36*(1), 1, 3–14. doi:10.2307/41410402

Ritter, Á. M., Borchardt, M., Vaccaro, G. L., Pereira, G. M., & Almeida, F. (2015). Motivations for promoting the consumption of green products in an emerging country: Exploring attitudes of Brazilian consumers. *Journal of Cleaner Production*, *106*, 507–520. doi:10.1016/j.jclepro.2014.11.066

Rival, A., & Levang, P. (2014). *Palms of controversies: Oil palm and development challenges*. CIFOR.

Rizkitysha, T. L., & Hananto, A. (2022). Do knowledge, perceived usefulness of halal label and religiosity affect attitude and intention to buy halal-labeled detergent? *Journal of Islamic Marketing*, *13*(3), 649–670. doi:10.1108/JIMA-03-2020-0070

Röd, I. (2016). Disentangling the family firm's innovation process: A systematic review. *Journal of Family Business Strategy*, *7*(3), 85–201. doi:10.1016/j.jfbs.2016.08.004

Rodríguez, E., Sánchez, L., & Megías, I. (2004). Jóvenes y publicidad. Valores en la comunicación publicitaria para jóvenes. *Injuve FAD*. http://www.injuve.es/ sites/default/files/completojovenesypublicidad.pdf

Rodriguez-Sanchez, C., & Sellers-Rubio, R. (2020). Sustainability in the beverage industry: A research agenda from the demand side. *Sustainability (Basel)*, *13*(1), 186. doi:10.3390/su13010186

Rodrik, D. (2018). What do trade agreements really do? *The Journal of Economic Perspectives*, *32*(2), 73–90. doi:10.1257/jep.32.2.73

Roessl, D., Fink, M., & Kraus, S. (2010). Are family firms fit for innovation? Towards an agenda for empirical research. *International Journal of Entrepreneurial Venturing*, *2*(3/4), 366–380. doi:10.1504/IJEV.2010.037118

Roldan, J., & Cepeda, G. (2017), Modelos de Ecuaciones basados en la Varianza: Partial Least Squares (PLS) para Investigadores en Ciencias Sociales (4a ed.), Universidad de Sevilla.

Roldan, J., & Cepeda, G. (2017), Modelos de Ecuaciones basados en la Varianza: Partial Least Squares (PLS) para Investigadores en Ciencias Sociales (4a ed.). Universidad de Sevilla.

Roldán, J. L., & Sánchez-Franco, M. J. (2012). Variance-based structural equation modeling: guidelines for using partial least squares in information systems research. In M. Mora, O. Gelman, & A. L. Steenkamp (Eds.), *Research Methodologies, Innovations and Philosophies in Software Systems Engineering and Information Systems*. IGI Global. doi:10.4018/978-1-4666-0179-6.ch010

Román-Sánchez, I. M., & Belmonte-Ureña, L. J. (2013). Araisal of environmental regulations on sustainable consumption of water in the wine-producing Spanish industry [EEMJ]. *Environmental Engineering and Management Journal*, *12*(10), 1979–1987. doi:10.30638/eemj.2013.247

Roseta, P., Sousa, B. B., & Roseta, L. (2020). Determiners in the consumer's purchase decision process in ecotourism contexts: A Portuguese case study. *Geosciences*, *10*(6), 224. doi:10.3390/geosciences10060224

Roy, M., & Khastagir, D. (2016). Exploring role of green management in enhancing organizational efficiency in petrochemical industry in India. *Journal of Cleaner Production*, *121*, 109–115. doi:10.1016/j.jclepro.2016.02.039

Rugani, B., & Lamastra, L. (2023). A common framework for sustainability indicators in the wine sector: Dream or reality? *Current Opinion in Environmental Science & Health*, *31*, 100408. doi:10.1016/j.coesh.2022.100408

Ruiz, W. (2014). Elementos para un Diagnóstico Económico de la Vitivinicultura en México I Revista de Economía, Facultad de Economía. *Universidad Autónoma de Yucatán.*, *31*(83), 9. doi:10.33937/reveco.2014.48

Sadik-Zada, E. R., Loewenstein, W., & Hasanli, Y. (2019). Commodity revenues, agricultural sector and the magnitude of deindustrialization: A novel multisector perspective. *Economies*, *7*(4), 113. doi:10.3390/economies7040113

Sadjadi, S. J., Yazdian, S. A., & Shahanaghi, K. (2012). Optimal pricing, lot-sizing and marketing planning in a capacitated and imperfect production system. *Computers & Industrial Engineering*, *62*(1), 349–358. doi:10.1016/j.cie.2011.10.006

Sahibzada, U. F., Jianfeng, C., Latif, K. F., Shah, S. A., & Sahibzada, H. F. (2020). Refuelling knowledge management processes towards organisational performance: Mediating role of creative organisational learning. *Knowledge Management Research and Practice*, 1–13.

Saint-Ges, V., & Bélis-Bergouignan, M.-C. (2009). Ways of reducing pesticides use in Bordeaux vineyards. *Journal of Cleaner Production*, *17*(18), 1644–1653. doi:10.1016/j.jclepro.2009.05.006

Saleh, M. M. A., Jawabreh, O., & Abu-Eker, E. F. M. (2023). Factors of applying creative accounting and its impact on the quality of financial statements in Jordanian hotels, sustainable practices. *Journal of Sustainable Finance & Investment*, *13*(1), 499–515. doi:10.1080/20430795.2021.1962662

San José, M. L. G. (2017). Enoturismo y entornos sostenibles. *Arbor: Ciencia, pensamiento y cultura, 193*(785), 8.

Sánchez, M. (2023). Bebidas alcohólicas: cuatro tendencias que marcan el rumbo. AEOC. https://www.aecoc.es/articulos/c84-bebidas-alcoholicas-4-tendencias-que-marcan-el-rumbo

Sánchez, C. M. (2000). Motives for Corporate Philanthropy in El Salvador: Altruism and Political Legitimacy. *Journal of Business Ethics*, *27*(4), 363–375. doi:10.1023/A:1006169005234

Sánchez-García, E., Marco-Lajara, B., Martínez-Falcó, J., & Poveda-Pareja, E. (2023a). Cognitive social capital for knowledge absorption in specialized environments: The path to innovation. *Heliyon*, *9*(3), e14223. doi:10.1016/j.heliyon.2023.e14223 PMID:36923853

Sánchez-García, E., Martínez-Falcó, J., Alcon-Vila, A., & Marco-Lajara, B. (2023b). Developing Green Innovations in the Wine Industry: An Applied Analysis. *Foods*, *12*(6), 1157. doi:10.3390/foods12061157 PMID:36981084

Sánchez, L., & Mungaray, A. (2010). Vino de calidad: Base de desarrollo endógeno en el Valle de Guadalupe, Baja California. *Frontera Norte*, *22*(44), 109–132.

Sánchez, R. (2002). Publicidad de bebidas alcohólicas. Algunas razones para establecer unos límites. *Adicciones*, *13*(1), 133–140.

Sandeepani, D. M. M., & Samaraweera, G. C. (2021). How green marketing tools shape consumer purchase behavior. *Tropical Agricultural Research and Extention*, *24*(3), 206. doi:10.4038/tare.v24i3.5523

SanJosé, M. L., Gómez-Miguel, V., & Sotés, V. (2017). La Cultura del Vino, motor del desarrollo sostenible de las regiones vitivinícolas. In *BIO Web of Conferences* (Vol. 9, p. 04003). EDP Sciences.

Santiago Guerrero, B. (2001). La industria vitivinícola en el Valle de Guadalupe, de 1956 a nuestros días. In P. R. David & A. S. O. José (Eds.), *Memoria del primer simposio Baja California en el siglo XX. Una reflexión histórica*. Universidad Autónoma de Baja California/Sociedad Histórica de Tijuana/Seminario de Historia de Baja California.

Santiago Guerrero, B. (2007). *Genealogía e la migración y la comunidad kumiai de San José de la Zorra. El Valle de Guadalupe, Ensenada, Baja California. Miguel Olmos (coord.) Antropología de las fronteras. Alteridad, historia e identidad más allá de la línea*. El Colegio de la Frontera Norte/Miguel Ángel Porrúa.

Santos, V., Ramos, P., Almeida, N., & Santos-Pavón, E. (2019). Wine and wine tourism experience: A theoretical and conceptual review. *Worldwide Hospitality and Tourism Themes, 11*(6), 718–730. doi:10.1108/WHATT-09-2019-0053

Santos, V., Ramos, P., Sousa, B., Almeida, N., & Valeri, M. (2022). Factors influencing touristic consumer behaviour. *Journal of Organizational Change Management, 35*(3), 409–429. doi:10.1108/JOCM-02-2021-0032

Santos, V., Ramos, P., Sousa, B., & Valeri, M. (2021). Towards a framework for the global wine tourism system. *Journal of Organizational Change Management, 35*(2), 348–360. doi:10.1108/JOCM-11-2020-0362

Santos, V., Sousa, B., Ramos, P., & Valeri, M. (2022). Emotions and in-volvement in tourism settings. *Current Issues in Tourism, 25*(10), 1526–1531. doi:10.1080/13683500.2021.1932769

Sarasa-Renedo, A., Sordo, L., Molist, G., Hoyos, J., Guitart, A. M., & Barrio, G. (2014). Principales daños sanitarios y sociales relacionados con el consumo de alcohol. *Revista Española de Salud Pública, 88*(4), 469–491. doi:10.4321/S1135-57272014000400004 PMID:25090405

Sargent, J. D., & Babor, T. F. (2020). The Relationship Between Exposure to Alcohol Marketing and Underage Drinking Is Causal. *Journal of Studies on Alcohol and Drugs, 19*(s19), 113–124. doi:10.15288/jsads.2020.s19.113 PMID:32079567

Sariego, M. M. M. (2019). Días de vino y rosas: el" carpe diem" convival y sus realizaciones literarias. In *Dionisio, el vino y la música: divino frenesí de ayer a hoy* (pp. 145–159). Editorial Cérix.

Sarkar, A. N. (2013). Promoting eco-innovations to leverage sustainable development of eco-industry and green growth. *European Journal of Sustainable Development, 2*(1), 171–171.

Sarkis, J., Gonzalez-Torre, P., & Adenso-Diaz, B. (2010). Stakeholder pressure and the adoption of environmental practices: The mediating effect of training. *Journal of Operations Management, 28*(2), 163–176. doi:10.1016/j.jom.2009.10.001

Sarkodie, S. A., & Strezov, V. (2019). Effect of foreign direct investments, economic development and energy consumption on greenhouse gas emissions in developing countries. *The Science of the Total Environment, 646*, 862–871. doi:10.1016/j.scitotenv.2018.07.365 PMID:30064112

Sarstedt, M., Bengart, P., Shaltoni, A. M., & Lehmann, S. (2018). The use of sampling methods in advertising research: A gap between theory and practice. *International Journal of Advertising, 37*(4), 650–663. doi:10.1080/02650487.2017.1348329

Sarstedt, M., Ringle, C. M., Henseler, J., & Hair, J. F. (2014). On the emancipation of PLS-SEM: A commentary on Rigdon (2012). *Long Range Planning, 47*(3), 154–160. doi:10.1016/j.lrp.2014.02.007

Schaper, M. T., & Savery, L. K. (2004). Entrepreneurship and philanthropy: The case of small Australian firms. *Journal of Developmental Entrepreneurship, 9*(3), 239–250.

Schäufele, I., & Hamm, U. (2017). Consumers' perceptions, preferences and willingness-to-pay for wine with sustainability characteristics: A review. *Journal of Cleaner Production, 147*, 379–394. doi:10.1016/j.jclepro.2017.01.118

Schiederig, T., Tietze, F., & Herstatt, C. (2012). Green innovation in technology and innovation management–an exploratory literature review. *R & D Management, 42*(2), 180–192. doi:10.1111/j.1467-9310.2011.00672.x

Schimmenti, E., Migliore, G., Di Franco, C. P., & Borsellino, V. (2016). Is there sustainable entrepreneurship in the wine industry? Exploring Sicilian wineries participating in the SOStain program. *Wine Economics and Policy, 5*(1), 14–23. doi:10.1016/j.wep.2016.05.001

Schlegelmilch, B. B., Bohlen, G. M., & Diamantopoulos, A. (1996). The link between green purchasing decisions and measures of environmental consciousness. *European Journal of Marketing, 30*(5), 35–55. doi:10.1108/03090569610118740

Scholer, A. A., & Miele, D. B. (2016). The role of metamotivation in creating task-motivation fit. *Motivation Science*, *2*(3), 171–197. doi:10.1037/mot0000043

Schumpeter, J. A. (1934). *The theory of economic development*. Harvard University Press.

Schumpeter, J. A. (1976). *Teoría del desenvolvimiento económico: Una investigación sobre ganancias, capital, crédito, interés y ciclo económico (1a* (E. Fondo de Cultura, Ed.).

Schuyt, T., Bekkers, R., & Smit, J. (2010). The philanthropy scale: A sociological perspective in measuring new forms of pro social behaviour. *Social Work & Society*, *8*(1), 121–135.

Sciascia, S., Nordqvist, M., Mazzola, P., & De Massis, A. (2015). Family ownership and RandD intensity in small and medium-sized firms. *Journal of Product Innovation Management*, *32*(3), 349–360. doi:10.1111/jpim.12204

Scorrano, P., Fait, M., Maizza, A., & Vrontis, D. (2019). Online branding strategy for wine tourism competitiveness. *International Journal of Wine Business Research*, *31*(2), 130–150. doi:10.1108/IJWBR-06-2017-0043

Scott, L., & Vigar-Ellis, D. (2014). Consumer understanding, perceptions and behaviours with regard to environmentally friendly packaging in a developing nation. *International Journal of Consumer Studies*, *38*(6), 642–649. doi:10.1111/ijcs.12136

Scott, W. R., & Davis, G. F. (2015). *Organizations and Organizing: Rational, Natural and Open Systems Perspectives* (1st ed.). Routledge., https://www.perlego.com/book/2192623/organizations-and-organizing-rational-natural-and-open-systems-perspectives-pdf doi:10.4324/9781315663371

Secinaro, S., & Calandra, D. (2021). Halal food: Structured literature review and research agenda. *British Food Journal*, *123*(1), 225–243. doi:10.1108/BFJ-03-2020-0234

Secretaría de Agricultura. Ganadería, Desarrollo Rural, Pesca y Alimentación [SAGARPA]. (2018). *Fomento a la Industria Vitivinícola, impulso y desarrollo del vino mexicano*. gob.mx. https://www.gob.mx/agricultura/es/articulos/fomento-a-la-industria-vitivinicola-impulso-y-desarrollo-del-vino-mexicano

Segaro, E. L., Larimo, J., & Jones, M. V. (2014). Internationalization of family small and medium sized enterprises: The role of stewardship orientation, family commitment culture and top management team. *International Business Review*, *23*(2), 381–395. doi:10.1016/j.ibusrev.2013.06.004

Seifert, B., Morris, S. A., & Bartkus, B. R. (2004). Having, giving, and getting: Slack resources, corporate philanthropy, and firm financial performance. *Business & Society*, *43*(2), 135–161. doi:10.1177/0007650304263919

Sekar, K. C., Thapliyal, N., Pandey, A., Joshi, B., Mukherjee, S., Bhojak, P., & Bahukhandi, A. (2023). *Plant species diversity and density patterns along altitude gradient covering high-altitude alpine regions of west Himalaya*. Geology, Ecology, and Landscapes. doi:10.1080/24749508.2022.2163606

Sellitto, M. A., Camfield, C. G., & Buzuku, S. (2020). Green innovation and competitive advantages in a furniture industrial cluster: A survey and structural model. *Sustainable Production and Consumption*, *23*, 94–104. doi:10.1016/j.spc.2020.04.007

Senna, P., Reis, A., Dias, A., Coelho, O., Guimaraes, J., & Eliana, S. (2023). Healthcare supply chain resilience framework: Antecedents, mediators, consequents. *Production Planning and Control*, *34*(3), 295–309. doi:10.1080/09537287.2021.1913525

Seo, J. Y., & Scammon, D. L. (2017). Do green packages lead to misperceptions? The influence of package colors on consumers' perceptions of brands with environmental claims. *Marketing Letters*, *28*(3), 357–369. doi:10.1007/s11002-017-9420-y

Seo, S., Ahn, H. K., Jeong, J., & Moon, J. (2016). Consumers' attitude toward sustainable food products: Ingredients vs. Packaging. *Sustainability (Basel)*, *8*(10), 1073. doi:10.3390/su8101073

Serenko, A., Bontis, N., & Hull, E. (2016). An application of the knowledge management maturity model: The case of credit unions. *Knowledge Management Research and Practice*, *14*(3), 338–352. doi:10.1057/kmrp.2014.37

Serra-Cantallops, A., Ramón-Cardona, J., & Vachiano, M. (2021). Increasing sustainability through wine tourism in mass tourism destinations. The case of the Balearic Islands. *Sustainability (Basel)*, *13*(5), 2481. doi:10.3390/su13052481

Sezen, B., & Cankaya, S. (2013). Effects of green manufacturing and eco-innovation on sustainability performance. *Procedia: Social and Behavioral Sciences*, *99*, 154–163. doi:10.1016/j.sbspro.2013.10.481

Shafie, F. A., & Rennie, D. (2012). Consumer perceptions towards organic food. *Procedia: Social and Behavioral Sciences*, *49*, 360–367. doi:10.1016/j.sbspro.2012.07.034

Shah, M. K. M. (2021). The Impact of Covid-19 Pandemic on Income and Employment in the Agriculture and Food Supply Industry. *Environment*, *6*(25), 171–188.

Shahzad, K., Arenius, P., Muller, A., Rasheed, M., & Bajwa, S. (2019). Unpacking the relationship between high-performance work systems and innovation performance in SMEs. *Personnel Review*, *48*(4), 977–1000. doi:10.1108/PR-10-2016-0271

Shahzad, M., Qu, Y., Zafar, A. U., Rehman, S., & Islam, T. (2020). Exploring the influence of knowledge management process on corporate sustainable performance through green innovation. *Journal of Knowledge Management*, *24*(9), 2079–2106. doi:10.1108/JKM-11-2019-0624

Shahzad, M., Qu, Y., Zafar, A., & Appolloni, A. (2021). Does the interaction between the knowledge management process and sustainable development practices boost corporate green innovation? *Business Strategy and the Environment*, *30*(8), 4206–4222. doi:10.1002/bse.2865

Shamsuddin, R., Singh, G., Kok, H. Y., Hakimi Rosli, M., Dawi Cahyono, N. A., Lam, M. K., & Low, A. (2021). Palm oil industry—processes, by-product treatment and value addition. *Sustainable Bioconversion of Waste to Value Added Products*, 121-143.

Sharma, P. (2008). Commentary: Familiness: Capital stocks and flows between family and business. *Entrepreneurship Theory and Practice*, *32*(6), 971–977. doi:10.1111/j.1540-6520.2008.00266.x

Sharma, P., & Sharma, S. (2011). Drivers of proactive environmental strategy in family firms. *Business Ethics Quarterly*, *21*(2), 309–334. doi:10.5840/beq201121218

Sharma, R., Kamble, S. S., Gunasekaran, A., Kumar, V., & Kumar, A. (2020). A systematic literature review on machine learning applications for sustainable agriculture supply chain performance. *Computers & Operations Research*, *119*, 104926. doi:10.1016/j.cor.2020.104926

Shehu, S., Salleh, M. A., & Ahmad, A. A. (2020). The sustainable palm oil policies in Malaysia. *The Journal of Management Theory and Practice (JMTP)*, 56-60.

Shehzad, M., Zhang, J., Dost, M., Ahmad, M., and Alam, S. (2022). Knowledge management enablers and knowledge management processes: a direct and configurational approach to stimulate green innovation. *European Journal of Innovation Management*. . doi:10.1108/EJIM-02-2022-0076

Siahaan, T. (2020). Indonesia environmental diplomacy in president Joko Widodo's era (2014-2019) of the issue rejection Indonesia's cpo by European Union. *Sociae Polites*, *21*(1), 73–94. doi:10.33541/sp.v21i1.1960

Sigala, M. (2019). The synergy of wine and culture: The case of Ariousios wine, Greece. In *Management and marketing of wine tourism business* (pp. 295–312). Palgrave Macmillan. doi:10.1007/978-3-319-75462-8_15

Sigala, M. (2023). Thriving in Wine Tourism Through Technology and Innovation: A Survival or a Competitiveness Need? In *Technology Advances and Innovation in Wine Tourism* (pp. 3–11). Springer. doi:10.1007/978-981-19-8277-4_1

Signori, P., Flint, D. J., & Golicic, S. L. (2017). Constrained innovation on sustainability in the global wine industry. *Journal of Wine Research*, *28*(2), 71–90. doi:10.1080/09571264.2017.1302413

Silvestre, B., & Ţîrca, D. (2019). Innovations for sustainable development: Moving toward a sustainable future. *Journal of Cleaner Production*, *208*, 325–332. doi:10.1016/j.jclepro.2018.09.244

Singh, A., Sharma, P. K., & Malviya, R. (2011). Eco friendly pharmaceutical packaging material. *World Applied Sciences Journal*, *14*(11), 1703–1716.

Singh, N., Cranage, D., & Lee, S. (2014). Green strategies for hotels: Estima-tion of recycling benefits. *International Journal of Hospitality Management*, *43*, 13–22. doi:10.1016/j.ijhm.2014.07.006

Singh, S. K., Gupta, S., Busso, D., & Kamboj, S. (2021). Top management knowledge value, knowledge sharing practices, open innovation and organizational performance. *Journal of Business Research*, *128*, 788–798. doi:10.1016/j.jbusres.2019.04.040

Sinha, P., Kumar, S., & Chandra, C. (2023). Strategies for ensuring required service level for COVID-19 herd immunity in Indian vaccine supply chain. *European Journal of Operational Research*, *304*(1), 339–352. doi:10.1016/j.ejor.2021.03.030 PMID:33776195

Smith, L. A., & Foxcroft, D. R. (2009). The effect of alcohol advertising, marketing and portrayal on drinking behaviour in young people: Systematic review of prospective cohort studies. *BMC Public Health*, *9*, 1–11. doi:10.1186/1471-2458-9-S1-S1 PMID:19200352

Smyczek, S., Festa, G., Rossi, M., & Monge, F. (2020). Economic sustainability of wine tourism services and direct sales performance–emergent profiles from Italy. *British Food Journal*, *122*(5), 1519–1529. doi:10.1108/BFJ-08-2019-0651

Šniepienė, G., & Jankauskienė, R. (2021). Organic personal care cosmetics: Behavior of choice and consumption. *Proceedings of CBU in Medicine and Pharmacy*, *2*, 158–168. doi:10.12955/pmp.v2.190

Souder, D., Zaheer, A., Sapienza, H., & Ranucci, R. (2017). How family influence, socioemotional wealth, and competitive conditions shape new technology adoption. *Strategic Management Journal*, *38*(9), 1774–1790. doi:10.1002/smj.2614

Stanković, M., Mrdak, G., & Stojanović, S. (2018). The importance of small and medium enterprises in modern economy. *KNOWLEDGE-International Journal*, *28*(5), 1619–1624. doi:10.35120/kij28051619M

Stanovcic, T., Pekovic, S., & Bouziri, A. (2015). The effect of knowledge management on environmental innovation: The empirical evidence from France. *Baltic Journal of Management, 10*, 413.

Stanovcic, T., Pekovic, S., & Bouziri, A. (2015). The effect of knowledge management on environmental innovation: The empirical evidence from France. *Baltic Journal of Management*, *10*(4), 413–431. doi:10.1108/BJM-01-2015-0012

Starik, M., & Kanashiro, P. (2013). Toward a theory of sustainability management: Uncovering and integrating the nearly obvious. *Organization & Environment*, *26*(1), 7–30. doi:10.1177/1086026612474958

Statista Research Department. (2022, October 5). *Malaysia palm oil share of GDP*. SRD.

Stechemesser, K., & Guenther, E. (2012). Carbon accounting: A systematic literature review. *Journal of Cleaner Production, 36*, 17–38. doi:10.1016/j.jclepro.2012.02.021

Stedman, R., Connelly, N., Heberlein, T., Decker, D., & Allred, S. (2019). The end of the (research) world as we know it? Understanding and coping with declining response rates to mail surveys. *Society & Natural Resources*, *32*(10), 1139–1154. doi:10.1080/08941920.2019.1587127

Steger, U., Ionescu-Somers, A., & Salzmann, O. (2007). The economic foundations of corporate sustainability. *Corporate Governance: The international journal of business in society, 7*(2), 162-177.

Steier, L. (2003). Variants of agency contracts in family-financed ventures as a continuum of familial altruistic and market rationalities. *Journal of Business Venturing*, *18*(5), 597–618. doi:10.1016/S0883-9026(03)00012-0

Strateji Geliştirme Başkanlığı. (2021).*Tarım Ürünleri Piyasaları, ÇAY, (Agricultural Products Markets, TEA).* Arastirma. https://arastirma.tarimorman.gov.tr/tepge/Belgeler/PDF%20Tar%C4%B1m%20%C3%9Cr%C3%BCnleri%20 Piyasalar%C4%B1/2021-Haziran%20Tar%C4%B1m%20%C3%9Cr%C3%BCnleri%20Raporu/%C3%87ay,%20Haziran-2021,%20Tar%C4%B1m%20%C3%9Cr%C3%BCnleri%20Piyasa%20Raporu,%20TEPGE.pdf

Su, D. N., Duong, T. H., Thanh, M., Dinh, T., Nguyen-phuoc, D. Q., & Johnson, L. W. (2020). Jo ur l P re of. *Journal of Cleaner Production, 123683*. Advance online publication. doi:10.1016/j.jclepro.2020.123683

Sudusinghe, J., & Seuring, S. (2021). Supply chain collaboration and sustainability performance in circular economy: A systematic literature review. *International Journal of Production Economics*, *245*, 1–19.

Sullivan, K., Thomas, S., & Rosano, M. (2018). Using industrial ecology and strategic management concepts to pursue the Sustainable Development Goals. *Journal of Cleaner Production*, *174*, 237–246. doi:10.1016/j.jclepro.2017.10.201

Šūmakaris, P., Ščeulovs, D., & Korsakienė, R. (2020). Current Research Trends on Interrelationships of Eco-Innovation and Internationalisation: A Bibliometric Analysis. *Journal of Risk and Financial Management*, *13*(5), 85. doi:10.3390/jrfm13050085

Sumarliah, E., & Al-hakeem, B. (2023). The effects of digital innovations and sustainable supply chain management on business competitive performance post-COVID-19. *Kybernetes*, *52*(7), 2568–2596. doi:10.1108/K-09-2022-1326

Sundaram, A. K., & Inkpen, A. C. (2004). Stakeholder Theory and 'The Corporate Objective Revisited': A Reply. *Organization Science*, *15*(3), 370–371. doi:10.1287/orsc.1040.0067

Sun, Y., & Drakeman, D. (2022). The double-edged sword of wine tourism: The economic and environmental impacts of wine tourism in Australia. *Journal of Sustainable Tourism*, *30*(4), 932–949. doi:10.1080/09669582.2021.1903018

Surjandari, I., Yusuf, H., Laoh, E., & Maulida, R. (2021). Designing a Permissioned Blockchain Network for the Halal Industry using Hyperledger Fabric with multiple channels and the raft consensus mechanism. *Journal of Big Data*, *8*(1), 10. doi:10.1186/s40537-020-00405-7

Surroca, J., Tribò, J. A., & Waddock, S. (2010). Corporate responsibility and financial performance: The role of intangible resources. *Strategic Management Journal*, *31*(5), 463–490. doi:10.1002/smj.820

Susanti, C. E. (2021). The effect of push motivational factors and pull motivational factors on tourist loyalty through satisfaction on halal tourists in east java. *WSEAS Transactions on Environment and Development*, *17*, 510–519. doi:10.37394/232015.2021.17.49

Swab, R. G., Sherlock, C., Markin, E., & Dibrell, C. (2020). SEW what do we know and where do we go? A review of socioemotional wealth and a way forward. *Family Business Review*, *33*(4), 424–445. doi:10.1177/0894486520961938

Szolnoki, G., & Tafel, M. (2022). Environmental Sustainability and Tourism—The Importance of Organic Wine Production for Wine Tourism in Germany. *Sustainability (Basel)*, *14*(19), 11831. doi:10.3390/su141911831

Takalo, S. K., & Tooranloo, H. S. (2021). Green innovation: A systematic literature review. *Journal of Cleaner Production, 279*, 122474. doi:10.1016/j.jclepro.2020.122474

Tamayo-Orbegozo, U., Vicente-Molina, M. A., & Villarreal-Larrinaga, O. (2017). Eco-innovation strategic model. A multiple-case study from a highly eco-innovative European region. *Journal of Cleaner Production, 142*, 1347–1367. doi:10.1016/j.jclepro.2016.11.174

Tan, A., Gligor, D., & Ngah, A. (2022). Applying Blockchain for Halal food traceability. *International Journal of Logistics, 25*(6), 947–964. doi:10.1080/13675567.2020.1825653

Tan, C., & McClements, D. J. (2021). Application of advanced emulsion technology in the food industry: A review and critical evaluation. *Foods, 10*(4), 812. doi:10.3390/foods10040812 PMID:33918596

Tariq, A., Badir, Y. F., Tariq, W., & Bhutta, U. S. (2017). Drivers and consequences of green product and process innovation: A systematic review, conceptual framework, and future outlook. *Technology in Society, 51*, 8–23. doi:10.1016/j.techsoc.2017.06.002

Tarkiainen, A., & Sundqvist, S. (2005). Subjective norms, attitudes and intentions of Finnish consumers in buying organic food. *British Food Journal, 107*(11), 808–822. doi:10.1108/00070700510629760

Tayob, S. (2021). Halal consumption as ethical practice: Negotiating halal certification in South Africa. *Islamic Africa, 11*(1), 71–93. doi:10.1163/21540993-01101006

Tea Association of the USA Inc. (2022). *Tea Fact Sheet – 2022.* Tea USA. https://www.teausa.com/teausa/images/Tea_Fact_2021.pdf

Tecnovino (2022, March). *Sosteniblidad y vino: ¿cómo influye en el consumidor el compromiso medioambiental?* https://www.tecnovino.com/sostenibilidad-y-vino-como-influye-en-el-consumidor-el-compromiso-medioambiental/

Teixeira, S., & Ferreira, J. (2018). Entrepreneurial artisan products as regional tourism competitiveness. *International Journal of Entrepreneurial Behaviour & Research, 25*(4), 652–673. doi:10.1108/IJEBR-01-2018-0023

Thakur, H.A. & N.S. Thakur, N.S.,(2021). Role of functional food components in COVID-19 pandemic: A review, *Annals of Phytomedicine*, Volume10, Special Issue1 (COVID-19): S240-S250, 2021

The Snack Haus. (n.d.). *Geleceğin Gidalari: Fonksiyonel Gidalar, (Foods of the Future: Functional Foods).* The Snack Haus. https://thesnackhaus.com/blog/fonksiyonel-gidalar/

Thrassou, A., Vrontis, D., Crescimanno, M., Giacomarra, M., & Galati, A. (2020). The requisite match between internal resources and network ties to cope with knowledge scarcity. *Journal of Knowledge Management, 24*(4), 861–880. doi:10.1108/JKM-06-2019-0291

Thulasiraman, V., Giri, M. S., Nandgopal, & Kothakota, A. (2020). *Need for a balance between short food supply chains and integrated food processing sectors: COVID 19 takeaways from India.* Springer. https://link.springer.com/article/10.1007/s13197-020-04942-0

Tobar, S. (2022). España, paraíso de la cerveza sin alcohol: ¿qué y quién está detrás del éxito de las 0,0? *El Español.* https://www.elespanol.com/invertia/empresas/distribucion/ 20220702/espana-paraiso-cerveza-sin-alcohol-detras-exito/684431923_0.html

Torrego, F. (2002). Las fiestas populares en la oferta turística cultural. In *Boletín de la Real Sociedad Geográfica* (pp. 325–339). Real Sociedad Geográfica., https://realsociedadgeografica.com/wp-content/uploads/2018/02/BOLETIN-RSG-2001-2002-CXXXVII-CXXXVIII.pdf

Tort, Ö. Ö., Vayvay, Ö., & Çobanoğlu, E. (2022). *A Systematic Review of Sustainable Fresh Fruit and Vegetable Supply Chains*. MDPI. . doi:10.3390/su14031573

Toubes, D. R., Araújo Vila, N., & Fraiz Brea, J. A. (2021). Changes in consumption patterns and tourist promotion after the COVID-19 pandemic. *Journal of Theoretical and Applied Electronic Commerce Research*, *16*(5), 1332–1352. doi:10.3390/jtaer16050075

Treiblmaier, H., & Garaus, M. (2023). Using blockchain to signal quality in the food supply chain: The impact on consumer purchase intentions and the moderating effect of brand familiarity. *International Journal of Information Management*, *68*, 102514. doi:10.1016/j.ijinfomgt.2022.102514

Trejo-Pech, C., Arellano-Sada, R., Coelho, A. M., & Weldon, R. (2012). *Is the Baja California, Mexico, Wine Industry a Cluster? - Trejo-Pech—2012—American Journal of Agricultural Economics—Wiley Online Library. 94*(1), 569–575.

Trigo, A., Marta-Costa, A., & Fragoso, R. (2023). Sustainability assessment: Testing and validating a hierarchical framework in the Portuguese wine sector context. In *BIO Web of Conferences* (*Vol. 68*, p. 03008). EDP Sciences. United Nations. https://www.un.org/en/academic-impact/sustainability

Trigo, A., & Silva, P. (2022). Sustainable Development Directions for Wine Tourism in Douro Wine Region, Portugal. *Sustainability (Basel)*, *14*(7), 3949. doi:10.3390/su14073949

Triguero, A., Fernández, S., & Sáez-Martinez, F. J. (2018). Inbound open innovative strategies and eco-innovation in the Spanish food and beverage industry. *Sustainable Production and Consumption*, *15*, 49–64. doi:10.1016/j.spc.2018.04.002

Triguero, A., Moreno-Mondéjar, L., & Davia, M. A. (2013). Drivers of different types of eco-innovation in European SMEs. *Ecological Economics*, *92*, 25–33. doi:10.1016/j.ecolecon.2013.04.009

Trišić, I. (2021). The Function of Protected Natural Areas of the Vojvodina Province in Sustainable Tourism Development. *TEME: Casopis Za Društvene Nauke*, *45*(1), 315–330. doi:10.22190/TEME200129017T

Tsakiridou, E., Boutsouki, C., Zotos, Y., & Mattas, K. (2008). Attitudes and behaviour towards organic products: An exploratory study. *International Journal of Retail & Distribution Management*, *36*(2), 158–175. doi:10.1108/09590550810853093

Tsang, S., Welford, R., & Brown, M. (2009). Reporting on community investment. *Corporate Social Responsibility and Environmental Management*, *16*(3), 123–136. doi:10.1002/csr.178

Tseng, M.-L., Ha, H. M., Tran, T. P. T., Bui, T.-D., Lim, M. K., Lin, C.-W., & Helmi Ali, M. (2022). Data-driven on sustainable food supply chain: A comparison on Halal and non-Halal food system. *Journal of Industrial and Production Engineering*, *39*(6), 430–457. doi:10.1080/21681015.2022.2040622

Turner, S. (2010). Networks of learning within the English wine industry. *Journal of Economic Geography*, *10*(5), 685–715. doi:10.1093/jeg/lbp053

Tu, Y., & Wu, W. (2021). How does green innovation improve enterprises' competitive advantage? The role of organizational learning. *Sustainable Production and Consumption*, *26*, 504–516. doi:10.1016/j.spc.2020.12.031

Tyler, B., Lahneman, B., Beukel, K., Cerrato, D., Minciullo, M., Spielmann, N., & Discua Cruz, A. (2018). SME Managers' Perceptions of Competitive Pressure and the Adoption of Environmental Practices in Fragmented Industries: A Multi-Country Study in the Wine Industry. *Organization & Environment*, *33*(3), 437–463. doi:10.1177/1086026618803720

Ugalde, C. (2014). Influencia de la actitud hacia la marca y su calidad percibida hacia sus anuncios: ¿afectan la intención de compra? *REDMARKA UIMA - Universidad de A Coruña – CIECID*, *13*, 43-62.

UNGC. (2018). *United Nations Global Compact*. United Nations.

Urbinati, A., Franzò, S., De Massis, A., & Frattini, F. (2017). Innovation in Family Firms: A Review of Prior Studies and a Framework for Future Research. In A. Brem & E. Viardot (Eds.), *Revolution of Innovation Management* (pp. 213–246). Palgrave Macmillan. doi:10.1057/978-1-349-95123-9_8

Usman, H., Chairy, C., & Projo, N. W. K. (2022). Impact of Muslim decision-making style and religiosity on intention to purchasing certified halal food. *Journal of Islamic Marketing*, *13*(11), 2268–2289. doi:10.1108/JIMA-01-2021-0027

Valero-Gil, J., Surroca, J. A., Tribo, J. A., Gutierrez, L., & Montiel, I. (2023). Innovation vs. standardization: The conjoint effects of eco-innovation and environmental management systems on environmental performance. *Research Policy*, *52*(4), 104737. doi:10.1016/j.respol.2023.104737

Vamuloh, V. V., Kozak, R. A., & Panwar, R. (2020). Voices unheard: Barriers to and opportunities for small farmers' participation in oil palm contract farming. *Journal of Cleaner Production*, *275*, 121955. doi:10.1016/j.jclepro.2020.121955

Van Eck, N., & Waltman, L. (2010). Software survey: VOSviewer, a computer program for bibliometric mapping. *Scientometrics*, *84*(2), 523–538. doi:10.1007/s11192-009-0146-3 PMID:20585380

Van Leeuwen, M. H., & Wiepking, P. (2013). National campaigns for charitable causes: A literature review. *Nonprofit and Voluntary Sector Quarterly*, *42*(2), 219–240. doi:10.1177/0899764012467084

Van Loo, E. J., Diem, M. N. H., Pieniak, Z., & Verbeke, W. (2013). Consumer attitudes, knowledge, and consumption of organic yogurt. *Journal of Dairy Science*, *96*(4), 2118–2129. doi:10.3168/jds.2012-6262 PMID:23415537

Van Wissen, L. (2000). SIMFIRMS: Simulating the spatial demography of firms, with an application in the Netherlands. Proceedings from Computing in Economics and Finance 2000, Barcelona, Spain.

Vaquero, D. (2013). Rutas del Vino de España, o el arte de conocer y experimentar el patrimonio de la vid y el vino. In S. Pérez & J. Blánquez (Eds.), *Patrimonio cultural de la vid y el vino* (pp. 293–305). Universidad Autónoma de Madrid.

Varshneya, G., & Das, G. (2017). Experiential value: Multi-item scale development and validation. *Journal of Retailing and Consumer Services*, *34*, 48–57. doi:10.1016/j.jretconser.2016.09.010

Vázquez-Vicente, G., Martín-Barroso, V., & Blanco-Jiménez, F. (2021). Sustainable tourism, economic growth and employment—The case of the wine routes of Spain. *Sustainability (Basel)*, *13*(13), 7164. doi:10.3390/su13137164

Veflen, N., Velasco, C., & Kraggerud, H. (2023). Signalling taste through packaging: The effects of shape and colour on consumers' perceptions of cheeses. *Food Quality and Preference*, *104*, 104742. doi:10.1016/j.foodqual.2022.104742

Vega San Sebastián, A. (1997). El alcohol en los medios de comunicación: La presión para su consumo-abuso. *Revista Científica Iberoamericana de Comunicación y Educación*, *9*, 105–110.

Vega-Bayo, A., Mariel, P., Meyerhoff, J., Corsi, A. M., & Chovan, M. (2023). Climate change adaptation preferences of winemakers from the Rioja wine appellation. *Journal of Choice Modelling*, *48*, 100434. doi:10.1016/j.jocm.2023.100434

Vega-Zamora, M., Torres-Ruiz, F. J., & Parras-Rosa, M. (2019). Towards sustainable consumption: Keys to communication for improving trust in organic foods. *Journal of Cleaner Production*, *216*, 511–519. doi:10.1016/j.jclepro.2018.12.129

Veleva, V., & Bodkin, G. (2018). Corporate-entrepreneur collaborations to advance a circular economy. *Journal of Cleaner Production*, *188*, 20–37. doi:10.1016/j.jclepro.2018.03.196

Vergamini, D., Bartolini, F., Prosperi, P., & Brunori, G. (2019). Explaining regional dynamics of marketing strategies: The experience of the Tuscan wine producers. *Journal of Rural Studies*, *72*, 136–152. doi:10.1016/j.jrurstud.2019.10.006

Vergura, D. T., Zerbini, C., & Luceri, B. (2020). Consumers' attitude and purchase intention towards organic personal care products. An application of the SOR model. *Sinergie Italian Journal of Management*, *38*(1), 121–137.

Vijayan, G., Kamarulzaman, N. H., Mohamed, Z. A., & Abdullah, A. M. (2014). Sustainability in food retail industry through reverse logistics. *International Journal of Supply Chain Management, 3*(2), 11–23.

Villanueva-Rey, P., Vázquez-Rowe, I., Moreira, M. T., & Feijoo, G. (2014). Comparative life cycle assessment in the wine sector: Biodynamic vs. conventional viticulture activities in NW Spain. *Journal of Cleaner Production, 65*, 330–341. doi:10.1016/j.jclepro.2013.08.026

Vinos de Castilla-La Mancha Media. (2022, May 20). *La sostenibilidad en el sector del vino: buenas prácticas*. Vinos de Castilla-La Mancha Media. https://vinosdecastillalamancha.es/la-sostenibilidad-en-el-sector-del-vino-buenas-practicas/

Vittersø, G., & Tangeland, T. (2015). The role of consumers in transitions towards sustainable food consumption. The case of organic food in Norway. *Journal of Cleaner Production, 92*, 91–99. doi:10.1016/j.jclepro.2014.12.055

Vollmer, I., Jenks, M. J. F., Roelands, M. C. P., White, R. J., van Harmelen, T., de Wild, P., van der Laan, G. P., Meirer, F., Keurentjes, J. T. F., & Weckhuysen, B. M. (2020). Beyond Mechanical Recycling: Giving New Life to Plastic Waste. *Angewandte Chemie International Edition, 59*(36), 15402–15423. doi:10.1002/anie.201915651 PMID:32160372

von Meyer-Hofer, M., Nitzko, S., & Spiller, A. (2015). Is there an expectation gap? Consumers' expectations towards organic: An exploratory survey in mature and emerging European organic food markets. *British Food Journal, 117*(5), 1527–1546. doi:10.1108/BFJ-07-2014-0252

von Philipsborn, P., Stratil, J., Burns, J., Busert, L., Pfadenhauer, L., Polus, S., Holzapfel, C., Hauner, H., & Rehfuess, E. (2016). Environmental interventions to reduce the consumption of sugar-sweetened beverages and their effects on health (Protocol). *Cochrane database of systematic reviews (Online)*.

Vrabcová, P., Urbancová, H., & Petříček, M. (2022). Knowledge and its transfer–key prerequisite for long-term competitive advantage and sustainable business. *Knowledge Management Research and Practice, 20*(4), 630–640. doi:10.1080/14778238.2021.2015262

Vranken, S., Beullens, K., Geyskens, D., & Matthes, J. (2023). Under the influence of (alcohol) influencers? A qualitative study examining Belgian adolescents' evaluations of alcohol-related Instagram images from influencers. *Journal of Children and Media, 17*(1), 134–153. doi:10.1080/17482798.2022.2157457

Vrontis, D., Bresciani, S., & Giacosa, E. (2016). Tradition and innovation in Italian wine family businesses. *British Food Journal, 118*(8), 1883–1897. doi:10.1108/BFJ-05-2016-0192

Vukovic, D., Maiti, M., Vujko, A., & Shams, R. (2020). Residents' perceptions of wine tourism on the rural destinations development. *British Food Journal, 122*(8), 2739–2753. doi:10.1108/BFJ-04-2019-0291

Wagner, M., Stanbury, P., Dietrich, T., Döring, J., Foerster, C., Freund, M., Friedel, M., Kammann, C., Koch, M., Owtram, T., Schultz, H. R., Voss-Fels, K., & Hanf, J. (2023). Developing a Sustainability Vision for the Global Wine Industry. *Sustainability (Basel), 15*(13), 10487. doi:10.3390/su151310487

Wahab, N. A., Hassan, L. F. A., Shahid, S. A. M., & Maon, S. N. (2016). The Relationship Between Marketing Mix And Customer Loyalty In Hijab Industry: The Mediating Effect Of Customer Satisfaction. *Procedia Economics and Finance, 37*, 366–371. doi:10.1016/S2212-5671(16)30138-1

Wamba-Taguimdje, S.-L., Fosso Wamba, S., Kala Kamdjoug, J. R., & Tchatchouang Wanko, C. E. (2020). Influence of artificial intelligence (AI) on firm performance: The business value of AI-based transformation projects. *Business Process Management Journal, 26*(7), 1893–1924. doi:10.1108/BPMJ-10-2019-0411

Wandosell, G., Parra-Meroño, M. C., Alcayde, A., & Baños, R. (2021). Green packaging from consumer and business perspectives. *Sustainability (Basel), 13*(3), 1356. doi:10.3390/su13031356

Wang, L., Elahi, E., Zhou, Y., Wang, L., & Zhang, S. (2022). A Review of Packaging Materials' Consumption Regulation and Pollution Control. *Sustainability (Basel), 14*(23), 15866. doi:10.3390/su142315866

Wang, W., Yu, B., Yan, X., Yao, X., & Liu, Y. (2017). Estimation of innovation's green performance: A range-adjusted measure aroach to assess the unified efficiency of China's manufacturing industry. *Journal of Cleaner Production, 149*, 919–924. doi:10.1016/j.jclepro.2017.02.174

Wang, Y., Li, Y., Sun, T., Milne, E., Yang, Y., Liu, K., Li, J., Yan, P., Zhao, C., Li, S., Duan, B., Li, J., & Wan, X. (2023). Environmental impact of organic and conventional wine grape production, a case study from Wuwei wine region, Gansu Province, China. *Ecological Indicators, 154*, 110730. doi:10.1016/j.ecolind.2023.110730

Wang, Z., & Wang, N. (2012). Knowledge sharing, innovation and firm performance. *Expert Systems with Applications, 39*(10), 8899–8908. doi:10.1016/j.eswa.2012.02.017

Waters, K., Altiparmak, S. O., Shutters, S. T., & Thies, C. (2024). The Green Mirage: The EU's Complex Relationship with Palm Oil Biodiesel in the Context of Environmental Narratives and Global Trade Dynamics. *Energies, 17*(2), 343. doi:10.3390/en17020343

Weber, O., & Saunders-Hogberg, G. (2018). Water management and corporate social performance in the food and beverage industry. *Journal of Cleaner Production, 195*, 963–977. doi:10.1016/j.jclepro.2018.05.269

Weng, H. H., Chen, J. S., & Chen, P. C. (2015). Effects of Green Innovation on Environmental and Corporate Performance: A Stakeholder Perspective. *Sustainability (Basel), 7*(5), 4997–5026. doi:10.3390/su7054997

Wen, Q., Wu, Y., & Long, J. (2021). Influence of ethical leadership on employees' innovative behavior: The role of organization-based self-esteem and flexible human resource management. *Sustainability (Basel), 13*(3), 1359. doi:10.3390/su13031359

Westhead, P., & Cowling, M. (1998). Family firm research: The need for a methodological rethink. *Entrepreneurship Theory and Practice, 23*(1), 31–56. doi:10.1177/104225879802300102

Westhead, P., & Howorth, C. (2007). Types of private family firms: An exploratory conceptual and empirical analysis. *Entrepreneurship and Regional Development, 19*(5), 405–431. doi:10.1080/08985620701552405

White, K., Habib, R., & Hardisty, D. J. (2019). How to SHIFT consumer behaviors to be more sustainable: A literature review and guiding framework. *Journal of Marketing, 83*(3), 22–49. doi:10.1177/0022242919825649

Widayat, W., Praharjo, A., Putri, V. P., Andharini, S. N., & Masudin, I. (2021). Responsible consumer behavior: Driving factors of pro-environmental behavior toward post-consumption plastic packaging. *Sustainability (Basel), 14*(1), 425. doi:10.3390/su14010425

Wier, M., Hansen, L. G., Andersen, L. M., & Millock, K. (2003). Consumer preferences for organic foods. *Organic agriculture: Sustainability, markets and policies*, 257-271.

Williams, K. (2021). Wine Tourism: From Winescape to Cellardoorscape. *Tourism Analysis, 26*(2), 245–248. doi:10.3727/108354221X16079839951529

Wine Australia. (2020). *Wine Tourism Snapshot 2018-2019*. Wine Australia. https://www.wineaustralia.com/market-insights/australian-wine-tourism-snapshot

Wine Institute. (2021), *Economic Impact of California Wine*. Wine Institute. http://www.wine-economy.com/

Wine Routes Tourism Observatory. (2021). *Informe de visitantes a bodegas y museos de las rutas del vino de españa. Año 2021*. WRTO. https://wineroutesofspain.com/observatorio-turistico-rve/

Wong, S. (2013). Environmental requirements, knowledge sharing and green innovation: Empirical evidence from the electronics industry in China. *Business Strategy and the Environment, 22*(5), 321–338. doi:10.1002/bse.1746

Wong, V., Turner, W., & Stoneman, P. (1996). Marketing strategies and market prospects for environmentally-friendly consumer products. *British Journal of Management, 7*(3), 263–281. doi:10.1111/j.1467-8551.1996.tb00119.x

Wong, W. P., Tseng, M., & Tan, K. H. (2013). A business process management capabilities perspective on organization performance. *Total Quality Management & Business Excellence, 25*, 5–6, 602–617.

Woodfield, P., & Husted, K. (2017). Intergenerational knowledge sharing in family firms: Case-based evidence from the New Zealand wine industry. *Journal of Family Business Strategy, 8*(1), 57–69. doi:10.1016/j.jfbs.2017.01.001

World Economic Forum Water Initiative. (2012). *Water security: the water-food-energy-climate nexus*. Island Press.

Wu, G., & Liang, L. (2020). Examining the effect of potential tourists' wine product involvement on wine tourism destination image and travel intention. *Current Issues in Tourism*, 1–16. doi:10.1080/13683500.2020.1828310

Wu, K., Wang, S., Song, W., Zhang, J., Wang, Y., Liu, Q., Yu, J., Ye, Y., Li, S., Chen, J., Zhao, Y., Wang, J., Wu, X., Wang, M., Zhang, Y., Liu, B., Wu, Y., Harberd, N. P., & Fu, X. (2020). Enhanced sustainable green revolution yield via nitrogen-responsive chromatin modulation in rice. *Science, 367*(6478), eaaz2046. Advance online publication. doi:10.1126/science.aaz2046 PMID:32029600

Wu, W., Sheng, L., Tang, F., Zhang, A., & Liu, J. (2021). A system dynamics model of green innovation and policy simulation with an application in Chinese manufacturing industry. *Sustainable Production and Consumption, 28*, 987–1005. doi:10.1016/j.spc.2021.07.007

Xia, Y., & Yan, B. (2022). Energy-food nexus scarcity risk and the synergic impact of climate policy: A global production network perspective. *Environmental Science & Policy, 135*, 26–35. doi:10.1016/j.envsci.2022.04.008

Yadav, R., & Pathak, G. S. (2017). Determinants of consumers' green purchase behavior in a developing nation: Applying and extending the theory of planned behavior. *Ecological Economics, 134*, 114–122. doi:10.1016/j.ecolecon.2016.12.019

Yaka, Z. (2022). The Effects Of Measures Taken In The Scope Of The Islamic Price Policy On Investment, Production, Employment, And Stability. *Ilahiyat Studies, 13*(1), 83–117. doi:10.12730/13091719.2022.131.234

Yang, F., Zhang, Y., Tariq, A., Jiang, X., Ahmed, Z., Zhihao, Z., Idrees, M., Azizullah, A., Adnan, M., & Bussmann, R. W. (2020). Food as medicine: A possible preventive measure against coronavirus disease (COVID-19). *Phytotherapy Research, 34*(12), 3124–3136. doi:10.1002/ptr.6770 PMID:32468635

Yang, Z., Nguyen, V., & Le, P. (2018). Knowledge sharing serves as a mediator between collaborative culture and innovation capability: An empirical research. *Journal of Business and Industrial Marketing, 33*(7), 958–969. doi:10.1108/JBIM-10-2017-0245

Ye, N., Kueh, T. B., Hou, L., Liu, Y., & Yu, H. (2020). A bibliometric analysis of corporate social responsibility in sustainable development. *Journal of Cleaner Production, 272*, 122679. doi:10.1016/j.jclepro.2020.122679

Yeon Kim, H., & Chung, J. E. (2011). Consumer purchase intention for organic personal care products. *Journal of Consumer Marketing, 28*(1), 40–47. doi:10.1108/07363761111101930

Yeo, S. F., Khoo, Y. H., Tan, C. L., & Lim, K. B. (2020). Product packaging: Impact on customers' purchase intention. *International Journal of Business and Society, 21*(2), 857–864. doi:10.33736/ijbs.3298.2020

Yıldırım, S. (2023). The Challenge of Self-diagnosis on Mental Health Through Social Media: A Qualitative Study. In G. Battineni, M. Mittal, & N. Chintalapudi (Eds.), *Computational Methods in Psychiatry*. Springer. doi:10.1007/978-981-99-6637-0_10

Yıldırım, S., Bostancı, S. H., Yıldırım, D. Ç., & Erdoğan, F. (2021). Rethinking mobility of international university students during COVID-19 pandemic. *Higher Education Evaluation and Development, 15*(2), 98–113. doi:10.1108/HEED-01-2021-0014

Yıldırım, S., Yildirim, D. C., & Calıskan, H. (2020). The influence of health on economic growth from the perspective of sustainable development: A case of OECD countries. *World Journal of Entrepreneurship, Management and Sustainable Development, 16*(3), 181–194. doi:10.1108/WJEMSD-09-2019-0071

Yin, Y. H., Sun, N., North, T. H., & Hu, S. S. (2010). Hook formation and mechanical properties in AZ31 friction stir spot welds. *Journal of Materials Processing Technology, 210*(14), 2062–2070. doi:10.1016/j.jmatprotec.2010.07.029

Yoo, B., Donthu, N., & Lee, S. (2000). An Examination of Selected Marketing Mix Elements and Brand Equity. *Journal of the Academy of Marketing Science, 28*(2), 195–211. doi:10.1177/0092070300282002

Yoon, Y., & Uysal, M. (2005). An examination of the effects of motivation and satisfaction on destination loyalty: A structural model. *Tourism Management, 26*(1), 45–56. doi:10.1016/j.tourman.2003.08.016

YuSheng, K., & Ibrahim, M.YuSheng. (2020). Innovation Capabilities, Innovation Types, and Firm Performance: Evidence From the Banking Sector of Ghana. *SAGE Open, 10*(2), 2158244020920892. doi:10.1177/2158244020920892

Zahra, S. A. (2005). Entrepreneurial Risk Taking in Family Firms. *Family Business Review, 18*(1), 23–40. doi:10.1111/j.1741-6248.2005.00028.x

Zahra, S. A. (2010). Harvesting family firms organizational social capital: A relational perspective. *Journal of Management Studies, 47*(2), 345–366. doi:10.1111/j.1467-6486.2009.00894.x

Zahra, S. A., Hayton, J. C., & Salvato, C. (2004). Entrepreneurship in family vs. non-family firms: A resource-based analysis of the effect of organizational culture. *Entrepreneurship Theory and Practice, 28*(4), 363–381. doi:10.1111/j.1540-6520.2004.00051.x

Zahra, S. A., Neubaum, D. O., & Larrañeta, B. (2007). Knowledge sharing and technological capabilities: The moderating role of family involvement. *Journal of Business Research, 60*(10), 1070–1079. doi:10.1016/j.jbusres.2006.12.014

Zakaria, N. Z. J., Rozali, S., Mubarak, N. M., & Ibrahim, S. (2024). A review of the recent trend in the synthesis of carbon nanomaterials derived from oil palm by-product materials. *Biomass Conversion and Biorefinery, 14*(1), 13–44. doi:10.1007/s13399-022-02430-3 PMID:35194538

Zamarreño-Aramendia, G., Cruz-Ruiz, E., & Ruiz-Romero de la Cruz, E. (2021). Sustainable economy and development of the rural territory: Proposal of wine tourism itineraries in La Axarquía of Malaga (Spain). *Economies, 9*(1), 29. doi:10.3390/economies9010029

Zarantonello, L., & Schmitt, B. (2010). Using the Brand Experience Scale to Profile Consumers and Predict Consumer Behavior. *Journal of Brand Management, 17*(7), 532–540. doi:10.1057/bm.2010.4

Zellweger, T. M., Eddleston, K. A., & Kellermanns, F. W. (2010). Exploring the concept of familiness: Introducing family firm identity *Journal of family business strategy, 1*, 54-63.

Zellweger, T. M., Nason, R. S., Nordqvist, M., & Brush, C. G. (2011). Why do family firms strive for nonfinancial goals? An organizational identity perspective. *Entrepreneurship Theory and Practice, 37*(2), 229–248. doi:10.1111/j.1540-6520.2011.00466.x

Zeng, T., & Durif, F. (2019). The influence of consumers' perceived risks towards eco-design packaging upon the purchasing decision process: An exploratory study. *Sustainability (Basel), 11*(21), 6131. doi:10.3390/su11216131

Zerbini, F. (2017). CSR initiatives as market signals: A review and research agenda. *Journal of Business Ethics, 146*(1), 1–23. doi:10.1007/s10551-015-2922-8

Zhang, L., Priestley, J., & Ni, X. (2018). Influence of the event rate on discrimination abilities of bankruptcy prediction models. *arXiv preprint arXiv:1803.03756.*

Zhang, D., Rong, Z., & Ji, Q. (2019). Green innovation and firm performance: Evidence from listed companies in China. *Resources, Conservation and Recycling, 144*, 48–55. doi:10.1016/j.resconrec.2019.01.023

Zhang, Q., & Ma, Y. (2021). The impact of environmental management on firm economic performance: The mediating effect of green innovation and the moderating effect of environmental leadership. *Journal of Cleaner Production, 292*, 126057. doi:10.1016/j.jclepro.2021.126057

Zhang, W., & Luo, B. (2021). Do environmental concern and perceived risk contribute to consumers ' intention toward buying remanufactured products? An empirical study from China. *Clean Technologies and Environmental Policy, 23*(2), 463–474. doi:10.1007/s10098-021-02061-8

Zhao, N., Liu, X., Pan, C., & Wang, C. (2021). The performance of green innovation: From an efficiency perspective. *Socio-Economic Planning Sciences, 78*, 101062. doi:10.1016/j.seps.2021.101062

Zheng, L., & Iatridis, K. (2022). Friends or foes? A systematic literature review and meta-analysis of the relationship between eco-innovation and firm performance. *Business Strategy and the Environment, 31*(4), 1838–1855. doi:10.1002/bse.2986

Zhou, M., Govindan, K., Xie, X., & Yan, L. (2021). How to drive green innovation in China's mining enterprises? Under the perspective of environmental legitimacy and green absorptive capacity. *Resources Policy, 72*, 102038. doi:10.1016/j.resourpol.2021.102038

Zollo, M. (2004). *Philanthropy or CSR: a strategic choice.* Paper presented at the London European Business Forum, London.

Zuraini, M. I., Muhammad Afiq, M., & Nurzulain, Z. (2019). The influence of cross-generation attitude on halal food products. *Malaysian Applied Biology, 48*(2), 41–46. https://www.scopus.com/inward/record.uri?eid=2-s2.0-85070731515&partnerID=40&md5=1c34445544f5c856f727f11789899a91

About the Contributors

Cristina Raluca Gh. Popescu is Full-Professor Habil. at University of Bucharest, PhD. Supervisor and Doctoral School Member at The Bucharest University of Economic Studies, Romania. She collaborates with University of Craiova and is scientific researcher at The National Institute of Research and Development for Environmental Protection and the National Institute for Research and Development Comoti Turbomotors. She is Public Policy Expert at Ministry of Research, Innovation and Digitization. She is Member of Chamber of Financial Auditors of Romania (CAFR), as Financial Auditor, and Member of Authority for the Public Oversight of the Statutory Audit Activity (ASPAAS), as Financial auditor. She is review board member: IBIMA Conferences and Journal of E-Government Studies and Best Practices, IBIMA Publishing, USA; IGI Global – Publishing House; International Journal of Health Economics (IJHE), University of Bucharest; Multidisciplinary Digital Publishing Institute (MDPI) (Basel, Switzerland) for Journal of Risk and Financial Management, Mathematics, Sustainability, Journal of Open Innovation: Technology, Market, and Complexity, Symmetry, Administrative Sciences, World, Informatics.

Javier Martínez-Falcó (PhD) is Assistant Professor at the Management Department of the University of Alicante and Research Fellow at Stellenbosch University. In the field of research, he focuses his interest in the wine business, specifically in the areas of wine tourism and intellectual capital of wineries, on which he has written hundreds of publications in the form of articles, book chapters and contributions to conferences. He has also participated in several national and international research projects, being lecturer of Strategic Management in the economics and business degrees of the University of Alicante.

Bartolomé Marco-Lajara is Professor of Business Organization at the University of Alicante (Spain). He holds a PhD in Economics and his doctoral dissertation focused in strategic alliances management. His research interests are on Strategic Management and Tourism Management. He is author of several books, book chapters and international articles related to teaching methodology and the areas above mentioned. On the other hand, he is member of the Tourism Research Institute at the University of Alicante since its foundation. He has participated in many public- and private-funded projects, being the main researcher in many of them. He was assistant dean of the Economics Faculty at the University of Alicante during eight years, holding now the position of Head of the Department of Business Organization at this University.

Eduardo Sánchez García (PhD) is an assistant professor in the Department of Business Organization at the University of Alicante (Spain). His research is in the field of strategic management of the company. Specifically, he focuses on the study of the territorial agglomeration of companies in clusters and the absorptive capacity, and its influence on the innovative performance and entrepreneurial orientation of companies. He is co-author of several papers presented at conferences, both national and international, as well as several articles and book chapters related to his field of research.

Luis Antonio Millán Tudela is Assistant Professor in the Department of Management at University of Alicante. MBA and Bachelor of Mechanical Engineering, his research focuses on business longevity, and more specifically on the factors that influence the survival of companies. This activity is developed within the research group "Dirección Estratégica, conocimiento e innovación en una economía global (DECI-GLOBAL)". He also teaches strategic management in the Degree of Business Administration.

***

Joshua Aboah is an applied economist with expertise in the application of system dynamics modelling for ex-ante impact assessment and foresight studies, specifically focused on sustainability and resilience in agrifood systems. He holds a PhD in Agricultural Economics and Management from Lincoln University, New Zealand and an M Sc. in Management Economics and Consumer Studies (Business Economics option) from Wageningen University, Netherlands. Currently, Joshua works as an Agrifood Systems Analyst at CSIRO in Australia.

Jorge Arranz (Almeria, 5 September 2000) is a graduate in Marketing and Market Research from the University of Almeria and European University of Lisbon since 2023. He is currently a student of the MSc of Marketing at the European University of Madrid since 2023.

Ömer Esen is an Assoc. Prof. in Public Finance at University of Tekirdag Namik Kemal, Turkey. His research interests are primarily in the areas of macroeconomics, energy economics and environmental economics with a particular focus on macroeconomic stability, sustainable growth, climate change and fiscal economics.

Sharon Forbes's research interests are centred on business and consumer studies in the wine and food sectors. In particular, she has led or participated in national and global studies which have examined consumer behaviour, supply chain management, disaster resilience, social media marketing, brand name perceptions, philanthropy, and the production and marketing of 'green' or 'sustainable' products.

Rosana Fuentes-Fernández is an associate Professor at the Faculty of Economics, Universidad de León. Her research focuses on CSR and sustainability in the wine sector. Her contributions have been published in reputable academic journals such as the International Journal of Wine Business Research or Wine Economics and Policy. She authored the monograph "Corporate Philanthropy: Influence on wine business management" (Dykinson). She participated in the Global Study on Philanthropy and Wine. This research was awarded at Fair'N'Green in 2018 and the Best Research Award for Social Sustainability in the Global Wine Industry by the International Organization of Vine and Wine (OIV) in 2020.

Armand Gilinsky, Jr. recently retired as Professor Emeritus of Business and as the F.J. Korbel and Bros. Professor of Wine Business at Sonoma State University, where he taught strategy and entrepreneurship since 1994. His most recent book is Business Strategy for a Better Normal (Springer, 2023). He was

Director of SSU's Entrepreneurship Center and Director of the Wine Business Institute. He previously held teaching appointments at the Harvard Business School, CSU East Bay, and Northeastern U. Dr. Gilinsky has extensive consulting experience in strategic planning, competitive strategy, and developing business and financial plans. He has authored over 50 published business case studies and articles on strategy and socially responsible entrepreneurship. In 2011, he was President of the North American Case Research Association, a group of some 500 case research professionals. In 2013, he received the University Award for Excellence in Scholarship from Sonoma State. He was the founding editor of the Wine Business Journal from 2014-2020. He holds a Ph.D. in Business Policy from Henley Business School/Brunel University (London), and the A.B. and A.M degrees rom Stanford U.

Martín Gómez-Ullate has a Ph.D. in Social Anthropology and Degree in Business and Administration. He has lectured in public universities and research centres in Portugal, France, Mexico and Spain where he has developed research in different fields and lines as identity, social representations and intercultural relationships, cultural heritage, qualitative methodology and shared musical heritage and cultural tourism. At the present, he is researcher in the University of Extremadura. Senior researcher, professor and project manager with more than ten years' experience in conducting and participating international, cross-border, national and local R+D projects in cultural management, applied anthropology, cooperation and local development. He has been selected in the Program of Attraction and Retention of Research Talent for the Region of Extremadura to develop research in the field of Immaterial Cultural Heritage Management for Sustainable Tourism in the University of Extremadura (Teacher Training College). He is coordinating CULTOUR+ Project Coordinator (Erasmus+ Strategic Partnership for Higher Education). He has directed the Scientific Committee in the International Conference. Cultural Management and Governance for European Pilgrimage Routes and Religious Tourism He has published several research works about pilgrims and pilgrimage and cultural routes. He has organized and directed international conferences as the 1st. International Conference on Musical Tourism and Festivals, The future of Rural Europe, or International Conference Cultural Heritage and Natural Heritage.

Coralie Haller is an associate-professor at EM Strasbourg Business School, University of Strasbourg. Director of the Corporate Chair in Wine and Tourism, she is also co-founder of the InvinoTECH® innovation cluster in the Grand Est region of France. Her research in entrepreneurship and information systems management has been published in academic and professional journals and books. With over 15 years' professional and academic experience in France, Germany, Australia and the United States, she has proven expertise in the wine, tourism and wine tourism industries.

Uttam Kaur is a research scholars of University School of Business, Chandigarh University, Mohali. Area of interest is Marketing Management. Expert in running software SPSS, PLS-SEM, AMOS, VoS Viewer, R studio.

Early Ridho Kismawadi, S.E.I, MA is a lecturer at the Department of Islamic Banking, Faculty of Islamic Economics and Business IAIN Langsa, Aceh, Indonesia, he has been a lecturer since 2013, he has completed a doctoral program in 2018 majoring in Sharia economics at the State Islamic University of North Sumatra. He was appointed head of the Islamic economics Law study program (2023) Islamic banking study program (2020) and Islamic financial management study program (2019) at Langsa State Islamic Institute (IAIN Langsa), Aceh, Indonesia. His research interests include financial economics, applied econometrics, Islamic economics, banking, and finance. He has published articles in national and international journals. In addition, he is also a reviewer of several reputable international journals such as Finance Research Letters, Financial Innovation, Cogent Business &; Management, Journal of Islamic Accounting and Business Research, Journal of Islamic Marketing. He has also presented his papers at various local and international seminars.

Umesh Kollimath is presently associated with SBSPM's APIMR, Landewadi as Associate Professor. He has been teaching subjects such as Economics, Ethics, Business Strategy, Corporate Governance, etc., to the Post Graduate Students of MBA affiliated to Savitribai Phule Pune University, Pune.

Ricardo Martinez-Cañas is an Associate Professor in Business Management at Castilla-La Mancha University (Spain). His research interest are Social Capital; Science Parks; Business Ethics; Wine Tourism; Innovation; Pay Satisfaction; Ethical Leadership; Educational Research; Entrepreneurial Intention; Value Co-creation

Nitish Kumar Minz is an exceptional Bachelor of Commerce student specializing in Business Administration and Management at K.R. Mangalam University. With an unwavering commitment to excellence and a remarkable work ethic, Mr. Minz has consistently demonstrated his dedication to academic and professional pursuits. His academic achievements extend beyond the classroom, as he has made significant contributions to several research papers and book chapters that are currently in the final stages of publication. His insightful contributions and research expertise have earned him recognition within his field of study. Nitish Kumar Minz, as the President of the Student Council at K.R. Mangalam University, holds a prestigious position. In this leadership role, he has demonstrated exceptional skills in managing various projects and strategic initiatives. His internship at KEIC (KRMU Entrepreneurship & Incubation Center) has allowed him to further refine his project management and strategic planning abilities, providing valuable hands-on experience in the field. Furthermore, he has been selected as NEP SAARTHI- Student Ambassador for Academic Reforms in Transforming Higher Education at K.R. Mangalam University. This esteemed role demonstrates his passion for educational reforms and his commitment to improving the quality of higher education. As a Student Ambassador, Mr. Minz actively engages with fellow students, faculty, and staff, promoting a culture of academic excellence and facilitating positive changes within the university. Recognizing his outstanding accomplishments and exceptional contributions, he has recently been honored with the prestigious CHANCELLOR'S EXCELLENCE AWARD. This esteemed award serves as a testament to his dedication, hard work, and exemplary performance throughout his academic journey. Mr. Nitish Kumar Minz's academic prowess, research contributions, leadership roles, and recognition through awards highlight his exceptional abilities and potential for future success. He continues to inspire and make a significant impact within the academic community, demonstrating his commitment to excellence in all his endeavors.

Prashant Kumar Siddhey is presently working as a Professor of Management at the University School of Business, Chandigarh University, Mohali. He is a master's and doctorate in supply chain management from Devi Ahilya University, Indore, Madhya Pradesh, India. His area of specialization is Supply Chain Management and General Management and has academic and research experience of 15 years. He has published 9 Research Papers, 5 Cases, and 1 Book in the area of supply chain management and general management.

Bruno Barbosa Sousa is Adjunct Professor of Marketing at Polytechnic Institute of Cávado and Ave (IPCA), Portugal and PhD in Marketing and Strategy in Universidade do Minho, Portugal. Head of Masters Program - Tourism Management and Marketing Tourism (IPCA); CiTUR – Center for Tourism Research, Development and Innovation and UNIAG research member. He has published in the Journal of Enterprising Communities, Tourism Management Perspectives, Current Issues in Tourism, Journal of Organizational Change Management, World Review of Entrepreneurship, Management and Sust. Development, among others.

Gerardo Vidal Gonçalves is an archaeologist and historian, member and researcher at CIDEHUS, completed a degree course in History at the University of Évora (pre-Bologna) and, subsequently, completed a Master's degree in Archeology and Environment at the same institution. He completed specializations in Archeology and Dendrochronology at several institutions such as the Swiss Federal Institute for Forest, Snow and Landscape Research, at Idiana State University and CONICET/IANIGLA in Mendoza, Argentina, for this last training he received a scholarship from CONICET and CIDEHUS. He also specialized in digital humanities and multidimensional surveys of architectural and archaeological heritage. For more than 20 years he dedicated himself to public and safeguard archaeology, digital archaeology, dendrochronology and historical research. He is currently a researcher at CIDEHUS- UÉ and collaborates with EROS Environment research on Science Consulting and with AHAS (Association of History and Archeology of Sabrosa and with the Society of Natural History, in Torres Vedras, being responsible and coordinator in the projects Pannonias Digital Old Lands, Touças old Paths, Touças Medieval Graveyard (multi-annual project approved by the DGPC) and the project to digitize the historical archive of the Mina do Vale das Gatas (Industrial archeology), in Sabrosa. He is also coordinator of the multi-annual project approved by the DGPC S. Lourenço dos Francos: between the Roman world, late antiquity and the Early Middle Ages, in the municipality of Lourinhã and the European Project Learning Villages "C": International Network, from the program "Citizens, Equality, Rights and Values Program (CERV). Dina Borges Pereira Dina Borges Pereira has a degree in archeology and a master's degree in archeology and environment, and has developed work in the areas of investigative archeology and preventive archeology for more than 18 years. She is the co-author of several scientific articles and co-responsible for several projects in the fields of public archeology. She is the founder of several cultural institutions, among which the Association of History and Archeology of Sabrosa stands out, of which she is currently president, and is also co-responsible for cultural and tourist projects such as the Panonnias Digital Old Lands project, financing by Turismo de Portugal and other projects on rural cultural heritage and education for culture.

Durmuş Çağrı Yıldırım works at Tekirdağ Namık Kemal University in Türkiye. He is an expert in economics. He studies on sustainable development, climate change, energy policies, education and health policies in general. He has many book chapter and book in IGI Global publishing. He has several publications in journal indexed by Web of Science and SCOPUS.

Seda Yıldırım currently works at Tekirdag Namık Kemal University in Turkey. She studies on sustainable development, 2030 sustainable development goals, sustainable consumption patterns, Islamic finance and banking, consumption patterns, environmental quality and food security. She is married and has two children She won Emerald literati award- Outstanding Paper Award 2022. #LiteratiAwards

Index

U

V

W

Z

www.ingramcontent.com/pod-product-compliance
Lightning Source LLC
LaVergne TN
LVHW080119011026
849160LV00013B/1135